D1528986

Jacob W. Kipp, 2016

Vietnam's
High Ground

MODERN WAR STUDIES

Theodore A. Wilson
General Editor

Raymond Callahan
Jacob W. Kipp
Allan R. Millett
Carol Reardon
Dennis Showalter
David R. Stone
James H. Willbanks
Series Editors

Vietnam's
High Ground

Armed Struggle for the
Central Highlands,
1954–1965

J. P. Harris

University Press of Kansas

© 2016 by the University Press of Kansas
All rights reserved

Published by the University Press of Kansas (Lawrence, Kansas 66045), which
was organized by the Kansas Board of Regents and is operated and funded by
Emporia State University, Fort Hays State University, Kansas State University,
Pittsburg State University, the University of Kansas, and Wichita State University

Library of Congress Cataloging-in-Publication Data
Names: Harris, J. P.
Title: Vietnam's high ground : armed struggle for the Central Highlands,
1954–1965 / J. P. Harris.
Description: Lawrence, Kansas : University Press of Kansas, 2016. | Series:
Modern war studies | Includes bibliographical references and index.
Identifiers: LCCN 2016014280| ISBN 9780700622832 (cloth : alk. paper) |
ISBN 9780700622849 (ebook)
Subjects: LCSH: Vietnam War, 1961–1975—Campaigns—Vietnam—Central
Highlands. | Central Highlands (Vietnam)—History, Military—20th century.
Classification: LCC DS557.8.C4 H37 2016 | DDC 959.704/342095976—dc23
LC record available at http://lccn.loc.gov/2016014280.

British Library Cataloguing-in-Publication Data is available.

Printed in the United States of America

10 9 8 7 6 5 4 3 2 1

The paper used in this publication is recycled and contains 30 percent
postconsumer waste. It is acid free and meets the minimum requirements of
the American National Standard for Permanence of Paper for Printed Library
Materials Z39.48-1992.

Contents

A photo gallery follows page 248.

Preface

The region that Americans and other Westerners generally call Vietnam's Central Highlands is the broader, southern end of the Truong Son or Annamite chain, the range of mountains that forms the boundary between Vietnam and Laos and part of the boundary between Vietnam and Cambodia. Over the years various other names have been used for the region. Today the Vietnamese government calls it the Tay Nguyen (Western Highlands), for although it was central to the old French Indochina, it is on Vietnam's western side.

Approximately 67,000 square km in area (450 km north–south and 150 km west–east), the Central Highlands constituted a large part of the landmass of the former South Vietnamese state (1954–1975), but it was by far the most sparsely populated region. Geologically, it is formed largely of granite and basalt, but there are sedimentary rocks too. Large parts of the region are too mountainous to support many people. There are, however, a number of plateau areas that are suitable for agriculture, and this is where the principal towns are situated. Among these plateaus are Kontum (elevation 545 m), Pleiku (800 m), and Ban Me Thuot (536 m). The highest peaks are Ngoc Linh (2,958 m), at the northern end of the region, and Chu Yang Sinh (2,410 m), in the east.

Because the Central Highlands is so topographically complex, the pattern of rainfall varies considerably. The dry season generally lasts from November to April, while rainfall from May to October is sufficiently heavy to permit the growth of tropical rain forest and thirsty commercial crops. The region is also watered by several sizable rivers and many smaller streams. For centuries the original inhabitants—the Highland ethnic groups, or Montagnards—had practiced simple subsistence farming on the more favorable terrain. By the early 1960s the Vietnamese were taking over increasing amounts of the best land and using it to grow a range of plantation crops, including coffee and tea.

Since 1975 large parts of the region have been drastically deforested. In the period covered by this book, however, a large proportion of it was still covered by jungle and grassland. Large, dangerous animals such as wild elephants, wild cattle, tigers, and leopards were present in some areas, and deer and wild pigs were abundant.

The aboriginal peoples of the Central Highlands, who were still a substantial majority of the region's inhabitants in 1954–1965, are discussed at some length in the main body of the book. It would be pointless to preempt that discussion here. It is important to understand from the outset, however, that although they lived in a state called the Republic of Vietnam, they did not see themselves as Vietnamese and generally were not seen as such by others. The Highland ethnic groups spoke a variety of different tongues. Although their traditional cultures had much in common with one another, they had little in common with that of the Vietnamese. Most Highlanders did not understand the Vietnamese language, and many were fearful and suspicious of the Vietnamese people. Yet many became active participants in (and all had their lives massively disrupted by) what was essentially a Vietnamese civil war.

A study of the political and military struggle for control of this region in 1954–1965 surely needs little justification. The Second Indochina War is generally acknowledged as one of the most important conflicts of the latter half of the twentieth century. Everyone with a basic knowledge of that conflict understands that the Central Highlands was a strategically vital region and that control of it was fiercely contested. It is generally appreciated that many branches of the Ho Chi Minh Trail entered South Vietnam through the Central Highlands and that American Special Forces worked there with Highland troops from an early stage in the war. It is also widely known that in November 1965 the US Army had its first major clashes with the North Vietnamese in the Central Highlands.

Serious students of the war also know that events in this region precipitated its end. The South Vietnamese defeat at Ban Me Thuot in April 1975 led to President Nguyen Van Thieu's ill-judged order to abandon the Central Highlands, a move for which no contingency plans had been made. Taking advantage of the chaotic retreat, the North Vietnamese were able to cross the narrow coastal plain, cut South Vietnam in two, and thereby envelop South Vietnamese troops in the northern section. For the anti-Communist side, this was a long-imagined nightmare scenario. Once it became reality, a final Communist victory could not be long delayed.

Even in the early 1960s, when guerrilla warfare was the norm, highly placed Vietnamese on both sides realized that the fighting in the Highlands would eventually assume a more high-intensity, "conventional" nature. To the Communist high command, the rugged terrain and dense vegetation of the Central Highlands offered the best chance of ambushing and annihilating major units of the South Vietnamese armed forces and of drawing in and destroying their strategic reserves. When large American units arrived in South Vietnam, the Central Highlands seemed to be the most suitable place to engage them, too. Both sides seemed to sense from an early stage in the war, moreover, that control of the high ground looming over South Vietnam's narrow coastal plain might ultimately prove decisive.

The Central Highlands was therefore strategically vital ground in one of recent history's major wars. The struggle to control this region seemed a worthwhile field of study, a point that first suggested itself when touring parts of it with Ed Flint, a Sandhurst colleague and friend, in December 2004 and January 2005. Covering the entire struggle, from 1954 to 1975, in a single monograph, however, always seemed more than could be managed effectively. From the outset, therefore, the intention was to stop at the end of 1965, after the US Army had fought its first battles in the region and after which, in the eyes of many Americans, the war entered a new phase.

Particular parts of the story told in this book have already been explored in print. There are memoirs and monographs concerning the US Special Forces and the counterinsurgency activities of the CIA. Specialist studies of the anthropology and ethnohistory of the Highlanders exist. One volume of the US Army's official history covers the Pleiku campaign of October–November 1965, and there are at least three other substantial studies of the role of the US 1st Cavalry Division in that fighting. The aim of this book, however, is to examine the struggle for the Central Highlands from 1954 to 1965 as a coherent whole. The intention has been to consider the perspectives of all the warring parties and, where possible, those of the civilians caught between them.

This was not the easiest of objectives. The great bulk of the secondary literature and the vast majority of the relevant primary source documents relating to this subject that are readily available to Western scholars were produced by Americans for Americans. Highlanders have left few written records of their experiences in these years. Relevant writings by Vietnamese who served on the anti-Communist side do exist and were consulted. But most significantly, perhaps, it has been possible to exploit a great deal of Vietnamese Communist historical writing, most of it never published in English. This literature, like all other sources, must be viewed critically and used cautiously. Yet some of the more recent Vietnamese accounts of the war contain breathtaking admissions of the Communist side's errors and disasters and the catastrophic collapse of morale at certain times in some Communist units. Even the older histories published in Hanoi contain information on matters such as unit identities and command arrangements that are impossible to find elsewhere. The painstaking efforts and great generosity of a single individual are responsible for translating most of this material and making it available to scholars. This book could not have been written in its present form without the help of Merle Pribbenow.

When the idea for this book was first mooted with American Vietnam specialists, they warned that the Central Highlands from 1954 to 1965 was the most obscure region of Vietnam at the most obscure period of the war. They doubted that sufficient primary sources could be found to make the project viable. It is certainly true that many records from the 1950s and early 1960s have gone missing. In particular, many of the papers of the Military Assistance and Advisory Group (MAAG), the American headquarters that preceded the Military Assistance Command Vietnam (MACV), have disappeared. Although South Vietnamese government forces mounted thousands of military operations of various sizes in the first half of the 1960s, and although the Americans were putting great effort into equipping and advising those armed forces, only a handful of after-action reports survive in American archives. Even the records of the US Army Special Forces are somewhat patchy for this period of the war.

Yet masses of documents from this early period of the struggle do exist, and a substantial number are related to the Central Highlands. The great majority of those used in the research for this book are accessible in American public archives. The US Army's official history of this period of the war is not yet completed, however, and some papers are still held at the Center of Military History in Washington, DC. Access to those records, graciously arranged by Dr. Andrew Birtle, was extremely important.

Even though the events considered here took place at least half a century ago, some participants are still very much with us and are willing to testify. Their evidence, too, was very important. Particular thanks are owed to Dave Nuttle, who, when still remarkably youthful, played a central role in important developments. His detailed recollections of distant events were repeatedly corroborated by documentary evidence that subsequently came to light.

Neither the accessible documents nor the surviving individuals can tell us everything we would ideally like to know. As with all histories, the account provided here is incomplete and grossly imperfect. This is especially true of the period up to the end of 1964. Yet a reasonably coherent picture of the struggle for the region in the decade after the Geneva Accords does emerge.

In 1965 the war in the Central Highlands changed. Though guerrilla actions persisted, there was also fighting on a significantly larger scale and of much greater intensity. As the Americans became increasingly involved, the quantity of records available to the historian expands dramatically. Both because of the increased scale and intensity of the fighting and because the greater availability of records allows more detailed analysis, a large part of this book deals with the events of that year.

Contrary to a common American perception, large North Vietnamese units were fighting major actions in the Central Highlands for several months before the US 1st Cavalry Division arrived there. As we shall see, the North Vietnamese did not always have these all their own way. Both in America and in Vietnam, however, by far the most famous series of military events in 1965 is the Plei Me–Ia Drang campaign of October–November. That campaign is explored in considerable detail in these pages. Largely as a result of a detailed comparison of American and Vietnamese Communist accounts, a revised narrative and new interpretations are presented.

It is hoped that this book sheds fresh light on a vital theater of operations in the crucial early years of one of the twentieth century's most important conflicts.

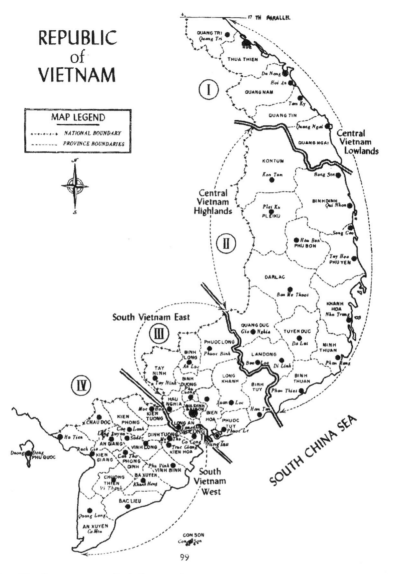

REPUBLIC
of
VIETNAM

MAP LEGEND
·—·—·—· NATIONAL BOUNDARY
·········· PROVINCE BOUNDARIES

17 TH PARALLEL

QUANG TRI
Quang Tri

HUE

THUA THIEN

I

Da Nang
Hoi An

QUANG NAM

Tam Ky

QUANG TIN

Quang Ngai

QUANG NGAI

Central
Vietnam
Lowlands

KONTUM

Kon Tum

Bong Son

Central
Vietnam
Highlands

BINH DINH
Qui Nhon

Plei Ku
PLEIKU

Song Cao

II

Hoa Bon
PHU BON

Tuy Hoa
PHU YEN

DARLAC

Ban Me Thuot

KHANH
HOA
Nha Trang

South Vietnam East

III

QUANG DUC
Gia Nghia

TUYEN DUC
Da Lat

PHUOC LONG
PHUOC LONG
Phuoc Binh

NINH
THUAN

LANDONG
Bao Loc Di Linh

Phan Rang

TAY
NINH
Tay Ninh

BINH
LONG
An Loc

BINH
DUONG
Phu Cuong

LONG
KHANH

BINH
THUAN

IV

HAU
NGHIA

BIEN
HOA

BINH
TUY
Xuan Loc

Phan Thiet

Phan Thiet

CHAU DOC

KIEN
TUONG

GIA DINH
SAIGON

Ham Tan

Moc Hoa

KIEN
HOA

PHUOC
TUY
Phuoc Le

LONG AN

Ha Tien

Cao Lanh

DINH TUONG

Vung Tau

AN GIANG
Long Xuyen
Sadec

My Tho
Truc Giang

Go Cong

KIEN HOA

Rach Gia

VINH LONG

KIEN
GIANG

CAN THO
PHONG
DINH

Phu Vinh
VINH BINH

South
Vietnam
West

Duong Dong
PHU QUOC

CHUONG
THIEN
Vi Thanh

BA XUYEN
Khanh Hung

BAC LIEU

Quan Long

AN XUYEN
Ca Mau

CON SON
Con Son

SOUTH CHINA SEA

99

Republic of Vietnam, 1965 (including South Vietnam's corps areas, provinces, and Central Highlands)

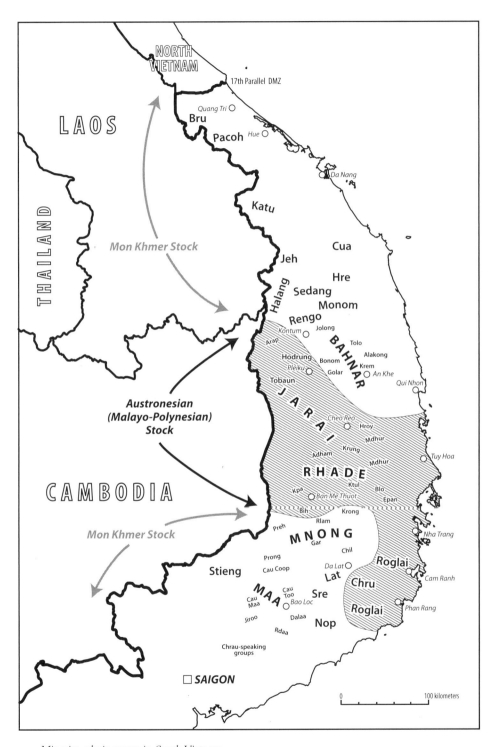

NORTH VIETNAM

17th Parallel DMZ

LAOS

THAILAND

CAMBODIA

Quang Tri ○

Bru

Pacoh   Hue ○

Da Nang

Katu

Cua

Jeh   Hre

Halang   Sedang   Monom

Rengo

Kontum ○   Jolong

Arap   BAHNAR   Tolo

Hodrung   Bonom   Alakong

Pleiku ○   Golar   Krem   An Khe

Tobaun   Qui Nhon

J A R A I

Cheo Reo ○   Hroy

Adham   Krung   Mdhur

Mdhur   Tuy Hoa

R H A D E

Ktul

Kpa   Blo

Bih   Ban Me Thuot   Epan

Krung

Rlam   Nha Trang

MNONG   Gar   Chil

Prong   Da Lat ○   Roglai

Stieng   Cau Coop   Lat   Chru   Cam Ranh

MAA   Cau   Sre   Roglai

Cau   Too   Phan Rang

Maa   Bao Loc

Jiroo   Dalaa   Nop

Rdaa

Chrau-speaking
groups

□ SAIGON

Mon Khmer Stock

Austronesian
(Malayo-Polynesian)
Stock

Mon Khmer Stock

0   100 kilometers

Minority ethnic groups in South Vietnam

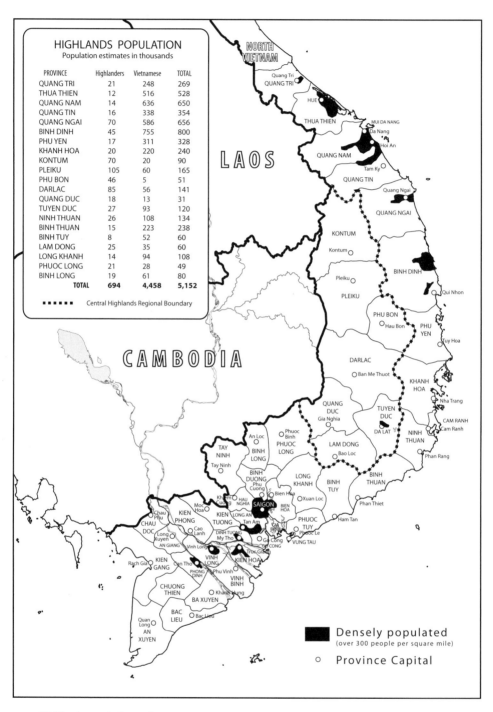

HIGHLANDS POPULATION
Population estimates in thousands

PROVINCE	Highlanders	Vietnamese	TOTAL
QUANG TRI	21	248	269
THUA THIEN	12	516	528
QUANG NAM	14	636	650
QUANG TIN	16	338	354
QUANG NGAI	70	586	656
BINH DINH	45	755	800
PHU YEN	17	311	328
KHANH HOA	20	220	240
KONTUM	70	20	90
PLEIKU	105	60	165
PHU BON	46	5	51
DARLAC	85	56	141
QUANG DUC	18	13	31
TUYEN DUC	27	93	120
NINH THUAN	26	108	134
BINH THUAN	15	223	238
BINH TUY	8	52	60
LAM DONG	25	35	60
LONG KHANH	14	94	108
PHUOC LONG	21	28	49
BINH LONG	19	61	80
TOTAL	**694**	**4,458**	**5,152**

■ ■ ■ ■ ■ ■ Central Highlands Regional Boundary

■ Densely populated
(over 300 people per square mile)

○ Province Capital

Highlands population, 1965

1

Vietnam and the Central Highlands to 1954

The Peoples Involved

The main participants in the struggle considered in the pages that follow were the Vietnamese, who became engaged in a civil war; the Highlanders (the original inhabitants of the region), who were sucked into it (in many cases against their will); and the Americans, who intervened because their leaders saw the conflict in Vietnam as part of a global struggle against communism. It is presumed that for most readers the Americans need no introduction. The provision of a little background on the Vietnamese and the Highlanders seems in order, if only to show why they were so different and why the relationships between them were often so fraught.

The Vietnamese before the French Conquest

For much of their history, the Vietnamese had little knowledge of the Central Highlands region. They as a distinct people and Vietnam as a political entity had originated hundreds of miles to the north in the region known as Tonkin, especially in the delta of the Hong (or Red) River. For about a thousand years, between the late second century BC and the early tenth century, the ancestors of the modern Vietnamese were under the control of the Chinese Empire. By the time they were able to break away and form a distinct kingdom in the early tenth century, the Chinese had exerted a very powerful—indeed, formative—influence on their language and culture.[1]

Over the centuries successive rulers of China attempted to regain control over the Vietnamese. It is important to the Vietnamese national consciousness that, in some very bloody wars, they ultimately defeated these efforts. Displaying impressive military prowess and great determination, they also expanded

1

their territory southward along the coastal plain between the Truong Son mountain range and the sea. By 1471 they had largely broken the power of the once mighty Champa, a group of Hindu kingdoms forged by the Cham ethnic group.[2]

Even though Vietnam was divided into northern and southern states for a lengthy period in the seventeenth and eighteenth centuries, its southward expansion continued. By the late eighteenth century the Vietnamese had conquered the Mekong Delta, taking it from Cambodia.[3] The Nguyen Dynasty, the last imperial dynasty in Vietnamese history, gained control of the whole of Vietnam in the early nineteenth century and ruled from Hue in central Vietnam. Initially it seemed powerful and splendid. But as that century wore on, like the Manchu Dynasty in China, it could neither isolate Vietnam from the European powers nor match their naval and military technology.[4]

The French Takeover of Indochina

In the second half of the nineteenth century Vietnam, Laos, and Cambodia all fell under French rule, and the Nguyen Dynasty's emperors became no more than puppets of the French. The French conquest began under Napoleon III, whose forces captured Saigon in 1859. By 1867 the French had taken control of the whole of Cochin China, roughly the southern third of Vietnam. They also secured a protectorate over Cambodia. The French conquest of Vietnam was completed under the Third Republic, after the fall of Napoleon III's Second Empire during the Franco-German War of 1870–1871. In 1883 France used military force to get Emperor Tu Duc to accept a protectorate over the rest of Vietnam. In 1893 the French rounded off their empire in Indochina by establishing a protectorate over Laos. Although Cochin China was technically a colony and the rest of Vietnam, Cambodia, and Laos were protectorates, the French endeavored to establish a fairly unified administrative system throughout the area they ruled.[5]

The Nguyen rulers had claimed a sort of suzerainty over the Central Highlands and had established settlements on the region's eastern edge. But the Vietnamese had not yet colonized it on a substantial scale. The reasons are not hard to understand. The main economic basis of Vietnamese life was wet rice agriculture. The main direction of their expansion over the centuries had therefore been south, along the coastal plain and into the wetlands of the Mekong Delta, where the terrain was particularly suitable for that activity. To many Vietnamese, the Central Highlands, by contrast, seemed distinctly alien—the abode of evil spirits. The French would explore the region thoroughly for the first time and open it, for better or worse, to development and colonization.[6]

The Traditional World of the Highlanders

Before they fell under French rule, the peoples of the Central Highlands were certainly primitive compared with the Vietnamese or the Cambodians. But they were Iron Age rather than Stone Age peoples and could not be considered "precontact" populations in the sense of having had no relations with more sophisticated societies outside their forests. Champa had in fact maintained outposts deep in the Highlands, had sought tribute from Highlanders, and had traded with them for a variety of commodities, including areca nuts, betel leaves, precious hardwoods such as ebony and eaglewood, cinnamon, elephant ivory, and rhinoceros horn.[7] After Champa's destruction the Vietnamese took over this trade. But the illiterate Highland societies seemed to the Vietnamese to fall well below their Chinese-influenced standards of what it meant to be civilized. Highlanders often wore little clothing, in some cases had darker skin, and practiced body modifications such as filing their teeth and plugging their earlobes. The Vietnamese called the Highlanders *Moi*, which means savages, and often made little effort to conceal their disdain.[8]

Although the Highlanders were not precontact peoples before the French arrived, they were to a large extent prehistoric. With the exception of the Chru, a small group that adopted the Cham script, they had no written language of their own, and what the lowland peoples of Indochina recorded about them was extremely limited. Linguistic research undertaken in the twentieth century indicates that some Highland peoples, such as the Rhade and the Jarai, speak Austronesian languages. The speech of other groups, the largest being the Bahnar, belongs to the Mon-Khmer group of Austroasiatic languages (which have rather more in common with Vietnamese).[9]

Western scholars have also undertaken ethnographic and anthropological studies, and a certain amount is known about the traditional customs and ways of life of the various Highland groups. Once French colonization gained pace after the First World War, however, these customs tended to change quite rapidly. With large-scale Vietnamese immigration to the Highlands from the second half of the 1950s and with war raging there from the early 1960s, it was very hard for traditional ways to survive.[10]

Even the most thorough and scholarly studies of the Highland peoples are strikingly vague on some issues. Little is known about when most of the groups arrived in the Highlands, where they came from (except in the most general terms), how they moved around over time, or the history of their relations with one another.[11] The Highland peoples are often regarded as divided into tribes, but the term "tribe" needs to be used cautiously. The Jarai, the most numerous of the Highland peoples, were certainly capable of identifying who among their neighbors was Jarai and who was not. But there were a number of Jarai subgroups that had different customs and spoke somewhat different dialects.[12] At the time of the Second Indochina War, the Jarai, like most other Highland groups, had no "tribal" chiefs or policy-making bodies above the village level.

The Jarai did have some priest-like or shamanic offices that, though not passed down from father to son, were held continuously over centuries. These shamans were called kings: the King of Fire, the King of Water, and the King of Wind. The first two commanded respect over a large area of the Highlands and apparently not just among the Jarai. But their authority involved primarily relations between human beings on the one hand and the spirit world and nature on the other. Though they may have exercised some form of political power on occasion, their primary function was not political in the sense that Westerners would understand it.[13]

A lack of centralized authority was the norm among the Highland ethnic groups in the mid-twentieth century, and in most respects, individual villages had probably always run their own affairs. In the nineteenth and early twentieth centuries, however, chiefs—in times of stress and for certain purposes—had authority over several villages and considerable geographic areas, raising war bands that were hundreds strong. Certain chiefdoms, though not necessarily passed from father to son, had endured within the same family or clan for several generations. The French tried to gain the cooperation of traditional chiefs and use them as intermediaries in running their administration in the Highlands.[14] The French administration was destroyed completely in 1945, and although it was revived thereafter, in many areas it had collapsed again by 1954. By the mid-1950s most Highlanders acknowledged the authority of a village chief or village council, but they did not recognize any tribal authority outside the village. As an American Special Forces handbook from the 1960s warned its readers:

> In Montagnard life, the village rather than the tribe is the important political, social, and economic unit. The villager's life is conditioned by the immediate environment; he knows that environment well—but little beyond. Thus, a really accurate picture of this complex culture would not deal only with a dozen or so tribal groups but also with the thousands of villages. Such an elaborate study is clearly impossible for reasons of space and insufficient information.[15]

As the village was the traditional center of Highland life, it needs attention here. Research suggests that villages of up to 180 houses were not unknown among the Bahnar in the precolonization period. Some traditional longhouses could house hundreds, so there may have been some villages with several thousand inhabitants. But the majority of Highland villages observed by Westerners or testified to by Highlanders in the twentieth century were much smaller. A village of 400 people appears to have been well above the average size.

Observers found it almost impossible to generalize about the way Highland villages were sited and laid out, there being much variation according to tribal custom and local circumstances. Naturally, it was rare for a village to be located far from a reliable source of fresh water. Usually surrounded by the fields tended by their inhabitants, villages were also rarely far from the edge of the forest, which served both as an additional source of food and as a refuge in case of danger. In some Highland cultures, particular areas of forest were regarded as integral to the villages that exploited them.

Traditional Highland longhouses were built of wood found locally, with bamboo usually playing a large part in their construction, and were thatched with dried long grass. The living quarters were well above the ground, supported on pilings, to keep the occupants safe from dangerous animals. A common arrangement was to have a long, central corridor dividing the interior, with compartments on each side, each compartment housing a nuclear family with its own hearth. The family groups sharing the longhouse depended on the kinship system observed in the particular village. Among those peoples observing a system of matrilineal descent (including the Rhade and the Jarai), a young married couple would likely live with the wife's parents; among those observing patrilineal descent, young couples normally lived with the husband's family. Most longhouses had a large common room for general gatherings and for the reception of guests. Many Highland groups also had a large "men's house" in the village that housed adolescent males and bachelors and served other communal functions. A smaller spirit house, where religious rituals were performed, was another feature of the villages of many Highland groups.[16]

Agriculture was based largely on the slash-and-burn system (in which trees were felled and burned to fertilize the soil), and rice was the main crop. In most cases this was "dry rice," which depended on rain for a healthy crop. But some Highland groups with access to sufficient water also practiced "wet rice" agriculture, involving paddies that were deliberately flooded. Manioc, maize, millet, sugarcane, and, by the twentieth century, tobacco were also cultivated. The Vietnamese sometimes labeled the Highlanders nomads. But for most Highland groups that cultivated essentially the same areas for generations, this was very misleading.

Chickens, pigs, goats, and buffalo were kept and eaten, although the last were normally reserved for special occasions. Women collected bamboo shoots, wild fruit, roots, herbs, and saffron from the forest. Men hunted deer, wild pigs, and other game and fished in the rivers. Highlanders used iron and steel to make farming implements, including machetes, and to fashion tips for spears and crossbow bolts. They had their own blacksmiths but apparently did not smelt their own iron, which they generally seemed to obtain through trade.[17]

The spiritual side of Highland life was intimately linked with social customs and social status. The Confucian and Buddhist beliefs held by the Vietnamese barely penetrated the Highlands, where religion remained animist. Spirits were associated with topographical features, trees, stones, and animals, as well as with dead people. As an American handbook put it: "These spirits make explicable to these people the inexplicable. The spirits themselves may be good, bad or neutral; they are usually ranked in some sort of hierarchy, and they are always present. They must be appeased."

Certain individuals were believed to have "more intimate contact with these spirits" than others and were considered particularly adept at appeasing them. Such magicians or shamans were awarded much respect. Most Highland groups also believed in witches who could use their spiritual powers to harm others. To keep the world in harmony, Highlanders believed it necessary to perform a variety of rituals and ceremonies. Sacrifice was an integral part of many of these. The sacrifice of a water buffalo had particular weight and brought social prestige to the person who provided the animal.

The consumption of alcohol and getting seriously drunk were important parts of many Highland rituals and festivals. A variety of home-brewed alcoholic drinks were consumed, but the most common was rice wine. Normally this was drunk through straws from large jars, allowing several people to imbibe at once. Among at least some Highland groups this sort of drinking was considered a recreational activity or social ritual that did not necessarily have religious significance.[18]

Given that the village was the basic sociopolitical unit, the village headman was an important individual. He was normally selected by a council of elders or by the adult population as a whole. The headman represented the village, officiated at rituals, took the lead in war, and helped settle disputes between families. The headman and village council arranged for the distribution of cultivable land among families in the village. Private ownership of land in the sense understood in the West was not common in Highland societies. Below the headman and the council of elders in terms of social status were the other married men in the village. Below them were bachelors and slaves; the latter were mostly debtors, prisoners of war, or the children of slaves. The French made an effort to stop the slave trade and ban slavery in the Highlands during the first half of the twentieth century, but it had not been completely eradicated by the end of French rule.[19]

Some elite Highlanders became members of the French administration, which eventually supplanted the role of the traditional chiefs. So by the mid-twentieth century the village headman was the most powerful traditional native authority figure with whom most Highlanders would have been acquainted. Although this meant that, for some Highlanders, their political world had narrowed, this was not true for all. Some Highlanders were capable of thinking outside the boundaries of their particular villages and even beyond their particular tribes.[20]

Vietnamese-Highlander Relations before the Twentieth Century

By the eighteenth century some Vietnamese had traveled up the river valleys from the coastal plain and founded villages in the Highland region. The military village of Tay Son in the An Khe valley, home of a famous family of rebels against the Nguyen lords, was one of these. The Vietnamese, like the Cham before them, also engaged in commerce with Highland peoples, trading for a variety of traditional Highland products.

From the Vietnamese point of view, it was important to have military posts on the edges of the Highlands. In addition to resenting Vietnamese encroachments, some Highland groups raided for and traded in Vietnamese slaves. Vietnam's rulers also sought to regulate contact between Vietnamese and Highlanders, fearing that Vietnamese customs and standards might be degraded by too much contact with barbarians. Daring Vietnamese itinerant traders sought profits by bartering for forest products in the Central Highlands. But before the twentieth century, much of the region had never been systematically explored or charted, and other than the Catholic mission station at Kontum (which was established by French missionaries rather than by the Vietnamese), there were no towns.

To what extent the Vietnamese exerted real sovereignty in the Central Highlands before the French takeover is not entirely clear. It is certain that the Jarai Kings of Fire and Kings of Water had been bringing presents to the Nguyen court on a regular basis at least since 1751 (while Vietnam was still divided into two states), and it is possible that this practice had started centuries earlier. It continued when the Nguyen Dynasty ruled a united Vietnam in the nineteenth century. When the French established control over the Vietnamese monarchy, they based their claim to administer and colonize the Central Highlands upon it. But as already noted, the Kings of Fire and Water were not kings in the Western sense. They lived modestly, like other Highlanders, and had little political authority as that concept was understood by the Vietnamese or Westerners. In the early nineteenth century the Nguyen Dynasty apparently regarded itself as having some sort of dominion over at least the Jarai Highlanders because of the tribute their kings paid. But based on the logic that they had received diplomatic gifts from those countries, they also liked to regard France, Britain, and Burma as tributaries.[21]

The French in the Highlands to 1940

It seems likely that before the French conquest, whatever its pretensions, the Nguyen Dynasty had little or no effective control over the lives of the vast majority of the peoples of the Central Highlands. By the 1880s, however, the French were actively exploring the region, and by the early twentieth century they were making fairly determined attempts at penetration, economic development, and, where necessary, "pacification."

French probing into the Highlands was accompanied, in some instances, by Vietnamese settlement. The Highlanders' reaction to both was sometimes violent. French Catholic missionaries had been based at Kontum since the mid-eighteenth century, so this was seen as a logical place to begin colonization and economic development. In 1900 and 1901, however, warriors of the Sedang tribe attacked and destroyed a number of Vietnamese villages north of Kontum. In early 1901 the French established a military post, with Vietnamese troops, on the Psi River near Kontum; its purpose was to protect Vietnamese villages and to prevent the Sedang from trading Vietnamese slaves to their Halang and Jarai neighbors. In May of that year, however, the Sedang overran the French post and inflicted twenty-four wounds on its commander; although he was taken to Kontum for medical help, he ultimately succumbed. In his absence the Sedang attacked the post again and burned it to the ground.

As late as 1914 some entire tribes (the Sedang and Mnong among them) were refusing to submit to French authority. On 5 August 1914 Henri Maitre, one of the most famous French explorers of the Highlands, was killed by a powerful Mnong chief whose warriors then overran a nearby military post. The following year a senior French official was ambushed and killed by warriors led by the same chief. Expanding their imperium in the Highlands clearly required considerable effort, and, faced with much more serious problems closer to home, the French largely stopped trying for the duration of the First World War.

Armed clashes were not the whole story of French involvement in the Central Highlands in the early twentieth century. Violence appears to have been only sporadic and small in scale. The Highland chief whose warriors killed Maitre may have had as many as 500 at his command at one time. But this was exceptional. Most chiefs probably commanded only a few score, and it quickly became obvious to the more intelligent of them that their warriors' crossbows and spears were no match for the rifles of French-controlled armed forces. However much they resented their intrusion, many Highland leaders saw the inevitability of some sort of accommodation with the French. By 1914 the French had organized a provincial administration in the Highlands, and in most areas their efforts at pacification were generally effective.

By 1914 French administrative centers at Kontum, Ban Me Thuot, and Dalat were growing into small towns, and French commercial firms were beginning to establish plantations. The French were also attempting to establish regular and reliable access from the coastal plain to their Highland towns. They were constructing roads and, in the case of Dalat, a railway branch from the main Hanoi-Saigon line. Rather than shattering preexisting leadership structures, the French approach was to identify local chiefs and use them as intermediaries between French officials and the bulk of the population. As some of the French demands were irksome, this did not always help the chiefs' images with their own people.

For most Highlanders the taxes imposed by the French were the first they ever had to pay. As in the rest of their empire in Indochina, the French also imposed the corvée, or compulsory labor, for several days each year. This normally consisted of building roads and other public works, but it might involve plantation work too. Many Highlanders were not particularly healthy or robust, as dietary deficiencies and tropical illnesses were fairly common. They often found this labor very hard. It could also be dangerous. There were some fatalities for which the French appear to have offered little or no compensation to the families concerned.[22]

On the positive side, the French made some real efforts to administer justice in local disputes. They attempted to learn and codify tribal law and used native chiefs as judges. The French also established schools and offered education to the children of the Highland elites. In many respects the model French administrator of the period was Leopold Sabatier, who took charge of the province of Darlac in 1914. Although this province had been in existence since 1899, it had undergone little development since then. By extracting greater tax revenue from the Highlanders, Sabatier expanded public works, putting particular stress on improving the roads. At the same time, he adopted a paternal and benevolent attitude toward the Rhade, the main Highland people in the area, and, in general, maintained fairly good relations with them.

Sabatier demonstrated respect for Rhade law and customs and sought positive Rhade cooperation in his efforts to develop the province. As part of his paternalism toward the Rhade, he severely restricted Vietnamese immigration. He believed that, with French education and training, the Rhade could develop a modern, productive economy that would be mutually beneficial for the Highlands and for France. He was instrumental in providing schooling for members of the Rhade elite at Ban Me Thuot, the settlement that served as his provincial capital. He took steps to develop a written Rhade language and to codify Rhade law in written form. He was also the first to create a Garde Indigene (militia) unit manned by Highland personnel.

Sabatier had critics among both Highlanders and Frenchmen. His style resembled that of an oriental potentate, and he could be arrogant. He apparently took several young Rhade girls as mistresses and fathered a daughter by one of them. He was not a devout Catholic, and the missionaries suspected him of Freemasonry, which they detested. In retrospect, Sabatier generally epitomized the most acceptable face of French imperialism in the Central Highlands. In 1926, however, he was relieved of his post and sent back to France. Darlac, like the rest of the Highlands, was opened to colonization.[23]

The 1920s and 1930s saw the granting of large blocks of land to French companies for use as tea, coffee, and rubber plantations. At the same time the French developed a more formal administrative system in which the traditional roles of Highland chiefs and village headmen were somewhat diminished, although Highlanders were brought into the French administrative system as "canton chiefs." Change led to discontent. Resentment of the land grants to French companies caused some members of the Highland elite to withdraw their children from French schools. The French, however, persisted in their educational efforts, and not without success. Some Highlanders educated in French schools became very effective teachers.

The French were always able to find educated, elite members of the largest and most important tribes—the Rhade, the Jarai, and the Bahnar—who were willing to work with them. Farther south, near the attractive, flourishing town of Dalat, which served as a recreational hill station for French officials employed on the hot, humid coastal plain, the French established particularly good relations with the leaders of the Chru, a small but exceptionally sophisticated tribe. By 1930 the French were able to form a regular military unit from Highlanders loyal to their regime.

Among many Highlanders, however, the corvée remained intensely unpopular. Colonization and the development of plantations made some tribesmen fear that their lands would be taken away and their traditional way of life destroyed. There was a renewed outbreak of violence northeast of Kontum in the late 1920s. Vehicles traveling on the new roads were ambushed, the roads themselves were cut, telegraph poles were felled and their wires removed, and Vietnamese colonists were attacked.

In March 1929 the Garde Indigène mounted a pacification effort aimed at the village of Kon Bar, a center of the insurgency. For the first time a Highland village was bombed from the air. In 1931 there was revolt in the southern part of the Highlands involving Mnong and Stieng tribesmen. French troops were ambushed, and French posts and plantations were attacked. The revolt lasted until June 1935, when a French military operation involving some loyal Highland troops reportedly killed the rebellion's Mnong leader, Pu Trang Lung. In the late 1930s a strange millenarian religion known as the Python God movement swept through much of the Highlands but did not inspire actual armed revolt.

While coping with dissidence in the Highlands, the French continued to open schools, including village schools designed (quite successfully) to address the Highlanders' reluctance to send their children to boarding schools in the towns. The town schools, however, continued to be very important. The French sent some graduates of their secondary schools, generally members of elite families, for more advanced study at colleges at Qui Nhon and Hué on the coastal plain. There, the Highland students mixed with Vietnamese youth and, in many cases, learned to speak Vietnamese.

These beneficiaries of French education became the next generation of Highland leaders. Like their Vietnamese counterparts, they learned to think independently of their French masters. Some later joined the Viet Minh, while others became involved in movements for Highland autonomy. Even so, the level of indigenous opposition to French rule in the Central Highlands before 1940 was well within the capacity of the French to contain and "pacify." External factors, particularly militant, Communist-directed Vietnamese nationalism, ultimately brought France's rule in this region to an end. Vietnamese nationalism became a serious threat mainly because of the impact on Indochina of the Second World War.[24]

The Impact of the Japanese, 1940–1945

After the defeat of France in the German military campaign of May–June 1940, the collaborationist Vichy regime became the effective government of France. The French colonial authorities in Indochina accepted the authority of that regime. But their willingness to align themselves with the Axis side in the Second World War did not save Indochina from Japanese intrusion. The French briefly tried to resist Japanese demands for military bases, but they were forced to accede. Even so, the Japanese left the administration of Indochina largely in French hands until 9 March 1945. At that point, realizing that the French authorities in Indochina were now trying to assist the Allies (by this time, clearly the winning side), the Japanese pounced. They shattered the French administration and imprisoned most French officials. In relation to the size of the region, the Japanese were not present in large numbers, but even a handful of them were capable of inspiring considerable awe. Over the next few months their authority was hardly challenged in the Highlands or elsewhere in Indochina.

The situation thus became rather favorable to those who militantly opposed the restoration of French rule. The Japanese were, at this stage, prepared to look benevolently on fellow oriental peoples who rejected European colonial rule. Indeed, on 10 March 1945 the Japanese officially informed Emperor Bao Dai, up to this point a puppet of the French, that Vietnam could celebrate its national independence. Bao Dai then formed a government under Tran Trong Kim that appeared to be progressive in its intentions but limited in terms of its real power and actual achievements.[25]

Most French officials in the Highlands were quickly rounded up, but others escaped into the jungle. It is impossible to generalize about the Highlanders' reaction to the Japanese coup. Most of those serving in French military and militia units seemed to try to remain loyal. Some were able to melt into the forest; others were imprisoned, and the Japanese reportedly beheaded at least one. Some units of troops from the Central Highlands then serving in northern Vietnam were able to flee into southern China, where the Chinese looked after them until the war was over. Other Highlanders who had done military service with the French were prepared to cooperate with the Japanese and joined military units under their control. Nor was the ordinary civilian population of the Highlands solidly loyal to the French. The Japanese offered rewards for French officials and officers who, after the coup of 9 March, had fled into the forest, and some Highlanders brought Frenchmen in and collected the rewards.[26]

The Rise of the Viet Minh, 1941–1946

The Vietnamese had never been entirely quiescent under French rule. There had been some major revolts, which the French had usually put down with great severity. By 1945 there was a wide variety of Vietnamese nationalist, anticolonial groups. The most skillful Vietnamese leader, however, was an individual who, beginning in 1943, called himself Ho Chi Minh. A committed Communist and long-term Comintern member, he had also always portrayed himself as a Vietnamese nationalist. Before he adopted the name Ho Chi Minh, his previous pseudonym had been Nguyen Ai Quoc: Quoc the Patriot. Like many twentieth-century Communist leaders, he apparently saw no contradiction between Marxism–Leninism and nationalism.

Ho Chi Minh spent most of the Second World War in China, where, in 1941, he managed to get a number of other Vietnamese political parties to join a Communist-dominated coalition called the Viet Nam Doc Lap Dong Minh (League for Vietnamese Independence), or Viet Minh for short. In 1942 Vo Nguyen Giap, a Communist colleague of Ho's, began to organize and train guerrilla groups in the Highlands of Tonkin, on the Chinese border. According to some reports, Ho Chi Minh returned to Vietnam from China in October 1944.

When Japan capitulated on 15 August 1945 the Viet Minh had a nationwide political network that was better organized than that of any competing nationalist group. The politically astute Viet Minh leadership curried favor with the Americans by offering the Office of Strategic Services (OSS), the forerunner of the Central Intelligence Agency (CIA), intelligence on the Japanese. In exchange the OSS supplied the Viet Minh with some weapons and radios. But the Viet Minh appear to have done very little, if any, actual fighting against the Japanese. The latter were extremely dangerous military opponents but, by 1945, were not a long-term problem for the Viet Minh; their ultimate defeat seemed inevitable. After their surrender in August of that year, the Japanese permitted fairly large quantities of their arms to fall into Viet Minh hands, further strengthening that organization's position.

In Hanoi the Viet Minh were able to take control. As soon as the Japanese capitulated, armed Viet Minh units made their presence felt in the city. The Viet Minh organized big demonstrations on 17 August, and some of their leaders appeared on a public platform there for the first time. The Viet Minh's Communist leadership never had the slightest compunction about using violence against rival Vietnamese nationalists, and within days such groups had largely been driven off the streets. Over the next few years the Viet Minh's domination of Vietnamese nationalism would be consolidated by assassination—the leaders of a Trotskyite group and of the armed Hoa Hao religious sect among their many victims.

The evident strength of the Viet Minh discouraged Tran Trong Kim, who in March had established a regime in Hue with Bao Dai's approval. But on 22 August he resigned. Bao Dai accepted his resignation and invited Ho Chi Minh to form a government. On 24 August Bao Dai abdicated. Ho Chi Minh announced the formation of a provisional government on 29 August and declared Vietnamese independence on 2 September, deliberately borrowing some of Thomas Jefferson's words from the comparable American declaration of 1776. He called the new state the Democratic Republic of Vietnam.[27]

The Allies, however, agreed that Vietnam should return to French rule. The British assumed responsibility for the country as far north as the sixteenth parallel, and the Chinese Nationalists assumed responsibility north of that. The British arrived in the South with a division of Indian troops on 12 September, and the first French troops arrived on British warships on 21 September. With British cooperation, the French commenced efforts to reestablish control of southern Vietnam, and street fighting broke out in Saigon almost immediately.

The Viet Minh had more armed forces at its command than any other Vietnamese nationalist group. Yet Ho Chi Minh did not consider his organization ready for an all-out war with a European power. He was very keen to avoid war, if possible, and hoped to secure the future of his regime by negotiation.

Although the French had gained control of the cities of Cochin China, their former colony in the South, by the end of 1945, they entered into negotiations with the Viet Minh before attempting to take the rest of the country. The details of these negotiations need not concern us. Suffice it to say that by the end of 1946 they had broken down, and an all-out war between France and the Viet Minh ensued.[28]

Early Stages of the First Indochina War, 1946–1950

The Viet Minh developed local militia forces and "regional force" units consisting of full-time light infantry troops operating in battalion strength across much of the country. But the principal seat of war was Tonkin. By the end of 1950 the Viet Minh were in control of much of northern Tonkin, including the Chinese border. This was crucial. From 1949, after a huge civil war, China had a Communist government. Mao Zedong, its leader, was ideologically committed to supporting his fellow revolutionaries in Vietnam.

With lavish Chinese military aid, the Viet Minh were able to develop, in northern Tonkin, a powerful, more or less conventional, "regular" army (the immediate predecessor of the People's Army of Vietnam [PAVN]). It consisted of several 10,000-man divisions, incorporating artillery and engineers as well as infantry, and was capable of taking on French forces in full-scale battle. It became part of the Viet Minh style of war to integrate the operations of local militia, regional force units, and "regulars."[29] The Vietnamese Communists would continue to employ this style in the Second Indochina War.

An early political development in the Highlands during the First Indochina War was the formation of the Pays Montagnard du Sud-Indochinois (PMSI) in 1946, which separated the administration of the Central Highlands from that of the rest of Vietnam. What the French intended to accomplish by this is not entirely clear. In any case, the arrangement did not last very long.

War in the Central Highlands, 1950–1954

The major battles of the Franco–Viet Minh War were fought in Tonkin. The Central Highlands region was always a backwater in comparison. There were still relatively few Vietnamese in the region, and for the first few years of the war, Viet Minh activity there was very low key. By 1950, however, French control of the region was increasingly contested as Viet Minh propaganda teams and small military units became active. Roads were frequently mined and ambushes laid. Outposts were attacked. The French were particularly concerned that the Viet Minh might seize the town of Ban Me Thuot, so they established defensive posts around it.

In 1949 the French had conceded a limited form of independence to Vietnam within the French Union. Bao Dai, who had briefly joined the Viet Minh government at one point, agreed to be its head of state. Despite his earlier abdication, he once again assumed the title of emperor, leaving the question of whether the new Vietnamese state would ultimately be a monarchy or a republic undecided. Bao Dai adopted the Highland town of Dalat as his place of residence, and the Central Highlands theoretically became his crown domain, although the region continued to be administered by French officials. In late 1950, with French backing, Bao Dai began to establish an army for the new Vietnamese state, which attracted some Vietnamese who were unhappy at the prospect of a Communist future. In March 1951 his military staff and its French mentors decided to establish the 4th Vietnamese Light Division to operate in the Highlands.[30] This unit became known as the Division Montagnarde, as most of its personnel were not ethnic Vietnamese but Highlanders from a variety of tribes, including the Rhade, Jarai, Bahnar, Mnong, Sedang, Maa, and Hre. Ultimately, the division numbered 9,000 men and operated four infantry battalions, in at least three of which the rank and file consisted entirely of Highlanders. Although most of the officers were French or Vietnamese, there were some Highlanders as well.

Some of the 4th Division's officers were trained at the Vietnamese army's principal military academy at Dalat (the equivalent of West Point) and others at the Ecole Militaire Regionale du Lac at Lac Thien in southern Darlac Province. One of the most senior officers was Touprong Ya Ba, commander of the 7th Battalion; a member of the Chru ethnic group, he had been serving in the French army since 1941. The formation of the 4th Division brought together Highlanders from many different ethnic groups and helped develop an increasing sense of Highland solidarity. The Rhade tended to be the most educated, sophisticated, and politically conscious of the major Highland groups, and the Rhade language became something of a lingua franca for this Pan-Highland elite.

The 4th Division's operational area was huge. In its first year of operations it claimed 1,000 Viet Minh killed and 600 captured. With no artillery or heavy weapons of its own, and with a relatively loose, informal style of discipline, the troops of the 4th Division could be effective in counterguerrilla operations but were less suited to more conventional, high-intensity fighting.

In addition to the 4th Division, there were a number of smaller Highland military and paramilitary units. Some of these were essentially home guard units providing security for towns and villages. But they also included the Detachements Legeres de Brousse (Light Brush Detachments), designed to be more mobile and play a more aggressive role, including performing reconnaissance in remote areas and ambushing small enemy units.

From mid-1951 the French also began to organize commando (or maquis) units, which were designed to remain in the field for long periods, gather intelligence, disrupt Viet Minh communications, and destroy weapons and food stocks. These units, which had a total strength of somewhere between 15,000 and 25,000 by the end of the war, operated in various parts of Indochina and were recruited from several ethnic groups. A substantial proportion, however, were Highlanders operating in the Central Highlands region. Commando units varied in size from 10 to 1,000 riflemen, with the average being about 400. A French officer or noncommissioned officer was normally in command. In mid-1952 these units were grouped for administrative purposes under an organization initially called the Groupement de Commandos Mixtes Aeroporte (Composite Airborne Commando Group); in December 1953 its name was changed to the Groupement Mixte d'Intervention. The overall commander was Major Roger Trinquier, who developed a reputation as one of France's foremost experts on unconventional warfare.

The French eventually considered some of their Highland troops capable of relatively high-intensity warfare. In the later years of the war the French high command began to establish mechanized formations known as Groupements Mobiles (GM), and two of these—GM-41 and GM-42—had predominantly Highland personnel. GM-42 was involved in very heavy fighting in the Central Highlands in the last few months of the war.[31]

During the First Indochina War, therefore, the French and Bao Dai made determined appeals for Highlander support, recruiting many into their armed forces and bringing a considerable number into their civil administration. It would be wrong to suppose, however, that all Highlanders rallied to them. The Viet Minh also directed propaganda at Highlanders and raised Highland troops.

Highlanders certainly had grievances that the Viet Minh could exploit. Many of these arose from the war itself. The corvée, sometimes known as the "leprosy" of the Highlands, had always been an unpopular aspect of French rule. This intensified in wartime, when Highland labor was used not only for road maintenance but also for cutting new trails through the forest, building emergency airstrips, and transporting supplies. Considerable numbers of Highlanders reportedly died during wartime corvée service, although there are no statistics available. As the British did in their counterinsurgency campaign in Malaya at the same time, and as the South Vietnamese and the Americans did later during the Second Indochina War, the French destroyed villages and displaced the inhabitants to control the population and deprive the enemy of resources. This was often intensely unpopular with Highlanders, especially when it involved the loss of rice stocks and animals and the abandonment of ancestral tombs.[32]

In the early 1950s the Viet Minh recruited a number of Highland units in Kontum Province, north of the provincial capital, and the French found them to be dangerous enemies.[33] By early 1953, however, the Viet Minh were shifting toward more conventional high-intensity operations even in the Central Highlands, and for these they placed little reliance on Highland troops. In mid-January of that year, using battalions brought in from Quang Ngai Province on the coastal plain, they feinted toward the town of Pleiku and then carried out a major attack toward An Khe, on the eastern edge of the Highlands on the road between Pleiku and the coast. Much of the 4th Division was sent to counter this threat. The French command, however, soon realized that this division could not cope on its own and rushed paratrooper, artillery, and air elements to support it. This prevented the 4th Division from disintegrating and, for the time being, contained the threat.[34]

By late 1953 the French found themselves stretched very thin across Indochina. At the same time they were concentrating a substantial proportion of their best-equipped forces at Dien Bien Phu, in a valley of the Thai highlands of western Tonkin, on the Laotian border. This was a somewhat desperate gambit designed to tempt the Viet Minh to commit its "regular" divisions to a large-scale battle in which the French, with their superior firepower and airpower, hoped to win an impressive victory and alter the course of the war. In early December 1953, therefore, the French high command began stripping forces out of the Central Highlands. This presented the Viet Minh with opportunities.

In January 1954 the Viet Minh mounted an offensive designed to take control of the northern part of the Central Highlands. The main effort was initially in the Kontum sector. The small town of Dak To, north of the town of Kontum, the provincial capital, fell to the Viet Minh on 1 February. The French soon realized they could not hold the provincial capital of Kontum and abandoned it on 7 February. Although the French organized the evacuation of all French civilians and Vietnamese civil servants, they did not make adequate provision for their Highland civil servants. According to testimony later given by one of these Highlanders, Philippe Yuk, to American anthropologist Gerald Hickey, panic gripped the town. Civil servants, schoolteachers, and their families, together with Catholic missionaries and priests, fled into the forest.

There were apparently few Highlanders in the Viet Minh force that occupied Kontum. Perhaps aware of the potential problems of using an overwhelmingly Vietnamese army of occupation to control a predominantly Highland population, the Viet Minh sent one of their ablest converts, Nay Der, a talented Jarai schoolteacher from Cheo Reo, to Kontum. In April 1954 Nay Der stayed for three days in the house of a Bahnar leader who had died in 1945.

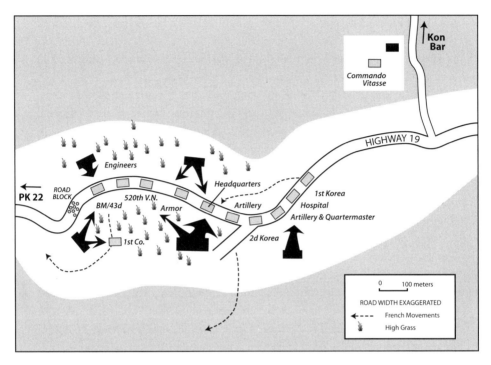

Ambush of GM-100 on Highway 19

According to Hickey: "He invited all the local highland leaders to attend a pig sacrifice in the front yard of the house. There, under the watchful eye of the Viet Minh guards, Nay Der extolled the virtues of the Viet Minh movement while all drank from the jars."[35]

While the Viet Minh occupied Kontum, the French concentrated their most powerful and mobile forces in the Highlands in and around the town of Pleiku. Among them were GM-11, which was predominantly Vietnamese; GM-42, which consisted mainly of Highland troops; and GM-100, a racially mixed force that included French troops who had fought in the Korean War. During the last few weeks of the First Indochina War, GM-100 would fight a series of bloody and desperate battles. Owing to the writings of journalist and historian Bernard Fall, the harrowing saga of GM-100 would become one of the better-known episodes of this war among educated American officers.[36] By May 1954 elements of GM-100 had already experienced some hard and bloody combat in the Highlands. But it seems particularly tragic that its grimmest wartime episodes occurred after the decisive battle of the First Indochina War was over. On 7 May 1954 the last French troops still resisting at Dien Bien Phu surrendered to the Viet Minh. While the French and the Viet Minh negotiated at Geneva, however, the war in the Highlands continued.

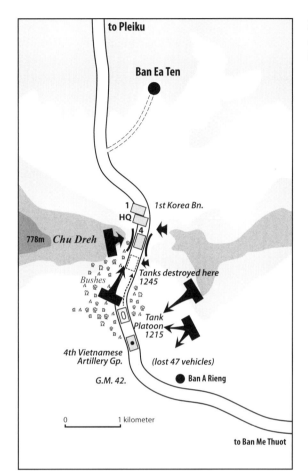

In late June the crisis point in the Highlands became the town of An Khe, on Route 19 between Pleiku and the coast, which was under threat from two Viet Minh regiments. The French decided to evacuate the town and pull back along the road to Pleiku, although they realized this would be a difficult operation. Between 24 June, when the evacuation commenced, and 28 June there was almost continuous fighting along Route 19, with GM-100 as well as the predominantly Highland GM-42 in the thick of it. Elements of the Viet Minh's 803d and 108th Regiments, the latter reinforced by the elite 30th Independent Battalion, mounted a series of fierce ambushes.

GM-100 suffered grievous casualties in a devastating ambush on 24 June but was not completely destroyed. Surviving elements linked up with GM-42 and other French forces retreating from An Khe. The last major ambush during the withdrawal to Pleiku occurred on 28 June 1954, at a point 30 km from Pleiku, where the jungle gave way to an open plain. The Viet Minh's 108th Regiment and 30th Independent Battalion were caught in the open by French B-26 fighter-bombers flying from bases in the coastal town of Nha Trang. Napalm strikes and strafing ripped through the Viet Minh forces, obliging them to abandon their attack and run for cover in the jungle. When the remnants of GM-100 limped into Pleiku on 29 June, however, the group had lost the bulk of its vehicles and heavy equipment and much of its personnel.

Even the retreat from An Khe, occurring a month and a half after the fall of Dien Bien Phu, was not the end of the ordeal. Some elements of GM-100, including the 1st Korea Battalion (a French unit that had fought in the Korean War before coming to Indochina), along with survivors of GM-42, formed a task force to clear Route 14 between Pleiku and Ban Me Thuot, an operation code-named Myosotis. The task force set off on 14 July. On 17 July the Viet Minh ambushed it at Chu Dreh Pass, inflicting especially heavy casualties on the luckless 1st Korea, which ceased to exist as a fighting unit. The final session of the Geneva conference was held on 21 July, the day the First Indochina War officially ended.[37]

By the end of the war the Viet Minh had conquered a substantial part of the northern Central Highlands, including the towns of Kontum and An Khe. The towns of Pleiku, Cheo Reo, Ban Me Thuot, and Dalat, however, were still occupied by French Union forces. Much of the rest of the region was a no-man's-land.

The Allegiance of Highlanders after the First Indochina War

The Viet Minh had adherents among the Highlanders and had raised some Highland military units but apparently did not rely on them heavily. In the most serious fighting that occurred in the Highlands, in the 1954 operations around Kontum and An Khe and in their campaign to destroy the forces retreating from An Khe to Pleiku, they used units of ethnic Vietnamese from outside the region. The French and the Bao Dai regime raised substantially larger Highland forces than did the Viet Minh and relied on them more heavily during the intense fighting of the last weeks of the war. Considerable numbers of Highlanders also served the anti-Communist regime in a civil capacity.

The Geneva Accords, which split Vietnam, at least temporarily, at the seventeenth parallel, left the Central Highlands in the South. Some Highlanders who had started their military or civil careers on the anti-Communist side preferred to stick with that side and continue their careers, although they would often find employment by the fiercely nationalistic and rather ethnocentric Vietnamese regime of Ngo Dinh Diem less congenial than working for the French.

The outcome of the First Indochina War, however, gave everyone good reason to believe that the Vietnamese Communists would eventually emerge as masters of the region. Regardless of whether Marxism-Leninism had an intrinsic appeal to them, some Highlanders thought it made sense to throw in their lot with the winning side. In the post-1954 period, moreover, the Communists initially appeared to be much more sensitive and respectful in their handling of the Highlanders than was the South Vietnamese regime. They certainly made bigger promises; however duplicitous these may have been, they probably gained some credence.

A third group of educated Highlanders, angry at Vietnamese colonization of their lands and at the loss of Highland life in Vietnamese quarrels, would call for a plague on both Vietnamese houses. Prepared to embrace Highlanders of all tribes as brothers, they would demand autonomy for their region and would be prepared to fight for it.[38]

Whatever their political views, all Highlanders and all Vietnamese living in the Highlands faced a grim future. They were cursed by strategic geography. The Central Highlands, a relative backwater for most of the First Indochina War, would become a major battleground in the second.

2

The Diem Regime and the Central Highlands, 1954–1960

The Geneva Accords and a Divided Vietnam

Few present on the last day of the Geneva Conference, 21 July 1954, could have felt confident that long-term peace had been restored to Indochina. The conference's final document, sometimes called the Geneva Accords, was divided into two parts. The first was titled "Agreement on the Cessation of Hostilities in Vietnam," which laid down the terms for a cease-fire. The military representatives of the Viet Minh and the French signed it, but their diplomatic representatives did not; nor did anyone else. This cease-fire agreement made the seventeenth parallel the dividing line between zones into which the opposing sides would regroup their forces—the Viet Minh north of it, the other side south of it. The second part of the document, entitled the "Final Declaration," contained a vaguely worded passage calling for nationwide elections to be held on 21 July 1956; these were apparently intended to allow all the people of Vietnam to choose a government for the country as a whole. Details of how the elections were to be held and procedures for monitoring them were not specified. Though diplomatic representatives of France, Britain, the United States, the Soviet Union, the People's Republic of China, Laos, Cambodia, and the two Vietnamese states were present, none of them signed the "Final Declaration," and it is not clear whether anyone really expected it to be acted on.[1]

The Central Highlands received no special attention at Geneva. As already noted, the great bulk of the region had not been part of any Vietnamese state before French colonization. From 1950 the French had considered most of the area to be part of a crown domain under Bao Dai's control but not an integral part of the state of Vietnam of which Bao Dai was head.[2] After 1954, however, successive regimes in Saigon treated it as part of Vietnam. No one in the international community seems to have protested this. From July 1956 the Vietnamese Communists regarded the anti-Communist regime in Saigon

22

as illegitimate everywhere and actively tried to bring it down. In so doing they were prepared to promise the indigenous peoples of the Central Highlands regional autonomy, even independence.[3] It is likely, however, that such promises on the part of the Communist leadership were no more than pure Machiavellian cynicism from the outset.

The Communists never denied in any international forum that the Central Highlands region was part of Vietnamese territory. Neither of the regimes in Vietnam, and no state in the international community, declared itself in favor of the Highlanders' right to secede from Vietnam. The Central Highlands was strategically vital to the conduct of the war in Vietnam, and both sides would try to manipulate and exploit the region's indigenous people for their own purposes. Yet it seems that only a handful of individuals from outside these ethnic groups seriously cared about their aspirations or their ultimate fate.

The French had not given up hope of exerting a substantial influence on the future of Indochina. Bao Dai, head of the old imperial family, was France's choice as head of the anti-Communist Vietnamese state. He remained in office after July 1954, as that state concentrated on making its authority effective south of the seventeenth parallel. The state's premier, however, Ngo Dinh Diem, a fifty-three-year-old bachelor from Nghe Anh Province in central Vietnam (also the birthplace of Ho Chi Minh), had a reputation for anti-French sentiments. A crucial factor in the situation was the United States. That superpower had been operating a military mission to the army of Bao Dai's state practically since its creation, and by 1954 the American taxpayer was funding most of the war against the Viet Minh.

Based on the logic that he who pays the piper calls the tune, it might be supposed that Diem was America's choice to lead South Vietnam. It would be more accurate to say that Diem was a choice the Americans endorsed, in some cases reluctantly. Their options were limited, their room for maneuver extremely restricted. Bao Dai offered Diem the premiership, and he accepted it on 19 June 1954. Although their relationship was uneasy, the two men had known each other for years. Bao Dai had made Diem the same offer in 1949 when the state was first established. Diem had rejected it then because, at that stage, he considered the regime insufficiently independent of France.[4]

The Rise of Ngo Dinh Diem

Though not as nationally famous as Ho Chi Minh, Diem had a certain stature in Vietnamese political circles. He came from a mandarin family, was reasonably well educated, and had served with some distinction as a province chief during the late 1920s and early 1930s. His family had been Catholic for two centuries, since before the French takeover, and he resented attempts by the French to manipulate Vietnam's Catholic minority to serve their interests. Though he chose not to become a priest, the devout Diem had apparently taken a vow of celibacy in his youth, with a view to devoting himself to God and his country. He accepted the post of Minister of the Interior from Emperor Bao Dai in 1933 but held it for only a few months. He reportedly resigned because the French would not delegate real power to Vietnamese officials. Thereafter he refused government employment for as long as the Vietnamese government was under French control.

In 1945, during the August Revolution, the Viet Minh kidnapped Diem and three of his brothers. The oldest brother, Khoi, who had been the province chief in Quang Nam, they beat to death. Diem's kidnappers took him from central Vietnam to Tonking. Ho Chi Minh interviewed him there and offered him a job in the Viet Minh government that was then in the process of forming. When Diem raised the issue of his older brother's recent murder, Ho tried to explain it away as one of those unfortunate occurrences that are bound to happen in revolutionary times. Diem was strongly influenced by Confucian as well by Catholic ethics. He reportedly told Ho Chi Minh that because Khoi had been the head of the family, his murder made it impossible for Diem to accept the offer.[5]

Ho Chi Minh had, of course, offered Diem a position in a Communist front organization, not real power. Yet the offer indicates that he took Diem seriously, not as a friend to be kept close but as an enemy to be kept closer. In many respects Diem deserved that sort of consideration. A genuine Vietnamese nationalist, he was brave, personally honest, not much interested in money, ambitious, fiercely determined, and, within limits, intelligent. He could also be enormously charming, and his good humor in the most trying of circumstances impressed many observers. His political career would end (as most do) in failure. In his case it would also terminate in premature and violent death, a murder perpetrated not by his avowed Communist enemies but by members of his own army in a coup backed by foreign erstwhile friends.

Diem had grave weaknesses that would contribute to this outcome. These flaws will emerge, with particular reference to the Central Highlands, in what follows. Yet it is perhaps more appropriate to view him as a tragic hero (with at least his fair share of hubris and blindness) rather than as a contemptible failure. Astute observers in the mid to late 1950s and early 1960s, Vietnamese and foreign, Catholic and non-Catholic, considered him South Vietnam's best hope for an independent future outside the "Bamboo Curtain."[6]

Establishing an effective regime that offered an alternative to communism in South Vietnam was a herculean labor, and it is perhaps unfair to blame Diem for not being, in the final analysis, Hercules. Observers in a good position to judge considered that the odds were stacked against him from the start. John Caswell, chief of the Central Intelligence Agency's Vietnam desk in July 1954, thought the Communists would be in control of South Vietnam within two years. The US ambassador, Donald Heath, seems to have been of the same opinion. John Foster Dulles, the US Secretary of State, put the chances of establishing a lasting anti-Communist regime in South Vietnam at one in ten.

Indeed, virtually all observers, foreign and domestic, gave Diem's regime little chance of surviving more than a few weeks and virtually no chance of making its authority effective. Paul Harwood, the chief of covert action in the CIA's Saigon station, was almost dismissive of the possibility of preventing a Communist takeover, observing that the "task is hopeless, but [the] effort must be made." Over much of South Vietnam there was no effective government in July 1954, and quite apart from the ambitions of the Communist Party, there were, at least in some parts of the country, massive obstacles to establishing one.[7]

One possible approach to developing an anti-Communist state in South Vietnam in 1954 was to build a coalition of groups with an interest in resisting a Communist takeover. South Vietnam was much more diverse than the North, with a substantial part of the population belonging to ethnic and religious minorities. Vietnam's Communist Party, which was overwhelmingly ethnically Vietnamese, was not disposed to be particularly tolerant of diverse belief systems, and it might have been possible to exploit minorities' fear of its rule. The Cao Dai and Hoa Hao religious sects, which had their own private armies and miniature state structures, had cooperated with the French against the Viet Minh. They almost certainly would have welcomed being invited to join an anti-Communist coalition government. The French had also worked closely with the Binh Xuyen, which sometimes posed as a religious sect but was really a sort of Vietnamese mafia with its own private army. Extraordinarily wealthy and powerful, it controlled not only large-scale opium, gambling, and prostitution operations in Saigon (including the House of Mirrors, reputedly the world's biggest brothel) but also the Saigon police.

The French, who still had more than 100,000 troops in South Vietnam in the second half of 1954, as well as some officials, thought the Saigon government should adopt an approach based on coalition building with such powerful groups and anyone else who might be prepared to resist a Communist takeover. Bao Dai and some senior Vietnamese army officers favored the same approach.[8]

This was not the road Diem wanted to take. He wanted to be a benevolent ruler for his people. But he wanted to be the *ruler*, not the first among equals in a broadly based coalition. Like a traditional Vietnamese or Chinese emperor, he placed great reliance on his family in running the state. He did not wish to persecute members of the Cao Dai or Hoa Hao sects or other minorities. He was content to have members of these minorities serve in his armed forces or in the civil service. But he intended to create a unitary state under his own authority. He was not inclined to tolerate states within his state. He wanted no autonomous areas. As far as the Central Highlands was concerned, it is critical to understand that Diem was a Vietnamese nationalist who wanted to create an essentially Vietnamese state. People from Highland ethnic groups could work within and serve that state, but only by assimilating themselves to its values and standards as Diem, the ruler, interpreted them.[9]

Consolidation of the Diem Regime

After a few rocky months in office, Diem fought a mini-war with the Binh Xuyen mafia in March–October 1955, the outcome of which greatly strengthened his position. Realizing that Diem was consolidating his control of the state, and that if his regime survived their days might be numbered, the Binh Xuyen mounted a preemptive strike in late March 1955, attacking government installations in various parts of Saigon. But most of the National Army remained loyal to Diem. He more than held his own in the first round of fighting. At the end of March, with the struggle clearly going against their former Binh Xuyen allies, the substantial French forces still present in Saigon at that time intervened to bring it to an end. When fighting was renewed in late April and May, however, the French were unable to prevent Diem's National Army from inflicting heavy damage on the Binh Xuyen. In July and August the Binh Xuyen mounted campaigns of terror bombing in Saigon, but thereafter its forces were driven out of the city altogether. By October, with the exception of small elements that had joined up with Communist forces, its resistance almost totally collapsed.[10]

Success against the Binh Xuyen saved Diem from imminent overthrow. For the time being, it made some of his American critics pipe down. The US ambassador, General "Lightning Joe" Collins, had so despaired of Diem that he had gone to Washington in April 1955 to try to persuade President Eisenhower to abandon him and look for someone else to run an anti-Communist administration in South Vietnam. Feeling obligated to support the views of the man on the spot, Eisenhower had reluctantly agreed. Dissent from Collins's position came mainly from the CIA, which had two separate offices in Saigon at this time, one under Paul Harwood and one under Edward Lansdale. Both provided detailed and timely reports of Diem's successes against the Binh Xuyen and advocated uncompromising support for Diem. Together they caused the Eisenhower administration to make a policy U-turn in Diem's favor.[11]

The defeat of the Binh Xuyen particularly strengthened the voice of Edward Lansdale in American councils. Having gained a good deal of credit for the defeat of Communist rebels in a recent campaign in the Philippines, he was regarded by some in the CIA as a counterinsurgency and nation-building expert. Allen Dulles, the Director of Central Intelligence, had sent him to Saigon on a mission independent of both the CIA's established station and the embassy. Lansdale had arrived in Saigon on 1 June 1954, and he quickly established a friendship with Diem, whom he came, within limits, to admire. Lansdale apparently agreed that Diem could not establish a viable, respectable state in South Vietnam while leaving the Saigon police and security apparatus in the hands of a local mafia; it was equally inappropriate for Diem to invite the illiterate river pirate who ran this mafia into a coalition government. Bao Dai and the French opposed Diem on these issues. In the aftermath of the Binh Xuyen's defeat, Lansdale encouraged Diem to break with both the ex-emperor and the former colonial power.

By late spring 1955 the Eisenhower administration, considerably influenced by Lansdale's reports, had become impatient with the continuing French involvement in Vietnamese affairs. Talks between Secretary of State John Foster Dulles and the French premier on 9–11 May led to an accelerated French military withdrawal. This might have become necessary in any case, given the intensifying war in Algeria. On 23 October 1955 Diem ran against Bao Dai in a referendum, which he probably rigged, to select the head of state. Declaring himself the winner by a very large majority, Diem made himself president, rather than just prime minister, of the embryonic state attempting to gain control of Vietnam south of the seventeenth parallel. On 26 October 1955, with Bao Dai now out of the political picture, Diem formally declared Vietnam a republic.[12]

While pushing Bao Dai and the French out of Vietnam, Diem was using the National Army to confront the Cao Dai and Hoa Hao sects. By mid-1956 the Cao Dai had come to terms without much actual fighting and allowed its armed forces to be absorbed into those of Diem's government. Against the Hoa Hao there was more actual combat, but apparently not of any great intensity or duration. The methods used by Diem's government in dealing with the Hoa Hao were not above reproach. His forces arrested one of their leaders, Le Van Ngo (also known as Ba Cut), during a parley, and he was promptly guillotined. According to some reports, this caused sufficient resentment on the part of a minority of Hoa Hao to make them throw in their lot with the Communists.

The Communist Party, indeed, at this particular time made a positive policy of embracing the sects. In general, however, it had limited success. Hoa Hao soldiers, like those of the Cao Dai, were absorbed into the Republic of Vietnam's armed forces, and most Hoa Hao fought on the anti-Communist side in the subsequent war. The Communists had more success making an alliance with some survivors of the Binh Xuyen's militia, and at least one of its leaders subsequently became a member of the Communist-organized National Liberation Front.[13]

At the same time, with no particular effort on the part of Diem's government, the essentially peacetime circumstances of 1954–1959 allowed South Vietnam's agriculture (much disrupted in 1941–1954) to bounce back to pre–Second World War levels of production. This benefited everyone in South Vietnam. By mid-1955 there seemed to be causes for optimism and reasons to applaud Diem. More Americans were added to his list of admirers. Diem was now sufficiently confident to refuse to have anything to do with nationwide elections in October 1956. He had not signed the "Final Declaration" at Geneva, and he insisted that any such elections could not possibly be fair in the North.

Perhaps surprisingly, in view of later events, protests of the Communist regime in the North over this issue were relatively muted during the next year or so. A brutally conducted Communist land reform program in North Vietnam had caused massive resentment and unrest, followed by considerable repression over much of the countryside. In Nghe Anh Province there was an actual peasants' revolt in autumn 1956. In these circumstances the prospect of international election monitors wandering around the North Vietnamese countryside was probably unappealing to the Communist regime. North Vietnam also had very little support from its Communist allies in the rest of the world for bringing this issue to a head at this time. It was too soon after the stresses and expenses of the Korean War and the First Indochina War. The Khrushchev regime in the Soviet Union was still trying to get established after Stalin's death and to deal with his appalling legacy. In 1956 there was serious unrest in parts of Communist eastern Europe.[14]

Diem versus the Communists on the Coastal Plain and the Mekong Delta, 1956–1960

Diem's regime was, nevertheless, now on a collision course with Ho Chi Minh and the Dang Lao Dong (Workers' Party), as the Vietnamese Communist Party now called itself. Agents of the Communist Party had never ceased operating in South Vietnam. But given the internal problems in the North and the lack of enthusiasm among Communist allies for another war at this time, Party policy from July 1954 had been one of opposing Diem's efforts to develop a viable anti-Communist state in South Vietnam while avoiding armed struggle. Diem, however, was far from naïve about that Party's long-term intentions toward him, and he took the initiative in attacking it. As early as July–August 1955, even before the struggle with the Binh Xuyen was over, Diem had begun phase one of an anti-Communist denunciation campaign in central Vietnam.

Judging by documents originating on the Communist side, Diem's campaign seems to have been remarkably effective in some areas. According to one source, half the Communist Party's Provincial Committee in Tay Ninh Province (which, incidentally, was a principal stronghold of the Cao Dai) was wiped out. The campaign was intensified in two later phases in 1955 and 1956. Hunting down and arresting Communist Party members so effectively must have required good intelligence on the part of Diem's security forces. At this stage, before a widespread and efficient Communist terror campaign imposed silence, such intelligence was apparently not lacking.

Obviously the Communists had to respond to the regime's countersubversion effort. In some areas they began to form armed gangs of thirty to forty members for self-defense and also, probably, to intimidate potential collaborators with the regime among the peasantry. But the manhunt became so intense that the Party found it necessary, in the short term, to virtually abandon some heavily populated areas. Its personnel in these areas retreated to former Viet Minh military bases in the Plain of Reeds southwest of Saigon; the U Minh forest, bordering the Gulf of Siam; and War Zones C and D, north of Saigon.[15]

According to Communist sources, during the Diem government's crackdown of 1955–1958, the Party lost 90 percent of its members in the South. The morale of the surviving members was inevitably low. It was made more so because the leadership in Hanoi would not authorize members to strike back by mounting a full-blown guerrilla war—the necessary Chinese and Soviet support was not yet forthcoming.

Yet from mid-1957 the Central Committee in Hanoi did authorize a program known as *Tru Gian*—killing tyrants. Its purpose was to curtail the power of the Diem regime by kidnapping and selective assassination. Assassination squads targeted government servants who presented a particular danger to the Party. Danger was construed in broad political, not narrow security, terms. A dedicated, charismatic schoolteacher who might win the hearts and minds of the young for the government was as likely to be targeted as an efficient officer of the Cong An, Diem's political police. Some sources indicate that, in general, honest, industrious, and respected officials (ultimately, the most dangerous) were disposed of quietly and deniably; the corrupt, arrogant, and unpopular were dealt with more publicly and agonizingly. The total number of assassinations carried out in 1957–1959 under this program is not certain. According to one analysis, however, there was an average of nineteen assassinations and twenty-eight abductions per month in 1959.[16]

Even at the peak of its apparent success in 1956–1957, Diem's regime had serious weaknesses. It lacked broadly based popular support, although it is not clear that any political movement had such support in South Vietnam at this time. Diem's rule was essentially a personal dictatorship. The National Assembly had no real power, and elections of legislators were obviously rigged. Of course, the bulk of Asia was run by dictatorships of one sort or another at this time. There was, in principle, no reason why Diem's regime should not survive, provided it ran an effective administration that addressed the country's economic and social problems. Most authorities agree, however, that Diem was not very successful in providing South Vietnam with an efficient, honest civil service and with reputable and effective local government.[17]

The regime undoubtedly had individual public servants of great energy, integrity, and ability.[18] But the evidence is overwhelming that it also had widespread, endemic corruption. For some officials, arrogance, aloofness, and even contempt characterized their approach to those they governed. This was a problem in their dealings with the Vietnamese peasantry and even more so in their relations with Highlanders. Diem's province and district chiefs were generally recruited from the educated classes and tended to be urbanites. Commonly they were not natives of the areas where they served.

The Communists pursued an opposite approach. They made a particular point of recruiting cadres from the peasantry, educating them to the necessary standard (usually in the North), and then sending them back to work in their home areas. This often gave the Communists a superior capacity to communicate with and motivate the poorer sections of the southern Vietnamese rural population, a crucial factor in the revolutionary struggle that gradually developed beginning in 1956. A similar approach gave them, as we shall see, greater initial success with Highlanders too.[19]

Some authorities have criticized Diem for the way he redrew the administrative map of South Vietnam. In 1954 there were thirty-two provinces south of the seventeenth parallel, varying in area from under 200 to over 8,000 square miles and varying in population from under 30,000 to over 1 million. Each province was divided into districts, numbering between two and ten. Diem increased the number of provinces by about a third (to forty-four) and the number of districts by a fifth. The main idea was apparently to achieve more rigorous and effective administration, although an increase in government patronage may have been a subsidiary aim. Some informed commentators have expressed doubt that the increase in administrative areas and officials made Diem's regime any more effective in the countryside, and they have suggested that, at the village level, the grip of the regime was weak over much of the country.[20]

Other historians, however, indicate that the problem was not that Diem's government failed, in the short term, to make its rule effective. The regime's writ did in fact run across most of the country by the end of 1956. The real problem, in this analysis, was that Diem pursued some inappropriate policies that ultimately played into the hands of the Communist Party. In other instances—for example, with regard to "land reform"—policy was headed in roughly the right direction but was not pursued vigorously enough.[21]

In some areas of South Vietnam, most notably the Mekong Delta, landholding was a very hot political and social issue. The Viet Minh had carried out major land redistribution in some areas during the First Indochina War. Landlords had fled the countryside—sometimes to the nearest Vietnamese city, and sometimes as far away as Paris. The apparent success of the Diem regime in reestablishing law and order brought these landlords back to the Vietnamese countryside. Some of them demanded just the current rents they were owed; others insisted on arrears going back several years—as far back as the First Indochina War. Although the Diem regime developed its own land reform policy, it was not sufficiently radical and was not executed with sufficient thoroughness and speed to defuse what was, at least in some areas of South Vietnam, a social time bomb.[22]

Diem regarded the demographic imbalance between the more populated North and the less populated South as a potential source of weakness, and he went to great lengths to promote the migration of a million or so anti-Communist Vietnamese, mostly Catholics, to the South. He also made great efforts to find these refugees land. Some of them were settled in the coastal plain or the Mekong Delta, and others were sent to the Central Highlands. Given the perpetual and insatiable land hunger of the rural Vietnamese and the Highlanders' great fear of being swamped by Vietnamese settlers, the refugee problem was bound to create jealousies and grievances that the Communists could exploit.[23]

Another issue the Communists were apparently able to utilize with considerable success was the anti-Communist manhunt that was terrifying their cadres in the South. Communist propaganda accused Diem's security forces of identifying all those who had served in the "Resistance" (i.e., with the Viet Minh in the First Indochina War) as enemies of the state. People who were widely regarded as heroes in their own communities were harassed, arrested, imprisoned, and sometimes tortured and killed.

It is impossible to know exactly how many former Viet Minh became innocent victims of Diem's anti-Communist witch hunt or to quantify this as a factor in the Communist Party's ability to rally peasant opinion against Diem's regime. The prejudice against former Viet Minh on the part of Diem's security forces was by no means total, and action against them was not as universal and indiscriminate as the Communists alleged. Some non-Communist former Viet Minh served Diem in civil and military capacities and gained considerable influence. Yet there is general agreement among historians that the hunt for

Communist agents resulted in many innocent victims and that outrage at their suffering helped real Communist cadres mobilize some sections of some rural communities against the regime.[24]

Another issue that, to a degree, played into the hands of the Communists was Diem's development of the Army of the Republic of Vietnam (ARVN) as a conscript army. In the early days of his regime the National Army had been largely a volunteer force, but by 1957, facing the possibility of active hostility by the Communist North, Diem saw the need for a large-scale expansion. Because the financial cost would otherwise be prohibitive, he thought it best to do this by conscription, which was enacted on 1 August 1957. Conscription, however, had serious political costs. There is little need to explain why it was unpopular. Family and local ties were very strong in Vietnamese society, and young men felt a particular wrench at the idea of being torn away from home. A serious war, moreover, seemed increasingly likely, and this prospect was frightening to any intelligent person with a healthy instinct for self-preservation.

Whereas the North was apparently able to enforce conscription successfully, in the South many young men absconded when they received their call-up notices. Often they remained close to home but in hiding. They were therefore outlaws as far as the Saigon government was concerned, and that made them very vulnerable to recruitment by the Communists. Service with Communist units would be no less dangerous, but it often allowed young men to remain in their own areas. Widespread draft evasion indicates that the Diem regime had not achieved full legitimacy in the eyes of many southern Vietnamese. These young men did not think the regime had an automatic right to their military services. Even more significantly, perhaps, they calculated that it did not have a sufficient grip, even by the late 1950s, to enforce its will in this matter.[25]

Thus the Communists had a raft of issues to exploit in their dealings with the Vietnamese of the coastal plain and the Mekong Delta. Certainly a large part of the population, probably a considerable majority, just wanted to avoid trouble and get on with everyday life. But as the new decade began, it seems that significantly greater numbers of people over large areas of the country were willing to risk their lives to oppose the Diem regime than to support it.

The Communist Party's Central Committee authorized a move to open armed struggle in the South during 1959. In most parts of the country Communist forces began this armed struggle—that is, serious guerrilla warfare as opposed to occasional assassinations—early in 1960. The results were dramatic. In some provinces there was a sudden and obvious collapse of government control over large areas of the countryside. Police, Civil Guard, and Self-Defense Force units became ineffective. Many of their arms fell into Communist hands. In some areas Communist leaders were rapidly establishing themselves as the real government. Vietnam was at war again, and the initiative seemed to be firmly in Communist hands.[26]

Diem's Government and the Central Highlands, 1954–1958

From July 1954 onward, new Vietnamese regimes North and South were confronted with the problem of dealing with Highland ethnic minorities. It seems fair to say that the Communist regime in Hanoi had the easier task. Its Highland minorities were smaller in relation to the total population of North Vietnam, and the areas they inhabited would be less crucial strategically in the Second Indochina War than the Central Highlands. Although some of the Thai groups of northern Vietnam had sided with the French against the Viet Minh in the First Indochina War, in general, as a CIA analysis of Highland politics noted, "the Highland minorities of the north were more used to central authority and less likely to express their discontent through armed resistance than their counter-parts in the south."[27]

The Hanoi government also demonstrated somewhat greater finesse in its dealings with Highland minorities compared with its counterpart in Saigon. It made an immediate effort to win the allegiance of the northern tribes, promised autonomy for tribal areas, claimed to respect minority languages and cultures, and offered minority peoples representation at the central government level. In May 1955 Hanoi announced the formation of the Thai-Meo Autonomous Region, later known as the Tay Bac Autonomous Region, which included part of Tonkin between the border with Laos and a line about twenty miles west of the Red River. It announced a similar region, the Viet Bac Autonomous Region, for the Tho and Nung minorities in June 1956.

There is little doubt that the degree of autonomy was nominal at best, and in the short run it did not satisfy all the minority peoples concerned. There was a revolt in the Dong Van District of Ha Giang Province, on the Chinese border, in December 1959, and according to a Communist history, it had the support of "tens of thousands of members of the H'Mong, Tay and Lolo tribes." Numerous local officials and members of the security apparatus were killed during the revolt, and its suppression involved substantial military forces, including the Viet Bac Military Region's 246th Regiment. Things settled down somewhat after this, however, and it is possible that even a nominal degree of local autonomy was useful in soothing the feelings of ethnic minorities.[28]

Preoccupied with the sects, the Communists, the French, Bao Dai, and the myriad other problems involved in establishing a viable state, Diem's administration in Saigon formulated no comparable political program to conciliate the indigenous peoples of the Central Highlands. One particular difficulty was the previously separate status of the Central Highlands as Bao Dai's crown domain. It took a year to integrate the Highlands, even on paper, into Diem's state. During that year there were overlapping authorities and much confusion.

In dealing with the refugee crisis and resettlement, the central government's delegate in the Highlands overrode the authority of the imperial delegate. Refugees from the North were moved into the Highlands before the formulation of a land policy that took into account the traditional Highlander land system and the Highlanders' natural concerns about the influx of additional Vietnamese into their ancestral areas. Diem visited Ban Me Thuot, the capital of Darlac Province, in June 1955 to accept an oath of allegiance from the Highland tribes. He did not, however, take the opportunity to grant them any special status or offer them any form of autonomy.

A CIA report on developments in the Central Highlands compiled in 1966 indicated that in the mid-1950s "some Western observers" (perhaps referring to its own analysts) believed that the loyalty and cooperation enjoyed by the French could be transferred to "any other authority" that offered the Highlanders "reasonable treatment." Much "would depend on the attitude adopted by the central government." In retrospect, however, CIA analysts clearly saw obstacles to such a happy outcome. On the one hand, the vast majority of Highlanders did not see themselves as Vietnamese, could not identify with Vietnamese nationalism, and were unused to central government control. On the other hand: "The Vietnamese disliked life in the Highlands for climatic reasons; few knew the local languages; they detested the general squalor of Highland life; they despised the Highlanders as backward barbarians; and they had no experience in administering the Highlanders." There was thus "a grave risk that the Highlands would become a dumping ground for the least efficient Vietnamese officials." But Western observers in the 1950s reportedly believed that, regardless of its policies and however its officials behaved, the Saigon government would experience only a limited amount of trouble from the Highlanders. The Highlanders' outlook was "so parochial," these observers believed, that they were unlikely to "unite to serve their common interests."[29]

While the climate and terrain of the Central Highlands did not strike most Vietnamese as ideal, the region represented much needed "new territory" for a ravenously land-hungry society. Settlers, encouraged by the Saigon government, moved in at an ever-increasing rate. In particular, Diem intended for the Central Highlands to absorb a substantial proportion of refugees from the North. Apparently he hoped to kill two birds with one stone: resolve the problem of finding land for refugees, and secure this strategically important region by colonizing it with known anti-Communists, his government's natural supporters.

Diem's policy toward the indigenous Highlanders, at least in the beginning, was not consciously harsh or exploitative. Rather, it was paternalistic and assimilatory. Diem's government wanted the Highlanders to improve their agricultural methods, take an active part in the economic development of their region, and participate in his government's administrative apparatus there. He wanted them to drop their traditional way of life (by Vietnamese standards, primitive and inferior) and become civilized. Ultimately he wanted them to abandon their separate tribal identities and to become culturally Vietnamese.

This was quite similar to the policy advocated by many of the most enlightened white Americans toward Indian tribes in the nineteenth century. There were also similar problems with implementation. First, many of the indigenous peoples were deeply attached to their traditional ways of life and tribal identities, and they strongly resisted assimilation. Second, a high proportion of the people from the dominant ethnic groups, including many soldiers and officials, had such strong racial and cultural prejudices against the minority tribes that they created their own obstacles to assimilation.

As more than one CIA study noted, a policy of benevolent assimilation of Highlanders was not really practiced on the ground by Vietnamese government officials, soldiers, and settlers in 1954–1958:

> There were numerous instances where government administrators and military forces treated the Highlanders with contempt and even with great brutality. The Highlanders were exploited by the military and by merchants [and] land was grabbed by settlers. There developed a deep sense of frustration among the Highlanders at not being able to do anything about the situation. Towns such as Ban Me Thuot and Pleiku doubled in size and the areas surrounding them were dotted with new [Vietnamese] villages and fields.[30]

The South Vietnamese administration in the Highlands was based in the towns, making it both mentally and physically remote from most of the indigenous population. Government personnel were generally ignorant of Highlander affairs and, according to American reports, made little effort to enlighten themselves. In extreme cases they did not even know the names of the tribes living in their areas, vaguely referring to all of them as *Moi* (Vietnamese for "savages") and insisting that they had no other names for themselves.

A CIA political history of the Central Highlands indicates that in 1956 the Diem government's Bureau of Ethnic Minorities in Hue "knew practically nothing about Highlanders' habits and customs. There was no clear idea where the Highland villages were [and no] accurate picture of the Highlanders' economy." The administration badly needed to know "the correct nomenclature, distribution and territorial arrangement of the major tribal groups, as well as have at its fingertips information regarding the economy, way of life and needs of the various tribal units and villages." Instead, it was operating in an almost total information vacuum in these respects. According to CIA analysts, Diem's government had made no serious efforts to gain this information, even though the French had left behind useful files in Hue. The Agency believed that Diem's government might have missed an opportunity by not trying to recruit some of the French administrators who had worked in the crown domain (apparently under contract to Bao Dai) during the First Indochina War. But the CIA recognized that difficult relations between Diem and the French would have made this awkward. Diem's government would have had to swallow its pride to ask for help from the former colonists, and French officials might have been reluctant to accept employment with a Vietnamese administration with distinctly anti-French attitudes. Moreover, whereas the French had sought to limit the influx of Vietnamese into the Central Highlands, Diem's policy was the reverse and was arguably the biggest obstacle to establishing favorable relations with the Highland peoples. It is doubtful that the French administrators could have adjusted to it.[31]

In conversations with Americans in 1957, Diem appeared to accept that his government faced growing problems in the Central Highlands and that he had to take immediate steps to address them. Diem's remarks indicate that he combined common Vietnamese prejudices about Highlanders with a spirit of paternal benevolence toward them. To what extent these benevolent noises were mere mood music played for the Americans' benefit is unclear. On balance, and despite a degree of racial arrogance, condescension, and irritation at the Highlanders' reluctance to conform to Vietnamese ways, it seems likely that Diem's benevolence was genuine enough at this stage.

On 9 July 1957 Diem told one American (unnamed in the CIA report) that he had appointed Lieutenant Colonel Huyn Cong Tinh to head an "Inspections and Special Studies" organization based in Dalat. Its purpose was to study tribal affairs and recommend measures to raise the standard of living and level of education of the Highland peoples. He said that dealing with Highlanders required psychology and patience. He was intensely critical of the French, whom he accused of exploiting the Highlanders while making a show of helping them. Diem said he considered the Highlanders to be intelligent and thought they could eventually be persuaded to adopt a more settled, Vietnamese-style village life.

Of all the tribes, Diem anticipated the most trouble with the Rhade, whom most observers regarded as the best educated and most politically sophisticated. He called the Rhade a "tricky people" who had a considerable amount of Cham blood in their veins—the Chams being, of course, a people involved in a centuries-long life-and-death struggle with the Vietnamese. He also compared them with the Thai, another ethnic group the Vietnamese had clashed with. Yet despite these prejudices, Diem was determined to integrate Highlanders into the Vietnamese state. He had started two schools in Dalat to train Civil Guards (militia) and government civic action cadres. Personnel trained by these programs would help improve tribal life.

Talking with US ambassador Eldridge Durbrow on 3 August 1957, Diem discussed at length his policy toward the indigenous peoples. Clearly, its key-note was assimilation; he intended to integrate the Highlanders into the Viet-namese economic system and culture. He told Durbrow that he had started a school for Highlanders at Dalat and intended to bring 200 students there for a four-month course in a variety of subjects. The idea was that they would then return to their villages and carry out civic action and community work. There were, Diem pointed out, "many fertile valleys in the Highlands where, with the construction of small dams and streams the Highlanders could be taught to raise water grown rather than dry rice, and thus raise their standard of living by raising more abundant crops." Diem reported that he had already talked with several Highland chiefs in the Ban Me Thuot and Pleiku areas about settling permanently on land his government had chosen for them. They had, he said, assented to this. But Diem's approach to government was authoritarian; it did not encourage the free and frank exchange of views. The Highland leaders would have at least sensed this, and they may have been afraid to object to his plans. Diem told the American ambassador that he knew Communist agents were active in the region. Getting Highlanders to settle in particular areas and adopt Vietnamese-style agriculture was his idea for stemming the Communist influence.[32]

CIA analysts were prepared to accept that in 1954–1958 Diem's "inten-tions were good" with regard to the Highlanders. But these intentions had been implemented halfheartedly at best. Diem's government had actually "ac-complished little" for the Highlanders. Government officials in the Central Highlands were, in general, very poorly prepared to work with the indige-nous peoples. Educational programs favored Vietnamese settlers rather than the indigenous population, and while ethnic Vietnamese expanded their land-holdings, talk of giving Highlanders definite titles to good-quality land suit-able for wet-rice agriculture remained just that—talk. Government influence over most Highlanders was extremely limited. Road building was hindered by a lack of funds, so much of the region remained physically inaccessible to government officials who were not prepared to trek long distances on foot. More important, few officials were trained or motivated to cross the cultural barrier and gain the trust of the Highlanders. The result was increasing hostil-ity to Diem's government. By the end of 1958: "Four years after the Saigon government came to power it was . . . faced with growing unrest among the tribal groups and subversion of these groups by the Viet Cong. Since the government had found itself incapable of implementing a political civic action program it resorted to a military program and oppressive action to control the Highlanders which further aggravated the situation."[33] Although the Communist Party already had dedicated cadres working among the Highland tribes, violence sometimes broke out between Highlanders and the government without Communist instigation and long before the Communist leadership thought the time was ripe for a serious armed struggle.

Faced with government attempts to control and resettle them: "Many highlanders chose to respond in the traditional way by withdrawing further upland away from Vietnamese control. When force or coercion was used against them they fought back, often with only primitive weapons. Throughout 1957 and 1958 most of the targets were RVN [Republic of Vietnam] officials. . . . In early 1957 members of the Katu [tribe] were responsible for killing several RVN officials in western Quang Nam."[34] A Communist history of the Party's armed forces in the Central Highlands mentions several other examples of violence between Highlanders and the Saigon government in the late 1950s. Some of these reportedly occurred before the Party leadership had formally authorized all-out armed struggle, and it seems likely that some incidents were spontaneous outbreaks neither instigated nor directed by the Communists.[35]

Communist Aims for and Activities among the Highland Tribes, 1954–1960

At the end of the First Indochina War ethnic minority peoples migrated in both directions—north and south of the seventeenth parallel. According to CIA figures, about 10,000 Muongs (members of a northern hill tribe) went south at the time of the Geneva Accords. The same was true of 55,000 Nungs; these were not primitive tribesmen but members of a group that originated in China and migrated to Vietnam in the seventeenth century. At the same time, the CIA estimated that approximately 10,000 indigenous people from the Central Highlands had regrouped north. About 5,000 of them were from the Rhade, generally considered the most educated and politically sophisticated of the Highland tribes; these migrants included four of the five qualified Rhade doctors.[36]

As they did throughout South Vietnam at the time of the cease-fire in July 1954, the Viet Minh left behind in the Central Highlands both some supply caches and a number of trained cadres. One Communist history indicates that Party officials in the Highlands realized that the "people's struggle for national liberation" was not yet complete and would not end simply because there was a truce. In fact, the war was "still continuing." In such circumstances, most Viet Minh forces were going north of the seventeenth parallel. However:

When everyone was turning toward the North and venerated and beloved Uncle Ho, wishing to see him and to hear his advice, a number of comrade cadres and party members were assigned to stay in the South to serve as activists of a new struggle movement. Repressing their burning desire to see Uncle Ho, these cadres and party members accepted hardships and sacrifices. Working side by side, ethnic Vietnamese and tribal cadres and party members assigned as reinforcements to local party organizations in the Highlands went to villages and hamlets to propagandize, agitate and awaken the masses. Filing their teeth, piercing their ear lobes and wearing loin cloths, these ethnic Vietnamese had become "undercover cadres," the sons and daughters, the trusted and beloved comrades of the Highland people.[37]

Soon after the end of the First Indochina War, Ho Chi Minh's government established the Central Minorities School in Hanoi to develop political cadres. There were special subschools for the Bahnar, Jarai, and Rhade, and by 1956 at the latest, products of these schools were being sent south to promote the Communist cause. A CIA report confirms that ethnic Vietnamese cadres arriving in the Highlands during this period came prepared to share the Highlanders' life for years at a time. "They dyed their skin to resemble the Highlanders, filled [*sic*] their teeth [and] learned the language."[38] For most ethnic Vietnamese, filing one's teeth, piercing one's ears, and dyeing one's skin in order to look like a savage (as they had long characterized Highlanders) would have been extremely demeaning. That these cadres were prepared to do this indicates their extreme discipline and dedication to the Communist cause.

By 1959, according to one report, the Minorities School was graduating "some 120 highlanders every nine months." Meanwhile, Radio Hanoi was broadcasting propaganda in the Rhade, Jarai, Bahnar, and Koho languages.[39]

A CIA study of what it called the "Viet Cong, Mountain Cong System" outlined both Communist objectives and the Communist modus operandi in the Highlands. Produced sometime before 1 March 1963, but not supplying any definite chronology of events, it gave the Agency's best estimate of how the Communists had been operating in the Highlands for the last several years:

I. Objective of the Mountain Cong System is to establish a control . . . base of operation in the . . . High Plateau region of South Vietnam. Tribal villages are remote and scattered, providing a perfect means of support for . . . communist guerrillas if tribesmen can be induced to cooperate.

Established cooperation with villages provides constant food supplies over a large area, plus intelligence and other factors vital to a guerrilla force.

Advanced development of the Mountain Cong System calls for agents in all villages and mountain guerrilla units effectively controlling all regions [of the

High Plateau]. These Mountain Cong Units shall be led by hare [*sic*] core Viet Cong, but large numbers of mountaineers shall be trained to follow and assist in all guerrilla actions.

II. Methods for establishing the Mountain Cong System is [*sic*] to press the already existing desire of the tribesmen to preserve the old way of life which is forever fading. To build this desire the Viet Cong build on certain existing facts. The first fact is that a great deal of assistance goes towards [Vietnamese land settlements in the Highlands] most of which are in tribal areas, on former tribal lands. Viet Cong point to these facts and tell the tribesmen that the government takes from them to give to the Vietnamese. They talk of the tractors, medical aid, seeds and plants given to the Vietnamese asking the tribesmen if they receive any of these things from the government. In most cases the answer is no.

The Viet Cong continue with this line of reasoning and begin to help the mountaineer to draw conclusions about these obvious facts. They contend that there is little doubt that the [Saigon] government intends to suppress the tribes by destroying their natural scheme of living with forest, field and stream.

It should therefore be obvious that an independent nation solely for and governed by the tribesmen would surely be better if the old ways are to be preserved. Viet Cong point out that unless this can be accomplished the mountaineer will be moulded into the Vietnamese way of life, which he does not like. They contend that the tribesmen will in effect [become] slaves of President Diem and his American partners in crime.[40]

The Communists proceeded to conduct propaganda meetings in each village they were trying to control. Cadres who spoke the tribal language of the area led these meetings, and they explained why the Communists sought to help the tribesmen against the Diem government—depicting the latter as oppressing virtually all its people, Vietnamese as well as Highlanders. The Communists, these cadres claimed, needed the help of the Highlanders to overthrow this tyranny. In return for their help, the Communists were prepared to aid the Highlanders in establishing an independent nation. They emphasized that the struggle would be hard and that some Highlanders would die, but some sacrifice was unavoidable in pursuit of a better life. The Communist cadres went on to explain that each family must pay taxes to support the cause and must follow certain rules. Those who broke the rules, they insisted, did great harm to the cause of building a Highlander nation and needed to be "dealt with in the worst possible manner." In exchange for full cooperation, the Communists agreed to adhere to certain standards themselves. They would treat all those who abided by their rules fairly and justly. They would levy taxes but would not steal. They would not rape women or force their attentions on them. In general, they would observe strict discipline and not allow individual self-interest to get in the way of the common cause.

Naturally, the Communists dedicated a large portion of their propaganda lectures to denouncing the Diem regime and the ARVN. The list of allegations was always long. "Key words in most cases," a CIA report noted, are "rape, steal, plunder, and enslave." Any instance of inappropriate behavior by the officials or troops of the Diem regime was grist for the Communist propaganda mill. Communist agents were not above twisting stories and grossly exaggerating incidents. But the CIA's own studies indicate that the Saigon government's conduct in the Highlands gave Communist propagandists a substantial amount of material to work with.[41]

The Communists also used demonstration teams to support their propaganda efforts. These teams were apparently peripatetic, moving between villages as required. Such teams might include a doctor with a supply of medicine. Two or three men might give small demonstrations in the use of explosives and in the setting of traps and go on to talk of their confidence in the ultimate Communist victory. In some cases teams carried transistor radios that could be tuned in to Radio Hanoi's broadcasts in the relevant tribal language. Radio Hanoi employed native speakers who had gone north during the First Indochina War or during the cease-fire that followed it. These Highlanders called on their families and friends to support the cause. Some of them told of their training as doctors, teachers, and government administrators for the new Highland nation that would be established when victory was achieved. Occasionally the Communists would hold mass meetings that drew people from many villages and different subregions of the Highlands. At one meeting near Buon Ho in Darlac Province in June 1961, speeches in nine tribal languages were reported.

It is clear that in the late 1950s and early 1960s the Communists were making a serious effort to gain the willing cooperation of Highlanders. A coercive element, however, was seldom far below the surface. The CIA reckoned that the recruitment and training of full-time guerrilla fighters for Communist forces in the Highlands were conducted "under the leadership of hard core Viet Cong with the support of mountaineers who have proven themselves loyal." But recruitment was not always voluntary. Kidnapping was routinely employed as a form of draft and was explained away on the grounds that extraordinary measures were needed if Highlanders were to obtain their freedom.

Highland guerrilla fighters were normally trained at a considerable distance from their home villages, although once they were fully trained and had proved their loyalty, they might be posted closer to home. In addition to receiving further Communist propaganda lectures, the trainees were taught how to make simple weapons and traps and how to move and fight in the jungle. Particular emphasis was given to the methods used in ambushes.

Central to the Communist effort in the Highlands was the relationship between the full-time guerrillas in the jungle and the populations of the villages. To provide itself with the best possible human intelligence, the Communist leadership in any given area would endeavor to plant an agent in every village. The agent's identity would be kept a secret, at least until the Communists felt confident that the majority of the village's population could be relied on to give their support.

The CIA apparently believed that the Communists had part-time guerrilla fighters living in the villages as well as full-time fighters living in jungle camps and that these part-time and full-time fighters could be directed to converge on a particular objective fairly rapidly. "For large objectives large numbers of Mountain Cong may gather and travel considerable distance[s] as a group. Most of this type of travel takes place at night. The group may form a simple camp during the daylight hours." If these Communist-directed Highland guerrillas encountered more powerful government forces than they were capable of fighting, they would, of course, run and hide. Various methods of dispersal and concealment were taught and practiced.[42]

In general, according to another CIA study, the Communist approach to the Highlanders was "soundly planned. The Highlanders would greet Communist agents as the first representatives of any authority in their experience who were prepared to learn their ways, treat them as equals, and who were sufficiently interested to give them advice and assistance." Without the introduction of proper countermeasures by the government, the CIA thought it inevitable that the Communists would gain control of large numbers of Highlanders. In fact, effective countermeasures were not developed until the early 1960s, by which time the Communists had "nearly accomplished their plan."[43]

To some extent, the government's failure to respond adequately before the 1960s can be ascribed to intelligence failure. The ARVN had little information about what was going on in the Highlands. This has been attributed, in part, to the attitude of the first two heads of the American Military Assistance and Advisory Group (MAAG), Lieutenant General Samuel T. "Hanging Sam" Williams and Lieutenant General Lionel C. McGarr. These generals reportedly wanted to train the ARVN as a conventional army and had relatively little interest in counterinsurgency. This is hearsay evidence, but CIA officer Lucien Conein claimed that the French officer who had handled the "intelligence organization embracing all the Montagnard tribes in the High Plateau and the Annamite Chaine" during the First Indochina War "offered to turn it all over to Williams. He was not interested. He didn't even look through the files. When things got tough on the High Plateau we didn't even know where to begin. We had to start all over again from the beginning."[44]

The Bajaraka Autonomy Movement, 1957–1958

The Communists were not the only problem the Diem regime faced in the Highlands. Diem's policy of promoting the immigration of ethnic Vietnamese had led to widespread fear among the indigenous people of being dispossessed and subjugated. While Highlanders living in the more remote areas were increasingly falling under Communist influence and control, some educated (mainly Rhade), urban Highlanders had begun to support an autonomy movement. Anthropologist Gerald Hickey dates its origins as far back as 1955, when some Rhade formed a secret organization called Le Front pour la Liberation des Montagnards (FLM), apparently in response to misbehavior by Vietnamese military units in the Highlands.[45]

Reports of a series of nasty racial incidents began to circulate widely in the Highlands in 1956. According to one such account, near a village forty miles south of Ban Me Thuot, South Vietnamese government troops had slaughtered Highlanders' buffalo and shot at Highland women for sport, seriously wounding at least one. Highlanders living at Buon Ho, north of Ban Me Thuot, alleged that ARVN troops routinely stole food from them, a very serious matter for people who lived close to the subsistence level. At about the same time, Mnong tribesmen in Darlac Province broke off all contact with 2,500 Vietnamese Catholic refugees in a resettlement camp at Dak Mil that had been built only two months earlier. They believed the refugees were responsible for bringing more Vietnamese troops into the Highlands and that these troops would commit atrocities against them.

Early in 1957 Highlander students attending a lycée in Dalat established a committee to investigate the possibility of organizing a Highlander autonomy movement. Eventually, Y–Bham Enoul, a member of a prestigious Rhade family born in 1913 and educated at the Ecole Nationale d'Agriculture at Tuyen Quang in northern Vietnam, became this movement's leader. According to reports that reached the ears of CIA officers, he called a meeting of representatives of all the Highland tribes in May 1957. The same reports indicated that leaders representing most of the tribes attended a conference at the village of Buon Trap in Darlac Province to air their grievances, but a later CIA study was skeptical, positing that this may have been a meeting of Rhade representatives only.

By 1958, however, the autonomy movement was developing real momentum. Its leaders were largely missionary-educated Rhade, but other tribes were becoming involved. "The organizers went amongst the villages soliciting support for their movement." They established an organization claiming to have the backing of some 200,000 people and with the aim of defending the rights of Highlanders and establishing autonomy for them.[46] In 1958 this movement started to call itself the Bajaraka autonomy movement—the name being an amalgamation and compression of the names of the tribes involved: Bahnar, Jarai, Rhade, and Koho. Some of its most active members were servants of the government from which they now sought autonomy, including teachers, militiamen, policemen, and even members of the ARVN. Among their many grievances was that Highland minorities were paid less than ethnic Vietnamese for the same work. Bajaraka's structure, at least in theory, was that four villages formed a commune over which a council presided. The commune council appointed provincial delegates, and the provincial delegates appointed a central committee. The four provincial committees, meeting in the towns of Kontum, Pleiku, Ban Me Thuot, and Dalat, had nine members each. The central committee had seven members.

According to a CIA report, "several tribal leaders talked in terms of using violent means, if necessary" to achieve autonomy. The Agency believed there were three factions within the movement. One of these, apparently supported by Y-Bham, wanted to work with the Saigon government and achieve autonomy within an anti-Communist Republic of (South) Vietnam. A second faction, apparently supported by French plantation owners still operating in the Highlands and by some French missionaries, wanted South Vietnam to be neutral in Cold War terms and the Highlands to be an autonomous area within a neutral state. The third faction favored Highland autonomy within a united Vietnam under a Communist government.

Considering that it represented relatively primitive people and that it was split into factions, the movement showed surprising political sophistication. It sent two representatives—both of whom appear to be Rhade, based on their names, Y-Ju and Y-Nam—to the US embassy in Saigon on 31 July 1958, where they aired grievances against the Diem government and sought American help in getting them rectified. Through the American, French, and British embassies in Saigon, they attempted to get letters signed by Highland leaders delivered to the United Nations Secretary-General. Although Ambassador Durbrow declined to accept a letter for transmission to the UN, he agreed to take up Highland grievances with the Diem government.

The Highlanders may have owed some of their political sophistication to advice from French missionaries. Father Roger Biancetti, whose parish was in Ban Me Thuot, counseled the leaders to be restrained in their demands, to ask for local autonomy rather than complete independence. He reportedly sent a petition for Highland autonomy to a variety of embassies and to the UN.[47]

By March 1958, Highlanders in government military units serving in Pleiku Province were reportedly deserting and crossing the border into Laos. One report put the number at 600. At this time, the ARVN had fewer than 200 officers and noncommissioned officers from the Highland minorities. But in a panic move, they were all arrested in August 1958 on suspicion of political unreliability and plotting to desert to Cambodia and link up with tribal elements that were hostile to the government in Saigon. The government subsequently released these military personnel, but its action against them increased restiveness and resentment among the Highlanders. Further inept government handling exacerbated the situation. On 8 September 1958 a group calling itself the Committee of Liberation stated its demands for autonomy in a letter to President Diem, signed by Y-Bham Enoul, president of the committee.

On 12 October 1958 the leaders of the autonomy movement addressed a petition to President Diem bearing approximately 1,000 signatures and requesting the release of Highlanders imprisoned in Pleiku. When Diem made no response, there were demonstrations in Kontum, Pleiku, Ban Me Thuot, and Di Lanh in Lam Dong Province on 15 October. The chief of Darlac Province, Nguyen Van Tich, organized a meeting of Vietnamese and Highland officials at the Lido Cinema in Ban Me Thuot, with the objective of dispelling the idea that there was any serious autonomy movement among Highlanders. But Y-Wing, a Rhade provincial official who was not actually a member of the autonomy movement, reportedly remarked that both the French and the Viet Cong had already claimed brotherhood with the Highlanders. Now the Saigon government was trying to sell the same political line. He went on to ask that these not be empty words but words proved by deeds.

In a Western democracy, suggesting that a government make good on its promises would hardly be regarded as a revolutionary outburst. But this relatively innocent statement by one of its own employees was enough to trigger a crackdown by Diem's regime. A military unit was despatched to Ban Me Thuot to arrest the leaders of the autonomy movement. Eventually, all the members of its Central Committee were arrested. These included the president of the movement, Y-Bham, a Rhade; Nay Luett, chairman of the Pleiku committee, which largely represented the Jarai; and Paul Nur, chairman of the Kontum committee, representing mainly the Bahnar. These leaders were sentenced to four years in prison, and some were not released until 1964. Most of these people were not committed to the Communist cause. If their ethnic groups had been treated with respect, they might well have been allies of the regime. Despite their imprisonment, both Nay Luett and Paul Nur ultimately proved willing to work with Saigon governments that succeeded Diem's. It is therefore difficult not to regard the Diem government's reaction to the Bajaraka movement as clumsy and excessive.

Bajaraka at this stage posed no military threat to Diem. Whatever strength it had was limited largely to the Rhade, and a CIA report considered it unlikely that a large number of Rhade would take up arms against the Saigon government under Bajaraka's leadership. The government's overreaction, however, had antagonized Highlanders, especially their educated elite, and this jeopardized rather than strengthened the government's grip on a strategically vital region.[48]

Even in discussions with Americans, however, the regime appeared to disregard the opinions of the Highland peoples. In an interview with Ambassador Durbrow in November 1958, Diem's brother Ngo Dinh Nhu stated that he regarded the Highland autonomy movement as just one part of the Communist effort against his brother's regime. But he did not believe the Communists could make a homogeneous force "out of these often antagonistic, aboriginal, ignorant peoples." The government was countering Communist influence by trying to get the Highlanders to settle in permanent fixed villages and to adopt the Vietnamese way of life. Nhu admitted these government policies were encountering resistance, and winning the loyalty of Highlanders would be "a very slow process requiring a great deal of patience." Yet he seemed to think the regime was following the right path and needed to make no fundamental change.[49]

Failure of the Highlander Resettlement Program, 1958–1960

From 1957, the Diem government's policy was to resettle Highlanders in permanent villages close enough to roads to allow it to exert strict control over them. By March 1959, however, this resettlement program was close to collapse, having achieved little. In that month the American consulate in Hue reported that the Communists had initiated a campaign of antigovernment propaganda and assassination in the Highlands. In fact, Communist cadres had been engaged in such propaganda for many years, but because Hue was somewhat remote from the Highlands, this may have been the first the consulate heard of it. The assassination program, directed against government officials of both Vietnamese and Highland ethnicity, was apparently a more recent development.

According to the Reverend Gordon Smith, an American missionary working with the Highlanders since 1929, the assassination program began in mountain districts of Quang Nam and Quang Ngai Provinces (north of the Central Highlands proper) in October or November 1958. The objective was clearly to paralyze the administration, and there was evidence that this was succeeding. Reports reaching the Hue consulate indicated that the Communists had considerable influence with Highlanders in all the provinces from Pleiku northward. They had supposedly established secret bases in northern Kontum and also in southern Quang Nam, an area that later became Quang Tin Province.[50]

As the consulate realized, the Communists' increasing influence in the Highlands grew out of the government's failings. By February 1959, the Diem government had created thirty-three resettlement centers (which it significantly referred to as "reservations") for the entire Highlands; these covered 13,000 hectares and supposedly had a population of 38,000 Highlanders. Ultimately, the government intended to house 88,000 Highlanders in eighty centers on 30,000 hectares of land, although even this would account for only 12 percent of the Highlander population.

The resettlement effort, however, was already in trouble before the Communist assassination program began to paralyze the government. The American consulate in Hué observed that the Highlanders on the "reservations" looked "sullen and unhappy," and Diem's brother Nhu admitted to American contacts that many refused to stay on them. In most cases, resettlement had been involuntary. In the process, tribal traditions and religious beliefs had been ignored. To take just one superficially trivial but psychologically important example, Highlanders were ordered to build their houses on the ground in the Vietnamese style, rather than on stilts, as was their custom.[51]

Even if they had made a determined effort to live and farm in the Vietnamese style, many resettled Highlanders would have had little or no chance of rising out of poverty. At the An My reservation in Pleiku and at Son Ha in Quang Ngai Province, Highlanders received only about a third of a hectare of land, whereas Vietnamese settlers in the Highlands normally got a full hectare. While they were making the transition to the new style of agriculture, Highlanders were supposed to be receiving some government aid. In some cases this aid scarcely materialized at all, and in other cases it dried up pretty quickly.

In 1959, rightly fearing Highlander disaffection, the government ordered the collection and destruction of the Highlanders' crossbows. This, of course, made it practically impossible for them to hunt for food to supplement that which they produced by cultivating their inadequate allocations of land. In such circumstances, Highlanders were leaving the reservations and fleeing to the most remote mountain areas. In at least a couple of cases, entire villages reportedly revolted and killed their Vietnamese guards so they could escape. This indicates, of course, that in the eyes of Highlanders, the reservations had become little more than prison camps, if they had ever been anything else.

The Hue consulate pointed out that Vietnamese officials sent to the Highlands were, in the majority of cases, given no proper training in dealing with Highlander affairs. In these circumstances, old racial and cultural prejudices were evident, presenting a massive obstacle to progress. A report by the Hué consulate indicated that derogatory remarks about Highlanders by government officials were commonplace: "The chief of Le Trung district [Pleiku Province] calls the Montagnards parasites; a Pleiku high school teacher says in front of her mixed class that Montagnards have less intelligence than Vietnamese; the Chief of Province [Pleiku] complains that they are hopelessly improvident and

drunkards to boot." Meanwhile, the Highlanders noted that the rice aid they
were supposed to receive from the Vietnamese government was being lost to
corruption, and the Vietnamese were taking the best land in the Highlands
without compensation.[52]

However badly it was executed, the Diem government's policy in the
Highlands had an element of what might be called integrationist idealism. In
Darlac Province in 1960, the government established a small number of experimental "New Life" villages where Vietnamese immigrants and Highlanders
were supposed to live together in harmony. The Diem government hoped the
Americans would help finance a larger program of such villages. But the ways
of life were so different and the racial prejudice on both sides so intense that
it quickly became evident to the Americans that this social experiment was a
dismal failure for all involved. They decided not to back it, and the program
soon folded.[53]

Outcome: The Security Situation in the Highlands, 1960

By 1960, the Diem government's policy toward the Highland tribes was clearly
failing. The priority given to settling Vietnamese in the Highlands, the prejudice and poor training of government personnel, the downright brutality toward Highlanders, the inadequate resources provided to resettled Highlanders,
and the misappropriation of such resources all contributed to a massive alienation from the government on the part of the indigenous population.

The government thought it had crushed the Highlander autonomy movement. But pro-autonomy sentiment was still alive and apparently growing fast.
American residents of Pleiku Province thought the Highlanders there would
revolt if they could arm themselves. At the same time, "The Viet Cong were
infiltrating the tribal villages establishing political cells, organising guerrillas,
propagandising against the government's resettlement program, and obtaining
a greater degree of control over the Highlanders than was even remotely suspected by the government."[54] As already noted, the Communists had started
a program of assassinating government officials in the Highlands in late 1958,
probably an extension of the *Tru Gian* (killing traitors) program initiated in
the lowlands in 1956, and certainly serving a similar purpose. In the lowlands
the assassination program lasted for three or four years before the Communists
moved to more open and general armed struggle. In the Highlands the process
was sharply accelerated. National Police reports indicated that "Viet Cong
incidents" in the Central Highlands increased from 22 in 1959 to 102 in 1960,
and the number continued to rise thereafter.[55]

By 1960, assassinations were not the only violent actions on the Communist agenda. In October 1960, in the northern part of Kontum Province, the Communists mounted a more substantial offensive apparently designed to "liberate" a base area large enough to sustain substantial military units. The Second Indochina War had finally arrived in the Central Highlands and would continue to rage there for the next decade and a half.

3

War in the Central Highlands, 1960–1961

The General Situation in South Vietnam
in the Second Half of 1960

Communist-led insurrection and an ensuing civil war convulsed much of South Vietnam's countryside in the course of 1960. Over large areas, particularly in the Mekong Delta and the southern part of the coastal plain, the Diem government's authority had practically collapsed by the middle of the year, its writ in these regions running only in provincial capitals and and other towns heavily garrisoned by government forces. By year end, the Communists had perhaps 10,000 full-time troops south of the seventeenth parallel.[1] Though still heavily outnumbered, the insurgents—the "Viet Cong," as their enemies called them—had so far had the better of the fighting.[2]

Diem had not lost his nerve. He was determined to hit back. But the regime's response to the insurgency up to this point had hardly been impressive. Diem had approved the creation, within the ARVN, of "Ranger" companies to combat Communist guerrillas with small-unit operations.[3] Rangers would ultimately play a significant role in the government's counteroffensive. But they had made relatively little impact by the end of 1960. In the meantime, Diem devoted a good deal of effort to demanding more money and military equipment from the Americans. Doubting that these things were really the answer, US Ambassador Elbridge Durbrow, always a severe critic of Diem, became even more negative about him. When officers of the elite ARVN Airborne Brigade attempted a coup in November 1960 (defeated after intense fighting in the middle of Saigon), Durbrow briefly toyed with the idea of supporting it.[4]

Hanoi's Intentions for the Central Highlands

Despite marked Communist gains and disarray on the other side, the Central Committee in Hanoi was not entirely satisfied with the Party's military achievements in the early part of 1960. In the spring of that year it sent a message to the committee coordinating the war effort in the South, stating, "We have seen no mention of the building of a base area in the mountain jungle region in the cables we have received." Hanoi demanded that the southern committee "devote a great deal of attention to this issue," considering it important to develop a base in the Highlands for "large military units."[5]

The Central Committee was obviously well aware that Party agents had, for several years, been at work among the Highland minorities and had recently mounted an assassination program against the Diem government's officials in the region. The wish to base "large military units" in the Highlands indicates, however, that the Hanoi leadership did not believe that assassination and guerrilla warfare were sufficient to bring about the collapse of the southern state. Party leaders evidently expected that, as in the war with the French, it would sooner or later become necessary to fight major battles. They may well have believed that controlling at least some parts of the Central Highlands might prove critical in such a phase of high-intensity fighting. Although the Central Committee did not spell out its collective reasoning, it probably saw the Central Highlands as vital in logistical terms; many branches of the evolving Ho Chi Minh Trail, which ran from the North down the Truong Son mountains in eastern Laos, eventually passed through that region. In addition, it may have hoped that if powerful Communist military units became established in the Central Highlands, they would be able to menace and perhaps ultimately to sever the enemy's communications along the narrow coastal plain.

The Communist Kontum Offensive of October 1960

The Central Committee's preoccupation with the development of a substantial base area in the Highlands may explain the Communist offensive in Kontum Province in October 1960. According to a dispatch from Joseph Mendenhall, counselor for political affairs at the US embassy in Saigon, to the State Department in Washington, the area north of the town of Kontum (the provincial capital) had previously been "relatively quiet," although for several months there had been "intermittent guerrilla and propaganda action by the Viet Cong (VC)." Early in October 1960 the Communists were reported to be "extremely active in spreading propaganda and preparing political groundwork"

in northern Kontum. The first round of major fighting in the Central Highlands during the Second Indochina War (over and above assassinations and
very minor guerrilla actions) commenced on 19 October 1960. Mendenhall's
account to his superiors in Washington was based largely on an earlier study
(now apparently lost) "compiled from numerous official sources" by MAAG.
Overloaded with detail in some respects, it lacks critical information in others
and is somewhat disjointed. But the story is important and worth recounting.[6]

To make sense of the campaign, it is important to have some appreciation of
the forces available to the two sides. In addition to armed National Police, Civil
Guard (full-time militia), and Self-Defense Corps (part-time militia) troops, all
of which were controlled by province chiefs, two of the seven ARVN infantry divisions routinely operated in the Central Highlands. The 22d Division,
commanded by Colonel Nguyen Bao Tri, had its headquarters in the town of
Kontum and operated in the northern half of the Highlands, in the provinces
of Kontum and Pleiku. The 23d Division, commanded by Lieutenant Colonel
Tran Thanh Phong, was based much farther south, having its headquarters at
Duc My in Khanh Hoa Province, on Route 2, which connected with Ban Me
Thuot in Darlac. The 23d Division was responsible for Darlac and the southern
provinces south of the Central Highlands. Its headquarters moved to Ban Me
Thuot in late 1960 and became formally established there in June 1961.

ARVN infantry divisions normally had three regiments, each with three
battalions. The 22d Division's regiments were the 40th based at Dak To, the
41st at Kontum, and the 42d at Phu Thanh, 15 km west of the city of Qui Nhon
on Highway 1. At this time, many of the 22d Division's troops came from the
Highland tribes, whereas the 23d Division, consisting of the 43d, 44th, and
45th Regiments, was overwhelmingly ethnically Vietnamese. ARVN divisions
were supposed to have 10,450 personnel, but most were understrength, and
this was particularly true of the 22d Division. A division's greatest firepower
came from its artillery battalion, equipped (in these particular divisions) with
105mm guns, and a mortar battalion, equipped with 4.2-inch mortars.

Both the 22d and 23d Divisions were part of II Corps, which also directly
controlled some smaller units such as the 3d Armored Reconnaissance Battalion.
Based in the town of Pleiku, II Corps, commanded by Brigadier General Ton
That Dinh, was responsible for the military security of the Central Highlands
and adjacent areas of the coastal plain. If the local militias and II Corps' ARVN
forces seemed inadequate to deal with an emergency in the Central Highlands,
the government could commit elements of its strategic reserve, which included
three Marine battalions and an Airborne Brigade of 4,500 troops.[7]

Information on the Communist order of battle for this campaign is less
detailed and is, in fact, very sketchy. It seems that the great majority of the
Communist forces in the Central Highlands at this time consisted of lightly

armed guerrillas, the great bulk of them recruited from the Highland tribes. But historical accounts published in Hanoi give little indication of their overall numerical strength, and the intelligence available to the South Vietnamese government and its American allies was sparse.

A history of the Communist Party's armed forces in the Central Highlands indicates that this offensive was part of an effort ordered by the Party Committee of Military Region 5 and that operations came "under the direct guidance of the Cong Tum [Kontum] Provincial Party Committee." But there may be an anachronism here. According to other Communist histories, Military Region 5, which became responsible for much of northern South Vietnam, including the northern part of the Central Highlands, did not exist until May 1961. Its predecessor was an organization called Inter-Zone 5, which had been organizing military activity in this part of the country since 20 October 1948 and may have planned this offensive.[8]

Playing a crucial part in the offensive (according to ARVN and American sources) were two recently created, well-armed Communist units, each with about a hundred men, based for the previous four months in the general area of Dak Dru in northwest Kontum Province. "The basic 40-man cadre for these two units were South Vietnamese who moved to North Viet-Nam for training in 1954. They moved to Sam Neua, Laos in late 1959 where they participated in training Pathet Lao insurgents. In July 1960 they moved to the Laos–South Viet-Nam border area near Dak Dru and set up a training base" where they trained Highland troops for the offensive mounted the following October. In addition to these two relatively hard-core hundred-man units, other forces of local guerrillas apparently joined in. Total numbers can only be guessed at, but given the large area over which the attacks were mounted, it seems probable that "at least 400 VC were involved." Actual numbers may have been considerably greater.[9]

Captured documents indicate that the Communists had established a "relatively firm Party organization" in Kontum Province north of the town of Kontum and along the boundary of Quang Ngai Province to the north. According to these sources, "the Viet Cong forces in the area were chiefly local people, trained by VC agents." One important piece of information missing from Mendenhall's report, but presumably available to ARVN intelligence, was the ethnicity of the Highlanders involved. The ethnic groups native to the area where the campaign took place were mainly the Halang, Sedang, Rengao, and Bahnar, but of course, that does not mean the Communist fighters were from these tribes. Mendenhall admitted to being unclear about the Communist leadership's aims for the operation, but he presented a number of theories, including the wish to test ARVN responses and the desire to distract attention from more critical areas that were closer to Saigon. His best guess was that:

The VC plan . . . may have been to weaken GVN [government of Vietnam—
i.e., South Vietnamese government] control in the area north of Kontum to
such an extent that their own control of the area would be facilitated, with a
view to establishing a base of operations accessible to the Lao border on the
west and Quang Ngai and Quang Nam provinces on the east. This could then
have been used to support autonomy movements amongst the highlanders,
and to facilitate infiltration via Laos from North Vietnam.[10]

Mendenhall did not explicitly suggest (which now appears to have been the
case) that Communist strategy included developing a base area in the Highlands that could be used by considerably larger military units.

On 17 October two companies of the 2d Battalion, 40th Regiment, ARVN
22d Division moved north from the regimental base at Dak To to Dak Pek
to provide security for government propaganda teams sent to explain to the
Highlanders what they might gain from a road linking Route 14 to the coast at
Da Nang. At 1000 hours on 19 October one of these companies clashed with
an estimated two Communist platoons in the hills west of Dak Se and became
pinned down by their fire. At 1900 this company, perhaps taking advantage of
nightfall, began to disengage and withdraw westward toward the village of Bon
Tul, about midway between Route 14 and the Lao border. There it clashed
with another Communist force, estimated at platoon strength. After a brief
exchange of fire, the Communist force retreated, and the ARVN entered Bon
Tul. During the afternoon of the following day, 20 October, a platoon of the
Reconnaissance Company of the 22d Division ran into an estimated 100 well-
armed Communist troops at Dak Lao, just north of Bon Tul. Under pressure,
the ARVN platoon withdrew.

The clashes on 19 and 20 October seem to have been encounter battles resulting from the largely accidental collisions of ARVN forces with Communist
troops getting ready for an offensive. That offensive actually began at 0300 on
21 October, when the Communists struck simultaneously at five government
posts: Bon Tul, Dak Se, Dak Gle, Dak Dru, and Dak Rotah—all on or immediately west of Route 14. Dak Dru, defended by only a Civil Guard militia
squad (perhaps a dozen men), fell immediately; Dak Se, defended by a Civil
Guard platoon, fell at 0600.

At Bon Tul a company of the 2d Battalion, 40th Regiment initially held
off the attack, but then 22d Division ordered it to fall back on Dak Rotah.
During the afternoon of 21 October, another company of the 2d Battalion,
40th Regiment at Dak Gle was also ordered to retreat to Dak Rotah, but the
latter post fell at about 1400 hours, apparently before that company reached
it. Meanwhile, the Communists had widened their offensive by attacking Dak
Pek (also on Route 14, about 10 km south of Dak Rotah) with an "unknown

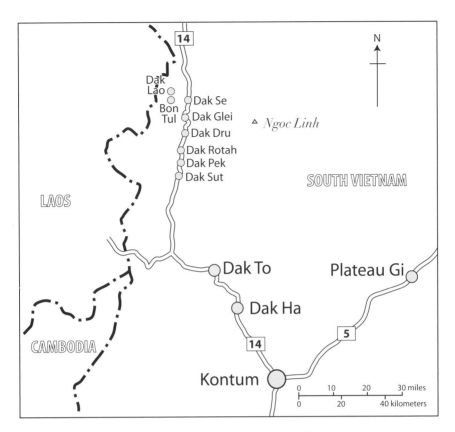

Highway 14 in Kontum Province, showing positions attacked by Communist forces in October 1960 and September 1961

number" of troops. Dak Pek was apparently the only government post in Kontum Province that the Communists attacked on 21 October 1960 but did not take.[11]

The loss of so many posts on a single day was a blow to the Diem government's prestige in this part of the country. But this was an extremely thinly populated area. In absolute terms, casualties among the government forces were not heavy. Five Civil Guards were killed or captured at Dak Se. Also killed was the assistant chief of Kontum Province, who happened to be spending the night there. At least two ARVN soldiers were killed at Dak Rotah, and another eight soldiers and eleven Civil Guards were wounded. Communist casualties may have been considerably heavier. The ARVN reckoned that it killed twenty at Dak Rotah alone, and civilians in the vicinity claimed to have seen Communist corpses in even greater numbers.

Mendenhall suggested that government forces had minimized their casualties by giving ground so readily. A judgment as to whether it was necessary to abandon all these positions, even temporarily, would be possible only if the size of the attacking forces was accurately known. That information is unavailable. The contemporary American assessment was that all the government posts north of Dak Pek had been assaulted by only 200 Communist troops and that the whole Communist offensive of October 1960 might have been mounted by just 400.[12] But a later CIA report that was not especially sympathetic to the Diem government or complimentary about the ARVN stated (on what evidence it did not say) that "1,000 crack Viet Cong troops" had taken part.[13]

Mendenhall's account lacks any reference to ARVN or South Vietnamese government personnel by name, and it is not clear who made the critical decisions. On the first day of the Communist offensive, however, the 22d Division, based at Kontum, reportedly formed a task force led by the division commander, Lieutenant Colonel Nguyen Bao Tri. The infantry component consisted of the 1st and 2d Battalions, 41st Regiment, with a company of the division's pioneer battalion, the mortar battalion, and two batteries of artillery in support. Setting off for the Dak Pek area at 1500 that afternoon, the task force recovered Dak Rotah at 1600 the following day, 22 October.

Indicative of the seriousness with which the authorities in Saigon took a Communist offensive in the Central Highlands is that they had the 1st Airborne Battalion airlifted to the town of Kontum, where it arrived at 1000 on 22 October before setting out for the combat zone at 1930 that evening. Additional reinforcements were on the way. The 2d Battalion, 44th Regiment, 23d Infantry Division and a squadron of the 3d Armored Reconnaissance Battalion, normally based at Pleiku, arrived at Kontum at 0340 on 23 October and proceeded northwest toward the operational area in the northern part of the province.[14]

The 22d Division's task force continued its counteroffensive on 23 October, attacking Communist forces north of Dak Gle and claiming twenty-six killed and six taken prisoner, with a loss of just two killed. The task force also rescued forty-three Civil Guards who, probably after fleeing from posts the Communists had overrun two days earlier, had been surrounded by Communist forces in the jungle. During their encirclement they had been hanging on to a strongbox containing a large sum of government money, perhaps intended as their pay.

Meanwhile, somewhat farther south, the Communist offensive continued with attacks on two other government posts. At 0400 on 23 October the Communists overran a post at Kannack, about 20 km north of Route 19 and 65 km east of the town of Pleiku. In so doing they killed at least eight members of the Civil Guard platoon defending the position and wounded eight more. Another eight were missing. At midnight on the same date Communist forces raided a district office at Chuong Nghia on Route 5, approximately 40 km northeast of the town of Kontum. In an action lasting about fifteen minutes, they killed the district chief and two Civil Guards and wounded three others before retreating.[15]

On 26 October the ARVN 1st Airborne Battalion overran a Communist training camp north of Bon Tul. On the same day government forces received intelligence of a Communist concentration in the Cordoc–Dak Bla area, east of Route 14 and about 10 km southeast of Dak Rotah. ARVN artillery (presumably the two batteries with the 22d Division's task force) shelled the area heavily, claiming fourteen Communists dead as a result.

By 28 October "the situation was again relatively quiet" in northern Kontum Province: "ARVN reconnaissance determined that a large part of the Viet Cong forces had withdrawn into Southern Laos, while the remainder had dispersed into the countryside." The first Communist offensive in the Central Highlands in the Second Indochina War was rapidly losing momentum, if not already over. Communist troops were unable to hold any of the posts they had captured a week earlier. On 29 October and 4 November ARVN vehicles on Route 14 between Kontum and Pleiku took some fire, but there were no casualties. Unspecified ARVN forces discovered "fairly large VC units" north of the town of An Khe in western Binh Dinh Province, on the eastern edge of the Highlands, in late October and called in artillery fire and air strikes against them. But if the Communists achieved any success, even of a temporary nature, in the An Khe sector, Mendenhall did not record it.[16]

Aftermath of the Kontum Offensive:
November 1960–August 1961

Perhaps as a result of the impatient urging of the Central Committee in Hanoi, and perhaps (though this is pure speculation) against the better judgment of the men on the ground, the Communists mounted an offensive in northern Kontum that was premature and dangerously overambitious, given the balance of forces. Their troops performed creditably but were overmatched in both numbers and firepower and suffered a definite defeat.

This put Diem in a bullish mood. In April he expressed his "satisfaction with the situation in the Highlands and among the Highlanders." He attributed "the success of the government campaign" to his "decision to utilize artillery and air forces in the region." In Diem's opinion, the Highlanders, "hearing and being subjected to such intense fire, quickly concluded that the government was much too strong and ejected the Viet Cong agents from their midst," gravitating "towards the greater force" exerted by the government. According to a CIA history of the politics of the Central Highlands, Diem told the Americans that whereas "many Highlanders had earlier objected to the

government's policy" of moving them into settled communities, now "many
. . . were coming forward and requesting it because of the protection afforded
against the Viet Cong."

The same CIA study indicated that Diem's interpretation of the Highlanders' response was open to question. At least in some cases, Highlanders had
probably abandoned their traditional villages and moved to government reservations not because they had made a conscious decision to reject the Communists but because they feared destruction by government bombing and
shelling.[17] Yet Diem's assessment that he had the upper hand, at least in the
northern provinces of the Central Highlands, in the first half of 1961 was by
no means delusional. A Communist official history of the Party's forces in that
region indicates that they were in great difficulty there for most of the year:

> During that time . . . the enemy assembled troops to attack our base areas and
> feverishly implemented plans to round up people. . . . Because of our eco-
> nomic difficulties and the revolutionary forces' weaknesses, the enemy was
> able to encroach on a number of "enclaves" we had obtained during the con-
> certed uprisings [of October 1960]. In the areas under his temporary control
> the enemy resorted to both enticement and terrorism to strike at the revolu-
> tionary bases. The political struggle, ruthlessly and bloodily suppressed by the
> enemy, stalled in some places.

Reading between the lines, in the northern Central Highlands, it became increasingly difficult for the Communists to recruit Highlanders into their military forces, much less to motivate such recruits to attack government posts or
ARVN field forces. The government seemed too strong, its troops too dangerous. It took very careful planning and a substantial concentration of Communist troops (the great majority of which seem to have been ethnic Vietnamese),
brought in with considerable difficulty from both North Vietnam and South
Vietnam's lowlands, to restore the Party's fortunes in the Central Highlands.[18]

In his report on the October 1960 offensive, Mendenhall concluded that
despite "successful counteraction by GVN forces [the] VC . . . retain . . . the
ability to conduct large scale coordinated attacks in Central Viet-Nam at times
and places of their choosing."[19] Though probably too pessimistic with regard
to its immediate aftermath, this assessment proved prescient in the medium
term. The Communists were building up a "liberated zone" that, according to
one account, included 557 hamlets in the southern Darlac–Quang Duc–Lam
Dong area, where they were apparently still able to recruit successfully. In the
words of a CIA study, "If Diem in the spring of 1961 thought he had contained
the Viet Cong advances in the Highlands, he was certainly not as confident in
September."[20]

Inside the map:

SOUTH VIETNAM

VIETNAM ARMY TROOP DISPOSITIONS (U)
1 July 1961

—— Corps Tactical Boundary

AFC   Army Field Command

0   50   100
Statute Miles

THAILAND

LAOS

CAMBODIA

DEMARCATION LINE

Cam Lo

Hué

Tourane

Dak To

Pleiku

Ban Me Thuot

PHNOM PENH

Bien Hoa

SAIGON

My Tho

Can Tho

Spec. Cap. Zone

SPECIAL CAPITAL ZONE

XXXX GHQ
XXXX
AFC
XXX
III
XXX

ARVN dispositions, 1 July 1961

The Dak Ha Offensive and the Crisis in
Kontum and Pleiku: Late 1961

At the beginning of September 1961 a Communist force that the ARVN estimated at 1,000 troops, including two or three battalions identified as "regular," attacked and occupied two government posts at Po Ko and Dak Ha (the district town) in the Dak Ha district of Kontum Province, 50 km north of the provincial capital.[21] Communist official histories indicate that Military Region 5 headquarters planned this offensive and confirm that "regular" or "main force" units were principally responsible for carrying it out.

One of these high-quality Communist units was the 200th Artillery Battalion. Composed of 148 "cadres and combatants" chosen from the artillery battalions of the 324th and 305th Divisions of the PAVN, and equipped with 75mm pack howitzers and 81mm and 61mm mortars, it had arrived in Kontum Province in mid-January 1961, becoming "the first main force unit of the Central Highlands." The 19th Battalion of the 108th Regiment of PAVN Division 305 came down the Ho Chi Minh Trail to participate in this operation, and another battalion, apparently recruited in the South, moved up from the coastal plain, undergoing considerable hardship in the process. "It was the middle of the heavy rainy season; the terrain was unfamiliar and there were many difficulties to be overcome."[22]

As well as capturing a district town, the Communist leadership apparently intended to ambush and annihilate government forces responding to that emergency. One Communist account claims:

> On 2 September 1961 two battalions of the puppet 22d Division moved down from Dak To to recapture Dak Ha. Our ambush force exploited the terrain and was able to divide the enemy force and attack it from many different directions. After one day of continuous fighting, we had almost completely annihilated the lead battalion and shattered and dispersed the second battalion. We captured more than 100 prisoners and almost a ton of weapons and ammunition.[23]

American sources indicate that Communist agents within the town helped the attacking force to capture Dak Ha. While there is no doubt that the Civil Guard force there suffered heavy casualties and disintegrated, Communist troops apparently had a much harder fight against ARVN forces moving to recapture the town. MAAG acknowledged that an understrength ARVN battalion of the 40th Regiment, 22d Division had suffered considerable losses in an ambush. Far from being annihilated, however, it had fought back hard, repelling four assaults by superior Communist forces until it was reinforced by elements of the 41st Regiment. Thirty-five ARVN soldiers were killed in this action, forty-nine wounded, and twenty-five missing, but Communist losses may have been considerably higher. Nevertheless, the situation was regarded as serious enough for one Airborne and one Marine battalion to be sent to the area from the South Vietnamese government's strategic reserve.[24]

It is not clear exactly how long either the battalions from the South Vietnamese strategic reserve or the hard-core, ethnic Vietnamese Communist infantry units, brought in especially for this offensive, remained in the Highlands, but probably not for much more than a few weeks. The personnel of the 200th Artillery Battalion did stay in the region on a long-term basis but were not kept together. Possibly because the supply of artillery ammunition was precarious, the unit was broken up and its members used for other tasks.

The Communist leadership regarded the Dak Ha offensive as "our biggest victory in the Highlands in 1961" and reckoned that it "helped consolidate and maintain the masses' faith in the face of the wave of enemy terrorism."[25] Indeed, it seems that this second Communist offensive in Kontum Province within a year achieved quite dramatic results. It shook the South Vietnamese government's confidence badly; made the ARVN nervous about operating on the high plateau, except in large units; revived Communist morale; and put the initiative back in Communist hands. It was followed by a widespread upsurge in guerrilla activity that included attacks on small government posts and road ambushes. The latter threatened to paralyze road traffic, and thus effective government control, over a large part of the Central Highlands and to jeopardize connections between the Central Highlands and the coast.

Commenting on the situation in Pleiku and Kontum in mid-October, John J. Helble, the American vice-consul in Hué, noted:

> The past several months have witnessed a general deterioration of the security situation in the highland provinces of Pleiku and Kontum. Roads leading out of the cities of Pleiku and Kontum are generally considered unsafe for daytime travel as well as night travel. In each province there are areas where the army (ARVN) has stopped patrolling simply because it is too hazardous. The towns themselves are considered to be threatened by night-time Viet Cong (VC) forays. Closely connected to the deterioration of the security situation is the problem of the tribespeoples of the two provinces. Totaling over 200,000 in Pleiku and Kontum these elements have been providing an increasing amount of support to the VC. As the Chief of Staff of the II Corps put it, "We have lost the Montagnards. Now we must start all over again and try to win them back."

Communist actions in these provinces had become much bolder. Government effectiveness had dramatically diminished as a result. Outside the provincial capital, no area in Pleiku was safe for government personnel or Americans at night, and "almost no areas . . . [were] safe in the daytime." On the newly reconstructed Route 19, connecting the town of Pleiku with the port city of Qui Nhon on the South China Sea, ambushes were extremely prevalent. Only "travel . . . by convoy of several military vehicles" was considered safe. "Route 14 south of Pleiku to Banmethuot [was] considered . . . just as unsafe as Route 19, if not more so. . . . North of Pleiku Route 14 to Kontum, only an hour's drive," was negotiable only by military convoys. Finally, the road running west of Pleiku to the Cambodian border was "entirely unsafe at night," and at a distance of 15 km or so out of Pleiku, it was "not regarded as secure in the daytime."[26]

A French tea planter who lived 16 km west of Pleiku, on the road to the Cambodian border, told the US vice-consul that Communist forces moved around "at will" on his plantation:

> GVN forces have been helpless in protecting it and he continues to be able
> to operate only because the VC have told the workers that as long as the
> plantation is French they will not bother it as the workers need their jobs. The
> planter expressed extreme pessimism regarding the future of Pleiku. He stated
> that only a complete change of attitudes and programs on the part of the GVN
> towards the tribespeople can save Pleiku. This particular planter has in the past
> not been noted for his pessimism. He feels that some time in 1962 all of the
> Plateau region will be lost to the VC.

Reading between the lines, it seems probable that this planter was paying "protection" money to the Communists and that his workers who were not active in the insurgency were contributing some sort of tax. As rural proletarians, plantation workers were obvious targets for recruitment into a Marxist movement, and it would be most surprising if at least some of this planter's employees had not been enrolled.

Talks with the ARVN II Corps chief of staff (not named by Helble, but probably Major Nguyen Van Minh) and with the MAAG team (commanded by Colonel Wilbur Wilson) in the town of Pleiku confirmed Helble's perception of the desperate security situation in that province. One of the greatest problems, according to II Corps' chief of staff, was the poor quality of the province's Civil Guard. The Pleiku province chief simply could not rely on this force. As a result, so much of the ARVN was tied down "in static guard duty and relief of CG forces" that little could be "done offensively against the VC." The same officer thought circumstances might improve once an extra ARVN regiment, formed specifically for use in the area, took up its duties in

January 1962. In the meantime, he expected an intensification of Communist activity with the onset of the dry season in November.

The clear skies of that season, however, would spell danger for Communist forces, exposing them to government air reconnaissance and air strikes by AD-6 fighter-bombers. Helble discovered that napalm and other munitions were being stocked in Pleiku for use by these aircraft. He expressed a hope "that use of these weapons will be carefully controlled" and that "indiscriminate use against the tribal villages which contain non-combattants [sic]" would be avoided. It was his "firm conviction" that if subjected to such bombardment, "only complete extermination of tribal elements in the area could prevent the tribespeoples from doing their utmost to aid the VC."[27]

Though not all military officers approved of such methods, it was already too late to hope that the Diem government would forgo using air strikes against Highland villages perceived to be under Communist control. How common this practice became is not clear, but it certainly caused widespread horror and outrage among the Highlanders. A struggle for control of the population is an intrinsic part of guerrilla warfare. To cite Mao's famous analogy, guerrillas are the fish and the people are the sea. Guerrillas usually require civilians to provide them with the basic necessities of life such as food, clothing, and shelter. Commonly, they also need a demographic base from which to draw fresh military recruits, nurses and paramedics, gatherers of intelligence, and laborers for a variety of tasks. In the Central Highlands in the early 1960s, government bombing was apparently used as a form of state terrorism to coerce the Highland peoples into abandoning villages in remote areas that were easily accessible to Communist cadres and to force them to resettle in districts closer to towns and roads and easier for the government to control, thus depriving the Communists of their services.[28]

This resettlement campaign served essentially the same purpose as the British "concentration camp" system in South Africa in 1901–1902, in which farms were destroyed and civilians rounded up to deny sustenance to the mounted guerrilla units known as *kommandos*. The "New Villages" system used by British authorities in Malaya in the 1950s to isolate Communist guerrillas from their civilian supporters and reduce them to virtual starvation was based on the same principle.[29]

The Diem government presumably used bombing to coerce the Highlanders into resettling mainly because it would be too difficult for ground forces to reach them and round them up in the mountains and jungles the Highlanders knew so intimately. Although such a ruthless exploitation of government airpower was not going to win Highlanders' hearts, there was no reason to doubt that it could be crudely effective in creating refugees and thus draining manpower from Communist-controlled areas. Bombing can certainly create resentment, hatred, and a desire for revenge, but the idea (apparently held by Helble) that it tends to strengthen the will to resist is prevalent mainly among people who have not been subjected to it.

Although the security situation in Pleiku was bad, Helble found it worse in Kontum. Large areas of the province had become virtual no-go areas for government forces. The chief of staff of the 22d Division admitted that the jungle-clad Tou Morong region, north-northeast of the town of Kontum, was "virtually inaccessible to ARVN troops," and the Communist forces used it "at will." The same was true of the area directly west of the provincial capital, later termed the "tri-border area," where Laos, Cambodia, and Vietnam meet. According to the commanding officer of the MAAG detachment there, the Civil Guard in the province was so weak that the Communists "continued to use small CG posts as sources . . . of weapons and supplies and, to some extent, even men." This officer also advised that the 22d Division was 2,000 men understrength; the rifle companies, which he regarded as the "guts of the division," were at only 60 or 70 percent of their authorized manpower. Intelligence had identified considerable concentrations of Communist troops on the other side of the Laotian border, and the MAAG commander believed that they "could probably take the city of Kontum if they were willing to pay a severe price," though they probably could not hold it for long. That town lived "under considerable threat from night to night of a VC attack." The MAAG officer thought the upcoming dry season in Kontum Province would tend to favor government forces, presumably because of the air factor. But no permanent improvement in the security situation could be expected until the ARVN was heavily reinforced, the Civil Guard completely overhauled, and a great deal of effort devoted to both resettling and aiding the Highlanders.[30]

Helble was convinced that finding an appropriate government policy for dealing with the Highlanders was the key to security in Kontum and Pleiku Provinces. There were, he believed, 80,000 Highland people in Kontum and 150,000 in Pleiku, making them a large majority of the region's population. He confirmed the accepted wisdom that "the tribal regions [were] fertile ground for the VC to exploit and gain support from." He drew up a list of Highlanders' grievances against the regime. Among these was the rationing of salt, rice, and kerosene, which required frequent and lengthy trips, often more than 15 km one way, to the nearest town. Another complaint was mistreatment at the hands of ARVN soldiers, who often took fowl, pigs, and other forms of food "with little or no payment." In some areas, the government had collected all crossbows, spears, and other traditional weapons, leaving the Highlanders defenseless and unable to hunt game.

Even when Highlanders were reluctant to cooperate with the Communists, or went so far as to inform the government of their presence, government forces often arrested them, "apparently hoping to extract more information" or else "suspecting them of being VC" because they had knowledge about the latter. But government ineptitude in handling cooperative Highlanders sometimes took a diametrically opposite course—publicizing such individuals as heroes and thus setting them up as targets for Communist retaliation. Another problem was that the Communists destroyed the Highlanders' government-issued identity passes, which the government generally refused to replace, making it difficult for Highlanders to move around, purchase rice or salt, or obtain work.[31]

Helble reported that, on the basis of "an almost unanimous consensus" among those to whom he had spoken, resettling the Highlanders in "larger communities accessible to CG and ARVN troops" was a necessary "first step" to gaining their loyalty and cooperation. Many of his informants had initially expressed a strong "distaste for the idea" of resettlement, but they now believed it would otherwise be impossible to break the Communist grip on the Highland peoples. A Sedang man to whom Helble had spoken in Kontum Province stated that "his people would be in favor of resettlement if it were handled properly, i.e. some good land was given them to settle on and aid in terms of rice, tools, medicine etc., was provided. He maintained that most of his people were forced to follow the communists though some did so voluntarily. Without protection from the VC, little [could] be done in terms of depriving the VC of tribal support in the Plateau area." Besides resettlement, which was already the policy of the Diem government, Helble had some other ideas:

ARVN patrols [might] reverse their present policy of taking from the tribespeople and instead carry with them small supplies of salt, kerosene and rice to distribute to the inhabitants when they visit a village. The people would then look forward to the visit of an ARVN patrol rather than fear it, and would probably be more co-operative in providing information about the VC. One ARVN CO has practiced this in his area without the knowledge of his superiors and feels the results are worth the personal risk he is taking.

Another suggestion is that a tribesman be appointed as province chief in one of the tribal provinces. As most of these provinces already have a tribesman as deputy province chief for tribal affairs and a couple of tribesmen are Deputies in the National Assembly, perhaps this propaganda gambit is already being exploited sufficiently. However it is worth noting that the VC operating in these areas usually have a tribesman as "CO," even though he may only be a figurehead.

Helble believed that the government had an opportunity to win the loyalty of the Highlanders in Kontum and Pleiku if it could offer them protection and was prepared to show a reasonable degree of kindness and consideration. He observed:

> The Jarai of Pleiku and the Sedangs of Kontum, the two largest groups in their respective provinces, feel that there is a real danger of their being exterminated in the war between the VC and the GVN. The GVN could do much to alleviate these fears by demonstrating to the tribespeople that it desires to protect them and succour them. While developing long-term loyalties to the GVN will require much time and education, it seems . . . that given the proper approach a short-term loyalty can be developed, or perhaps "purchased," would be a more accurate term.[32]

The Communist Challenge in Darlac: Late 1961

Kontum and Pleiku Provinces in the Central Highlands saw the most Communist activity in 1961, but the Communists were also contending for control of Darlac Province, immediately south of Pleiku. Geographically, this province had two types of terrain. Much of the land in the north and southeast was mountainous and forested, while in the south-central zone, the Darlac Plateau, the land not under cultivation was generally covered by low brush. Route 14, the main north-south route through the Highlands, connected the provincial capital, Ban Me Thuot, with Saigon and with the towns of Pleiku and Kontum. More important in terms of the economy was the recently rebuilt Route 21, connecting Ban Me Thuot with the South China Sea at Ninh Hoa, 30 km north of Nha Trang.

Darlac was the focus of a government land development program. About 35,000 people had already been moved, mostly from the lowland provinces of central Vietnam, into twenty-two centers in Darlac. It was an enormously expensive program, costing about VN$40,000 per family (each family averaging five persons). The overall intent was "to establish a belt of loyal Vietnamese settlements in this sparsely settled area that was previously a virtual reservation for the aboriginal montagnards." In addition, there were three particular aims: (1) It was hoped that these villages would form "a barrier to Communist infiltration." (2) The government planned to "increase and diversify agricultural production by encouraging the settlers to cultivate industrial crops such as fibers and rubber" and thus boost the national economy, even though it was known that such crops tended to deplete the soil rapidly. (3) The government intended "to reduce the population pressure in the lowland deltas along the coast of Central Viet-Nam by moving families into the plateau area."[33]

Reporting to the State Department, the US embassy in Saigon was, in broad terms, willing to look favorably on the land development program, seeing it as "among the most forward-looking activities of the GVN." But it also ran the risk of seriously alienating the Highlanders and thus playing into Communist hands. Only two of the nineteen resettlement centers so far established in the province were for Highlanders; the rest were for Vietnamese. Plans to establish centers in 1962 (ten in Darlac Province) contemplated no new ones for Highlanders. This tended "to strengthen the VC propaganda line" that the government did "not really care about their problems" and was "uninterested in helping them." In security terms, this was potentially serious. Highlanders constituted about 90,000 of the 140,751 people then living in Darlac, according to government records. Of the five main tribes, by far the largest and most dominant was the Rhade, estimated at 30,000 people. Many people of the other tribes spoke Rhade, which served as a sort of lingua franca in the area.

As in Kontum and Pleiku, the security situation in Darlac had worsened considerably since late 1960. Whereas the number of Communist troops in the province was "believed to be negligible at the end of 1960," by the end of June 1961, ARVN intelligence "estimated armed VC in Darlac at 270." This was "still a small force in a province of 63 villages and 397 hamlets," but the Communists' presence and activity had been "enough to hamper normal administration to a serious extent."

The Communists "made their presence felt" in a "spectacular way" when, on 24 July 1961, they "killed two members of the National Assembly" who were "inspecting a village development project . . . some 25 kilometers south of Banmethuot." Officials had apparently heard reports that the Communists intended to disrupt this village inspection, but having provided themselves with an armed guard, they went ahead with it. The Communists then mounted an extremely well-organized, well-executed road ambush on the small military convoy escorting the inspectors, killing nearly all the personnel in the convoy.

In general, security was now very uncertain outside the province's main towns. Officials of the local branch of the national Agricultural Credit Office, for example, were willing to visit only "five or six" villages in the entire province without an armed guard. The two most dangerous areas were the southern sector around Lac Thien and the heavily forested northeastern sector, adjacent to the Cheo Reo area of Pleiku Province. But officials at the embassy thought the Communists were probably also in control of the western third of the province, along the Cambodian border, as the Saigon government had "never exercised effective jurisdiction in that area."

Darlac's provincial officials were, in many cases, trying to do their duty despite the insurgency. They still visited "outlying areas of the province, though generally only with an armed escort." But because travel was difficult and sometimes dangerous, there were a significant number of areas that government officials visited only rarely. The US embassy's view was that "this loss of contact between the people and the government" played "into the hands of the VC." Highlanders, in particular, reportedly felt "abandoned by the government" and so had been "driven to come to terms with the VC organization in the province."[34]

The estimate of only 270 Communist troops in Darlac had to be revised sharply upward when the embassy received news of an offensive, "reportedly involving up to two regular VC battalions accompanied by several hundred additional local guerrillas," mounted about 20 km southeast of Ban Me Thuot on 18 September 1961. The objective was apparently to seize rice and other supplies from newly established Vietnamese villages at Ban Ti Srenh, Ban Yang Bong, and Ban Kron Kmar. Having overrun a Civil Guard post in the area, the Communists occupied these villages for several days, burned schoolhouses and administration buildings, and "terrorised people." The villagers had received some warning of the approach of Communist troops and, according to some reports, had managed to hide much of their rice while the heavily outnumbered Self-Defense Corps hid its weapons and uniforms. Unspecified government troops, probably elements of the 23d Division then based at Ban Me Thuot, were sent to the area, but the Communists withdrew into a nearby "mountain redoubt" before they arrived. Air strikes were mounted, but if these caused any Communist casualties they were not reported.[35]

Much of the news from Darlac, therefore, made grim reading for the Saigon government and its American backers. From their points of view, however, there was also a somewhat lighter side to the picture. Of the major Highland provinces, Darlac was making the greatest economic progress, and of all the Highland tribes, the Rhade had the greatest number of well-educated people, some of them holding "positions of some importance in [its] administration." For instance, Y-Djap ("Y," the Rhade word for males, is used here as the equivalent of "Mr.") had been assistant province chief since early 1961, when his predecessor, Y-Blong, had gone to Saigon to work for the Directorate of Psychological Warfare. In 1961 Y-Djap was fifty-three years old. He came from a small village about 25 km from Ban Me Thuot and had served in the French army from about 1930 until 1947; he had joined the civil administration of the South Vietnamese state in 1957. Another Rhade, Y-Klong, was chief of malaria eradication in Darlac. At the Darlac Office of Information, five of the forty-one information officers were Rhade, and the Ban Me Thuot government radio station, scheduled to begin transmission soon, was intended to concentrate on programs in the two principal regional languages: Rhade and Jarai.

The Vietnamese Communist Party evidently regarded the active involvement of Highlanders in the southern state, even if confined to a relatively small number of individuals, as a serious threat to its interests. Y-Gue, the chief of Montagnard education in Darlac, was killed in the 24 July ambush mentioned earlier. Y-Ut Nie Buon Rit, a member of the National Assembly and perhaps the most distinguished member of his ethnic group, died with him. Y-Ut had reputedly been the first Rhade to learn to read and write and had worked with the French to develop a Rhade alphabet.[36] Killing a man of his distinction made two related points: First, the Communist Party would not tolerate cooperation with the Saigon regime by any Highlander. Second, none was so eminent as to escape its vengeance.

Yet, while such acts would put fear into the mind of any rational person, they were probably not best designed to win Rhade hearts. Both Diem and some American observers believed that most of the Rhade were fundamentally mistrustful of the Communists.[37] The Communists, moreover, did not yet have the same military strength in Darlac that they had in Pleiku and Kontum. Such factors apparently played a major part in the decision to launch in Darlac, and among the Rhade, an imaginative initiative designed to win Highlanders over to the anti-Communist side.

Renewed CIA Involvement with Counterinsurgency

Some factors remote from the Central Highlands also contributed to the counterinsurgency program that began in October 1961 in the village of Buon Enao. It is relevant that a new American president took office that year. John F. Kennedy had an interest in covert action and the use of Special Forces. He was concerned about the accusation of being "soft on Communism" and was smarting from the fiasco of the Bay of Pigs intervention in Cuba. He now perceived Indochina to be at or very near the top of the list of Cold War challenges facing the United States.

In National Security Action Memorandum 52, dated 11 May 1961, he authorized a "program for covert action to be carried out by the Central Intelligence Agency which would precede and remain in force" even if it were ultimately decided to commit forces of a more conventional nature to South Vietnam. In October Kennedy also sent policy advisers General Maxwell Taylor and Walt W. Rostow to Saigon to make an on-the-spot assessment. They advocated a massive new commitment, including 8,000 US troops. Kennedy was not ready to go that far, but he did approve the dispatch of additional war material and more advisers. It was against this background that, on 26 October 1961, Allen Dulles, the Director of Central Intelligence, authorized the CIA to run a major new counterinsurgency program in the Central Highlands.[38]

The program that Dulles endorsed had some of its roots in the American Country Team in Saigon and others in the handful of Americans in Darlac Province. It had been in the making for several months. Under Edward Lansdale, a keen supporter and personal friend of Ngo Dinh Diem, the CIA had been actively involved in operations in support of the regime. According to a recent Agency history, however, after Lansdale's departure in December 1956, "the CIA Station in Saigon played no active role in village-level counterinsurgency in South Vietnam until early 1961."

Ambassador Durbrow and his team, however, considered the security situation so desperate by mid-1960 that the CIA's direct operational involvement was again deemed necessary. By the end of 1960, they had drawn up a rather uninspired but (at 234 pages) distinctly bulky counterinsurgency plan. Over the course of 1961 the Agency began looking for operational initiatives that might reduce Communist momentum. Early that year, a young American aid worker based in Darlac Province had suggested to Colonel Gilbert Layton, commander of the CIA's Military Operations Section, that action was needed to prevent the Rhade from falling under Communist domination, and this might mean arming some of them.[39]

The Genesis of the Rhade Project

The aid worker in question was David A. Nuttle.[40] Brought up on a mixed crop and livestock farm in Kansas, Nuttle had graduated from college with a degree in agriculture and had gone to Vietnam in late 1959, at the age of twenty-three, to work with the International Voluntary Service (IVS), a non-governmental organization that was the precursor of the Peace Corps. Nuttle's contract with IVS stipulated that he would "provide agricultural and community services" in South Vietnam. IVS volunteers assisted the South Vietnamese government in resettling refugees from North Vietnam as well as in general agricultural development and technical education. The headquarters of the operation was at Tan Son Nhut, near Saigon's international airport.

The IVS helped run ten experimental agricultural stations scattered over the country. The oldest, known as Ea Kmat, was at Ban Me Thuot, the capital of Darlac Province. When Nuttle arrived, Ea Kmat had already been working, under the direction of the Saigon government's Ministry of Agriculture, for three years. It employed nine Vietnamese graduates of the new National

College of Agriculture at Bao Lac, as well as two American IVS volunteers. Ea Kmat was particularly concerned with boosting the production of fiber crops, upland rice, livestock, and vegetables. The station was widely considered a big success, and Nuttle was proud of its record.[41]

Nuttle worked with ethnic Vietnamese and Chinese refugees in Darlac too, but he forged a particularly close relationship with the Rhade. He respected their culture and customs and managed to acquire some of their language. He became sufficiently interested in the Rhade to conduct an ethnological study, which he passed on to American officials working in embassy circles. Like many Americans brought up in the countryside, Nuttle was an enthusiastic hunter. He used this skill to provide meat, mostly deer and wild pig, for the Rhade villages with which he worked. This was significant, given that the government, out of fear of the Bajaraka autonomy movement, had confiscated the Rhade's crossbows and spears, making it practically impossible for them to hunt for themselves. Nuttle also disposed of at least one tiger and one leopard perceived to be threats to Rhade villages.

The Rhade had a strong hunting tradition. They respected successful hunters and appreciated Nuttle's efforts on their behalf.[42] Nuttle's practical skills, the success of the agricultural methods he advocated, and "his evident commitment to their welfare" made him many friends among the Rhade, and these friends repeatedly warned him that the Communists were trying to kill him. In part, Nuttle attributes his survival to a hunter's knowledge and instincts. He quickly learned not to adopt a set routine, not to make definite appointments, and always to vary the times and routes of journeys. His Rhade friends talked to him quite freely about the local political situation, as they perceived it. The Communists were gaining steadily increasing influence with their people, but this was mainly because of their difficult relations with the Diem government. In general, the Rhade feared rather than liked the Communists.[13]

Though based at Ban Me Thuot, Nuttle went to Saigon from time to time for both professional and social reasons. There, in February 1961, he began to date Bonnie Layton, a young American woman he met through US embassy contacts. Her parents sometimes invited him to their Saigon residence for "a home cooked meal" and, initially, perhaps to check his suitability as their daughter's boyfriend. Bonnie Layton's father was Colonel Gilbert Layton of the CIA's Military Operations Section. Nuttle and Gil Layton got on well, and a series of approximately eight after-dinner conversations from February to April 1961 ultimately led to what became known as the Buon Enao experiment, which involved arming the Rhade to defend themselves against Communist forces. That in turn led to the wider Citizens' (later Civilian) Irregular Defense Group project (CIDG)—the principal way in which US Special Forces contributed to the war in Vietnam.

Nuttle's version is that he and Layton "agreed that the Montagnards would not fight for . . . South Viet-Nam per se. The Montagnards had no concept of nation or national defense. . . . We further agreed that they would probably fight for family, home and village if the ARVN would stay off their backs" and if the government "provided some social and political benefits." The Rhade, Nuttle emphasized, had learned to appreciate some of the benefits of modern medicine, education, and agricultural improvement under the French administration. They now had a taste for these things, and in order to gain and maintain the Rhade's loyalty, they would have to be adequately provided.[44]

On 5 May 1961 Layton raised the Highlander question with William Colby, the CIA station chief in Saigon, suggesting that the government arm up to 1,000 tribesmen. In response, Colby submitted a paper to his Country Team colleagues on 25 May. He followed this up with discussions with Ngo Dinh Nhu, Diem's brother, who was now playing a major role in organizing the government's counterinsurgency effort. At some point Colby and Nhu visited Darlac together, and Colby emphasized the need to win the Rhade over to the anti-Communist side.

To deal with any concerns it might have about arming Highlanders, Colby suggested to Nhu that the government be directly involved in any such project through the agency of the South Vietnamese Special Forces, over which Diem had a high degree of personal control through his Presidential Survey Office (PSO)—the nearest thing South Vietnam had to the CIA. Experience had given the CIA some reason to doubt the general standard of efficiency of the Vietnamese Special Forces, whose officers were picked more for their personal loyalty to Diem than their military skill. But Colby apparently believed their involvement would reassure Diem that he could maintain control of whatever program were ultimately adopted for the Rhade, without interfering too much with its implementation.[45] In the long run, as we shall see, this would prove overly optimistic, although a widespread breakdown in relations between Vietnamese Special Forces and Highland fighters occurred only after the CIA had lost control of the program and the government in Saigon had suffered a massive collapse of its willingness to trust Highlanders, which was fundamental to the program as originally conceived.

The process by which the CIA (with Colby apparently taking the lead) gained consent from both the US embassy and the South Vietnamese government to arm the Rhade was long and involved. It seems to have taken from late May or early June to early October. Although Layton tried to keep Nuttle informed, at least in broad terms, of what was going on, some of the steps in this process are obscure, and our chronology is vague. At some point in late July or early August 1961, however, Nuttle was summoned from his IVS post in Ban Me Thuot for a meeting with Ambassador Frederick E. Nolting at the

US embassy in Saigon.[46] Nolting, who had an academic background in history and international affairs and spoke good French, had arrived in Saigon to replace Elbridge Durbrow in May 1961. President Kennedy tasked him with establishing better relations with the Diem regime than his predecessor had managed. He was to do everything in his power to aid Diem and to prevent the fall of South Vietnam to the Communists.[47]

Nolting's meeting with Nuttle also involved a large part of the Country Team, which advised the ambassador on relations with Diem's government and on the prosecution of the war. Arthur Gardiner, the director of the United States Operations Mission (USOM); Lieutenant General L. C. McGarr and Colonel M. P. Ward from MAAG; William Colby; and Douglas Pike of the United States Information Agency (USIA) were among those attending. Nolting opened the meeting by indicating that the Country Team wanted Nuttle's views on "how best to stop a possible VC takeover of the Highlands." His ideas were being sought because of his "knowledge and experience of the area." Nolting indicated that a number of approaches to security in the Highlands were already under consideration. The one favored by MAAG (and, apparently, much of the ARVN) was to force Highlanders onto "reservations." Any Highlanders moving off these reservations could be regarded as hostile and attacked by government forces. All the Highlands not clearly under government control would thus be considered a "free-fire zone."

According to his own account, Nuttle attacked the reservation, free-fire zone approach. "The Montagnards would resist forced relocation and would be alienated against those attempting it. If relocated the Montagnards could and would escape any reservations by slipping away into the jungle. The rugged terrain, dense vegetation and many trails would make it easy for the Montagnards to elude capture. Living in the jungle the Montagnards would probably come under VC control. General McGarr interrupted, saying that while my arguments [might] have some credibility, there seemed to be no other realistic alternative." In response to a question by Colby, Nuttle launched into the proposal he and Layton had worked out for Rhade self-defense, determined, in his words, "to find a way to save my Rhade friends from a horrible fate." He pointed out that the Rhade would not fight for South Vietnam as such but would "fight to defend family, home and village" and would "indirectly support" the South Vietnamese government "by resisting VC control, taxation and conscription of young men." A small pilot project could be used to test these concepts.[48]

During August and September, however, the project seems again to have hung fire. Although the CIA had found it relatively easy to win over Ngo Dinh Nhu, it probably had a more difficult time selling the concept to his brother the president. From what Nuttle heard, "This sales effort was accomplished by the CIA Station Chief William Colby. Colby was aided in his efforts by Sir

Robert Thompson, the British adviser to Viet-Nam. . . . Diem agreed to 'experiment' with a Montagnard defended village as a last hope to save the Highlands." Once Diem had been won over, there was no difficulty convincing Colonel Le Quang Tung, head of the PSO, which controlled the Vietnamese Special Forces, or Major Nguyen Van Bang, the province chief in Darlac. The Americans regarded Bang as very enlightened, but he was initially (and predictably) cautious about the large-scale arming of Highlanders. Colby had been in negotiation with Tung on the Rhade issue since July. A devoted, trusted Diem loyalist, there is evidence that Tung was won over long before the president and that he played an important part in gaining that latter's consent.[49]

On 3 October 1961 Nuttle was back in Saigon, where Layton dispatched him to a dinner appointment at the house of Jack Benefiel, one of Layton's subordinates in the CIA's Military Operations Section. At that dinner, Colby and Benefiel told Nuttle that they wanted him "to go forth and help the military create a pilot model of a Montagnard defended village." Nuttle agreed to this. The following day, while still in Saigon, he resigned from IVS, an organization he did not want to involve in a warlike project. Nuttle's IVS superiors, having been briefed in advance by the CIA, were expecting the resignation and raised no objection. Nuttle signed a contract with the CIA later the same day.

On 5 October Nuttle and Colby met Nhu in the latter's Saigon office, where Nhu formally gave his blessing to the project but imposed tight limits. It would begin with a single village, and initially, Rhade self-defense forces would be armed only with traditional weapons: crossbows and spears. Firearms would be issued, and villagers would be trained in their use, only when they had erected a fence around the village and posted signs declaring their allegiance to the South Vietnamese government and threatening any Communist forces entering it with death.

Major Bang, the Darlac province chief, would oversee the project on behalf of the regime. Captain Phu of the PSO was assigned to work closely with Nuttle and would handle liaison with Bang and with ARVN headquarters in the area, including Colonel Le Quang Trong's 23d Division at Ban Me Thuot and Brigadier General Ton That Dinh's II Corps at Pleiku. On 8 October Nuttle flew on a CIA aircraft from Saigon to Ban Me Thuot, where Phu, making his own travel arrangements, agreed to join him the following day.[50]

The Buon Enao Experiment Begins

Over the next few weeks, Jack Benefiel would play a major role in supervising the project for the CIA, dividing his time between Saigon, where he was based, and Darlac. Hugh Murray, who arrived in Darlac in mid-October, was the CIA officer who worked most closely with Nuttle, helping to run the project on a day-to-day basis. Y-Rit, a Rhade colleague of Nuttle's from the agricultural station at Ban Me Thuot, was vital to the project from the outset. His command of all three relevant languages—Rhade, Vietnamese, and English—was crucial for negotiations and planning.

Also sent to work with Nuttle was Sergeant First Class Paul Campbell, a US Army Special Forces medic who had come to Vietnam to train his Vietnamese counterparts. Commencing on or about 10 October, Nuttle and Campbell (the latter working in civilian dress) approached Rhade villages. Introducing themselves as "Mr. Dave" and "Dr. Paul," respectively, they toured villages up to 70 km from Ban Me Thuot. Campbell treated sick people while Nuttle talked politics and defense with village elders.[51]

The villagers were courteous but also very wary. They sensed that, like the French before them and the Vietnamese on both sides, the Americans had a particular agenda and were trying to manipulate the Rhade to further it. Nuttle and Campbell soon decided that the project of arming the Rhade should start at Buon Enao, a village of about 400 people just 6 km from Ban Me Thuot. Buon Enao was not under direct Communist threat at this time and could thus become a "firm base" for further development. Nuttle knew the village well and regarded its chief, Y-Ju, as a personal friend. Sometime during the first half of October 1961, Campbell "assisted" Buon Enao's traditional sorcerer in curing Y-Ju's daughter, who had fallen ill with dysentery. Even this, however, did not make the village defense concept an easy sell. Negotiations involving Phu, Murray, Nuttle, Campbell, and Y-Rit on the one hand and Y-Ju and the Buon Enao village elders on the other took up much of the second half of October.[52]

The author of a recent CIA history finds it strange that the village elders of Buon Enao were extremely hesitant about acceding to the scheme. Nuttle's and Campbell's initial proposals, he points out, were modest: "a perimeter fence for security and a dispensary to care for the inhabitants of Buon Enao and surrounding villages." But as the elders surely realized, agreeing to these things would be the start of a process of turning Buon Enao into a "combat village" for the anti-Communist side. The Communists would, quite correctly, see the Buon Enao elders as having declared war against them. This would convert the village from a potential object of Communist infiltration, propaganda, and subversion into a target for Communist military assault. The elders would thus be risking their own lives, and those of their wives and children. Their hesitation is best seen not as a symptom of primitive suspicion of the outside world but rather as the product of a realistic politico-military appreciation of the peril of their position, a position that would be frightening to any rational group.

Ultimately, it seems that a rather brutal argument swung their decision. They had to choose sides, the Americans told them, because otherwise they were likely to be caught in the cross fire and destroyed. As Nuttle put it, "When elephants fight the grass gets trampled." At Buon Enao, the villagers were closer to Ban Me Thuot, a center of the Saigon government and (by proxy) American power, than they were to any substantial Communist force. In the final analysis, perhaps, they had little choice.[53]

The village elders nevertheless showed themselves to be tough negotiators with a keen sense of their own interests and those of their ethnic group. They would resist the Communists, they said, but only on certain conditions. First, all attacks on Rhade and Jarai villages by government forces, even if these villages were perceived to be cooperating with the Communists, must cease. Second, Rhade "who had been forced to train with or support the VC would be given an amnesty upon declaring their allegiance" to the government. Third, the government would guarantee the Rhade medical, educational, and agricultural assistance. If the government accepted these conditions, Buon Enao would act as the test village. Once a self-defense force, initially armed with crossbows and spears, had been trained, the villagers would erect a fence around the village and display notices announcing their allegiance to the government and forbidding entry to the Communists. Underground shelters would be dug for the women and children; village medics would be trained and a dispensary built. After that, they would expect the self-defense force to be issued modern firearms.

Captain Phu played a vital role in convincing Major Bang, the province chief, and Colonel Trong, commander of the ARVN 23d Division (whose tactical area of responsibility encompassed Buon Enao), that virtually all these terms should be accepted. The only caveat the authorities introduced at this stage was this: "Any Rhade who had co-operated with the VC in any way was to be identified, re-educated to the government cause, and carefully observed. Amnesty would not be granted immediately."

Such was the agreement made between the village elders of Buon Enao and the South Vietnamese government. Concluded on or about 4 November, it was an entirely oral agreement, but because of the importance of what was at stake, it was taken seriously by all parties. The negotiators and the village as a whole celebrated the deal in the traditional Rhade manner with drums, a feast, and plenty of rice wine.[54]

Special Forces at Buon Enao: Arming and Expanding

Two or three days after the agreement was concluded, Captain Khoai of the Vietnamese Special Forces arrived with ten soldiers from the 77th Observation Group. About half were Rhade and half Jarai. Khoai was a native of

Darlac Province and, according to some reports, was Jarai himself. He understood Highlanders and their problems. He was also a skillful fighter and commander and proved to be a major military asset to the project. He and his men commenced the training of a thirty-man village defense force while Sergeant Campbell trained four Rhade paramedics.

Also in early November, work began on the dispensary, the civilian shelters, and the bamboo fence around Buon Enao. The Americans paid the villagers and other Rhade from the surrounding area 35 piastres (about 50 cents American) per day for their labor. A trail-watch system was established to warn of approaching Communist forces. Though still armed only with crossbows and spears, the Village Defenders patrolled and set ambushes. As promised, pro-government, anti-Communist notices were placed on the fence, and South Vietnamese flags were flown. The villagers were drilled in the use of the shelters in the event of attack.

The village chief, Y-Ju, identified three villagers who had attended Communist training camps. Nuttle and Phu organized "reeducation" for them, and this was effective. These individuals subsequently identified other Rhade who had attended Communist camps. From the outset, the village defense leadership team, consisting of Nuttle, Phu, Khoai, Murray, Campbell, and Y-Rit, gave intelligence and security a high priority. To maintain security, they asked Y-Ju to certify the loyalty of each villager. During inspections, each man in the defense force was asked to vouch for the loyalty of the man to his right.[55]

In mid-November, after completion of the dispensary, a government inspection team led by Colonel Tung of the PSO and accompanied by Layton came from Saigon to review Buon Enao. The inspectors recognized that the villagers had completely fulfilled their part of the bargain and responded by authorizing the immediate issuance of firearms to the self-defense force. A shipment of arms consisting of a mixture of 1903 vintage Springfield rifles, M2 carbines, and Madsen 9mm submachine guns was received soon after the inspection. Training in their use began without delay, ending the most dangerous period of the experiment. (Up to mid-November, only the village defense leadership team and Khoai's ten-man Vietnamese Special Forces team had firearms.[56] If a substantial force of well-armed Communist troops had attacked before then, the results could have been catastrophic for the villagers.)

Sometime in the first half of December (possibly on 4 December) the village was reinforced with half a US Special Forces A-detachment: a dozen soldiers from A-35 under Captain Larry Arritola, flown in through Ban Me Thuot from Okinawa via Saigon.[57] Unpaid volunteer Village Defenders had already been trained, and work began on the creation of a Strike Force of paid volunteers that could patrol beyond the village and, to a degree, hit back at the Communists.

In mid-December there was another inspection, this time involving Ngo Dinh Nhu, accompanied by both Colby and Layton. Nhu was greatly impressed by what he saw and authorized the inclusion of other Rhade villages in the project. What Colby had now christened the Citizens' Irregular Defense Group program began to expand rapidly, with Buon Enao becoming the first CIDG Area Development Center. Over the next few months the project grew with astonishing speed, incorporating scores of villages until it became, at least in part, the victim of its own success.[58] But these events belong largely to 1962 and are covered in the next chapter.

Diem's Highland Pacification Plan and the Mountain Scouts Program

Diem's attitude toward Highlanders seems to have been deeply ambivalent. The better angels of his intensely religious nature impelled him to be benevolently paternalistic toward them, to integrate them into his state as fully as possible and help them attain what the Vietnamese regarded as a decent, civilized life. But he found it difficult to rid himself of prejudices against those traditionally regarded as *Moi* (savages). He saw the Central Highlands as a vitally important resource to be developed by his Vietnamese state without giving its original inhabitants much say in the matter. Authoritarian by nature, impatient with any opposition from any quarter, he tended to be particularly short with Highlanders who refused to fit in with his plans. As already noted, he reacted to their demands for autonomy with repression. And any aid they gave to the Communists, whether voluntary or not, was met with often brutal and indiscriminate violence.

There can be little doubt that Diem understood the strategic importance of the Central Highlands. At some point in 1961, most likely in the immediate aftermath of the Communist Dak Ha offensive in early September, he asked his Highlands Social Action Directorate (which dealt with the administration of the Highland tribes) to prepare a pacification plan for the region. Exemplifying the danger of making crude generalizations about the Diem regime, it seems that Captain Ngo Van Hung, the head of that office, was intellectually honest, enlightened, and courageous. He was not afraid to criticize the attitudes and behavior of his own ethnic group and was willing to tell the president uncomfortable truths about the conduct of his own administration and its armed forces.

In a report submitted in late September Hung made the same complaints and accusations heard many times from Highlanders themselves: everything from unequal pay and limited opportunities for Highlanders in government service, cultural insensitivity, bullying, and theft to murder and the burning of villages. Hung believed the Highlanders were falling under Communist influence and that reversing this process required fairly drastic reform. The government would need to choose its representatives carefully, promote loyal tribesmen, isolate dissidents, and guarantee the physical security of the model villages it needed to establish. Hung advocated revitalizing the Highlander resettlement program, which had stalled in 1960, and make it more attractive to Highlanders by putting serious money (92.3 million piastres) into it, this to be spent on food, clothing, medicine, and books for Highland schoolchildren. Hung also wanted to recruit Highlanders both as intelligence operatives to run agent networks in the Highland provinces and as paramilitary forces to carry out operations against the Communists.

In the emergency atmosphere of late 1961, when the imminent loss of a large part of the Central Highlands seemed a real possibility, Diem approved, at least in principle, much of this. He backed a plan developed by II Corps commander, Brigadier General Ton That Dinh, to relocate Highland villages along highways, and he consented to Hung's scheme, enthusiastically endorsed by his brother Ngo Dinh Can (in effect, Diem's viceroy in the northern half of South Vietnam), to recruit more Highlanders as intelligence operatives and specialist small-unit fighters. Colby, the CIA station chief, was impressed with Captain Hung's analysis and plan and expressed a willingness to finance what became known as the "Mountain Scouts" project.

The Mountain Scouts program was approved by the American Country Team and sponsored by the Political Operations Section of the CIA, with Ralph Johnson, a World War II bomber pilot, organizing the CIA's contribution. It began a little later than the Buon Enao experiment, with the first 350 Mountain Scout recruits beginning their training in December 1961 at a purpose-built camp funded by the CIA near Hué. Captain Hung had gone to great lengths to acquire good instructors: many of them were from the ARVN's 1st Division, widely regarded as its best. The program became operational in January 1962 and was most important in the northern part of the Central Highlands, especially Kontum Province. Estimates of its effectiveness vary widely, but some accounts give the Mountain Scouts considerable credit for their contribution to an impressive government fight-back in Kontum Province in 1962.[59]

The General Situation at the End of 1961

In 1960 and 1961, over large parts of South Vietnam, the initiative was in Communist hands. By the end of 1961, the Diem regime faced an intense crisis. By November 1961, the US embassy reckoned there were 20,000 "hard-core" Communist troops in Vietnam south of the seventeenth parallel, roughly double the Communist strength at the same time the previous year.[60]

In the Central Highlands major armed struggle began later than it did in the Mekong Delta or the coastal plain. When the Communists initiated major attacks in October 1960, these met with initial defeat. In the last quarter of 1961, however, the impact of a renewed Communist offensive in Kontum, Pleiku, much of Darlac, and the highland parts of Binh Dinh was dramatic. Over a big section of the Central Highlands, the Communists seemed to have Diem's government on the ropes.

American military advisers reckoned the Communists had between 4,000 and 5,000 troops in Kontum Province alone (many of them brought in from the North) and that they were opposed by just 6,700 government troops. By November 1961, Wilbur Wilson was expressing fear that the Communists might mount a drive across the Central Highlands "to the coast," with the "goal of separating I Corps Tactical Zone from the rest of South Vietnam," thereby cutting South Vietnam into two separate pieces.[61]

In the Central Highlands south of Darlac, there was not as much of a military challenge, but the Communists were hard at work in some places agitating, disseminating propaganda, and developing a political infrastructure. By early 1962, the National Police in Tuyen Duc Province, containing the town of Dalat, one of the biggest in the Highlands, believed that the "Viet Cong controlled all the Highlanders living in the mountains of that province and that there was little chance of the government establishing effective control over these Highlanders in the near future."[62]

Yet Diem, for all his faults, was a fighter, and once Frederick Nolting took over as US ambassador, he had, at least for the time being, the earnest and virtually unequivocal backing of a superpower. By late 1961, both the Americans and the Republic of Vietnam's government and armed forces had conceived and were beginning to develop some bold, imaginative, and remarkably enlightened initiatives. The following year would see the anti-Communist side engaged in an active counteroffensive over much of the country. In the Highlands, as elsewhere, the Communists in 1962 would experience serious difficulties and sustain significant defeats.

4

Buon Enao and the Civilian Irregular Defense Group Program, 1962

An Eventful Year

In the Central Highlands, 1962 was an eventful year, and one about which we are relatively well informed. Two chapters are devoted to it here. This chapter examines events in the Central Highlands in the context of the war as a whole, traces the rise of the Buon Enao experiment to its remarkable apogee, analyzes the factors that ultimately led to its dissolution, and sketches the early development of the CIDG program that emerged from it. The next chapter examines the subsistence crisis that faced the Communists in the Central Highlands, the movement of substantial numbers of Highlanders from Communist- to government-controlled areas, plans for the Strategic Hamlet Program in the region, and ARVN activity and its impact.

The Government Fight-back

In the immediate aftermath of the Dak Ha offensive of early September 1961, Communist momentum in the Central Highlands appeared unstoppable. It looked as though the entire region might be under their control by mid-1962. Beginning in early 1962, however, and continuing for more than a year, their surge in the region was checked and in some places seriously reversed.

There was, indeed, a major counteroffensive by the Diem government's forces, strongly aided by American money, equipment, and personnel, across much of South Vietnam.[1] Its success should not be exaggerated. Neither the regime nor its most optimistic American backers claimed victory at this time. For the anti-Communist side, some adverse trends and worrying problems continued. Levels of infiltration from the North remained high and may have tended to increase. Though intelligence was imprecise, the number of

Communist troops in the South did not seem to diminish significantly, and in some areas may have continued to grow.[2]

Although there were effective units and commanders, it seems that practically no one on the anti-Communist side was satisfied with the general quality, performance, and combat activeness of South Vietnamese government troops.[3] Desertion rates, at least in some units, were worryingly high, and although American advisers made much effort to develop training programs, these could barely keep up with the rapid expansion of the armed forces and the pressure of operational commitments.[4]

The armed forces' loyalty to Diem was by no means universal. There continued to be many rumors of assassination plots or coups, as well as some actual attempts of this nature.[5] In these circumstances it was hardly surprising that promotions tended "to be based on presumed loyalty to Diem rather than upon professional competence." In addition, much of the ARVN officer corps perceived that closeness to Saigon rather than contact with the enemy was the key to career success, and officers gravitated toward the technical arms and headquarters appointments, leaving the infantry, which did most of the fighting, seriously short of leadership.[6] In the Central Highlands there was the additional problem of ethnic tensions between Highlanders and Vietnamese, a constant drag on the anti-Communist war effort. The seriousness of its impact varied from time to time and place to place, but the underlying problem of race relations simply would not go away.[7]

Yet, despite all these difficulties, by the second half of 1962, the mood of the majority of senior American military advisers in Vietnam, not always shared by their juniors, can best be described as cautiously sanguine.[8] Not everyone who held such views was an incorrigible optimist like General Paul Harkins, the first head of the new Military Assistance Command Vietnam (MACV), which, from its inception in February 1962, gradually superseded and replaced MAAG.[9] They included the hard-bitten, notoriously irascible Colonel Wilbur Wilson, the senior American adviser to II Corps (and later III Corps).[10]

Some non-American observers and advisers shared this positive outlook. These included British counterinsurgency expert Robert Thompson and his Australian counterpart Colonel "Ted" Serong, both of whom became so intellectually, emotionally, and professionally involved with this war that they came to see it as their own.[11] At least one Communist sympathizer from the developed world, Australian journalist Wilfred Burchett, also thought the war was going Diem's way in 1962. We now know that these assessments were not mere delusion. The cautious optimism of some senior personnel on the anti-Communist side was reflected in a deep sense of frustration, alarm, and even crisis on the part of those directing the Communist war effort in the South.[12]

If American military advisers had had their way, they would have wanted to see on the part of South Vietnamese government forces, especially the ARVN, a stronger emphasis on bringing Communist forces to battle. Plans the Americans drew up and offered to Diem's government did not ignore the need to secure the rural population. But they placed more stress on the traditional business of finding, fixing, and destroying enemy troops than Diem's regime ultimately endorsed or that the bulk of his armed forces attempted to implement.[13] Although the Rangers were something of an exception in this respect,[14] and the ARVN as a whole was not as passive as is sometimes suggested,[15] the primary focus of the Saigon government's counterinsurgency effort in this period was not so much seeking combat with and inflicting casualties on Communist forces but rather gaining control of South Vietnam's rural population and breaking contact between it and the Communist Party's apparatus, both military and political.

The principal means of doing this was called the Strategic Hamlet Program. The idea seems to have been conceived within the regime itself, though to some degree it was influenced by a study of what the British had done in Malaya.[16] The main emphasis was on securing the rural masses and, by implication, their economic output—most importantly, food. Feeding its troops was an issue for the Communist side throughout South Vietnam, and this was particularly true in the thinly populated, not very productive Central Highlands. As in the Communist insurrection in Malaya, population control and the control of food were very closely linked. In both Malaya and South Vietnam the government side considered starving the Communist enemy a significant part of its strategy.[17]

The Strategic Hamlet Program involved establishing defended settlements that were, in many cases (and not necessarily with the consent of their inhabitants), relocated and reorganized in the interests of defense, or, to be more exact, in the interests of making contact between Communist forces and the settlements' inhabitants more difficult. By far the greatest numbers of strategic hamlets were established in the fertile rice lands of the coastal plain and the Mekong Delta. In 1962 they were constructed at a slower rate in the Central Highlands, although they were important in parts of that region too.[18] In one Highland province there was also, as already noted, a village defense program that operated on different principles, relying very much on voluntary action and encouraging people to defend their villages as traditionally located.

Buon Enao: Philosophy and Management

It seems fair to say that the Buon Enao experiment, which began in Darlac Province near Ban Me Thuot in October 1961, was the most remarkable and successful initiative by the anti-Communist side in the Central Highlands in 1962. This was true to such an extent that it became a showpiece for the anti-Communist war effort in South Vietnam: a sort of Mecca for important visitors.[19] Not merely did the Buon Enao experiment check the Communist advance in Darlac; over a large part of that province, it rolled the Communists back.

Whereas the Strategic Hamlet Program frequently involved the forcible removal of villages or, particularly in the Central Highlands, the establishment of refugee villages, the fundamental idea of the Buon Enao experiment was to allow people to reject Communist influence and defend their own homes as traditionally located. By October 1962, within a year of its inception, the experiment was nearing the peak of its prodigious success. Its expansion was not accomplished without much hard fighting. But to a remarkable degree, combat against Communist troops of all types, apparently including ethnic Vietnamese units recruited and trained in the North, went in favor of paramilitary forces that the program itself generated.

Fundamental to the program's combat effectiveness was an extraordinarily sophisticated, remarkably holistic approach to counterinsurgency that provided a mainspring of motivation for its participants to fight on the anti-Communist side. The Buon Enao experiment was not conceived by conventional military men as a purely military response to military threats. Rather, it was developed by an aid worker, operating in conjunction with an intelligence agency, as a solution to the problems, considered in the broadest terms (political, military, social, economic, educational, medical, and psychological), of an entire people: the Rhade.

Indeed, the experiment's prime movers and principal promoters, Dave Nuttle, Gilbert Layton, and William Colby, appeared to have a still wider vision. They considered the approach adopted at Buon Enao a possible solution to the dilemmas facing the Highland tribes in general. Ultimately, rather less than half the Highlanders involved in the Buon Enao project were Rhade. The project involved people from all the Highland groups in Darlac (including Jarai and Mnong) and seems to have developed great symbolic and emotional significance for politically aware Highlanders more widely.[20]

That Nuttle's work with the Rhade might have implications for other Highlanders was grasped, even before the Buon Enao project got off the ground, by at least one high-status, politically aware individual from another tribe. This was Rcom H'un, daughter of the Jarai leader Nay Moul and a member of the educated Highland elite.[21] Knowing of Nuttle's work with the Rhade, with whom her own people had a cultural affinity, she had introduced herself to him in Ban Me Thuot in July 1961, seeking his aid to stop government air strikes against Jarai villages in the Cheo Reo area, her family's home. Through his CIA and embassy contacts, Nuttle did intercede, although he was unable to halt the bombing immediately and completely. Nevertheless, Nuttle's relationship with Bonnie Layton having somewhat cooled, and Bonnie having returned to the United States to go to college, Nuttle and H'un soon became close. H'un proposed marriage, and they had a simple wedding, although they never lived together continuously for any length of time. In the short term, H'un spent much of her time with her family in Cheo Reo, and Nuttle continued to reside in Ban Me Thuot.

When Buon Enao began to be developed into a defended village in October 1961, however, Communist forces renewed their efforts to assassinate Nuttle, and there were indications they had identified the house where he and Hugh Murray of the CIA lived. Realizing that it would be safer to live in Buon Enao than to stay in Ban Me Thuot, Nuttle asked permission from Y-Ju, the chief, to reside in the village full time. Y-Ju agreed but indicated that it would be most appropriate for Nuttle to have a Highland wife in residence with him.[22] Rcom H'un never became a fixed resident of Buon Enao, her attachment to her own people being too strong, but she was a frequent visitor. American anthropologist and historian Gerald Hickey notes the involvement of this high-status Jarai woman with the Buon Enao project as a matter of some significance in the politics of the Central Highlands in 1962.[23]

The term most commonly associated with the Buon Enao project is Civilian Irregular Defense Group Program (CIDG), a modified version of Citizens' Irregular Defense Group Program, the name CIA station chief Colby had originally given it.[24] In Darlac Province in 1962, however, the Buon Enao project was most commonly called the Village Defense Program, or VDP. The command and control element of the project, initially called the village defense leadership team, was also most commonly referred to simply as the VDP. In overall command of the project, at least nominally, was Darlac's province chief, Major Bang. Bang did not reside at Buon Enao, but his office in the provincial capital at Ban Me Thuot was close enough for the three key decision makers—Nuttle, Captain Phu of the Presidential Survey Office, and Y-Ju—to attend weekly planning sessions there with him. Between such meetings this three-man group made most of the important day-to-day management decisions.

There were seven or eight other members of the VDP's directing staff, including the commanders of the Special Forces teams (Vietnamese and American); Hugh Murray, who ran intelligence and counterintelligence; Y-Rit, who, as both an agricultural expert and a gifted linguist, ran the agricultural improvement program, the interpreter training program, and a radio school (for propaganda broadcasts); Y-Cha, who, with the help of Paul Katz of USOM, ran the program's early-warning radio network and provided training in the use of HT-1 and HT-2 radio sets for the program's militias; another man named Y-Ju (not the Buon Enao village chief), who ran Information Teams (more about these later); and Dr. Ksor Dun, who ran the medical programs and the dispensary, which also functioned as a field hospital. Ksor Dun, a Jarai, was reportedly the first Highlander to qualify as a medical doctor. An exceptionally gifted man, his presence at Buon Enao added prestige to the project. His wife, Georgia, who spoke seven languages, became the VDP's office manager. Other Rhade members of the VDP management team ran the educational, commercial, and industrial microenterprise parts of the program.[25]

The various aspects of the VDP were closely linked and ran simultaneously. It seems fitting, however, first to discuss the nonmilitary aspects of the program, activities sometimes described as "civic action." Nuttle, of course, had been helping with the economic welfare of the Rhade, mainly through agriculture, long before he became involved with paramilitary matters. Efforts to improve agriculture, the economic basis of Rhade life, continued under Y-Rit's direction. In mid-1961 Nuttle, with financial aid from the CIA obtained through Layton, had started a seed farm to encourage the Rhade to experiment with new crops. This continued to be useful. Peppers, cucumbers, watermelons, and beans were all grown successfully and proved popular. The use of better fertilizer greatly improved the productivity of the soil, which assisted in generating a significant food surplus. Surplus rice was purchased by the project's leadership team and used to feed refugees and prisoners.[26]

The VDP, backed financially by the CIA, also initiated a number of commercial and industrial enterprises. One of the first was a village store that operated on a nonprofit basis and sold basic goods at reasonable prices, undercutting Vietnamese itinerant traders who charged exorbitant rates and were, in some cases, suspected of being spies for the Communists. The expanding Buon Enao complex also developed a cottage industry of making clothing from discarded ARVN uniforms. Rhade women used sewing machines powered by treadles in order to avoid dependence on an electricity supply that might not survive the American presence. Nuttle and his CIA backers also encouraged the development of a blacksmithing industry, using scrap metal from vehicles in ARVN dumps to manufacture simple tools such as machetes. Within a short time, the success of the Buon Enao project attracted a substantial number of visitors. Some of them were interested in purchasing traditionally manufactured articles such as weaving, jewelry, and crossbows. A trading post was established to sell such items and bring in much-needed cash.[27]

One of the VDP's most powerful draws for the Rhade was its stress on improving their health. This included both public health and preventive medicine on the one hand and the actual treatment of illness on the other. Vital to the preventive side were clean water and good sanitation. The project provided drills for digging wells and expertise in constructing them. In keeping with the emphasis on being self-sustaining and using local resources, in one village that became part of the Buon Enao complex, bamboo was employed for the pipes and buffalo hide for the valves. Sanitation was also improved through the building of proper latrines and insistence on their use.

With the support of Major Bang and Dr. Niem, the provincial medical officer, the VDP also mounted an attack on malaria, which was endemic in the region, through the use of DDT on standing water. In early 1962, with the dispensary at Buon Enao already completed, a training program commenced for village health workers. It was so successful and expanded so rapidly that by July 1962, eighty-eight Rhade villages within the complex had at least one such worker. As the VDP expanded and additional Area Development Centers were established as satellites of Buon Enao, each was provided with a modest, austere dispensary, "which as far as the Highlanders were concerned, was a magnificent leap forward over their previous way of life."[28]

The Communists knew that the health services run by the Buon Enao project were among its most powerful propaganda weapons. They tried to counteract them with their own propaganda, stating, for example, that the DDT used to kill mosquitoes would ultimately poison the Rhade too. This seems to have had little impact. The Communists, quite correctly, saw the health visits paid to outlying villages as exercises in propaganda for the Buon Enao program. They set ambushes for health workers and, in two separate cases, reportedly executed an old man and a child for betraying these ambushes to their intended victims. Such atrocious acts, however, did not seem to diminish the Rhade's enthusiasm for Western-style health care, which many of them came to value more than the traditional medicine administered by their sorcerers.[29]

Because ARVN military hospitals were sometimes reluctant to treat Highlanders, and because speedy treatment was crucial to the survival and recovery of casualties, the dispensary at Buon Enao soon started to function as a field hospital. The absence of formally qualified field surgeons meant that locally trained combat medics sometimes carried out major surgery, including amputations. Reports of this got out, and the American Medical Association persuaded the US surgeon general's office to investigate. The inspector who was sent seems to have understood that wartime exigencies forced combat medics to perform work for which they were not strictly qualified. He took a broad-minded approach and pronounced both the administration of the hospital and the medical and surgical practices he witnessed admirable. There was no further trouble on this score.[30]

There was an educational dimension to the program too. The Rhade, the most advanced of the Highland tribes, had, with French assistance, devised a method of writing their own language. Many had a desire for literacy and a broader education. The VDP organized not just elementary schools to teach the village children reading, writing, and basic arithmetic but also home economics classes for women and language classes for all interested adults. Although, for political reasons, it might have been better to teach the Rhade Vietnamese, they often showed a greater interest in learning English. English was indeed useful in facilitating communication with American Special Forces personnel, few of whom spoke Rhade. Soon substantial numbers of the Rhade spoke some English, and quite a few spoke it fluently.[31]

In a sense, the entire Buon Enao project can be seen as a psychological exercise: an effort to change the collective mood, attitude, and behavior of Darlac's Highlanders, transforming them from downtrodden minority peoples living in poverty and in fear of all Vietnamese into a self-confident, healthy, assertive population committed, through an accurate perception of their own interests, to the anti-Communist side in the war raging around them. Fundamental to this transformation was the matter of arms. It seems reasonable to suggest that, given their traditional roles as hunters and warriors, Highland men felt emasculated by the government's confiscation of their spears and crossbows. Even getting these relatively primitive weapons back was of great benefit, both practically and psychologically. The issuance of modern firearms was greeted with positive delight. With these weapons, along with proper training and American support, Highland men could lose their fear of their enemies and regain their self-respect.[32]

The VDP also made sophisticated use of modern media for propaganda purposes. When a new village joined the project, the chief was given a transistor radio as a gift. Only a minority of the Rhade could understand broadcasts in English or Vietnamese, but Radio Darlac and Radio Ban Me Thuot also broadcast in Rhade. The VDP provided suitable material for broadcast and, under Y-Rit's direction, established a radio school that trained local people in giving radio interviews and talks.[33] Colonel Wilbur Wilson, the senior MAAG adviser at II Corps, may have been more perceptive and open-minded than his often curmudgeonly manner suggested. He appreciated the VDP's efforts in this area, crediting Nuttle personally.[34]

Films, whether overtly propagandistic, educational (on such topics as agriculture, health, and hygiene), or purely entertaining, proved popular with villagers and were good for morale. The VDP obtained two trucks to carry mobile movie-showing equipment that Rhade personnel were trained to use; however, these operated only in areas declared "white" (secure) and even there were protected by Strike Force teams.[35] Live performances, carried out by the Information Teams, were perhaps an even more effective form of propaganda. Captain Ron Shackleton, who commanded A-113, the A-team that arrived in February 1962 to help expand the project, describes watching a rehearsal:

Their first act was a group of singers who sang Rhade songs and encouraged the audience to sing along with them to stimulate their interest. A skit followed where in the first scene the VC are supported by the villagers. The SF [Strike Force], on patrol, questions the villagers who indicate that they don't know where the VC are. The second scene depicts the VC demanding more support from the villagers. When this is denied, the villagers are manhandled and forced to provide additional food. After the VC depart a villager is seen leaving the village. The third scene again shows the VC taking food from the villagers only to be surrounded and killed by the SF who were informed by one of the villagers. The cheer of the audience was deafening. . . .

The third act was the delivery of a message on the care and protection of weapons. An instrumental number followed. Then a political message called for the support of all Rhade to unite behind the VDP [Village Defense Project] and to denounce the VC. The benefits the VDP brought these people were cited. A fire-power demonstration was next on the program which concluded with a pep rally.[36]

Buon Enao's Militias and Their Enemies

The potential material and psychological benefits of the Buon Enao project would have been of no use to the Rhade had its armed forces failed. The overriding missions of these forces were to protect people already in the program and to influence others to join it, rather than to seek and destroy enemy troops, although that did not stop them from attacking Communist forces in the VDP's immediate vicinity.

The forces employed were of three types. Unpaid but reasonably well-trained and well-armed units of Village Defenders were the first to be raised. As the program developed, some of these units were issued automatic rifles and light machine guns as well as carbines, rifles, and submachine guns. Each new village entering the program developed its own village defense group trained by Vietnamese or American Special Forces. Essentially just a home guard sub-unit, each group was intended primarily to resist attacks on its village and to summon reinforcements if necessary. In some circumstances a group might go to the assistance of a neighboring village in trouble. Even in defense of their own villages, however, these groups were supposed to exercise discretion. Preserving life was far more important than protecting buildings or holding ground. If they were facing an attack too powerful to repel with their own resources and could not be reinforced quickly enough, they were instructed to organize a controlled evacuation. A village could always be rebuilt.[37]

The second type of unit was the Strike Force. Strike Force personnel were full-time paid professionals supplied with the normal range of infantry weapons, including heavier types of machine guns, grenades, and mortars. The Strike Force's principal function was to act as a reserve, going to the rescue of villages under Communist attack in its area of responsibility. It also patrolled the perimeter of its area and sometimes probed further, looking for opportunities to bring new villages into the VDP. The basic subunit of the Strike Force was the section, the equivalent of an infantry platoon.[38]

The third type of VDP armed force was the Information Team, which also consisted of full-time, well-armed, paid professionals. The first Information Team was raised not long after the first Strike Force. These teams were composed entirely of Highlanders, the great majority of them Rhade. They were essentially armed propaganda teams, about thirty strong and predominantly male, but including some female singers and performers. They visited villages within the defended area of the VDP as well as adjacent villages, where they encouraged the inhabitants to declare against the Communists and become part of the program. They became crucial intelligence gatherers, carefully observing and listening during their conversations with villagers. Sometimes they helped recruit agents, who would then be handled by Murray and his Rhade intelligence staff. These teams did a significant proportion of all the VDP's fighting and suffered the heaviest casualties among the VDP's militias. But because they never operated with Americans, there is practically no record of their endeavors, and their contributions have been lost to history.[39]

What was the VDP up against? The intelligence picture was never totally clear. In 1962 things were changing fast. But, as in other parts of Vietnam, there were three basic types of Communist troops: village militia, local force troops, and regular or main force troops. Village militiamen, who, in the vicinity of Ban Me Thuot, were normally ethnically Rhade, were unpaid, part-time troops who spent much of their time farming or performing other civilian work. In the Highlands there were normally half a dozen such militiamen per Communist-controlled village. Their role consisted largely of village control on behalf of a Communist leadership that depended on villagers to grow food to support its troops, for recruits, and for simple munitions such as panji (sharpened bamboo) stakes used in booby traps.

The next category of Communist troops consisted of local force units. These were full-timers. When the Buon Enao project started, those in central Darlac were racially mixed and usually more than 50 percent Rhade, although the leadership was mostly Vietnamese. They operated from jungle bases and were organized as local battalions and companies. Their numerical strength varied, as did their equipment. There was no standardization, and both weapons and ammunition were in short supply. French MATS-36 rifles were common;

MAS-49 automatic rifles rather less so. Captured American carbines were also found, as were many other types of weapons. An interrogation report of a Communist soldier captured on 10 May 1962 read:

> The group that I was with numbered 100 men: 60 were Rhade and 40 were Vietnamese. About 50 men were armed with a mixture of French rifles and American carbines. They had one 60mm mortar and four British Bren guns. The cadre wore pistols and carried grenades. Our area of operation was always within 10–15 km of Buon Knoup (village). We had no uniforms and we wore mixed clothing.[40]

Communist regular troops or main force units, as they were referred to later in the war, first made an appearance in Darlac in late 1961. Indeed, one of the CIA's reasons for developing the Buon Enao venture was its assessment that a major branch of the Ho Chi Minh Trail (along which whole units sometimes traveled) led directly into this area. The presence of such troops was again sometimes felt in 1962. They normally operated only in company or battalion strength but were far better armed than the local force units. Their weapons, commonly a mixture of French and Chinese, were more standardized within the unit than was the case with local forces. They normally had a variety of crew-served weapons, including machine guns, mortars, and recoilless rifles, as well as small arms. They were usually uniformed. Those operating against the VDP in 1962 were thought to be predominantly ethnic Vietnamese, and in some cases at least, raised and trained in the North.

It appears that with the growing success of the VDP in early 1962, the motivation to fight of Rhade personnel in the Communist ranks, never especially strong in most cases, declined markedly. Unable to rely on locally recruited Highlanders, later in the year the Communist leadership reacted by using regular, largely ethnically Vietnamese units to assault VDP villages and try to wreck or at least disrupt the program.[41]

The Expansion of the Buon Enao Program

The program started to expand as soon as it began. As soon as the first Village Defenders and Strike Force personnel completed their training, forty neighboring villages elected to join the program. This happened even before the first American Special Forces A-team arrived, circa 4 December 1961. By April 1962, there were 972 trained Village Defenders and a 300-strong Strike Force to protect forty villages with a total of 14,000 inhabitants. Up to that point, the only Area Development Center was the village of Buon Enao, where the

Strike Force was based. The defense of the other villages was organized from there.

Continued expansion from April to October 1962 involved the creation of Area Development Centers at Buon Ho, Buon Krong, Ea Ana, Lac Thien, and Buon Tah. Each of these became a hub for both civic and paramilitary action, and each had a small number of US Special Forces soldiers—usually not a complete A-detachment and rarely even half a detachment, but usually a four-man group. The whole Buon Enao complex contained, by October 1960, about 60,000 people in 200 villages defended by 10,600 Village Defenders and 1,500 Strike Force members.

Although the first year of the project saw dramatically successful growth, inevitably there were some setbacks along the way. In May, two small villages that had joined the VDP, Buon Cu Bong and Buon Tong Dok, fell to Communist forces with little resistance and the loss of some weapons—the indications being that the Communists had inside help. These villages were forcibly evacuated and their inhabitants dispersed to other villages within the VDP.[42]

Buon Enao's Battles

The VDP expanded mainly by a kind of magnetism. The inhabitants of nearby villages saw its benefits and were drawn in. Village elders and chiefs expressed a wish to join, erected fences as a symbol of this desire, and requested that some of their men be trained as Village Defenders. Unlike the Strategic Hamlet Program in other parts of the country, the VDP never forced a village to join. Expansion, however, was not achieved without violence. Military or paramilitary activity in and around the VDP was continuous. By May 1962, substantial firefights (lasting thirty minutes or more and involving the expenditure of hundreds of rounds) averaged about two per week.

No American died or (to the best of Dave Nuttle's recollection) even sustained a wound up to the beginning of October 1962, although several dozen served there during that time. Nuttle can remember no fatalities among Vietnamese Special Forces personnel either. He recollects that there were somewhere between seventy and eighty fatalities among the project's Highlanders up to October 1962, and about 10 percent of them were civilians not enrolled in any of the militias.[43] These losses were undoubtedly serious for the Rhade, but the program's continuing expansion indicates that they were not considered disastrous in relation to the many thousands of people involved.

Losses on the Communist side can only be estimated. A CIA report from 1966 indicates that by September 1962, "At least 160 Viet Cong had been killed, 90 wounded and 400 captured or surrendered." The credibility of this

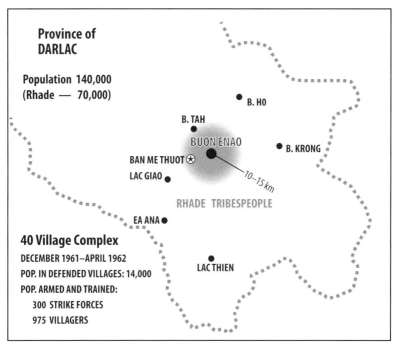

Province of DARLAC

Population 140,000
(Rhade — 70,000)

B. HO

B. TAH

BUON ENAO

B. KRONG

BAN ME THUOT ⊗

LAC GIAO

10–15 km

RHADE TRIBESPEOPLE

EA ANA

40 Village Complex

DECEMBER 1961–APRIL 1962

POP. IN DEFENDED VILLAGES: 14,000

POP. ARMED AND TRAINED:

   300 STRIKE FORCES

   975 VILLAGERS

LAC THIEN

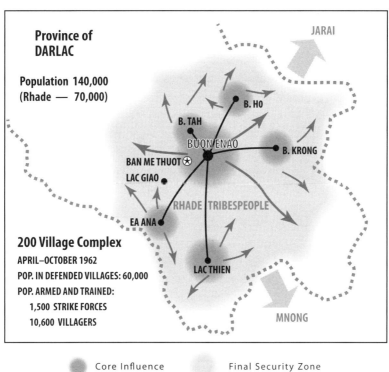

JARAI

Province of DARLAC

Population 140,000
(Rhade — 70,000)

B. HO

B. TAH

BUON ENAO

B. KRONG

BAN ME THUOT ⊗

LAC GIAO

RHADE TRIBESPEOPLE

EA ANA

200 Village Complex

APRIL–OCTOBER 1962

POP. IN DEFENDED VILLAGES: 60,000

POP. ARMED AND TRAINED:

   1,500 STRIKE FORCES

   10,600 VILLAGERS

LAC THIEN

MNONG

Core Influence   Final Security Zone

Province Boundary   Expanding Influence

Expansion of the Buon Enao complex

report is somewhat damaged by the claim that the Rhade lost only 15 killed over the same period, a figure that Nuttle, a surviving witness in a good position to know, indicates to be far too low.[44] A recent account based on CIA sources indicates that the VDP captured 460 enemy personnel over the course of 1962 and killed more than 200.[45]

The surviving records of all this combat activity are patchy. We have, however, reasonably detailed accounts of some actions, and these must suffice to give an impression of the VDP's war. One fairly minor incident occurred on 16 May 1962 and involved the village of Buon Ea Khit, about 10 km south of Buon Enao as the crow flies or 15 km by road. At 1100 hours the village came under attack, probably by elements of a local Communist company based in the mountains immediately to the east. To reach the village as rapidly as possible, the Strike Force based at Buon Enao used its World War II vintage trucks to transport one section part of the way. Road ambush being a common Communist tactic, there was, however, a standing order against moving by vehicle within 2 km of a "red" (enemy-controlled) area.

Buon Ea Khit was in an area normally coded "pink"—that is, neither secure nor totally under enemy control. Once a locality came under attack, however, its classification immediately changed to red. Consequently, the Strike Force convoy did not drive all the way to Buon Ea Khit but halted about 3 km west of the village and moved the rest of the distance tactically and on foot. They still arrived in time to relieve the village before the attackers penetrated its defenses (if, indeed, that was ever their intention). No casualties were reported on either side. While scouting around later, however, the Strike Force section found a Communist ambush position about 1.5 km from Buon Ea Khit on the road they would have used had they not dismounted from their vehicles. Because the village fences were never broken and the attack took place in daylight (unusual for a Communist assault on a village), there is a good chance that ambushing the Strike Force convoy was the real Communist aim.[46]

More typical in terms of its timing was the assault on the village of Buon Tang Ju at 0300 on 10 July 1962. The attack took place during heavy rain and in complete darkness. The VDP's intelligence branch later assessed that the attacking force had been a Communist company. Perhaps judging by their equipment and lack of definite uniform, it categorized the Communist troops as "irregulars." But they were not locals. A company dossier captured at the end of the engagement indicated that they were all ethnic Vietnamese who had recently been operating in War Zone D, near Saigon.

Just prior to the attack, the Communists had yelled into the village (perhaps demanding surrender in Vietnamese, a language few villagers would have understood) and rattled the fence. Then they cut a hole in it. One Communist soldier entered the village, and a Village Defender called Y-Ao shot him dead,

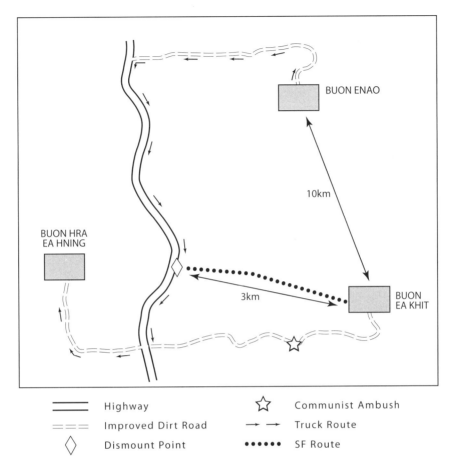

━━━━	Highway	☆	Communist Ambush
═══	Improved Dirt Road	→ →	Truck Route
◇	Dismount Point	••••••	SF Route

Action at Buon Ea Khit

reportedly with a single carbine bullet fired from his foxhole. After that, the Communists realized they were not going to get an easy capitulation. They opened an intense fire into the village from a number of angles. More Communist troops entered through the same hole in the fence and managed to kill Y-Ao and capture his weapon.

In this instance, however, the Communists had bitten off much more than they could chew. There normally would have been thirty-six Village Defenders at Buon Tang Ju, and even that number might have been difficult to overwhelm before first light, when Strike Force reinforcements were likely to arrive. But a Strike Force section had been conducting operations south of the village and had stayed there overnight, waiting for pickup by motor transport the following morning. Another section had been conducting a psychological operation in the village itself and had also remained overnight. There were thus an additional sixty-eight armed men defending the village, with thirty

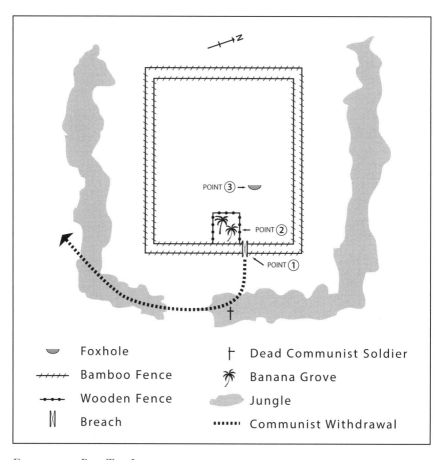

Engagement at Buon Tang Ju

extra submachine guns, twenty-six extra carbines, and six extra automatic rifles among them. Altogether, more than a hundred well-armed men defended Buon Tang Ju. Under such circumstances, it is surprising the Communist troops sustained the attack as long as they did. The fight went on for three hours, and the defenders fired approximately 15,000 rounds.

The VDP base at Buon Enao knew that Buon Tang Ju was under attack, but reinforcements were not dispatched until 0500. The intention was for them to arrive at first light. Past experience had taught that trying to relieve a village in darkness entailed too great a risk of fratricide through "friendly fire." But by first light, the fight was practically over. The village had lost only one man (Y-Ao) killed and one carbine captured. (Y-Ao's widow was later compensated financially for his loss.) There were no Strike Force casualties. While the fight was in progress, the women, children, and old people of the village had taken refuge in the shelters and came to no harm. Inspection of the battle area revealed that the Communists had tried to carry away a considerable number of casualties, but overburdened and in haste, they left behind two corpses, two MATS-36 rifles, 100 rounds of MAS-36 ammunition, one grenade, two flashlights, one aid kit, three Bren gun magazines, three canteens, two knives, one hammock, some clothing, and some documents. The VDP's estimate that the Communists suffered fifty casualties might have been high, but a small victory had undoubtedly been won.[47]

By July 1962, the Communists were sending regular elements against outlying villages of the Buon Enao complex, which probably indicates that the project's success had them worried. One such village was Buon Trap. It had only recently joined the program, and its Village Defenders had returned from training at Buon Enao just two weeks prior to a heavy Communist attack on the early morning of 24 July. The Village Defenders put up a good fight, assisted by those of some neighboring villages, until their ammunition ran low and they organized a withdrawal into the jungle.

A Strike Force section sent out from Buon Enao was ambushed 8 km from Buon Trap but reacted vigorously, overrunning the ambush positions and killing a number of ambushers. The Strike Force and Village Defenders reoccupied Buon Trap on 25 July. The Communists continued their harassing attacks over the next two days and then, on the night of 26–27 July, mounted a further determined assault with a force estimated at two companies. On this occasion they met such stiff resistance that they abandoned the attack after just ten minutes.[48] The VDP had won this trial of strength, and the village remained in the program.

The least satisfactory aspect of this mini-battle was the behavior of a South Vietnamese Marine company that was in the immediate vicinity and could have mounted a counterattack but stood by doing little or nothing. On hearing reports of the incident, Nuttle attributed it to the old racial antipathy, considering that the Marines might have found the spectacle of the Rhade militia and the Communists battling it out merely amusing.[49]

The Communists continued their efforts to disrupt the Buon Enao project with large-scale attacks by regular units. At about 0500 on the morning of 1 August, the inhabitants of Buon Trea Mman heard noises outside the village, and the Village Defenders manned their positions. A Communist soldier was killed trying to get in through the north gate. At this point a bugle sounded, and heavy fire tore through the village from a number of directions. VDP villages normally had inner and outer bamboo fences a few yards apart, with the bamboo poles sharpened at the top and punji stakes fixed in the ground between them. This was the case at Buon Trea Mman. Within minutes of the start of the attack, there was a loud explosion on the northwest side of the village as the Communists used crude Bangalore torpedoes to demolish part of the outer fence. The firefight continued for about an hour before the Communists managed to demolish a section of the inner fence with more Bangalores. A force estimated at battalion strength stormed in through the breach at approximately 0630. The eighty-nine Village Defenders at Buon Trea Mman were compelled to retreat. Leaving behind a three-man covering force, all members of which were killed, they scattered into the jungle and then made their way to nearby villages within the VDP.

Buon Trea Mman was not yet equipped with a radio. Strike Force headquarters at Buon Enao therefore knew nothing of the attack until 0900, by which time fleeing Village Defenders had reached other villages. At that point, the Strike Force headquarters instructed Village Defenders in Buon Ea Huk, the nearest village with a radio, to send a patrol to Buon Trea Mman to assess the situation and report back. At the same time, a Strike Force section with four American Special Forces personnel attached went out from Buon Enao. The ARVN was also contacted, and aerial surveillance was requested. A South Vietnamese L-19 spotter aircraft was immediately dispatched, and a company of the ARVN 45th Regiment was placed on stand-by.

At 1100 the spotter aircraft reported that the patrol from Buon Ea Huk was entering Buon Trea Mman, that the Strike Force section was near the village, and that the Communist troops had withdrawn. The Communist troops had apparently not harmed the women and children left behind in the shelters, but they had destroyed large sections of the fences, taken all the livestock and all the food and clothing they could carry, and done a good deal of damage to buildings. Strike Force personnel helped rally Buon Trea Mman's Village Defenders and bring them back to the village. They reported that their attackers had been dressed in khaki or black uniforms and that many wore pith helmets. Their clothing, combined with their use of bugle calls, suggested the presence of PAVN elements or even a complete PAVN unit. If the latter, it would not (as already noted) have been the first in the Highlands.

In midafternoon patrols spotted Communist forces again surrounding Buon Trea Mman. The VDP requested that MAAG air-drop more ammunition into the village. Remarkably, this arrived within an hour. A South Vietnamese Marine company (whether the same one that had so conspicuously failed to distinguish itself at Buon Trap a week earlier is not clear) reinforced the Village Defenders and Strike Force personnel. The Communists mounted a number of probes on the night of 1–2 August, but none got closer than the outer fence. By morning they had gone. The Village Defenders of Buon Trea Mman lost three men killed and seventeen wounded in this action, as well as four weapons. On this occasion the Communists had plenty of opportunity to remove any casualties they had sustained, and their losses are unknown. Even then, the Communists did not give up on Buon Trea Mman. They mounted a night attack about forty-eight hours later but were repelled with the assistance of air-dropped flares, followed by an air strike.[50]

Air support could, of course, make an enormous difference. For a few months in late 1962 and early 1963, the Buon Enao complex had, in effect, its own private branch of the mighty United States Air Force (USAF).

Air Commandos, Farm Gate, and Buon Enao's Airpower

In view of the scale of attack by Communist regular units by August 1962, co-operation from the air was increasingly important for the Buon Enao project. Presumably owing to the persuasive skills of Captain Phu and the power of the PSO, the program was sometimes able to procure Vietnamese Air Force (VNAF) helicopters to give its Strike Force greater mobility and to help it avoid Communist ambushes.[51] As already noted, the VNAF also provided spotter aircraft from time to time. Sometimes, however, the VDP wanted close air support with more substantial firepower.

In 1962 the USAF was becoming an increasing presence in the war. As well as providing increased airlift for ground forces, the USAF ran a program called Farm Gate that carried out both "interdiction" bombing and close tactical support to ground forces.[52] Farm Gate's aircraft were piston-engine machines, mostly of Second World War vintage, including C-47 flare ships, T-28 fighter-bombers, and B-26 bombers. They were flown by a USAF Special Forces branch known as the Air Commandos.

The Air Commandos were seeking missions, and according to the CIA's own semiofficial account, Layton was quick to seize on their potential for supporting his CIDG program. At least initially, that meant mainly Buon Enao. The Air Commandos found this work much to their taste and developed an affinity with their US Army Special Forces colleagues. At this point in the war, neither the Army Special Forces nor their Air Commando counterparts wore uniforms, and some Farm Gate pilots reportedly flew in cowboy boots rather than regulation footwear.[53]

Air strikes by the T-28 fighter-bombers and Douglas B-26 bombers were coordinated by forward air controllers or combat control team members flying in U-10 D (L-28) Helio Super Courier light airplanes or operating with Special Forces A-team personnel on the ground. A small number of Air Commando noncommissioned officers lived full time within the Buon Enao complex to help direct the airpower assigned to it.[54] Communist attacks on villages belonging to the VDP most commonly occurred at night, and organizing effective air support in the dark was not easy. Even dropping flares in the wrong place could be disastrous. One technique to avoid this problem was the "underground fire arrow." A large bamboo arrow was placed in a shallow, circular pit in a village; the arrow could pivot like a compass needle, and pots containing combustible material could be hung from it. In the event of an attack, Village Defenders pointed the arrow in the direction from which the main threat was coming and ignited the combustible material. Because the arrow itself was in a pit, it did not illuminate the Village Defenders on the ground but could be seen from the air. Air Commando pilots and crews would know how far from the arrow it was safe to drop bombs or flares.[55]

The Air Commandos' support for the Buon Enao project was not without sacrifice. On 15 October 1962 elements of US Special Forces A-223 (based in the village of Buon Tah Mo) and Strike Force troops they had trained mounted an operation code-named Powder Blue against a Communist training camp in the foothills of the Cu Ken Mountains, near Ban Don along the Song Srepok River. Disturbed by the expansion of the Buon Enao project, the Communists had forcibly evacuated villages adjacent to Buon Tah Mo and compelled their residents to join them at this camp.

US Special Forces and Rhade Strike Force troops were brought to the battlefield by three H-21 Shawnee "Flying Banana" helicopters (each of which flew two lifts) belonging to the 81st Transportation Company of the US Army based at Holloway Field near the town of Pleiku. A Douglas B-26 bomber then bombed the Communist training camp—a ruthless act, considering that many of those in it, including women and children, were not there by choice. Two T-28s flew air cover for the Strike Force personnel as they moved to seize the camp and pursue the Communist troops fleeing from it. Flying overhead in a Helio U-10 spotter plane and directing the operation were Captain Terry D. Cordell, the senior Special Forces officer at Buon Enao at this time; the pilot, Captain Herbert Booth; and Sergeant Richard L. Foxx, whose mission was to direct air strikes. The U-10 was shot down in flames, reportedly by a Communist team with a Browning automatic rifle, and crashed into the jungle, killing all three Americans.

As if this were not bad enough from the American perspective, the Communists brought down a T-28 the following day during the same operation, although that pilot survived. US Special Forces nevertheless claimed that the operation was generally successful and that later on 16 October the Strike Force from Buon Tah Mo surrounded and destroyed the team thought responsible for downing both aircraft.[56] But losing three Americans on a single day was, at this stage of the war, quite exceptional. It was a hard blow and an ill omen.

Both the rather conventional military approach to this operation (with its relative disregard for the likelihood of civilian casualties) and the deaths of three Americans on one day (when none participating in this project had previously suffered a wound) might suggest that something significant had changed at

Buon Enao. It is probably no coincidence that Dave Nuttle, the prime mover and, up to the beginning of October 1962, principal day-to-day director of the project, had left Vietnam a couple of weeks previously.

Public Relations

Success on the scale achieved by the Buon Enao experiment, especially when such success has hitherto been so rare, inevitably attracts attention. Many people wanted to associate themselves with this success. As the complex expanded, the village of Buon Enao itself became a fairly safe rear-area location. Increasingly it functioned as a tourist center for VIP visitors.

Diem's brother Nhu had been the most important of these visitors in the initial stages of the project. A substantial number of ministers in the Diem government visited Buon Enao at one time or another, as did Ambassador Nolting. Australian counterinsurgency guru Ted Serong and Richard Noone, a British intelligence officer who had served during the Malayan emergency, paid multiple visits in 1962. The US Marine Corps' counterinsurgency specialist and adviser on the subject to the Joint Chiefs of Staff, Lieutenant General Victor H. "Brute" Krulak, had been to Buon Enao on at least three occasions by the end of September. Many of the most senior US Army officers serving in Vietnam, including the MAAG chief, Major General Charles Timmes, and General Paul Harkins, who commanded MACV, also visited.

Nuttle was very conscious of the VDP's public relations and gave such visits careful attention. In organizing them, he had the assistance of the efficient and highly regarded Major George Patton Jr., son of the renowned World War II commander and MAAG's liaison officer with Buon Enao at the time. They worked out a standard tour that included the VDP headquarters building, the industrial and commercial projects, the hospital, and the dispensary. Special Forces officers were always on hand to discuss military training and operations. For those with an interest in such things, village chief Y-Ju was available to show visitors his longhouse.[57]

The Kennedy administration itself took an interest in Buon Enao. Chalmers B. Wood, deputy director of the administration's Task Force Viet-Nam, paid a visit in May 1962. Wood recognized Nuttle as the driving force behind the project but also perceived that the support of the enlightened province chief, Major Nguyen Dinh Bang, was vital to its success. Bang was still supportive, despite his concern that some Rhade members of the province's Self-Defense Corps were slipping away to join Buon Enao's paramilitary forces. Wood perceptively commented: "Liaison is maintained with the Presidency at Saigon and so far the GVN attitude has been laissez-faire . . . [but] Buon Enao's very success will undoubtedly require increased co-ordination with local authorities."[58]

Nuttle and the patient, diplomatic Captain Phu of Diem's PSO had worked extremely hard to achieve such coordination. Ultimately, however, conflicts within the apparatus of the South Vietnamese state, politicking between and within the various (now rapidly expanding) American agencies in Vietnam, and, above all, racial tensions between Highlanders and Vietnamese combined to defeat them.

Storm Clouds over Buon Enao

Nuttle had long been aware that the Buon Enao project was meeting with suspicion, even hostility, in quarters from which it might have expected to draw support. Colonel Wilson, MAAG chief at II Corps in Pleiku, was generally most helpful, but Lieutenant Colonel Frederick, senior American adviser to the ARVN 23d Infantry Division, made no secret of his distaste for Special Forces and unconventional warfare.[59] Colonel Le Quang Trong, commanding the 23d Division, appears to have been deeply duplicitous in this matter. On the one hand, he expressed admiration for Nuttle's work at Buon Enao and personally presented Nuttle with an award from the South Vietnamese government. On the other hand, he was engaged in a bitter power struggle with Major Bang, the Darlac province chief, over who should run the war effort in Darlac and seemed determined to wrest control of Buon Enao from Bang; he was also intensely suspicious of both Rhade political aspirations and Buon Enao's militias.[60] Trong reportedly used his influence to have Bang removed from office in the summer of 1962. According to a CIA history of the politics of the Central Highlands:

> Some Rhade leaders believed that . . . Trong . . . had removed . . . Bang . . . because Bang was helping the Rhade, whereas Trong was attempting to provoke incidents between ARVN and the Rhade and was arresting Rhade he thought favored autonomy. He had obtained several Rhade prisoners and had coerced them into being prepared to [make] statements on the Rhade autonomy movement, which one high ranking military intelligence officer believed Trong would use as an excuse to enforce strict control measures.[61]

To Trong, Buon Enao's militias probably seemed to be outside the effective control of the South Vietnamese government. He probably considered them too likely to side with Bajaraka, the Highland autonomy movement, in any conflict between it and the regime.

Trong was not the only one to harbor such suspicions. General Ton That Dinh, commanding ARVN II Corps, was also anxious. Buon Enao was, in reality, outside Dinh's chain of command. Captain Phu, the highest-ranking Vietnamese officer based at Buon Enao, carried out liaison work with II Corps, but he was primarily responsible to his immediate superior in the PSO, Colonel Le Quang Tung, who apparently remained a supporter of the VDP. In this context, it is relevant that Jack Benefiel, the CIA case officer for the Buon Enao project, noted a marked hostility between Colonel Le Quang Trong, the 23d Division commander, and Colonel Le Quang Tung, head of the PSO.[62]

In his ethnohistory of the Central Highlands, American anthropologist Gerald Hickey recounts a story told to him in 1977 by Lucien Conein of the CIA: At some unspecified date (apparently in the summer of 1962), Colonel Tung invited both General Dinh and President Diem's brother, Ngo Dinh Nhu, to a celebration at Buon Enao involving the usual buffalo sacrifice, banging of gongs, and consumption of rice wine. At one point Dinh took Nhu aside and complained, "The Americans have put an army at my back." They had, he said, armed 18,000 Highlanders in the II Corps area—a fairly accurate figure. Nhu, according to this story, turned back toward the Rhade crowd wearing "a coldly impassive expression."[63]

This account is based on a story told some fifteen years after the event it describes and set down in print even later. The event, moreover, is not precisely dated, and it is apparently contradicted by a statement made by Colonel Wilbur Wilson, the senior American adviser at II Corps, who reported, "General Dinh is most enthusiastic in regard to the Buon Enao program and is backing it 100%."[64] Despite these caveats, Hickey's account has the ring of truth. There is no doubt that, from the midsummer of 1962, the Diem regime became increasingly suspicious of Buon Enao, an experiment it had authorized as recently as October of the previous year.

The outrage of many Highlanders (and of the Americans working with them) at what became a Saigon government U-turn on Buon Enao in 1962 is easy to understand. In the interest of historical balance, some effort must be made to see the matter from the government's viewpoint. Within a few months, the Americans had, in terms of weapons per head, made the Rhade of Darlac the most heavily armed population group in South Vietnam. Yet this group had no real allegiance to the Diem regime (or to any other conceivable government in Saigon). The Rhade were so suspicious of all Vietnamese that they regarded their villages as "no-go" areas for all but a tiny number of people from that ethnic group.

The Diem regime, as noted, did not favor developing the South Vietnamese economy by throwing the country wide open to foreign commercial and industrial investment. Diem was almost as suspicious of the exploitative tendencies of foreign capitalism as the Communists were. As part of his brand of nationalism, he wanted the southern Vietnamese to develop their country by their own efforts, using its indigenous resources to the fullest. In this scheme of things, the Central Highlands region was vital. Vietnamese who were en-countering economic and social frustration on the coastal plain should go west, the regime indicated, to this land of opportunity. The scattered populations of primitives who were its original inhabitants should not be allowed to interfere with Vietnam's manifest destiny in the region.[65]

The expanded VDP of late 1962 covered a large part of Darlac Province and constituted one of the most economically promising parts of the high plateau region. It was an area from which the Highlanders involved in the Buon Enao project had largely expelled the Communists. Clearly, this was a plus from the Diem regime's point of view. But the area covered by the VDP was also one where the Rhade showed every sign of wanting to exclude further Vietnamese settlement and within which they seemed (tacitly and in practice, rather than overtly and by law) set on restricting the control of the South Vietnamese government.

To Diem, his brother Nhu, and others who shared their outlook (which, on this specific issue, probably included the vast majority of Vietnamese), this was unacceptable. In other parts of the Highlands, Highlanders were being resettled in government-controlled areas and, in some cases, enrolled in the government's armed forces (see chapter 5). These processes, however, were being carried out in ways that left the government very much in control and gave the Highlanders no encouragement to believe that they could achieve autonomy. This approach was, from Diem's point of view, vastly safer than what was happening at Buon Enao.

Even so, it can be argued that the regime was foolish to turn on the VDP at this stage. It could afford only one enemy at a time, and the Communists were by far the main threat. In any case, the full potential of the Highlands for colo-nization and economic development could not be achieved until the Commu-nists had been defeated. In the meantime, any group willing to kill Communist troops should have been accepted as an ally. But one of the regime's concerns seems to have been that although the VDP's armed forces had proved highly effective in expelling the Communists from much of the "home range" of the Rhade people, they had no obligation (or inclination) to go after Communist forces beyond it. As the war receded from Rhade lands, therefore, the VDP's militias might become a well-armed but largely idle rear-area force—"an army at my back" as Dinh, the II Corps commander, allegedly put it.

In the summer of 1962 the Diem government started to demand that the VDP's Strike Force personnel be enrolled in the ARVN or turned over to the province chief as Civil Guard. In the regime's view, as the Communist threat receded in central Darlac, the arms issued to Village Defenders were no longer necessary and should be withdrawn. Though almost certainly exaggerated, the regime's anxiety about arms distribution to the Rhade was probably not mere paranoia. There is evidence that the Bajaraka movement was regaining strength, and there were reports that it had covert support within the VDP.[66]

Despite the increasing disapproval of the Diem regime, the Buon Enao experiment might have survived if the growing American establishment in Vietnam, on which Diem was heavily dependent, had been united in its support. But this was not the case. The Military Operations Section of the CIA in Vietnam, which, along with Nuttle, had initiated the program, remained solidly behind it. Layton and Benefiel had not lost faith in the project, and they continued to have supporters in CIA headquarters at Langley. John Richardson, however, who had replaced Colby as the station chief in Saigon, had not been involved in the initiation of Buon Enao, and he tended to see the war in rather conventional military terms. He offered little or no support for continued CIA involvement with the VDP.[67]

Meanwhile, MACV, established under General Paul D. Harkins in February 1962, was gradually taking over the direction of the American war effort. As the CIDG program expanded massively in 1962 to parts of the Central Highlands outside Darlac and to ethnic and religious minority groups in other regions, CIA headquarters realized that CIDG's administration and costs would eventually exceed the Agency's resources, and the military would ultimately have to take control. As a step in that direction, in May 1962 MACV acquired joint control of CIDG with the CIA.

CIA officers like Layton and Benefiel who had helped establish CIDG apparently hoped to continue their involvement with it, in some capacity, on a long-term basis. But it gradually became clear that this was unlikely to happen. In July the Department of Defense in Washington decided that MACV should take complete control of all US Army Special Forces in Vietnam. This was to be done in stages. By 1 July 1963, however, CIDG would be entirely under MACV control, and CIA involvement would cease. The code name for this transfer of authority and responsibility was Operation Switchback. It soon became apparent that the holistic, population-centric approach to counterinsurgency that had characterized the VDP up to October 1962 was unlikely to survive the change.[68]

MACV's J-3 staff included a small Special Warfare section. In charge of that section from July 1962 was Colonel George C. Morton. Morton's mission, as he saw it, was to assume both formal command and effective control of US Army Special Forces in Vietnam on behalf of MACV. He proceeded to do this by establishing a Special Forces headquarters that was initially based in Saigon and later at Nha Trang. Even though the first US Special Forces A-team had arrived at Buon Enao only on 4 December 1961, after the project had been up and running for about a month, Morton saw CIDG as essentially a US Special Forces program. He came to perceive CIA personnel such as Gil Layton and Jack Benefiel as institutional enemies and resented their rearguard action against the CIA's expulsion from CIDG under Switchback. He was also jealous of the credit given to the Air Commandos for their support of Buon Enao and apparently wanted them out of CIDG too.

Morton was a qualified Special Forces officer with broad experience. He had served as an enlisted man in the US Navy from 1932 to 1934, as an officer in the US Army in both the European and Pacific theaters in the Second World War, in the Philippines during the Communist Hukbalahap insurgency, and in Greece during the civil war there. But based on surviving documents, he seems to have been a fundamentally conventional individual with a rigidly military outlook. Irritated by the tendency of US Army Special Forces before Switchback to don informal attire suited to local conditions, he wanted his men to wear their proper uniforms, even though at least one item—the iconic green beret—was proving quite unsuitable for operations in the Central Highlands.[69]

As Morton was based in Saigon, he depended on Captain Ronald Shackleton, commanding A-113, which had arrived at Buon Enao in February 1962, to study and learn its principles and lessons so that the Special Forces could apply them to the CIDG program elsewhere. To give Shackleton the credit he deserves, his report did suggest that the nonmilitary elements of the VDP (especially agricultural development, industrial and commercial enterprises, and health care) were significant. He also observed that it was important for Special Forces to have the assistance of an "area specialist" who might be a civilian and might take on the role of "project supervisor." Clearly, Shackleton had Nuttle in mind, but he did not indicate how to find such a person everywhere a CIDG program was initiated. Shackleton gave only a limited account of the Buon Enao project's origins and inception and omitted to mention the CIA's crucial role in all this.

It is perhaps indicative of Shackleton's institutional agenda that although he was certainly aware of Nuttle's role as the principal American director of the VDP, he failed to mention his name and failed to acknowledge the pivotal role played by Nuttle's unique combination of professional expertise, local knowledge, and charisma in the project's conception, development, and success. Shackleton's report indicated, misleadingly, that most of the skills necessary to replicate the Buon Enao project in other areas were intrinsic to Special Forces A-teams.[70] Reports on the CIDG program written later in the war, however, admitted that its subsequent manifestations did not achieve the same widespread, committed support shown by the Rhade and other Highlanders to the Buon Enao experiment in the Nuttle era.[71]

In view of the Diem government's growing hostility toward the Buon Enao experiment, the lack of effort by American authorities to preserve it, and the ongoing process of the military takeover of CIDG, Nuttle decided to leave Vietnam. He first discussed the possibility of his departure with his CIA superiors in August and broached the subject with his Highland colleagues in September. Both the Americans and the Highlanders tried to dissuade him, but he could see no way of preserving the project. He also sensed that, given its capacity to make enemies out of potential allies, the Diem regime was doomed. In addition, he believed that, with its limited grasp of the type of war being waged in Vietnam, the American military could not prevent Communist victory there in the long run.

One of Nuttle's last and saddest duties before leaving Vietnam was to participate in negotiations with 23d Division commander Colonel Le Quang Trong, whom he clearly did not trust, for an orderly handover of the Buon Enao project to the South Vietnamese provincial authorities. A critical conference was held in Trong's office in Ban Me Thuot on 8 September 1962, involving representatives of the PSO, the CIA, and the US ambassador. There were further discussions on 11 September involving Trong, Nuttle, Wilson, and Lieutenant Colonel R. J. Billado, who had replaced Frederick as the senior American adviser at 23d Division. (In contrast with his predecessor, Billado became a passionate supporter of the VDP and a bitter opponent of plans to dismantle the project.) An agreement was concluded on 12 September 1962, with Nuttle, Captain Phu, Colonel Trong, and Major Hoang Thong, who had replaced Major Bang as Darlac's province chief, as signatories. Nuttle was under no illusion that this would preserve the essence of the Buon Enao experiment. At best, he hoped to ease the pain of the handover and minimize the damage to Rhade prospects and to security in Darlac.

The handover would occur in three phases. The first phase represented more or less the status quo in mid-September 1962, with the VDP still in control of its constituent villages and Strike Force operations but coordinating the latter more tightly with the 23d Division commander. In the second phase, control of the villages would gradually be transferred from the VDP to the province chief, at which point they would be regarded as part of the Strategic Hamlet Program. In the final phase, the Strike Force troops, paid for through the VDP, would be transferred to Darlac's Self-Defense Corps and continue to defend their local area, sent to work with CIDG in other areas, enrolled in ARVN commando units, or assigned to the Border Scouts.

It is noteworthy that the agreement was, at this stage, extremely vague, with no definite time frame for the phases of transfer and no specific statement as to the number of Strike Force personnel to be enrolled in the various branches of the Republic of Vietnam's armed forces. There was no mention at all of the arms provided to the part-time Village Defenders—the main concern of Diem's government and the main source of friction between it and the Americans.[72]

In late September Nuttle submitted his resignation from the CIA, making it clear that this was an act of protest against what he saw as the betrayal of the Buon Enao project. On 1 October the Rhade gave a huge all-day farewell feast in Nuttle's honor in a jungle clearing near Buon Enao. That evening, having said his farewells, he flew from Ban Me Thuot to Saigon. There, on 2 October, he had his final interviews with Layton and Richardson, the CIA station chief. Richardson demanded that he go immediately to CIA headquarters at Langley to give an account of himself. Nuttle replied that the Agency no longer owned him. He had resigned. Now a free agent, he intended to travel before returning to the United States. He flew from Saigon to Bangkok on 3 October. After roaming parts of Asia, the Middle East, and southern Europe, he returned to the United States only in mid-December 1962.

On his arrival at the airport in New York, a customs officer handed Nuttle a note politely requesting that he report immediately to Langley. On this occasion he decided to comply. Still heavily bearded and in his traveling clothes, he was greeted at Langley by Don Gregg, chief of the CIA's Vietnam desk. Gregg took him directly to meet with DCI John McCone, who had taken a strong interest in Buon Enao and talked with Nuttle about it knowledgeably and at some length. A few days later McCone personally escorted Nuttle to the Department of Defense, where they met the Joint Chiefs of Staff. Nuttle was later asked to appear before President Kennedy's Special Group for Counter-Insurgency, and together with the DCI, he attended meetings at the Old Executive Building, near the White House, in February, March, and April 1963. During these meetings at the Pentagon and the Old Executive Building, Nuttle's views on the Buon Enao experiment and on the prognosis for the American effort in Vietnam were sought and given. The main thrust of his advice was against the large-scale commitment of US ground troops. Nuttle would subsequently work under contract for the CIA on a number of occasions and in several countries, including Laos. To this day, however, he has never returned to Vietnam.[73]

Nuttle's leaving Vietnam did not, of course, put an immediate end to the Buon Enao program. It had always been a collective enterprise with a collective management. Although the provincial authorities were supposed to take control of the first thirty-one villages from the VDP in September 1962, nothing much happened at this stage. The writing was very much on the wall with regard to its long-term future, but in the short term the VDP continued to grow. It is a tribute to Nuttle's direction during the project's critical first year that, at the beginning of 1963, US advisers regarded Buon Enao as still going strong and as one of the greatest successes in the II Corps area throughout 1962.[74]

The Expansion of CIDG

It is one of the many strange paradoxes of this war that while the American authorities in Vietnam were failing to resist the dissolution of the Buon Enao project—the starting point of CIDG and by far its most successful element— they were vigorously promoting its expansion into other parts of the country. By November 1962, there were twenty-six US Special Forces A-detachments in Vietnam. Although CIDG was their core business, it was not the only pro- gram with which US Special Forces were involved. In the Central Highlands such programs included training Highland troops in border surveillance and mountain scout roles. For command and control and for administrative support of the A-detachments involved in these programs, as well as for liaison with the South Vietnamese, the Special Forces began to establish B-detachments at this time. They set up the one for the 2d Tactical Zone in the town of Pleiku.

At the same time, CIDG camps, including all or part of an A-detachment, were established at Dak Pek and Tanh Canh in Kontum Province; Plei Mrong in Pleiku Province; Cheo Reo in Phu Bon Province; Ban Don, Buon Dan Bak, and the Krong No Valley (as well as Buon Enao) in Darlac Province; and the Serignac Valley in Tuyen Duc Province. The A-detachments employed were sent to Vietnam on temporary duty from 1st Special Forces Group on Okinawa and from 5th and 7th Special Forces Groups based at Fort Bragg, North Carolina. While in Vietnam they were under the overall control of the headquarters called "US Army Special Forces (Provisional) Vietnam," which was initially based in Saigon but moved to a more geographically central loca- tion at Nha Trang in February 1963.[75]

In retrospect, some aspects of the administration of US Army Special Forces in Vietnam in this period appear deeply unsatisfactory. Special Forces person- nel did six-month tours of duty only, and if they returned for a subsequent tour, as many did, they usually went to a completely different location. Even if they did two successive tours in the Central Highlands, they would usually be operating in different areas and with different tribes. It was equally likely that, after serving with an A-detachment in the Highlands, a Special Forces officer or soldier would do his next tour on the coastal plain or in the Mekong Delta. This made it difficult for Special Forces personnel to achieve real area exper- tise, even in terms of local geography. The level of knowledge of language, culture, and customs and the range and intimacy of contacts with local people that Nuttle had attained in Darlac was, in these circumstances, practically im- possible for Special Forces personnel to acquire.[76]

Serious weaknesses in the rapidly expanding CIDG program of late 1962 and early 1963 were frankly admitted in the official US Army study. To a con- siderable degree, the emphasis shifted from classic counterinsurgency (efforts to win the allegiance of population groups and to protect them from insurgent penetration and harassment) to a more conventional military approach that focused on finding and killing enemy soldiers. There were, in addition, obvious indications of the handiwork of haste:

> The expansion of the CIDG program from 1 November 1962 to 1 July 1963, the end of Operation Switchback, was fairly rapid. Approximately forty CIDG camps were opened and eight closed. The rapidity of this expansion did not permit the kind of developments that took place at Buon Enao, where a great deal of time was taken to prepare the area and the people . . . this time the emphasis was on speed. The usual approach was to establish security first, undertake civic action later, and work through province and district chiefs rather than tribal leaders. In general these projects were not as successful as the Buon Enao experiment. In many areas Viet Cong control was stronger than at Buon Enao, making recruitment difficult. Often the tribal groups were not as advanced as the Rhade. Strike forces often had to be moved from their home areas to establish a new camp. It was also during this period that emphasis was shifted from the establishment of mutually supporting village defense systems to carrying out offensive strike operations in order to open up and then secure an area. Finally, increased emphasis was placed on selecting area development camp sites near the border so that strike forces could be assigned a border security mission in addition to the task of clearing and securing the assigned operational area.[77]

It is commonly hoped that, in wartime, armed forces will exhibit a learning curve and improve with experience. For US Special Forces in Vietnam, however, arguably the most sophisticated, holistic, and successful example of counterinsurgency practice came not toward the end of that lengthy conflict but quite close to its beginning. Buon Enao represented a sort of counterinsurgency Garden of Eden prepared for them by a remarkable collection of ministering angels, including Dave Nuttle, Gil Layton, and William Colby, not to mention a number of exceptionally broad-minded Vietnamese and a larger group of extremely capable Highlanders. Finding this relative paradise terminated by the darker forces on their own side and themselves expelled from it, they could never quite re-create it elsewhere. The consequences of its closure would be serious not only for them but also for the future of the anti-Communist war effort in the Central Highlands.

5

Refugees, Strategic Hamlets, and ARVN Operations, 1962

The Communist Subsistence Crisis

From early 1962 (sooner in some places), Communist forces in the Central Highlands hit a crisis. They began to suffer a desperate food shortage exacerbated by a tendency for Highlanders to abandon traditional villages and take refuge in government-controlled areas. Apparently, the main cause of this crisis was that, over the last couple of years, the Communist Party had greatly increased the number of full-time troops in the Highlands, partly by local recruitment and partly by bringing in ethnically Vietnamese units through Laos or from the coastal plain.[1] The available evidence does not allow us to be specific about the numbers involved, but somewhere between 5,000 and 10,000 seems a reasonable guess.

It was normal in most parts of South Vietnam for the Communists to feed their troops from local resources, often making demands on the same communities from which personnel were recruited. Over much of the coastal plain and the Mekong Delta, food was plentiful, by Asian standards, and such a policy was quite feasible.[2] It was a different story in the Central Highlands. Highland villages generally lived pretty close to the subsistence level. It needed a major psychological warfare effort, backed by at least the implicit threat of force, to get them to bear the strain of supporting full-time Communist troops.[3] In the first half of 1962, at least in some communities, the elastic limit of toleration seems to have been reached and passed.

While most accounts attribute the mass migration of Highlanders at this period primarily to Communist pressure, it seems certain that the Saigon government's own policies and actions contributed. On the positive side, these policies included active proselytizing, allocating land for Highlanders' use in some areas, and recruiting, arming, and paying Highland military and paramilitary

111

forces.[4] Darker aspects included harassment from the ground and bombing from the air of Highland villages perceived to be under Communist control and the destruction of crops belonging to such villages.[5]

When put together, these factors led to a fair-sized flood of refugees. As a CIA history of political developments in the Highlands put it:

> The upsurge of Viet Cong infiltration into the Highlands from Laos in late 1960 and continued heavy infiltration in 1961, which had forced the Vietnamese government to take up a program of arming the Highlanders, also caused the Viet Cong to increase their demands for support and assistance from the Highlanders to a point where the latter could no longer stand the pressure and the effect it was having on their subsistence economy. By the summer months they were fleeing their villages to government-controlled areas in such numbers that the government had to initiate crash relief programs. By August 1962 the number of refugees was estimated to range between 100,000 and 150,000, with most observers tending to favor the higher figure.[6]

Refugees

Although the flood of refugees peaked in the summer of 1962, it had, according to Ton That Chu, the province chief in Pleiku, begun a year or so earlier, in mid-1961.[7] John Helble, the American consul in Hue, reported in April 1962 that large numbers of Highlanders had already been resettled in both Kontum and Pleiku. In most cases this migration appeared to be largely voluntary:

> According to the Deputy Province Chief for Administration in Kontum a total of about 15,000 (of about 80,000 total) tribesmen have been resettled since January 1. Of these, 11,900 have been located in the northern districts of Dak Sut and Dak To, most of them in existing villages and in about 36 new villages, and some along the route from Dak To northeast towards Toumorong district. Only a few have been resettled in Toumorong. The remaining 3,000 have been placed in Kontum district, west of Kontum city.[8]

Helble did not make it clear from exactly which areas all these people were fleeing, and he did not specify which tribal groups were contributing to the refugee surge and in what numbers, though it seems likely that a high proportion of them came from the westernmost areas, adjacent to the Laotian border, and from the northernmost Toumorong district—areas inhabited mainly by the Halang and Sedang peoples. The only district in the province unaffected by the movement of Highland refugees was Chuong Nghia in the east, an area containing about 2,500 people of the "fierce" Bahnar tribe. According to the ARVN garrison commander at Plateau Gi (apparently, the government's only real outpost in the area), at best, 800 of the Bahnar in this district could be regarded as neutral. The rest, he believed, were actively pro-Communist.

Up to April 1962, much of the effort involved in resettling the refugees in Kontum Province had been carried out by the 40th Regiment of the ARVN's 22d Division. The 40th Regiment's commander, Major Quy, who reportedly came from one of the Highland minorities of North Vietnam, was acting intelligently and constructively in this matter:

> In resettling the 11,900 Sedang in his regimental area, Quy has started by conducting collection operations in the mountain areas near Route 14. First he sends one of his four psychological warfare teams, composed of two ARVN members, two Civil Guard members, two Self Defense Corps members, a medic, and sometimes two Civic Action cadres, which advises the tribesmen that they will have an opportunity to relocate nearer the road and which outlines the advantages which may accrue to them if they choose to do so. His unit then sweeps the area and brings back all the people who choose to come down to the road. There they are given ground, usually made available by the district chief and instructed how to lay out their village and construct their defenses for protection against VC depredations. Each village is also usually provided with 10 to 20 rifles (598 have been passed out in Quy's area) for a "home guard" (not Self Defense Corps), which Quy has established. According to Quy he has found many more volunteers for the guard than he has rifles to pass out and thus some have been armed with bows, spears etc.
>
> Quy states that he has had no food, clothing, medicine, seeds or agricultural tools to pass out to the villagers, though many left behind rice stocks, animals and other possessions when they came down to resettle. In a few cases the district chief has been able to offer a little help, through the resources of the Province Chief's office. In the Kontum district program, ARVN and the district chief have joined to pass out food. Quy's psywar teams are sometimes left in a village after it is established to educate the tribespeople in certain rudimentary practices of hygiene and defense techniques.[9]

Helble accompanied Quy on a visit to the village of Dak Bron, 55 km north of Kontum city, which he understood to be "typical of those newly created in northern Kontum." Having about 400 "fairly well constructed" houses, it was inhabited by people who had come down from the mountains in about mid-March and was defended by twenty "home guards." Except for a psywar team that happened to be in the village at the time, "no government services were in evidence."[10]

The same sort of internal migration was taking place in Pleiku Province. From the beginning of January through late April, some 20,000 of the 125,000 Highlanders in that province had been resettled. The bulk of the refugees made their new homes "east of Pleiku city along the principal east-west communication axis, Route 19, just south of Pleiku city along Route 14, and along the road branching off from Route 14 south of the city towards the Cambodian border." A substantial number had also been resettled "on Route 14 north of Cheo Reo, in the southern part of the province." In general, the refugees' new homes were located in areas considered to be largely under government control.

There were problems with the reception of refugees in some areas. At least in some parts of Pleiku, the local authorities insisted that the Jarai fortify their new villages quite heavily, issuing very detailed instructions on how defenses were to be built. But they offered no help with the actual labor. Some refugees "found that building fences round each house as well as around the entire village, digging trenches and planting gardens, plus the work of constructing the new houses was too much for them." Missionaries reported an incident in which fifty Jarai young men went into the town of Pleiku and volunteered for the army rather than perform this heavy labor. Given that they were probably severely undernourished and might reasonably have expected the ARVN to feed its recruits, their decision was understandable.

Yet some sort of fortification was necessary if the new villages were to survive. The flight of Highlanders from areas the Communists controlled was causing the Party in Pleiku Province severe problems with "labor, recruitment, intelligence and supplies." Frustrated and angry, the Party leadership tried hard to regain control of these people and was prepared to use violence to do so. Helble reported that one Jarai village near the provincial capital had "been attacked by the VC three times recently." On each occasion, however, "the local SDC [Self-Defense Corps] drove the attackers off" before they could "destroy the village fence."[11]

There was no doubt that the migrations of Highlanders occurring in Kontum and Pleiku (as well as in the northern provinces of Quang Tri, Quang Nam, and Quang Ngai in ARVN I Corps' area) were potentially of great benefit to the government. As far as Helble could see, ARVN units and provincial authorities were reasonably willing to help the refugees—at least enough to encourage them to remain in their new locations and to encourage others to make similar moves. The central government, however, was not rising to the challenge: it was not fully exploiting opportunities to win Highlanders over to its side. Far more needed to be done in terms of aiding the resettled populations with food, clothing, medicine, seed, and tools.[12]

Diem's government seemed to be sending mixed messages. On the one hand, it definitely wanted to encourage the flight of Highlanders from Communist-controlled areas. On the other hand, Diem was fiscally conservative, and spending money on the welfare of Highlanders was not high on his list of priorities.[13] He is reported to have said that if the government gave the Highlanders rice, they would be too improvident to cultivate their own[14]—an attitude rather typical of the condescending racial prejudice exhibited by many Vietnamese toward their less sophisticated neighbors. Helble commented:

> It appears essential that some aid . . . be given to those resettled as they have had to leave behind much of what little they possessed in the mountains, and it will take them at least four to eight months to harvest their first crop in their new location. If aid is not provided them, desertion of many back to the mountains, and the VC, seems likely. On the other hand, given some material assistance it is probable most of those resettled will stay in their new homes, and the word of their content will reach their compatriots still in the mountains and entice the latter to give the new life a try.[15]

Chalmers B. Wood, deputy director of the Kennedy administration's Task Force Viet-Nam, reported on Kontum and Pleiku Provinces in late May 1962. By that time, the province chief in Pleiku claimed that a total of fifty-six strategic hamlets had been built, including twenty-five for Highlanders. In addition, he was gradually arming Highland refugees, although on a much smaller scale than had happened with the Buon Enao project in Darlac. The situation in Kontum had also changed somewhat since April. Helble's report for that month had mentioned no Bahnar refugees and had given the impression that the Bahnar (at least those living in the eastern part of the province) were overwhelmingly pro-Communist. Wood, however, reported visiting a relocation center called Polei Kleng, west of the town of Kontum and about 25 km east of the Cambodian frontier. At Polei Kleng there were 1,287 Bahnar, all of them from four villages about 10 km from Cambodia. Without specifying why he was so unimpressed, Wood described them as "less than noble savages." He noted that they "lined up enthusiastically with some weapons but their defenses seemed to consist mainly of mud pillboxes and zigzag trenches inside the village perimeter, a sort of mudpie Maginot." The provincial authorities intended that when adequately organized and trained, these home guard troops would patrol beyond their villages. In their present state of training, however, Wood thought that Communist forces would easily overmatch them.[16]

By July, the Americans had noticed that Highlanders were also fleeing from Communist- to government-controlled areas in provinces farther south, in Darlac, Tuyen Duc, and Lam Dong. A "Montagnard Group" consisting of representatives of the Saigon government's land development agency and a variety of American agencies visited these provinces in late June. Neither the ethnicities of the refugees nor the exact locations from which they were fleeing were specified in the embassy's communication to the State Department. But of a total Highlander population of about 165,000 in these provinces, it was estimated that some 18,000 (about 11 percent) had left their normal living areas in the last few months. There was "general agreement amongst provincial officials, U.S. military advisers, and missionaries" that this movement was "principally due to increasingly harsh VC pressures on montagnards." But government action had played a role in some instances. The movement of "4,500 of 11,000 montagnards in Tuyen Duc," for example, had been "made at [the] invitation of provincial officials into areas which had been prepared in advance."

In general, the welfare of this wave of refugees was not an immediate cause for alarm. But the Americans were concerned that the central government was doing far too little and that everything depended on the provincial authorities. Although most of the province chiefs in the Highlands seemed willing to encourage resettlement and to aid refugees, there were exceptions. The embassy reported that the province chief in "Lam Duc" (probably a careless rendering of Lam Dong) "estimated 7,000 or 8,000 additional montagnards would move if he would permit it. However, he was opposed to such movement, since he preferred [to] have them remain in former locations as [a] source of information about VC." Consequently, he was doing whatever he could to discourage the exodus.[17]

By the end of July, the population shift under way in the Central Highlands was attracting attention at the highest levels of policy making in both South Vietnam and the United States. Diem's brother Nhu, who had assumed responsibility for the affairs of the Central Highlands, was very excited by the development, and Diem himself went to the Highlands to address some groups. The US Joint Chiefs of Staff noted toward the end of the month: "The Montagnards . . . are leaving their tribal areas because of VC levies on them for food, forced labor and other support. They are fleeing to Government of Vietnam controlled areas."[18] Some people on the anti-Communist side were now prepared to use drastic measures to hurry this process along. The Joint Chiefs, Ambassador Nolting, and much of the American military hierarchy in Vietnam now supported Diem's frequently expressed desire to use defoliants to destroy crops in Communist-controlled areas of the Highlands and thereby increase Communist supply problems and the pressure on Highlanders to move. The State Department, however, obviously concerned about the United States' image in the world, came out strongly against US involvement in any such activity.[19]

At the same time, some American officers and officials were still concerned that Diem was not doing enough to look after Highland refugees. Reporting on a conference held at Honolulu in late July, Marine Corps Major General

V. H. "Brute" Krulak, special assistant to the Joint Chiefs for counterinsurgency and special activities, noted that one important matter considered "was the care of the Montagnards, some of whom are hungary [*sic*], most of whom need assistance in some form. The GVN, for many reasons, has done less than they might have to care for these people, despite the great importance of their good will and their potential usefulness as combatants."[20]

In August, with the number of refugee or recently resettled Highlanders somewhere between 100,000 and 150,000, the Americans arranged (ostensibly at the request of the Diem government, but more likely on their own initiative) for their aid mission in Saigon to release 50 million piastres for the Highlanders' assistance. The Americans also tried to develop the CIDG program in such a way as to aid Highland refugees. A US Special Forces A-team established a CIDG camp at Dum Pau in Tuyen Duc Province in September 1962 to provide security and economic assistance to 4,000 refugees of the Koho tribe, who had started to come out of the mountains and settle in the area the previous April. Prior to the establishment of the CIDG camp, these Koho refugees had been receiving assistance from "local missionaries, members of the International Voluntary Service and the US AID provincial officer with medical supplies and training, agricultural programs and material."[21]

Planning a Strategic Hamlet Program for the Highlands

In the Central Highlands there was an obvious link between the movement of refugees and the development of the Strategic Hamlet Program. Refugees were often placed in defended villages that were regarded as part of that program.[22]

In 1962 the Central Highlands was part of the ARVN II Corps' area, known as the 2d Tactical Zone. It was divided between the divisional tactical areas (DTAs) of the 22d and 23d Divisions, with the 22d Division responsible for roughly the northern half of the Central Highlands and the 23d Division for the southern half. Up to late 1962, the main emphasis of the Strategic Hamlet Program in the 2d Tactical Zone was on the coastal plain, and the development of strategic hamlets in the Central Highlands appears to have been a low priority. Plans drawn up by the 22d and 23d Divisions in late 1962, however, anticipated that the vast majority of inhabitants of the Central Highlands provinces would be in strategic hamlets or government-controlled towns by some point in 1963.

The 22d Division's plan was so ambitious in relation to what had been achieved up to that point that its realism may seriously be doubted. The intention was to bring 95 percent of the population of Kontum Province under government control in 171 strategic hamlets within six months of the start of the program. But by the division's own reckoning, only 55 strategic hamlets actually existed in that province at the end of 1962. The situation in Pleiku Province, which was considered a lower priority, was even less developed. To bring 92 percent of the population there under effective government control would require an estimated 197 strategic hamlets. However, the 22d Division staff reckoned that only 26 existed at the end of 1962—a figure far lower than that given to Wood in May and one of many indications that, to put it mildly, historians need to exercise great caution when dealing with South Vietnamese government statistics on strategic hamlets.[23]

Whereas the 22d Division's Strategic Hamlets Program for its Highland provinces appears excessively ambitious, the 23d Division's is difficult to follow. This may be because it was poorly explained in the original Vietnamese, because it was poorly translated from Vietnamese into English, or a combination of the two. Its commander claimed that, at the end of 1962, there were 551 completed strategic hamlets in his divisional area (including coastal provinces), with 225 more under construction, but he did not specify in which provinces they could be found. Highland provinces in the 23d Division's area included Darlac, Quang Duc, Tuyen Duc, and Lam Dong, as well as the city of Dalat, which was within the boundaries of Tuyen Duc but treated separately for some purposes. By the end of the first six months of the program, the intention was to have 114 strategic hamlets in Darlac housing 86,488 persons, or 49 percent of the population; 43 strategic hamlets in Quang Duc housing 31,158 people, or 99 percent of the population; 81 strategic hamlets in Lam Dong housing 41,007 people, or 67 percent; and 26 strategic hamlets in Tuyen Duc (excluding Dalat) housing 26,116 people, or 44 percent. It is not clear how many of these strategic hamlets already existed or were deemed to exist.

It gives the 23d Division's program an even greater air of unreality that nothing was mentioned about the Buon Enao program in Darlac Province.[24] By the end of 1962, those directing the Buon Enao experiment had organized approximately 60,000 people in the most concentrated, sophisticated, and successful system of defended villages anywhere in South Vietnam.[25] But we know from other sources that the Diem government was not intending to build on that system; instead, apparently at the urging of the 23d Division's commander, it was planning its virtual dissolution.[26]

ARVN II Corps and Its Enemies: The Balance of Forces

From mid-1961 to the end of 1962, Colonel Wilbur Wilson was the senior American adviser to ARVN II Corps, which had its headquarters at Pleiku. Born in Oklahoma in 1909, Wilson had served as an army officer both in the

Second World War and in Korea, where he won the Silver Star while commanding the 9th Infantry Regiment. A controversial and somewhat acerbic personality, Wilson was undoubtedly an extremely forceful and industrious staff officer, determined to improve II Corps' organization, efficiency, and performance.[27] According to some reports, however, he had a very difficult relationship with Brigadier General Ton That Dinh, the youngest of Diem's corps commanders and widely regarded as an arrogant and incompetent political general. Having little patience for stern lectures from irascible foreigners, Dinh could take Wilson's company only in small doses, a frailty he apparently shared with some Americans.[28]

Yet, despite this difficult relationship at the top, Wilson thought II Corps was making substantial progress in 1962. He was cautiously optimistic about the way the war was going in the 2d Tactical Zone. However, he considered 1962 predominantly a year of organization, training, planning, and preparation for which the payoff would come in 1963.

Over the course of the year, II Corps, which already had the 22d and 23d Infantry Divisions, was reinforced with the 9th Infantry Division and the 47th (independent) Infantry Regiment. In accordance with the somewhat more positive policy toward Highlanders initiated in late 1961, thirteen scout companies, seventeen psywar platoons, and seventeen intelligence platoons were raised from among these ethnic groups in the II Corps Tactical Zone by December 1962. The 3d Armored Cavalry Squadron, which had been based at Pleiku for some time, was reorganized and strengthened by adding two mechanized troops mounted in M-113 armored personnel carriers to an existing tank troop. As part of an ambitious training regime that Wilson worked hard to develop and initiate, the 44th and 42d Regiments went through seventeen-week programs at the II Corps Training Center. There were also serious efforts to strengthen and improve the training of Civil Guard and Self-Defense Corps troops within the 2d Tactical Zone.[29]

At the beginning of 1962 both ARVN and US intelligence officers believed that South Vietnam's 2d Tactical Zone fell in the southern half of the Communist command known as Inter-Sector 5, an area that included South Vietnam's 1st and 2d Tactical Zones, in which ARVN I Corps and II Corps, respectively, operated. The southernmost part of the country, including the Saigon area and the Mekong Delta, they believed, fell within the Communists' Nambo Region, which largely coincided with the 3d Tactical Zone, or ARVN III Corps' area. Partway through 1962, however, MACV's intelligence staff received reports (apparently from ARVN intelligence) that the Communists had reorganized and divided Inter-Sector 5 into two areas: Military Region 5 and Military Region 6. As late as October 1962, the intelligence branch of MACV was still not ready to confirm this reorganization,[30] though by December 1962 the staffs at ARVN 22d and 23d Divisions were certain of it. The 22d Division believed its area fell mainly within the Communists' Military Region 5, while 23d Division reckoned that its troops faced forces belonging to Military Region 6.[31]

Even ARVN intelligence had been slow to pick up on this very real Communist reorganization. According to histories published in Hanoi since the war, Military Regions 5 and 6 had replaced Inter-Zone 5 back in mid-1961. MACV's reluctance to adjust its order of battle intelligence indicates how little the Americans really knew about Vietnamese Communist military organization at this time.[32]

II Corps' intelligence gave a figure of 10,824 Communist armed insurgents in the 2d Tactical Zone (including both the Central Highlands and the lowland provinces immediately to the east) on 1 January 1962. This figure had risen to 18,113 by the end of the year. But if such an expansion really took place, it seems likely that it occurred largely on the coastal plain. Given the acute supply problems in the Highlands, the number of Communist troops there probably declined. II Corps' intelligence officers reckoned that throughout the year, Communist forces in II Corps as a whole remained badly equipped and very precariously supplied by ARVN standards.[33]

It is difficult to find estimates of Communist strength in the Central Highlands specifically (as opposed to in the 2d Tactical Zone as a whole) in early 1962. In October, however, MACV's J-2 (intelligence) staff produced a detailed breakdown of Communist military strength province by province and tried also to identify Communist interprovince forces throughout South Vietnam. MACV's intelligence officers admitted that the great bulk of their information came from the Republic of Vietnam Armed Forces (RVNAF), although they analyzed it differently from (and, in their eyes, more rigorously than) their suppliers. According to MACV's analysts, in the Central Highlands provinces of Kontum, Pleiku, Phu Bon, Darlac, Tuyen Duc, Quang Duc, and Lam Dong combined, there were thirteen Communist companies and thirteen independent platoons with a total of 1,465 personnel among them. The picture was complicated by the existence, within the 2d Tactical Zone, of three Communist interprovince battalions and four interprovince companies, with an estimated 1,450 personnel among them, more than half of which seemed to be operating in the Central Highlands at least some of the time.[34]

The situation was made even more complex by the fact that most Central Highlands provinces (except for Phu Bon, Tuyen Duc, and Lam Dong) had a border with either Laos or Cambodia. There was a substantial Vietnamese Communist military presence in Laos in particular, and a strong possibility of units crossing the border from there. This was especially relevant in Kontum Province. According to MACV, in October 1962 Kontum contained three Communist infantry companies and three independent platoons, for a total of

360 full-time Communist military personnel based permanently in the province. This represented a big decline since late 1961, when ARVN intelligence had estimated that up to 5,000 Communist troops were present there. Presumably the food crisis had forced the Communist command to withdraw large numbers into Laos, to disperse them to other areas of South Vietnam, or to adopt some combination of these courses.

MACV's intelligence gave a unit designation and strength for each of the Communist forces believed to be in Kontum in 1962, its approximate location or area of operations, and, in most cases, even the commander's name or nom de guerre. The real intelligence picture for Kontum, however, was much more complicated and confused than this might make it appear. It was pretty certain that a 500-man unit, known as the U/i Battalion and commanded by an officer known as "Hoa," operated in the southwestern part of the province from time to time. In addition, three other units with strengths of between 500 and 1,000 had reportedly entered the province at some point in 1962 but apparently had not stayed.[35]

Throughout the 2d Tactical Zone, and especially in the Central Highlands provinces, it seems that the RVNAF considered as a whole (including the Civil Guard, the Self-Defense Corps, the Vietnamese Air Force, and the ARVN) had the Communists heavily outnumbered and outgunned in 1962, although it would be difficult to quantify this with any degree of precision. There can be no doubt that the firepower advantage was particularly marked. Whereas government forces had substantial field artillery and an increasingly formidable airpower, the Communists had to rely on mortars and a few recoilless rifles. In the Central Highlands the number of such weapons and the ammunition supply for them were very limited.

The government's military advantages in numbers and firepower were not in themselves decisive. Communist units were extremely difficult to trap and destroy, particularly in the mountainous and jungle-covered terrain of much of the Central Highlands. With their interprovince units, their foot-propelled cross-country mobility, and their flexibility of approach, the Communists could still, on occasion, achieve temporary local superiority.[36] Even such local superiority, however, was becoming difficult to maintain for any length of time (especially in the dry season), given the government's growing airpower and the increasing availability of helicopters to ferry combat troops.

Changing the Defensive Layout

Early in 1962 II Corps carried out a careful review of the layout of forces in its zone. Communist action in the Central Highlands in 1960–1961 had exposed

the "extreme vulnerability" of "numerous outposts guarding avenues of infiltration, axes of communication and isolated settlements." It found that, "during
the rainy season, in particular, the Viet Cong would attack these outposts and
often overrun them, inflicting large number[s] of casualties and capturing large
numbers of weapons, ammunition and medical supplies." The Communists
gained a further advantage when they "ambushed the relief columns, which
they knew had to proceed generally from one direction along one route." The
loss of several outposts in this manner in September 1961 during the Dak Ha
offensive had produced a "highly demoralising effect on ARVN units."

In the early part of 1962, therefore, all outposts within the 2d Tactical Zone
were surveyed, with detailed consideration given to the "type and strength
of [the] unit manning [each] post, communications, weapons and basic loads
of ammunition, food supply routes to the outpost, artillery support and fire-
plans, status of training, previous attacks directed against the outpost by the
Viet Cong, and location of nearest reinforcing units." This initial survey was
followed by a series of inspections carried out by "local commanders accompanied by their US Advisers," and "corrective action was taken where required."
The reorganization was regarded as highly successful: "Three outposts were
severely hit during the rainy season and several others less violently. Not one
outpost was lost during 1962 and the Viet Cong suffered heavy casualties in all
attacks. This has been one area of significant improvement during the year."[37]

ARVN Offensives in II Corps' Area

For most of 1962 the main emphasis throughout the 2d Tactical Zone, as
elsewhere in South Vietnam, was on population resettlement and population
control, the latter usually achieved through the mechanism of strategic hamlets.
The Strategic Hamlet Program involved many small-scale ARVN operations
to relocate people (sometimes with their consent, and sometimes without) into
areas the government could control more easily. Such operations were sometimes conducted in cooperation with the Civil Guard and the Self-Defense
Corps, such as those carried out by Major Quy and the 40th Regiment in
Kontum Province.

On occasion, military operations had to be mounted in relief of strategic
hamlets that had come under attack. American advisers considered that, over
the course of the year, population resettlement and strategic hamlets had "accomplished a great deal by isolating a large segment of the population from
Viet Cong influence or domination." Although the main emphasis for strategic
hamlet development in 1962 was the coastal plain and the Delta, it was not
without significance in the Central Highlands too. In July the Communists

conducted a series of attacks on defended villages in Pleiku, Kontum, and Darlac. On 14 July the village of Dak Rode, west of the city of Kontum, was overrun. In the majority of cases, however, the attackers were beaten off, sometimes with considerable losses. Communist activity dropped markedly in August compared with the previous month. II Corps' intelligence attributed this to the enemy's need for rest, reorganization, retraining, and the rebuilding of morale, probably with the aid of additional cadres from North Vietnam.[38]

II Corps' biggest and most ambitious undertakings in 1962 were three province-wide "clear and hold" operations. These began on 8 May 1962 with Operation Hai Yen in Phu Yen Province (a coastal, predominantly lowland province) and continued on 15 October with Operation Dong Tien in Binh Dinh (another predominantly lowland province, but with mountains on the eastern edge of the high-plateau provinces of Kontum and Pleiku). Then, on 6 November, Operation Nhan Hoa began in the recently created Phu Bon Province, an area of the Central Highlands surrounded by Binh Dinh, Pleiku, Darlac, Khan Hoa, and Phu Yen Provinces and believed to be largely under Communist control. Nhan Hoa was the first effort to clear and hold an entire province of the Central Highlands.

Operations designated "clear and hold" were defined as being "extensive" in terms of both ground and time and were intended to combine "military and civic action to clear [areas] of Viet Cong through offensive operations and hold [them] through civic action, backed by Civil Guard, Self-Defense Corps and other para-military defense forces." At times, Colonel Wilson was evidently frustrated at the slowness with which these operations progressed. They often seemed to be little more than programs for the large-scale construction of strategic hamlets, with far less in the way of direct offensive action against Communist units than he had hoped. Yet an American assessment conducted at the beginning of 1963 indicated that "results to date have been encouraging." II Corps staff expected Operation Hai Yen in Phu Yen to be completed in mid-1963, but Operation Dong Tien in Binh Dinh and Operation Nhan Hoa in Phu Bon would continue indefinitely.[39]

During 1962 II Corps also carried out offensive operations in the Central Highlands with less ambitious objectives than the clearance of an entire province. One aim of such operations was to bring Communist units to battle and inflict casualties on them, but this was not normally their only and, in the minds of ARVN commanders, rarely their primary purpose. At least as important was to disrupt Communist recruitment, training, and logistics by penetrating base areas they had hitherto considered secure, while at the same time increasing the experience and confidence levels of ARVN troops for operations deep in jungle-covered and mountainous areas. According to an American analysis, "During 1962, the tenor of [ARVN offensive] operations has changed from the unsuccessful, large, regimental, slow plodding ground sweeps to the more successful small unit, rapid heliborne operations. Although the Viet Cong have not been significantly hurt militarily and are still a formidable foe, these operations have succeeded in hurting them logistically and psychologically. The initiative has been transferred from the Viet Cong to ARVN forces." This American assessment found most commendable operations that involved substantial contact with the enemy and inflicted serious casualties by kinetic means. Operations that did not inflict casualties in this way did not, in this analysis, hurt the enemy "militarily," although they might do so "logistically and psychologically."[40] ARVN officers might have replied that destroying the enemy's crops, driving off or slaughtering his livestock, removing or disrupting his recruitment and labor base, and thus restricting his food supply and manpower pool could damage the Communists' military potential as much as inflicting casualties in firefights, a point at least partially conceded later in the same American report:

> ARVN operations deep into Viet Cong areas continue to be successful, although without large concrete results. The fact that the ARVN has taken the initiative away from the Viet Cong is the greatest single factor in the reduced incident rate and for a feeling of cautious optimism. During 1962, ARVN conducted operations in areas where they had not been in years and in a few cases where they had never been. This intrusion into so called Viet Cong inviolable areas, although not resulting in large numbers of Viet Cong casualties, has accomplished many rewarding side effects, namely: the Viet Cong have been kept moving, off balance and on the defensive; their logistical, training and secret base areas have been seriously disrupted; Viet Cong morale has been lowered; the population is regaining its faith in ARVN (and therefore GVN); intelligence is being generated upon which to base future and progressively more successful operations.[41]

Whether the bulk of the Vietnamese peasantry in the coastal areas of the 2d Tactical Zone had faith in the Diem government was still very much open to question.[42] It is even more doubtful that significant numbers of Highlanders felt much loyalty to the regime.[43] In any civil war, however, there is a tendency for people to cooperate with the side that looks stronger and seems more likely to win. In 1962 the Republic of Vietnam and its armed forces certainly looked more potent and effective than they had the previous year, and Communist prospects looked correspondingly poorer. Communist morale, which was somewhat lower over much of South Vietnam in 1962, was especially badly affected in the Central Highlands. Documents captured by the 23d Division indicated:

(1) A large number of Viet Cong troops have attempted suicide because they were sick and not being treated properly. Viet Cong regional hospitals and provincial dispensaries have refused to admit additional patients due to a lack of means to care for them. (2) Many veteran Viet Cong are requesting to return to their home areas. Morale of recruits is extremely low due to deprivations, poor and antiquated equipment and lack of combat experience. (3) A number of Viet Cong have refused to undergo training in order to use the time to repair their shabby equipment and to seek food. (4) Many Viet Cong dislike being assigned to agricultural production agencies, thus agricultural production is suffering. Montagnards who are used by the Viet Cong to grow crops are reluctant to work their lands due to continued ARVN operations, which destroy or confiscate their crops. (5) The Viet Cong are short of critical items such as medicine and MAS 36 [French rifle] ammunition.[44]

A 22d Division analysis confirmed some of these points, noting that enemy forces in its area suffered from:

1) Exceedingly poor logistical support. Many different types of weapons, insufficient quantities of ammunition and lack of an adequate road network for re-supply all combine to limit the duration of time Viet Cong forces can engage. An average engagement normally terminates 30 to 40 minutes after initiation, by the withdrawal of Viet Cong forces.

2) The general poverty of the area. The low standard of living of Montagnard tribesmen severely limits the capability of the Viet Cong to live off the populace. This has forced them to divert a considerable portion of time, effort and personnel to the growth and production of food. Such a requirement has markedly lessened the combat potential of their forces.[45]

Although the Communists suffered serious problems with the supply of weapons, ammunition, and medicine too, ARVN intelligence personnel and American advisers had no doubt that "food was the Viet Cong's biggest problem" in the Central Highlands in 1962. In Quang Duc and Lam Dong Provinces, prisoners of war had been described as "living skeletons." Communist units in Phu Bon Province, "already on short rations were ordered to cut food consumption by one third"—condemning their troops to a near-starvation diet. Miscalculation on the part of the Communist high command, which had tried to base more troops in the Central Highlands than the local economy could bear, was the main cause of these privations. But the operations of the Republic of Vietnam's forces both exploited and exacerbated them.[46]

The surviving record is fragmentary, but it is clear that both the 22d and 23d Divisions undertook offensive operations against Communist bases in the

Central Highlands, including remote jungle strongholds, from early in 1962. From 19 February to 9 March the ARVN 40th Infantry Regiment undertook the first phase of Operation Jungle Jim, directed at a 500-square-km area regarded as a Communist stronghold in the Dak Bron Valley of Kontum Province. That regiment (minus one battalion) plus one Ranger company and two additional Ranger platoons was supported by one battery of 155mm guns and one of 105mm guns, eight civic action teams, two psychological warfare platoons, one company of US helicopters, and two AD-6 fighter-bombers. The mission was to kill or capture Communist personnel; destroy installations, equipment, and food supplies; relocate Highlanders; obtain volunteers to serve as part of an intelligence network; and assist district chiefs in assuming control of newly cleared areas.

The plan was simple. Two battalion-strength task forces would converge— one from the north and the other from the south. Each battalion was given a designated area to occupy, and each company was assigned a zone of responsibility within it. Artillery was used primarily to interdict Communist routes of withdrawal, and each company had a forward observer so that it could be called in quickly and efficiently. Helicopters were used for some troop movements and for resupply, medical evacuations, and aerial reconnaissance. Jungle Jim led to no substantial battle and thus could not be considered a military victory in the normal sense, yet it could still be counted as a success for the anti-Communist side.

Communist casualties were fewer than fifty killed, wounded, and captured, but government losses were just two killed and six wounded. For this modest cost in life, 1,000 kilograms of Communist-controlled rice was destroyed, 300 Highlanders relocated, a small number of weapons captured, and, reportedly, a network of informants established in the area. Over a period of eighteen days, an American report noted, the ARVN had not only occupied a previously Communist-controlled area but, by "aggressive small unit patrols" accompanied by civic action and psychological warfare teams, had broken the Communists' control over the population. "The VC potential was reduced to a point where local forces could assume responsibility [for] the area."[47]

From 12 to 27 April the 23d Division directed a fairly large-scale operation code-named Tiger Hunt against a Communist stronghold 40 km northwest of the city of Dalat on the boundary of Darlac, Tuyen Duc, and Quang Duc Provinces. Units participating included two infantry regiment headquarters, three infantry battalions, one separate Ranger company, a divisional reconnaissance company, "military sector forces" (presumably Civil Guard and Self-Defense Corps troops) belonging to the provinces involved, two H-21 helicopters, and two B-26 aircraft, all under 23d Division's operational control. The operation was supposed to be some sort of converging movement, but it was not well executed and "only partially successful." The movements of ARVN forces were too slow and clumsy to trap any Communist troops, although some documents and supplies were captured.

The seizure of the Communist base area was only temporary in this instance. There were no plans to hold it on a long-term basis. Stay-behind parties, most likely consisting of Rangers, inflicted the only Communist casualties (ten killed and three captured) as the Communists returned to the area after the main ARVN forces had left. It seems most likely that the eight Communist weapons captured were also taken at this stage. No casualties to government forces were recorded, so the operation can be regarded as a sort of victory for the government side, albeit a very modest one in relation to the effort expended.[48]

In August 1962 the ARVN 42d Infantry Regiment moved to Kontum and there conducted a series of operations designed to find, fix, and destroy Communist units. As with most ARVN operations at this period of the war, we have no details about its conduct or outcome. Communist accounts make it clear, however, that ARVN activity in the Central Highlands in 1962 put some of their forces under extreme stress.[49] This was most definitely the case with the An Lac campaign.

The An Lac Campaign, October–December 1962: A Communist Perspective on ARVN Operations

The history of the Communists' Military Region 6 (which included the southern part of the Central Highlands) refers to a series of especially dangerous operations mounted in early October at the junction of Darlac, Tuyen Duc, and Quang Duc Provinces. The An Lac area, which was the focus of these operations, contained a major Communist military base and several way stations on an important branch of the Ho Chi Minh Trail.[50]

Sufficient American records survive to confirm that the An Lac campaign was real and important. Giving 4 October as the start date for the operation, one source states:

> Operation An Lac . . . was conceived by President Diem and the mission given to the 23d Division (ARVN). The 44th Regiment, 23d Division was:
>
> To destroy enemy in zone and deny VC entrance to South Vietnam from the north through this area. Also destroy VC economic and political holds now established in this zone.
>
> To concentrate in the Krong Kno Valley the 12,000 Montagnard people located in this zone. Also to establish security and help them build a better way of life for themselves.

To establish Strategic Hamlets and initially organize administrative district for the Montagnard people.

To repair and open highway from Dalat to Lac Thien.

Transfer responsibility for security and control of this administrative district [to] civilian control.[51]

The history of Military Region 6 indicates that, starting in October 1962, elements of the ARVN 23d Division, Civil Guard troops, Rangers, and occasionally Marines were used to surround and attack the Communist base area centered on the watershed of the Krong No River. At the outset of the campaign, ARVN forces established two military strongpoints deep inside the Communist base: the Phi Di-da strongpoint in the Phi Co area on an extension of Route 21, southwest of Military Region 6 headquarters, and the Dam Roong strongpoint on the left bank of the Krong No River, south of headquarters. A reinforced battalion supported by 105mm artillery held each strongpoint.

Government forces surrounding the base area then mounted thirteen waves of attack, each involving two or three ARVN battalions "along with commandos, reconnaissance elements and air strikes," and each focusing on one sector of the base area. "In between these waves the enemy sent out commandos to conduct searches, arrest and detain the civilian residents and attack our headquarters installations, supply caches, rice fields, commo-liaison stations etc."[52] The Communist narrative confirms ARVN and US accounts of the state to which Communist forces in the Highlands were often reduced at this period:

We fought back against these sweeps under extremely difficult conditions. We had just finished building our bases, our people's guerrilla movement had just begun to develop among the ethnic tribes-people, and we were short of food supplies and had to produce our own food. Sometimes for a month at a time all we had to eat was flour made from sabu tree-trunks, leaves and jungle roots. In spite of these hardships, the Regional Party Committee resolutely instructed all headquarters, agencies and units to cling to the land, fight back against the enemy, and firmly defend our bases and our strategic transport corridor.

The account notes that the 186th Battalion (apparently a "regular" or "main force" unit) had to be recalled from another area to meet the emergency. Its mission was:

[To] help guerrillas and headquarters personnel combat sweeps, instruct guerrilla self-defense forces in the hamlets how to deploy their forces, set up guard posts and fight to protect the people. Our troops clung to the enemy and fought him to protect the civilian population while . . . they made time to collect rice for their daily meals. We assigned our own troops to those tribal minority villages where our guerrilla units were weak, to directly protect the people, to escort the people away from the enemy, and to help provide food to the people.[53]

Reading between the lines, it seems that during the An Lac campaign the Communists used their main force troops to herd Highlanders (predominantly of the Mnong and Koho ethnic groups) "away from the enemy" in order to hold on to them as a source of agricultural and military manpower, just as the ARVN tried to herd them into government-controlled areas to deny the Communists this resource. But the notion that Communist troops helped provide food for Highland communities, as suggested in this passage, rather than being parasitic upon them, seems distinctly improbable.

The Communist account continues:

Every day enemy artillery . . . shelled the areas where our headquarters staff and our troops were located and . . . fired support missions for . . . enemy troops conducting search operations. When the enemy troops clashed with our forces, enemy bombers would be sent to provide air support and helicopters would be used to land troops to conduct surprise assaults. The enemy also collected the residents of tribal minority villages and resettled them at Dam Roong and in the area surrounding a number of military strong points south of Ho Lac. Hundreds of hectares of ripened rice stalks either could not be harvested or were destroyed by the enemy.

The situation was so serious that, despite the importance of the strategic transport corridor running through it, the local Communist leadership considered abandoning this base area. Comrade Tran Le, secretary of the Regional Party Committee, is principally credited with the decision to stay. Many cadres "became discouraged, wavered and wanted to retreat." But Tran Le met with the Party chapter in each headquarters organization and each unit to "bolster their morale and strengthen their resolve." In these circumstances:

The vast bulk of our cadres and soldiers held their ground, working shoulder to shoulder to defend against the enemy, to protect the civilian population, to help our communication-liaison way-stations, cut new trails for guests and visitors and to transport supplies, to harvest and cache the rice crops and to go down to [the coastal provinces of] Ninh Thuan–Khanh Hoa to obtain salt for our meals. For almost two months our forces resolutely clung to the base area fighting against the enemy. The enemy decided to extend their sweep operations to destroy us or force us out of the area so they could collect the local population and destroy our transportation corridor. The situation was extremely tense.[54]

In mid-November 1962 the Communist authorities in the area (the Regional Party Current Affairs Committee and Military Region 6 headquarters) decided on a counteroffensive, intending to "mass . . . forces to attack and destroy the Dam Roong operations base." The Dam Roong base, according to the Communist history, was held by a forward headquarters of the 44th Regiment of 23d Division, one ARVN battalion, a Ranger company, two 105mm guns, a mortar section with three 81mm mortars, and three American advisers. The Communist planners apparently reckoned there were six fortified defensive positions integral to the base, with other "fortifications, obstacles, mines etc." around it. To attack this position, Military Region 6 headquarters decided to concentrate the recently redesignated 840th Battalion (formerly the 120th Battalion), the 1st Company of the 186th Battalion, the military region's separate 143d Company, a sapper company, a heavy weapons company (with three 81mm mortars, two 57mm recoilless rifles, and two medium machine guns), one reconnaissance unit, and a signals platoon for an attack on the night of 4–5 December 1962.

Only part of the 840th Battalion actually showed up in time for the operation. Nevertheless, "after 55 minutes of savage and courageous combat," Communist forces allegedly captured the central compound at Dam Roong, destroyed the command post, caused some 300 ARVN casualties (including the regimental commander, who was killed), wrecked a massive amount of equipment, and carried other material away with them. The account makes no statement about casualties on the Communist side and no claim that the Dam Roong base remained in Communist hands, indicating that the operation was conceived and executed as a "raid."

It seems likely that some such raid did take place. It was probably rather less successful than this Communist account claims. Vietnamese Communist histories routinely exaggerate, often quite massively, casualties inflicted on the enemy, while ignoring casualties to Communist forces. The death in combat of an ARVN regimental commander and 300 casualties in a single battle would have been big news at this stage in the war and practically impossible to conceal. But no reference to such a disaster has been found in American sources.

The Military Region 6 history admits that the ARVN reinforced the base heavily after the attack and that the campaign continued. Nevertheless, it claims that the Dam Roong "victory" made an "enormous impact," earning the military region a "cable of commendation" from the Ministry of Defense in Hanoi and having a "good effect on the civilian population living in the southern portion of the Central Highlands," presumably by convincing them of the continuing potency of Communist forces in that area.[55]

For the rest of December, serious fighting continued in and around the An Lac base area. Communist forces, including the 2d Company of the 186th Battalion, the 141st and 143d Companies (apparently independent main force subunits), and some local guerrilla forces known collectively as the B8 unit, fought back vigorously. By the end of the year, the base area and the forces within it were still functioning. Personnel were still being escorted and supplies were still being transported along this "strategic corridor."[56]

This Communist account of the An Lac campaign indicates that at least some of the major operations of South Vietnamese government forces in the Highlands in 1962 were no joke from a Communist viewpoint and that they could impose extreme, agonizing pressure on Communist troops. But it is also probably true that very few such operations achieved truly decisive results. The branch of the Ho Chi Minh Trail that ran through the An Lac area almost certainly was, as the Military Region 6 history indicates, kept open, at least to some degree. Government forces continued their operations in this area well into 1963, presumably in the belief that they had not yet eliminated the Communist base.

The General Situation in the Central Highlands in Late 1962

Although the Communists were clearly experiencing difficulties throughout the Republic of Vietnam's 2d Tactical Zone, and especially in the Central Highlands, no one suggested that they were anywhere near final defeat. Indeed, "1962 was characterized by a steady increase in Viet Cong activity during the early part of the year and into the rainy season." Whereas II Corps' G-2 (intelligence) staff had estimated 10,824 armed Communist insurgents in the area on 1 January 1962, its estimate for the same zone at the end of the year was 18,113. The larger year-end figure may have been as attributable to an increased volume of intelligence reports as to an actual increase in Communist military manpower, but it was hardly indicative of an enemy on the ropes.[57]

II Corps' intelligence staff also attempted a province-by-province breakdown of Communist numerical strength in its tactical zone at the end of 1962. The estimates for the Central Highlands provinces in December 1962 were as follows: The senior ARVN intelligence officer in Kontum counted 3,127 Communist troops in that province, "broken down into 896 confirmed and 2,231 unconfirmed." For Pleiku, the figures were 620 confirmed and 1,080 unconfirmed, and for Phu Bon, there were approximately 1,100 altogether.

The Communist strength at the end of the year was estimated at 2,700 in Darlac and approximately 1,000 in Quang Duc. In the two remaining provinces
of the Central Highlands, Communist forces were thought to be significantly
weaker: just 250 in Tuyen Duc and 200 in Lam Dong. These figures (however unreliable) suggest that there were somewhere between 6,000 and 10,000
Communist troops (of various sorts) in the Central Highlands alone by the end
of 1962.[58]

As noted previously, MACV's estimates for October, just two months earlier, had suggested far lower totals. But MACV tended to count only full-time
Communist troops, not part-time guerrillas, and its estimates always tended to
be rather conservative. ARVN corps and divisions, in contrast, had a vested
interest in playing up the opposition they faced in an effort to obtain greater
resources and to excuse their failures.

An educated guess might be that there were between 3,000 and 4,000 full-
time Communist troops based in the Central Highlands on a long-term basis
at the end of 1962, in addition to a large number of part-time guerrillas. Other
full-time Communist troops would enter the region from time to time to undertake special missions or just to pass through, having come down the Trail
through Laos. Once the distinction between full-time and part-time Communist troops is taken into consideration, and once the focus is on the "confirmed" rather than "unconfirmed" figures, the historian's guess offered here
does not diverge greatly from contemporary ARVN intelligence estimates. It
is likely that the vast majority of Communist troops based in the Highlands in
1962, even the full-timers, had very little firepower and could not be regarded
as suitable for serious battles with ARVN troops or for assaults on fortified
positions.

Though the coastal plain, rather than the Highlands, saw the most bloodshed, the intensity of the insurgency as a whole is indicated by the admission
of 548 killed in action for the ARVN alone (not including other government
forces) in just the seven provinces of the 23d Division's tactical area in 1962.
In the same area over the same period, there were 230 ARVN soldiers missing
in action and a total ARVN casualty figure of 2,144. The Communists in the
same area suffered 3,246 fatal casualties in 1962 and a total of 6,180 casualties.
But these figures apparently included 1,547 detained "suspects" who were not
even verified as enemy personnel. Another important caveat is that whereas it
is a relatively simple matter for an army to record its own casualties, the figures
it provides for those of the enemy are always more speculative. A tendency
toward optimism and exaggeration in that regard is a widespread and well-
known phenomenon.

Given that the government side started with more troops, it seems likely
that the attrition in the 2d Tactical Zone in 1962 favored it, but not decisively.

Indeed, the statistics as a whole give a mixed impression. The Communists were still showing a fair amount of fight relatively late in the year. For the ARVN in the 23d Division's tactical area, October was indeed the second bloodiest month in 1962.[59] It was, however, encouraging for II Corps and its advisers that, after peaking in May, the total number of "incidents" caused by Communist forces in the 2d Tactical Zone dropped quite steeply after July. After October this figure again dropped—to the lowest level since the war began.[60]

II Corps' staff and its US advisers, however, clearly regarded the particular weakness the Communists had shown in the Central Highlands for much of 1962 as a short-term phenomenon, largely attributable to problems with food supply. The food shortage had resulted not only in malnutrition and low morale for the Communist forces but also in the diversion of their efforts from military operations to agriculture and foraging. Harvests in the Central Highlands in 1962 appeared to be good, and there was every possibility that Communist fortunes would revive in 1963. II Corps indeed anticipated an upsurge of Communist military activity early that year and considered that any significant military success their forces then achieved would lead to a rapid recovery of their morale.[61]

Though the abuse of Highlanders by government forces (some of it probably officially sanctioned and some not) had never entirely ceased,[62] certain developments in 1962 seemed to indicate that better relations between the government and the Highland ethnic minorities were possible. Some Highlanders had elected to leave Communist-controlled areas, some had established defended villages in government-controlled areas, and some had voluntarily enrolled in the government's armed forces.

Above all, the Buon Enao project indicated that, given the right conditions, Highlanders (working in conjunction with the Americans, sympathetic province chiefs, and Diem's own Presidential Survey Office) might declare for the government side and expel the Communists from their areas. But with the closing down of the Buon Enao experiment, the government's opportunity to develop a real working partnership with South Vietnam's Highland minorities was on the point of being renounced. This would cause some Highlanders to feel a strong sense of betrayal and contribute to the renewal of militant demands for Highland autonomy. These factors, in turn, would contribute to a loss of initiative for the anti-Communist side and eventually to a reversal of military fortunes in the Central Highlands in 1963.

6

Reversal of Fortune, 1963

Dramatic Year

The year 1963 brought high drama to Vietnam. At its outset the Communists were in great difficulty in the Central Highlands and in much of the rest of the South. The government's Strategic Hamlet Program was gripping an increasing proportion of the rural population, and its armed forces were penetrating and disrupting Communist base areas with greater frequency and force.[1] Though elements of the ARVN 7th Division suffered bloody frustration attacking Communist troops at Ap Bac in the Mekong Delta in early January, this episode has been blown out of proportion in some histories. Just one of many large firefights, Ap Bac was untypical of the general course of operations during this period of the war.[2] In early 1963 government forces were generally in the ascendancy.

By July, however, the war effort of the southern state was faltering, and by year end it was in crisis. The Communists were making impressive gains in high plateau areas and across most of the rest of the country. Was this reversal of fortune entirely owing, as some have alleged, to America's progressive abandonment and ultimate betrayal of Ngo Dinh Diem?[3] Or, with particular regard to the Central Highlands, are other explanations appropriate?

ARVN Reorganization, November 1962–January 1963

Between November 1962 and January 1963 the Joint General Staff (JGS) in Saigon carried out a major reorganization of ARVN corps areas and made some key appointments. The number of corps increased ·from three to four, with IV Corps, established in November 1962, taking charge of the Mekong Delta, the area that had seen the most intense fighting up to this time. IV Corps gained the 7th and 21st Divisions from III Corps. III Corps, which had previously been responsible for the Delta, in effect shifted northward. It

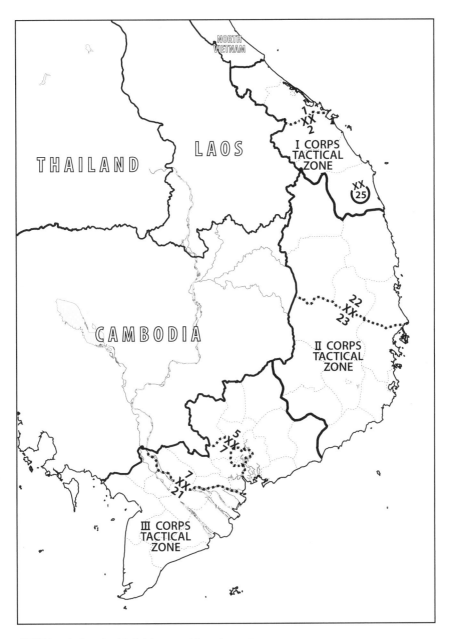

ARVN tactical territorial division, pre–November 1962

took over from II Corps much of the Central Highlands (Darlac, Tuyen Duc, Quang Duc, and Lam Dong) and adjacent provinces on the coastal plain, while continuing to have responsibilities for provinces immediately east of Saigon and between Saigon and the Cambodian border. III Corps gained the 23d Division, based at Ban Me Thuot, from II Corps and retained the 5th Division, with its headquarters at Bien Hoa.

II Corps' area of responsibility also shifted northward, and while it lost the 23d Division to III Corps, it gained the newly formed 25th Division, with its headquarters in the city of Quang Ngai. II Corps took responsibility for the coastal Quang Ngai Province, previously in I Corps. II Corps, which had three divisions after the reorganization—the 25th, 22d, and 9th—ended up with a smaller zone than in 1962 and with more troops to control it. II Corps' overriding mission was to control the vital northern half of the Central Highlands—preventing the Communists from driving from there to the coast and thus cutting the country in two. In 1963 I Corps retained just two divisions, the 1st and 2d, and it was responsible for the security of the provinces between the seventeenth parallel in the north and the northern borders of Kontum and Quang Ngai in the south.

After the reorganization, therefore, there were four ARVN corps, each having two divisions, except II Corps, which had three.[4]

A further change in late 1962 (and one potentially confusing to students of the war) was the division of the country into numbered divisional tactical areas (DTAs), the numbering of which had an internal logic but did not correspond with the numbers of the divisions occupying them. III Corps' zone, for example, was divided into the 31st DTA (III Corps' first DTA) and the 32d DTA (III Corps' second DTA). In 1963 the 23d Division occupied the 31st DTA and the 5th Division occupied the 32d. To make this even more confusing, the 23d Division was put back under II Corps' control on 20 August, reuniting the whole Central Highlands area under a single command, but as late as 30 September 1963, the 23d Division's area of operations was still being described as the 31st DTA.[5]

Despite all these developments, the situation of ARVN forces in the Central Highlands was, in some respects, hardly altered. The provinces in the southern half of the region continued to be the responsibility of the 23d Division, which remained in essentially the same geographic location as in 1962, with its headquarters at Ban Me Thuot. The 22d Division, which remained in II Corps, continued to be responsible for the northern Central Highlands, including the provinces of Kontum, Pleiku, and Phu Bon, and its headquarters remained in the town of Kontum. So the same divisions were responsible for basically the same areas of the Highlands in 1963 as in 1962. The division commanders were also unchanged. Lieutenant Colonel Nguyen Bao Tri commanded the 22d

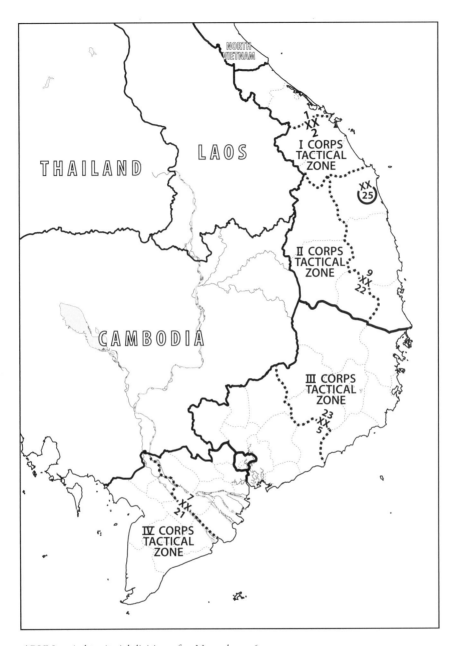

ARVN tactical territorial division, after November 1962

Division, a post he had held since September 1959, until the November 1963 coup against Diem. Colonel Le Quang Trong, who had commanded the 23d Division since May 1961, continued in that position until mid-December 1963.[6]

There were, however, significant personnel changes at the corps level. General Ton That Dinh moved from II Corps' headquarters at Pleiku to take command of III Corps, which had its headquarters in Saigon. At least one commentator considered it bizarre (given their obviously strained personal relationship) that Colonel Wilbur Wilson, who had been senior adviser at II Corps in 1961–1962, was paired with Dinh in this shift to III Corps.[7] But Wilson remained Dinh's principal American adviser up to the time of the coup in November 1963.[8]

Lieutenant General Nguyen Khanh (who tended to impress Americans because he spoke good English and appeared to appreciate their advice) filled Dinh's former slot at Pleiku, commanding II Corps between 20 December 1962 and 12 December 1963. Khanh's senior US adviser at II Corps up to 13 August 1963 was Colonel Hal McCown. McCown clearly liked and admired Khanh and remained extraordinarily optimistic about developments in II Corps' area up to the time he left the country.[9]

ARVN Pressure and the Communist Response, January–June 1963

For Communist forces in the Central Highlands, 1962 had generally been a nightmarish year. Accounts published in Hanoi since the war indicate that, in South Vietnam as a whole, 1963 began with the initiative firmly in the Diem government's hands and with morale in many Communist units severely depressed. In the first half of 1963, moreover, the anti-Communist war effort intensified rather than diminished. A multivolume general history of the war written from a Communist perspective notes:

> As 1963 began, the enemy strove to finish the network of strategic hamlets in the areas they controlled while at the same time they massed their forces to launch a large number of operations striking deep into our base areas to force us to defend against them in order to give them time to carry out their plan to move people into strategic hamlets. The enemy doubled both the number and the size of his operations as compared with those he conducted during 1962. During the first six months of 1963 the enemy conducted 109 sweep operations ranging in size from three to ten battalions each.[10]

During the first days of 1963, Military Region 5 headquarters (which dealt with the northern part of South Vietnam, including the northern half of the

Central Highlands) held a wave of political meetings for local Communist Party chapters and armed units in an effort to get a grip on people's fears and restore morale. In 1962 many Communist units had been intimidated by the other side's use of modern weapon systems, especially M-113 armored personnel carriers (which, especially in the Delta, the ARVN often used like tanks) and armed helicopters. As well as holding pep talks to allay such fears, the Military Region 5 Party Committee apparently intended to wrest the initiative from the Diem regime by winning a significant military victory early in 1963. To this end, it reassembled the 200th Artillery Battalion as an elite strike force, apparently in late 1962. The first regular Communist unit in the Central Highlands in the Second Indochina War, this battalion had played a key role in the Dak Ha offensive of October 1961 but had subsequently been dispersed. Neither an exact order of battle nor details of the equipment of the reconstituted 200th Battalion are available, but it seems to have had both 81mm mortars and 57mm recoilless rifles.[11]

Communist histories indicate that an ambitious, carefully planned assault on the CIDG camp at Plei Mrong on the night of 2–3 January involved both the 200th Artillery Battalion and another regular unit, the 407th Sapper Battalion. This action (discussed in more detail in the section on CIDG below) was, however, only a partial success. Although the breach of the camp's defenses and the severe mauling of its defenders represented a reverse for the CIDG program, the Plei Mrong action was not the signal victory with which the Communist leadership had hoped to open the new year. For the time being, the strategic initiative in the Central Highlands remained with government forces.[12]

ARVN forces in the first half of 1963 were almost continuously involved in a series of offensive operations designed to ensure that the Communists were not left undisturbed, even in base areas they had hitherto considered secure. "Fix and destroy" operations were supposedly based on intelligence and were designed to destroy specific Communist units or installations. "Search and clear" operations involved searching specific areas for evidence of Communist activity and then either destroying Communist forces in that area or driving them out of it. Not necessarily based on hard intelligence or aimed at establishing a permanent government presence in a given area, this type of operation was intended to disrupt and damage the enemy by killing troops or destroying vital resources. "Clear and hold" operations were normally mounted in conjunction with the Strategic Hamlet Program or with the resettlement of Highlanders and were designed not only to clear the Communists out of particular areas but also to secure those areas for the government on a long-term basis.[13]

A high proportion of ARVN operations in the Central Highlands in the first half of 1963 resulted in little or no contact with Communist forces. As in 1962, however, operations that did not involve major armed clashes should not necessarily be dismissed as useless. The destruction or disruption of Communist organization, logistics, and supply and the removal of populations from Communist control were potentially as significant as the infliction of casualties by kinetic means. Major ARVN penetrations into Communist base areas inevitably disrupted Communist planning and preparation and helped keep the initiative with the anti-Communist side. On a few occasions, however, Communist forces in the northern half of the Central Highlands not only evaded contact with government troops that were too powerful to engage but also struck back with some success at times and places of their own choosing.

Perhaps the biggest ARVN undertaking in the region in early 1963 was a province-wide clear and hold operation, code-named Nhan Hoa, in Phu Bon. This province, which had been established only on 1 September 1962, was situated in the center of the high plateau area and contained portions of Phu Yen, Binh Dinh, Pleiku, and Darlac. The purpose of creating the new province was apparently to focus government action on an area that had become a Communist stronghold but was hitherto, for all existing government authorities, both remote and peripheral.

An area of 4,800 square km, two-thirds of Phu Bon consisted of mountainous, densely forested terrain. Out of a recorded population of 32,546, the great majority—more than 22,000—were Highlanders. These were largely Jarai, with 4,000 to 5,000 Trung and small pockets of Bahnar and M'Dhur. With the partial exception of a corridor along Route 7, which ran west to east through Phu Bon from Pleiku Province to Phu Yen, the area had been under Communist control for years.

The plan was that, over a period of four months, from mid-December to mid-April, forces coordinated by the 22d Division's commander would attack Communist forces in the province and, with assistance of other troops, block their escape to other provinces, reopen Route 7 and Route 2 (which ran from Route 7 northward to the border with Binh Dinh), and resettle 10,000 Highlanders in thirty-four strategic hamlets located along Route 7 and in the Ba River Valley in the Phu Tuc district of the province. The ultimate aim—which, it was accepted, might take longer than four months—was to develop local security forces to the point that they could deal with security problems without depending on ARVN troops.

Communist forces in Phu Bon were believed to amount to at least five companies (possibly two battalions), with a total of around 900 troops. Each company had a "secret" base area, although the ARVN had a fair idea where these were located. The main ARVN units would be the 41st Infantry Regiment, the 207th Ranger Company, and the 402d Scout Company, backed by an artillery battery and a mortar platoon. Phu Bon provincial forces participating in the operation included the 50th Civil Guard Battalion, a separate Civil

Guard Rifle Company, and ten Self-Defense Corps platoons. Modest amounts of helicopter and fighter-bomber support were available.[14]

Evidence as to the outcome of Nhan Hoa is sparse. What is available suggests only limited success. The intrusion of government forces into secure strongholds in Phu Bon must have been disruptive for the Communists, but reports of Communist combat losses are hard to find. Given the size of the province in relation to the government forces operating in it, and given the nature of the terrain and vegetation, it was always likely that the Communists would be able to evade contact if they wished to do so. Nearly three months into the operation, Route 7 was still not secure. At 1945 on 9 March, a Communist force with an estimated strength of 200 men ambushed a convoy of eight military vehicles on that road before withdrawing under cover of darkness, "direction unknown." The ARVN lost seven killed, ten wounded, and one missing, together with a medium machine gun, six carbines, an M1 rifle, two Thompson submachine guns, two pistols, and two radios, with no evidence of loss on the Communist side.[15]

The armed forces' Joint Operations Center (JOC) in Saigon reported in September 1963 that only 31 percent of Phu Bon's population was in strategic hamlets; the rest was presumably at least accessible to Communist forces, if not actually under their control.[16] Yet JOC maps showed only 350 Communist main force and regional force troops in Phu Bon by the middle of 1963, and no whole regiments or battalions.[17] The province remained relatively quiet in late 1963 and 1964, though this may have been because its main significance to the Communists was the communication routes running through it. It is possible they were content to live and let live if these routes were not seriously disturbed. During the Communist monsoon offensive of 1965, Phu Bon would be the scene of fierce battles. But most of the Communist troops involved in them were not Highlanders and not locally recruited. They were either PAVN units that had recently come down the Trail or ethnic Vietnamese recruited on the coastal plain and sent to the Highlands for specific missions.[18]

Some ARVN operations in the northern half of the Central Highlands did result in successful firefights. During Operation Dan Thang 301, a search and clear effort in Kontum Province, the 22d Ranger Company clashed with a force estimated at 100 Communist troops on the late afternoon of 16 February. In the early hours of 17 February American helicopters of the 81st Transport Company moved the 1st Company of the 2d Battalion of the 40th Infantry Regiment (22d Division) into blocking positions to cut off the Communist retreat. The effort to envelop and annihilate this force failed, but the ARVN claimed nineteen enemy dead without loss to its own men.[19] An armed clash on a similar scale occurred on the afternoon of 10 March 1963. Elements of the 1st Battalion of the 42d Infantry Regiment, 22d Division, were taking part in Dan Thang 303, another search and clear operation in Kontum Province, when they clashed with an estimated two Communist companies. They lost two killed and twelve wounded but claimed to have counted the bodies of ten Communist soldiers and captured a submachine gun, three magazines, and two grenades.[20]

It seems likely that the steady attrition of small-scale actions in II Corps' area of the Central Highlands in the early months of 1963 generally favored the anti-Communist side. This pattern, however, was somewhat disrupted when, just after midnight on 27 April (Saigon time), the Communists mounted their biggest attack in this region since the assault on Plei Mrong in early January. In the aftermath of Dan Thang 313, yet another ARVN search and clear operation, elements of the 22d Engineer Battalion and part of the 2d Battalion of the 41st Regiment (22d Division) were located at a work site called Vic Klum, their mission being to repair and improve the road from Kon Plong to Cia Vuc and to restore the airfield at Plateau Gi. One of the standard Communist histories of the war states:

> On 26 April the 409th Sapper Battalion and two infantry companies from the 95th Battalion/2d Regiment, under the command of Comrade Ho Van Tri, the 2d Regiment Chief of Staff, mounted a surprise attack that annihilated the puppet engineers who [were] building a road between Gia Vut and Mang Den. During two hours of fighting we overran and destroyed the battalion headquarters, one company of infantry and one artillery platoon and we captured two 105mm howitzers.[21]

The use of the term "annihilated" in the Communist account seems to be an exaggeration. In other respects, it agrees remarkably well with accounts from South Vietnamese and American sources. It should be noted that the Communists normally operated on Hanoi time, which was an hour behind Saigon time, the time used by the ARVN and the Americans. Also, the two sides often used different names for the same places. Accounts from both sides agree, however, that in this action the ARVN fought stubbornly, despite being surprised. The South Vietnamese JOC in Saigon admitted "sizable losses in lives, heavy equipment and weapons," including thirty-two ARVN fatalities. A later American report estimated "40 ARVN KIA [killed in action], 1 US advisor KIA, 25 WIA [wounded in action], unknown MIA [missing in action]." II Corps responded with a pursuit operation at 0800 the same day. The work site was reoccupied at 1000, but no contact was made with the Communist forces that had mounted the assault.[22]

Though Vic Klum was a setback for government forces, it was a relatively small one and did not wrest the strategic initiative from the anti-Communist side, even in the northern half of the Central Highlands. On 4 May II Corps mounted a major operation, Dan Thang 099, at the junction of Kontum, Quang Ngai, and Quang Tin Provinces, where the Communists had one of their four main "war zones" in South Vietnam. The intent was to destroy installations and facilities in major Communist bases at Do Xa and Dang Hong, bring the population in these areas under government control, and establish secure government military bases for further operations. Intended to last for thirty days, the operation involved substantial elements of the 2d, 22d, and 25th Infantry Divisions, as well as the 2d and 4th Battalions of the Marine Brigade, the 3d Armored Cavalry Brigade, and other units. The Marines arrived at Do Xa at the start of the operation in a major helicopter lift, a type of operation that was becoming increasingly common for South Vietnamese forces.[23]

Initially, Communist troops avoided contact. Government troops captured an arsenal containing five tons of iron, communications equipment, administrative supplies, and large quantities of paddy and livestock. Eleven days into the operation, however, Communist forces struck back, attacking the 22d Artillery Battalion and overrunning the headquarters of the 41st Regiment (22d Division). Also on 15 May, just before midday, a Communist force of about company strength ambushed a ten-vehicle convoy belonging to the 1st Battalion of the 41st Regiment on the road between Kontum and Plateau Gi, killing twenty-one ARVN soldiers and wounding twenty-five before fleeing northward.[24]

The ARVN credited local Communist forces with the vehicle ambush. It is possible, however, that the assault on the 41st Regiment's headquarters involved elements of the main force 200th and 407th Battalions. Communist accounts state that these units were in the northern part of the Central Highlands in May, where they "eliminated hundreds of enemy troops from the field of battle and captured large quantities of weapons, ammunition and military equipment."[25]

In reality, these impressive little victories for the Communists in northern Kontum, while signaling the determination of their leadership and the resilience of at least some of their forces, had little effect on the overall situation. The initiative in this region remained with the ARVN.

On 4 June II Corps mounted a twenty-day operation, code-named Dan Thang 888, involving elements of the 9th, 22d, and 25th Divisions, intended to surround and disrupt the Communists' "secret zones" of Kon Hannung, Nuon Yen, and Ba Nam. Employing an average of thirty-two rifle companies at any given time, government forces encountered little effective resistance in their task of wrecking these Communist "liaison, economical and logistical bases." While recording three of its own troops killed and twenty-four wounded, II Corps claimed forty-two Communist soldiers killed and two captured, along with sixteen individual weapons and "a large assortment of small arms ammunition and grenades." The Communists also lost forty-six tons of crops and 934 head of livestock, as well as clothing, drugs, and documents. According to II Corps, these losses, coupled with "the return to RVN control of 1744 Montagnards," had "materially reduced the VC influence in the area."[26]

Although MACV's intelligence staff believed that Military Region 6 had a heavy weapons battalion in Darlac,[27] there were no major assaults on government positions in the southern Central Highlands in the first half of 1963 to compare with those that occurred in Kontum. The 23d Division did mount operations aimed at Communist base areas in its part of the Highlands,[28] but firefights with Communist troops in that sector were rare. Indeed, they were so rare that Colonel Wilbur Wilson, the senior American adviser at III Corps, was convinced that Colonel Le Quang Trong, the 23d Division commander, was deliberately avoiding contact with the enemy, mounting few of the small-unit operations that were most likely to achieve it.[29]

Despite Trong's apparent weakness as ARVN commander in the southern part of the region, and despite the small Communist victories achieved in Kontum, government forces generally continued to hold the strategic initiative in the Central Highlands in the first half of 1963. The harvest of late 1962 had apparently been a good one, and reports of Communist troops actually starving were not common in 1963. But with the incursion of government troops into their base areas and the resulting destruction or removal of food supplies and the relocation of Highland populations on whom they depended, Communist units generally subsisted on meager rations. Medicines, too, continued to be scarce.[30] In these circumstances, physical and psychological recovery from the extreme hardship of 1962 was bound to be a slow process.

Yet some full-time Communist forces remained in the Central Highlands in mid-1963. Their numbers were not particularly great, and most of them had very limited combat power. A few elite, apparently ethnic Vietnamese main force units were, however, able to inflict some nasty little defeats on the ARVN, thus keeping Communist hopes for this region alive.

Organizational Changes to
US and South Vietnamese Special Forces

In 1963 US Special Forces had a growing presence in the Central Highlands, sometimes establishing camps in areas so remote that the ARVN seldom reached them in any strength. Both the administration of these forces and the ways in which they were employed were, however, undergoing rapid change. On 1 September 1962, as part of Operation Switchback, Colonel George C. Morton, formerly chief of the Special Warfare Branch, J-3 MACV, had become commander of all US Special Forces in South Vietnam. Over the next few months he developed a formal military hierarchy to take control of operations previously controlled and financed by the CIA. On 8 November 1962, using extra administrative personnel brought in from Fort Bragg, he established the Headquarters US Army Special Forces Vietnam (Provisional) in the Cholon district of Saigon. In February 1963 he moved it to Nha Trang, close to the center of South Vietnam's coast. By the beginning of 1963, four B-detachments (each with seven officers and seventeen men) had arrived to help administer and control the twenty-eight A-detachments (each with two officers and ten enlisted men). Each ARVN corps area had one B-detachment. The B-detachment at Pleiku supervised the A-detachments in II Corps' area, and the one in Saigon looked after those in III Corps.[31]

By the time Switchback was completed in July 1963, Morton's Nha Trang headquarters had assumed (under MACV's umbrella) effective control of almost all US Army Special Forces activity in Vietnam. Four Special Forces A-detachments doing surveillance work on the Laotian frontier were the only exceptions. These, and the Highland troops working with them, remained under CIA control until October 1963, when they were integrated into CIDG.

Until late 1963, when the program was finally shut down, the CIA also remained involved with the Mountain Scouts, to which no US Special Forces A-detachments were assigned. The CIA claimed that in the twelve months prior to the program's closure, the Mountain Scouts, working in fifteen-man teams and responsible to provincial governors, had killed 251 Communist personnel and captured 103, while losing only 18 killed and 2 missing. Perhaps more significantly, they had generated a great many reports on Communist troop strengths, locations, and activities. Like the Buon Enao experiment, the Mountain Scout program fell victim to Diem's anxiety about armed Highlanders not being under close South Vietnamese government control. Despite the protests of province chiefs in Kontum, Pleiku, and Quang Duc, all of whom had found the Mountain Scouts very useful, the central government ordered these troops to report to CIDG camps, where most were integrated into Strike Forces.[32]

Vietnamese Special Forces too were evolving fast in 1963. Those sent to participate in CIDG when it began in late 1961 belonged to the 77th Observation Group, a paramilitary force that was under the control of Diem's Presidential Survey Office. The PSO had carefully selected the personnel sent to Buon Enao, and they performed well there. As CIDG rapidly expanded, however, it was more difficult to find suitable personnel. At the same time, Diem became increasingly anxious about the program because few of the minorities it was arming had much positive loyalty to his regime. If it were to continue, he wanted it under better control. To that end, Vietnamese Special Forces personnel were to serve alongside their American counterparts in all CIDG camps, with a Vietnamese officer as camp commander. This necessitated a rapid expansion, so the government established the 31st Observation Group. On 15 January the 77th and 31st Observation Groups were formally designated the Vietnamese Special Forces (VNSF) and, under a Special Forces command initially held by Colonel Le Quang Tung (who remained head of the PSO), they were integrated into the Republic of Vietnam Armed Forces (RVNAF).[33]

The very rapid expansion of the VNSF from late 1962 almost inevitably diminished their general quality. The government's anxieties about CIDG meant that when selecting officers for the program, political loyalty was considered more important than military skills or the ability to relate to people of other cultures, and this compounded the problem. In 1963 and 1964, therefore, the VNSF developed a distinctly poor reputation with their US counterparts.[34]

Plei Mrong and After: CIDG Outside the Buon Enao Complex

While the Buon Enao complex was in the process of being dissolved, a development examined in some detail later in this chapter, CIDG was expanding outside Darlac. It was no longer the policy to begin with the active consent of local people in a relatively secure area and work outward. Instead, US Special Forces were building camps, with little or no prior exploration of local attitudes, on the edge of areas of intense Communist activity.[35] The approach was intrinsically and obviously dangerous, and in early January one camp came close to being completely overrun.

Plei Mrong was about 20 km northwest of the town of Pleiku. The locals were Jarai Highlanders whose traditional lifestyle was quite similar to that of the Rhade further south. A-314, commanded by Captain William P. Grace III, arrived on 1 November 1962. In contrast to the situation at Buon Enao the previous year, no friendly villages had asked the Americans to help defend them. Grace's men arrived uninvited and without prior consultation with the locals. They first constructed and fortified a camp and then started recruiting a Strike Force from a population about which they knew almost nothing. Poor relations with their VNSF counterparts in the camp and with the local government compounded their difficulties. Grace considered Aspirant Hanh, the notional camp commandant, irresponsible and incompetent, and he apparently held almost equally negative opinions of both the district chief and the province chief. Although A-314 attempted to use a local "Highlander Affairs" officer to screen out Communist infiltrators, it soon became apparent that the man was out of his depth. Virtually from the outset, there were insurgents on the Strike Force at Plei Mrong, and the Americans apparently suspected as much.

In contrast with Buon Enao, the recruitment of defenders for local villages seems to have been something of an afterthought with the US Special Forces at Plei Mrong. The process commenced only on 27 December. By that time, it was obvious that the Communists were active in the area and had influence in the villages. During the first two months, patrols had six skirmishes, and one vehicle hit a mine. Most of the local Communist fighters were evidently Jarai, so when A-314 started recruiting Jarai village defense trainees, there was good reason to be concerned about their allegiance. Yet, instead of training them in and around their home villages, the Americans brought them inside their own camp.

The camp's perimeter defenses were quite strong by the standards of this period of the war. Two double barbed-wire fences surrounded the camp; the outer fence was reinforced with broken glass and three-inch-high steel spikes, and the gap between the fences was filled with antipersonnel mines and punji stakes. A ring of trenches and fighting positions lay within the wire, interrupted only at the two gates. Given the very limited firepower of local Communist troops, this may have seemed sufficient. But having an enemy within the camp greatly diminished the value of the perimeter defenses, and the Communist command would deploy heavier hitters than A-314 had hitherto encountered to strike from without.[36]

Under MACV's overall direction, A-detachment commanders were pressed to act aggressively, always keeping a substantial part of their Strike Forces outside the wire. On 30 December 1962 Grace received a report from a local South Vietnamese government official that there were 3,000 Communist troops in the mountains northwest of Plei Mrong. Patrols sent out on 31 December went as far as Plei Hiep on the Krong Bolah River, but upon receiving fire from the far bank, they proceeded no further. On 2 January 1963 Grace mounted an operation in which 3 members of his A-detachment and 123 members of the Strike Force were lifted by helicopter to the other side of the Krong Bolah River. Grace left his executive officer, Lieutenant Leary, in command of the half detachment remaining in camp.

In contrast with their poisonous relations with the VNSF and with the Vietnamese local government, the Americans at Plei Mrong had achieved a degree of cooperation with ARVN 22d Division forces in their area, and this probably saved some of their lives. Grace's operation had the support of two 155mm guns of the 37th ARVN Artillery Battalion. At 1830 on 2 January the battery commander, apparently feeling that his guns were excessively exposed, asked for greater infantry protection to supplement the eighteen Strike Force soldiers with him. Believing that he could spare no more men for the defense of the guns, Leary invited the ARVN officer to bring them inside the camp— an offer he accepted. The eighteen Strike Force troops accompanied him. On the night of 2–3 January the total force inside the camp consisted of eight US Special Forces personnel, the ARVN crews of the two 155mm howitzers, the Vietnamese camp commander and his assistant, two companies of Strike Force troops totaling 191 men, and 171 village defense trainees.

At 0130 on 3 January 1963 the firing of a 57mm recoilless rifle on the west side of the camp awakened its personnel, who ran to their assigned defensive positions. Supported by the fire of mortars and recoilless rifles, a Communist force estimated at 100 men was attacking through a twelve-foot gap cut in the thirty-three-strand double-apron fence on the southwest perimeter. The gap had been made with wire cutters, mostly from the outside, but with the aid or passive assistance of the village defense trainees on guard inside that portion of the fence. Another Communist force, also estimated at 100 men, was attacking the north side of the camp, and small-arms fire appeared to be coming from all sides. The ARVN artillery battery, which had taken up position near the north gate, was largely responsible for averting total disaster. The gunners lowered howitzer tubes to minimum elevation and fired eight to ten rounds of high-explosive point-blank. They and the Strike Force troops with them also opened up with one 50-caliber machine gun, one 30-caliber machine gun, and a number of 45-caliber submachine guns, quite quickly defeating the Communist attack from the north.

The Communist penetration from the southwest, however, was extremely serious. Communist troops stormed in, throwing grenades and blocks of TNT. Chaos reigned as about thirty of the village defense trainees joined the Communists, while others joined the defenders and a third group merely panicked. The Americans then realized that a number of their Strike Force soldiers were also fighting on the Communist side, adding to the general pandemonium.

Lieutenant Leary was unable to alert the B-detachment (B-210) in Pleiku because the attackers had broken the camp's radio antenna, and according to one account, it was Second Lieutenant Bao, the ARVN liaison officer, who raised the alarm and summoned help. Bao had been trained at the British jungle warfare school in Malaya and spoke good English. He used the ARVN artillery net to alert II Corps headquarters at Pleiku, and II Corps relayed requests for air support to both the Vietnamese and American air forces. For those defending the camp, the worst was over by 0400. Up to that point, no air support of any kind had materialized, but at 0510 a C-47 started dropping flares. Communist troops mounted a final probe from the east at approximately 0600, but that quickly broke down. ARVN reinforcements arrived at 0615 and commenced a pursuit. About an hour later helicopters arrived to evacuate the wounded.

Though there were no American fatalities, the little battle at Plei Mrong was perhaps the greatest ordeal endured by US Special Forces up to this point in the war. It was later estimated that (not including those who had already

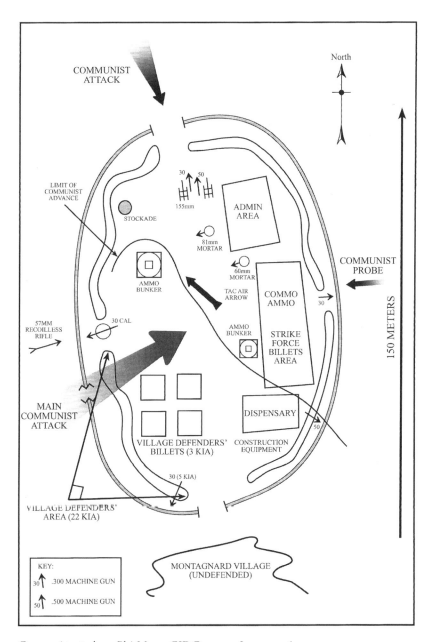

Communist attack on Plei Mrong CIDG camp, 3 January 1963

infiltrated) up to 450 Communist troops may have been involved in the attack on the camp, the majority of them ethnic Vietnamese from regular units but accompanied by some Highlanders. While they had not succeeded in overrunning the camp completely, the battle was a limited Communist victory and a significant setback (or at least a grave warning) for the CIDG program.

Communist forces carried away nearly all their casualties, so these cannot be determined with any accuracy. Thirty-nine of the defenders were killed: one ARVN soldier and thirty-eight Strike Force members. Thirty village defense trainees also died, although it was unclear on which side many of them had fought, if they fought at all. One American, one ARVN soldier, eight Strike Force members, and thirty village defense trainees were wounded. More than sixty personnel (all village defense trainees) were missing, although it can be assumed that many of them left voluntarily. A total of 114 small arms, mostly carbines but including 5 Browning automatic rifles, was also lost. A subsequent inquiry estimated that at the time of the attack there were at least thirty-three Communist infiltrators on Plei Mrong's Strike Force, as well as those among the village defense trainees.[37]

The assault on Plei Mrong was by far the most dramatic incident involving the CIDG program in the Central Highlands during 1963. At 2300 on 16 August, two small outposts belonging to a camp called Polei Jar in Kontum Province fell to Communist forces, with the loss of six lives and a few weapons; the camp was closed shortly afterward.[38] In terms of the intensity of the fighting, however, the rest of the year was an anticlimax for Special Forces in the region.

Most CIDG Strike Forces in the Central Highlands conducted patrols, where they encountered punji stakes and booby traps, attracted sniping and occasional ambushes, and engaged in occasional small-scale firefights. Where they penetrated Communist bases, they, like the ARVN, destroyed food stocks and buildings, killed or rounded up livestock, and herded away Highlanders perceived to be aiding the Communist war effort.

A holistic, population-centric approach to counterinsurgency no longer governed US Special Forces operations in the CIDG program. Often the families of Strike Force soldiers were the only civilians offered protection, and sometimes this did not amount to much. Medical aid was sometimes given to neighboring villages, but this was only a sideline. MACV's emphasis on border surveillance and offensive operations rather than village defense and civic action made the development of intimate relations with Highland communities difficult. In many cases A-detachments encountered suspicion from both Highland civilians and Vietnamese local authorities, and they were unable to form much of an intelligence picture of events going on around them. Plei Mrong in late 1962–1963 was the classic example of this, but the same pattern occurred elsewhere.[39]

In December 1963 Special Forces camps in the Central Highlands, all controlled by the B-detachment at Pleiku, included Dak Pek, Dak To, and Polei Krong in Kontum Province; Buon Beng in Phu Bon Province; Chu Dron (also known as Duc Co), Plei Do Lim, and Plei Mei in Pleiku Province; Ban Don, Bon Sar Pa, and Buon Mi Ga in Darlac; and Dam Pau in Tuyen Duc.[40] The Civilian Irregular Defense Groups based in such camps were neither civilian nor irregular nor primarily defensive. No longer did the program comprise networks of defended villages. It was becoming a scattering of paramilitary forts. Strike Forces were no longer essentially defenders of minority communities against Communist exactions. They were becoming indigenous mercenaries in American pay.[41]

By the time he was relieved as commander of US Special Forces in Vietnam in early November 1963, Colonel George Morton was in a gloomy mood. His opinion of the Diem government echoed that of Colonel Gil Layton of the CIA, who had run CIDG before him. Both had found it intensely obstructive of nearly everything they had tried to do. In his final report Morton declared the regime virtually devoid of popular support.[42] With regard to most of the minorities with which CIDG worked, that may have been accurate.

Morton's own record in Vietnam, however, was not above criticism. His victories were bureaucratic ones won over people on his own side. If he was not entirely responsible for the dubious direction CIDG took in late 1962 and 1963, he did little or nothing to correct the steering. By the time he left Vietnam, the Buon Enao complex, which embodied CIDG's initial spirit, had ceased to exist. Morton's part in its final demise was both distinctly inglorious and rather bizarre.

Dissolution of the Buon Enao Complex

As already noted, the Buon Enao project was the most impressive element of the counterinsurgency effort in the Central Highlands and perhaps anywhere in South Vietnam in 1962. Yet the Diem government, possibly at the instigation of 23d Division commander Colonel Le Quang Trong, and certainly with his active encouragement, decided to terminate the experiment, apparently because Buon Enao encouraged the Rhade and other Highlanders to aspire to the kind of autonomy the government was determined to deny them. In September 1962 a rather vague agreement was sketched out for the handover of villages to Darlac's provincial authorities and for the gradual dispersal of its Strike Force.[43] On paper, implementation of this agreement began almost immediately. Major Hoang Thong, Darlac's province chief, took control of the first thirty-one villages from the Buon Enao project in the second half of the month. In reality, little changed at that stage. The provincial authorities lacked the resources to defend or support these villages, and as late as April 1963 they were still relying on the Buon Enao complex for both defense and medical support.[44]

The Diem government, indeed, showed no enthusiasm for providing anything to Highlanders who had been involved in the Buon Enao program. Its overriding obsession was with taking things away—specifically, weapons, and especially automatic weapons. At some point in the last quarter of 1962, Diem ordered that the total number of weapons held by Highland Village Defenders in Darlac be reduced to 3,500, and he wanted this done quickly. Colonel Layton of the CIA reckoned that this meant collecting about 7,000 weapons, but the actual figure might have been even higher.[45]

The idea of disarming most of those involved in the Buon Enao complex caused intense dismay among the Highlanders, Dave Nuttle and his CIA employers, and others on the anti-Communist side. The Australian counterinsurgency guru Colonel Ted Serong protested the intended disarmament in October 1962, probably as soon as he heard about it and before the process actually began. In a memorandum to General Paul Harkins, commander of MACV, Serong extolled Buon Enao's achievements:

> The Boun Enou [sic] project is rolling. It has momentum. It is like a big snow-ball getting bigger and better. Already its center is quiet, and the fighting is being pushed further away as the periphery expands. All this is based on the confidence of the people who continue to come in for training and arming then return to fight for, or in, the villages. . . . The project is a whole. Its strength lies in its unity. . . . That is basic.

Serong acknowledged that the issuance of weapons to Highlanders had been insufficiently conditional and inadequately controlled. Presumably, he thought that Nuttle and his CIA backers should have made it clear that the weapons provided to Village Defenders were on loan to meet a particular emergency and might be withdrawn if the crisis diminished. Yet he also thought that disarming the Highlanders while the war was still going on was extremely ill advised:

> The current position is that 10,000 Montagnards are armed, and most are making good use of their arms. The weapon in the hands of the Montagnard is a status symbol. He is a king. He is a friend of the Americans. The Montagnard dislikes the Vietnamese. The Vietnamese fear the Montagnard. Both have reasons . . . I suggest that this is a matter going far beyond the apparently simple matter of lining up a few hundred tribesmen, patting them on the

head for a job well done, and relieving them of their weapons. However we may regret the facts of the original distribution (or, more important, what the Montagnards believe to be the facts) we cannot escape the conclusion that, [in] the eyes of the Montagnards, this act is a breach of faith by their friends the Americans, at the instigation of their enemies (I hesitate to use the expression) the Vietnamese; and we expect the Montagnards to do a lot more fighting for us before this thing is over. Suggestion—forget the weapons, count our blessings, and try to organize the distribution better next time.[46] •

Despite Serong's strictures, the Americans found it impossible to resist the Diem government's demands to start taking weapons from the Highlanders in Darlac. In early November 1962 Jack Benefiel, the CIA case officer responsible for Buon Enao, instructed Captain Curtis D. Terry, commander of detachment A-334 and the senior US Army Special Forces officer involved in the project, to begin collecting weapons from the thirty-one villages that had been transferred, at least in theory, to the province chief's control. Benefiel told Terry to take charge of this personally. Terry queried his orders, asking why the Vietnamese authorities did not undertake this task. Benefiel told him that because Americans had issued the arms in the first place, it was considered more appropriate that they should collect them. The Rhade might prove a lot less compliant if the Vietnamese authorities handled the disarmament.

Probably with great reluctance, Terry obeyed. By Christmas 1962, he had collected 499 weapons. After Christmas, however, he began to meet increasing resistance, and the Rhade expressed concerns that their villages would be left too weak to repel a Communist attack. On 10 January 1963 Terry suspended the operation. By that stage, he had taken in about 600 weapons.[47]

By mid-January, Operation Switchback, transferring control of the whole CIDG program from the CIA to MACV, was well under way. Colonel Morton was due to take operational control of the Special Forces in Darlac on 15 January. On 14 January, however, Layton warned him that a massive crisis might be brewing in Darlac. Layton was particularly worried that Terry was due to leave Vietnam, and he wanted that departure delayed. Layton wrote:

As you know it has always been my strong feeling that this is a war of people and not of IBM machines and . . . numbers. Captain Terry's importance to the project is not because he is a Captain of the US Special Forces with certain military qualifications but that he has established a certain rapport with the Rhade and they like, trust and believe in him. He has also managed to accomplish the far more difficult exercise of adjusting himself to the peculiarities of the Vietnamese and establishing himself as a buffer between the two unfriendly ethnic groups.

Although control of the Buon Enao project now rested with Morton, Layton pointed out that it was at a critical stage:

> There [has been] continuous and serious ill-feeling between the Vietnamese and the Rhade and attempts to disarm the Rhade, if poorly handled, could easily lead to a massive revolt which, as we know, might spread through the . . . tribes. Such a revolt could well result in the loss of the entire Highlands. This would be a serious, if not fatal, blow to the US effort here in Vietnam. It would almost certainly destroy immediately the CIDG program.[48]

It is not clear what effect, if any, Layton's pleas had.

It was not just CIA and Special Forces personnel who were dismayed about developments in Darlac. In mid-January Lieutenant Colonel R. J. Billado, the 23d Division's senior adviser, expressed his alarm in a highly articulate, passionately argued memorandum to his immediate superior, Wilbur Wilson. Billado attributed the Diem government's anxiety about the Buon Enao program to "the desire of the Montagnards for autonomy" and to the belief that "the Montagnard cannot be trusted." He discounted the government's worries about a Highlander revolt while insisting that the Communist threat in Darlac was still very real. The number of Communist troops in the province had not dropped appreciably, and it was still a "runway" for Communist personnel moving down from the North. While it was true that the incident rate had dropped dramatically, this was largely owing to "the Buon Enao concept of defended villages," which Billado considered "the most effective anti–Viet Cong action in Darlac." Disarming Village Defenders would provide "the VC with powerful anti-government propaganda, and conceivably recruits, based on the Montagnard becoming . . . disenchanted with the government because of its apparent lack of consideration for their welfare and security." Rhade village chiefs had declared their intention "to tear down their protective fences and assume a position of strict neutrality" if the government stripped their villages of the bulk of their weapons. Billado concluded that the rapid dissolution of the Buon Enao project would be dangerous to the point of recklessness. "VC incidents will increase rapidly once the VC learn that their previous sources of food . . . and freedom of movement can be obtained without combat against a strongly defended village system. . . . Without the support of the defended villages, ARVN does not have the capability to control and eventually eliminate the VC from Darlac Province." He urged that the authorities in Darlac "discontinue the collection of weapons until such time as government control has been firmly established and the VC eliminated as a threat to law and order," which meant, of course, indefinitely.[49]

Wilson forwarded Billado's memorandum to Paul Harkins at MACV with a note expressing his fundamental agreement. By November 1962: "As a consequence of the success of the Buon Enao Program as implemented by the US Special Forces the pacification of Darlac Province was considered to be well along toward success." Like Billado, Wilson considered the dismantling of the program extremely ill advised, but he realized that "the decision to re-cover weapons previously issued to Rhade Tribesmen was made by President Diem" and that in the long run it might be very difficult to resist. According to Wilson, III Corps commander General Ton That Dinh, whom he had earlier characterized as a firm supporter of the Buon Enao project, had be-come "virtually incoherent on the subject," probably because he was "under considerable pressure from the President." Dinh was raving that the Rhade "wanted autonomy," that they "could not be trusted," and that "they were undisciplined if they refused to turn in the weapons in question." For his part, Wilson thought:

> The recovery of the weapons previously issued to the Rhade Tribesmen by the US Special Forces at Buon Enao is a particularly delicate operation and . . . can be accomplished only at considerable personal risk to the US officers charged with the mission. . . . I want to point out that the rapid implemen-tation of any decision to withdraw weapons from the Rhade could in a few days destroy over a year's hard work by Special Forces at Buon Enao.

Wilson recommended that if US military personnel were charged with dis-arming the Rhade, they should deliberately go slowly, and a policy of "foot-dragging" was apparently adopted.[50]

On 21 January 1963 three officers from Morton's Special Forces command, including Terry, visited one of the villages that had resisted disarmament. The village chief insisted that his people could not afford to give up any weapons. When his American visitors pointed out that no insurgents had bothered the village lately, the chief responded that this offered no guarantee for the future. The last words of the villagers were, "Please do not forget us." Their fear of being left naked before their enemies was quite evident.[51]

It seems important, in trying to give a balanced account of Buon Enao, to emphasize that enlightened Vietnamese officers played positive roles virtually throughout the program. In early 1963 Captain Hy replaced Captain Phu (a pillar of the project) as the PSO representative at Buon Enao. Hy held the title of camp commander or commandant. He recognized the Rhade's apprehen-sion about handing over Buon Enao to Vietnamese provincial authorities and was reluctant to upset them further by pressing for their disarmament. Colonel Tung, head of the PSO, had been an early backer of Buon Enao, and al-though President Diem had turned against the project, Tung seemed reluctant to abandon it. At some point in mid-January Captain Hy received orders from PSO headqurters (i.e., from Tung) to stop all arms collection until further notice. As late as March 1963, at least six months after Diem had decided to close the program, Hy was still speaking in its favor: "Buon Enao is a symbol; it means a great deal to the Montagnards. Its name and spirit should not die." Hy was working with Major Thong, the Darlac province chief, to ensure that the villages would enjoy similar degrees of protection and welfare under provincial control as they had as part of the Buon Enao complex. Yet, despite American attempts to put a brave face on the situation, it became apparent that all the project's achievements were in the process of being thrown away. The state of security in Darlac seemed likely to deteriorate catastrophically as a result.[52]

In spring 1963 at least two very strongly worded protests on this issue went to the very top of the US chain of command in Vietnam. In March, Harkins's extremely blunt Australian adviser sent him another general survey on the course of the war—this one a good deal more pessimistic than its October 1962 predecessor. Again Serong condemned the Diem regime's policies in the Highlands—policies that seemed completely at odds with the CIDG program:

> Many of these . . . stem directly from the President himself and the remainder certainly have his approval and the support of Counsellor Nhu. These men are not fools. While I believe that neither of them fully appreciates the mechanics of the CIDG program, I have no reason to doubt that they understand it in outline. Why then do they authorise and . . . direct activities patently damaging to the concept?
>
> The reason is that their aim is not our aim. Our aim is the . . . destruction of the VC Com Z [communications zone] in the High Plateau and eventually control of the border. There is ample evidence to suggest that President Diem and Counsellor Nhu do not share that aim, or at best regard it as secondary. Their aim in the High Plateau is the subjugation of the Montagnard, their destruction as an ethnic entity, and the incorporation of the Montagnard people and the Montagnard land in an integrated Vietnamese community.

Accepting that Diem did not intend the physical extermination of the Highland peoples, only their forcible integration with the Vietnamese, Serong nevertheless characterized this as a form of "genocide" and opined that it was inappropriate for the Americans to associate themselves with it.[53]

Though Serong's comments were the most acerbic, George Morton now joined the list of those complaining to Harkins about developments in Darlac. Morton had been determined to take complete control of CIDG from the CIA and had falsely claimed virtually all credit for its successes for his own service branch. But having finally got the CIA out of the way, he was now finding that the much-vaunted achievements of the Buon Enao complex, by far CIDG's biggest and most successful component, were in danger of vanishing in a matter of weeks. All 214 villages that were, or had been, part of the complex were due to be handed over to provincial authorities by 30 June 1963. Some 31 or 32 villages (sources differ) had theoretically been transferred in September 1962 and another 107 in March 1963. But, as Morton now argued, the notion that provincial authorities were going to organize these villages as strategic hamlets had no basis in reality:

> While the Province Chief has agreed to accept responsibility for the villages turned over to him, he is in fact not physically capable of supporting [them] logistically . . . medically or operationally. This turnover of villages is at present simply a play of words and does not provide the villages under Province control with anything but moral support. Special Forces elements continue to provide medical assistance and support . . . resupply, weapons repair and/or exchange and conduct periodic inspection of village defense facilities. Strike Force elements throughout Darlac Province conduct patrol activities . . . and are prepared to go to the assistance of any village under VC attack. Air support and control are effected through the Buon Enao Special Forces.

In principle, Morton had no objection to turning over villages located in reasonably safe areas to the provincial authorities. Indeed, he favored such a policy. It would allow his Special Forces to be concentrated in more dangerous areas where they were needed. But stripping villages of the bulk of their weapons, while offering them practically no external help, was unacceptable.

The area in which the Buon Enao project had been operating was divided into three zones—A, B, and C—with Zone A being the most secure and Zone C the least secure. The Diem government's intention at this stage was to leave just twelve weapons for villages in Zone A, twenty-four for those in Zone B, and thirty-six for those in Zone C. Morton described this plan as "completely unrealistic and . . . unacceptable to the Montagnard villagers. A village in the Zone 'C' area containing only 36 weapons would do nothing other than provide the VC with a lucrative target." With the provincial authorities offering nothing to former VDP villages, Morton opposed efforts to reduce the number of weapons they held. Given that the Diem government seemed particularly worried about the automatic weapons (mostly 9mm submachine guns) in Highlanders' hands, Morton was prepared to encourage Village Defenders to swap these for semiautomatic M1 carbines. The ARVN used M1 carbines but not 9mm submachine guns, so this would make ammunition supply easier. But Morton thought this was as far as US Special Forces should go in reducing the firepower of Highlanders in Darlac.[54]

The matter of arms was still unresolved on 4 June when Morton had a conference on the handover process with Major Thong and some of his staff. Judging by the rather ragged transcript that survives, Morton knew he had few, if any, cards left to play. He could salvage little of substance from the impending wreck of Buon Enao. The stridency of his April position paper to Harkins was gone. His performance was not only unimpressive but also distinctly weird. Initially, he tried to insist that the disarmament of Highlanders should be carried out slowly and sensitively, with a lot of psychological preparation. Then, perhaps because the provincial authorities seemed determined to settle the arms issue quickly, and in an effort to lighten the mood, he suggested another plan of action: Before their final departure from Buon Enao, US Special Forces would hold "a gigantic marksmanship contest for the Rhade" and "give prizes to them." They would expend "every round of 9mm ammunition" so that, after the contest, there would be "no more ammo." He suggested that the competition be held "on the 4th of July, Independence Day," although why American Independence Day would have significance for the Highlanders he did not explain. The Special Forces would provide 214 turkeys—one for every village in the complex—and have "a turkey shoot." After the contest everybody would "have a good feast and go home happy."

By this stage, MACV had decided that 1,024 members of the Buon Enao Strike Force could be retained by CIDG for use elsewhere, leaving 604 in the hands of Darlac's provincial authorities. Thong indicated that he intended to use these as "Province Special Forces" but admitted, "We don't have the money to pay them . . . and because of this we will lose some." Thong also divulged that the now famous hospital at Buon Enao, the centerpiece of the health service for Highlanders created by the Buon Enao program in Darlac, would soon close. In the future Highlanders in that vicinity would have to seek medical attention at the hospital in Ban Me Thuot. This evidently dismayed Morton, who stated that the Americans "would not like to see the Buon Enao dispensary go down." For the Rhade, the hospital was the "proudest symbol" of the whole Buon Enao enterprise, and Morton thought there ought to be "as little change as possible at present." There is no indication his objection had any effect.

By the end of this meeting, Morton obviously wanted to wash his hands of Buon Enao as quickly as possible, and he seemed to change his tune again:

> Many people in Saigon [Vietnamese and American] feel that we are working too fast in the turnover of Buon Enao, however I don't think so. We should have de-emphasized Buon Enao some time ago. This turnover must be approved by MACV per orders of Gen. Harkins. We must present to the Unconventional Warfare Committee and tell them [that] all officials think

the turnover is going well and that it is time to pull US Special Forces out of Buon Enao . . . I will advise [the] Committee to [get both American and Vietnamese personnel] in Saigon to quit worrying about the Rhade and Buon Enao.[55]

Morton's suggestion that many people in Saigon objected to the speed of the transfer is intriguing, especially because he apparently believed they included a considerable number of Vietnamese. Who these people were is not entirely clear. It seems likely that they included some CIA officers, some American embassy officials, and Colonel Le Quang Tung and some of his PSO officers. There is a suggestion of tension between General Harkins, who apparently wanted to hand over Buon Enao quickly, and other members of the American Country Team, who were opposed to doing so or at least very doubtful about it.

Despite any doubts that may have existed in Vietnamese PSO and American embassy circles, all CIA support for CIDG ceased at the beginning of July, and all 214 villages were consigned to the care of Darlac's provincial administration. This left an atmosphere of disillusionment and disaffection among Highlanders and dramatically diminished the strength of the anti-Communist side in Darlac.[56] The Communists were not slow to take advantage.

Rising Racial Tensions: The Resurgence of Bajaraka

Some senior officials of the Diem government were sympathetic to the native cultures of the Central Highlands and were open to a certain degree of Highlander self-determination within an essentially Vietnamese state. Politically aware Highlanders recognized Major Hoang Van Dinh, province chief in Kontum, and Major Ngo Nhu Bich, who became province chief in Tuyen Duc in April 1963, as belonging to this category. Most officials in the region, however, were unwilling or unable to relate to most of the people they governed. The arrival of increasing numbers of ethnic Vietnamese, Highlanders' consequent fear of losing their traditional lands, and their rough treatment by government troops remained contentious issues.[57] By late 1962, there was another sharp deterioration in the relationship between Highlanders and the Saigon government. This became a serious security issue in 1963 and a critical one in 1964. The dissolution of the Buon Enao complex, an important symbol to Highlanders and an embodiment of their hopes for the future, played a crucial part in these developments.

It may be no coincidence that October 1962, the same month Dave Nuttle left Vietnam, was pivotal in the resurgence of the Bajaraka autonomy movement. In the middle of that month four Rhade, some of them apparently junior officials in Darlac's provincial administration, contacted a Rhade-speaking American in Ban Me Thuot and asked for US help. Claiming the existence of a Vietnamese plot to exterminate Highlanders, they referred to an ancient legend: The Rhade had first arrived in Darlac after an underground migration from a cave near Dalat. They had emerged through a small aperture known as the Hole of Drung (a real geological feature located about halfway between the city of Ban Me Thuot and Lac Thien). According to the legend, when the Hole of Drung closed, the Rhade people would face extinction. The Rhade spokesmen told the American that their people feared this was happening now. They wanted the Americans to intercede with the Diem government to have their grievances addressed.

A second meeting was scheduled for later that month, but Y-Thinh Eban was the only Rhade to show up. The others, believing they were already under government surveillance, had taken fright. Y-Thinh had been arrested for his part in the Bajaraka autonomy movement in 1958 and imprisoned until May 1962, after which he was employed as a translator at Buon Enao. He now declared himself to be the general secretary of the Bajaraka Central Committee, based at Ban Me Thuot. The tone of this meeting was far less apocalyptic than the previous one. Y-Thinh's remarks were rational and constructive, leading the Americans to believe that a useful dialogue was possible.

The experience of the Buon Enao project, Y-Thinh indicated, had made some Highland leaders rethink the necessity of striving for autonomy. Bajaraka was now contemplating limiting its demands to racial equality within the southern Vietnamese state. A proposal of particular interest to both the Americans and the Saigon government was that Y-Bih, a Rhade leader actively involved in the Communist insurgency, be approached. Convincing Y-Bih to "rally" to the government side, it was generally agreed, would be a major blow to the Communists in Darlac. Some in the Bajaraka movement thought his involvement in negotiations with the government offered the best hope of a successful and lasting settlement of Highlanders' grievances.[58]

On 29 October 1962 the CIA informed Ngo Dinh Nhu and Colonel Le Quang Tung about these meetings. Colonel Tung told the CIA on 13 December 1962 that he had the authority (presumably from his immediate superior, President Diem) to approach Y-Bih and offer him amnesty. Tung's only caveat was that a member of the PSO should be present at any meetings between CIA officers and Y-Bih. The CIA made a concerted effort to contact Y-Bih and recruited Y-Bham, chairman of the Bajaraka Central Committee and still imprisoned in Ban Me Thuot, to help with the negotiations. Y-Bham wrote several letters to Y-Bih, encouraging him to surrender. Such efforts assumed a particular urgency by a development in mid-January. Y-Preh, a

Rhade associated with the Ban Me Thuot Bajaraka committee, informed the CIA that the Kontum and Pleiku committees had sent an oral message to their comrades in Darlac proposing a general Highlander revolt against the government. The authenticity of this message was suspect; some Bajaraka members and some CIA officers believed it might have been a Communist plot. If so, it failed. The Americans told the Ban Me Thuot committee that neither they nor Y-Bham would support such a revolt.

On 18 January 1963 Layton addressed a letter to the Pleiku Bajaraka committee suggesting that its members meet with General Nguyen Khanh, commander of II Corps. In a separate development, on 1 February a message was received from Y-Bih, who stated that he was willing to meet representatives of the Saigon government provided Y-Bham was released from prison. Given the CIA's judgment that Y-Bham's influence was needed to head off a revolt in Pleiku, it used its influence to secure his temporary release.

Preliminary discussions involving Layton's people, some Highlanders, and General Khanh occurred on 6 February. A more formal meeting involving Khanh, representatives of the Pleiku Bajaraka committee, and Y-Bham (flown to Pleiku from Ban Me Thuot for this purpose) took place eight days later. The CIA personnel present deemed this meeting a success, later claiming: "The prospective revolt was thwarted." Reading between the lines, however, it seems that the CIA had only a vague idea of what was going on among politically active Highlanders in Kontum and Pleiku. Whether an armed uprising there was ever a real possibility is not certain.

Events that spring gave Highlanders further cause to doubt the benevolence and trustworthiness of the Saigon government. Y-Bham, who had never been promised a permanent release, was returned to prison by the end of February. The effort to bring Y-Bih into talks collapsed when, on 15 March, elements of the ARVN 23d Division, possibly taking advantage of information supplied by Bajaraka to assist negotiations, mounted an operation to capture him. Apparently, division commander Colonel Le Quang Trong intended to have Y-Bih summarily executed, but the operation failed. Y-Bih then broke off all communication with the CIA and the South Vietnamese government. Having already played a substantial role in wrecking the Buon Enao project, Trong had now severely damaged the prospect of addressing Highlanders' grievances more broadly. Whether he was motivated purely by racial prejudice, perceived some personal advantage in exacerbating tensions between Highlanders and ethnic Vietnamese, or was following secret orders from Saigon remains unclear.

As early as February 1963, it seems the Diem government was having second thoughts about working with Bajaraka, fearing that its Central Committee wanted to use American support and money to rebuild its organization. On

13 April the Minister of Defense, Nguyen Thuan, informed the embassy that his government wanted the Americans immediately to cease all involvement in matters connected with the autonomy of Highlanders. On 17 April Layton met with government ministers and Colonel Tung of the PSO and agreed, probably with extreme reluctance, to break off all contact with Bajaraka and to cease all efforts to mediate between Highland leaders and the Vietnamese government.

During May, members of the Bajaraka committee in Ban Me Thuot, no longer protected by the Americans and fearing arrest, dispersed to their villages. That same month, the CIA heard rumors of a revolt by CIDG Strike Force personnel in the Highlands. Although no such insurrection took place at this time, some of the camps rumored to be involved participated in a real rebellion the following year.[59]

Communist Numerical Strength in the Central Highlands, Mid-1963

In the first half of 1963 the initiative in the Central Highlands was in the hands of the Diem government. The Communists were on the receiving end of military operations during that time, and according to histories written in Hanoi since 1975, it was principally the existence of a number of small, unusually well-equipped elite units that allowed them to strike back impressively from time to time. These Communist official accounts, however, give no indication of the numerical strength of the Party's armed forces in the Central Highlands in 1963, and estimates produced by the other side differ widely.

The lowest estimates came from MACV's intelligence analysis branch (J-2). Practically all of MACV's information on the strength of Communist forces originated with South Vietnamese government forces, but MACV J-2 demanded a lot of corroboration before it would credit the existence of a new Communist unit or make any other change to an existing order of battle assessment. Although MACV J-2 was aware of the existence of what it called "Irregular Elements" among Communist forces (part-time guerrillas and political and internal security personnel), and although it judged that these accounted for a large majority of the total number of Communist personnel, it did not give them much military status. They did not appear at all on some MACV maps and charts, which included only what MACV called "Main Force" units. At this stage in the war, however, MACV counted all full-time Communist units as main force.[60]

Maps produced by the South Vietnamese JOC in Saigon credited the Communists with significantly greater military strength (although they too showed

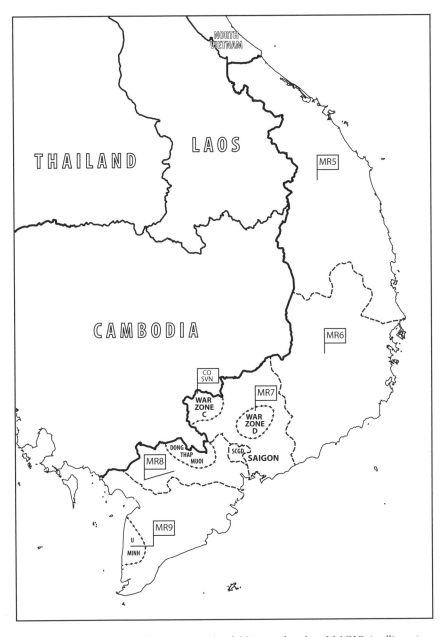

Communist organizations and war zones in South Vietnam (based on MACV's intelligence),
October 1963

only main force and regional force units, not part-time guerrillas).[61] Figures provided by the intelligence staffs at ARVN corps headquarters were a good deal higher—or at least that is the case for those produced by III Corps.[62] Thanks to the meticulous record keeping of Wilbur Wilson at III Corps (and his retention of corps records in his private papers when he left Vietnam), we have some detailed assessments of the Communist order of battle in the southern half of the Central Highlands in mid-1963. Information for the northern half of the region is much sparser, and we must rely on JOC figures. At the end of June 1963, the JOC gave the combined numerical strength of Communist main force (controlled by military regions) and regional (controlled at the provincial or district level) units in the Central Highlands provinces as follows: Kontum, 705; Pleiku, 350; Phu Bon, 305; Darlac, 460; Quang Duc, 675; Tuyen Duc, 120; and Lam Don, 300. According to the JOC, Kontum, Pleiku, and Darlac were the only Central Highlands provinces that contained, at this time, whole Communist battalions, as opposed to mere companies.[63]

At the end of June a special evaluation team, organized by Wilson and composed of American advisers under his command, provided the III Corps commander and his staff with a brief report on the situation in each province in the corps' area. Each report contained the current III Corps intelligence estimate of Communist numerical strength in three categories: main force, regional, and guerrilla (i.e., part time). Each report listed the various government forces present and their strength and provided a numerical evaluation of the balance of forces. Each also contained the MACV assessment of Communist strength in these provinces, allowing direct comparisons between ARVN III Corps and MACV figures.

In late June 1963 MACV assessed Communist military strength in Darlac at 738. But the ARVN III Corps figure, 3,153, was more than four times higher. The III Corps figure was broken down as follows: main force, 1,373; regional, 1,180; guerrilla, 600. Like the JOC, III Corps' intelligence staff defined main force units more narrowly than did MACV J-2, putting only troops directly subordinate to Communist military regions (in this case, Military Region 6) into this class. Regional troops were those controlled at the provincial or district level, and guerrillas were controlled by the part-time Communist hamlet militia. Even on the basis of the III Corps intelligence assessment, however, government forces in Darlac had a numerical advantage of 6.3:1 over their enemies, with the ARVN alone outnumbering Communist forces of all types.

In Tuyen Duc III Corps assessed that the Communists had 48 main force, 300 regional, and 380 guerrilla troops, for a total of 728 (almost three times the MACV figure of 250). Even accepting III Corps' figures, however, government forces in Tuyen Duc had a numerical advantage of approximately 5.6:1. In Quang Duc, on the Cambodian border, III Corps estimated a Communist strength of 1,160 troops (60 main force, 500 regional, and 600 guerrilla), compared with the MACV reckoning of 242; however, even the III Corps figure gave government forces a 3:1 superiority. In Lam Dong, the southernmost high plateau province, III Corps estimated there were 1,764 Communist military personnel in June 1963 (164 main force, 700 regional, and 900 guerrilla), versus the MACV figure of just 200. The III Corps figures, however, still gave the government a 3.5:1 superiority.[64]

These statistics, considered as a whole, indicate that, in the southern half of the Central Highlands in mid-1963, the government had the upper hand, even if it was not in a position to win a decisive victory. This seemed particularly true in Darlac, where the numerical superiority of its forces was reported to be the greatest. With regard to revolutionary warfare, however, there is much that cannot be conveyed in statistics. It was in Darlac more than any other province in the Central Highlands that the government's position deteriorated most dramatically in July–December 1963.

Communist Resurgence, July–December 1963

On the high plateau, as in other regions of the country, there was a Communist resurgence in the second half of 1963. A CIA analysis from mid-November 1963, based on official military reports compiled in Saigon, placed the turning point for South Vietnam as a whole in July. Statistics on the loss of weapons gave a crude indication of how fortunes were changing; "The ratio of weapons losses which favored the government earlier this year has turned dramatically in favor of the Viet Cong. . . . The 1,800 weapons lost by government forces since June would be enough to arm either six [Communist] 'main force' battalions, 22 district companies, or 70 village platoons."[65] This marked change in the war occurred during a wave of antigovernment protests organized and led by militant Buddhists that began in May. Militant Buddhism might seem like an oxymoron, but in Vietnam in the 1960s it was an important political phenomenon. The protest movement (by no means supported by all of Vietnam's Buddhists) condemned human rights violations by the Diem government and the favoritism it allegedly showed to Catholics. The movement had a vaguely neutralist, anti-American political agenda that was potentially useful to the Communists, so there have always been suspicions that Hanoi had a hand in it.

Though there were big marches and demonstrations, some of which turned into riots, it was the self-immolation of Buddhist monks that caught the world's attention. Organizers were sufficiently media aware to ensure that some of these incidents were caught by television cameras.[66] Overwhelmingly urban, the Buddhist protest movement had little direct impact in the Central

Highlands, where the native population was largely animist or Christian. It was, however, a serious development for South Vietnam as a whole. The government declared a state of siege on 21 August and used substantial armed forces in a crackdown on the militants.[67]

The Buddhist protests exacerbated the growing discontent of some American politicians and officials with the Diem government. By late August, the Americans had a new ambassador in Henry Cabot Lodge, and they were sounding out ARVN generals about the possibility of a coup.[68] There is no doubt that, in the fevered atmosphere of conspiracy and suspicion that developed over the next few months, some senior ARVN officers became distracted from the war against the Communists. General Ton That Dinh, the III Corps commander, was among them. Encountering him in a Saigon restaurant in mid-October, noticeably inebriated and evidently plotting with other ARVN generals, an American adviser asked Dinh why he was wearing no fewer than three pistols under his civilian clothes. He pronounced that these were "dangerous times."[69]

During a counteroffensive that began in July, the Communists mounted the vast majority of their attacks where they had the greatest military strength and where their efforts would have the greatest political impact: in the heavily populated lowlands. Through the end of August, their attacks focused principally on strategic hamlets and small posts; by September, they were also mounting large-scale ambushes of government forces and, in the Mekong Delta, assaults on ARVN bases.[70]

Even though the Central Highlands was not the main focus of their efforts, the Communists tried to seize the local initiative in parts of the region, taking full advantage of the weakened security and widespread disaffection in central Darlac following the termination of the Buon Enao project. About an hour before midnight on 23 July 1963:

> A complex of strategic hamlets . . . approximately ten km south of Ban Me Thuot was the target of VC pressure. . . . An estimated VC company, augmented by two regional platoons . . . accosted 4 hamlets and a leper colony . . . in an apparent attempt to discredit the strategic hamlet program in the area. One of the hamlets (Buon Nuoi), after receiving harassing fire from the VC, requested and received 155mm howitzer support, which forced the VC to withdraw. The hamlet militia defenders of three other hamlets (Buon Draith, Buon Kia, Buon Eana/B) surrendered to the VC without offering resistance. The VC entered the hamlets unopposed and confiscated 70 individual weapons (SMG's, M1's and Carbines). The fifth village (Buon Eana/A, a leper colony) resisted the VC attack and suffered the only friendly casualties (1 KIA and 5 WIA) before being entered.

From all these villages, including the leper colony, Communist forces acquired a total of thirty-one submachine guns, twenty-three carbines, and forty-three rifles—ninety-seven weapons in all—enough to equip a small company.[71] This episode marked the beginning of a sharp deterioration of security in Darlac.[72]

Communist forces in the Highlands, however, did not have it all their own way that week. On 22 July the 22d Division mounted a search and clear operation called Dan Thang 325 in an area 25 km southwest of Mang Buk in Kontum Province. Designed to destroy the 131st Company of the Communists' 120th Battalion and to resettle Highlanders in the area, it involved four battalions—2d Battalion, 42d Regiment, and all three battalions of 41st Regiment—and terminated on 9 August. The ARVN suffered six fatalities and seven wounded but claimed twenty-seven enemy killed and two prisoners.[73]

In early August the intensity of the Communist offensive declined somewhat. But while there were few reports of major fighting in the Central Highlands, across the country as a whole, the government's position deteriorated significantly in the second half of the month. The major military crackdown on the militant Buddhists, however necessary in the circumstances, temporarily diverted efforts away from fighting the main enemy, and the Communists were able to seize the initiative. As a JOC report frankly put it:

> On 21 August 63, the President of the Republic of Vietnam invoked a state of military siege that encompassed the whole country. . . . This week RVNAF [Republic of Vietnam Armed Forces] . . . activity against the VC was overshadowed by the armed forces' assigned objectives in carrying out the President's proclamation. RVNAF offensive operations declined . . . VC initiated activity of all types increased . . . and continued on the ascendency for the second straight week.[74]

After something of a pause in the Communist offensive during the first week of September, that month was even worse for the government side. The JOC report for 6–13 September stated frankly: "Audacious acts of Viet Cong aggression early in the week controlled the pulse and force of ground activity for the rest of the period."[75]

As had been the case virtually all year, the greatest concentration of fighting was in the Mekong Delta, where the Communists launched twenty-eight of their forty-two attacks. But they were also active throughout I Corps' and II Corps' areas, with a particular concentration of "attacks and harassments in Pleiku province," about which, unfortunately, no details were recorded.

The war in the Highlands was not one-sided, however, and the ARVN won a small victory in Kontum. At 1530 on 10 September, during a search and clear operation, a platoon of the 42d Reconnaissance Company of the 42d

Regiment (22d Division) ambushed about a hundred men from the Communist A-20 Company, killing twenty-eight and capturing a considerable number of weapons without loss to its own personnel.[76] Toward the end of the month Communist forces tried to seize the initiative in Kontum by attacking the strategic hamlet system, with simultaneous assaults on three hamlets in the early hours of 24 September and on two more between 0300 and 0330 on 26 September. It is not clear whether any of these hamlets was overrun.[77]

The intensity of the fighting across South Vietnam dropped markedly in October, possibly because Communist forces had temporarily exhausted themselves or were getting low on ammunition. By the middle of the month, casualties on the two sides were evening out.[78] There were even some signs that government forces were beginning to recover their equilibrium, although in general they seemed too dazed by the violence of the Communist offensive of July–September (and perhaps, in the case of some senior officers, too preoccupied with plans for the upcoming coup) to regain the initiative fully.

It illustrates the danger of excessive generalization, however, that ARVN reaction to the loss of two strategic hamlets in Pleiku was vigorous and effective. At 0245 on 30 September Communist forces in Pleiku attacked and overran the strategic hamlets of De Groi and De Haroh (not far from the intersection of Pleiku's border with Binh Dinh and Phu Bon), killing three Civil Guards and two members of the Self-Defense Corps, capturing seventy-seven individual weapons, and removing 2,468 of the 2,482 inhabitants. Within hours of the attack, the 40th Regiment had mounted an operation to find and destroy the Communist force that had conducted it. The 22d Division soon took over the operation and expanded it, bringing in more troops and establishing a cordon, approximately 20 km in radius, around the two hamlets, with many of the forces moved into place by helicopter. The South Vietnamese air force then dropped leaflets and used airborne loudspeakers with "taped aerial broadcasts which contained appeals to the former hamlet occupants, recorded by their respective hamlet chiefs," to return to their villages under ARVN protection. By 21 October, government forces claimed they had killed twenty-five Communist troops, taken two prisoners, and captured some weapons, at a cost of just sixteen men wounded, mostly by booby traps. More significantly, 2,023 of the 2,468 villagers that the Communists had herded away had returned to their hamlets and to government control. In this instance, it seems that the Highlanders, probably acting on instincts of self-preservation, responded rather passively, acceding to the wishes of whichever side demonstrated the greater military power in their immediate vicinity at a particular moment.[79]

The most dramatic weakening of the government position in the Central Highlands, as in the rest of the country, occurred in the last two months of the year, following the military coup of 1–2 November that killed Diem.

Communist forces renewed their offensive across the country within days of the coup. The government's weekly losses reached unprecedented levels, greatly exceeding those of their opponents. For the new military regime, the most worrying aspect of the casualty figures was the very large number of "missing." Clearly, many in this category had simply deserted, perhaps in the belief that all authority on the anti-Communist side was in a state of collapse.[80] There was undoubtedly massive disruption to chains of command, with sweeping changes in leadership at the corps and division levels and in the offices of provincial and district chiefs.[81]

Information on military events in the Central Highland in November and December 1963 is sparse. There is little in the JOC reports.[82] One Communist account, however, refers to troops from two elite Communist main force units infiltrating and disrupting strategic hamlets "along Route 14" and on "the outskirts of Kontum city." The overall strategic situation now favored the Communists, and they evidently tried hard to capitalize on it in Kontum and other Highland provinces:

> Exploiting the tide of major victories won by our forces and the November 1963 coup against Ngo Dinh Diem, both of which spread fear and confusion among enemy civil guard, militia and police personnel at the local level, local party chapters in the Central Highlands incited the masses to rise up, to kill enemy thugs, destroy the enemy's apparatus of oppression and return to their home villages. . . . The entire northern portion of Kontum province was liberated.[83]

In reality, the anti-Communist side continued to hold some posts in the northern half of Kontum in December 1963, although it seems likely that most of that area was under Communist control. While JOC weekly reports provide very little narrative or analysis of events in the Central Highlands during November and December, the maps they contain indicate that Kontum, Pleiku, and Darlac were considered the least secure, most Communist-infested provinces in the entire country by the end of the year. The official history of Communist forces in the Central Highlands indicates that they were able to expand and consolidate "liberated areas" in northern Kontum, western Gia Lai (Pleiku), and southern Darlac.[84]

It took Diem's fall, probably accompanied by accelerating infiltration from the North, to bring things to such a pass.[85] But there had been something of a Communist resurgence on the high plateau in the second half of the year, especially in Darlac, even before the coup. Decisions by the Diem government and its American backers during Operation Switchback had alienated Highlanders there, causing some to have apocalyptic fears for the future. Educated

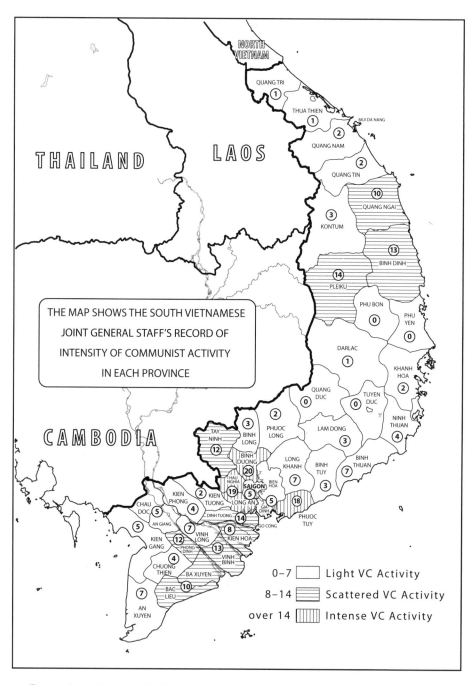

THE MAP SHOWS THE SOUTH VIETNAMESE JOINT GENERAL STAFF'S RECORD OF INTENSITY OF COMMUNIST ACTIVITY IN EACH PROVINCE

0–7 ☐ Light VC Activity
8–14 ☰ Scattered VC Activity
over 14 ⫼ Intense VC Activity

Communist activity across South Vietnam, June 1963

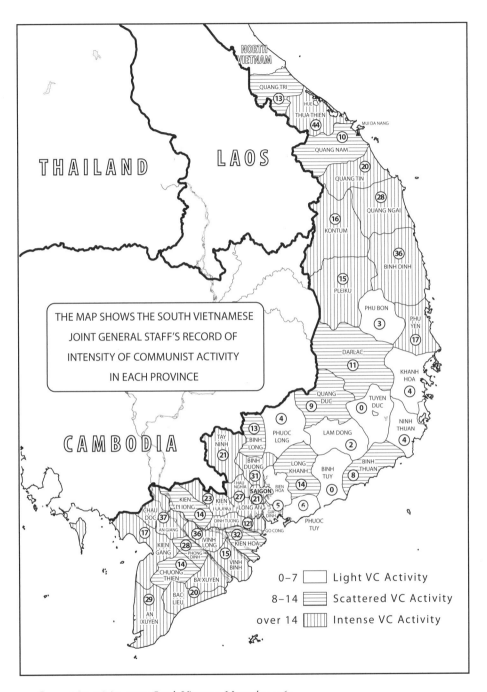

THE MAP SHOWS THE SOUTH VIETNAMESE
JOINT GENERAL STAFF'S RECORD OF
INTENSITY OF COMMUNIST ACTIVITY
IN EACH PROVINCE

THAILAND

LAOS

CAMBODIA

NORTH VIETNAM

QUANG TRI — 13
HUE
THUA THIEN — 44
MUI DA NANG
10
QUANG NAM
20
QUANG TIN
28
QUANG NGAI
16
KONTUM
36
BINH DINH
15
PLEIKU
PHU BON
3
PHU YEN — 17
DARLAC
11
KHANH HOA — 4
QUANG DUC — 9
TUYEN DUC — 0
NINH THUAN — 4
4
PHUOC LONG
13
TAY NINH — 21
BINH LONG
LAM DONG — 2
BINH DUONG — 31
LONG KHANH — 14
BINH TUY — 8
BINH THUAN
HAU NGHIA
SAIGON
BIEN HOA
27
21
KIEN TUONG — 23
KIEN PHONG
CHAU DOC — 37
AN GIANG — 17
14
DINH TUONG
LONG AN — 5
GIA DINH
6
PHUOC TUY
12
GO CONG
KIEN GIANG — 28
VINH LONG — 36
KIEN HOA — 32
PHONG DINH
15
VINH BINH
14
CHUONG THIEN
BA XUYEN — 20
BAC LIEU
29
AN XUYEN

0–7 Light VC Activity
8–14 Scattered VC Activity
over 14 Intense VC Activity

Communist activity across South Vietnam, November 1963

Highlanders communicated across tribal and provincial boundaries. Rhade dismay over the closure of Buon Enao was linked with other issues, such as the security of land tenure and the impact of institutional racism within the Diem government, that were deeply felt across the Highlands.

In 1963 the South Vietnamese government turned its back on the possibility of negotiating a general settlement of Highlanders' grievances and thereby enlisting Highland peoples as willing partners in the war against the Communists. In such circumstances, Highlanders could hardly be blamed for lacking the will to risk their lives for the government cause and merely complying with the demands of whichever side applied the greater pressure at a particular place and time.

7

The Central Highlands,
January–June 1964

Communist Strategy and Command Arrangements

The coup of 1–2 November 1963 plunged South Vietnam into a protracted period of internal political disorder that lasted throughout 1964 and for the first half of 1965.[1] In the Central Highlands, as in the rest of the country, the Communists exploited the situation as best they could. Although they continued to experience particular difficulties and frustrations in the region, the Central Highlands had special importance in their strategy as it developed at this period.

With the fall of Diem, the key figures in the Communist leadership in Hanoi believed the war had entered a new phase. The confusion and partial paralysis in the enemy camp following the coup presented a great opportunity. Certainly there was a risk of increased American involvement, and it was important to be psychologically prepared for protracted war. But there was also real hope that such drawn-out agony could be avoided. By making strenuous efforts in the immediate future, the Party and its armed forces might bring the southern state to the point of collapse before the Americans were ready to intervene on a large scale.[2]

A Communist official history of the war summarizes the main decision of the Ninth Plenum of the Party Central Committee (elected by the Third Party Congress) in December 1963 as being to "step up infiltration and seek a quick victory." As the Ninth Plenum itself expressed it: "The key issue at present is for the entire Party and the entire population to make a maximum effort to rapidly strengthen our armed forces in order to achieve a basic shift in the balance of forces between ourselves and the enemy in South Vietnam." While recognizing that guerrilla and local force troops would continue to be important, the Party leadership now emphasized "expanding our main force troops." Over the next year, there would be a shift to "mobile attacks" (more or less

conventional operations) in which "puppet regulars" were annihilated in "decisive . . . massed combat operations."[3]

The strategy adopted was one of "general offensive and general uprising"—
abbreviated as GO-GU. The Central Office for South Vietnam (COSVN),
the Communist headquarters for the southern part of South Vietnam, was intended to "incite a mass movement that will co-operate with [Communist]
armed forces to conduct insurrections." In this scheme of things, a series of
dramatic victories in fairly major battles would "spark a mass political uprising,
combining the force of the troops with the power of the people to topple the
already fragile Saigon regime." The GO-GU strategy de-emphasized the Mekong Delta, where Communist guerrilla operations had been most frequent
and successful. Instead, it involved "a major build up of conventional military
force in the Central Highlands and the area northwest of Saigon" and the employment of those forces in major battles to bring about the collapse of the
southern republic before the Americans could intervene on a large scale. The
Party leadership replaced a strategy of protracted war with a strategy of "going
for broke" in 1964.[4]

The GO-GU strategy was not endorsed by all senior Party members. It
represented an agenda pushed by Le Duan, acting first secretary of the Party
since 1959, who had emerged, over the last few years, as the dominant man
in Hanoi, and by his close associate and second in command Le Duc Tho.
Born in Quang Tri Province (in central Vietnam, immediately below the seventeenth parallel) in 1907, Le Duan had been a key figure in organizing the
southernmost part of the country during the war against the French. Le Duc
Tho, born in Ha Nam Province in 1911, had also served in the South during
the First Indochina War. He became the Party's organizational chief in 1956.

By 1963, the "Comrades Le" had managed to greatly reduce the practical
influence of some famous Party figures, including Ho Chi Minh (now an old
man and in poor health), Vo Nguyen Giap, and Pham Van Dong, all of whom
appear to have favored a more cautious, long-term approach to the struggle in
the South. Partly through the establishment of a powerful police state under
bosses who were personally loyal to them, they were also able to intimidate,
marginalize, and demote a large number of less famous Party members who
wanted to give priority to developing a successful, prosperous socialist state in
the North rather than fighting a war in the South.[5]

The war did indeed intensify in 1964, though, particularly in the first half of
the year, not anything like as much as the Hanoi leadership wanted. In addition
to incidents of assassination, sniping, sabotage, and mortar and grenade attacks,
fierce little battles (company- and occasionally battalion-sized actions) raged
somewhere in the country most weeks. During the first six months of 1964
the war seemed to be killing a couple of hundred people a week on average.

Then in July, on the instructions of the Hanoi leadership, there was a further dramatic escalation. Yet relatively little of this fighting happened in the Central Highlands. In terms of major armed clashes, the region remained, with only occasional exceptions, a relative backwater in the war for most of 1964, as it had been during the big Communist offensive of July–October 1963. The rarity of major military actions in the Central Highlands, however, was not a function of Communist strategic priorities. Indeed, in the Ninth Plenum's strategy of decisive "massed combat actions" outlined in December 1963, the Central Highlands was considered crucial, and it was to this region that Hanoi directed the large PAVN units it began to send south in late 1964.[6]

The memoirs of Colonel General Dang Vu Hiep, who served in the PAVN in the Highlands for much of the war, help explain Hanoi's perception of the importance of the region. Hiep indicates that "in the new strategic situation" of early 1964, in which the "American 'special war' strategy" was "failing and . . . faced with total collapse," Communist forces were "confronted with a new situation: Revolutionary warfare's law of armed struggle is that [it] begins with guerrilla warfare and then advances to conduct conventional warfare while closely combining and coordinating the guerrilla war with conventional war. Beginning from a foundation of guerrilla war that gradually expands step-by-step, the struggle must develop into conventional warfare in order to maintain the offensive initiative, annihilate large numbers of enemy forces and liberate territory." From an early stage in the war, the Communist leadership had selected "the mountain jungles as the battlefield in which we could conduct conventional warfare, as the place where our main force units could fight."[7]

Up to 1964, however, the number of Communist victories in major actions (involving whole battalions or more) in the Central Highlands had been modest. Reading between the lines of Communist histories, this theater of operations, for which it had such high hopes, had so far been a source of frustration for the high command in Hanoi. To appreciate this, it seems appropriate to review developments over the previous three years from a Communist strategic standpoint.

As noted earlier, the Communist command had mounted its first major Highland offensive in northern Kontum in October 1960—the intention apparently being to create a substantial "liberated zone" where large units could be based. This offensive gained initial successes but was ultimately defeated, with serious losses. Most of the troops used in this first offensive were Highlanders. In subsequent offensives, however, the Communists placed less reliance on Highland units, particularly for major assaults. Instead, they employed ethnic Vietnamese troops brought to the Highlands specifically for such tasks, as in the much more successful Dak Ha offensive of September 1961. This may have been because they considered ethnic Vietnamese forces intrinsically superior. Or it may have been that, after October 1960, Highlanders recruited into their armed forces demonstrated obvious reluctance to be employed as shock troops in what was, after all, essentially a Vietnamese civil war.

With the Dak Ha offensive of September 1961, Communist forces had again seized the initiative and had seemed likely to take control of much of the northern half of the Central Highlands in the immediate future. In 1962, however, they had suffered a food supply crisis. Many Highlanders, finding Communist demands on them for food, labor, and military service exorbitant, had migrated from Communist-controlled to government-controlled areas. As a result, the Communist troops suffered widespread malnutrition, even starvation. The same year the Communists encountered a reinvigorated, American-aided counterinsurgency effort. Their war effort in the region stalled and in some places was rolled back.

There was a significant, if slow, Communist recovery in 1963, helped by a good harvest in 1962, by the dissolution of the Buon Enao program in Darlac, and, most significantly, by the near paralysis of the anti-Communist side that accompanied the plotting against Diem and intensified with his fall. By the end of 1963, Communist forces could regard substantial parts of northern Kontum, western Pleiku, and southern Darlac as relatively safe base areas.[8] Nevertheless, the total number of full-time Communist troops in the Central Highlands in 1964 remained modest.[9] Although these forces were active enough to make much of Kontum, Pleiku, and Darlac Provinces seem extremely insecure from a South Vietnamese government perspective, the Communist high command judged the real striking power of most of them to be very limited.

The only units the Communist leadership considered main force were the 200th Artillery Battalion, 407th Sapper Battalion, and 303d Antiaircraft Machine Gun Battalion. The 200th Artillery Battalion, the first main force unit in the Central Highlands, had arrived in early 1961, but after the Dak Ha offensive, it had been dispersed for more than a year, reforming only in late 1962. The 407th Sapper Battalion, which, together with the 200th Artillery Battalion, reportedly attacked the Special Forces–CIDG base at Plei Mrong in early January 1963, probably arrived sometime in late 1962. The 303d Antiaircraft Machine Gun Battalion, the last of these units to reach the region, apparently did so sometime during the first half of 1964.[10] Although the 200th Artillery Battalion originally contained a number of Highlanders who had gone to the North in 1954, all these main force units were organized and trained in North Vietnam. All consisted predominantly or entirely of ethnic Vietnamese. According to Colonel General Dang Vu Hiep:

> Although they were not recruited and trained locally, our main force troops
> utilized the revolutionary character of the Heroic People's Army of Vietnam.

Loved, supported and protected by the people, our Central Highlands main force troops truly became the sons and brothers of the ethnic minority peoples of the Central Highlands, sharing their pains and pleasures, their hardships and their joys.[11]

To what extent the "ethnic minority peoples" shared this PAVN perception remains open to question, little direct testimony being available. Attitudes surely varied. But the 1962 mass migration of Highlanders from Communist-controlled areas to areas controlled by the Diem government (a government the Highlanders had little reason to love) suggests that their relations with Communist forces were, to put it mildly, not always characterized by sweetness and light.

Despite the relative weakness of its military forces in the Central Highlands in the first half of 1964, the Hanoi leadership clearly regarded the region as vital to its strategy as the war moved toward a climax. On 1 May 1964 the Politburo formally established a special command organization for the region: the Central Highlands Front (CHF), also known as the B3 Front or B3 Battlefield.[12] For many purposes, the CHF worked under the close supervision of Military Region (MR) 5, and the Front's first commander, Ha Vi Tung, and its senior political officer, Duong Lien, were apparently appointed by General Nguyen Don, who commanded MR 5 up to mid-1964. Shortly thereafter, however, Nguyen Don was relieved at MR 5 (ostensibly due to ill health) by General Chu Huy Man—a rising star in the PAVN who would play a crucial role in the Highlands in 1965. Chu Huy Man began to move his own people into key positions, and Nguyen Chanh soon succeeded Ha Vi Tung as CHF commander, and Doan Khue replaced Duong Lien as the senior political officer.[13]

Chanh and Khue were a formidable pair. Chanh was born in Binh Dinh Province in 1917 and had been a Party member since 1946. He had a distinguished military record in the First Indochina War, during which he held commands in both Laos and Cochin China. Earlier in 1964 he had been deputy director of the Combat Operations Department of the General Staff in North Vietnam. He would survive the Second Indochina War, rise to be director of the General Department of Rear Services in 1985, and was living in retirement in 1996. Doan Khue was born in Quang Tri in 1923 and had been a Party member since 1945, serving as a political officer in the Party's military forces in the First Indochina War and subsequently. At one point in the 1980s he would command the Vietnamese army in Cambodia and would later serve on the Party's Central Committee and Politburo. Khue was Deputy Minister of Defense from 1987 to 1991 and finished his career as a four-star general; he was apparently still alive in the mid-1990s.[14]

The CHF was responsible for Kontum, the area the Communists called Gia Lai (essentially Pleiku and some adjacent areas of Binh Dinh and Phu Bon), and Darlac, but not for Quang Duc, Tuyen Duc, or Lam Dong. The Military Mission of the Communist Party's Central Committee and the military high command in Hanoi defined the task of the new Front as follows:

> [To] build the Highlands into a theater ready for large-scale . . . combat, equipped with a strong main force army . . . annihilate and wear down enemy strength and war means . . . draw in and pin down the U.S.-puppet mobile main forces . . . develop the theater's direct rear into a steady base of the southern and Indochinese revolutions . . . build and protect the strategic corridor linking the great rear with the great front . . . upset the enemy's plan to split up our forces, and . . . advance to split up the enemy's forces.[15]

Some of this seems strangely expressed and in need of interpretation, but it is clear that the intention was to develop the Central Highlands into a theater of war where powerful main force units (probably including entire PAVN regiments) could be sustained. These units would engage in major offensive operations to destroy substantial parts of the ARVN and draw in and pin down others (including some of the most mobile and effective), thus helping other Communist forces achieve final victory in the lowlands. The Party leadership and the military high command appreciated, however, that sustaining large main force units in the Central Highlands would require a great deal of attention to problems of logistics and supply. (As already noted, supply problems had frustrated its ambitions in this region in the recent past.) This meant attention to the theater's "direct rear"—adjacent areas of Laos and Cambodia. Thus, the "southern revolution" (the war in South Vietnam) had to be considered in relation to developments in other parts of Indochina.[16] Just as Laos and Cambodia were crucial rear areas for the Communist effort in the Central Highlands, the Ho Chi Minh Trail ("the strategic corridor linking the great rear [North Vietnam] with the great front [South Vietnam]") was crucial to the overall progress of the war. Sections of the Trail running through the Central Highlands needed to be maintained and protected.

The CHF's place in the Communist chain of command was complex and somewhat confused. In some respects and for some purposes, it was considered subordinate to MR 5, but in other situations it was directly subordinate to the military high command in Hanoi. As General Hiep seemed to realize, his attempt to explain the system in his military memoirs likely only added to readers' confusion:

> In the political arena . . . the Front received political and Party guidance from both the Region 5 Party Committee and from the Central Party Committee. However the High Command exercised direct command over and provided

direct support to the Front in the military and logistics areas. Military Region 5 assisted in these areas by producing recommendations and suggestions. As for the three provincial military Party Committees for the three provinces of Kontum, Gia Lai and Darlac, the Central Highlands Front Party Committee worked closely with them. . . . Military Region 5 [sometimes] turned direct command over the province military units to the Front, while sometimes [the] Military Region exerted direct command over [them] with the Front simply providing combat co-ordination arrangements. Although there were some aspects of the organizational arrangements that did not make much sense [a refreshing admission!], the relationships between the Front and the three provincial military units were always extremely close [and they helped one another in the achievement of their respective missions].[17]

Perhaps the CHF's most critical problem, together with the PAVN's logisticians, was to find the means to feed the entire North Vietnamese regiments Hanoi intended to send to the region. But given that such units did not start to arrive until very late 1964 at the earliest, and possibly not until early 1965, a discussion of the arrangements for their sustenance is deferred to a later chapter.

South Vietnamese and US Command Arrangements

On 30 January 1964 General Nguyen Khanh, who had supported the overthrow of Diem, mounted a largely bloodless coup against the group of officers who had run the country since then. It was the substitution of one military regime for another. Khanh remained a central figure in the South Vietnamese government throughout 1964 but never established anything close to the degree of control Diem had once exerted. Throughout 1964 there was continuous infighting and incessant reshuffling of posts both in the armed forces and in the general administration. There was no consistency of policy at the top and considerable confusion at lower levels of the armed forces and in the provincial administration.[18]

By the beginning of 1964, almost the entire Central Highlands, which had been divided between the ARVN's II Corps and III Corps tactical zones for much of 1963, was back within II Corps' area of responsibility. The only exception was the southernmost province of the region, Lam Dong, which was assigned to the Binh Lam Special Zone in III Corps.[19] The most important personnel change in the II Corps area after the coup against Diem was the replacement of Lieutenant General Nguyen Khanh by Lieutenant General Do Cao Tri as the commander of II Corps. Tri, born in 1929, came from a wealthy landowning family and had served in the French army before transferring to the Vietnamese National Army upon its establishment in 1947. He had risen rapidly under the Diem regime. From August to December 1963 he commanded I Corps. During this period he clamped down on the Buddhist militants in Hue with a degree of severity that even some Diem supporters regarded as excessive. Yet Tri evidently had an eye for the main chance. While continuing to hammer Diem's Buddhist opponents, by October 1963 he had joined the plot against the president. Probably as a result of this timely change of allegiance, and despite his unpopularity with many of Diem's opponents, Tri was not dismissed or demoted after the coup but was given a lateral transfer to II Corps, of which he assumed command on 12 December 1963.

Meanwhile, within days of the coup against Diem, Colonel Nguyen Thanh Sang (a thirty-seven-year-old infantry officer from central Vietnam who had attended the American Command and General Staff College at Leavenworth) had replaced Lieutenant Colonel Nguyen Bao Tri as commander of the 22d Division, still based at Kontum and still responsible for the northern half of the Central Highlands. In December 1963 Brigadier General Hoan Xuan Lam, a thirty-five-year-old specialist in armored cavalry from Quang Tri Province, replaced Colonel Le Quang Trong at the 23d Division, still based at Ban Me Thuot and charged with holding the southern half of the region. The other division in II Corps for most of 1964 was Colonel Nguyen Viet Dam's 25th Division, which operated mainly on the coastal plain, especially in Binh Dinh Province.[20]

Do Cao Tri, II Corps' commander for most of 1964, later gained a reputation for questionable business dealings, and some people found his flamboyance and his rather princely lifestyle irritating. Yet he was also widely seen as a fighting general with leadership qualities and a fair degree of military competence. In relation to the rights of the Highland tribes and their treatment by the Vietnamese, moreover, his attitudes appear to have been remarkably humanitarian and liberal. The two division commanders who served under Tri in the Highlands in early 1964 were a rather undistinguished pair, and the continuing political instability meant that they would soon be replaced. Sang lasted only three months as commander of 22d Division, that division having a total of four commanders during 1964. The 23d Division had only two; Lam was replaced by Brigadier General Lu Lan on 14 October.[21]

These ARVN divisions were not, of course, the only South Vietnamese government forces in the Highlands. During 1964 there was a reorganization of local forces. Regional Forces gradually replaced the earlier Civil Guard, although these paid, full-time, province-based troops continued to perform similar functions. Likewise, Popular Forces gradually replaced the Self-Defense Corps and were increasingly regularized, becoming paid, full-time forces with the task of defending particular districts. At the same time, the term "Combat Youth" was increasingly used to refer to various groups of unpaid village and hamlet defenders.[22]

The American military apparatus in Vietnam also underwent considerable changes in 1964. Colonel Charles E. Balthis Jr., who had replaced Colonel McCown as senior adviser to II Corps on 30 October 1963, was replaced by Colonel Theodore C. Mataxis on 7 October 1964. Balthis had graduated from West Point in 1940 and had been on the staff of the 102d Division during the fighting in Germany in the closing months of the Second World War. Having served with MAAG in the early 1950s during the First Indochina War, he was not unfamiliar with Vietnam, and this should have been an advantage at II Corps. We know practically nothing about his relationship with corps commander Do Cao Tri, however, and it is very difficult to gauge his impact on operations. Perhaps because he already had his bags packed by the time it erupted, he seems to have played no part in responding to the CIDG uprising that commenced on the night of 19 September, perhaps the most dramatic crisis in the Highlands in 1964.[23] Balthis's successor, Mataxis, would leave a more distinct imprint, but his influence would be felt mainly in 1965.

Since February 1962, there had been two major American military headquarters in Saigon: MAAG's and MACV's. Although they were initially supposed to have somewhat different areas of responsibility, their coexistence was always an awkward arrangement. MACV gradually superseded MAAG, and MAAG's last chief, Major General Charles J. Timmes (July 1962–May 1964), found himself progressively marginalized by General Paul Harkins, commanding MACV. After Timmes left Vietnam, MACV absorbed MAAG. When Harkins left the following month, Lieutenant General William C. Westmoreland succeeded him, initially as acting commander of MACV before formally becoming commander on 1 August 1964 when he was promoted to four-star general.[24]

A South Carolinian, Westmoreland was born in 1914, educated at the Citadel and West Point, and commissioned into the artillery, and he had a good combat record in the European theater in the Second World War. Today he is sometimes criticized for having limited intellect and various character defects. But that is with the benefit of hindsight. Though not generally regarded as an academically oriented officer, he was responsible for introducing counterinsurgency to the West Point curriculum. When he took over MACV, however, the Vietnamese Communists were, in an effort to complete the destruction of the South Vietnamese quickly, consciously moving toward conventional warfare. When, in 1965, large American ground forces arrived in Vietnam, Westmoreland therefore wanted them to focus on fighting the big-unit war. Westmoreland gave an impression of determination, confidence, and physical and psychological robustness that was not, for the most part, misleading. It was by no means obvious, up to the end of 1965, that he was the wrong man for the job.[25]

Westmoreland worked closely with Maxwell Taylor, who succeeded Henry Cabot Lodge as US ambassador in Vietnam in July. Taylor, who had commanded the celebrated 101st Airborne Division in the Second World War, had just stepped down as chairman of the Joint Chiefs of Staff. At least to begin with, Taylor seems to have treated Westmoreland as a military subordinate, a relationship that Westmoreland initially (but only initially) accepted. Taken together, Taylor and Westmoreland may be regarded as the key Vietnam appointments of President Lyndon B. Johnson's administration.

Johnson, who had succeeded to the presidency after Kennedy's assassination on 22 November 1963, was primarily interested in domestic rather than foreign policy. Johnson seems to have feared that a Communist takeover of South Vietnam early in his administration would brand him as weak and ineffective in the eyes of the American political establishment and the public, thus crippling his presidency. Arguably it was this fear more than any positive enthusiasm for involvement that drove his policy on Vietnam.[26]

Post-Diem Political Instability

In 1964 the South Vietnamese state continued to maintain substantial numbers of troops in the Central Highlands. Certainly into the middle of the year, the balance of forces there continued to be heavily weighted against the Communists. Yet, at least in the provinces of Kontum, Pleiku, and Darlac, the degree of government control outside the towns was in sharp decline as early as January, continuing a trend that had started with the November 1963 coup. The coup resulted in sweeping changes in South Vietnam's administrative personnel. With ongoing political instability in Saigon, such changes were not a one-off event but occurred with remarkable frequency. As Hanoi's history of its armed forces in the Central Highlands puts it:

> After Ngo Dinh Diem was killed, the lackeys in the South repeatedly staged military coups, engaged in power struggles and purged one another, causing deep rifts and serious disarray in their administrative and military apparatus from the central to the local level.[27]

In May 1964, in Binh Dinh Province on the eastern edge of the Central Highlands, Colonel Xuan became the fourth province chief since the November 1963 coup, as was Major Ba in Pleiku. Major Be was the fifth province chief in Kontum since Diem's overthrow, while Lieutenant Colonel De in Tuyen Duc Province was its third. This extreme turbulence in key appointments inevitably caused a massive dislocation of the process of government.[28]

Even more than the Vietnamese, Highlanders saw government in personal terms. Relationships established by particular province and district officials were not easily transferred to their successors. In the Central Highlands, therefore, patron-client relationships collapsed, and intelligence networks were degraded perhaps even more rapidly than in other parts of the country.[29] Naturally, the Communists took advantage.

Military Operations, January–April 1964

Even though incidents were generally scattered and small scale, and few details were given, the South Vietnamese Joint Operations Center reported in January 1964 that "overall VC activity substantially increased in the highlands . . . over the previous month."[30] A series of incidents in Pleiku Province between 18 and 20 January is indicative of the strength of the Communist resurgence in the northern part of the Central Highlands and the fragility of government control: The Communists placed "effective pressure" on a group of ten "Montagnard communities astride the main highway some 35 miles south" of the town of Pleiku. Five of these were "new rural life hamlets," the new name for strategic hamlets. Communist troops moved into these settlements at night and "stripped them of 1611 civilian inhabitants, including two village chiefs, plus 21 Combat Youth and 43 weapons." Most worrying from the government's point of view was the lack of resistance on the part of the inhabitants. No casualties were reported on either side. Though government forces mounted some sort of operation "to pursue the VC in mountains to the east of the highway," they apparently achieved no useful results. It was, perhaps, a little more encouraging that some of the Highlanders involved did not want to remain under Communist control and "in several cases reportedly returned to their former homes."[31]

By mid-March, a pattern was emerging of Communist "harassment" of ostensibly government-controlled hamlets across a great swath of territory from the foothills north and west of the provincial capital of Quang Ngai (in I Corps) in the north to Darlac in the south:

> In many of these harassments against hamlets, there appeared to be no effective defense against the VC. At one hamlet, the VC entered and forced the inhabitants to destroy the security fences. In other incidents the VC entered and destroyed fences. In yet others they entered, destroyed fences and kidnapped the hamlet chief. At several locations they gave propaganda lectures, seized weapons, kidnapped officials and civilians, seized rice supplies and destroyed hamlet offices, houses and watchtowers. Perhaps the best example occurred in Darlac Province where a VC platoon entered [an] NRL [new rural life]

hamlet defended by Combat Youth, killed a hamlet official, seized weapons and a radio, kidnapped Combat Youth and [other] hamlet officials and dispersed the other inhabitants, all without any apparent resistance.[32]

A series of Communist incursions into hamlets in Phu Bon Province during the week of 15–21 March was not sustained and was apparently regarded as aberrant. In Kontum, Pleiku, and Darlac, however, comparable incidents were viewed as almost commonplace.

Since the end of the Buon Enao project, the emphasis of the CIDG program had shifted away from the defense of Highland communities and toward aggressive action and long-range patrols in an effort to control infiltration across South Vietnam's borders. Highland villagers were commonly left with relatively few weapons, and given their difficult relations with the Vietnamese provincial authorities, they were not inclined to risk their lives by using those weapons against the Communists. Meanwhile, the MACV border-control mission was proving largely unsuccessful. There was just too much border, and Communist infiltrators generally found it fairly easy to evade CIDG camps and the patrols sent out from them. The MACV report for the week of 22–28 March did, however, record a relatively rare success. An operation mounted jointly from two (unspecified) CIDG camps in II Corps "resulted in 3 VC killed, 5 wounded and 13 captured." The infiltrating force, estimated at twenty-nine personnel, had evidently passed through Laos, as "the equipment captured contained Laotian currency and other items of Laotian origin."

Such minor successes reinforced MACV's emphasis on CIDG Strike Forces mounting long-range, long-duration patrols. MACV wanted "a more aggressive guerrilla type role for US/VN Special Forces." Preparations "to transfer responsibility for two area development sites [previously under CIDG control] to province officials in Darlac province" were nearing completion.[33] The problem of poor security in Darlac villages that were supposedly under the control of provincial authorities was, however, underlined in mid-April, when "in an action reminiscent of the VC 'weapons supply' raids of last winter, a VC platoon aided by three traitors from among the Combat Youth entered two NRL [new rural life] hamlets and seized 41 weapons and a radio set. Apparently no resistance to the VC action was offered by hamlet defenders."[34]

Much of the news from the Central Highlands in the early months of 1964 was thus very depressing for the anti-Communist side. But government forces were making some efforts to regain the initiative. On 15 March the 22d Division mounted "an extensive clear and hold operation" called Campaign Binh Tri in an area straddling the Kontum-Pleiku provincial boundary. The operation involved two of 22d Division's infantry battalions and two Civil Guard battalions, supported by a platoon of 105mm howitzers. It targeted two "VC

Main Force companies" believed to be operating in this zone. After negligible contact with Communist forces in the southern part of this area, 22d Division decided to concentrate efforts "in Kontum Province to the east of the village of Daksut, just to the south of the VC Secret Area of Bong Hong." There, from 5 to 7 April, the forces under 22d Division's command attempted to envelop and destroy a Communist force of perhaps company strength, using air mobility, weight of numbers, and the superior firepower provided, in part, by four T-28 combat aircraft of the VNAF. The fighting, which became hand-to-hand at times, reportedly caused more than seventy fatalities on the Communist side, but only one killed and twenty-six wounded among the government forces; the latter also captured a radio, forty rounds of mortar ammunition, and forty grenades. Officers and men of the 1st Battalion, 42d Regiment (transported by helicopters from the US Army's 52d Aviation Battalion), gained particular praise from II Corps commander General Tri for their aggressive conduct on the battlefield.[35]

Since 1962, the increasing use of helicopters by the anti-Communist side had become a major feature of this war. On occasion, the ARVN consciously aimed at the vertical envelopment of Communist troops. By mid-1964, Communist forces had given considerable thought to countering the heliborne threat and in some instances, such as at Ap Bac in January 1963, had already done so very effectively. This is a point worth remembering when considering operations of the US 1st Cavalry Division in Pleiku Province in late 1965, operations that have somewhat misleadingly been described as the "dawn of helicopter warfare in Vietnam."[36]

Also in early April, in the course of the Binh Tri operation, a Communist force estimated at battalion strength mounted a determined attack on an unspecified ARVN battalion in western Kontum Province. Though details are lacking, the ARVN battalion reportedly resisted effectively and inflicted serious losses on its attackers.[37]

Balance of Forces, May 1964

In May MACV produced a series of "fact sheets" on each of the provinces of South Vietnam, apparently in an effort to get a better picture of the war as a whole. Each sheet gave basic information about the province concerned, including its physical size and population, an analysis of the balance of military forces between the government and the Communists, and a few paragraphs on what the government was supposed to be doing to win the war there. The fact sheets on the provinces of the Central Highlands are obviously worth reviewing here.

Kontum, the northernmost of the Central Highlands provinces, was the third largest in the country, but with only 102,616 people, according to government records, it was one of the least populous. MACV at this stage judged it to have just one weak main force Communist battalion with only 100 soldiers, plus three separate local force companies with 240 personnel among them and 770 part-time guerrillas, for a total of 1,110 Communist troops in the province. These were very heavily outnumbered by 6,217 ARVN troops (in six battalions and seven separate companies), 1,166 Civil Guard troops in eleven companies, 2,077 Self-Defense Corps troops in thirty platoons, 1,364 CIDG troops in ten companies, and 2,899 armed Combat Youth. Even when the CIDG and Combat Youth personnel were left out of the equation, the government forces had an 8.5:1 advantage over the Communists, based on MACV's reckoning.

The government appeared to be making considerable efforts to conduct psychological operations and civic action in this province. A special psywar–civic action team had been organized. "With an emergency supply of relief items this team is dispatched to any hamlet immediately following a VC attack to treat the wounded, issue blankets, clothing and food and to encourage the people to continue to resist the VC." This team apparently had an excellent interpreter who spoke five of the local languages and dialects. The province chief, Major Be, had been in office only eight weeks, but MACV found him to be energetic and industrious. There was, however, no definite statement about the proportions of the Kontum population under the control of the government, under the control of the Communists, and still in contention between the warring sides.[38]

Also in the 22d Division's sector was Pleiku, the country's fourth biggest province in area but, with a mere 162,563 inhabitants, only twenty-ninth out of forty-two in terms of population. MACV's estimate of Communist military strength in the province seems extraordinarily low. It reckoned there were no main force units at all, one weak company of local force troops with 80 personnel, plus 500 guerrillas, for a total of 580 Communist troops in the province. Stacked against them were 6,421 ARVN troops belonging to five battalions and one independent company, 1,307 Civil Guards in eleven companies, and 1,326 Self-Defense Corps troops in thirty-two platoons. This gave the government side (by MACV's estimate) a 15.6:1 numerical advantage over the Communists, not counting the 1,951 CIDG troops in fourteen companies and the 801 armed Combat Youth. During the last two months, the government side had mounted two battalion-sized search and clear operations, as well as sixteen small-unit operations that achieved contact with Communist forces.

At this time, reports indicated that province chief Major Ba, another newcomer, was working hard and that the psyops–civic aid effort was being vigorously directed by an officer who was himself a Highlander and who, "in his many contacts with the people [had] given the Montagnard population a sense of belonging, and a feeling of having someone to help them with their problems." Even in a relatively optimistic MACV assessment, however, it was clear that much remained to be done to make this province secure for the government side.[39]

Phu Bon, the recently established province in the Cheo Reo area, was fifteenth in the country in terms of physical size but, with a mere 52,843 known inhabitants, one of the smallest in terms of population. MACV thought there were just 780 Communist troops operating in the whole province, consisting of 550 local force troops in five separate companies and 230 part-time guerrillas. These Communist forces faced an ARVN company of 124 personnel, 904 Civil Guards in seven companies, and 1,135 Self-Defense Corps troops in fifty-nine platoons. Based on MACV's calculations, the Communists were outnumbered 2.8:1, leaving 673 CIDG personnel and 444 Combat Youth personnel out of the equation. Yet MACV did not find that the war was going well for the government side in Phu Bon. Ninety-two percent of the population consisted of Highlanders, and the government's psywar and civic action program was "hampered considerably by the language barrier and the illiteracy of the Montagnard population." Despite "effective civic action performed by Engineer units, and quick reaction on the part of the Province Chief to aid needy families after extensive destruction to hamlets by fire and VC attack," MACV reported that "the Montagnard population [has shown] little desire to resist VC aggression." Because of "an extensive loss of weapons to the VC," the government was reluctant to issue additional arms to the Combat Youth units that were meant to defend the new rural life hamlets. Morale among these Highland hamlet defenders was low. Meanwhile, of the 4,000 Vietnamese people the government had encouraged to settle in nine "land development centers" in Phu Bon, 500 had apparently become fed up with life in this alien land and "returned to their homes along the coast."[40]

A little farther to the south, Darlac, in the 23d Division's sector, was the largest province in the country (10,552 square km), but with only 176,243 inhabitants, it was one of the least densely populated. There were thought to be 920 full-time Communist troops in the province, including three main force battalions and two separate main force companies, plus one local force company, as well as 500 part-time guerrillas, for a total of 1,420 Communist troops. ARVN forces were present in Darlac in exceptionally large numbers, with 6,955 in six battalions and seven independent companies. There were also 1,116 Civil Guard troops in nine companies and 1,374 Self-Defense Corps personnel in thirty-three platoons. By MACV's reckoning, these government forces outnumbered Communist forces in the province 6.6:1, leaving aside the 1,846 CIDG troops in twelve companies and the 11,140 Combat Youth also present. Yet this large mass of government forces seemed somewhat inert. In the past two months, there had been only one battalion-sized operation, and since the beginning of March, only fifteen smaller operations mounted by government troops had achieved any contact with Communist forces. MACV had been unable to carry out any meaningful evaluation of the post–November 1963 pacification effort in this province, but it was clear that race relations were a continuing problem, with "discrimination" still "evident in the treatment of Montagnards." MACV, however, expressed confidence (on what basis, it is not clear) that "this situation" was "gradually improving."[41]

In the Central Highlands south of Darlac, Communist forces appeared to be quite thin on the ground. In the relatively small, lightly populated province of Tuyen Duc, which contained the city of Dalat, where the ARVN's equivalent of West Point was located, MACV recognized the existence of only one company of Communist local forces with 80 personnel. An additional 200 part-time guerrillas were thought to be operating in the province. To deal with these modest Communist forces, the ARVN had a single company of 136 troops, 741 Civil Guard troops in eleven companies, and 870 Self-Defense Corps troops in twenty-two platoons. This total of 1,747 government troops outnumbered Communist forces by 6.2:1, according to MACV's figures, not including 636 CIDG troops and 1,198 Combat Youth in the province. Communist forces in Tuyen Duc were not particularly active at this time. However, the government was not using its hefty numerical superiority there very vigorously or effectively. No battalion-sized operation had been conducted in the last two months, and none of the smaller operations mounted had achieved any contact with Communist forces. In general, however, MACV judged the security situation in the province to be favorable, with the great majority of the population under government control.[42]

MACV reckoned that the Communists had a single local battalion of some 320 full-time soldiers in Quang Duc and about 150 part-time guerrillas. This province was the least populated in the entire country, with only 33,309 people. Government forces there, too, were sparse. The province was in the 23d Division's sector, but no ARVN combat troops were based there. Government military forces included 727 Civil Guards and 613 Self-Defense Corps troops. Leaving aside the 1,010 CIDG troops and 1,052 Combat Youth, the government's margin of numerical superiority was not exceptionally great: just 2.8:1. Having a border with Cambodia (which Tuyen Duc lacked) made this province more important to the Communists in terms of "supply routes and way stations." MACV did not consider that government forces in Quang Duc were attacking the enemy's logistical system with real energy, although small-unit operations had resulted in eleven contacts since March—eleven more than in neighboring Tuyen Duc. Like Phu Bon, Quang Duc was having difficulty retaining the ethnic Vietnamese people the government had encouraged to migrate there. About 20 percent of an estimated 7,000 people moved into the nine land development centers had "left to return to their old homes" or go to other locations.[43]

Lam Dong, the southernmost province of the Central Highlands, ranked seventeenth in physical size but, with only 61,011 known inhabitants, was one of the smallest (thirty-eighth) in terms of population. The name of the province, which means "immense jungle" in Vietnamese, suggests its lack of development at this time. Either the Highlanders in this province were exceptionally thin on the ground or many of them had managed to avoid government census takers, as they amounted to only 37 percent of the population. Lam Dong was the only province of the Central Highlands not part of II Corps' tactical zone, being assigned to the Binh Lam Special Zone in III Corps. It was one of the quietest provinces in the country, with "VC activity" being "light" and Communist military strength considered "low." MACV did not believe there were any Communist main force units present, and it was aware of only one local force company with perhaps 150 personnel, along with an estimated 75 part-time guerrillas. Against these were three battalions and an independent company of ARVN troops in Lam Dong, plus twelve companies of Civil Guard and twenty-seven Self-Defense Corps platoons. These 3,822 government troops outnumbered Communist forces 17:1, excluding the part-time Combat Youth.[44]

MACV's assessments in early May 1964 suggest that none of the provinces of the Central Highlands was likely to fall under complete Communist control in the near future. So far, the Communists held no town in the region, and MACV's fact sheets indicated that the numerical balance of military forces still markedly favored the government. But how seriously can these assessments be taken?

MACV had reasonably accurate knowledge of the numerical strength of government forces in each province. It did not, in these brief summaries, systematically evaluate the morale, motivation, or combat effectiveness of these forces, but some inferences can be drawn. On the basis of the number of large operations mounted and the number of small operations that achieved contact, the effectiveness of Republic of Vietnam troops at this period was distinctly low in many of the Highland provinces. In general, they were not very active or effective in hunting down and destroying Communist troops.

With regard to the numerical strength of Communist forces within the provinces, we must accept not only that MACV's knowledge was much less certain but also that its estimates were probably on the low side. MACV's provincial assessments put the total number of full-time Communist troops in the Central Highlands at less than 2,300, with less than 1,800 in the critical provinces of Kontum, Pleiku, Phu Bon, and Darlac. Recall that in 1963 MACV, the South Vietnamese Joint Operations Center, and the individual

ARVN corps all produced different sets of figures on Communist strength in the Central Highlands, and MACV's were consistently the lowest. They were lower than III Corps' figures for the southern half of the Central Highlands by very wide margins. Unfortunately, MACV's estimates of Communist forces in the Central Highlands are the only ones available for 1964.

In assessing the quality of Communist forces in the Highlands, however, MACV seems to have erred on the side of generosity. It counted more of them as main force (i.e., capable of fairly intense and sustained fighting) than did the Communist leadership. There can, moreover, be little doubt that the total number of armed men serving on the Saigon government's side in the Central Highlands greatly exceeded the number of those involved in the Communist-led insurgency. The fragility of government control outside the towns in the provinces of Kontum, Pleiku, and Darlac, which is apparent from MACV's weekly reports, may suggest a generally higher standard of leadership and initiative among the numerically inferior Communist forces. It also seems to suggest a lack of commitment to the government cause on the part of the majority of civilian Highlanders, although there was probably very little enthusiasm for the Communists either.

Despite their general lack of effectiveness in hunting Communist troops and securing Highlanders' villages against Communist penetration, the bulk of Saigon government forces in the Central Highlands in mid-1964 would probably not have disintegrated readily if attacked. Attacking ARVN or even Civil Guard–Regional Force troops in their own bases was probably beyond the capability of the vast majority of Communist units in this region in mid-1964. There was thus little immediate danger of the Communists seizing the towns or gaining full control of the road network. It was to break this regional stalemate that the Communist leadership in Hanoi was preparing to bring in powerful PAVN units from the North—units that would have to be largely fed, as they had been recruited, from sources outside the Highlands.

Military Operations, May–June 1964

In mid-1964 MACV was well aware that the war as a whole was not going well for the South Vietnamese state. The report for 9–16 May 1964 states frankly: "The pacification program throughout SVN [South Vietnam] continues to make little progress. The latest GVN [government of Vietnam] statistical reports indicate a deterioration of GVN control. . . . Only 55% of the total population is now reported as being in hamlets constructed or under construction under government control whereas in November 1963 the total was 85%. Further deterioration is expected." MACV argued that a large part of this apparent deterioration since the coup was attributable to more realistic reporting: the government's own estimates were now more in line with those of American advisers. But there is little doubt that the actual situation had deteriorated. To monitor developments, MACV came up with a list of "critical provinces" on which it would provide regular updates, but it is interesting that none of these was in the Central Highlands. MACV's focus was on the more densely populated provinces of the coastal plain and the Mekong Delta.[45]

The week of 9–16 May saw an upsurge in Communist activity in the II Corps area, with twice the number of attacks compared with the previous week. Most of this activity was in the coastal provinces, but small-scale Communist attacks were reported even in the normally quiet Tuyen Duc Province. In one of the Special Forces camps in Pleiku, a grenade was thrown into the mess hall (presumably by a Communist agent who had infiltrated the camp), injuring three Americans.[46]

The ARVN was not entirely passive in the face of this increased Communist military activity. Indeed, II Corps was trying to disrupt the Communist war effort by making major incursions into the most important Communist base areas it could identify. On 27 April an ambitious operation code-named Quyet Thang 202 had been mounted against the Communist Do Xa base area in the western part of Quang Ngai Province. This campaign, involving four "battle groups" consisting mainly of troops belonging to 22d Division, was designed to inflict maximum damage on the base and destroy or massively disrupt MR 5 headquarters, which was believed to lie within it. Although Quang Ngai was not regarded as a Central Highlands province, the Do Xa base was in the foothills immediately east of the Central Highlands proper, and much of the population in the vicinity consisted of Highlanders. Most significantly, MR 5 was the Communist command organization for a large part of the Central Highlands, including the provinces of Kontum, Pleiku, and Darlac.

Against the generally gloomy background of military events in the first half of 1964, MACV viewed Quyet Thang 202 with some satisfaction, considering that it "seized the initiative against a major VC stronghold in order to impose [their] will on the enemy." MACV admitted that "the VC reacted against the initial heliborne operations," in which two battle groups were inserted into Do Xa, with "well directed and concentrated anti-aircraft machine gun fire," but "despite this the airlift" conducted by American helicopter units "was completed in a highly successful manner." Though "no large scale engagement developed, the VC regional command and communications systems were disrupted [and] their food sources destroyed."

The operation lasted a month, with ARVN units conducting "day and night operations continually throughout this period." Government forces destroyed a "considerable number of structures" and a "large quantity of crops."

Much of the crop destruction (some 122 acres) was achieved through chemical spraying by VNAF H-34 helicopters. Throughout the operation, the VNAF used A-1 H Skyraider strike aircraft for close support to ground troops and H-34 helicopters for medical evacuation. MACV believed that "the pressure of operations" had "caused the VC Fifth Regional Headquarters and at least three VC radio stations to relocate." Sixty-two Communist troops had been killed, seventeen captured, and one persuaded to defect. The haul of captured war material included four machine guns, four automatic rifles, sixty-five personal weapons, and substantial quantities of grenades, mines, explosives, and documents. At the end of the operation, according to US advisory staff with II Corps, "219 Montagnard families were returned to government control."

The cost, however, was far from negligible. Government forces lost twenty-three killed and eighty-seven wounded. The Communists also managed to destroy six aircraft, including one A-1 H Skyraider. So even by its own calculations, the anti-Communist side had lost roughly one aircraft for every thirteen enemy soldiers put out of action. When the operation terminated, it was considered too dangerous to leave in the area the three CIDG Strike Force companies originally intended to secure it on a long-term basis, a tacit admission that powerful Communist units remained in the vicinity.[47]

Whereas the official history of MR 5 acknowledges that this operation took place (dating it 23 April to 22 May), it quickly dismisses it as a failure. "We blocked the enemy attacks, caused many enemy casualties, shot down 42 aircraft and defeated the enemy plot to attack our headquarters organization."[48] The claim as to number of aircraft destroyed is surely a gross exaggeration, but the truth, as acknowledged by the anti-Communist side, was impressive enough. The implication that MR 5 headquarters was not forced to evacuate the area, or that it left for only a short period, seems credible. Nevertheless, a large-scale ARVN attack on the base area containing this major headquarters must have distressed the Communists, and at least temporarily, it must have wrested the initiative from them. The damage done to this important base, especially in terms of lost foodstuffs, crops, and labor (which were never in plentiful supply in the Highlands), must have caused serious concern.

On 31 May the 22d Division mounted a follow-up operation, Quyet Thang 303, into the western Do Xa and Hong Bong base areas in northeastern Kontum Province. The mission's goal was "to destroy VC political, military and economic organizations and influence within the operational area," including the "destruction of VC headquarters and units, crops, installations, disruption of . . . routes of infiltration and relocation of Montagnards living in the area." The operation was based on "numerous intelligence reports" that "located a VC infiltration route across northern Kontum Province and confirmed VC main force location." Consideration was also given to "the probability of encountering the VC 5th Regional Headquarters with its support and security units, estimated strength of 500, which were driven to the west by Operation Quyet Thang 202." The ARVN's intelligence also revealed that the Communist province committee and a district committee were located in this area, together with the 20th and 80th Main Force Battalions, "with estimated strength[s] of 300 and 200 respectively," five local force platoons with a total strength of 150, and a reconnaissance platoon. It is not possible to judge the accuracy of this intelligence. There is no doubt that the Communists had important base areas in northern Kontum, as indicated by their own postwar accounts; however, they recognized the existence of only three main force battalions in the Central Highlands, and none of them was the 20th or 80th. Because Communist units were known by different names at different times, it is by no means impossible that actual Communist main force units were in the operational area. But it is equally likely that units identified by ARVN intelligence as "main force" were regarded as provincial or local troops by the Communists themselves.

The operation involved mainly troops of the 41st and 42d Regiments, 22d Division, supported by artillery and engineers. The scheme of maneuver called for three infantry battalions to march north into the operational area to seize three objectives along a northwest-to-southeast diagonal, with the northernmost point designated the main objective. A fourth infantry battalion was to be lifted by US Army and US Marine Corps helicopters to the main objective on the fourth day.

The three battalions traveling on foot began the maneuver on the morning of 31 May and had just nine minor contacts in their march north. The fourth battalion, the 3d Battalion of the 42d Regiment, arrived by helicopter on the main objective, as planned, on 3 June. It was accompanied by the regimental headquarters and captured two prisoners shortly after landing. These two admitted to being from an infiltration group that had just arrived from North Vietnam.

There were apparently no other Communist forces to be dealt with, so the ARVN battalion commander commenced a hunt for the rest of the infiltration group. "Late in the afternoon [on 4 June] two of its companies set up ambushes on adjacent ridges. At 1800 hours two platoons of VC were trapped between these companies." The report does not make it clear whether this was the infiltration group that had been targeted or whether another Communist force had wandered into the trap set for that group. Whoever it was came off badly. A "firefight developed but the VC were outmatched. The results . . . were 28 killed, 5 rifles, 2 French ARs, 1 US BAR and some small arms ammunition captured." Only five ARVN soldiers were wounded and none killed.

Although the operation lasted a month, its subsequent results were relatively limited. Fifty-nine Communist personnel were reported killed altogether, and six captured; three automatic rifles and twenty-three individual weapons were taken. Eleven ARVN soldiers were reported killed and sixteen wounded—half of the latter by spike traps.

The casualties the ARVN inflicted were obviously modest in relation both to the scale and duration of the operation and to the number of Communist troops believed (rightly or wrongly) to be in the area. Only in terms of the destruction of food stocks, livestock, and crops (which was apparently considerable) did the operation have much impact. Although MACV praised "a well-planned scheme of maneuver,"[49] given the size of the area and the mountainous and jungle-covered terrain, it was probably easy enough, in most cases, for Communist forces to evade contact if they wished to do so. The only real combat success for the ARVN was the 4 June ambush in an area where ARVN troops had recently arrived by helicopter and where Communist forces may not have been aware of their presence.

The General Situation in Mid-1964

In the most critical provinces of the Central Highlands in mid-1964, the Saigon government exerted little control outside the provincial capitals, the district towns, and its military bases. Few Highlanders' villages in Kontum, Pleiku, or Darlac were really secure against penetration by Communist forces. The Communists were often able to remove personnel and weaponry from such settlements with little or no loss to themselves. Yet it is important not to exaggerate either the military strength or the popular support the Communists enjoyed in the region at this time. Neither in numbers nor in striking power were Communist forces in the Highlands particularly strong, and the proportion of the population under long-term Communist control was quite modest. Given the evident attitudes of most Highlanders by this stage of the war, neither the recruitment of substantially larger Communist forces in the region nor the sustenance of such forces from the region's resources would be easy for the high command in Hanoi.

From the mid-1950s onward the Communists worked hard among the native peoples in some of the more remote parts of the Highlands.[50] In general, they put more effort into understanding the Highlanders' cultures and aspirations than did those who served the Diem regime. The Communists also placed far more emphasis than Diem or subsequent Saigon governments on the military recruitment of the native Highlanders, and in some localities they established a modus vivendi with Highland villages that provided Communist troops with food, labor, and personnel. By 1964, however, the great majority of Highlanders had little enthusiasm for supplying these Communist needs.

In the vast majority of cases, Highlanders certainly had little liking for successive Saigon governments. These regimes sponsored Vietnamese colonization of the Highlands; they took good land and offered little in the way of compensation. Yet no regime in Saigon demanded as much from the Highlanders in terms of military service, labor, and food as did the Communists. As early as 1962, Highlanders found those demands exorbitant, leading to their substantial voluntary movement from Communist-controlled areas to those controlled by the South Vietnamese government. In the absence of adequate armament, Highlanders were often reluctant to risk their lives trying to prevent Communist troops from entering their villages, whether these were traditionally located or refugee settlements. When Communist troops tried to herd them away from their villages and toward the insurgency's base areas, however, they sometimes attempted to escape and go home.

The Communist leadership in Hanoi wanted its forces to win major battles in the Central Highlands, to destroy the government forces' bases, and to establish "liberated zones" much larger than the base areas they held in late 1963.[51] In mid-1964, however, they had yet to achieve these aims. The military balance in the region, in terms of numbers and firepower, still strongly favored the anti-Communist side. The majority of the Saigon government forces in the Central Highlands may have been somewhat unadventurous and combat-averse, but the same might be said of much of the Communist military personnel in the region.

In the first half of 1964, it seems quite clear that most Communist units in the Central Highlands, though led by Vietnamese, consisted largely of Highlanders. Communist command organizations such as MR 5 and CHF, however, had only limited confidence in such units, regarding none of them as main force. They were fine for harassing villages, taking weapons from Village Defenders, kidnapping or killing minor officials, and herding civilians. Sometimes they could successfully carry out ambushes of modest size. But they were not considered reliable for assaults on fortified positions or for major firefights.

The Communists, by their own reckoning, had only three main force units in the whole of the Central Highlands, all of which were ethnically Vietnamese.[52] It seems likely that these units had no more than a few hundred personnel each. In these circumstances it is hardly surprising that major attacks on towns, on government forces' bases, and even on substantial government forces in the field were rare in the Central Highlands in the first half of 1964. Up to the end of June, moreover, ARVN troops were, from time to time, penetrating major Communist base areas in the Highlands in considerable strength. Such operations might not always have been conducted very efficiently, but while they continued, the initiative could not be said to be wholly in Communist hands.

8

Crisis in the Highlands,
July–December 1964

The Communists Plan a July Offensive

In early July 1964 Communist forces in South Vietnam mounted a major offensive designed to put Le Duan's GO-GU strategy into effect. The offensive was planned and organized by COSVN, the Communist general headquarters for the southern part of the country. Established in mid-1961, COSVN was located in Tay Ninh Province near the Cambodian border and had been commanded by Nguyen Van Linh since its inception. Born in Hung Yen near Hanoi in 1915, possibly into a bourgeois family, Linh was a protégé of Le Duan, having served with him in the Mekong Delta in the First Indochina War. COSVN's writ did not normally run as far north as the Central Highlands, and it did not normally give orders to MR 5, but the July 1964 offensive seems to have been an exception. COSVN's apparent intent was to seize the initiative throughout South Vietnam and, perhaps, to initiate an endgame that would bring about, in a matter of months, the final collapse of the southern state. It is unclear exactly when COSVN issued its orders for this offensive or how they were transmitted. But MR 5 was left in no doubt that it had a particularly vital part to play and that COSVN and the high command in Hanoi expected substantial victories in the Central Highlands as well as on the coastal plain.[1]

We do not know whether the July operations in the Central Highlands were planned by MR 5 itself, delegated to the newly created Central Highlands Front, or given to some sort of special task force. But whichever group of officers received the assignment must have realized that the Party had trusted them with a mission of the utmost importance. They were expected to achieve at least one dramatic, signal victory somewhere in the Highlands. But, given the general weakness of the Party's military forces in the region, how could they accomplish this?

The Highway 19 Ambush and the Assault on Polei Krong

Whoever did the planning demonstrated military professionalism of a high order. Communist forces struck two hard blows in quick succession. The first was a large ambush sprung by the 93d Battalion of the 2d Regiment against a forty-one-vehicle ARVN artillery ammunition convoy on Highway 19 near the An Khe pass in Binh Dinh Province on 1 July. Efficiently planned and executed, the ambush cost the ARVN twenty-seven killed and twenty-five wounded, as well as the loss of some small arms and damage to twenty-nine trucks. Having struck hard, the ambushers promptly withdrew without trying to capture or destroy the ammunition the convoy carried. Hasty departure seems to have kept their casualties to a minimum. They left just three bodies behind.

The South Vietnamese and Americans did not normally consider Binh Dinh a Central Highlands province, but its western side did incorporate part of the eastern edge of the Highlands and fell within the area the Communists called Gia Lai, which also included Pleiku and much of Phu Bon. The Communist battalion that executed the ambush was ethnically Vietnamese and not normally based in the Highlands. The 2d Regiment's usual stamping ground was Quang Ngai, the coastal province immediately north of Binh Dinh.[2]

The affair on Highway 19 was, however, merely a vehicle ambush. For their major assault (a much more difficult, dangerous, and dramatic operation), the Communist planners chose a substantial fortified camp that looked impressive but, as their intelligence almost certainly indicated, was so dysfunctional as to make it a fairly easy target. In an exemplary application of the principle of concentration of force, they decided to use all the main force units normally based in the Highlands against this one, carefully selected point. They also achieved a high degree of surprise.

US Special Forces had established the Polei Krong camp during a phase of rapid expansion of the CIDG program in February 1963. It was one of twenty or so CIDG–Special Forces camps in II Corps in mid-1964.[3] It lay in Kontum Province, northwest of the provincial capital and on the western side of the river Krong Poko, not far from the Cambodian border—an area described as "90% occupied by mountains . . . up to an altitude of 1,500 feet above sea level."[4] The camp was in an ethnically mixed area with nearby villages or hamlets occupied by Jarai, Halang, and Rongao people. Many of these were refugee settlements—the traditional villages being still closer to the border, in areas that were largely under Communist control.

Twenty-eight villages lay within a 10 km "area of influence" around the camp. But the relationship of the CIDG Strike Force at Polei Krong with these villages was ill defined and half-baked. Border surveillance, not the defense and welfare of Highland villages, was Polei Krong's designated mission. The villagers had supposedly been armed and trained by the South Vietnamese provincial authorities. In reality, arms had generally been issued on a very modest scale, and only a handful of people had been trained in their use. At least in some cases, village fortifications were decrepit and porous.[5]

The US Special Forces A-detachment serving at Polei Krong from 9 December 1963 to 22 May 1964 was Captain John Williamson's A-134. Williamson wrote a fascinating final report that combined a frank, highly perceptive account of the camp's gross ineffectiveness, internal conflicts, and weaknesses with an apparent complacency that, in hindsight, was grossly inappropriate. Williamson believed that although local Highlanders were, in general, favorably disposed toward the Americans, they were also in at least intermittent communication with the Communists. Communist forces had easy access to some of their villages and could forcibly evacuate them in a matter of minutes.[6] Williamson also knew that the intelligence available to his detachment was grossly inadequate and that the camp's counterintelligence effort was completely ineffective. He considered it "an assured fact that there are VC in the camp" and that "information is going out of the camp to the VC. . . . From all indicators in the field, it is suspected that the VC are on the distribution list for all operations orders." No intelligence agency operating in the area had proved capable of vetting CIDG personnel effectively. American Special Forces had, on their own initiative, removed some individuals from the camp, but the leakage of military information had continued.[7]

Relations between the Special Forces at Polei Krong and the ARVN 22d Division were extremely poor. Indeed, Williamson rated all non-CIDG government forces in the vicinity as "of little or no assistance and dangerous, due to the tendency to send their troops into our area without our knowledge. It is only due to luck that they have become involved in firefights or ambushes with our patrols."[8] He indicated that attempts at joint operations with Vietnamese forces had been a fiasco owing to "the difficulty of getting the Vietnamese to listen to us" and "the fact" that the Vietnamese units concerned had "no desire to find VC." Local Self-Defense Corps personnel had also exhibited extreme (presumably racially motivated) hostility toward CIDG Strike Force troops. "In . . . one co-ordinated effort with an SDC unit we were delibertly [*sic*] fired on with automatic weapons, small arms and 81mm mortar. The only reason we were not hit is because we did not spend the night where we told the ARVIN [*sic*] officer we would be."[9] There were racial tensions in the camp too. The Vietnamese apparently wanted the camp turned over entirely to their control. But Williamson was convinced that if this were done, "all the Mountainard [*sic*] soldiers would leave with the Americans. It is impossible in any short time to change the age-old hatered [*sic*] the soldiers have for the Vietnamese. This is as much the Viet. fault as anyones [*sic*] due to their attitudes towards the Mountainard."[10] Williamson thought the local ARVN units were so intensely suspicious of the camp that some ARVN officers had infiltrated it, perhaps to try to identify Communist agents, but perhaps also to spy on the Americans.[11]

Williamson and his team had done their best. Communist forces seemed to be giving the camp a wider berth than before. At the time of his detachment's arrival, patrols reported punji and spear traps on trails just 5 km from the camp. Six months later, these had been pushed back to a distance of 10 km. Williamson admitted, however, that the "VC seem to have no fear of being surprised beyond this limit."[12]

Yet, despite his frank admissions of the camp's very limited effectiveness and numerous problems, Williamson did not ring alarm bells that might have alerted his superiors to the camp's real and present danger. Indeed, he strongly implied that no such danger existed:

> There has been no offensive action by the VC in the past six months with the exception of half hearted attempts at infiltration into Strike Force companies within camp. . . . The VC within our area have the capability of massing at least a battalion force but to mass any unit larger than a platoon takes a formidable amount of time and [it] is normally easy to determine a build up is taking place. . . . Within our area the VC seem to have very poor medical facilities, little re-supply of ammunition or weapons and little or no use of munitions, mines etc. . . . From all intelligence indications the VC are losing large numbers of followers due to lack of food and inability to pay or provide medical treatment. There is little to indicate a build up or increased activity in the near future.[13]

Williamson came to the "obvious conclusion . . . that the maximum VC effort is in the South and that only enough VC are present to keep [this] province in . . . need [of] troops. It is thought that the small VC units in this area are for this purpose and to maintain infiltration routes from Laos and Cambodia."[14]

Williamson had considerably underestimated the importance of the Central Highlands in Communist strategy. As a captain, strategic analysis was arguably "above his pay grade," but he was doing it anyway. Getting it wrong led him to underestimate the threat to his base. It also perhaps led to the neglect of certain vital tactical matters that were in fact appropriate to his rank and station. So little did he fear an assault that he made practically no comment on the camp's physical security, including its fortifications, the layout of its buildings, its sentry system and passwords, its emergency drills, its defensive fire plan, or its arrangements for summoning reinforcements. Given that the camp had been selected for a "battle of annihilation" early in the Communist July offensive, some of these matters soon proved critical.

The Communist 200th Artillery Battalion, the 407th Sapper Battalion, and at least part of the 303d Antiaircraft Battalion all took part in the attack on Po-lei Krong.[15] Where these units were based before the operation is not clearly stated in the Communist histories. For the first two, it is reasonable to speculate that they were further north in Kontum Province, where we know the Com-munists had some of their biggest base areas. The 303d Antiaircraft Battalion may have been at the Do Xa base in Quang Ngai, protecting MR 5 headquar-ters. (Its presence in that area would help account for the exceptionally heavy aircraft losses during the ARVN's operation Quyet Thang 202 in May.)

Wherever they had been beforehand, getting them into position for the assault on Polei Krong was clearly something of a logistical nightmare: "The rainy season had already begun. The ground in the jungles was soggy and slippery. Civilian laborers were mobilized . . . having no nylon sheets for protection against the rain the laborers and troops cut wild banana leaves and used them to cover supplies, weapons and ammunition. Despite difficulties and hardships nobody was discouraged or lost heart because they fully understood the . . . significance of this opening battle."[16]

Captain William Johnson commanded A-122, the A-detachment that re-placed John Williamson's at Polei Krong. (The similarity of the commanders' names was either a bizarre coincidence or an odd joke on the part of whoever did the posting.) According to Johnson, on 27 June 1964, a company-sized patrol led by Sergeant Akuna had spotted "two (2) VC Companies" in the vi-cinity of the camp. Upon his return, Akuna reported that these appeared "well armed and organized"—too strong for him to mount an attack against them with a single Strike Force company. Yet, despite the fact that two of Polei Krong's four companies were absent from the camp at this time, there does not seem to have been any particular anxiety about its safety. Rather, over the next few days, the discussion focused on mounting some sort of attack against these Communist forces. But all attempts to arrange combined operations with the CIDG Strike Force at Plei Mrong and with the ARVN 22d Division for this purpose ended in failure.[17]

From 1 to 3 July Lieutenant Tan, the camp's Vietnamese commander, was away from Polei Krong, trying to find a new campsite for the border surveil-lance program. In Tan's absence, the American Special Forces at Polei Krong noticed that his subordinates failed to send out ambush patrols to help secure the camp at night. On the evening of 3 July, Tan returned to Polei Krong. Johnson's report indicates that he considered Tan a competent and conscien-tious officer. Johnson thus believed Tan when he said he had sent out ambush patrols on the night of 3 July. In reality, no such patrols had gone. There were, however, ten guard posts around the camp perimeter, each with five men, one of whom was supposed to be awake at all times. Johnson claimed that at midnight on 3 July he had personally checked all the posts on the perimeter and found everything in order.[18]

Very early on 4 July, unknown to the Americans, a force of seventy sappers from the Communist 407th Battalion began clearing paths through the minefields and barbed wire defending the camp. The Communists also had a substantial group of infiltrators inside the camp whose primary mission was to neutralize Polei Krong's command and control. According to the American after-action report, at about 0150, an interpreter working for the Americans was awakened by voices. Picking up his weapon, he moved toward the troop mess to investigate. Someone demanded in Vietnamese, "Where are the Americans, take us to them." The interpreter realized that the speaker must be an enemy soldier and responded by emptying a thirty-round magazine from his M2 carbine in his direction. This unleashed pandemonium.

Bullets seemed to sweep the camp from all directions, and mortar rounds fell on the key buildings, wounding at least four of the Americans within minutes of the start of the battle. The Americans then heard an explosion, thought to be a Bangalore torpedo, on the camp's southern perimeter. Soon Communist troops had breached the perimeter in fourteen places (the main breaches being on the northeastern and southeastern sectors of the perimeter) and were charging into the camp throwing grenades and satchel charges. Because the camp had been heavily infiltrated, CIDG defenders in some cases found themselves attacked simultaneously from without and from within, in the latter case by people they had hitherto regarded as comrades.[19]

According to Johnson's after-action report, the Americans and a group of Nung mercenaries (on whom Americans in CIDG camps now routinely relied) initially offered fierce resistance. But at 0303, believing that all resistance other than their own had ended, they began to withdraw to the riverbank. Some of the wounded, finding that being carried was too painful, were reduced to crawling. Because some of the Nungs could not swim, and because there was a reluctance to abandon the severely wounded, none of them crossed the river. At 0330 a flare ship aircraft appeared over the camp, but their one radio had been damaged and proved inoperable. It was only because the Communists made no detailed search of the riverbank that any of them survived.

Communist troops were in possession of the camp between 0315 and 0445, before commencing an evacuation. By 0515 that was complete. The Communists seem to have been preoccupied with evacuating their wounded (and perhaps their dead) and did not carry off or destroy as much materiel as might have been expected. Only one building in the camp was destroyed after its capture. Of the six ammunition bunkers, the Communist forces attempted to destroy

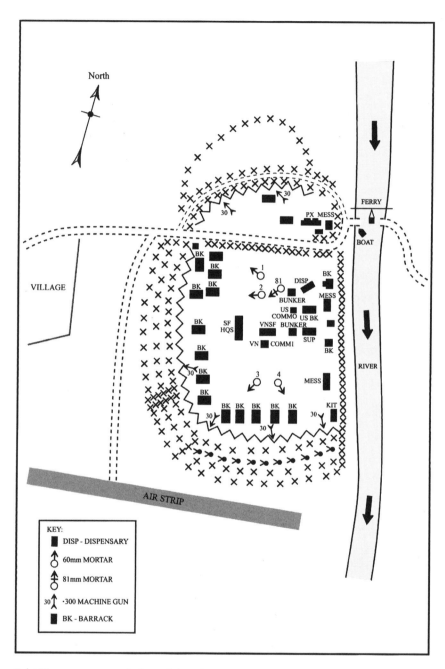

Polei Krong camp as attacked on 4 July 1964

only three, and because the explosives they used were inadequate, these were largely undamaged. Little ammunition was carried off, although a couple of hundred weapons of various sorts, including two 6omm mortars, were taken.[20]

The attack killed at least thirty of the camp's defenders and wounded fifty-six; some sixty-six were reported as captured or missing.[21] The setback to morale was perhaps the most serious result—this being reflected in a substantial number of desertions in the few days following the attack and the failure of many of those who had been absent during the attack to return to duty.[22]

This was a worrying defeat for the anti-Communist side, but its scale is exaggerated in Communist accounts. These claimed that a fortified camp of four companies was "completely destroyed" and nine Americans were killed.[23] In reality, one of the CIDG companies was on a mission elsewhere, and much of another was out on patrol. Significant numbers of CIDG personnel had been allowed to sleep in local villages that night, and others were absent without leave. Indeed, there seem to have been fewer than 200 military personnel on the anti-Communist side in the camp when the attack started. No Americans died. Communist accounts, moreover, fail to indicate the extent of their own losses, which may have been heavy. Johnson reported 105 Communist dead and 63 wounded, though there is no indication as to how he arrived at these figures.

Subsequent inquiries and interrogations revealed that "Lt Tan's CIDG clerk was a VC officer who took all correspondence to his home to work on it. Lt Tan's personal driver and the camp tailor are VC. One of the men working with the food contractor is VC. The executive officer of the 4th company is VC."[24]

Johnson's account of the fall of Polei Krong is not the only one available from the anti-Communist side. Major Thon That Hung prepared a lessons-learned report for II Corps that included blistering criticisms of both the standards of security and the quality of leadership at Polei Krong. Thick vegetation, Hung indicated, had been allowed to grow up near the camp's edges, limiting fields of fire. Contractors' employees had access to the camp at night. There was no proper system of passwords. Some Strike Force personnel had fought hard against the Communist assault, but they ran out of ammunition and grenades. The bulk of the camp's stocks of these items were locked away and inaccessible. Most controversially, Hung's account contradicted Johnson's story of determined American and Nung resistance, accusing all the camp's command elements of having panicked and fled almost as soon as the attack began. Despite the fact that the signals shelter had not been hit in the opening bombardment, they failed to provide timely and accurate information about the attack to 22d Division or II Corps. As a passage underlined in the original puts it: "The loss of communication right at the first gun shot is a defect of Vietnamese and American commanding levels who lost their heads and ran away."[25]

ARVN mistrust of the CIDG program may have prejudiced Hung's report to some degree. It certainly cannot be reconciled with Johnson's. A later American assessment, however, admitted that there was much truth in the ARVN account.[26]

At Polei Krong on 4 July 1964 the Communists won an impressive little victory based on excellent intelligence, the skillful use of a fifth column, and an exemplary application of the principle of concentration of force. But it was only a little victory. The Communist high command realized as much. The units involved were awarded the Liberation Order of Military Exploit Third Class. It was the first award of its kind bestowed on main force units in this region. But it was still only a third-class award.[27]

The CIDG Strike Force at Polei Krong was soon reorganized and the camp rebuilt, although it would be abandoned a few months later. That this was the Communists' biggest victory in the Central Highlands in 1964 (a year in which they are usually considered to have been in the ascendancy in South Vietnam as a whole) is indicative of the peculiar difficulties they faced in this region.

Other Military Operations, July–September 1964

The Polei Krong attack was part of a general Communist offensive across South Vietnam. Its scale and intensity are worth emphasizing. At the beginning of August DCI John McCone reported:

> During July, the Viet Cong made twelve major attacks using at least one battalion—more such attacks in July alone than were in the first five months this year, or in the first nine months of 1963. The twelve battalion attacks, combined with eight attacks by one or more companies of Viet Cong regulars, represent the most aggressive level of Viet Cong military activity to date. The high rate of terrorism, sabotage and harassment was maintained at the same time.

The CIA thought that this intensification of the fighting might have been partly "intended to welcome General Taylor" (the new ambassador). But it was obviously also timed to coincide with "the onset of the summer monsoon season, when the rains hamper guerrilla movement less than they slow down government reaction."[28] The latter point was certainly valid. The Communists had also commenced their big 1963 offensive in July.

The Agency noted that in their July 1964 offensive the Communists had particularly targeted Special Forces–CIDG camps. On 6 July they launched a major assault on Nam Dong in Thua Thien Province in I Corps' area, a camp reportedly almost as dysfunctional as Polei Krong. They were, however, unable to overrun it completely and withdrew after suffering heavy losses. At 0215 on 9 July, an estimated two companies of Communist troops probed the CIDG base at Polei Djereng in Kontum Province, about 30 km northwest of the town of Pleiku. But the probe met significant resistance and never developed into an all-out assault.[29]

On 15 July in the Phu Nhon district of Pleiku, Communist troops ambushed a convoy of vehicles belonging to an unspecified ARVN engineer battalion, wounding a couple of soldiers. But the ARVN engineers reacted aggressively and claimed to have killed seven of their attackers. Later the same day, in the Le Trung district of the same province, a group of armored cars belonging to the Regional Forces (RF) and a truckload of Rangers escaped a Communist ambush, reportedly killing a further five Communist troops in the process. But while Communist attacks on ARVN and RF troops in the Highlands were quite likely to meet with defeat, their intensified harassment of Highland villages brought greater success. Their handful of main force units could not be everywhere at once, and harassing villages was a type of action more suited to the capabilities of the bulk of the troops they had in the region. Their local force units, while exposing themselves to little risk, were often able to seize arms and kidnap villagers. In so doing they created a general climate of insecurity that undermined government authority.[30]

Even in terms of population control, however, the Communists were not having it all their way in the Highlands in July 1964. US Special Forces achieved a small victory in Pleiku Province in the middle of that month, making contact with Highland civilians living in an area under Communist control and persuading them to leave. "They had been used by the VC to grow food and perform labor. Additionally the VC levied taxes and had 'taken over' in the villages." Special Forces escorted these people to government-controlled territory. MACV reported:

> Homes, rice and all belongings that could not be carried were destroyed so that they could not be used by the VC. The people are destitute and suffering from malnutrition. The province chief paid them a personal visit and he is providing them with everything that is within his capability. In addition, all VN and US sources are being exploited to supply them with clothes, bedding and other needed items. A new hamlet site is being selected, and construction will start as soon as possible.[31]

On 24 July Special Forces–CIDG suffered a minor disaster when a convoy was ambushed in the vicinity of Camp Buon Brieng in Darlac Province. The convoy was carrying families as well as soldiers. Nineteen CIDG personnel and

dependents and one US Special Forces enlisted man died, and a similar number were wounded. In the last few days of the month, however, CIDG forces
had some minor successes in the same province. A patrol from Camp Bu Mi
Ga made contact with Communist forces approximately 10 km southeast of
the camp; three Communist soldiers were killed, and a rifle and submachine
gun were captured, with no loss to CIDG personnel. On 31 July a patrol
from Camp Buon Brieng, whose personnel had suffered heavy casualties in
the ambush a week earlier, engaged a company-sized Communist force and
recaptured two Browning automatic rifles and two light machine guns lost in
the earlier action.[32]

The big vehicle ambush on Highway 19 and Polei Krong were the Communists' only "main force" victories in the Highlands in mid-1964. But a CIA
political history of this period (written in 1966) states:

> Viet Cong activity among Highland villages was on the upsurge. Quietly the
> Viet Cong infiltrated the hamlets, conducted propaganda lectures, recruited
> supporters and set the stage for taking control of the hamlets . . . the Viet Cong
> were mounting an increasing number of attacks . . . and with the coming of
> the rainy season in July, started . . . collecting all weapons in outlying hamlets.
> . . . The Viet Cong began pressing closer and closer to the district towns and
> provincial capitals, slowly cutting them off from road communications with
> other towns and the lowlands. The Highlands were being effectively isolated.[33]

It is certainly true that the Republic of Vietnam's armed forces were frequently
failing to secure Highlanders' villages from Communist penetration and that
many of these villages had been left inadequately armed to defend themselves.
Yet the impression given in this CIA report of the strength and ubiquity of
Communist forces in the Highlands in July 1964 is probably somewhat exaggerated. It more accurately reflects the radically changed situation in early
1965, after II Corps had been weakened by the withdrawal of 25th Division
and whole PAVN regiments had arrived in the region.

In the last week of July there was a substantial drop in Communist military activity throughout South Vietnam. The decline continued into August,
despite the clash between American and North Vietnamese ships in the Gulf
of Tonkin early that month and the violent American reaction to it.[34] In the
Highlands, Communist forces continued to target CIDG, but with little success. At 0210 on 3 August Communist forces harassed Camp Plei Ta Nangle,
60 km southwest of Pleiku, with small-arms fire but caused no casualties. At
2030 on 6 August a Communist company with mortar support attacked a two-
platoon outpost of Camp Bu Prang, 60 km southwest of Pleiku, but inflicted
no casualties and withdrew forty-five minutes later.[35]

In South Vietnam as a whole, Communist warlike activity began to rise again in early September. The Communist leadership was apparently trying to take advantage of the acute political disturbance that would culminate in an attempted coup against General Khanh's government in the week commencing 12 September. The Central Highlands, however, remained quieter than most other areas, with Phu Bon, Darlac, Quang Duc, and Tuyen Duc all reporting "no VC initiated actions" for the week of 29 August–5 September. A Communist attack on a fortified hamlet in Kontum Province on 2 September, however, caused three fatalities and the loss of five weapons. The ambush of an RF unit in Phu Bon on 5 September 1962 (apparently occurring too late to be reported for that week) resulted in at least sixteen RF fatalities.[36] On 6 September a combat patrol from the CIDG camp at Plei Mrong, 20 km northwest of Pleiku, clashed with a number of Highlanders in Communist service, killing one and capturing ten without incurring any casualties. On the same day in Lam Dong, a normally quiet province, a well-armed Communist squad ambushed an RF squad, killing one RF soldier but withdrawing after a ten-minute exchange of fire.[37] The general pattern of activity only tends to reinforce the notion that, throughout 1964, the striking power of most Communist troops in the Highlands was rather limited.

The "Montagnard Revolt" of September 1964

The week of 12–19 September saw both an attempted coup against General Khanh's regime and the year's highest rate of Communist military activity up to that point across South Vietnam as a whole. But again, there was relatively little fighting in the Central Highlands, and the following week the Communist effort slackened markedly throughout the country.[38]

Far and away the most important event in the Central Highlands in the second half of September was a CIDG mutiny that the Americans generally called the Montagnard Revolt. On the night of 19 September, a group of mainly Rhade Strike Force troops began an open rebellion. What triggered the revolt? The grievances of Highland communities and individuals against the Diem regime have already been explored at some length. Most politically aware Highlanders probably welcomed the coup of November 1963. General Nguyen Khanh's second coup in January 1964 initially appeared to offer them significant hope of more favorable treatment and some recognition of their political aspirations. On 10 February 1964 the Khanh regime released Y-Bham and other leaders of the Bajaraka movement from prison and gave them government posts in the Highlands. Y-Bham became deputy province chief for Highlander affairs in Darlac. Paul Nur gained the same position in Kontum, while Nay Luett became an interpreter for the Americans in Phu Bon Province and later liaison officer for the Directorate of Highlander Affairs in Saigon.

The II Corps commander, Lieutenant General Do Cao Tri (who had been the hammer against Buddhist militants in I Corps' area under the Diem regime), was apparently one of the driving forces behind the Khanh regime's new liberal attitude toward Highlanders:

> He called for the release and acceptance of imprisoned and self-exiled leaders of the Bajaraka Autonomy Movement, the assignment of these leaders to government positions at their former civil service grades, and the creation of a school of public administration for Highlanders to train them for civil service positions in their own areas. The government policy was to assign a Highlander as deputy district chief where more than 50 per cent of the population was Highlander; as of April 1964 there were five Highlanders assigned as deputy province chiefs.[39]

But if Khanh's government and some of its senior military personnel were relatively enlightened in their attitude toward Highlanders, this enlightenment did not extend to a majority of local officials or to a high proportion of ARVN officers. In March 1964 there was a major meeting, apparently held at Pleiku, of the ARVN II Corps staff, representatives of all three ARVN divisions in II Corps at the time, and Highland leaders. Some ARVN officers either were not properly briefed on the new government policy on the treatment of Highlanders or simply chose to ignore the briefing. One said: "I feel that we can solve the Highlander problem the same way the Americans solved their Indian problem. We should form Highlander reservations as the Americans formed Indian reservations." This remark created a strong sense of alienation among the Highland leaders, and the meeting resulted in little progress.[40]

In the same month Lieutenant Colonel Le Dinh Hien, director of social action for the Highlands, told American contacts that tribal elements in the Highlands had become even more alienated from the South Vietnamese government after Diem's overthrow. He cited the following reasons:

> (1) there continued to be an absence of a central program for the Highlanders; (2) changes of district and province chiefs brought in new officials ignorant of the Highlanders and activities concerning them; (3) the Highlanders traditionally were loyal to district chiefs rather than the central government, and the changes in the district chiefs left the Highlanders with no one to trust; (4) broad promises made to the Highlanders by the government were not kept; and, (5) Highlanders regrouped to defended villages were not receiving the basic necessities.[41]

An American embassy official reporting on Phu Bon Province in July 1964 stated that many of the Vietnamese provincial staff continued to treat "Highlanders . . . unsympathetically." He observed:

> Refugees had not always received their required food supplies, due only in part to the lack of transportation. Care for Highlanders at the outpatient dispensary in Cheoreo (there was no hospital) was often given grudgingly, if at all. Coupled with the discrimination the Highlanders suffer at the hands of the local Vietnamese civilian population, these acts of provincial neglect continue to alienate the Highlanders from the Vietnamese and the government.[42]

In these circumstances, some elements of the Bajaraka organization (which had never ceased to exist) planned an armed revolt. The obvious gap between government rhetoric and the actual treatment of Highlanders was clearly part of the motivation for the uprising. But many Highlanders wanted more than the government was offering—formal autonomy. Perhaps even more significantly, some Highlanders had convinced themselves that, in the government's weakened state following the coup against Diem, a revolt might have some chance of success. Success in this context might mean not an outright military victory but rather an American intervention (in the interests of the anti-Communist war effort) that would bring about an early cease-fire and force the South Vietnamese government to concede a high degree of autonomy for the Highlands.

For months before the revolt started, Highland leaders had been actively wooing the Americans. American Special Forces heard a great deal about the Highlanders' discontents:

> The commander of the US Special Forces B Team in Pleiku met with several key Highlander leaders in April 1964. During this meeting, the Highlanders stated that General Khanh was only the leader of the Vietnamese; the Highlanders had their own leader. They wanted all village, district and province chiefs in the Highlands to be Highlanders; a Highland army of 50,000 with its own Highlander officers and men and advised by US Special Forces; representation in the Vietnamese legislature and direct aid from the US.[43]

Rumors of a revolt reached both US Special Forces and the CIA, which passed them on to Vietnamese Special Forces. But some of the details were wildly exaggerated or just plain inaccurate, diminishing their credibility.

In April 1964 Y-Bham sent a letter to a member of the CIA in which he reviewed Highlander grievances since the creation of the South Vietnamese state in 1954. He stated: "In 1958 we asked the U.S. to support us as a free world power. It is certain that we cannot exist alone, but we want to have a just settlement. . . . We want to be Highlanders forever. There is no reason why our race should die out under the very eyes of the Americans and the UN. We count on the Americans to help us and give us our liberty." The reward for American support of Highlander rights and autonomy would be committed Highlander support in the war against the Communists: "If our plan is realized we will do everything possible to pacify our territory. We will pacify our country first and if possible we will later help our Vietnamese friends." Y-Bham pursued the same argument in contacts with American officials during May. He made it clear that he "desired some type of autonomy for the Highlanders and said that if he was in charge of the Highlands, the war against the Viet Cong would be over in six months. He wanted to encourage Highlanders to consolidate into larger hamlets for better protection and to have more weapons and U.S. Special Forces personnel to help defend the hamlets."[44]

Voices in favor of compromise from both the South Vietnamese government and Highland leaders continued to be heard. On 25 and 26 August forty-five prominent Highlanders as well as representatives from all the South Vietnamese and US government departments and agencies in the country attended a conference in Pleiku. The mood was reportedly constructive, but there were no promises of autonomy for the Highlands. Highland hard-liners continued to prepare their revolt.

On the night of 19–20 September Highland troops in the CIDG camps at Bu Prang and Buon Sar Pa in Quang Duc Province and Ban Don and Buon Mi Ga in Darlac Province revolted:

> They disarmed and restricted their U.S. Special Forces (USSF) advisors.
> The Bu Prang force killed approximately 15 Vietnamese (VN) Strike Force
> troop leaders in their camp and killed 19 Self-Defense Corps (SDC) at Three
> Frontiers, including the Post Commander, his wife and child. The Bon Sar
> Pa (BSP) force (augmented by one company of CIDG from Bu Prang) killed
> eleven VN at BSP, seized the district seat at Dak Mil, and moved towards
> Ban Me Thuot (BMT). The Buon Mi Ga (BMG) force killed ten VN Special
> Forces men (LLDB) and moved toward BMT. The Ban Don force bound
> their LLDB with rope and likewise moved toward BMT.[45]

Those planning the revolt intended for two additional CIDG camps to join it: Buon Brieng and Truong Son, the latter near the village of Buon Enao, where the CIDG program had begun. But the personnel in those camps remained neutral. In the case of Buon Brieng, this was owing, at least in part, to the work of Captain Vernon Gillespie, who led the American A-detachment there and enjoyed an exceptionally close and cordial relationship with the senior Highlander in the Strike Force.[46]

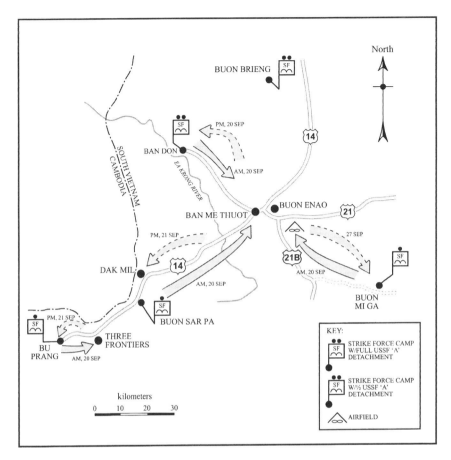

Rebel troop movements during the CIDG revolt

Even though some other Highland military and paramilitary personnel joined the mutinous CIDG personnel en route to Ban Me Thuot, the total size of the Highland rebel army was only 2,000 to 3,000. By 0700 on 20 September, these forces (mainly Rhade, but including some Mnong), moving by truck, had converged from three sides on the town of Ban Me Thuot. They took control of a radio station on its southwestern outskirts that morning but did not move to seize the town itself. Ban Me Thuot remained garrisoned by troops of the 23d Division, who established roadblocks on its approaches. The rebels proved unable to broadcast from the radio station because the province chief had removed some critical equipment. They were unable to completely invest Ban Me Thuot, and their position deteriorated by the hour as the 23d Division rapidly reinforced the town. "By midday, Brig Gen Nguyen Huu Co (II ARVN Corps CG), Sub-Brig Gen Hoang Xuan Lam (23rd ARVN Inf Div CG), Col John 'Fritz' Freund (II Corps Deputy Senior Advisor), and

Col Donald A. Kersting (23rd Division Senior Advisor) arrived on the scene and were co-ordinating activities in BMT."[47] Nguyen Huu Co had taken over as II Corps commander only on 14 September. He had played an important role in the coup against Diem and later gained a reputation as one of the most corrupt generals in the ARVN; he acquired vast wealth that evidently did not derive directly from his military salary. In 1964–1965, however, the Americans regarded him highly. He demonstrated a fair degree of restraint and common sense in response to the Rhade revolt. Skeptical and suspicious of CIDG, as were many ARVN officers, he allowed the Americans reasonable room for maneuver in their efforts to defuse a crisis that, in his opinion, was largely of their own making.[48]

The CIDG mutiny occurred in a sort of interregnum between senior American advisers at II Corps. Colonel Balthis was clearly on his way out, and Colonel Mataxis had not yet arrived. In these circumstances, the deputy senior adviser, Lieutenant Colonel John Frederick "Fritz" Freund, was instrumental in bringing the situation under control. A New Yorker who had graduated from the Naval Academy in 1940, Freund had a distinguished record with the US Army in the European theater in 1943–1945.[49] On the afternoon of Sunday, 20 September, with General Co's agreement, Freund proceeded to the rebel command post located at Buon Mbre, a village 10 km southwest of Ban Me Thuot, and opened negotiations with the rebels. Freund had the advantage of speaking French—a language that some Highland leaders understood better than English. Perhaps largely owing to his moderating influence, no major military clashes took place between the rebels and the ARVN around Ban Me Thuot.[50] It is not true, however, as a CIA report would later claim, that the ARVN never fired a shot during the revolt.[51] At approximately 2100 on the evening of 20 September the rebels suffered some ten casualties in a clash with an ARVN roadblock approximately 40 km east of town.[52]

Y-Bham was the most famous Highland leader, so it is important to examine his actions and attitudes during the early stages of the revolt. It seems that he played no part in its planning and that, at least initially, he disapproved of it. On the morning of 20 September, before it was seized by the rebels, he was with the Darlac province chief at the Ban Me Thuot radio station appealing for calm and trying to talk the CIDG rebels into returning to their camps. Some commentators considered that Y-Bham's position was undermined by the revolt and that it greatly annoyed him. He had been "close to gaining concessions from the Vietnamese Government and . . . the actions by more radical elements had upset these negotiations, tarnished the Rhade image and caused the Rhade to lose face." After the radio broadcast in the morning, Y-Bham returned to his home in Ban Me Thuot. The military situation was still very fluid, and at "about noon on 20 September, two or three jeeps full of CIDG troops from Buon Sar Pa entered Ban Me Thuot (apparently having evaded ARVN roadblocks) and took Y-Bham away to the rebel headquarters" south of town. (According to General Westmoreland's memoirs, an American Special Forces captain—who was, in effect, a hostage—was in one of the jeeps. This may have confused South Vietnamese troops and officials in Ban Me Thuot and prevented them from stopping the jeeps.)

The American and South Vietnamese authorities did not know whether Y-Bham left willingly. But from that point onward, he remained with the Highland autonomy movement, which now called itself the Front Uni de Lutte des Races Opprimées (FULRO)—the United Front for the Struggle of the Oppressed Race—and soon became its president. One theory was that, although the revolt had started against his will, he remained with the rebels in order to moderate their violence and negotiate a truce.[53]

On the morning of Monday, 21 September, the rebels at Buon Mbre, having witnessed a low flyover of fighter aircraft, realized that their prospects of winning any military action against government forces near Ban Me Thuot were negligible. They fell back to the CIDG camp at Buon Sar Pa. Freund went with them, although it is unclear whether he did so of his own volition or had become a hostage.[54] The situation remained extremely tense. The South Vietnamese authorities and, to a slightly lesser extent, the American authorities in Vietnam were losing patience with the rebels. The South Vietnamese government's anxiety focused on the sixty Vietnamese hostages held at Buon Sar Pa, most of them civilians picked up in the early stages of the uprising.

By 27 September, an American heliborne rescue mission under the control of Brigadier General William E. DePuy, Westmoreland's J-3 (operations chief) at MACV, had been prepared to release Vietnamese and American hostages held at Buon Sar Pa. The ARVN was also getting ready for a ground assault on that camp. Only desperate last-minute negotiations by Freund and DePuy's restraining influence on the ARVN averted further bloodshed. Freund (whom DePuy considered very brave but with a flair for melodrama) insisted that the rebels either release their Vietnamese prisoners or kill him, and he pointed out that only their leader should assume the responsibility of taking an American life. This argument and the passion with which it was expressed apparently did the trick. At about 1100 on Sunday, 27 September, the rebels allowed Freund personally to release their sixty Vietnamese hostages (many of whom had been taken during the capture of the district town of Dak Mil) just in time to prevent the American helicopter task force from assaulting the camp. The helicopters landed peacefully. They had flown out the last of the hostages by about 1125 that morning. By midday:

Col Freund had the situation in hand. After the departure of the prisoners, the Rhade troops mustered in military formation. To show good faith and take the rebels' minds off the prisoner release, General De Puy landed at 1125 hours and entered the camp. After a brief introduction by Col Freund, General De Puy addressed the troops. At 1141 hours, Gen De Puy was again airborne and returning to BMT.

It seemed that the worst of the crisis was over. Certainly the senior US authorities in Vietnam thought so. "Ambassador Taylor and General West-moreland sent their congratulations. General Westmoreland came to BMT for several hours of conferences in the afternoon." The sense of relief expressed by Taylor and Westmoreland indicates how serious the crisis had been. Indeed, it could have undermined much of what remained of the anti-Communist position in the Central Highlands. Taylor and Westmoreland had been formally briefed on the situation on the afternoon of Tuesday, 22 September, by, among others, Colonel John H. Spears, head of US Army Special Forces in Vietnam, and anthropologist Gerald C. Hickey, whose field research on the Highland peoples was being financed by the Rand Corporation. The general and the ambassador had been monitoring the crisis continuously since then.

In reality, even after the release of the sixty Vietnamese hostages at Buon Sar Pa, the situation remained extremely tense and dangerous. On Monday, 28 September, the South Vietnamese authorities were still planning to attack Buon Sar Pa, but American pressure apparently delayed the assault. In his memoirs, Westmoreland claims credit for intervening directly with Khanh. That morning, "Maj Y-Aba, an ARVN officer of Montagnard nationality, entered the BSP camp with Gen De Puy and stayed to negotiate with the rebels." The negotiations were successful, and South Vietnamese government forces were allowed to take control of the camp peacefully:

> Not a single shot was fired. By 1400 hours, the rebels agreed to lay aside their weapons. . . . At 1500 hours, General Khanh entered the camp for an impressive ceremony. General Khanh and Y-Tlur [the rebel leader at Buon Sar Pa] exchanged speeches of peace and co-operation. Before departure for BMT at 1540 hours, General Khanh left 10,000 piasters for the families of CIDG troops living in the camp.

The CIDG revolt of 1964 was now practically at an end, although the underlying causes remained. Khanh's very direct personal involvement underlines the seriousness of this episode for the South Vietnamese state.[55]

Throughout the crisis, American negotiators apparently refused to endorse the Highlanders' demand for autonomy, indicating that they were acting as intermediaries for the Saigon government and not on their own account.[56] The Americans, however, may have given the rebels some sort of unofficial assurance that they would use their leverage to prevent the Vietnamese from exacting a bloody revenge. Without this, it is difficult to imagine the mutineers climbing down as tamely as they did.

The CIA concluded in the revolt's aftermath that its "primary military leader" had been YDhon Adrong, "a Rhade intellectual and militant" who had been prominent in Bajaraka. FULRO had become more militant under the influence of Prince Sihanouk's Cambodian government, which had encouraged South Vietnam's Highlanders to make common cause with its substantial Khmer (ethnic Cambodian) and Cham minorities. It was to Cambodia that the leaders fled when the revolt petered out. There, on 17 October 1964, they formed what they described as "the Provisional Government for the High Plateau."[57]

The CIA reported, contrary to MACV's assessment, that prior to the revolt there had been some communication between its organizers and the Communists:

> Indications are that the Viet Cong may have sought to influence the organization of the revolt. Apparently the Viet Cong had agreed not to attack the CIDG camps during the revolt, preferring to sit back and let disintegrating forces go to work. Limited information indicates that the Viet Cong hoped that CIDG and ARVN elements would engage in combat destroying the effectiveness of each other and then the Viet Cong could move in and destroy the remaining elements of both ARVN and the CIDG. . . . It is possible that the rapid action on the part of the US Special Forces to get the revolting CIDG troops back to their camps and the restraint of ARVN commanders not to engage the rebels in combat negated Viet Cong plans.[58]

While the revolt was in progress there had been serious tensions between American and South Vietnamese military and political authorities. Some Vietnamese blamed the Americans for arming the Highlanders in the first place; Nguyen Huu Co, the II Corps commander, was apparently among them. Yet generally the South Vietnamese authorities, perhaps mainly because of American influence, demonstrated great restraint in the revolt's aftermath. Despite the fact that some Vietnamese had been murdered, there were apparently no acts of vengeance. Indeed, there seemed to be no concerted effort to identify the murderers and bring them to justice.

A later CIA report characterized the Khanh government's postrevolt policy as one of appeasement. Khanh did not concede autonomy for the Highlands or allow Highland military units to use their own flag. But at a conference of Highland leaders in Pleiku on 15–17 October, he did promise that his government would recognize Highlanders' ownership of land, establish agricultural and rural development programs, improve communications and commerce for the Highlands, and provide better health care, education, career opportunities, and political representation for Highlanders.[59] Khanh, however, was scarcely in control of the South Vietnamese government apparatus, and that apparatus, facing not only violent Communist attacks but also revived Buddhist protests and a wave of labor unrest and strikes in some of the coastal cities, had only very limited control of South Vietnam.[60]

Communist Strategy and Personnel Changes in Late 1964

Even though the war seemed to be going its way during 1964, the leadership in Hanoi was not satisfied with the pace of progress. In the opinion of Le Duan and his clique, the Communist command apparatus in the South had not fully implemented the GO-GU strategy. It was indeed the case that many southern Communist leaders had been reluctant to switch from predominantly guerrilla operations to main force battles and were unwilling to give up locally recruited manpower to form main force units under COSVN's control. These were tough, determined men, and their resistance had been difficult to overcome. Although the July offensive represented a significant increase in the intensity of military operations, it had not delivered the knockout blow to the Saigon government that the Hanoi leadership was seeking.

To overcome this resistance and to more effectively implement its chosen strategy, the Politburo met 25–26 September and decided to send General Nguyen Chi Thanh south to take command of COSVN, replacing Nguyen Van Linh, who had headed that organization since its inception in 1961. Linh would remain in the South doing important work. But the Hanoi leadership seems to have considered that, as a Politburo member who had run the PAVN's General Political Department (which ensured ideological correctness and Party discipline in the army), Thanh would have a better chance of overcoming southern Communist leaders' opposition to Hanoi's strategy.[61]

"Also sent south at the same time were Major-General Tran Do, Major-General Le Trong Tran, Senior Colonel Hoang Cam and many other mid and high-level officers with experience in training and building regular forces and in commanding large battles." On 11 October 1964 the Central Military Party Committee and the high command ordered "a wave of military operations throughout all of South Vietnam aimed at: destroying a portion of the puppets' main force army in combination with inflicting widespread casualties in order to further stimulate the disintegration of the puppet forces . . . and at stepping up the political struggle in order to heighten the state of the enemy's political crisis." This was, of course, a reaffirmation of the GO-GU strategy launched in December 1963.[62]

Military Operations, October–December 1964

Even before the new Communist military leadership arrived in the South, the war was intensifying and things were looking even worse for the southern state. During the week of 3–10 October the level of Communist-initiated military activity, in excess of 700 incidents per week for the fourth successive week, reached a new high plateau of intensity. Some South Vietnamese government forces were buckling under the pressure. Senior American advisers rated a large part of them, including four infantry battalions, two Ranger battalions, and one Marine battalion, as combat ineffective.

By the standards of the country as a whole, the Central Highlands was relatively quiet in October. However, in the aftermath of the CIDG mutiny, the atmosphere remained tense, and there were rumors of a second revolt in early November. Communist activity was most serious in Pleiku, where, on 10 October, ten government-controlled villages near the CIDG camp of Plei Do Lim were simultaneously burned. In the northeast corner of the same province Communist forces ambushed an RF company on 20 October, killing three and wounding six.[63]

A radical shift in the balance of forces in the Central Highlands commenced with the 25th Division's move from II Corps to III Corps in early October. The transfer had been planned for several months, and the division had received a warning order on 8 April. The northern part of the Mekong Delta and the areas around Saigon had seen intense Communist military activity and were in serious need of reinforcement. In April 1964 II Corps had looked relatively well off in terms of troops and perhaps somewhat overinsured in some parts of the Central Highlands. When the move actually occurred, however (the new headquarters officially became operational at Cay Diep, west of Saigon on Highway 1 in Gia Dinh Province, on 8 October), the situation was bad everywhere for the anti-Communist side.

The 25th Division had operated largely in II Corps' coastal provinces. It left behind one of its three regiments, the 51st, which became an independent unit.[64] But its withdrawal left II Corps as a whole seriously weakened, and forces had to be pulled out of the Highlands to fill gaps in the more populated adjacent provinces. The 22d Division shifted its headquarters and some of its troops from Kontum to the coastal plain, and in November three ARVN battalions were withdrawn from Darlac. Also in that month, because "security forces [were] spread so thin in II CTZ," General Co was "assigned an economy of force mission" and "instructed to hold what he now controls." For the time being, major offensive operations by the ARVN anywhere in II Corps, including the Highlands, were off the table.[65]

A devastating mortar attack on the American air base at Bien Hoa, north of Saigon, on 1 November was a sort of prelude to the Communist high command's "Winter-Spring Offensive."[66] Commencing on 2 December, the offensive's first campaign was fought around the strongly anti-Communist, predominantly Catholic village of Binh Gia in the coastal province of Phuoc Tuy, due east of Saigon. COSVN concentrated the equivalent of a division's worth of main force troops around this village. The idea was to draw in and destroy the major government forces in the vicinity, gain control of this part of Phuoc Tuy, and thus connect base areas with the coast, allowing ease of supply from the sea. During a month of intense fighting, Communist forces inflicted crippling casualties on the 33d Ranger Battalion and the 4th Marine Battalion and destroyed substantial numbers of armored vehicles and helicopters. But casualties on the Communist side were also very heavy, and when the campaign ended on 3 January 1965, Binh Gia was in government hands. Many of the Communist main force troops retreated into War Zone D, northeast of Saigon, where they had been before mounting this campaign.[67]

The Binh Gia campaign was a major step in the Communist transition to high-intensity warfare, but it was fought at some distance from the Central Highlands and did not affect the situation there directly. The Communists were, however, simultaneously trying to take full advantage of II Corps' weakness. On 7 December MR 5 began a campaign in the An Lao district of western Binh Dinh Province; the district town of An Lao was some 96 km north of the coastal city of Qui Nhon. MR 5 targeted the area partly because the Saigon government's counterinsurgency effort there had been annoyingly successful, partly to get control of the rice-rich river valley, and partly to improve communications between its forces in Quang Ngai and Binh Dinh. MR 5 used the 2d Regiment and the 409th Sapper Battalion (both main force units normally based in Quang Ngai), as well as local troops.

The An Lao campaign, like that in Binh Gia, was very hard fought, with heavy losses on both sides; it too lasted about a month. After an impressive start, the Communists met stiff resistance as II Corps rushed elements of the ARVN 22d Division to the area. Communist forces were unable to take the district town, and by early January 1965 they had withdrawn their main force units from the district. But they had shattered the government Regional Forces and Popular Forces units that had hitherto controlled the area successfully. By January 1965 the ARVN was so dangerously overextended in II Corps that, in order to concentrate his remaining forces and avoid defeat in detail, General Co soon felt obliged to abandon the district.[68]

The Communists also stepped up offensive operations in the Highlands, where they mounted three substantial attacks (one of them perhaps in battalion strength) and four ambushes in the week of 5–12 December alone. Three of the ambushes were in Pleiku. The rapidly declining security of that province was becoming particularly worrisome to MACV. The situation in Darlac was little better. On 7 and 9 December Communist troops reportedly entered several villages, taking away both weapons and personnel. In the same week there were rumors of a Highland revolt centering on the Ban Me Thuot area. During Christmas week "122 weapons were lost to the VC from five hamlets" in the same province. MACV attributed the ARVN's ineffectiveness in responding to Communist military activity across South Vietnam at this time at least in part to the extreme political instability and to officers' consequent preoccupation with internal politics.[69]

The General Situation in Late 1964

There was no indication that the acute political disorder in South Vietnam since Diem's overthrow was getting any better by the end of 1964. Indeed, it seemed to be getting worse on a weekly basis. The military situation was also deteriorating fast. Although the Communists had achieved less success in the Central Highlands than in other parts of the country, most notably the Mekong Delta, the Saigon government's position was declining drastically in the Highlands too. The removal of 25th Division from II Corps in early October had adverse effects in that region. To make matters worse, powerful PAVN forces were on their way down the Ho Chi Minh Trail to the Central Highlands in the last months of 1964.[70] With II Corps down to just two divisions to hold the largest of the four tactical zones, there was a real risk that entire Highland provinces would fall under Communist control early in 1965.

9

An Escalating War, January–March 1965

The January Lull

Although the South Vietnamese state was under acute pressure by the beginning of 1965, it had not reached the point of collapse. The Communists were not yet achieving easy or overwhelming successes in major battles. The December campaigns in the Binh Gia area of Phuoc Tuy Province and the An Lao district of Binh Dinh Province had been very hard fought. In both campaigns South Vietnamese government forces had sustained serious losses. But by the end of the first week of 1965, Communist main force units had retreated from both areas, evidently having suffered very heavy casualties of their own. While Le Duan hailed the achievements of the Party's forces in the Binh Gia campaign,[1] neither that episode nor the An Lao fighting had ended in the sort of clear-cut, decisive victory he was so clearly seeking. Since the Gulf of Tonkin Resolutions there was, moreover, an increasing likelihood of much greater American involvement in the war. One historian has argued that by the end of 1964, Le Duan's GO-GU strategy was, if not already bankrupt, in very serious trouble.[2]

In January 1965, while the level of Communist guerrilla activity remained fairly high, there was a lull in offensive operations by main force units, some of which seemed to be trying to regroup, recuperate, and learn lessons from their recent battle experience. According to MACV, the ARVN mounted eight substantial offensive operations that month, all of which the Americans considered reasonably successful. In an operation of 28–29 January, for example, even the severely overstretched II Corps managed to recapture the heavily defended Phu Lac peninsula in Phu Yen Province, inflicting considerable casualties on Communist troops at a modest cost to its own. MACV's monthly evaluation went so far as to suggest that the southern republic's armed forces might be in the process of regaining the strategic initiative.[3] This was, however, far too sanguine, especially as far as II Corps was concerned. By the middle of January, indeed, II Corps' commander had realized that his tactical zone would soon be the focus of a powerful Communist onslaught..In order to avoid defeat in detail he would have to consolidate his overstretched forces, abandoning some areas in the process.[4]

PAVN Regiments Move to the Central Highlands, 1964–1965

As part of the escalation of the war intrinsic to the GO-GU quick victory strategy, a strategy reaffirmed by the Politburo in September 1964, the high command in Hanoi sent whole PAVN regiments down the Ho Chi Minh Trail in the last quarter of that year. The first to make the journey was probably the 320th (aka 32d) Regiment.[5]

According to an American study based on prisoner interrogations, the 334th Battalion, the first unit of the 320th Regiment to go down the Trail, left its home station sometime during early September 1964. It was followed almost immediately by the 635th Battalion and the regimental headquarters. The last element of the regiment to begin the journey was the 966th Battalion, which departed in late October. The 320th Regiment's "infiltration route began in Na Nam Province, North Vietnam, crossed the NVN-Laos border, continued through Laos and terminated in Kontum Province. . . . By the end of January 1965 all elements of the regiment had completed infiltration."[6]

We have little specific information about the 320th Regiment's trek down the Trail. But at this period of the war, PAVN troops seem to have entered the first circle of hell almost as soon as they crossed the Laotian border. The 320th was not a lucky regiment; its journey down the Truong Son mountain range would be just the beginning of a nightmare year of extreme privation, acute suffering, and appalling loss of life.

The 325th Division, the next formation to make the trip, traveled south between late November 1964 and February 1965. While still in the North, to confuse enemy intelligence, the division was "cloned." There would be two 325th Divisions: 325A and 325B. According to the division's history, "The first 325th Division (325A) would prepare to march off to fight on the battlefields of South Vietnam. This unit would have a light, compact table of organization. Its forces would consist of three infantry regiments (18A, 95A and 101A), division headquarters and a number of separate subordinate battalions and companies." The 325B Division, meanwhile, would remain in the North and continue the mission of force building and training, being prepared to move to the southern

battlefields whenever required. Enemy intelligence officers who picked up indications that this division had gone to South Vietnam would have to contend
with others who had credible evidence that it was still in the North.[7]

The General Staff had initially intended to send the 325A Division south
in September 1964, but its departure was delayed until late November, at least
partly out of fear that the Americans would detect the move and escalate their
intervention in the war. By mid-November the division commander knew
that his force would depart soon and that its destination was "the Central
Highlands of South Vietnam." But even in late November, when the move
was about to begin, the high command still considered it "a matter of strategic
importance" that it should not be detected and that political deniability should
be maintained. As part of the security and deception planning, Regiments
95A, 101A, and 18A were given cover names as Agricultural Worksites 10, 11,
and 12.

On 20 November 1964 the division held a ceremony for the 95A Regiment,
the first to depart. This regiment, together with an advance party of division
headquarters, went by truck to the "Commo-Liaison Station 1" at Lang Ho
before commencing the arduous journey down the Ho Chi Minh Trail on
foot. The division historians explained:

> Group 559 [the logistical organization that ran the Ho Chi Minh Trail] was
> not yet able to support a heavy concentration of troops. . . . For this reason
> the division sent only one battalion at a time. . . . In early December the units
> of Regiment 101A and the division headquarters began their march down the
> Trail. Finally, in early February 1965 the last elements of Regiment 18A were
> transported to Lang Ho to enter the commo-liaison trail network and begin
> their journey south.[8]

Although the division had originated in the South during the First Indochina War, by 1965, very few of its members had ties "to the land on the other
side of the Ben Hai River," south of the seventeenth parallel. Its historians
considered it a matter of pride that "the ranks of the division were filled almost
entirely by young soldiers from . . . North Vietnam—the generation born during the August revolution and which had grown up under socialism." These
men were intensely indoctrinated:

> Educated and honed by the Party, and having been steeped in the revolution-
> ary virtues of our army and in the glorious traditions of our division, they set
> out filled with a sacred spirit of hope that the South would soon be liberated
> and that the entire nation would soon be unified and would march forward
> together to build socialism.

In addition to their ideological soundness and rigorous training, their recent combat experience as part of the North Vietnamese intervention in the civil war in Laos gave the Hanoi leadership great confidence in the capacity of these troops.[9]

They would, however, need all their zeal and toughness to get through the next few months. The trek down the Truong Son was an extraordinary feat of endurance. The paths were slippery and dangerous and in some places nonexistent. "There were many sheer cliffs and steep slopes that had not been developed into an actual path. These took great strength to overcome." At many of the way stations along the Trail there was virtually nothing to eat. The division's history attributes the near starvation of its troops, at least in part, to the destruction of food caches by enemy "commandos."[10] William Westmoreland's memoirs confirm that MACV/SOG (a secret organization employing both American and indigenous personnel) was operating along the Trail by early 1965 and that it made efforts to destroy such supplies.[11] But it seems likely that most of the extreme privation suffered by troops going down the Trail in late 1964 and early 1965 was the result of inadequate quantities of rice being stockpiled in the first place or stocks being inexpertly stored so that they rotted or were consumed by the local fauna.

Indeed, the 325A Division commander's memoirs suggest that mildew and worms in the rice stocks were the main issues. "Towards the end of the journey when the soldiers attempted to scrub off the worm and the mildew the rice turned to powder. In these cases the regimental cooks mixed unscrubbed rice with all the mildew and worms, together with wild jungle vegetables, to make a smelly, mushy green soup."[12] Sometimes even this repellent mush was in short supply. For weeks at a time the troops had to try to live off the meager resources of the land:

> Roots and jungle vegetables . . . are not always easy to find and many times there was only enough to make gruel to feed our sick, while the soldiers had to go hungry.
>
> Every soldier had to carry an average load of 35 to 45 kilograms of weapons and equipment on his back. The longer the march the deeper this equipment dug into the shoulders of our troops. Without careful prior training and the honing of their will, it would be difficult for anyone to endure this effort.
>
> The jungles were wild, some still showing evidence that they had never been touched by human hands, and were filled with disease-bearing germs. Before our . . . units ever reached the battlefield many cadres [i.e., officers] and soldiers had already been struck down by disease.
>
> In many units marching down the trail the percentage of sick rose to two-thirds of the unit. There were not enough able-bodied men left to carry the

litters of the sick and support one another as they marched forward. More than a few soldiers died of acute attacks of fever.[13]

The march down the Ho Chi Minh Trail took the 95A Regiment, the first of the regiments of the 325A Division to make the journey, sixty-three days. Given that it started out on 20 November, it would have arrived in the Central Highlands on or about 22 January 1965.[14] The 325A Division as a whole completed its move to the South in March.[15] It is not clear where its various units were initially based, though northern Kontum was probably the principal concentration area. The division's history provides no numerical strengths for its regiments at the time of their arrival in the Highlands, but almost certainly they all suffered serious loss of life coming down the Trail and arrived exhausted and debilitated.

According to the memoirs of Nguyen Huu An, 325A's division commander (best known in the West as the senior North Vietnamese officer present during the battle for LZ X-Ray in the Ia Drang in mid-November 1965), he and his men were allowed a few days' rest and recuperation upon arrival. During these few days they received a reasonable amount of rice but: "As for other foods we had to find them for ourselves in the jungle. It was mostly bamboo shoots and potatoes and occasionally fish the soldiers caught in the streams."[16]

Further to confuse the other side's intelligence, each regiment was given a new number upon its arrival in the South: the 95th, 101st, and 18th Regiments became the 10th, 11th, and 12th, respectively.[17] These regiments, however, would never fight together as a division. Shortly after its arrival in the Central Highlands, the high command decided (evidently to An's considerable surprise and disappointment) to break his division up. The Central Highlands Front took control of his regiments. He and some of his officers, who might otherwise have been redundant, joined its staff.[18]

The Sustenance of PAVN Troops

Clearly, arrangements for the sustenance of the PAVN regiments arriving in the Central Highlands in early January were utterly inadequate by Western (and even by normal Vietnamese) standards. But given the extreme difficulty the Communist leadership had experienced in feeding quite modest forces in the Central Highlands earlier in the war, it might seem extraordinary that they thought they could maintain multiple PAVN regiments in that region in early 1965. Doubtless the Party's apparatus in the Highlands continued to put great pressure to provide food on the communities it controlled, but it was surely quite obvious that nothing like enough could be obtained that way.

In fact, the problem of supplying its troops in the Central Highlands had worried the Communist high command for years, and it had put great effort into finding a solution. Back in the summer of 1963, the Minister of Defense, General Vo Nguyen Giap, had picked Colonel Nguyen Duc Phuong, then chief of rear services for the 308th Division, to play the leading role in this. Given command of Working Group 763, formed in July 1963, Phuong was tasked to set up a supply base in northern Kontum, in the triborder area where Vietnam meets Laos and Cambodia. He was able to obtain some of the rice to be stockpiled at this base in Laos, but nowhere near enough. Laos was a poor country racked by civil war. Instead, "neutral" Cambodia, its government under Prince Sihanouk favorably disposed toward the Vietnamese Communists, became the main focus of the procurement effort.

A "large, heavy-set man with dark skin and a receding hair line," Phuong looked convincing as a capitalist entrepreneur, in the opinion of his superiors. Posing as such, he established a bogus trading company in Cambodia. Using North Vietnamese gold and foreign currency, he bribed the right people and was permitted not only to buy rice and medicines but also to build a road on which to truck them to the triborder area. For transportation he employed not only Vietnamese residents in Cambodia with their own trucks but also officers and men of the Cambodian army driving Cambodian military vehicles. Initially, perhaps, the North Vietnamese paid market price for their rice. Later they appear to have made compulsory purchases at fixed prices—"requisition purchase," as one Vietnamese history calls it.[19] By 1966, the Vietnamese Communists were reportedly using about a quarter of Cambodia's rice crop to feed their forces in South Vietnam.[20]

Despite all these efforts, in 1965 the provision of food and medicine for PAVN troops operating in the Central Highlands would prove desperately inadequate. They would suffer serious malnutrition and very high levels of sickness throughout that year's fighting.

II Corps during the January Lull

After the loss of the 25th Division in October 1964, the ARVN was thin on the ground in II Corps' area. Responsible for an exceptionally large territory constituting nearly 50 percent of South Vietnam's total land area, II Corps now had only two full divisions, the 22d and 23d, compared with three divisions each in III Corps' and IV Corps' much smaller tactical zones.

How much he knew about the movement of PAVN troops down the Ho Chi Minh Trail is unclear, but by the middle of the month, Brigadier General Nguyen Huu Co, II Corps' commander, had apparently realized that his area was likely to become the focus of a major Communist offensive after the Tet truce. Appreciating how overstretched his forces were, he began to consolidate them, sacrificing territory in the process. After the heavy fighting in that district in December, Co's troops had managed to fully reoccupy only the upper An Lao valley by the first week in January. But he decided to withdraw them again as part of a fairly comprehensive administrative and military reorganization in Binh Dinh Province, where he considered the threat to be particularly acute.

Redeployments were not confined to Binh Dinh. According to Colonel Theodore Mataxis, the senior American adviser to II Corps, Co not only anticipated that his area was about to be hit hard but also perceived that the Communists intended to implement a concept of operations similar to the one the Viet Minh had used back in 1954. Then they had largely isolated the Central Highlands by cutting the major roads running into the region from the coastal plain before mounting an offensive in which they took control of a large part of it, attacking and crippling the most mobile and combat-effective enemy forces there in the process.

Mataxis quotes Co as saying: "This is just like the Viet-Minh winter-spring campaign of 1954. They will strike in the plains of northern Binh Dinh to force us to rush our reserves over to the seacoast. Once this is done, they will then try to cut Highway 19 and isolate the highlands. This time we will be ready for them."[21] Co and his staff freed several infantry battalions from static security missions and turned them into mobile reserves. Helicopter landing zones and airstrips in the Highlands and along Highway 19 were surveyed, and ammunition, fuel, and other supplies were stocked in key areas. At the same time, the mobile reserves "were trained in the techniques of movement by helicopter and fixed wing transport, Caribous as well as C-123s."[22]

With the agreement of MACV, II Corps also opened two new CIDG camps on Highway 19, the road that connected the Highland town of Pleiku with the coastal town of Qui Nhon. One of the new camps was at Suoi Doi, near the Mang Yang Pass, and the other was at An Khe by the pass of the same name, near the eastern edge of the Highlands. Partly to free up Strike Force personnel to man them, four other CIDG camps at Dak To, Polei Krong, Bu Prang, and Ban Don were closed.[23] Given the buildup of Communist main force troops in northern Kontum, Dak To may have been considered too isolated and vulnerable. Polei Krong, as already noted, had been a very dysfunctional camp and had been overrun the previous July. It was, perhaps, still considered rather ineffective. Ban Don and Bu Prang were both in Rhade areas and garrisoned largely by Rhade troops. Ban Don had been actively involved in the CIDG mutiny of September 1964, and FULRO sentiment was still strong in its garrison.

Shifting Rhade troops away from the Rhade heartland did indeed have the ulterior motive of making another FULRO rebellion less feasible. Predictably, the order to move was badly received by the Ban Don Strike Force. Much influenced by FULRO ideology, these troops did not like the idea of being shifted from their home territory to be used as cannon fodder in a Vietnamese civil war. Those familiar with the grizzly saga of French Groupe Mobile 100 would have known that Highway 19 had been a bloody battleground in the First Indochina War, and they might well have anticipated that it would be so again. By the end of January, a total of 159 CIDG personnel had deserted, taking forty-seven weapons with them. Even those who remained and grudgingly accepted removal from Ban Don to Suoi Doi were clearly somewhat demoralized and of questionable reliability. Members of the Strike Force at An Khe, however, most of whom came from Bu Prang, a camp that had played no part in the FULRO mutiny, were still disciplined and loyal.[24]

Clearly, relations between Highlanders and the Saigon government remained tense. Trying to improve them was more important than ever. The Communists were about to make a determined effort to take complete control of much of the Central Highlands, and the South Vietnamese state needed the cooperation of its Highland troops. It definitely did not want Highlanders rallying to the Communist cause or participating in another FULRO-inspired CIDG mutiny. Apparently realizing how much was at stake, some of those on the anti-Communist side were trying to address Highlanders' grievances in a constructive manner.

Following the FULRO uprising, Rhade Popular Forces platoons charged with village defense in Darlac Province (apparently considering themselves inadequately armed, and unwilling to risk their lives for a government that did little for them) had surrendered a great many weapons to the Communists. In an effort to address this problem, the province chief devised a ceremony (perhaps similar to that used during the heyday of the Buon Enao experiment) "designed to increase the solidarity of the local forces and to strengthen the bonds between these forces and the local government." MACV reported: "Within the past 4 weeks, three such ceremonies were held in Lac Thien, Buon Ho and Ban Me Thuot Districts. In each case, the distinguished guests have included the II Corps CG [commanding general], SA [senior adviser] II Corps and CG 23d Division. A total of over 8,000 Montagnards have participated." In further efforts to achieve better relations with Highlanders, on 6 January 1965 local authorities in Pleiku began work on two projects: a trade school for Highlanders and the Pleiku Junior Military Academy for the children of Highlanders serving in the Republic of Vietnam's armed forces. The Junior Military Academy had been agreed upon in October negotiations between the Khanh government and Highland leaders, but the central government had not provided funds to build it. Brigadier General

Co, not previously known for his enlightened views on Highlanders and perhaps influenced by his senior American adviser, Ted Mataxis, decided to use money from II Corps' engineering budget. The project went ahead.[25]

Some such efforts may have borne fruit. According to an MACV report of early February: "In II CTZ the montagnard defenders of Darlac Province who earlier underwent the oath ceremony acquitted themselves well against [probes] initiated by the VC. In a two-week period there was only one weapon lost and none of the six montagnard hamlets attacked was entered by the VC. The VC have apparently shifted tactics and are harassing the Vietnamese land development centers instead of the montagnard hamlets."[26]

The Storm Breaks, February 1965

In 1965 Tet, the Vietnamese New Year, fell in the first week of February. Up to a point, both sides observed the traditional truce, and the level of violence dropped markedly. In the second week of February, however, the Communists renewed their winter-spring offensive with dramatic effect. The main focus of the Communist effort was MR 5, which included much of ARVN II Corps' tactical zone. "There," according to an American report, "large and . . . extremely well equipped VC units conducted a major campaign."[27]

In the Central Highlands that campaign commenced at "approximately 0200 hours on 7 February 1965 [when] the VC simultaneously attacked the II Corps US MACV Compound and the Camp Holloway airfield at Pleiku." Camp Holloway, the base of the US Army's 52d Aviation Battalion, and the MACV compound were approximately 6.5 km apart. The attacks lasted just ten to fifteen minutes. The casualties inflicted and the damage done in that short time (especially at the airfield) were a tribute to the thoroughness of Communist planning and the small assault teams' skill in carrying out their missions. The attack on the airfield was by far the more destructive, killing 7 Americans and wounding 104, destroying five aircraft completely, and damaging another seventeen. The assault on the MACV compound killed just one American and wounded another twenty-four, but it made the point that Americans were not safe even in a fortified area within a town that contained a corps headquarters.

The methods used were extremely simple. For the attack on the MACV compound in the town of Pleiku, a subsequent American inquiry determined that the Communists had employed the following:

A small force of 6 to 10 personnel armed with automatic weapons and small demolition charges with 4 to 5 second delay fuzes. The VC gained entry by penetrating the barbed wire perimeter fence and attacked the compound

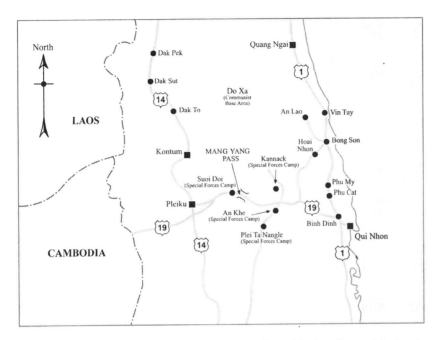

Key locations during Communist offensive operations in the Highlands, February–March 1965

building from close range with demolitions and small arms fire. US personnel at the compound responded immediately with small arms fire from the windows of the billeting area. This rapid response probably stopped the VC from entering the inner court of the compound thereby reducing the effectiveness of the VC attack.

The same American inquiry concluded that the attack on the 52d Aviation Battalion at Camp Holloway was:

A co-ordinated effort of two assault teams (5 to 6 men each) armed with small demolition charges and supported by 81mm mortars. The assault and fire support elements launched their attack simultaneously. Demolition teams entered the runway and aircraft parking ramp by two routes. One team entered along the runway from the northeast, gained access to the fixed wing parking area and placed demolition charges on the landing gear and under the fuselages of aircraft. The other team breached the barbed wire perimeter fence generally south of the airstrip in the vicinity of the helicopter parking ramp and placed demolition charges on the landing skids of the helicopters. The mortar attack was directed primarily at the troop billeting area [and this] pinned down US personnel in the billeting area until the attack ceased. . . . A Vietnamese guard post engaged the VC as they withdrew along the runway. This guard post was brought under fire by a VC covering force deployed in the vicinity of the northeast approach to the airfield.[28]

The official history of the PAVN credits these attacks to the 409th Sapper Battalion,[29] a unit formed on 20 May 1964 out of two preexisting sapper companies in a Communist base area in western Quang Ngai Province.[30] The history of MR 5 sapper troops indicates that the Camp Holloway attack was the work of the 409th Sapper Battalion's 30th Company, supported by a sapper platoon recruited in the town of Pleiku, a Gia Lai Province sapper cell, part of a mortar company from 2d Regiment (with four 82mm mortars), and a Gia Lai Province infantry company.[31] The 2d Regiment normally operated in Quang Ngai Province but had moved south to Binh Dinh for the winter-spring offensive.[32] Though some Highlanders undoubtedly participated in these attacks, the Communist planners evidently relied mainly on ethnic Vietnamese brought into the area from the coastal plain specifically for these missions, a pattern we have noted before.

The attacks in Pleiku were raids. Having hit, the attackers ran. ARVN II Corps' conventional ground troops could not move fast enough to intercept their retreat. But an "Eagle Flight," a fast-reaction force trained to operate from helicopters, put 140 ARVN troops into blocking positions on what were considered the most likely escape routes northeast of Pleiku. By 0930 some of these troops had clashed with "VC elements" and captured a notebook that apparently contained "a copy of a Viet Cong operations order for an attack on Camp Holloway."[33] It seems, however, that only a handful of the retreating Communist troops were intercepted. The bulk of them, having accomplished their mission, got clean away.

The MACV compound and Camp Holloway raids led to the opening of an American bombing campaign against the North code-named Flaming Dart.[34] But these initial Communist raids were mere pinpricks compared with what was happening elsewhere in II Corps. Communist attacks in Kontum, western Pleiku, and northern Binh Dinh were much more serious.[35] The February 1965 fighting in western Pleiku and northern Kontum is poorly documented in American sources. According to a Communist source, however, "on the night of 7 February the 407th Sapper Battalion and the 334th Battalion of the 320th Regiment attacked and captured a line of RF outposts west of Pleiku City." The same history mentions an attack on the Plei Mrong CIDG camp (west and slightly north of the town of Pleiku) but makes no claim that the camp fell into Communist hands.[36]

The 101st Regiment, which had come down the Trail as part of the 325A Division, also saw action immediately after Tet. Commanded by Nguyen Van Mot, with Vo Duy as his political commissar, this regiment overran the Dak

Giao military strongpoint in northern Kontum and attacked the base at Dak Pek. At this point, according to a Communist history, the 3d Battalion of the ARVN's 42d Regiment moved north to try to retake Dak Giao, but as it reached Dak Long, the PAVN 101st Regiment's 3rd Battalion ambushed it, inflicting heavy losses. The 101A Regiment next received orders to "exploit this tide of victory by destroying the strongpoint at Dak Long." Its success there caused the anti-Communist side to abandon a large number of other positions in northern Kontum. By the beginning of March, the South Vietnamese government had largely lost control of Kontum Province north of Dak To.[37]

The MACV report for the second week of February frankly admitted that in Binh Dinh, "the VC dealt the 40th Regiment and other units a series of serious defeats." It appeared that the Communists were "rapidly consolidating their power in An Lao, Hoai Nhon, Phu My and Hoai An districts," where government control was "limited to the immediate vicinity of the district towns." MACV's evaluation was that village-level counterinsurgency and the winning of "hearts and minds" was now practically suspended in Binh Dinh and jeopardized virtually throughout II Corps. As one report expressed it, "Until the military situation in Binh Dinh is brought under control, there will be no possibility of making any meaningful progress there in pacification. The II Corps as a whole is now conducting a holding operation."[38] In northern Binh Dinh, by mid-February the anti-Communist side held only enclaves around some of the district towns such as Bong Son and Phu My, and these had to be supplied by air. Always sensitive to the possibility of the country being cut in half, the southern republic's Joint General Staff considered northern Binh Dinh too important to be given up easily. It sent two reinforced Marine battalions with "a tactical command element from the brigade headquarters" (a substantial part of its vital strategic reserve) to Bong Son on 11 February.[39]

Known as Task Force Alpha, the Marine force based at Bong Son commenced a series of operations to relieve the pressure on that town and other government enclaves and to reopen Highway 1—operations that continued until June 1965. Task Force Alpha fought some hard actions with Communist forces in which it gave at least as good as it got. But it had only limited success in carrying out its missions.[40] MACV noted during the last week of February that while Highway 1 (the country's main north-south road) was precariously open throughout I Corps' tactical zone, it remained closed through most of II Corps'. In addition, Highway 19 was cut between Pleiku and the coastal city of Qui Nhon, while Highway 14 north of the town of Kontum had been repeatedly severed. In summary:

Pacification efforts in II CTZ continued to decline in the face of significant VC gains. ARVN remained very much on the defensive as intensified VC activities prohibited the assignment of troops to clearing and securing missions. An acute refugee problem has developed in Binh Dinh Province. Successful VC operations have driven nearly 56,000 people into 31 refugee centers . . . operating as of 25 February. The majority of these refugees came from An Lao and Hoai Nhon in the north and Binh Khe and An Tuc in the west.[41]

Mang Yang Pass and Highway 19,
Mid-February to Early March 1965

Some of the most intense (and some of the best documented) fighting in II Corps in the second half of February was for control of Highway 19, the road linking Pleiku with the coastal city of Qui Nhon. By this time, Colonel Theodore Mataxis had settled in at II Corps' headquarters in Pleiku. Having served in the Washington National Guard, he was commissioned into the army from the ROTC in 1940. He had fought in the final phase of the Second World War in northwestern Europe with the 276th Infantry Regiment and had won the Silver Star. Since the Second World War he had served in various capacities in Asian countries, including India. He had also fought in Korea, where he participated with the 17th Infantry Regiment in a number of notable actions, including the one at Pork Chop Hill. Having been with II Corps since September 1964, he had established a degree of trust with General Co and had considerable influence in directing the latter stages of the campaign on Highway 19.[42] In Mataxis's words:

> [The Communist conquest of northern Binh Dinh was] quickly followed by an operation in central Binh Dinh to cut Highway 19, the main supply route between the major port in the area (Qui Nhon) and the highlands. If successful this attack would have isolated the highland provinces of Kontum and Pleiku. Cut off from supplies by road they would have depended . . . on air for resupply. This would have further weakened morale and put the VC in an excellent position for a later offensive during the rainy season, against Kontum and Pleiku.[43]

At 1045 on the morning of 14 February, the understrength 144th RF Company was moving by truck convoy from Pleiku along Highway 19 to occupy positions in the Mang Yang Pass. Just west of the pass it ran into an ambush by a force initially estimated to be at least two companies. The 144th RF suffered thirty-two dead and eight wounded. A couple of armored cars that had been escorting the convoy were destroyed, four trucks damaged, and some weapons lost. Some of the survivors radioed for help, and a rescue operation involving

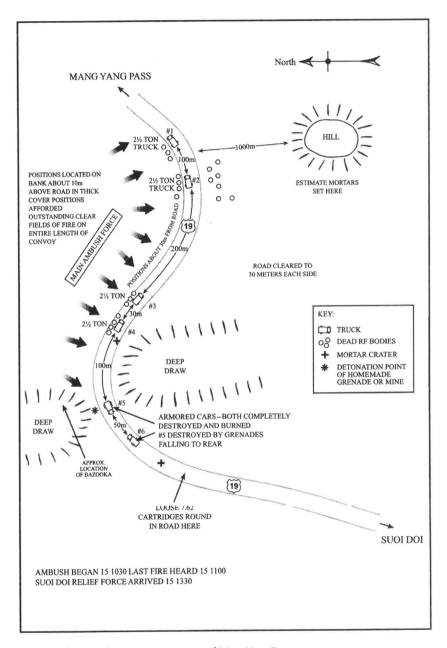

Ambush of Regional Forces company west of Mang Yang Pass

the 3d Battalion of the 42d Regiment, two CIDG platoons from Suoi Doi, and an RF platoon was hurriedly improvised with an L-19 spotter aircraft in support. The aircraft came under machine gun fire near the ambush site, but the ground troops in the rescue force made no contact with the ambushers.[44] Survivors of the ambush reported that their attackers were "armed with Chinese copies of the latest Soviet family of infantry weapons: SKS rifle, AK assault rifle, and RPD light machine gun as well as a copy of the new Soviet RPG-2 antitank rocket launcher."[45]

At the time, neither American nor South Vietnamese intelligence was able to identify this Communist force. From histories written in Hanoi since 1975, however, it seems certain that the 95A Regiment (aka 10th Regiment), which had come down the Trail as part of the 325A Division, was responsible. Under the leadership of regimental commander Nguyen Quang Cu and political commissar Than Ngoc Sang, 95A's task at this time was to sever Highway 19.[46] According to the regiment's own history: "The most exemplary battle in this initial [post-Tet 1965] wave of operations was the attack at Mang Giang. There the regiment's officers and enlisted men patiently waited in ambush positions for 19 days and nights and then fought courageously in a battle in which they destroyed a convoy of military vehicles and one enemy company."[47]

In the early months of 1965, American intelligence, confused by North Vietnamese deception, persistently and greatly underestimated the PAVN presence in the South.[48] The Americans serving in II Corps assumed that there was, at most, a single North Vietnamese battalion operating on Highway 19 in the second half of February, a belief evident in an article Mataxis published on the campaign a few months later. It now seems that this belief was inaccurate. The 95th Regiment's own history suggests that its entire force was operating in the area. American underestimation of PAVN strength appears to have led to some bad decision making during the Highway 19 campaign and to a number of unnecessary reverses for the anti-Communist side.

In reaction to the ambush of the 144th RF Company, II Corps ordered its forces to intensify their activity along the highway between the Mang Yang Pass and An Khe. At 1400 on 17 February, a convoy containing 143 CIDG troops, accompanied by 2 American and 2 Vietnamese Special Forces personnel and an interpreter, drove west from the camp at An Khe along Highway 19 and established two forward operating bases (FOBs) on the eastern side of the pass. FOB 1, the base nearer to the pass, was garrisoned with 69 CIDG troops and a Vietnamese Special Forces officer. FOB 2, a little farther east, was manned by 74 CIDG troops, 2 members of the American A-team, and an interpreter.

The first contact between these CIDG troops and the North Vietnamese in this sector occurred when a patrol from FOB 2 engaged "an estimated VC squad" with small arms shortly after midday on 18 February. There were no

casualties on either side, and patrols from both FOBs continued the following day without further contact. At 1600 on 20 February, however, FOB 1
reported receiving mortar fire from the west. After about fifteen minutes the
mortar fire lifted, and PAVN infantry attacked from the northwest and southwest simultaneously, overrunning the FOB, killing eight CIDG personnel,
wounding eleven, and scattering the others. The PAVN followed up by mor-
taring FOB 2 heavily at 1800 and making a series of probes during the night.
CIDG troops at FOB 2 resisted the probes, however, and Communist forces
delivered no real assault.

When Captain Em of the Vietnamese Special Forces and Captain Hendricks
of the US Special Forces, in command at the CIDG camp at An Khe, received
reports that FOBs 1 and 2 were under attack, they formed a task force to assist
their men at these sites. Commanded by Hendricks, Relief Force Alpha consisted of 100 CIDG troops, 3 members of the American Special Forces, and
2 of the South Vietnamese Special Forces. It left Camp An Khe in a seven-
vehicle convoy and moved along Highway 19 to the vicinity of FOB 2. At that
point, the force dismounted and continued on foot.

At approximately 2000 on 20 February, as Relief Force Alpha approached
FOB 1, the PAVN sprang an ambush. The Rhade troops reacted with an anti-
ambush assault that put the North Vietnamese to flight. Relief Force Alpha lost
two killed and nine wounded, "but when the VC withdrew, they left behind
9 bodies, 3 SKS carbines, 5 AK assault rifles and one RPG-2 rocket launcher.
All the VC bodies were dressed in light khaki uniforms with leather cartridge
belts" and were identified as North Vietnamese. Having defeated this ambush,
the CIDG troops "established a perimeter defense and awaited first light before
proceeding to FOB1."[49]

Upon arriving at FOB 1 on the morning of 21 February, Relief Force Alpha
discovered eight dead and eleven wounded CIDG Strike Force soldiers, as well
as four Communist dead from the previous day's fighting. Once he had collected most of the CIDG survivors of the assault on FOB 1, Captain Hendricks
radioed the camp at An Khe requesting that Captain Em form a second relief
force to assist in searching for about twenty soldiers who were still missing.

In response, Em and 120 CIDG troops (designated Relief Force Bravo) left
the camp at An Khe by convoy at 1400 on 21 February and relieved Hendricks
at FOB 1. Hendricks then returned to An Khe with the CIDG dead and
wounded and, apparently, all or most of Relief Force Alpha. At 1630 on 21
February, having completed his search for missing personnel around FOB 1,
Em's convoy set off back to An Khe, stopping to deposit a reinforcement of 70
CIDG troops at FOB 2. It is not clear whether any sort of garrison was left at
FOB 1, but probably not, as there is no further mention of it as a functioning
outpost.[50]

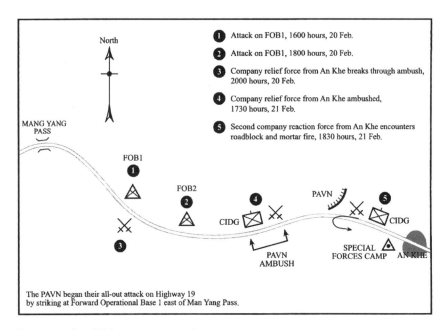

The PAVN began their all-out attack on Highway 19
by striking at Forward Operational Base 1 east of Man Yang Pass.

Operations along Highway 19, 20–21 February 1965

En route to An Khe at 1730 on 21 February, Captain Em's Relief Force
Bravo ran into an ambush involving about two companies of North Vietnamese. The ambushers opened fire from both sides of Highway 19 with "an unknown number of 81mm and 60mm mortars, automatic weapons, small arms
and hand grenades." The convoy was halted, its troops became somewhat dispersed, and communication with the camp at An Khe was lost. Three CIDG
Strike Force troops were killed, fourteen were wounded, and a Vietnamese
Special Forces officer, Lieutenant Ngan, was captured. But with the rest of his
men, the wounded Captain Em was able to establish a crude perimeter and
held out against occasional PAVN probes for the next two days.

By 1745 on 21 February, Captain Hendricks at An Khe was aware that Em's
force had been ambushed, possibly because a contact report had been sent
before the convoy's radios were put out of action. Hendricks organized Relief
Force Charlie, comprising seventy CIDG Strike Force troops, and headed for
the ambush site in a four-vehicle convoy. The North Vietnamese, however,
had anticipated this move and organized a force to block it. At 1839 Relief
Force Charlie started taking small-arms and mortar fire, and its lead truck was
disabled. Its troops dismounted and sought cover, but within five or six minutes about twenty mortar rounds fell among them. Three CIDG soldiers and
a civilian driver were killed and two soldiers wounded. Relief Force Charlie

got into the two vehicles that remained operable and drove back to An Khe, reaching camp at around 2030.[51]

On 21 February Lieutenant Colonel Lindsey W. Hale, commanding Special Forces Detachment C-2 at Pleiku, decided to send the Strike Force at Suoi Doi, already severely disaffected, to assist their comrades from An Khe. He gave an order to that effect to Captain Mireau, who commanded the US Special Forces A-detachment at Suoi Doi. Just before midnight on 21 February, Lieutenant Y-Lang, commanding 269th Company of the Camp Suoi Doi Strike Force, received orders to prepare his company for a five-day operation. Y-Lang was instructed to move east along Highway 19 through the Mang Yang Pass to the area where Relief Force Bravo had been ambushed. He was to collect survivors and take them to An Khe, clearing the road of enemy troops in the process.

At 1245 on 22 February Y-Lang's CIDG company from Suoi Doi, designated Relief Force Delta, left camp in a six-vehicle convoy carrying 3 American and 2 Vietnamese Special Forces personnel and 167 CIDG troops. It was escorted by armed helicopters, and arrangements had been made for an Eagle Flight, a 40-man CIDG heliborne reinforcement, should this prove necessary. Nevertheless, sending a single company from a demoralized force in soft-skinned vehicles down a stretch of highway where a substantial, well-equipped PAVN force was known to be operating appears, with the benefit of hindsight, a strange move. Admittedly, the troops from Suoi Doi were supposed to get some cooperation from the An Khe Strike Force as they approached the site where Em's convoy had been ambushed. But they never got that far.

Relief Force Delta dismounted as it approached the Mang Yang Pass and proceeded very cautiously on foot, returning to its vehicles only when it had cleared that defile. But at 1550, about halfway between the Mang Yang Pass and FOB 2, it was ambushed by North Vietnamese troops firing small arms, mortars, and rocket-propelled grenades from both sides of the road. The CIDG troops left their vehicles and sought cover. American advisers who reportedly tried to lead counterattacks quickly became casualties. Many of the CIDG soldiers soon expended all their ammunition (whether because of poor fire discipline or inadequate supplies is not clear) and then tried to surrender. It quickly became apparent, however, that the North Vietnamese were not taking prisoners. This caused the CIDG troops to rally to some degree. Using bayonets and knives (and presumably whatever ammunition they had left), 112 CIDG personnel managed to break out of the ambush and escape toward the Mang Yang Pass. The close-quarters fighting was extremely savage, and one CIDG soldier who survived the ambush suffered a North Vietnamese bite wound in his calf.

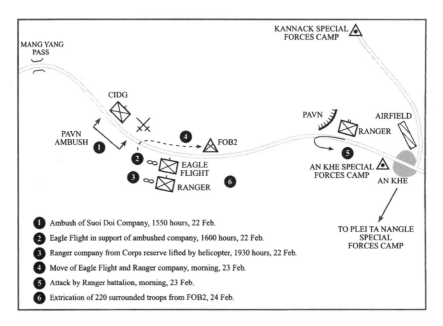

Operations along Highway 19, 22–24 February 1965

Lieutenant Griggs, a member of the American A-detachment with Relief Force Delta, had been badly wounded and left for dead by the PAVN, but he regained consciousness and, finding a radio concealed under the dead body of its operator, used it to direct the fire of the armed helicopters that had been escorting the convoy before asking to be picked up for medical treatment. As a helicopter descended to collect him, however, it received a number of hits, and the pilot was wounded in the right thigh. Abandoning the rescue attempt, the pilot diverted to Suoi Doi, where he made an emergency landing and had an engine fire extinguished. Another helicopter soon rescued both Griggs and Sergeant Long, another wounded survivor.[52]

By 1550 on 22 February, the American and Vietnamese Special Forces at Camp Suoi Doi, which had been monitoring the air-ground frequency, were aware that Relief Force Delta was under attack, and they alerted the Eagle Flight. At 1608 eight UH1B helicopters arrived at Suoi Doi and picked up forty CIDG soldiers, who were landed southwest of the ambush site at 1620. As they moved toward that site, however, they were hit by fire from armed helicopters that were meant to be supporting them, and one man was wounded. This had a demoralizing effect and, for the time being, halted their advance.

After dark, at 1930, thirteen UH1B helicopters brought sixty men of the 2d Company of the 22d Ranger Battalion from Pleiku to reinforce them. The

Rangers and the CIDG Eagle Flight proceeded together toward the ambush site, where they encountered some resistance and took casualties, including one Ranger killed. The Rangers thought they had killed four Communist troops but decided to proceed no further in darkness. The combined Ranger-CIDG force established a protective perimeter and waited for morning.

On the morning of 23 February the combined Ranger-CIDG force pushed on toward the ambush site, reaching it at 0700. They found the bodies of sixteen CIDG soldiers, three wounded CIDG personnel, and a dead American. The North Vietnamese had left behind a number of weapons and two unburied bodies of their own soldiers. Six badly burned civilian corpses lay beside a burnt-out civilian bus and motorcycle. But some wounded civilians still survived, as did a baby, apparently unharmed, clinging to the body of a dead woman. Helicopters removed the wounded and the baby at 0910.[53]

The combined Ranger-CIDG force proceeded east down Highway 19 and found survivors of Captain Em's Relief Force Bravo, which had been ambushed at 1700 on 21 February. Although the original intention had been to link up with the rest of the 22d Ranger Battalion as it advanced west from An Khe, that advance met stiff resistance, and any linkup was postponed. On 23 February the 2d Company of the 22d Rangers, the CIDG Eagle Flight, and the survivors of Relief Force Bravo took up defensive positions at FOB 2.

Just before midnight on 22 February, the bulk of the 22d Ranger Battalion, apparently on II Corps' instructions, had landed in Caribou transport aircraft at the An Khe airstrip. The battalion's mission was to advance west along Highway 19 on the morning of 23 February, clearing Communist forces from the road and linking up with the CIDG Eagle Flight and the men of its own 2d Company. But when the main body of the 22d Ranger Battalion set out from An Khe, it encountered stiff resistance near the point where Captain Hendricks's Relief Force Charlie had come under fire on 21 February.[54] The Rangers mounted a vigorous assault on this roadblock. But the North Vietnamese force confronting them was well dug in, with an all-around defense. The Rangers were unable to penetrate the position. During the course of the day, they lost 9 killed and 21 wounded, with another 12 missing. They claimed they killed 12 North Vietnamese in close combat and estimated the PAVN lost an additional 100 to 150 to air attack. By evening, however, the Rangers were very low on ammunition. At 1800, under the cover of strikes by A-1E aircraft, they broke contact and pulled back a short distance before taking up defensive positions for the night.[55]

On the afternoon of 23 February, the II Corps chief of staff, Colonel Nguyen Van Hieu, and the senior American adviser, Colonel Ted Mataxis, made a joint reconnaissance of the battle area on behalf of General Co. According to Mataxis:

They found that the VC troops were in battalion strength [were] well
equipped and had used conventional infantry tactics. . . . In addition, the VC
had been well trained in the techniques of anti-aircraft fire against helicopter
gunships. Those being fired at directly would seek cover, but those in the
flanks would continue firing at the choppers. [Co and Hieu had no doubt
about the presence of] large numbers of hard-core Viet Cong troops. After
learning this General Co, II Corps' commander, immediately called for reinforcements from units of the general reserve at Saigon.[56]

Control of operations along Highway 19, which had theoretically been in
the hands of II Corps (but in practice had been left to the Special Forces
C-detachment in Pleiku), was transferred to the headquarters of the 40th Infantry Regiment on the night of 23 February. At 1600 on 24 February the 22d
Ranger Battalion received an order to fall back on An Khe.[57]

Before conducting decisive operations to clear Communist troops from
Highway 19, Mataxis and Hieu apparently considered it crucial to extract the
mixed body of troops at FOB 2 (including the 2d Company of the 22d Ranger
Battalion and members of both the Suoi Doi and An Khe Strike Forces—some
220 personnel altogether). They were reportedly surrounded, and it was feared
that "if . . . not relieved they would soon be overrun." To solve this problem:

A plan was drawn up and approved by General Westmoreland for the first use
of jet aircraft in support of operations in Vietnam. The plan called for the use
of US jets on the flanks of the helicopters to provide suppressive fires by strafing and bombing while the helicopter gunships flew shotgun on the immediate flanks of the "slick" [i.e., troop-carrying] choppers. This scheme—trying
to match helicopters, F-100s and A-1E and B-57 bombers, all of different
speeds and characteristics, in a single integrated operation required careful
planning and split-second execution. Fortunately it went off like a charm.
Almost without incident 220 ARVN and CIDG troops were [removed] in
three lifts on the afternoon of 24 February. On the last lift the choppers began
meeting mortar fire and sporadic small-arms fire near the land zone, but fortunately only one chopper was hit and one man wounded.[58]

An account written by Mataxis and published just a few months later indicates that ARVN Airborne troops were arriving in the An Khe area while the
extraction from FOB 2 was in progress. In fact, there was apparently about a
week's hiatus in the struggle for Highway 19, with the 8th Airborne Battalion relieving the 22d Rangers only on 2 March.[59] No after-action report for
the 8th Airborne Battalion's operation on Highway 19 has come to light, but
according to Mataxis: "The airborne task force soon . . . launched an attack

against the VC battalion [*sic*] . . . and mauled it severely. It was estimated that the VC lost more than 200 in this engagement. They were punished so badly that they left many weapons and bodies on the battlefield."[60] The PAVN 95th Regiment's history acknowledges that this battle took place. Claiming that 95A inflicted heavy losses on the ARVN 8th Airborne, this Communist history does not mention the regiment's own casualties and neither confirms nor denies that the roadblock attacked by the 8th Airborne was broken up.[61]

The officers and men of the PAVN 95A Regiment, sent to close Highway 19, had fought with impressive determination and skill and sometimes with extraordinary savagery, refusing to take prisoners (possibly because they could not spare the resources to deal with them) and slaughtering civilians (presumably to make the point that the road was closed to all traffic, not just military convoys). The cost to South Vietnamese government forces had been considerable. In addition to the heavy losses, including more than thirty killed, inflicted on the RF company ambushed on 14 February, some thirty-two CIDG troops and one of their American advisers died, another fourteen CIDG personnel were missing, and seventy-six had been wounded. The 22d Ranger Battalion had twenty-two killed in action and about thirty wounded. If we presume that some of the missing were killed, then the anti-Communist side suffered about ninety fatalities along the stretch of Highway 19 from just west of the Mang Yang Pass to An Khe, in the second half of February 1965. This does not include whatever losses the 8th Airborne Battalion had in its subsequent operation.[62]

These statistics, moreover, somewhat underestimate the damage done to II Corps' strength. The CIDG force transferred from Ban Don to Suoi Doi, perceiving, not without reason, that it had been used as "cannon fodder," became so demoralized, angry, and mutinous that it had to be disbanded. Admittedly, it had been highly politicized and of dubious loyalty before being sent to Highway 19. But the Highway 19 campaign destroyed any chance of restoring its allegiance.

As a CIDG report put it: "Since this action these troops have been lethargical [*sic*], uncooperative and undisciplined, and on 10 March refused to participate in any future combat operations. The decision was therefore made to discharge these troops and turn Camp Suoi Doi over to 3rd Bn, 42nd Inf Regt. This was accomplished on 24 March 1965."[63]

II Corps' handling of the situation on Highway 19, at least initially, had not been particularly efficient. For several days it had allowed the whole campaign to be dealt with by the Special Forces C-detachment in Pleiku. Probably owing to a faulty appreciation of enemy strength, headquarters had sent CIDG troops (some of them already demoralized and disaffected) in penny packets against a significantly larger, exceptionally well-equipped and well-trained, highly motivated enemy force. On the positive side, II Corps had refused to give up on Highway 19 and had subjected the Communist force blocking it to unrelenting pressure. After its sixty-three-day nightmare on the Ho Chi Minh Trail, the PAVN 95A Regiment had experienced a tough first campaign in the South. We do not know its casualties, but they were likely heavy. On 8 March a large part of the same regiment would experience further severe trauma (and clear-cut defeat) in an action a little farther north.

The Attack on Camp Kannack, 8 March 1965

According to their official history, the US Special Forces opened Camp Kannack, "a CIDG camp located in Binh Dinh Province, II CTZ," in February 1964. In March 1965 it had four Strike Force companies with an approximate overall strength of 520, plus 7 Vietnamese Special Forces and the 9 Americans of Detachment A-231 of the 5th Special Force Group (Airborne) under Captain Wallace E. Viau. The Highlanders living around Camp Kannack were predominantly of the Rhe (Hre) ethnic group. According to a US Special Forces after-action report on the March attack, the ethnically mixed Strike Force consisted of a Vietnamese platoon of 29 soldiers recruited in the local area; the 241st Company, which consisted of 19 locally recruited Vietnamese and 128 local Rhe; the 242d Company, with 106 Bahnar recruited in Pleiku; the 243d Company, with 118 Rhade recruited in Darlac; and the 244th Company, consisting of 120 Muong, also recruited in Darlac.

The camp was on Provincial Route 508 about 20 km north of the town of An Khe and 20 km north of the nearest section of Highway 19.[64] According to an account in the postwar Vietnamese press:

> It lay on a vital road artery that ran into Route 19, the road that ran down to the vital coastal port city of Quy [sic] Nhon. . . . From their Kanak [sic] base the enemy constantly sent out sweep operations, constantly forcibly settled people into strategic hamlets and sent ambush teams to block the movement of our armed forces marching from eastern Gia Lai [a Communist administrative unit including Pleiku Province and some adjacent areas] down into Binh Dinh and from western Binh Dinh into western Phu Yen.
>
> Determined to overrun and destroy the Kanak base in order to expand our area of operations . . . between the mountain jungle zone and the lowlands . . . in early February 1965 the Military Region 5 forward headquarters and the Central Highlands Front, which was commanded by Comrade Giap Van Cuong, directed combat forces in the Kanak area consisting of the 10th Infantry Regiment [aka the 95A Regiment], the 409th Sapper Battalion and two Gia Lai Province local companies to make preparations to attack.[65]

Ultimately, the forces chosen to do the job were the 409th Sapper Battalion; the 95A Regiment, minus one battalion; two Gia Lai local force companies; and more than 100 civilian coolie laborers from Gia Lai and Binh Dinh Provinces. One source specifically mentions the 4th Battalion of the 10th (95A) Regiment as taking part. Elements of the 409th Sapper Battalion had played a crucial part in the 7 February attacks in Pleiku and at Camp Holloway. For the Kannack operation, battalion commander Nguyen Thanh Tan and political officer Ngo Trong Dai took personal charge of this unit.[66] We know neither the exact routes taken by the 409th Sapper Battalion, the 95A Regiment, or any of the other units nor where they assembled. We do know that the attack was launched principally from the east.

Camp Kannack's forces at the time of the attack consisted of one CIDG company located in an outlying position 1.5 km south of the main camp (a position the Communist forces apparently ignored); one company divided between two outpost positions that were much closer in, between the inner and outer wires, north and south of the main camp; three squad-sized security patrols operating outside the camp area; and two CIDG companies inside the main camp, with two platoons actually manning positions in the main camp while, presumably, the rest of these companies slept. One of the two companies inside the camp had returned from an operation on the afternoon of 7 March.

Camp Kannack was 550 meters long and from 50 to 80 meters wide. Its defensive layout, according to American sources, consisted of an outer concertina wire barrier; an inner protective wire system consisting of a double-apron fence and concertina; a four-foot-deep dry moat with punji stakes at the bottom; and claymore M-18A1 mines, trip flares, and punji stakes within the inner protective wire system. There were three 81mm and three 60mm mortars within the main camp and one 60mm mortar in each of the two close-in outpost positions (a total of three 81mm and five 60mm mortars). There were light machine gun positions on each corner of the main camp's defensive perimeter and the two main entrances into the camp, plus two in each of the close-in outpost positions. The inner camp defensive perimeter consisted of sixteen sandbagged automatic weapons bunkers with overhead cover and reinforced firing positions and a four-foot-high earth berm.[67]

One account from the Communist side indicates that the ground on which the base was located was between 15 and 30 meters higher than the surrounding area. The attacking forces had the sensation of being looked down on from commanding ground as they approached their objective. According to the most detailed account from the Communist side, officers involved in planning the attack, guided by local guerrillas, conducted numerous reconnaissance missions from mid-February to early March. The final plan called for the 409th

Sapper Battalion (330 troops) to mount a surprise attack supported by the fire
of its own mortars, recoilless rifle, and machine guns and by the more powerful weapons belonging to the 10th (95A) Regiment. If the initial assault by
the 409th failed, there would be a second-echelon attack by the 4th Battalion
of the 95A Regiment. Before finally settling on the plan, senior officers from
Military Region 5's forward headquarters, the Central Highlands Front, the
409th Battalion, and the 4th Battalion all conducted personal reconnaissance.[68]

A consensus has clearly developed among those who have studied the battle from the Communist side that some of this reconnaissance was carelessly
conducted and traces left behind that the enemy picked up. As a result, the
element of surprise was largely lost, and the base was heavily reinforced before
the attack started. There is, however, no confirmation of this in American
reports,[69] and it may be a myth used to explain the failure of an elite, ethnic
Vietnamese, Communist force to take a position defended largely by mere
Highlanders in American pay.

Communist accounts indicate that any remaining surprise was lost when, at
2330 on 7 March (Hanoi-PAVN time, which was 0030 on 8 March by Saigon-
US Army time), soldiers of the 409th Battalion's "40th Company's Attack
Spearhead 1, led by Platoon Commander Vinh did not properly carry out mine
defuzing procedures" as they were approaching the northern outpost. They
triggered a flare. Within minutes the defenders were bringing down heavy fire
from mortars and M-79 grenade launchers.[70] Again, no confirmation can be
found in American accounts.

Reports by US Special Forces indicate that the first they knew of the presence of Communist troops was a heavy mortar and recoilless rifle bombardment falling within their perimeter at 0145 on 8 March. Initially stunned by the
bombardment, the CIDG troops soon recovered their wits, left their sleeping
accommodation, and manned fighting positions. Fortunately for the defenders,
the initial bombardment did not put the camp's radios out of action. Communications with the B-detachment at An Khe were established immediately and
were never lost while the battle lasted. The US A-detachment at Kannack requested an aircraft to drop flares, and this arrived at 0400.[71] Before then, Kannack's defenders apparently sent up plenty of flares of their own, and ARVN
artillery in the area fired illumination rounds, for at least one Communist veteran recalled that the sky was brilliantly lit for most of the battle. That level of
illumination would have greatly increased Communist casualties.[72]

Having cut the outer wire on the eastern side of the camp, Communist
forces breached the inner wire using "chicom [Chinese Communist] and
home-made Bangalore torpedoes" and charged into the camp. The northern outpost was overrun quickly, but the defenders were able to hold part of
the southern outpost and bring to bear the fire of sixteen mortars, nineteen

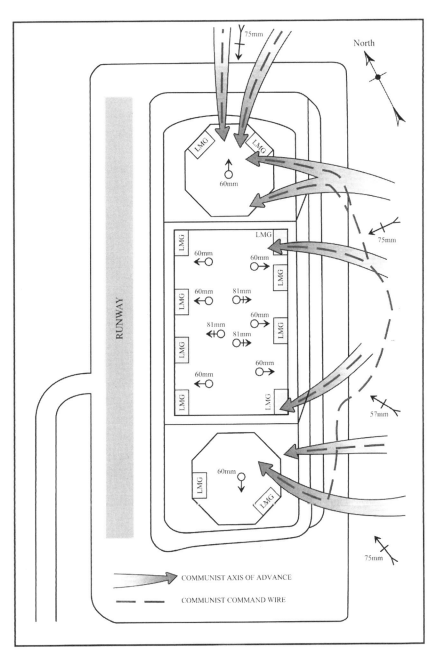

Defense of Camp Kannack, 8 March 1965

machine guns, and one recoilless rifle, establishing fire superiority from an early stage in the action. The formal American after-action report suggests that all elements in the garrison, including the Vietnamese Special Forces (with whom Americans in other camps often had issues), performed well. It is indicative of the fury of the fighting that, in the main body of the compound, twenty-one Communist soldiers' corpses were later counted around a single machine gun post and twenty-nine around another. By first light, the defenders had the upper hand and were driving their attackers out of the inner defenses of the camp and the northern outpost. "After day break, A1E fighter bombers strafed and bombed the withdrawing VC while the CIDG with USSF advisors counterattacked the southern outpost forceing [*sic*] the VC to withdraw."

There were thirty-four killed and thirty-two wounded among CIDG Strike Force personnel. Three US Special Forces personnel were wounded, and three of their dependents (perhaps indigenous girlfriends or members of girlfriends' families) were killed. One member of the Vietnamese Special Forces was also wounded. The American A-detachment reported: "The VC sustained a body-count of 129 killed within the periphery of the camp and suspected loss of over 100 killed and wounded during airstrike. A total of 74 individual and crew served weapons were captured from the VC during the attack."[73]

Strangely, the air strikes are not mentioned in Communist accounts, perhaps because they did not happen until the battle was practically over and did not do as much damage as the Americans thought. The most detailed Communist accounts, however, strongly emphasize that, virtually throughout the action, their troops were subjected to converging and quite devastating mortar and artillery fire, apparently from nearby South Vietnamese government posts.[74] This is not mentioned in American Special Forces' reports, perhaps because they did not want to share the credit for a CIDG victory with the South Vietnamese.

Communist accounts attribute some of the blame for the attack's ultimate failure and heavy casualties to a breakdown of their command and control arrangements when the initial assault got stuck: second-echelon forces from the 4th Battalion of the 95A Regiment did not go in rapidly enough to maintain the momentum. Making matters worse for the sappers in the first echelon, they were hard hit by "friendly fire" from mortars and recoilless rifles meant to be supporting them.[75] In the final analysis, in the absence of the sort of fifth column inside the camp that had been available at Polei Krong in July 1964, Kannack was just too tough a nut to crack for the Communist forces sent against it.

The Kannack battle was a morale-lifting success for the anti-Communist side at a key moment. Coming in the immediate aftermath of the fighting along Highway 19, during which some Strike Force personnel had proved less than enthusiastic and during which some had mutinied, Kannack also put Special Forces and CIDG in a vastly better light. US Special Forces carefully photographed the Communist dead and both photographed and minutely documented the impressive amount of Communist weaponry, including machine guns, mortars, and recoilless rifles of modern design and recent manufacture, left behind when the battle was over.[76] They also went into public relations mode—trumpeting the victory to higher headquarters and preparing a lecture with slides for interested audiences.

It is usually appropriate for historians to be skeptical of claims of enemy casualties in battle reports. In the case of the Camp Kannack battle, however, American estimates seem not to have been exaggerated. Older Communist official histories do not even admit defeat at Kannack. Recent accounts are far franker. In an article entitled "The Attack on the Ka Nak Outpost . . . Heroic Saga in the Vast Jungle," published on 24 July 2009, the *Gia Lai* newspaper admits, "By the time the battle ended almost 200 of our soldiers had heroically sacrificed their lives."[77] This figure more or less equals American estimates in the battle's immediate aftermath, but it may still be too low—possibly much too low.

The history of Military Region 5's sapper troops indicates, "By the time the attack was over, the entire [409th] battalion had little over 100 officers and men left" out of some 330 at the start of the battle; it is clear that casualties in the 95A Regiment were also severe.[78] According to a newspaper article published on 1 August 2008 reporting the establishment of a Communist war memorial at Kannack, while it was "still not possible to obtain the precise number of martyrs who were killed in the attack," surviving officers estimated the number at around 400.[79] If that figure is accurate, it probably means that more Communist main force troops lost their lives in the attack on Kannack than at either LZ X-Ray or LZ Albany—the far more famous battles, involving US 1st Cavalry Division troops, in the Ia Drang valley the following November.

At some point after the fighting at Kannack (the regimental history is not precise), the 95A Regiment was sent south to what the South Vietnamese government called Phu Bon Province but the Communists regarded as part of Darlac. There it would cooperate with the 18A Regiment as part of the monsoon offensive in the Highlands.[80] The 95A Regiment's withdrawal was probably crucial to the success of a road clearance operation that elements of the ARVN 22d Division conducted from 14 to 21 March and, at least for a while, allowed Highway 19 to be reopened.[81]

II Corps Fails to Recover Northern Kontum, March 1965

Though the clear-cut defensive victory at Camp Kannack was a morale lifter for II Corps, in general the news was more depressing. By the end of February, the Communists had essentially seized control of both northern Binh Dinh and northern Kontum, leaving only small enclaves in those areas held by Saigon government forces. Task Force Alpha, the force of South Vietnamese Marines airlifted to Bong Son to expand that enclave and open Highway 1, had fought bravely and inflicted some serious casualties on Communist forces but had little effect on the general situation in northern Binh Dinh.[82]

Starting on 26 March, II Corps attempted to strengthen the government's military position in northern Kontum with an operation called Quyet Thang 109, in which it employed elements of the ARVN 40th and 42d Regiments and the 21st Ranger Battalion. Communist histories acknowledge a hard, back-and-forth struggle in which their strongest force in the area, the 101A (aka the 11th) Regiment, was put under great pressure. The men of 101A were fighting half-starved, existing on 250 grams of food per man per day. Communist histories nevertheless claim that, in ferocious fighting on 29–30 March, elements of the 101A Regiment not only defeated the 21st Ranger Battalion's attempt to retake Dak Long but practically destroyed that Ranger unit. No corroboration has been found in American or South Vietnamese sources for this claim.[83] Yet it does appear that Communist forces remained in control of most of northern Kontum at the end of March and that II Corps had no certainty that it could hold any part of that province in the long run. Indeed, back in early March that headquarters had started to develop contingency plans to abandon Kontum as a whole.[84]

The General Situation at the End of March 1965

A small number of US Marines had landed at Da Nang, and American bombing of the North was already in progress. Yet there is limited evidence that these things were having any effect on the general situation in South Vietnam. The southern republic seemed no nearer to finding any kind of post-Diem political stability. Indeed, in that respect, things seemed worse than ever. Though much of the fighting was fierce, and the Communists were not winning all the battles, MACV's assessment, by the end of February, was that the strategic initiative in South Vietnam as a whole was firmly in Communist hands. That month, the number of operations mounted by South Vietnamese government troops had declined, but their "personnel and weapon losses [had reached] a new monthly high for the war."[85] In March there was another relative lull in offensive activity by Communist main force units, but there was no indication that government forces were regaining the initiative.

Highlanders on the Communist side preparing spike traps. (Getty Images)

Highlanders on the Communist side aiming crossbows—in an obviously posed photo. (Getty Images)

The village of Buon Enao, late 1961. (US Army Center of Military History)

Another view of Buon Enao, March 1962. (US Army Center of Military History)

Y-Ju, Buon Enao's village chief, with Dave Nuttle. (Courtesy of David Nuttle)

Nuttle with Captain Phu of Diem's Presidential Survey Office. (Courtesy of David Nuttle)

Fortifying a village in the Buon Enao complex. (Vietnam Archive, Texas Tech University)

A Highland Village Defender in the CIDG program, 1963. (US Army Center of Military History)

Strike Force troops in training, 1963. (US Army Center of Military History)

US Special Forces medics in a Highland village, 1963. (US Army Center of Military History)

A Strike Force soldier and Highland civilians on the porch of a Highland hut. (Eddie Adams/AP/Press Association Images)

Strike Force soldiers and civilians in a Highland village. (Eddie Adams/AP/Press Association Images)

A US Special Forces sergeant briefing a Highland Strike Force, 1964. (US Army Center of Military History)

A Strike Force patrol crossing a crude bridge, 1964. (Larry Burrows/The LIFE *Picture Collection/Getty Images)*

A massive truck convoy on Highway 19 during the monsoon season, 1965. (Eddie Adams/AP/ Press Association Images)

South Vietnamese troops advancing to relieve Duc Co, August 1965. (Rick Merron/AP/Press Association Images)

The triangular Plei Me CIDG–Special Forces camp seen from the air. (US Army Center of Military History)

*Major Norman Schwarzkopf marching with ARVN airborne troops after the relief of Duc Co.
(Bettmann/CORBIS)*

A US Special Forces soldier with Highland troops in a mortar pit at Plei Me. (Eddie Adams/ AP/Press Association Images)

Captain Harold Moore ordering a radio operator to call for an air strike during the siege of Plei Me, October 1965. (Eddie Adams/AP/Press Association Images)

An air strike as seen by the defenders during the siege of Plei Me. (TopFoto)

South Vietnamese Airborne Rangers defending Plei Me. (TopFoto)

US 1st Cavalry Division soldiers in action at LZ X-Ray, November 1965. (US Army Center of Military History)

Second Lieutenant Rick Rescorla at LZ X-Ray. Originally from Cornwall in the United Kingdom, Rescorla died in the Twin Towers on 11 September 2001 and performed heroically during that disaster as well as at Ia Drang. (Peter Arnett/AP/Press Association Images)

Lieutenant Colonel Harold Moore with a dead North Vietnamese soldier immediately after the fighting at LZ X-Ray. (US Army Center of Military History)

American wounded at LZ Albany. (TopFoto)

American corpses being removed after the fight at LZ Albany. (US Army Center of Military History)

General William Westmoreland. (US Army Center of Military History)

Major General Harry Kinnard, commander of the US 1st Cavalry Division. (US Army Center of Military History)

10

The Monsoon Offensive,
April–August 1965

The Politico-Strategic Picture in Early April 1965

As we saw at the end of the last chapter, at the end of February 1965 the situation in South Vietnam looked extremely worrying from an official American perspective. Yet the Vietnamese Communists also had cause for concern. Despite continuing political turmoil and weak leadership in Saigon and a serious loss of control in the countryside, the South Vietnamese state had still not collapsed by the beginning of April. The performance of the southern republic's armed forces in late 1964 and early 1965 had been mixed. There had been some debacles, but in general, from the start of the winter-spring offensive, Communist main force units had encountered serious resistance and experienced arduous and bloody fighting.

The Binh Gia campaign of December 1964 to January 1965, which the Communist leadership in Hanoi hailed as a signal victory,[1] was, as previously noted, a very hard fought, rather inconclusive affair with punishing losses on both sides. Much the same could be said of the An Lao campaign in the II Corps area.[2] There had been important Communist successes in battalion-sized actions in northern Binh Dinh in February 1965.[3] But recently arrived, exceptionally well-equipped PAVN units committed to battle in the Central Highlands in the same month, though able to capture small government posts and execute ambushes against RF troops, had so far failed to win really dramatic victories over the ARVN. Indeed, by 8 March, in western Binh Dinh on the eastern edge of the Central Highlands, one such unit, the 95A Regiment, had suffered in quick succession a protracted battering on Highway 19 and a clear-cut defeat at Camp Kannack.[4] Meanwhile, the involvement of US armed forces in the war was gradually but, from a Communist point of view, ominously increasing.

After the discovery of a 100-ton North Vietnamese trawler carrying arms for Communist forces in Vung Ro Bay in February 1965, the US Navy and Coast Guard greatly increased their patrolling of the South Vietnamese coast in an operation that became known as "Market Time."[5] After two brief Flaming Dart air campaigns earlier in the year, in response to attacks on US personnel, the Americans commenced a more sustained bombing of the North, code-named Operation Rolling Thunder, on 2 March 1965.[6] Most worrying from a Vietnamese Communist viewpoint, in response to requests from General William Westmoreland, the Johnson administration had started to send mainstream American ground troops, not just advisers or Special Forces. Two battalions of US Marines had landed near Da Nang on 8 March.[7]

Admittedly, this force was not large enough to make much of a real difference to the military balance, and the role of American ground troops in Vietnam remained undecided. Some American planners intended them merely to defend enclaves that contained American facilities and thereby release South Vietnamese forces for mobile operations. Others, such as Westmoreland himself, wanted them to assume a more aggressive role.[8] No one in America's political and military leadership had, at this stage, any definite idea how many troops were likely to be sent to Vietnam or when. Inevitably, Vietnamese Communist leaders were also in the dark on those issues.

Nevertheless, if Le Duan's "go for broke" strategy was already in great difficulty by the end of 1964, as at least one historian has argued,[9] it was facing even more acute challenges in the spring of 1965. The southern state's armed forces were not disintegrating as fast as the Hanoi leadership had hoped. Substantial parts of them were still fighting back with a fair degree of determination. Hopes for a true mass uprising against the Saigon government, in urban as well as rural areas, were proving chimerical.[10] Getting large PAVN forces into South Vietnam without the appearance of a blatant invasion was turning out to be a slow and extremely difficult process. Conditions on the Ho Chi Minh Trail—the covered path down the Truong Son mountain range by which North Vietnamese troops could reach the Central Highlands unobserved— were positively nightmarish for big units.[11] Although no one knew when or in what quantity American ground troops would reinforce the South, there was certainly a possibility—perhaps even a likelihood—that they would do so soon enough and on a sufficient scale to prevent a final Communist victory in 1965.

Despite all this, there is little evidence that Le Duan's position or policies were seriously challenged in Hanoi that spring. The initial popular response in the North to American strategic bombing and the growing American ground force commitment to the South was a patriotic rallying behind the war effort, a short-lived war fever during which considerable numbers of people volunteered for military service. At the Vietnamese Communist Party's Eleventh

Plenum in March, the leadership expressed its intent to respond to growing American military involvement by stepping up its offensive efforts in the South. Letters between Le Duan in Hanoi and General Thanh at COSVN at this time indicate that both parties intended to match any American buildup and were still hoping that big-unit offensive action would bring a speedy victory.[12]

This response to the events of November 1964 to March 1965 was not necessarily irrational. Counterbalancing the negatives, there were some legitimate grounds for optimism in the Communist camp. There was some reason to believe that, with some additional hard blows, the southern state might disintegrate before the Americans reinforced it too strongly. The Americans themselves were worried that the South Vietnamese armed forces were taking losses faster than these could be replaced and that their morale was brittle.[13] While the Communists had not, for the most part, been winning the larger military clashes as decisively as they had hoped, the concern expressed by some southern Communist commanders—that emphasizing the creation of big units and fighting major battles might weaken the Party at the local level—had not, so far and for the most part, proved justified. The Communist big-unit offensive had already caused, and was continuing to cause, South Vietnamese government forces to concentrate and consolidate in order to avoid defeat in detail. In the process, they had already, over large rural areas, abandoned efforts at village-level counterinsurgency.

Across great swaths of the countryside, therefore, the South Vietnamese government's authority had collapsed or was on the brink of collapse. Systems of defended villages had already been or were in the process of being ripped apart by Communist forces, sometimes with the aid of their residents. In some areas, much of the peasantry seemed increasingly convinced that the Communists were going to win. Recruitment for the Party's armed forces became fairly easy. A considerable amount of this recruitment was voluntary (always the best sort), but in areas where they became the effective government, the Communists could, in effect, conscript people too. Given the paucity of enlistment in and the high levels of desertion from the Saigon government's armed forces, the manpower balance was shifting quite substantially in the Communists' favor.[14]

When combined with the factors considered above, perhaps the best hope for a swift Communist victory was the extreme political instability in Saigon. Weak, constantly changing governments were tending to enfeeble the ARVN by the frequent reshuffling of command appointments and distracting its officers from their war tasks by presenting them with opportunities for internal power plays. It was reasonable to doubt that such feeble governments could manage an increasingly high-intensity war for much longer without a catastrophic breakdown. This is not the place for a detailed analysis of Saigon politics. But given that, in the spring of 1965, instability at the top was having a detrimental effect on the southern republic's armed forces throughout the country, the topic cannot be wholly ignored.

From late January 1964, when he mounted a successful military coup, General Nguyen Khanh became the most important figure in Saigon politics. But given his different roles in governments whose composition was constantly shifting, he never attained the authority Diem had enjoyed at the peak of his fortunes. Not a natural politician, Khanh had initially tried to adopt a populist style, but he ultimately came across as inconsistent and indecisive. One of Khanh's problems was a revived militant Buddhist movement led by Tri Quang, whom some alleged to be a Communist agent. Although Khanh's policy fluctuated, it was generally one of appeasing political Buddhism, a policy with which some generals and nationalist politicians strongly disagreed. Khanh had uneasy relations with both some of the older generals who had helped engineer the coup against Diem and a younger group known as the Young Turks, which included Air Marshal Nguyen Cao Ky and Lieutenant General Nguyen Van Thieu.

In late September 1964 Khanh and some senior officers in his junta, under considerable pressure from the Americans to restore civilian rule, had appointed a group of mainly older nationalist politicians as a High National Council (HNC). The HNC selected Phan Khac Suu, an elderly but reasonably well-respected politician, as president and head of state. Suu selected Tran Van Huong, a veteran conservative nationalist politician, as prime minister. Huong wanted to strengthen the war effort against the Communists and take a tough stand against militant political Buddhism.

In December 1964 Khanh and the Young Turks prevailed on Huong to pass a law forcing ARVN officers with more than twenty-five years service to retire. The real purpose was to get rid of generals such as "Big" Minh and Tran Van Don, who had planned the coup against Diem and now spent much of their time planning fresh coups, thus tending to destabilize the state. Huong sent this measure to Suu for presidential approval. Suu sent it to the HNC, whose members were themselves mostly men of the older generation, and they turned it down. At this point, Khanh and the Young Turks decided to get rid of the HNC. They mounted a coup on 19 December 1964 to accomplish this and to arrest Minh, Don, and their associates. The coup threw Maxwell Taylor, the US ambassador, into a violent temper. He summoned members of Khanh's junta to the embassy and denounced their action in extremely blunt terms. This gave the impression that the United States was trying to dictate South Vietnam's internal affairs and caused a crisis in the relationship between Taylor and Khanh.[15]

In December 1964 there was some evidence that Huong's tough, conservative civilian government was raising the morale of anti-Communist nationalists and even stimulating recruitment to the armed forces. In late January 1965, however, new measures introduced by Huong to put the country on a more effective war footing triggered a protest movement organized mainly by political Buddhists and by militant student groups whose members feared being conscripted into the armed forces. One of the worst incidents occurred in the city of Hue, where militant Buddhist demonstrators attacked the US Information Service's library, burning 8,000 books.[16]

On 27 January 1965 Khanh organized another military coup and bloodlessly removed Huong (though not Suu), replacing him with Nguyen Xuan Oanh, a civilian economist. Oanh lasted in that post only until 16 February, when Khanh replaced him with Dr. Phan Huy Quat. By this time, however, Khanh's days as kingmaker were numbered. He had made too many enemies. After some complicated politico-military maneuvers, he was obliged to leave the country on 25 February, ostensibly to become a "roving ambassador." After his departure he quickly lost any remaining political influence. He would never regain power.

Phan Huy Quat was intelligent and cultured. A qualified physician, he had held ministerial posts in the French-sponsored State of Vietnam and had briefly been acting prime minister before Diem. He may well have been an honest politician, committed to the service of his country, as William Westmoreland evidently believed. But his premiership (February–June 1965) was not a success in terms of managing the southern republic's war effort. His government tended to appease the militant Buddhists by releasing political prisoners who sought to undermine the state and, under Buddhist influence, engaged in another round of political purges of the armed forces. The purges removed some officers who were dedicated anti-Communists and competent military professionals. With the strain of war intensifying, an acute sense of crisis continued throughout Quat's time in office.[17]

It was against this background that, in mid-March, President Lyndon Johnson sent General Harold K. Johnson, the US Army Chief of Staff, on a whirlwind trip to Vietnam. Upon his return, General Johnson reported to the president, on 15 March, that four US divisions would be required just to hold the line of the seventeenth parallel across both Laos and South Vietnam. This was necessary to prevent additional Communist troops and supplies from getting into South Vietnam by overland routes. Securing victory in this war would take half a million US troops and five years—a scale and duration of commitment the president was not ready to contemplate. Yet, when American intelligence realized, toward the end of March, that elements of the PAVN 101A Regiment (and perhaps many more North Vietnamese troops) had been operating in South Vietnam for weeks, analysts concluded that the Communist leadership intended to precipitate the fall of the southern state in 1965. That gave urgency to the commitment of American ground troops to combat.[18]

II Corps' Spring Respite, Mid-March to Late May 1965

A serious weakness of the Communist military effort from November 1964 through October 1965 was that bouts of intense offensive action in particular regions of the country, which pushed the southern republic's forces in those regions to the breaking point, were followed by longish lulls that allowed them some opportunity to recover. The Communists seemed unable to sustain sufficient offensive effort in any one major region for long enough to get their opponents' forces there to collapse completely.

For II Corps, for example, after the An Lao campaign in December, much of January had been relatively quiet.[19] Then, after Tet, February had been frantic—indeed, desperate—with defeats in northern Binh Dinh and smaller-scale, but still serious, reverses in northern Kontum, leaving those areas largely under Communist control. II Corps was in so much trouble in February that substantial elements of South Vietnam's strategic reserve were committed to its area of operations. Marine Task Force Alpha went to northern Binh Dinh, and an Airborne task force was sent to open Highway 19. But after the Highway 19–Camp Kannack fighting ended on 8 March with the Communist defeat in the attack on the CIDG camp, the crisis in II Corps subsided.[20] Except for a few days in late March, when there was a flurry of fairly intense but apparently not very decisive fighting in Kontum,[21] the pressure was off until mid-May. II Corps was allowed a couple of months' breathing space.[22]

Indeed, as the CIA noted, Communist offensive efforts with main force units slackened significantly across South Vietnam during March and April 1965. The reasons for this hiatus were not entirely clear to the Agency at the time (although its analysts were prepared to make educated guesses),[23] and they remain largely a matter of speculation for historians today. It seems probable, however, that some Communist main force units had fought themselves into a state of depletion and exhaustion and desperately needed rest, reorganization, and the induction and training of new personnel before they could renew their efforts. It also seems highly likely that there were logistical problems in some parts of the country. Communist sources claim that Group 559, which ran the Ho Chi Minh Trail, had delivered 700 tons of weapons to the Central Highlands by the spring of 1965. But despite requisition-purchase in Cambodia, the long-standing problem of food supply for Communist forces in this region had still not been solved.[24]

According to Colonel Ted Mataxis, the senior American adviser at II Corps, General Co, the corps commander, and his staff were not complacent about the March–May lull. They realized that "large-scale infiltration was continuing, the enemy moving battalions initially into Kontum Province and then continuing the move to the south and southeast into Pleiku and Phu Bon

Provinces." It was obvious that Communist forces "were increasing their build up for an offensive which it was estimated would begin during the bad weather of the summer monsoon."

The weather could have a huge impact on military operations in Vietnam, especially in the Central Highlands:

> When the southwest monsoon began during the latter part of May . . . the weather worsened as the warm moist winds blowing from the Gulf of Siam brought the rainy season to the highland plateau of Central Vietnam. Low clouds and fog in the morning combined with tropical thunderstorms in the afternoon not only hampered the use of high performance Air Force planes, but Army aircraft as well. At times during severe tropical storms, which lasted from two to three days, even helicopter flight was limited. This problem of bad weather was particularly critical in the highlands. On the coastal plains thunderstorms could be flown around with relative ease. In the hills and mountains of the central highlands low cloud cover and rainstorms obscuring the peaks of the higher hills and mountains could frequently cause a mission to be aborted or planes to fly so low that enemy ground fire [became an extreme hazard].[25]

Good flying weather was defined as a cloud ceiling of 1,000 feet or more, with visibility extending to two and a half miles. During the spring, favorable weather was the rule, with an average of twenty-five good days per month. In the summer monsoon in Pleiku Province, the average was only six days per month. Bad weather did not totally eliminate the anti-Communist side's air support, but it forced pilots to fly in difficult and dangerous conditions and made airpower far less effective. It certainly made sense for the Communists to intensify their efforts in the Central Highlands in the rainy season—a pattern fairly well established in previous years. The monsoon months of 1965, however, would be the most dramatic of the war so far.

The Early Stages of the Monsoon Offensive, May–June 1965

Communist offensive operations in the Central Highlands from May to August 1965 bear some signs of a campaign planned and coordinated for the region as a whole. But if so, it remains uncertain who planned it and how it was coordinated. The Central Highlands Front had existed since 1 May 1964, commanded in May and June by Colonel Nguyen Chanh with Colonel Doan Khue as his senior political officer.[26] But it is not certain whether, at the start of the 1965 monsoon season, that organization was the principal headquarters giving orders to the major military units in the region. It is also unclear whether, during the summer of 1965, the CHF was taking orders from COSVN, from MR 5, directly from Hanoi, or from some combination of them. We do know that in July General Chu Huy Man assumed command of the CHF, replacing Chanh. Highly regarded in Hanoi, Man may have been appointed to give the CHF greater authority. In October 1965 he would have two PAVN regiments (the 320th/32d and the 33d) directly under his command, and in November (with the 66th arriving in the Highlands) he would gain a third.[27] Command arrangements for the May–August period are, however, far less clear.

Whichever headquarters directed them, and whatever the chain of command, in the second half of May 1965 the Vietnamese Communists launched a series of attacks apparently designed to take control of outlying areas of the Central Highlands—places that were distant from the main towns. They began with the "harassment of road traffic by raids on major lines of communication including Highways 1, 7, 14, 19 and 21." There was a particular effort to make communications between the Central Highlands and the coastal plain as precarious as possible. Internal communications within the provinces of Kontum, Pleiku, Phu Bon, and Darlac were also attacked. Communist troops destroyed bridges and dug ditches across major roads. The Central Highlands was increasingly cut off from the coastal plain, and the provincial capitals in the Highlands were progressively cut off from one another.

According to Mataxis: "The VC next extended their attacks to secondary roads leading from the provincial capitals in an effort to isolate the subordinate district towns. It wasn't long before all administrative centers in the outlying district towns and Special Forces outposts were also completely isolated from provincial capitals." Soon, all supplies coming into the Highlands from the coastal plain, and even supplies moving between towns within the Highlands, depended on airlifts. If the only issue had been keeping military forces supplied, the problem would have been more manageable, but it was also necessary to feed the civilian populations of the towns:

> This was important because the corps commander wore two hats: one as corps commander, the other as government delegate. While wearing his second hat he became the senior Vietnamese government official in II Corps and as such was charged with supplying . . . foodstuffs in the highlands. . . . Fortunately USAID joined with MACV to help provide the air shipment of foodstuffs and critical supplies to civilians in isolated highland towns. Here a factor stressed in so many histories of beleaguered garrisons again proved valid: the close relationship of the morale of civilians in a surrounded town and that of its military garrison.[28]

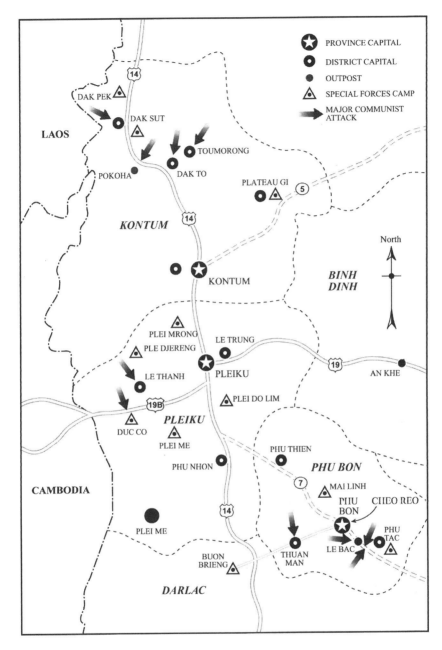

Monsoon offensive in the Highlands, 1965

Communist attacks on lines of communication were accompanied by a renewed campaign of terror, including assassinations of government officials and raids against Vietnamese land development centers and Highland villages friendly to the government side. These attacks were designed to "seize control of the rural populace, which the VC could then use not only as porters to move their ammunition and supplies, but also as fillers to replace their battle losses." The wave of assassinations "so terrorised the people that normal sources of government intelligence dried up. In addition, many refugees . . . soon flooded the provincial and district towns where they became an additional drain on the already scanty rice supply in marketplaces."

The next stage in the Communist effort to take over the region was "to unleash their newly infiltrated PAVN regiments in a series of attacks on . . . isolated district towns, outposts and Special Forces camps." In conjunction with these attacks, the Communists laid large-scale ambushes to destroy ARVN mobile reaction forces on relief missions. It was obviously their intention to take control of entire districts—district towns and headquarters and all—within the provinces of Kontum, Pleiku, and Phu Bon.[29]

The first series of major attacks began on 26 May along Highway 7, in a district called Phu Tuc in southeastern Phu Bon Province. It started when Communist forces, possibly from the PAVN 18A Regiment or 95A Regiment, both of which were operating along Highway 7 at this time, attacked the village of Buon Mroc (aka Ama Hrok), driving out the local Popular Forces (PF) troops. When the Phu Tuc district chief heard of this attack he sent one of his Regional Forces (RF) companies to help the PF platoon regain the village. As the RF company reached Buon Mroc, it came under heavy fire and radioed for reinforcements. A CIDG Strike Force patrol from the nearby Phu Tuc Special Forces camp went to assist, but the combined RF-CIDG force made no progress. The CIDG patrol called for reinforcements, but the reinforcing Strike Force troops were ambushed and fell back to their camp. The Communists had effectively severed the road from Phu Tuc to Buon Mroc. The RF commander again used his radio to call district headquarters for help. This time, he indicated that the confidence of his troops had been so badly shaken that he could not get them to move.[30]

Requests for help from the CIDG camp commander and the district commander were relayed through Phu Bon's province chief, Lieutenant Colonel Dong, to the headquarters of the 24th Special Tactical Zone (24 STZ) at Kontum and from there to II Corps at Pleiku. Aircraft were sent to attack the ambush site, while II Corps' Eagle Flight—a highly trained, thirty-six man airmobile platoon consisting of Highland troops led by an American Special Forces captain and three American Special Forces noncommissioned officers—went by helicopter to support the troops cut off near Buon Mroc. At about the same time, someone at II Corps headquarters (possibly Mataxis or Hieu) developed a plan: the reinforced company near Buon Mroc would attack toward Phu Tuc, supported by air strikes, and the CIDG troops at Phu Tuc, supported by mortars, would attack toward the Communist ambush position blocking the road.

The plan worked. In the face of the air strikes and the converging ground attacks, the Communist troops abandoned their roadblock. As one of Hanoi's official histories admits, Communist troops "were unable to destroy the enemy relief units as they moved up Route 7." The converging CIDG and RF troops linked up near the site where the CIDG troops had been ambushed and then fell back to Phu Tuc, where they took up defensive positions. The incident is noteworthy because the RF and CIDG troops, admittedly with substantial air support, ultimately defeated a major PAVN ambush.[31]

With perhaps two PAVN regiments operating in Phu Bon Province, however, the security situation there continued to deteriorate rapidly. Reports of sightings of battalion- and company-sized Communist units poured in from all points of the compass. Road traffic was paralyzed, and the provincial capital at Cheo Reo was cut off from the district towns. To stem the deterioration of morale in the province, General Co sent a battalion of the ARVN's 40th Regiment from Kontum to Cheo Reo by air.[32]

The next step in the Communist monsoon offensive in the Central Highlands consisted of two simultaneous but widely separated blows. In northern Kontum and southern Phu Bon Provinces, Communist forces struck key bridges on the roads between provincial capitals and outlying district towns. At 2300 hours on 28 May, the defenders of the key bridge at Pokoha in Kontum reported that it was under attack by a battalion-strength force. Postwar Communist accounts indicate that this was the work of elements of Regiment 101A, the most powerful military force the Communists had in Kontum at the time. 24 STZ and II Corps headquarters lost contact with the Pokoha garrison at this point and assumed it had been overrun.

Half an hour later, II Corps' tactical operations center received a report from the Phu Bon province chief that a Communist force was attacking the RF unit holding the bridge at Le Bac on Highway 7, between Cheo Reo and Phu Tuc. The RF troops there soon reported that while they had been pinned down by recoilless rifle, mortar, and machine gun fire, a Communist demolition party had blown up and partially destroyed the bridge. It is difficult to identify positively the Communist unit involved in the Le Bac bridge action. It may have been an element of the PAVN 18A or 95A Regiment, both of which appear to have been operating in the general area at this time.[33]

The loss of these bridges was serious. Losing the one at Pokoha cut Highway 14 between the provincial capital and government garrisons in northwestern

Kontum Province, including the Dak Pek Special Forces camp, the district town of Dak Sut, and the Dak Sut Special Forces training camp. These posts were "added to the growing list" of those that had to be supplied by air. The damage to the bridge at Le Bac on Highway 7, together with other Communist military activity in that area, isolated the district garrison and Special Forces camp at Phu Tuc in southeastern Phu Bon Province from the provincial capital at Cheo Reo. Government troops in the Phu Tuc area also became dependent on air supply.

Pressing their advantage, Communist forces in the Phu Tuc district began to probe defended villages and other outlying military posts. The district chief sent another plea for reinforcements to Lieutenant Colonel Dong, the province chief at Cheo Reo, indicating that he was surrounded and that the morale of his RF and PF troops had fallen to a dangerously low level. In response, on 31 May Dong sent a battalion of the 40th Regiment, which had arrived in Cheo Reo from Kontum a few days earlier, to Phu Tuc by air. From Phu Tuc, this ARVN battalion pushed north toward Buon Mroc and started to clear Communist forces from that area.[34]

The Le Thanh Campaign, 31 May–2 June 1965

The next Communist offensive developed in western Pleiku. On 1 June Lieutenant Colonel Vo Van Ba, the Pleiku province chief, was scheduled to pay a visit, accompanied by both provincial and national government officials, to the Le Thanh district headquarters and the surrounding land development centers. The people living in these land development centers were ethnic Vietnamese migrants to the Highlands. They were trusted by the Saigon government and important to it in terms of expanding its political control in the region and developing the region's economy. The Pleiku sector military headquarters (which controlled military forces under the province chief's command) had organized a convoy to escort Ba and his party, protected by sufficient RF troops to deal with the guerrillas who normally operated in the area. Early that morning it drove west from the town of Pleiku on a 63-km trip to Le Thanh.

Shortly after the convoy's departure, the Pleiku sector headquarters got no response from the Le Thanh district headquarters during a routine morning radio check. Concerned, personnel at the headquarters dispatched a reconnaissance aircraft. The aircraft's crew could not make radio contact with Le Thanh either, and as they flew over the district headquarters, they found it and the surrounding buildings in ruins.[35]

The devastation was the result of a joint attack by a battalion of the PAVN 32d/320th Regiment and the 925th Sapper Battalion on the night of 31 May–1

June. The 32d/320th Regiment had been based in western Pleiku since December 1964. The 925th Sapper Battalion had been formed in early 1965 from the 407th Battalion, which had been operating in the Highlands since 1961 but had been reduced to only about 100 men, and the 545th Company, which had arrived in the region in late 1964. It was controlled directly by the CHF, which presumably directed the Le Thanh campaign. Small but well equipped, the 925th had a total of 240 personnel, four 81mm mortars, four 60mm mortars, four 57mm recoilless rifles, and four medium machine guns, as well as light machine guns, shoulder-fired rocket launchers, AK 47 and SKS rifles, flare guns, satchel charges, wire cutters, and both field telephones and radios.[36]

The crew of the reconnaissance aircraft radioed news of the disaster at Le Thanh to Pleiku. The Pleiku sector headquarters tried to relay the information to the province chief's convoy but could not get a message through in time to prevent it from running into an ambush mounted by elements of the 32d/320th Regiment. The RF troops defending the convoy did not panic. They fought back with determination, buying time for air strikes to be called in against the ambushers. The air strikes were remarkably accurate, inflicting heavy losses on the Communist troops. With the ambushers' fire temporarily suppressed, the province chief and some of the other survivors turned their vehicles around and headed back to Pleiku.

On hearing news of the ambush, II Corps dispatched its heliborne reaction force. The Eagle Flight landed on the road at the ambush site, where its personnel rescued some of the wounded survivors. At about the same time, another reaction force headed west by road from the town of Pleiku to link up with the portion of the convoy that had escaped the ambush and was now heading back east, toward the provincial capital. Linkup was accomplished,[37] but it occurred at a pass where elements of the PAVN 32d/320th Regiment had prepared another large ambush.[38] According to Mataxis: "Soon 57mm recoilless rifle fire and rocket launcher fire from enemy positions in the hills left the trucks burning and the survivors scattered."[39] The helicopter gunships of the US 52d Aviation Battalion (based at Camp Holloway) attempted to help the survivors by suppressing the fire of the Communist ambushers, but the helicopters took heavy fire, and two were shot down. A Hanoi official history claims 300 RF troops and an entire inspection team from the Saigon Ministry of the Interior were killed and Pleiku's deputy province chief, Major Le Van Cu, captured.

Though Communist histories are prone to exaggerate their military successes, it is clear that this was a nasty defeat for the South Vietnamese government. It would have crowned the Communist victory if they had been able to kill or capture the province chief. But Ba managed to escape this second ambush by running uphill from the road into the jungle. He was missing for a few days before being found by CIDG Strike Force troops from Duc Co, after which he returned to Pleiku and resumed his duties.[40]

Meanwhile, survivors of the first ambush whom the Eagle Flight had rescued reported that their attackers were "regular PAVN forces armed with Chinese copies of the new Soviet family of 7.62 weapons." The presence of PAVN troops in western Pleiku in early June came as a surprise to II Corps headquarters, even though elements of the 32d/320th Regiment had been in the Central Highlands since late 1964 and the regiment had conducted a number of small operations in western Pleiku in February. Now that the presence of a PAVN regiment in this area was finally recognized, however, an Airborne task force was immediately dispatched. Mataxis provides no details as to the composition of this force and no information as to where it came from, but its mission was to retake Le Thanh and rally the RF and PF troops that the PAVN assault had scattered and driven into the jungle. If there were any PAVN troops still in the town of Le Thanh when the ARVN paratroops arrived, they refused combat. The Airborne force quickly reoccupied the wrecked district headquarters, and the RF and PF troops, most of them still in possession of their personal weapons, came out of the jungle to join them.[41]

Ambush on Highway 7 in Phu Bon, 3 June 1965

The scene of the most intense action then shifted to southern Phu Bon Province, where a battalion of the ARVN's 40th Regiment was operating in the vicinity of Buon Mroc. On 3 June the battalion mounted an operation along Highway 7 northwest of Buon Mroc to clear the road to the bridge at Le Bac and thus restore land communications with the provincial capital. Halfway to the bridge, the battalion was caught in a very big ambush, apparently involving a large part of the PAVN 18A (aka 12th) Regiment, which stretched several kilometers along the road. The ARVN battalion suffered serious losses and fled. The survivors regrouped at Phu Tuc and were flown from there to the provincial capital at Cheo Reo, where they manned some of that town's defenses.

Mataxis frankly admits that this disastrous action broke the back of resistance by South Vietnamese government forces in the Phu Tuc district of Phu Bon. Almost the whole district fell under Communist control. The district chief and the government's remaining forces there concentrated on holding the CIDG camp, the airfield, and some positions within the district town. Even air supply became difficult as Communist forces tightened their hold on Phu Tuc, establishing positions near the airfield from which they could fire on supply planes as they landed and took off.[42]

A Change of Government and a
New II Corps Commander, June 1965

After some very heavy and bloody fighting in many parts of the country and, in particular, some significant defeats for the ARVN in the Dong Xoai and Ba Gia campaigns, there was a crisis in Saigon in mid-June. Dr. Quat, the prime minister, wanted to remove some ministers, but President Suu opposed this. The disagreement paralyzed the government. After an angry meeting of political and military leaders in Saigon on 9 June, Quat tendered his resignation.

At this point, there was a bloodless military takeover. Air Marshal Nguyen Cao Ky and General Nguyen Van Thieu, leaders of the Young Turks in the officer corps, emerged as the new strongmen. Ky became the premier, and Thieu the head of state. Ky, who sometimes came across as conceited, narcissistic, impetuous, and politically immature, appeared to be the main leader at this stage. But the less flamboyant Thieu arguably gave greater ballast to the administration. In the long run, Thieu would edge Ky out. Some degree of political stability was restored to Saigon in the second half of 1965, though it was not clear that this would be the case when Ky and Thieu first came to power.[43]

In the short term, the change of government produced more military upheaval. General Co went to Saigon to become chief of the Joint General Staff. He was replaced at II Corps by Brigadier General Nguyen Phuoc Vinh Loc (soon to be promoted to major general). Vinh Loc was a controversial, larger-than-life figure. A member of the old imperial family and a cousin of Bao Dai, he was a wealthy man who tended to live a princely lifestyle. He sometimes gave the impression of being an old-fashioned warlord rather than a modern general. He fancied himself something of an intellectual and, over the years, had published a number of books, all printed at his own expense. One of these was a polemic about FULRO—a denunciation of the movement for Highland autonomy. He generally seemed lacking in the sympathetic understanding of Highlanders' grievances that was so important in a II Corps commander.

Vinh Loc's air of imperial grandeur and his condescending attitude toward Highlanders generally did not play well with the Americans. Westmoreland greatly distrusted him and tried, without initial success, to get the Saigon government to remove him.[44] Vinh Loc lost his command only after what was generally deemed a poor performance in the Tet Offensive of 1968. Within the ARVN officer corps, at least up to that point, his reputation was not a bad one, although he was rumored to be overly fond of the bottle.[45] In 1965 Vinh Loc was lucky to have some dependable people to help him. Colonel Nguyen Van Hieu, the chief of staff;[46] Major Hung, the assistant chief of staff; and Colonel Mataxis, the senior American adviser, provided continuity at II Corps. Control of major operations in the Highlands was, moreover, sometimes delegated to the 24th Special Tactical Zone, the headquarters, normally based in the town of Kontum, that had been established to take responsibility for military operations in Kontum, Pleiku, and Phu Bon Provinces when, in March 1965, the 22d Division moved its headquarters from Kontum to Qui Nhon on the coast.

ARVN Strategy, June–August 1965

Mataxis reports that soon after Vinh Loc took command at II Corps, probably in late June:

> A meeting was held at II Corps headquarters in Pleiku by representatives of General William C. Westmoreland's staff headed by Brigadier General William DePuy, then J-3, and the ARVN Joint Chiefs of the General Staff headed by General Nguyen Huu Co, former II Corps commander who had been appointed head of the ARVN military forces. It was agreed that due to the increased build-up of enemy troops II Corps during the rainy season would adopt an essentially defensive posture in the highlands. The new II Corps commander, Major General Vinh Loc, in line with the defensive posture taken by his corps analysed the military worth of all key outposts and district towns.

Vinh Loc decided to hang on to a large number of outlying positions, fortifying them and making arrangements for their reinforcement. Apparently, he reasoned that it was preferable for the Communists to expend their effort and resources trying to take outlying posts rather than immediately focusing their attention on vital places. As Mataxis put it:

> He decided that [some] posts in exposed positions would be held as long as possible in order to cause the highest casualties to the attacking Communist forces. If after an attack it was determined that it would be to our military disadvantage to reinforce at that time, due to lack of troops or air support, the [troops in the] posts would [be] ordered to withdraw, using escape and evasion tactics if necessary. [But posts] earmarked as keys to the defense of vital areas within each province were to be held at all costs. Contingency plans were drawn up and ARVN general reserve troops and [US and South Vietnamese] Air Force airlift and fighter planes were earmarked as the nucleus of a "fire brigade" which could be rushed to critical areas in the highlands. It was hoped that our superior mobility would allow the rapid concentration of

troops by air from all over the corps area and then to return these troops to their normal defensive assignments before the VC were able to react.[47]

Some positions, however, were abandoned almost immediately. The old Le Thanh district headquarters, which had been destroyed by the PAVN but recently repossessed by an Airborne task force, was now considered untenable. A new district headquarters was established somewhat closer to Pleiku. At the same time, II Corps decided to hold the Duc Co Special Forces camp (in the same general area) because of its strategic position blocking the approach along Highway 19 from the Cambodian border to Pleiku. Some of the RF troops formerly stationed in the old Le Thanh district were ordered to reinforce the Duc Co camp, while the rest were withdrawn to Pleiku for reorganization and retraining. The Airborne task force at Le Thanh was ordered back into mobile reserve at Pleiku, where it would be ready to respond to the next Communist attack.[48]

Toumorong, 24–25 June 1965

The next major Communist move was against the isolated district town of Toumorong, in the mountains of northern Kontum. On the night of 24–25 June elements of the PAVN 101A Regiment mounted a well-planned attack that quickly overran the town and scattered the RF troops defending it. The weather was extremely bad, which made aerial reconnaissance difficult. As the provincial headquarters tried to get accurate information about what had happened at Toumorong, the RF survivors drifted into Dak To district and nearby Tan Canh, the main base of the ARVN 42d Regiment. Meanwhile, civilian refugees from the area indicated that PAVN forces, possibly two battalions strong, were positioned along the road between Dak To and Toumorong, waiting to ambush the expected relief column.

Since this was one of the districts designated only marginally important, Vinh Loc and his staff decided not to launch a reaction force. He considered it more important "to conserve his troops to meet the next enemy attack under more favourable conditions of weather and terrain where he could utilize his helicopter mobility and superior firepower to better advantage." But "troops were maneuvered as if they were going to attempt a relief operation. This ruse was designed to cause the PAVN troops to stay in their ambush positions along the road. Heavy air strikes were then scheduled not only against the abandoned district town and the platoon of 105s [artillery pieces] that had been overrun, but also against the reported PAVN ambush sites along the road from Dak To to Toumorong."[49]

The Thuan Man Campaign, 27 June–2 July 1965

At the same time, the position of South Vietnamese government forces in western Phu Bon was deteriorating rapidly. The PAVN 95A Regiment was increasing the pressure on the district town of Thuan Man.[50] The outposts of RF troops defending the town were completely cut off from the provincial capital at Cheo Reo. In late June, Thuan Man's district chief reported to the province chief that his men were running out of food and ammunition, and if they were not relieved soon, the town would fall. Lacking troops to relieve them, the province chief again called on 24 STZ for assistance. Because all its troops were tied up in Kontum and Pleiku, 24 STZ passed the request on to II Corps.[51]

With the benefit of hindsight, this was clearly a Communist "lure and ambush" type of operation. The screw was being tightened on Thuan Man to lure in high-quality ARVN reserve forces that could then be destroyed in a major ambush. The strategic idea behind this plan was that the progressive destruction of its elite forces would demoralize the ARVN, rob it of its strategic reserves, and ultimately cause its collapse.

To deal with the situation at Thuan Man, II Corps was given use of the 1st Airborne Task Force, commanded by Lieutenant Colonel Kha, with Captain William N. Ciccolo as his senior American adviser. For this operation, the 1st Airborne Task Force had two Airborne battalions (the 1st and 5th), plus the 2d Battalion of the 40th Regiment (reinforced with a company of the 1st Battalion), an engineer platoon, and a Marine artillery battery with four 105mm guns. The mission was not to restore Thuan Man district to government control but merely to extract RF and PF troops trapped in the district capital, which, given II Corps' overstretched resources, would have to be abandoned for the time being.[52]

On 27 and 28 June American C-130 and C-123 aircraft flew the task force from Pleiku to Cheo Reo. On 29 June it headed from Cheo Reo toward Thuan Man along Highway 7B, moving in an essentially westward direction. Three Communist battalions had been reported in the Thuan Man area, so the movement was cautious. Highway 7B was a dirt road running along a valley with rough, hilly terrain on either side. This terrain was "heavily overgrown by thick vegetation which generally limited observation to 10 yards." Kha, the task force commander, wanted to be sure to control the high ground on either side of the road as the task force advanced. While the 1st Airborne Battalion proceeded down the road itself, the 5th Airborne Battalion moved on the left flank, south of the road, and the 2d Battalion of the 40th Regiment moved on the right flank, north of it. The task force made good progress, and in the late afternoon it began to establish defensive positions for the night, registering defensive fires from supporting artillery at Cheo Reo.

The advance resumed at 0740 on 30 June. By 0830, elements of the force were coming under fire. Heavy mortar, recoilless rifle, and small-arms fire was soon being received from a number of directions. Apparently trying to save his battalion from the major Communist ambush that was clearly developing, the officer commanding the reinforced 2d Battalion of the 40th Regiment, on the task force's right flank, ordered a withdrawal to high ground to the east. In the process, his battalion not only broke contact with the attacking Communist forces but also lost touch with the rest of the task force. Continuing to move east, away from the fighting, the great bulk of the 2d Battalion was back at Cheo Reo by 1800.[53]

The two Airborne battalions neither retreated nor disintegrated but fought back hard. Their supporting Marine artillery battery, located toward the rear of the task force, was also fiercely engaged that morning. Hit by mortar fire, the battery's ammunition trucks exploded, but the gunners used the ammunition they had at hand to engage the attacking Communist forces with direct fire until the intensity of incoming mortar and small-arms fire forced them to abandon their guns temporarily.

Radio communication between the 1st Airborne Task Force and Cheo Reo broke down that morning, making it impossible to get fire support from the artillery there. At 1000 on 30 June, however, through an American forward air controller accompanying the task force, its commander was able to make an urgent request for air support. The request was fairly quickly and very fully answered. From 1045 to 2000 there were eighty-four expertly controlled close-support air strikes. The attacking Communist forces were "bombed and strafed so heavily that the assault slackened." Communist attacks drove a wedge between the two Airborne battalions that morning. By 1430, however, they were able to link up, and by 1700 they had reached the Marine artillery position and cleared it of Communist troops. The Marine gunners got three of their guns operating again and commenced firing the approximately 150 rounds they had left.

At some point that afternoon, the 1st Airborne Task Force was able to inform II Corps that it was under attack by a Communist force, estimated to be a reinforced regiment, and that its line of retreat to Cheo Reo had been severed.[54] That assessment was essentially correct. We now know that the principal force mounting these attacks was the Communist 2d Regiment. Composed mainly of personnel recruited on South Vietnam's coastal plain, particularly Quang Ngai, it was an exceptionally powerful unit with four infantry battalions, an artillery-mortar battalion, and a sapper company.[55] Elements of the PAVN 95A (aka 10th) Regiment, which was conducting the siege of Thuan Man,[56] may have participated in the attacks on the task force. The PAVN 18A (aka 12th) Regiment appears to have been in the same general area awaiting developments and acting as the Communists' reserve for this campaign.[57]

In a relatively rare compliment to the fighting spirit of enemy forces, a Communist multivolume history of the war observes of the ARVN Airborne in this action: "The enemy troops fought back ferociously and launched many counter-attacks. . . . The battle lasted until nightfall without our being able to finish the enemy off."[58] By evening, the task force's two Airborne battalions, together with the Marine artillery, had been able to form a coherent defensive perimeter and beat off the Communist attacks, but they were getting low on ammunition and had many wounded who needed to be taken to hospitals. II Corps sent helicopters to fulfill these needs, but antiaircraft fire from machine guns on the hills overlooking the beleaguered task force prevented them from landing.

The situation now confronting the II Corps commander and his staff appeared grim. In addition to the Communist regiment (which, at this stage, II Corps had not yet identified) attacking the 1st Airborne Task Force, ARVN intelligence now indicated that "a second regiment was located south of Cheo Reo within reinforcing distance of the current engagement."[59] This may well have been the PAVN 18A Regiment.

As a corps reserve, II Corps still had Marine Task Force Alpha, commanded by Lieutenant Colonel W. T. Yen, with two Marine battalions (the 2d and 5th), a force that had been committed to II Corps since February. But in view of the estimated Communist strength in Phu Bon, it was not clear that this would be enough. Vinh Loc called on the Joint General Staff for additional reinforcements from the general reserve in Saigon. It was perhaps indicative of the strategic importance of the Central Highlands in the JGS's collective mind that the request was granted. II Corps ordered Task Force Alpha to fly immediately from Kontum to Cheo Reo. The lift commenced at 1430 on 30 June and was completed by 2000. The ARVN Airborne Brigade headquarters and another Airborne task force flew up from Saigon immediately afterward.[60]

Believing the situation to be grave, with a substantial ARVN force surrounded and in danger of being destroyed, the US Air Force did excellent work transporting these reinforcements: "They flew troops and supplies into the Cheo Reo airfield in a steady stream, around the clock. The pilots of the planes being unloaded took over traffic control until their ships were emptied. When the unloaded planes taxied off, the mission would be picked up by succeeding pilots. This continued throughout the night."[61] On the morning of 1 July, while Airborne troops from the general reserve in Saigon were still flying into Cheo Reo, Marine Task Force Alpha moved west from Cheo Reo toward Thuan Man. According to Task Force Alpha's senior adviser, the celebrated Major William Leftwich, the Marines were frustrated by II Corps' repeated change of plans that resulted in some marching and countermarching in unseasonably hot weather. In the early evening of 2 July, however, the

Marines linked up with the Airborne battalions of 1st Airborne Task Force without making contact with Communist forces.[62]

The Communist 2d Regiment had ceased any serious attacks on the 1st Airborne Task Force by nightfall on 30 June. On 1 July the pressure was off, and helicopters were able to take out the wounded and replenish ammunition and food. The battle on 30 June had cost the ARVN 26 dead, 12 missing, and 56 wounded. Four Americans were also killed and 4 wounded. American advisers gave figures of 122 Communist dead (apparently based on body count) and 3 captured. Interrogation reports indicated that up to 300 more had been killed in air strikes. The latter figure certainly cannot be taken as gospel, but presumably the 2d Regiment would have continued its efforts to annihilate the task force had it not been pretty badly hurt.[63] By dawn, the 2d Regiment had broken contact and disappeared. No further reports were heard of it in the Highlands in 1965. But at the time, the ARVN had to assume that it might still be lurking somewhere in the vicinity of Thuan Man.[64]

The 1st Airborne Task Force had not achieved its original mission of extracting beleaguered government forces from the district town of Thuan Man. Late on the afternoon of 1 July, the district chief at Thuan Man reported by radio that his troops were almost out of food and ammunition and would be unable to hold out another night. Even once the Marines and the Airborne task forces had linked up, II Corps reckoned it might take them another two days to fight through to Thuan Man. It was therefore decided to try to lift the RF troops out by helicopter that afternoon. But as soon as the lead helicopters touched down, they came under intense mortar fire. The Communist mortars were too well hidden for the fixed-wing aircraft supporting the operation to suppress them, and although the helicopters were able to lift off again without loss, the mission had to be aborted.

When the Thuan Man district chief was informed that his troops could not be rescued by helicopter that day, he asked permission to attempt a breakout to the west during the night. II Corps gave permission and hurriedly organized support for the intended maneuver, making arrangements through the ARVN 23d Division for CIDG troops from the camp at Buon Brieng to move east to link up with the RF troops breaking out from Thuan Man. II Corps also improvised a simple deception plan, transmitting orders in the clear for the garrison to stay put until the relief column broke through to them the next day. It arranged for strike aircraft to pound Communist positions all around the beleaguered garrison during the early evening on 1 July and provided for helicopter gunship and fighter cover along the Thuan Man garrison's escape route at first light on 2 July. The breakout was successful. The RF troops linked up with the Buon Brieng CIDG troops and accompanied them back to their camp; from there, they were flown to Cheo Reo.

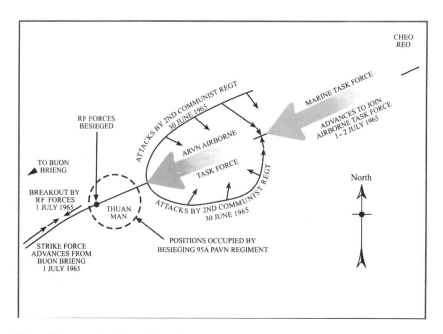

Thuan Man campaign, June–July 1965

For the time being, II Corps abandoned Thuan Man to the PAVN 95A Regiment. The Marine and Airborne task forces brought in to deal with the emergency in Phu Bon did not stay long in that province.[65]

Assessing the Monsoon Offensive in Phu Bon, May–July 1965

How should the monsoon season fighting in Phu Bon be evaluated? The picture in early July was mixed. It is clear that the Communists' main strategy at this time was to pursue a decisive victory by destroying the southern republic's armed forces. A particular feature of that strategy was to lure the most capable elements of those armed forces into the Central Highlands and use the best-equipped and best-trained Communist units to destroy them. The three Communist main force regiments that operated in Phu Bon during the monsoon offensive (18A, 95A, and 2d), while able to shatter one battalion of the ARVN 40th Regiment, did not deal crippling blows to the elite of the South Vietnamese government forces. Certainly, they placed two ARVN Airborne battalions in a perilous position for a short time. The destruction of those battalions would have represented exactly the sort of dramatic victory that Le Duan and the Communist high command were seeking. But this remained a might-have-been. It did not happen. In attempting to make it happen, both the PAVN 95A Regiment and the 2d Regiment were severely battered.

Although it was still monsoon season, Communist forces had bad luck with the weather in late June and early July. It was unseasonably hot and dry.[66] Clear skies much of the time allowed the opposition to exploit to the fullest its advantages of airpower and airlift. Close air support was critical in blunting PAVN attacks on the 1st Airborne Task Force. In airlifting two more task forces of elite troops into Phu Bon, the Republic of Vietnam's forces and their American backers rather overinsured against disaster. By nightfall on 30 June, the Communist 2d Regiment had apparently accepted its inability to destroy the two Airborne battalions and backed off. But the sheer size of its airlift capacity allowed the anti-Communist side the luxury of overinsurance. The extra task forces could quickly be redeployed.

Despite failing to achieve their primary purpose—inflicting a major defeat on large, elite elements of the Saigon government's armed forces—the Communists achieved other secondary goals. As Mataxis openly admitted: "While Cheo Reo itself was saved, the VC had made many gains in Phu Bon. . . . The government forces had lost not only the entire district of Thuan Man, but the majority of the villages scattered throughout the province. By the end of June in Phu Bon ARVN held only the area immediately around the provincial capital and its two remaining district towns."[67]

Dak To, 7–8 July 1965

On 7 July 1965 the main Communist effort in the Central Highlands shifted north to Kontum, where the district town of Dak To became the target. The PAVN 101A Regiment attacked the Dak To district headquarters in the middle of the night. The RF garrison's morale was already shaky after the loss of Toumorong and other recent setbacks in northern Kontum, and the troops apparently offered little resistance—fleeing to the protection of the nearby ARVN 42d Regiment garrison at Tan Canh.

Lieutenant Colonel Lai Van Chu, the 42d Regiment's commander, organized an attempt to retake Dak To early the following morning, using the garrison at Tan Canh. It was the wrong move. The Communists were almost certainly expecting it. The ambush of 42d Regiment troops from Tan Canh, rather than holding on to Dak To, was likely their main aim. Just 2 km from their camp the ARVN troops ran into a PAVN roadblock and were almost immediately subjected to a flank attack. Although their casualties were not particularly heavy, both the regimental commander, Colonel Chu, and his senior

American adviser, Major John Black, were seriously wounded. Discouraged by the loss of its commander, the ARVN force fell back to its camp at Tan Canh. Chu, in Mataxis's judgment, was "one of the outstanding regimental commanders" of the ARVN. His death from his wounds a short time later caused the morale of his regiment, which had been "built around his charismatic leadership," to "sink appreciably."

At this point, II Corps commander Vinh Loc flew to Kontum to evaluate the situation and, according to Mataxis, saw that drastic action was needed to restore the morale of government forces in northern Kontum. In particular, the 42d Regiment needed an "experienced and dynamic commander." Vinh Loc found such a man in Colonel Dam Van Qui. Qui was reunited with Lieutenant Colonel Thomas Perkins, an American adviser with whom he had enjoyed a successful partnership in a previous command. II Corps also sent a Ranger battalion, probably the 21st, to Tan Canh as reinforcement.[68]

Having recently returned from Phu Bon, where it had been sent to rescue 1st Airborne Task Force, Marine Task Force Alpha flew from Kontum to Tan Canh on 8 July. From there, on the morning of 9 July, the Marines were sent to retake Dak To. They did so without opposition. The Communist troops there apparently declined to fight a force of that size and quality and made a hasty getaway.[69]

Highway 19 Again: Operation Free Way

II Corps was trying to organize the emergency provision of rice to civilians in the towns, but by the beginning of July, the supply situation in the northern half of the Central Highlands had become critical. According to Mataxis, as "the prices of scarce products skyrocketed . . . civilian morale plummeted."[70] In an article published in an American military journal in 1966, Vinh Loc noted that the "price of food and commodities rose steadily, in some cases more than doubling in six months. . . . The scarcity of food and the increasing enemy pressure forced many people to evacuate their families to Saigon. . . . By the first days of July, the populations of Pleiku and Kontum were near panic."[71]

To alleviate this problem, II Corps mounted its second large campaign along Highway 19. Planning for Operation Free Way began on 8 July. It was an elaborate and quite sophisticated affair, the basic concept being to deploy overwhelming force along Highway 19 for just a few days to allow carefully prepared convoys to deliver a large quantity of supplies from the coastal city of Qui Nhon to Pleiku. After a number of diversions to confuse their enemies, powerful South Vietnamese government ground forces (with massive American and South Vietnamese air support) would move onto and along Highway

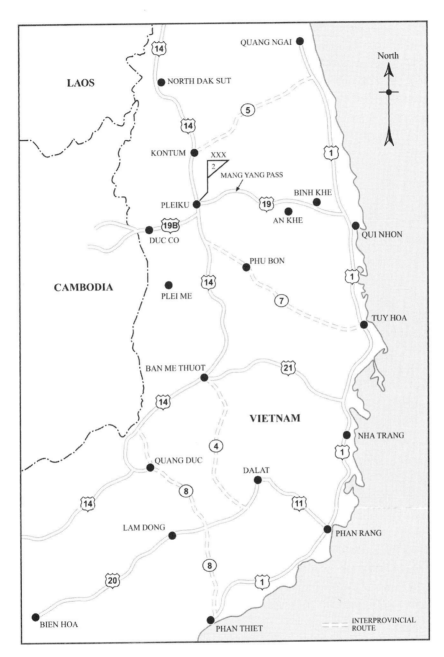

Highways in the Highlands

19 from different directions. The idea was to keep the Communist forces off balance, confused, and distracted as II Corps carried out its main purpose—bringing supplies to the Central Highlands.

During the planning and buildup phase, strict secrecy was maintained—applying a need-to-know approach even within the II Corps staff. Once the operation began, a high tempo would be maintained, and the forces taking part would be organized and distributed in such a way that a successful Communist ambush of any substantial part of them would be a virtual impossibility. It was to be a three-phase operation. From D minus 6 to D plus 2, II Corps would launch a number of diversions, position troops along Highway 19, and repair bridges and sections of the road. From D plus 3 to D plus 7, it would move its convoys. On D plus 8 and D plus 9, most of the participating forces would be withdrawn. D-day was set for 16 July.

The diversionary operations all had some intrinsic purpose. They were not mere feints. Elements of 22d Division and the 3d Armored Battalion pushed south along Highway 1, opening at least temporarily the section between Qui Nhon and Tuy Hoa. The 2d Airborne Task Force pushed from Pleiku down Highway 19 in the direction of Duc Co. Marine Task Force Alpha, with the 2d and 5th Marine Battalions operating together with the 42d Regiment, pushed north from Kontum, reopening Highway 14 as far north as Dak Sut. The 20th Engineering Group pushed southeast from the vicinity of Pleiku down Highway 7, reopening at least temporarily one section of that road.

The section of Highway 19 between Qui Nhon on the coast and a point just east of An Khe was the responsibility of 22d Division, which, on 15 July, dispatched two task forces, one advancing on either side of the road. On 15 July Task Force Alpha, consisting of the 2d and 5th Marine Battalions and commanded by Lieutenant Colonel Yen, flew from Tan Canh in Kontum Province to the town of Pleiku and from there moved east to its line of departure for the operation, in the vicinity of Dak Quan, between Pleiku and the Mang Yang Pass. At 1100 on 16 July Task Force Alpha crossed its start line and advanced on both sides of the road to clear the stretch of Highway 19 up to and including the Mang Yang Pass.[72]

The most critical part of the road, however, where big ambushes had occurred in the recent past, was between the Mang Yang Pass and An Khe. That area was dealt with by two ARVN Airborne task forces. The 1st Airborne Task Force consisted of the 1st and 5th Airborne Battalions, with the 6th Airborne Battalion as a reserve; it was flown up from Saigon for this operation. The 2d Airborne Task Force, consisting of the 3d and 8th Airborne Battalions, was already in the Highlands on loan to II Corps. The American after-action report for this operation does not name the Vietnamese Airborne task force or Airborne battalion commanders, but the senior American adviser to

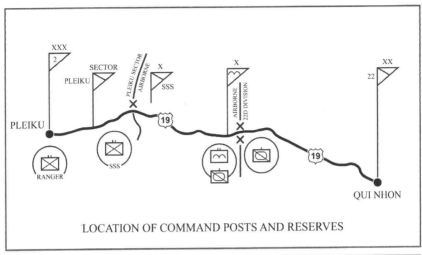

LOCATION OF COMMAND POSTS AND RESERVES

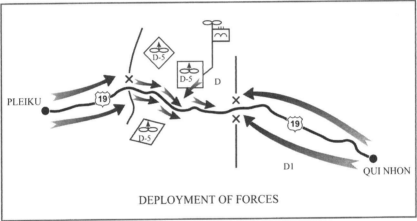

DEPLOYMENT OF FORCES

Road clearing operations on Highway 19, July 1965

the 1st Airborne Task Force was Captain Donald Wells, and Major Norman Schwarzkopf held that position with the 2d Airborne Task Force.

On 15 July the 1st Airborne Task Force flew from Saigon to An Khe. The bulk of the 6th Airborne Battalion followed it on 16 July. The 6th Airborne Battalion remained at An Khe, where it formed a local reserve. Between 1053 and 1140 on 16 July, the 1,050 personnel of the 1st Airborne Task Force were lifted by helicopter to an area approximately 10 km northwest of An Khe. They then advanced south toward Highway 19, ready to deal with any enemy force that might be preparing an ambush in that vicinity and securing both sides of that stretch of road. At 1230 on 16 July the 2d Airborne Task Force departed Pleiku, linking up with Marine Task Force Alpha just west of the Mang Yang Pass at 1610.[73]

The whole operation received lavish air support, with fighter-bombers attacking suspected Communist positions during daylight hours throughout. At 0730 on 17 July, thirty B-52s pounded a suspected Communist position near the Mang Yang Pass south of Highway 19. In one of the few mishaps of the operation, a technical malfunction with a bomb rack "resulted in twelve 750 pound bombs falling 200 meters from the Marine Task Force command post."[74] It could have been a massive disaster, but just four Marines were slightly wounded. At 0930 on 17 July, the 2d Airborne Task Force crossed its line of departure near the Mang Yang Pass and moved east along Highway 19. Once the two Airborne task forces had secured the section of road between the Mang Yang Pass and An Khe, on 17 and 18 July ARVN engineers went to work repairing bridges and finished their task ahead of schedule. Paradoxically, their efficiency in this respect had a somewhat disorganizing impact on II Corps' plan and provided American advisers with one of their few complaints about the operation:

> The Corps order contained a convoy movement schedule for all planned movements from D+3 to D+8 but due to the early opening of the road, one convoy was able to move on D+2 [18 July]. During the succeeding days, the original movement order was not followed. Information on the new movement schedule of the convoys was not well disseminated to the units securing the road. Because of this . . . it was difficult to plan the use of covering gunships. . . . Air ground communication[s] with the convoy[s] were non-existent because of the absence of radios in the convoy[s].[75]

For South Vietnamese government forces, this was a "no contact" operation. They suffered just a handful of casualties, and these were mostly owing to accidents. Despite lots of air strikes and artillery fire directed at locations where aerial surveillance and Special Forces Delta teams had indicated Communist forces to be, Communist casualties were stated as "unknown." But that was largely irrelevant. The infliction of casualties was not the principal purpose. Convoys had delivered 5,365 tons of supplies from Qui Nhon to Pleiku during the course of the operation. Vinh Loc's summary of its results for the American military press had a somewhat triumphalist tone: "The convoys transfused new life into the Highlands. Along with an immediate drop of 25 to 30 per cent in the price of food and commodities, the population regained their feelings of security, confidence and hope. Schoolboys in Pleiku voluntarily helped the troops in unloading the cargoes and people who had started to evacuate now returned to their homesteads."[76] In reality, the July operation on Highway 19 had brought Pleiku and other Highland towns only partial and temporary relief. Yet participating American advisers, not normally slow to criticize errors in South Vietnamese planning and execution, reckoned this II Corps operation a sophisticated and successful enterprise that could be exploited for propaganda purposes.[77]

The Duc Co Campaign, July–August 1965

Perhaps the fiercest battle during the Communist monsoon offensive in the Central Highlands took place in the first half of August around the CIDG–Special Forces camp at Duc Co in western Pleiku Province. Opened in May 1963, the Duc Co (aka Chu Dron) camp lay on Highway 19, 55 km from the provincial capital and only 13 km from the Cambodian border. Its garrison in August 1965 consisted of Captain Richard B. Johnson's detachment A-215, with a dozen men; a similar number of Vietnamese Special Forces; 200 Highland troops, mainly from the Jarai ethnic group; and 200 Nungs.[78]

Duc Co had been experiencing a high desertion rate from its Strike Force since at least February 1965. The PAVN 320th/32d Regiment was in western Pleiku, and Highlanders in the area sensed the growing power of the Communists. Since the loss of the district town at Le Thanh in early June, most of the surrounding Jarai villages and Vietnamese land development had fallen under Communist control. The Duc Co camp was increasingly isolated, and starting at the end of June it was effectively besieged. By mid-July, morale in the camp was dropping, and the desertion rate was becoming critical. The camp's patrols were driven back within the perimeter wire. Day by day the pressure increased. By the end of July, in spite of numerous air strikes, Communist forces, as yet unidentified, were using carefully emplaced mortars and recoilless rifles to bombard the camp. Under the cover of this fire, Communist troops were moving closer and closer to the perimeter. Helicopters could not land, and it became almost impossible to supply the camp with food and ammunition or to take out its wounded.[79]

By the last week in July, II Corps had tasked 24 STZ to mount an operation to relieve Duc Co, intending to use the 2d Airborne Task Force, already with II Corps, for this purpose. Composed of the 3d and 8th Airborne Battalions, the 2d Airborne Task Force was commanded by Major Nghi, with Major Schwarzkopf as his senior American adviser. According to 24 STZ's plan, Nghi's paratroopers would land in a jungle clearing near Duc Co. Once they had reinforced the camp, they would break the siege by aggressive operations outside the wire. The plan looked impressive on paper. But according to Schwarzkopf's memoirs, his own reconnaissance indicated that there was no clearing in the jungle where the force could land, and although the helicopter landing was supposed to be preceded by air strikes and with artillery support on call, no such support had been arranged. He and Nghi therefore insisted on delaying the operation until proper support had been arranged.

Again according to Schwarzkopf's memoirs, he and Nghi were summoned to Vinh Loc's palatial residence in Pleiku, where they were both berated for making unnecessary difficulties—Nghi by Vinh Loc, and Schwarzkopf by an unnamed American, apparently Mataxis. Because their task force really belonged to the Airborne Brigade (normally part of the JGS reserve) and was only on loan to II Corps, Nghi and Schwarzkopf were able to bypass the II Corps chain of command and appeal to their superiors in the Airborne Brigade, who supported them.[80] The operation to relieve Duc Co was thus delayed for a few days and became a good deal more sophisticated.

Between 30 July and 17 August, 24 STZ coordinated a series of connected operations (Dan Thang 4–7) intended to execute two related missions. A new district headquarters for Le Thanh was to be established at Thanh Binh, and pressure on the Duc Co Special Forces camp was to be relieved by finding and destroying Communist units and installations in that vicinity.[81]

On 29 July a command group from 24 STZ, including the commanding general, Brigadier General Cao Hao Hon, moved from Kontum to Pleiku. Operation Dan Thang 4 commenced at 0900 on 30 July when the 3d Armored Task Force, commanded by Major Nguyen Truong Luat and consisting of fifteen M-41 Walker Bulldog tanks, fifteen M-113 armored personnel carriers, the 21st Ranger Battalion, the 201st Engineer Company, and two 105mm howitzers of the 221st Artillery Battalion, began its advance from Pleiku to Thanh Binh. Its mission, to secure that section of Highway 19 and the town of Thanh Binh itself, was completed that afternoon, no contact with Communist forces being reported.[82]

Operation Dan Thang 5 began at 0312 on 3 August when the US 52d Aviation Battalion, based at Camp Holloway, began lifting the 2d Airborne Task Force (3d and 8th Airborne Battalions) by helicopter from Pleiku to an airfield on the edge of the camp at Duc Co. A "heavy air strike to suppress VC fire" preceded the first helicopter landings. The last of six lifts was completed by 1715. The first two encountered no resistance. After that, the approaching helicopters met a growing volume of small-arms and machine gun fire. Two were hit, but none crashed.[83]

The 2d Airborne Task Force's efforts to clear Communist forces from the environs of the camp, however, soon met serious resistance, and by 1245 on 3 August the operation had largely ground to a halt. Schwarzkopf, for whom Duc Co was his first combat experience, did not consider Nghi a dynamic commander but agreed with him that it was impossible to break the siege from within the camp. Indeed, Schwarzkopf was unsure that the presence of the paratroopers would save the camp from being overrun. During its abortive effort to break out from Duc Co, the 2d Airborne Task Force suffered losses of thirteen killed and sixty wounded. "Sixty-two VC were reported dead by ARVN body count, but only twenty-two of the bodies were counted by advisors. Eleven VC weapons were captured."[84] Schwarzkopf's memoirs indicate that superiors pressed him to provide figures for enemy casualties, even though they were bound to be pure speculation.[85]

Reinforcing Duc Co without relieving it only made the camp's supply problems more acute. Communist forces still had it too closely invested to allow helicopters to land safely, and medical supplies parachuted in at 0428 on 6 August landed partly inside and partly outside the wire. It seemed likely that this would happen with subsequent drops as well.[86]

At this point, it became clear at II Corps headquarters that it would need to commit both the 3d Armored Task Force and its one substantial remaining mobile force, Task Force Alpha, to relieve Duc Co. The latter was "pulled off operations in Kontum" and transported by air to Pleiku, this move being completed by 1800 on 6 August.[87]

II Corps planned an operation (Dan Thang 6) to shift Task Force Alpha (2d and 5th Marine Battalions) by helicopter to a landing zone 4 km southwest of the Special Forces camp at Duc Co on the afternoon of 7 August. Bad weather delayed this operation, however, and it was ultimately abandoned. Instead, the Marines moved by road to join the 3d Armored Task Force at Thanh Binh. In Operation Dan Thang 7, commencing at 0800 on 8 August, the armored and Marine task forces were to advance west along Highway 19 toward Duc Co, with the intention of relieving the camp and smashing the Communist forces besieging it.[88]

Committing both task forces to Duc Co's relief, however, would leave II Corps almost devoid of reserves. That prospect clearly worried Vinh Loc. He therefore requested help from the JGS General Reserve but was turned down. The JGS had nothing more available, but it passed on the request to General Westmoreland, asking him to send American troops to Pleiku Province to act as a reserve for II Corps. Their mission would be not to fight but to release South Vietnamese forces to do so. Westmoreland approved the move. The US 173d Airborne Brigade arrived at Camp Holloway airfield near Pleiku on 11 August and immediately moved west to Thanh Binh on Highway 19, where it fulfilled the dual missions of securing the district headquarters and acting as the main corps reserve. During the period 12–16 August, the 173d conducted foot, motorized, and heliborne patrols. Meanwhile, the 22d Ranger Battalion, based at Pleiku, secured that town and acted as II Corps' final reserve.[89]

On 8 August the 3d Armored Task Force and Task Force Alpha made an uncontested move as far as a small town on Highway 19 called Plei Rongol Dogrong. A bridge there had been blown, however, and reconnaissance reported many obstacles on the road beyond it. Having repaired the bridge, the two forces pushed on toward Duc Co on the morning of 9 August. That afternoon, the 3d Armored Task Force, which was leading the advance, met opposition centering on a ridge 500 meters southwest of the town of Colon. Communist forces opened up with heavy machine guns and 57mm recoilless rifles, as well as small arms. Supported by air strikes, the 5th Marine Battalion took the ridge by 1700, finding numerous Communist dead and a considerable number of abandoned weapons. Shortly after the ridge was taken, two substantial groups of PAVN troops were spotted from the air advancing rapidly on Highway 19 from the south. Each group apparently seized part of the road and formed a roadblock. The South Vietnamese were fragmented, and there was a good deal of confusion.[90]

After a brief, unsuccessful attempt to clear the roadblock, the bulk of the South Vietnamese forces fell back to the east, looking for better ground to defend during the night. There was considerable confusion: "The front of the Armored Task Force doubled back on the rear of its column, which was still moving west. The result . . . was an immense traffic jam. The Marine battalions further congested the area as they started their movement to the east." The South Vietnamese soon found that there were also Communist troops blocking their retreat eastward along Highway 19, and hurriedly improvised attacks failed to shift them. After that, the bulk of "the Armored and Marine Task Forces coiled into a perimeter for the night." Only 800 meters long and 200 meters broad, it was congested, and in the opinion of the American advisers, the troops inside it were not particularly well organized. Though the bulk of the Marines and armored vehicles were inside this perimeter, the 21st Ranger Battalion and the artillery, protected by one Marine company, were cut off in other, separate defensive positions.[91]

Apparently surrounded, Duc Co's fragmented relief forces seemed to be in considerable danger. But despite a lot of shooting that night, there were no real Communist assaults. We now know that only two North Vietnamese battalions (already badly battered, half starved, and sick) were involved in attacking the two South Vietnamese task forces going to the relief of Duc Co, which had three battalions between them plus armor and artillery. Just one PAVN battalion had been left to besiege Duc Co. Therefore, both around Duc Co itself and on the road approaching it, North Vietnamese besiegers and attackers were heavily outnumbered by the South Vietnamese defenders. The South Vietnamese, moreover, enjoyed excellent air support. Air-dropped flares illuminated the battlefield virtually all night, and tracer fire from the tanks helped indicate the relative positions of the opposing forces. "A1E aircraft delivered a series of five strikes against the VC," and these were devastatingly effective.[92]

At 0510 on 10 August the PAVN finally launched an infantry assault, supported by mortar and recoilless rifle fire, on the main South Vietnamese position. Given the balance of forces, this stood little chance. The South Vietnamese fired all the weapons available to them and again were well supported by air strikes. After about fifteen minutes the North Vietnamese assault collapsed without even denting the perimeter. Some twenty-five rounds of Communist 81mm mortar fire, however, landed within it and, given the cramped conditions, caused considerable casualties.[93]

With their attack stopped dead, the bulk of the two North Vietnamese battalions withdrew from the battlefield. A few troops, however, hung around, firing at South Vietnamese forces for the rest of the day. The South Vietnamese remained extremely cautious. They did not seize the initiative and drive the enemy off, which they almost certainly could have done. Although the 21st Rangers managed to link up with the artillery on 10 August, those troops remained separated from the defensive position containing the bulk of the Marines and the armor. Over the course of the day, however, the South Vietnamese troops' ammunition and food were replenished by parachute drop and helicopter lift, and helicopters picked up their casualties. Also on 10 August, helicopters flew the 5th Airborne Battalion into Duc Co, where it reinforced the 2d Airborne Task Force in an already overcrowded camp.

In the fighting of 9–10 August, the South Vietnamese lost at least 44 killed and 94 wounded. North Vietnamese losses were much higher. US advisers confirmed at least 152 Communist dead by body count and 59 weapons captured. "Later," an American after-action report noted, "reports from the Montagnards indicated that 200 VC were buried in 40 graves dug by the villagers. The bodies were reportedly buried five to a grave. An additional 70 bodies were reported as being carried away." The official estimate provided by 24 STZ was 434 Communist soldiers killed in the fighting of 9–10 August, although this might have been on the high side.[94] Nevertheless, when the casualties of the heavy bombing during the lengthy siege prior to 9 August are added, it seems likely that the PAVN 32d Regiment would have been psychologically shattered as well as physically diminished for at least several weeks.

The following day, 11 August, the ARVN 2d Airborne Task Force struck east from Duc Co in an effort to link up with the forces advancing to relieve the camp. According to Mataxis, "Threatened with entrapment between these two attacking forces, the enemy broke contact and withdrew leaving only small delaying forces, snipers and mines along the road."[95] The linkup took place 2 km east of the camp. The forty-eight-day siege at Duc Co was over.[96] There was no fighting in this sector on 12 August. After some largely fruitless searches of the area for Communist forces and supply caches, the task forces fell back on the town of Pleiku.[97]

Considering the appalling condition (which ARVN intelligence was about to reveal) of the heavily outnumbered PAVN 32d Regiment, the performance of South Vietnamese ground troops in the Duc Co campaign had not been especially impressive. There had been no disasters or routs, but their movements had been pedestrian and ultra-cautious. Nevertheless, the anti-Communist side had won a significant victory. As Mataxis expressed it:

> The battle of Duc Co ended with the VC defeated with heavy losses and the government forces in control of the battlefield. [It] raised the morale of ARVN troops. They had taken the worst the VC could throw at them and had not only held on, but made the enemy break contact and flee, leaving his weapons and dead on the battlefield. This significant victory was celebrated by visits of General Westmoreland and the principal Vietnamese government officials headed by General Thieu, the Head of State, to the Duc Co camp.
>
> This battle had its effects on the PAVN's morale also . . . PAVN troops became depressed by their losses and the disparity between their firepower and that of the [South Vietnamese] government forces. PAVN prisoners captured during the summer's fighting all stressed the high incidence of malaria due to living in the jungle and the heavy losses they had suffered from air strikes and artillery.

Mataxis recounts that during the Duc Co fighting, the ARVN found on the body of a North Vietnamese political officer a letter of remonstrance, apparently written to his battalion commander on behalf of the officers and men of his company. It described the 32d/320th Regiment's nightmarish existence since its arrival in the South and the low morale that had inevitably resulted. A translation (probably by an ARVN intelligence officer and in rather odd English) is quoted directly in Mataxis's memoir: "It is miserable and terrible—fighting situation is too serious and difficult—enemy mortars shelled day and night and airplanes come to bomb and strike freely. There is a little low spirit because of the difficulty and terrible conditions and hunger." Health was a huge problem, with half the unit sick, a third seriously so. Cadres (i.e., officers) were as prone to sickness as everyone else, and at times there were none fit for duty. The supply of drugs was totally inadequate, and little could be done for the sick. A high rate of illness was perhaps inevitable, given the appalling state of the rations: "The rice is too bad so when we brought it to the front after cooking it becomes sour. . . . Our comrades groaned while they were working, some cried while cooking." The company commissar ended with a plea to the battalion commander that he should try to find some way of getting the unit relieved or temporarily withdrawn for a period of rest and recuperation.

"Information of this nature," according to Mataxis, "was most heartening to the ARVN troops and their morale rose correspondingly."[98]

Actions at Dak Sut, 18–19 August 1965

This serious defeat in Pleiku did not cause the Communists to abandon their monsoon offensive in the Highlands. Their final effort, and a much more successful one, came at Dak Sut in northern Kontum. As Mataxis put it:

> This district town had been under . . . pressure since early June when the enemy seized the area surrounding the Pokaha bridge and cut off Dak Sut's land communications with Kontum. There was no question that the VC were methodically preparing to attack the district headquarters. Since isolating the garrison, the enemy steadily increased his harassment of Dak Sut. Raids and attacks on the Sedang Montagnard villages in northwestern Kontum gradually destroyed government influence outside the range of the weapons of the isolated garrison at Dak Sut and the CIDG camp to the north, Dak Pek. The VC stepped up their detailed preparation for the attack to such an extent that a patrol from Dak Sut even ambushed a VC artillery survey party [actually from the 200th Artillery Battalion, the oldest Communist main force unit in the Highlands] who, with their surveying equipment, had been making an extremely accurate sketch of the garrison's defensive bunkers and trenches. A study of the captured firing tables indicated that these troops were from a 75mm pack artillery unit.[99]

Just after dark on 18 August, the PAVN 101A Regiment, acting on orders from the CHF and commanded by Colonel Ha Huu Thua (deputy chief of staff of the 325th Division), launched its long-expected attack on Dak Sut, with fire support provided by the 200th Artillery Battalion. According to the official history of Communist forces in the Central Highlands, "This was the first regimental-level coordinated assault between artillery and infantry on an enemy stronghold."[100] The attack came much earlier in the evening than was typical for this sort of operation and gained a degree of surprise. The RF district garrison "soon reported that their perimeter wire had been breached and hand-to-hand fighting was taking place. Shortly after this their radio went dead and it was presumed that their position had been overrun."[101]

Communist forces made a virtually simultaneous strike on the nearby Dak Sut CIDG training camp, established the previous May. But their initial assaults against this objective failed, and the action "slackened off for a couple of hours." In the early hours of 19 August, however, the North Vietnamese were able to focus all their efforts on the CIDG camp. After a fierce struggle that lasted a total of four hours, the camp fell before dawn. According to Mataxis:

> The Special Forces "A" team commander [Captain Cook of detachment
> A-218] . . . reported that his defensive perimeter had been penetrated and that
> the defenders were falling back from the northern wall. . . . The next message
> reported that they were breaking up into small groups, destroying their radio,
> and were going to attempt to filter through the enemy. Early next morning
> contact was regained with the Special Forces team. Helicopters were sent to
> pick up some of the American and Vietnamese Special Forces who had man-
> aged to escape . . . in the course of the night. . . . For the next several days,
> small groups of CIDG and RF [troops] who had successfully filtered through
> the enemy positions appeared at the outposts of the 42d Regiment at Tan
> Canh. They were reorganized and incorporated into the defense of Dak To.[102]

Only some 230 of the 474 CIDG soldiers at the Dak Sut camp managed to escape.[103]

Road Clearance Again, Late August 1965

The assaults at Dak Sut were the last significant Communist offensive moves during the monsoon season in the Central Highlands. Before the rainy season ended, however, II Corps mounted two more road opening campaigns, similar to the one on Highway 19 in July. In the second half of August, the prob-lem of keeping the towns supplied with food and other necessities once again "reached a critical state"; with "prices constantly rising," the morale of ordinary civilians and soldiers' dependents was "constantly sinking." The situation in the southern half of the Highlands had also become perilous, with the city of Ban Me Thuot, as well as Pleiku and Kontum, "feeling the pinch of VC road interdiction." Toward the end of the month, II Corps mounted simultaneous operations along Highway 19 from Qui Nhon to Pleiku and along Highway 21 from Nha Trang to Ban Me Thuot. According to Mataxis, "Both . . . were highly successful and restocked the highlands for the rest of the rainy season."[104]

Assessment

What was the politico-military situation in the Central Highlands as the rainy season came to an end? How had the two sides performed in this round of fighting?

In the short run, the Communist side had made some significant gains. Of the five district capitals they had seized, four were still under their control when the monsoon season ended in October.[105] They had virtually paralyzed road transport within the Central Highlands, forcing the anti-Communist side to keep the Highland towns and garrisons supplied by air. Enormously expensive, this also placed aviation assets under great stress. Supplementing air supply with occasional road opening operations to allow big truck convoys to deliver masses of supplies over short periods had staved off disaster. But the difficulty of keeping the towns supplied was somewhat demoralizing for the government's troops and for the civilians who were inclined to support it.

Saigon's control outside the towns in the Central Highlands had greatly diminished. But the notion that in August 1965 the Central Highlands was a Communist sea in which the Saigon government held merely a scattering of islands is somewhat misleading. Much of the region consisted of mountains and jungles with very little population, and Communist power and influence extended only as far as their increasingly starved, sick, and battered main force units could make their presence felt. The South Vietnamese state continued to hold all the provincial capitals and the majority of district towns. Even in the district of western Pleiku, adjacent to the Communists' Chu Pong base area where they had strong main force units, their histories admit that at least until October 1965, they did not hold all the villages. Mataxis reckoned that at the end of the Communists' 1965 monsoon offensives the Saigon government continued to control more of the population of the Central Highlands than the Communists did.[106] Though a participant in and therefore not an unbiased observer of these events, Mataxis generally seems to have taken a balanced, professional view.

The number of Highlander villages under Communist control undoubtedly increased substantially in the summer of 1965.[107] But rather than reflecting the aspirations of Highlanders, this was a result of the military initiative having been in Communist hands for the last few months. The Communists' ability to seize the military initiative was largely owing to the actions of main force military units recruited from outside the Highlands, especially PAVN regiments. Communist local force and militia units comprising mainly indigenous Highlanders continued to exist, and their actions were critical in closing some of the lesser roads and in getting local civilians to meet Communist demands for food and labor. Yet little is reported of the participation of Highland units on the Communist side in the major actions of this period, whereas Highland troops on the other side were sometimes pivotal to the struggle, especially when Communist forces chose to target CIDG camps.

American writing on the struggle for the Central Highlands in 1965 has tended to focus on the last quarter of the year, when US ground troops fought their first battles there. By then, however, the Communists' best chance of major military success in the region had already passed. It was during the monsoon season that the Communists stood the best chance of winning decisive battles in the Highlands that would cripple the South Vietnamese armed forces and trigger the collapse of the South Vietnamese state. They knew this and concentrated a high proportion of their elite forces in the region. In late June they had four PAVN regiments plus the main force 2d Regiment from the coastal plain in the Central Highlands. At least two main force Communist regiments took an active part in the Thuan Man campaign, with a third apparently acting as a reserve. This force was as substantial as that assembled for the Plei Me–Ia Drang campaign of October–November.

Yet the Communists repeatedly failed to win the crushing victories they sought over South Vietnam's elite troops. American airpower and strategic airlift and the airmobility conferred by American helicopters played a significant role in frustrating their ambitions. Although an American brigade served for a time as ARVN II Corps' reserve, no US ground unit had yet fought a battle in the region. It is only reasonable, therefore, to attribute this partial Communist failure at least in part to armed forces of the Republic of Vietnam, especially to the elite units the Communists were so keen to destroy.

11

Plei Me: Background, Siege, and Relief, August–October 1965

The August–October Lull

The attacks on the district headquarters and the Special Forces training camp at Dak Sut in Kontum Province in mid-August were the last substantial Communist attacks in the Central Highlands during the 1965 monsoon season.[1] There followed a two-month lull. From the Communist viewpoint, the monsoon season was by far the best time to mount major attacks in this region. Why, then, was there a pause from mid-August until the latter half of October, when the season was virtually over?

Lengthy pauses had been characteristic of the Communist "win the war" offensives commencing in November 1964. In some cases, logistical issues (main force units waiting to be resupplied) were probably the main factor, but sheer physical and psychological exhaustion must also have played a part. In the Central Highlands the Communist war effort depended very heavily on the PAVN, as no main force units had been recruited in the region. Sustaining big PAVN units in the Highlands, however, presented particular problems. Despite requisition-purchase in Cambodia, food supply remained extremely precarious. There is evidence of regiments being half starved long after they emerged from the Ho Chi Minh Trail. Malnutrition was accompanied by high rates of illness and serious shortages of medicine.[2] Although no figures are available, it is clear that all the PAVN regiments operating in the Highlands from February to August 1965 (320th/32d, 95A, 18A, and 101A) suffered substantial battle casualties. Two of them, the 95A Regiment (at Kannack) and the 320th/32d (at Duc Co), had also tasted the bitterness of clear-cut defeats.[3] By August, therefore, a high degree of weariness, both physical and psychological, was probably affecting most PAVN troops in the Central Highlands. That alone may have necessitated some sort of lull.

Supply issues and exhaustion, however, were not the only factors at work, and they may not have been the principal cause of this lengthy hiatus. It is notable that none of the regiments that had come down the Trail with the 325A Division (95A, 18A, and 101A) participated in the campaign in western Pleiku Province in October–November. All of them had left the Highlands by then.[4] Hanoi's assessment of the strategic importance of this region had apparently not diminished. The high command dispatched other regiments (the 33d and 66th) to the Central Highlands, these arriving in western Pleiku between mid-September and mid-November.[5] So why send the former 325A Division regiments elsewhere? The most likely explanation is that the intervention of significant numbers of American ground troops had created acute and immediate problems for the Communists in other regions, necessitating their urgent reinforcement. The diversion of PAVN regiments to other parts of the country, coupled with a time lag before new regiments arrived in the Central Highlands, was almost certainly the principal reason for the operational pause of August–October.

The only PAVN regiment that had already been in the Highlands for any length of time and that would participate in the October–November Pleiku campaign was the 320th/32d. Having arrived in the theater in December 1964–January 1965 (before 325A Division), the 320th's greatest success had been the Le Thanh campaign in early June. Since then, it had been severely battered and definitely defeated around Duc Co in July and early August. The Duc Co failure had occurred in the face of overwhelming odds but had left the regiment in a severely depleted and distinctly wretched condition, both physically and in terms of morale. Nevertheless, after a period of rest, it was to be employed, together with the newly arrived 33d Regiment, in another extremely difficult operation. At least the 320th/32d would have the advantage of operating in familiar territory—western Pleiku, where it had spent its entire fighting career so far.[6]

The Plei Me Campaign and Communist Strategy

In some American literature, the Communist campaign in western Pleiku, commencing on 19 October 1965, has been presented as part of a sophisticated grand strategic conception. General Nguyen Chi Thanh, commanding COSVN, is alleged to have developed a scheme for a Dong Xuan (winter-spring) series of offensives that would gain control of much of the northern part of South Vietnam by summer 1966, disrupt the American buildup, and cause the Americans such serious casualties that public opinion would force President Johnson to open negotiations. One part of this master plan was a Tay Nguyen (Western

Plateau) campaign to seize complete control of Kontum and Pleiku Provinces and parts of Binh Dinh and Phu Bon. The attack on the Special Forces camp at Plei Me was merely the opening move in this much larger game.[7]

Postwar Communist publications, however, describe no such grandiose strategic scheme, and the evidence for its existence is flimsy.[8] In August, when Major General Chu Huy Man apparently began planning his Plei Me campaign, the Communist high command was adjusting to the intervention of substantial numbers of US ground forces and just coming to terms with its inability to win the war in 1965. It was wondering how to respond strategically to American intervention and how its forces could cope tactically with American military technology.[9] It was a little early for a new master plan.

It seems more probable that the campaign that commenced around Plei Me on 19 October was a relatively ad hoc measure designed to reassert some strategic initiative and regain a degree of operational momentum in the Central Highlands after the monsoon offensives had fizzled out. A Communist history written in the mid-1990s states the goals of the campaign as follows: "to destroy a portion of the enemy's regular army, to lure in and destroy a portion of the American forces, to consolidate and expand our liberated zone, to hone and train our troops and our campaign headquarters staff . . . to improve our armed forces, to feel out and gain a better understanding of the American forces and to co-ordinate with . . . the rest of our forces in South Vietnam."[10]

Communist commanders certainly anticipated that American ground troops might become involved, and they might have thought this campaign would help them assess the strengths and weaknesses of American tactics and technology in the particular conditions of terrain and vegetation found in the Central Highlands. But that consideration was probably less important during the planning stages than has been suggested in some Communist histories.[11]

Chu Huy Man, the PAVN, and the Plei Me Target

Chu Huy Man, who had been in command of the Central Highlands Front since July, was well respected by the Party leadership and high command in Hanoi. Man probably knew at the end of September that, within the next month or two, he would have three PAVN regiments under his command—the 32d, 33d, and 66th—plus support units including a battalion of 120mm mortars and a battalion of 14.5mm machine guns. Each of these PAVN regiments had an authorized strength of 2,200 men and consisted of the usual three battalions, each with an authorized strength of 550 men. Each also had a 75mm recoilless rifle company, an 82mm mortar company, a 12.7mm antiaircraft machine gun company, and company-sized groups of medics, engineers, transportation troops, and signalers. However, substantial attrition rates during the journey down the Ho Chi Minh Trail, coupled with sickness and casualties after arriving in the Central Highlands, meant that Man's regiments would never operate at anything like full strength.[12]

The 32d was the only PAVN regiment physically present in western Pleiku when the planning for the Plei Me campaign began in mid to late September. On 12 October the regimental headquarters was reportedly in the vicinity of Plei Lao Chin, just north of the Ia Drang and about 2 km east of the Cambodian border. The 33d Regiment was still on its way down the Trail; its first elements did not reach Pleiku until 10 September, and the regiment as a whole did not arrive until about 2 October. Upon arrival, it took up residence around a Highland village the Communists called Anta, at the foot of the Chu Pong massif and adjacent to the Ia Drang valley on the Cambodian border. The 66th Regiment reportedly started moving south from its peacetime base in Thanh Hoa Province in North Vietnam between 10 and 18 August but only started to arrive in the area of the Chu Pong massif on or about 1 November.[13]

General Man's basic concept of operations for the use of these forces (or at least his opening gambit) was to attack another of Pleiku's Special Forces–CIDG camps and ambush the expected relief force. The target picked on this occasion was the camp at Plei Me, about 45 km south and slightly west of the town of Pleiku. This type of operation, sometimes called "lure and ambush," was a standard part of the repertoire for Communist main force units in South Vietnam. Indeed, it was already somewhat hackneyed—a deadly game with which both sides were all too familiar.[14] What had happened in the Duc Co campaign in July–August 1965 proved that this method held no guarantee of success for the Communist side. After their Duc Co experience, some members of the 32d Regiment had serious doubts about whether the same approach could work in and around Plei Me. One history written in Hanoi in the 1990s describes "heated arguments and tense debates between . . . those who were resolute and those who were wavering."[15]

General Man and his staff, however, apparently hoped to get better results by employing greater force against a better chosen target. The 33d Regiment's mission was to attack and besiege Plei Me. The 32d Regiment, with its greater experience, would then ambush the ARVN forces sent to relieve the camp. The employment of two whole PAVN regiments seemed to reduce the risk of the ARVN responding with forces so numerically superior that neither the besiegers nor the ambushers could cope, as had happened at Duc Co.

The Special Forces camp at Plei Me was also somewhat more favorably situated geographically, from the Communist point of view, than Duc Co had been. Duc Co was on Highway 19, a fairly major, all-weather, two-lane road connecting the Central Highlands with the coast. Plei Me, by contrast, was on

Provincial Route 5 (known to Communist forces as Route 211), a one-lane dirt road that connected, at two points, with Highway 14, the main north-south route through the Highlands. If Plei Me were under attack, major reinforcements from Pleiku would have to go down this road, which was a better place to spring an ambush. Being narrower, it stretched convoys out further, and whereas the terrain around Highway 19 near Duc Co permitted tracked vehicles considerable freedom to move off road, the rougher ground and dense vegetation along some sections of Provincial Route 5 greatly constrained them. On the negative side, because the road was at a higher level than the ground on either side of it, Communist forces would have to attack uphill.[16]

A US military intelligence section undertook a "target analysis" of Plei Me in October 1965, apparently just before it was hit. The camp lay 21 km west of Highway 14 and 25 km south of Highway 19. It was at an elevation of 320 meters in a sparsely forested, generally level area. The camp was shaped like an equilateral triangle, surrounded by two strands of barbed wire fencing within which there were two concentric, triangular trench systems: an outer system and an inner system. There were twenty-four bunkers altogether. There was a 0.5-inch machine gun in each of the three major bunkers at the corners of the triangle. The camp also had at least two 81mm mortars and a 4.2-inch mortar. There was an airstrip 96 feet wide and approximately 1,500 feet long, capable of handling C-123 transport aircraft, immediately south of the camp and a helipad just to its eastern side.[17] In mid-October 1965 Plei Me had a garrison of some 12 US and 14 Vietnamese Special Forces personnel and 415 CIDG soldiers, the latter largely recruited from the Jarai tribe, local to the area. The camp had two main outposts, one of them 1 km northeast and the other 2 km south of the main camp, each of them containing 20 soldiers. The normal practice was to have five smaller pickets or ambush patrols, each consisting of 8 men, outside the wire at night.[18] Postwar accounts published in Hanoi indicate that, for weeks prior to the attack on the camp, Communist forces were performing close target reconnaissance of Plei Me and almost certainly would have been in possession of this information by then.[19]

Communist Logistics and Provincial Support for the PAVN

Organizing a campaign involving two entire PAVN regiments (in addition to provincial and local forces) that would be concentrated for weeks in a remote part of western Pleiku undoubtedly presented the Communist planners with serious supply problems. Keeping the troops fed was almost certainly the biggest of these. A document captured by the ARVN in the Duc Co campaign indicated that in August the men of the 320th/32d Regiment were in a bad state of malnutrition and sickness. It surely would have required weeks of proper feeding to get them physically healthy enough to undertake another demanding campaign. In early September General Man and his staff were, moreover, expecting the 33d Regiment to emerge from the Ho Chi Minh Trail, and its men too were likely to be suffering from malnutrition and disease. Indeed, according to one source, 40 percent of the men in the 33d Regiment's rifle companies were sick when the siege of Plei Me began.[20]

Inadequate stocks of basic medicines probably limited the ability to treat malaria and other tropical diseases in the PAVN regiments. But the Communist Party in this part of the country, operating in conjunction with the PAVN's logistical services, went to enormous lengths to ensure that its soldiers from the North were adequately fed and in other respects fully supported before and during the Plei Me campaign. The Rear Services (logistics) branch of the Central Highlands Front, which had existed for a little over a year, had organized two rear services sectors—a northern one near the triborder area, north of the town of Kontum, and a southern sector (relevant to the Plei Me campaign) along the Cambodian border, southwest of the town of Pleiku. Supplies reached the southern sector via both purchasing and collection centers in Cambodia and "a transportation corridor for use by porters that linked into the Group 559 strategic military transportation corridor [i.e., the Ho Chi Minh Trail] which brought supplies down from the North." When planning for this campaign began, the CHF's rear services had stockpiled only 202 tons of supplies altogether, and the 50 tons of ammunition in stock were judged to be only 30 percent of the campaign's requirements. Thus, a huge effort had to be made to boost supplies. The forward supply base for the Plei Me campaign was established in the H5–Ba Bi area on the banks of the river Drang, northwest of Plei Me. All supplies moving within South Vietnam had to be carried by human porters, and most of this work was undertaken by civilian Highlanders under Communist control.[21]

A postwar history by the Gia Lai Province Party Committee (Gia Lai being the Communist name for Pleiku Province and the adjacent areas of Binh Dinh and Phu Bon) indicates that in September 1965 the Communists controlled a large majority of the villages in Gia Lai's Chu Pong district (aka the 5th District or Area 5), where Plei Me was situated. At the same time, the Communists reckoned they controlled 80 percent of the physical area of Gia Lai and about 60 percent of its people.[22] Communist accounts, of course, tend to exaggerate Party success. Much of the area the Communists called Gia Lai consisted of sparsely populated mountains and jungles. It would be misleading to claim that either side controlled this sort of terrain more than a few hundred yards from where its troops were present at any given time. Yet it seems quite possible that in the autumn of 1965 the Communists controlled more than half of Gia Lai's population. The claim of 60 percent may, indeed, be pretty close to the mark.

One Communist account gives a fair degree of statistical detail, reckoning that the Party controlled 226,000 people in Gia Lai at this time, "including 117,000 liberated during the spring of 1965, 50,000 liberated in the summer of 1965 and 59,000 living in our base areas."[23]

Communist Party histories also give considerable detail as to how the people it controlled were used to support the Plei Me campaign. The most remarkable statistic is that, "during the fall of 1965 the people of the province managed to collect 1,200 tons of food."[24] This amount seems incredibly high, given that most of the population lived close to subsistence level. Extracting this amount of food must have caused extreme hardship. Food was not the only thing the Party required from those it ruled. The most unpopular aspect of French rule in the Highlands had been corvée—forced labor.[25] But in Gia Lai in autumn 1965, the Communist Party's corvée was just as demanding and oppressive as that of the French at their worst—and probably a good deal more so. "During the peak period the province provided as many as 2,500 coolie laborers and 'Determined-to-Win Youth' to provide support to the front lines. This is not counting the tens of thousands of days of labor organized by the Liberation Women's Association in directing members to mill rice all night. Sometimes even the old men of the ethnic minority tribes in the villages helped to mill rice to keep up with the need to support combat operations. This was a job that for generations the men of the tribes had never done before." The Party obviously allowed neither concern for the nutritional needs of the civilian population nor respect for its social customs to get in the way of supporting the military operations of its soldiers from the North. It is very difficult to imagine so much food and labor being obtained from these relatively primitive people without coercion. One Party history gives definite indications as to how its coercive apparatus was brought to bear:

> Among the ranks of the civilian coolie laborers transporting supplies and weapons were always 60 members of the Province's Determined-to-Win Youth Unit serving as a hard core for the conduct of this work. The security network in our base area, and especially along the Cambodian border, was strengthened and perfected, establishing a total of 52 village security sections within the province, with a total of 482 security cadre at the hamlet level.[26]

How exactly the "Determined-to-Win Youth Unit" worked in Pleiku–Gia Lai we do not know, but the twentieth century offers several examples of organizations in which ideologically imbued youths were used to further the ends of radical parties, regimes, or factions—the Hitler Youth and Mao's Red Guard being obvious examples. It is conceivable that young, ambitious Highlanders, perhaps from families of relatively low status, were attracted to a movement that offered them authority over people who had previously been above them in the social hierarchy. The "security sections" referred to here were the ultimate Communist political police at the village level throughout South Vietnam. Their mission was to enforce discipline, liquidating any form of collaboration with the enemy or resistance to the Party's will.

At the same time, the Communist district troops in Chu Pong, commanded by an individual known as Comrade Y-Gir or Nghi, tried to eliminate the remaining government-defended villages in the district and to interdict Highway 19 and Highway 14. Village militia (the lowliest and least well-equipped Communist personnel) in this district were split into three groups to assist the PAVN's Plei Me campaign: "Group A: Strong healthy individuals assigned to serve as guides, to reconnoiter the enemy situation and to transport rice and ammunition from the [Cambodian] border to the battle area. Group B: Responsible for protecting and dispersing the civilian population during the battle and for keeping the population safe. Group C: Provide food and water, transport the wounded and bury the dead on the battlefield." In Chu Pong, "each village collected three to five water buffalo and more than twenty pigs and chickens . . . to supply to the troops during the battle."[27]

It was not merely district troops, village militia, and civilian labor that the Party in Gia Lai mobilized in support of the PAVN for this campaign. In October 1965 its military command created, for the first time, a fully fledged provincial battalion: H-15. With four companies (and about 375 personnel according to an American estimate), it replaced a proto-battalion called Inter-Company 45 that had apparently existed for some years. No details are given in Communist histories about H-15's ethnic composition, strength, or equipment. For the Plei Me campaign, it was based "east of Route 14 to operate from the My Thach area to the area west of the Ayun River to provide co-ordination and support."[28]

While the Party authorities in Gia Lai obviously mobilized a massive civilian effort in support of the PAVN in the Plei Me campaign, the claim in one Communist account that "the mountain jungles of Gia Lai burned with enthusiasm for fighting the Americans" needs to be treated with considerable caution.[29] It is clear from its own histories that the Party applied a high degree of coercion to get what it wanted. And most of those against whom the initial PAVN blows in this campaign were struck were not in fact Americans but Highlanders and Vietnamese.

The PAVN's Final Plan and Preparations

According to an American analysis based on the interrogation of captured North Vietnamese personnel, the plan for the attack on Plei Me consisted of three phases: "First the 33rd Regiment would surround Plei Me and harass the defenders, exerting enough pressure to force the Army of the Republic of Vietnam (ARVN) to send a reaction force. In the second phase, the 32nd Regiment would ambush the relief column and destroy it. Finally both regiments would combine forces to overrun and destroy the camp itself."[30]

Some odd decisions were made with regard to the distribution of forces. Perhaps because the really decisive mission was the 320th/32d Regiment's ambush, and the greatest threat to the success of that mission was enemy airpower, General Man decided that the 32d Regiment should have at least the bulk of the 33d Regiment's antiaircraft company (equipped with 12.7mm machine guns), as well as its own. The decision proved a dubious one; the 33d Regiment would bear the brunt of the American air attack of 20–25 October. Leaving the 33d Regiment with a 75mm recoilless rifle company was also questionable. This company seems to have been little used in the siege, but the 32d Regiment, conducting an ambush against an armored force, might have found additional recoilless rifles very useful.[31]

The 32d Regiment reportedly began its detailed planning and preparation for the attack as early as 19 September, about a month ahead of the event. First, the intended ambush site was reconnoitred and the area around it and the approaches to it carefully explored. These areas were reconstructed on sand tables, and exercises and rehearsals were carried out by each unit. At the same time, the regiment's transportation company, assisted by local labor, was stockpiling food and ammunition where it would be required. Even before the entire 33d Regiment had arrived in western Pleiku, its staff became heavily engaged in planning its role in the Plei Me campaign. But because the regiment was still arriving in the theater, its actual battle preparations were reduced to a mere ten days. The regimental commander reportedly did not regard this as enough.

The two regiments started moving to their assembly areas for the attack on 10 October. By 17 October, the 32d Regiment had completed its concentration in its main regimental assembly area 2 to 3 km west of the road on which the ambush would be sprung. The regiment proceeded to construct robust, carefully camouflaged bunkers where it could await the approach of Plei Me's relief force. The intention was to conduct a "maneuver ambush." A series of assaults would cut the road both in front of and behind the ARVN column, break the column into fragments, and destroy it piecemeal. The ambush site was about 4 km long and located about 30 km south of the town of Pleiku and 10 km north of Plei Me camp. A reconnaissance, lookout, and communication system was organized to keep commanders informed of enemy movements. Until battle was joined, this system would rely largely on field telephones and runners. Radio silence would be maintained until the fighting commenced. As the ARVN column approached, the attacking PAVN companies would move forward along carefully prepared and camouflaged paths from their bunkers in the assembly area to their firing and assault positions. The 32d Regiment had to construct both the paths and the final assault positions. Given that there were swift streams running parallel to the road and on either side of it, it was also necessary to build bridges. To avoid detection, most of this work had to be done at night.

While the 32d Regiment was doing all this, the 33d Regiment gradually moved into position around the Special Forces camp at Plei Me. Despite their extensive preparations and rehearsals for the attack, the majority of the troops did not know the name or location of their objective until 15 October. Only the regimental staff, the regimental reconnaissance element, and the battalion commanders knew beforehand that the objective was Plei Me. From 15 to 19 October the 33d Regiment constructed assault positions and made final battle preparations.[32]

A remarkable degree of surprise was achieved. Special Forces and CIDG personnel at Plei Me had "not encountered any Viet Cong activity that indicated a major attack was pending."[33] Given that reconnaissance was a large part of their role, they were perhaps culpable for not finding these large PAVN units in their vicinity and alerting higher authorities to their presence. Major South Vietnamese headquarters in the Highlands, such as 24 STZ and II Corps, had apparently received some warning that an attack was pending, but reports were vague or unconfirmed and difficult to evaluate: "Commencing on 27 September 1965, agent reports were periodically received of VC battalion sightings from 10 to 20 km to the North and North-West of the Plei Me Special Forces Camp. Early in October an agent reported that the Plei Me Special Forces Camp was to be the target of a VC attack. This report was evaluated C2 (doubtful) by the [South] Vietnamese."[34] An intelligence history of the campaign, apparently written in its immediate aftermath at MACV, indicates:

> Prior to the attack on Plei Me Special Forces Camp on 20 October there were a number of indications that a force build-up had taken place in Western Pleiku Province. Between 1 and 20 October 65, MACV J2 received 18 separate reports which indicated that units up to regimental size were in Western Pleiku Province. These reports also indicated that a training center existed 10 km north of Duc Co. The 32d NVA [North Vietnamese Army] Regiment was first identified after the attack on Duc Co on 9 August and was carried in order of battle as a possible unit located in the vicinity of Chu Pong. The H-15 Local Force Battalion was also carried as a confirmed unit, with a strength of 375, located northwest of Chu Pong.[35]

Yet it does not seem that MACV's analysts predicted a Communist offensive in western Pleiku in the second half of October. If they did, they failed to give timely warning to those who needed to know.

The Campaign Commences, 19–20 October

On the night of 19 October 1965 a combat patrol from Plei Me, consisting of 85 CIDG personnel and 2 members of the American A-detachment (A-217), was on a mission 15 km northwest of the camp. A total of some 40 CIDG soldiers were holding the camp's two outposts (northern and southern), and another 40 were manning local pickets or ambushes outside the wire. That left approximately 250 CIDG personnel, 14 Vietnamese Special Forces, and 8 to 10 American Special Forces personnel (accounts differ) inside the main camp.[36] The officer commanding the A-detachment was Captain Harold H. Moore, a twenty-four-year-old from Pekin, Illinois, who had been at Plei Me for about two weeks.[37]

The weapons carried by CIDG personnel at Plei Me were mostly older-generation American equipment: M2 carbines, M1 rifles, and Browning automatic rifles.[38] The camp also had some crew-served machine guns and some mortars. Even with the advantage of fortifications, however, the camp's garrison did not constitute a particularly powerful force to be confronting a PAVN regiment. It may be that most of its personnel survived not only because of the close air support provided, mainly by the US Air Force, but also because it was not the Communists' intention, in the short run, to capture the camp.[39]

There are conflicting accounts as to when the attack on the camp started, probably because it was difficult to distinguish clashes between the PAVN and patrols from the attack on the camp itself. According to a report by US Special Forces:

> The camp started receiving small arms fire from the southwest at 1915 hours on 19 October 1965. It was determined later that one of the local ambush patrols was involved in a fire fight with a PAVN unit of unknown strength. At 2200 hours the outpost to the south was attacked by approximately forty PAVN soldiers. At the same time the camp had been receiving 81mm mortar and 57mm recoilless rifle fire. Twenty minutes later contact with the outpost was lost.[40]

According to this report, the PAVN forces launched their attack on the camp itself at 0030 on Wednesday, 20 October, the main thrusts coming from the north and northwest. Over the next forty minutes, attacks came from a variety of directions. By 0110 hours, "the PAVN were within the defensive wire barriers to the south, on the east near the main gate and to the north near the corner bunker. They made a determined attempt to overrun the corner bunker but the defenders in the vicinity . . . repulsed the attack." North Vietnamese attacks continued throughout the night. At approximately 0600 on 20 October, the north corner bunker was hit and badly damaged, possibly by recoilless rifle fire. But surviving defenders apparently continued to fight, and the PAVN did not take the position.[41]

According to one report, at 2300 on Tuesday, 19 October, before the attack on the main camp developed, Captain Moore requested the assistance of a flare helicopter. At about the same time this Bell Iroquois HUIB "Huey" took off (apparently from one of the airfields at Pleiku), a C-123 Provider (fixed-wing) flare ship piloted by Major Howard Pierson of the 309th Air Commando Squadron flew from Bien Hoa toward the New Pleiku Air Base, just north of the town of Pleiku, where it picked up a forward air controller, Captain Dick Shortridge, to help direct air strikes. Flares, probably from the helicopter, were falling around the beleaguered camp by 0215 on 20 October. The C-123 arrived on station at 0340 and was joined, about ten minutes later, by two A-1E strike aircraft. Reports differ as to when the air strikes began, but 0410 on 20 October is the latest estimate. Between then and 0600 on 21 October, no fewer than 109 strike sorties were reportedly flown in support of the camp.[42]

A medical evacuation helicopter from Pleiku arrived at Plei Me at 0730 on Wednesday, 20 October, and left at 0900 carrying four wounded CIDG personnel. Captain Lanny Hunter, a surgeon attached to the Special Forces C-detachment at Pleiku, arrived in this helicopter and remained throughout the siege, treating the wounded. During the course of the siege, Hunter himself was reportedly wounded three times, but he patched himself up on each occasion "without slowing his pace in looking after the other wounded." A helicopter flying in support of this first medical rescue mission was shot down. An attempt to reach the crashed aircraft from Plei Me was unsuccessful, and an American Special Forces staff sergeant, Joseph Bailey, was badly wounded in the attempt. He died when North Vietnamese fire pinned the patrol down as it was trying to get back to camp.[43]

Reinforcements for Plei Me, 20–22 October

On the morning of Wednesday, 20 October, both the South Vietnamese and American Special Forces at Plei Me requested reinforcement, each through their own channels. By 0518, the request had reached II Corps headquarters at Pleiku.[44] But II Corps was very short of reserves at this particular time and was hesitant to commit all it had. Rather more rapid assistance came from Special Forces resources. Colonel William McKean, the commanding officer of the 5th Special Forces Group (overall US Army Special Forces commander in Vietnam), and the head of South Vietnamese Special Forces, Colonel Doan Van Quang, decided to send some American Project Delta personnel and two

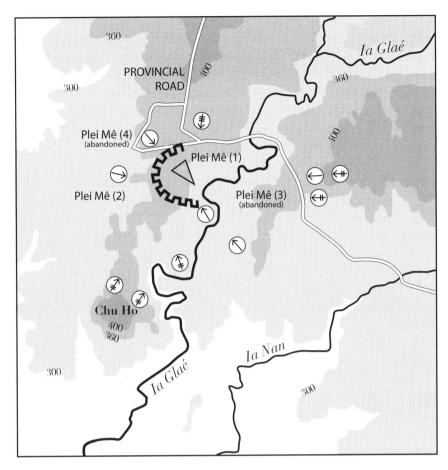

PAVN antiaircraft and trench positions around Plei Me camp, 20 October 1965

companies (about 150 officers and men) of the South Vietnamese 91st Airborne Ranger Battalion. The normal job of the 91st Airborne Ranger Battalion was to support Project Delta reconnaissance missions designed to locate concentrations of Communist troops.

Two Vietnamese Airborne Ranger companies, commanded by Major Thut, together with some fifteen US Special Forces personnel from Project Delta, commanded by Major Charles "Charlie" Beckwith, assembled at an airfield in the coastal city of Qui Nhon by 1530 on 20 October. American fixed-wing transport aircraft (one C-123 Provider and one C-130) then flew them from Qui Nhon to Pleiku, a move completed by 1700 the same day. Also on 20 October, II Corps commander Vinh Loc, with the encouragement of American advisers, decided to send an armored task force by road to relieve Plei Me. But disputes about the composition of this force delayed its dispatch.[45]

Plei Me's earliest reinforcement came from the substantial part of its own Strike Force that had been on patrol northwest of the camp when the attack began. Although the camp "was under continuous small arms and mortar fire from 1200 hours on the 20th until 0400 hours on the 21st," the North Vietnamese clearly did not have it completely surrounded. At 2130 on 20 October this large patrol managed to get back in "without encountering any major action," adding between eighty and ninety combatants to the garrison.[46] Further reinforcement was not long delayed.

Major Beckwith was the senior American with the joint American–South Vietnamese Special Forces task force intended to reinforce Plei Me. Born in Atlanta in 1929, he had gone to the University of Georgia on a football scholarship and joined the ROTC program there. When a career in professional football did not seem feasible, he joined the army and commanded a rifle company in Korea toward the end of the war there. Six feet two inches tall, powerfully built, and with a fierce temper, he was an exceptionally zealous, tough, and determined officer. Beckwith had transferred to the US Army Special Forces in 1958 but was in some respects critical of that organization. Having served on attachment to the British Special Air Service in 1962–1963, one of his principal military ambitions became the development of a comparable elite force in his own army.[47]

Beckwith arrived at the New Airfield at Pleiku at about 1700 on 20 October. A little later that evening he met with Lieutenant Colonel John Bennett, deputy commander of the US 5th Special Forces Group, in the Pleiku sector headquarters. Bennett announced that the Airborne Ranger companies and accompanying Project Delta personnel would parachute into the besieged camp that very evening, just before last light. According to Beckwith's rather idiosyncratic (and very idiomatic) memoirs, previous experience had made him mistrustful of Bennett's judgment. He regarded the prospect of being parachuted into Plei Me with grave reservations. "Hey man, I said to myself, this ain't the way to go. I couldn't see [myself] hanging from a parachute and being shot at by the Communists as I floated into that little old camp. I thought other courses of action were open to us." Again according to Beckwith, Colonel Ted Mataxis, the senior American adviser at II Corps, agreed with him. Mataxis overruled Bennett, declaring, according to Beckwith, "There won't be no parachute operation this evening. In fact there won't be one at all."[48]

By the evening of Wednesday, 20 October, the siege of Plei Me was clearly becoming, in the minds of senior American officers, the biggest event in Vietnam. Colonel McKean flew to Pleiku to involve himself in planning the camp's reinforcement. After intensive discussions between 1800 and 2000 that evening, a scheme "was devised to make a helicopter assault seven km north of Plei Me, infiltrate through the jungle and reinforce" the camp. At 0630 the following day, McKean and Beckwith climbed aboard a Huey helicopter at Camp Holloway air base and flew over the area to select the precise landing zone (LZ). They ended up picking a spot about 5 km north of Plei Me. On the way back to Camp Holloway, they were reminded how potentially dangerous helicopter flight was in those days, even in the absence of enemy action. According to Beckwith's memoirs, a gunship escorting them suffered a catastrophic mechanical failure, crashed into the jungle, and exploded.[49]

At 0730 on Thursday, 21 October, the US Air Force strafed the intended LZ. (The logic behind this is difficult to understand. "Prepping" the LZ in this way might have signaled its location to the North Vietnamese, and the air strike occurred too long before the first helicopter landed to have any useful suppressive effect.) Helicopters were in short supply in II Corps at this time, and it was necessary to use a rather mixed bag, including Hueys from the 52d Aviation Battalion at Pleiku and H-34s from the US Marine Corps' 363d Medium Helicopter Squadron. The first of three helicopter lifts, which would carry the fifteen Project Delta personnel and two companies of South Vietnamese Airborne Rangers, left the Camp Holloway airfield at 0805. By 1030, the move to the LZ was complete. At 1100 the assembled force departed the LZ for Plei Me.[50]

Owing to the density of the jungle, which in this sector was mostly tall elephant grass, movement was very slow and in single file. About 80 percent of the time it was necessary to hack their way forward. At approximately 1500 on 21 October, the front of the Delta–Airborne Ranger file ran into three North Vietnamese soldiers, one of whom was carrying a box of recoilless rifle ammunition. That man was killed, but the others got away. Major Thut, commanding the Airborne Ranger companies, apparently believed the element of surprise had now been lost, and trying to get into the camp would involve excessive risk. According to Beckwith's memoirs, Thut wanted to abort the mission. Beckwith insisted that his Project Delta personnel would proceed to reinforce Plei Me with or without their Airborne Ranger counterparts. Rather than head directly for the camp, however, he decided first to turn east, going deeper into the jungle. After some delay, and apparently fearing loss of face, Major Thut decided that he and his men should follow Beckwith.[51]

Though no account says so directly, it seems probable that the Delta–Airborne Ranger force led by Beckwith became lost, at least for a time. Upon making radio contact with the camp that evening, Beckwith was invited "to come in and join the party," a phrase he later claimed to have taken strong objection to, finding it too flippant in the grim circumstances. He requested a patrol from Plei Me to act as guides. A patrol went out but failed to find the prospective reinforcements, possibly because they were not where Beckwith had indicated. Beckwith later claimed that he had, in any case, changed his mind about trying to get into the camp that night. At 2100 on Thursday, 21 October, with Beckwith reckoning he was about 1,000 meters north of the camp, the Delta-Ranger force formed a defensive perimeter and waited until morning.[52]

At some point between 0500 and 0600 on Friday, 22 October (his subsequent accounts differ), Beckwith's people started moving again. Pushing approximately 400 meters to the east, they found a road that obviously led to the camp. Up to this point, they had taken a circuitous route through dense jungle, but Beckwith's after-action report indicates: "To expedite movement into the camp the road was utilized the remainder of the way." Yet, according to the same report, it took until 0900 to get within 400 meters of the camp. This makes little sense unless the Delta-Ranger force had been much further from Plei Me on the night of 21 October than Beckwith realized.

When his force was about 400 meters from the camp, Beckwith gave the order to run straight down the road and through the main gate. It was broad daylight by this time. Inevitably, the large body of running men attracted fire. An Airborne Ranger lieutenant was killed, and two American soldiers and at least two Vietnamese were slightly wounded. A civilian newsman accompanying the force, Charles Burnett of KTLA-TV in Los Angeles, suffered an ultimately fatal head wound. The rest of the force apparently reached the camp intact. It had been twenty-three hours since helicopters first inserted the force just 5 km to the north.[53]

Plei Me under Beckwith's Command, 22–25 October

It may be inferred that Beckwith was not in the best of moods by the time he reached the camp. His memoirs relate that what he witnessed upon arrival greatly concerned him: "The first thing I noticed on going through the gate was the Montagnard tribesmen who had been killed while defending the camp; they were still lying in the wire, I mean everywhere. . . . Oh shit, I thought, there's going to be a lack of discipline in here . . . there's some problems in here." In addition to the dead defenders lying "everywhere" in the wire, Beckwith's memoirs indicate there were "about sixty other dead Montagnard soldiers stuffed into body bags and stacked up like cordwood. The smell was terrible." Nor did Beckwith like the overcrowding in the camp, caused in part by sheltering CIDG soldiers' families as well as the soldiers themselves. (The arrival of Beckwith's Project Delta personnel and the Airborne Rangers had, of course, greatly exacerbated rather than relieved this problem.) Beckwith was further perturbed, he later claimed, by the camp's "dirty" appearance. "A thick red dust covered everything."

Again according to Beckwith, the notional camp commander, a Vietnamese Special Forces captain, never left his "deep bunker." (This is credible, as no report on Plei Me ascribes any role in the siege to this officer. His name is not even mentioned in any account that has come to light during research for this book.) The effective camp commander since the start of the siege had been Captain Harold H. Moore, leading A-217, the American Special Forces detachment. Upon his arrival, Beckwith became the senior American officer present, so it was perfectly natural for him to supersede Moore. By his own account, however, he did so brusquely: "I let him know that I was the new mayor of Plei Me."[54] Beckwith's memoirs record that he experienced continuing friction with Moore and that he eventually had to become "physical" with him.[55]

It is difficult, on the basis of the relatively slender evidence available, to know whether Beckwith's strongly implied condemnation of Moore's leadership is justified. That a camp under fairly intense bombardment for a couple of days had become covered in the red dust characteristic of Vietnam is scarcely surprising, and Beckwith apparently did little to remedy that during his time in command.[56] On the matter of CIDG corpses left lying around (an issue that does not figure in Beckwith's after-action report), there is a conflict of evidence between his memoirs and other records. One set of official American statistics lists just fourteen CIDG personnel killed in the siege of Plei Me itself (20–25 October), although that figure clearly does not include those who died on 19 October when the southern outpost was overrun. Several of those fourteen evidently died after Beckwith took over.[57]

The bodies Beckwith remembered seeing lying on the edges of the camp when he wrote his memoirs in the 1980s would have been covered in dust, partially decomposed, and perhaps, in some cases, burned by napalm. It seems probable that most if not all of these corpses were those of North Vietnamese soldiers, who were far more likely than their CIDG opponents to have been caught in the wire. Assuming they did not critically obstruct the defenders' fields of fire, was it worth Moore's risking the lives of members of the garrison to remove them?

William Westmoreland apparently received reports of Harold Moore's conduct of the defense of Plei Me from sources other than Charlie Beckwith. The day after the siege ended, the commanding general met the young captain and congratulated him.[58]

Judging by the official statistics, a very substantial proportion of the fatal casualties among the camp's defenders occurred after Beckwith assumed command. Under Moore's direction, the Plei Me garrison had made sorties for limited purposes. They had attempted to rescue downed aircrews (sometimes successfully and sometimes not) and had tried, unsuccessfully, to find and guide Beckwith's force as it sought to reinforce the camp. They had incurred at least one fatal casualty (Sergeant Bailey) in such sorties, but apparently not many. Under Beckwith, there would be larger and more aggressive sorties, and these would incur far greater casualties, with little or nothing to show in the way of positive results.[59]

Beckwith's memoirs indicate that his real intention was to strengthen the camp's fortifications rather than to go on the offensive. He claimed that he radioed this intention to Pleiku but was overruled by Bill McKean, his immediate superior. McKean ordered him to get outside the wire, "rummage around," and try to clear Communist forces away from the camp. Beckwith further claims that he told McKean this was "not a good idea," but McKean ignored him and gave him a direct order to mount an aggressive sortie.[60] This, however, is not the version of events found in Beckwith's after-action report, which indicates that upon arrival in the camp, "Delta CO [Beckwith] and counterpart [Thut] determined that the area immediately around the camp must be cleared." There is no mention of this decision being imposed from above.[61]

Presumably with the assent of Major Thut, Beckwith decided to use the two Airborne Ranger companies as well as one CIDG company (but apparently not his Project Delta personnel) in an effort to clear a hill approximately 400 meters north of the camp. Beckwith, or whoever did the detailed planning for this operation, apparently sent the Airborne Rangers out through the main gate in broad daylight sometime between 1300 and 1400 on Friday, 22 October. The North Vietnamese were in bunkers and foxholes. As might have been expected, they offered fierce resistance. According to Beckwith's after-action report, the troops conducting the sortie had a particular problem with a North Vietnamese machine gun team that was dug in very near the camp. As they advanced on their objective, they passed this machine gun without realizing it was there. Its fire took them in the flank and rear and seriously disorganized them. Although some of them turned to deal with it, they were unsuccessful. The companies involved in the sortie became pinned down for several hours. They did not get back inside the wire until 1840. Possibly they waited for dark before attempting a move. Thirteen of them had been killed: eleven enlisted men (Airborne Rangers and CIDG); Captain Thomas W. Pusser, American adviser to the Airborne Rangers; and a Vietnamese Special Forces lieutenant. Another twenty-six men were wounded.[62]

At some point that day, Beckwith requested that Plei Me be resupplied by parachute, asking for a couple of hundred five-gallon water cans and a basic load of ammunition plus "a couple of boxes of cigars, some cigarettes and a case of whiskey." Apparently concerned that he not be thought too demanding, he added that he was not fussy about the brand of the whiskey. Beckwith's immediate superior, Bill McKean, was not amused by the demands for luxury goods but nevertheless complied. Beckwith's memoirs record three parachute drops that day. The first fell outside the wire, but the others were absolutely accurate.[63]

Official records confirm that the first airdrops for Plei Me happened on Friday, 22 October, the day Beckwith took over. Beckwith deserves credit for the extra security and comfort they afforded the garrison, but the cost, in terms of damage to aircraft, was considerable. According to the official US Army Special Forces report, "During the period 22 through 25 October 1965 a total of 313,000 pounds of supplies were air dropped to besieged Plei Mei," and despite the camp's small size, "304,000 pounds of the supplies landed inside. . . . There were 41 missions flown, 25 by C-123 [Provider] type aircraft from the 310th Air Commando Squadron and 16 by CV2B [Caribou] type aircraft from the 92d Army Aviation company. Nineteen of the C-123 and two CV2B were hit by ground fire." None of the supply aircraft crashed, but "the two CV2B and seven of the C-123's remained out of service as a result of the hits received." It is interesting to note the continuing importance of the Air Commandos, who had been providing support for Special Forces ground operations since the days of Dave Nuttle and the Buon Enao experiment.[64]

Plei Me also received massive close tactical air support. This, however, started within hours of the initial North Vietnamese attack, long before Beckwith took over. One report indicates that over ten days beginning on 20 October, "in 696 day and night sorties, B-57s, A1-Es, F 100s, and F-8s rained 866,300 pounds of GP [general purpose] bombs, 250,380 pounds of frag bombs, 485,880 pounds of napalm, plus rockets, CBUs and cannon fire on VC positions as close as 35 meters from the outpost walls." Some of these munitions were clearly expended in support of the column that II Corps sent for the relief of Plei Me, rather than in direct support of the camp, and given that the siege effectively ended on 25 October, some were obviously expended against the PAVN forces in its immediate aftermath. The US Air Force official history indicates, "This was the largest air-supported combat operation of the war so far using almost 600 strikes. Two-thirds of these were flown by the Air Force, with the Navy, Marines and Vietnamese providing the rest." One of the principal groups of intended beneficiaries, the American A-detachment in Plei Me, thought the air effort was magnificent and recorded that, on at least one occasion (apparently during one of the early assaults), napalm had been dropped right along the edge of the wire.[65]

The cost was far from negligible. One B-57 (Canberra) bomber was damaged by ground fire on the morning of Wednesday, 20 October, and diverted to Camp Holloway, not its normal station, to land. It crashed before getting there, although the crew survived. Another aircraft of the same type was shot down later the same day; that crew bailed out and was rescued. Two A-1E strike aircraft crashed on Friday, 22 October. In both cases the pilots survived.

At least two helicopters also crashed and were totally wrecked. In financial terms, all this irreparable damage to aircraft (both transport and strike) was a considerable price to pay for a few days' fighting against a light infantry foe equipped with no antiaircraft weapon more powerful than a heavy machine gun. Perhaps only US forces could accept such material losses so lightly, while writing up the campaign as a major success for airpower.[66]

Despite the prodigious hammering they were taking from the air, on 22 October, the day Beckwith arrived in camp, the besieging North Vietnamese showed no sign of giving up. Though there was no major assault during his period in command, the camp continued to receive mortar, machine gun, and small-arms fire. Beckwith's memoirs indicate that his instincts as to how to handle the situation at Plei Me remained defensive; that the big sortie mounted on Friday, 22 October, was on McKean's orders and against Beckwith's better judgment; and that Beckwith reverted to a defensive stance when it failed.[67] But it is clear from contemporary records (including Beckwith's own after-action report) that on both Saturday, 23 October, and Monday, 25 October, he ordered further aggressive sorties, in broad daylight and in the absence of artillery support, against a well dug in, numerically superior enemy. According to Beckwith's after-action report:

> At 0900 [on Saturday, 23 October] a platoon of CIDG and one platoon of Airborne Rangers made an attempt to knock out two known machine gun positions. This attack was supported by mortar and machine gun fire from the camp. This force moved into position, laid down a base of fire and the maneuver element moved forward to assault the position. At this time one VC came out of his hole and ran the CIDG–Abn Ranger force out of the area. This VC was killed by supporting fires from within the camp. The force withdrew.[68]

Beckwith was evidently disappointed and frustrated by the failure of the second attack he had ordered within twenty-four hours. Strongly implying that only cowardice or panic on the part of the indigenous troops under his command could explain it, he did not enumerate the casualties they had sustained. Nor did he desist from ordering additional daylight attacks, in the absence of armor and artillery support, on an entrenched, alert, numerically superior, extremely determined enemy. Indeed, on the afternoon or evening of 23 October, he asked for flamethrowers to be dropped into the camp "to attack bunkers." They arrived the following day.[69]

In a version of events given orally to TV journalist John Laurence at the end of the siege, Beckwith (and some of the other Americans present) strongly implied that Americans had done all the real fighting in defense of Plei Me. The Vietnamese in the Plei Me garrison (leaving aside the CIDG Highlanders,

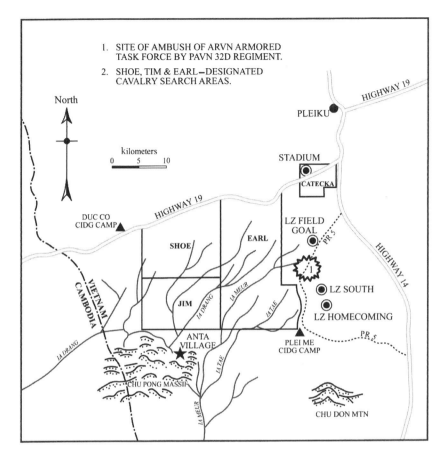

Operations in the Plei Me area, 23–31 October 1965

many of whom had chosen to return to the camp while it was under siege) were dismissed as cowardly, incompetent, or both. Though not made explicit, the same thing is clearly implied in Beckwith's TV interview with Laurence, broadcast to the American public shortly after the conclusion of the siege and now accessible on the Internet.[70]

It may well be true that most members of the original Vietnamese Special Forces group at Plei Me (the counterpart of the American A-detachment) played little or no part in the camp's defense. Such groups generally had bad reputations with their American opposite numbers. Their main function, from the Saigon government's point of view, seems to have been to watch the Americans and their Highland troops for signs of FULRO-style subversive, pro-autonomy activity. Yet a lieutenant from this group died on 22 October in the first of Beckwith's ill-fated sorties, and two of its other members were wounded during the siege.[71]

With regard to the Airborne Rangers who accompanied Beckwith to Plei Me, the suggestion of cowardice and incompetence scarcely holds up. It is indeed contradicted in some parts of Beckwith's own, rather inconsistent, accounts of these events. On 23 October, according to his memoirs, Beckwith grew concerned about the body of Captain Thomas Pusser, the Airborne Rangers' adviser killed in the previous day's sortie. Beckwith wanted to send a third sortie on Sunday, 24 October, to retrieve it. When he asked for volunteers, Major Thut said, "The Vietnamese will get his body for you. We want to do this."[72] Thut gave the job to the commander of the 1st Airborne Ranger Company, who apparently decided to retrieve all the bodies left behind after the first sortie, not just Pusser's. In his after-action report, Beckwith noted that this complex little operation, which involved organizing fire support and sending out both a reconnaissance party and a carrying party, was conducted in "a very professional manner." All the bodies were recovered.[73]

American official statistics indicate that 15 of Thut's 135 to 150 Airborne Rangers were killed and 29 wounded during the siege. Of the three American Special Forces personnel killed serving as part of the Plei Me garrison,[74] one was Thomas Pusser, who died fighting alongside these troops. The Airborne Rangers thus appear to have suffered a 10 or 11 percent fatality rate in three or four days—extraordinarily heavy losses, given that there were no PAVN assaults or even substantial probes during this period. The great majority of these deaths almost certainly occurred during Beckwith's repeated daylight attacks on a well-prepared enemy in carefully concealed, mutually supporting bunkers, machine gun nests, and foxholes[75]—attacks that Thut surely should have vetoed and Beckwith should never have ordered.

For the morning of Monday, 25 October, Beckwith developed a plan "to attack machine gun bunkers with one commando type squad and two Americans with flame throwers." The sortie went ahead at 0930. The flamethrowers reportedly malfunctioned and proved ineffective. Beckwith's after-action report indicates, "The commando squad successfully knocked out one light machine gun bunker." Another report merely notes, "The operation met stiff resistance and was forced back to the camp."[76]

This appears to have been the last attack Beckwith ordered while in command at Plei Me. Again, his report does not enumerate the casualties among the indigenous troops acting under his orders. Again, it is far from clear that anything useful was achieved. The siege would end later that day. But that had nothing to do with any of the attacks Beckwith launched from within the camp. The repeated failure of these ill-conceived and unnecessary ventures may well have contributed to Beckwith's ugly mood when relief finally came from without.

Organizing the Relief Force, 20–22 October

At II Corps headquarters and at 24 STZ headquarters, which had operational responsibility for this part of the Central Highlands, the intelligence picture of events at Plei Me took a couple of days to evolve. Initially, the attack against the camp was perceived to be "a one Battalion size attack by fire only"; the two subsequent "VC probes" were "estimated to be by 30–40 men each." By the second day, however, the assessment had changed somewhat:

> On the morning of 21 October 1965, as intelligence information and VC activities continued to be evaluated in conjunction with previous reports, it was estimated that in addition to the VC battalion committed against the Special Forces Camp, two to three VC battalions were available for employment against any friendly relief force.
>
> On Friday 22 October the intelligence estimate was [again] revised. At that time it was believed that two VC regiments were operating in the Plei Me area. It became apparent that the VC were capable of mounting an attack to destroy the Plei Me camp while simultaneously attacking a relief force; or the VC could position only sufficient force to harass the camp and commit their main force to destroy the relief column. The second course of action appeared the most valid. . . . Based upon that evaluation two areas along the route of approach of the relief column were determined to be ideal sites from which an attack could be mounted.[77]

On Wednesday, 20 October, II Corps had very few reserves, and this clearly worried the corps commander, Major General Vinh Loc. For the relief of Duc Co, II Corps had used both a two-battalion Airborne task force and a two-battalion Marine task force. The Airborne task force, however, was now committed on the coastal plain, taking part in operations designed to gain control of the rice harvest. Marine Task Force Alpha was engaged in operations in Darlac, from which there was apparently some reluctance to withdraw it. Vinh Loc's corps reserve essentially consisted of only an armored cavalry squadron and two Ranger battalions. On 20 October 1965, the first day of the siege, Vinh Loc released most of that reserve to Brigadier General Cao Hao Hon, commander of 24 STZ, for use in the relief of Plei Me.

Considered in more detail, the forces Vinh Loc made available for Plei Me's relief consisted of the 3d Armored Cavalry Squadron headquarters under Lieutenant Colonel Nguyen Trong Luat; Armored Personnel Carrier Troop 2/6 (with fifteen M-113s), commanded by Captain Du Ngoc Thanh; Tank Troop 3/5 (with sixteen M41 Walker Bulldog tanks), commanded by Captain Nguyen

Manh Lam; one platoon of the 222d Artillery; a platoon of the 201st Engineers; and the 21st Ranger Battalion. This conglomeration, designated the Armored Task Force (ATF), was placed under Lieutenant Colonel Luat's command.

At some point on 20 October, Brigadier General Hon flew from Kontum, where 24 STZ had its headquarters, to Pleiku, where he established a forward command post to take charge of Plei Me's relief. Hon ordered Luat to move the ATF from Pleiku down Highway 14 to the junction with Provincial Route 5 at Phu My. From there, he was to "execute aggressive patrolling" up to 5 km to the south, the patrols being intended as "feints" in "an effort to divert the attention of the VC from Plei Me." Luat moved the ATF to Phu My by 1945 on 20 October and began patrols the following day.[78]

Both Hon and his American adviser, Lieutenant Colonel Archie Hyle, evidently thought the ATF, as initially constituted, was insufficient for its purpose. They were in no rush to send it into the chosen killing ground of a large-scale Communist ambush. On 21 October, therefore, Luat's force confined itself to patrols within 5 km of Phu My, none of which made contact with Communist forces. At noon that day, at II Corps headquarters in Pleiku, there was a conference on Plei Me involving both Vietnamese and American officers. Mataxis and Hyle apparently tried to persuade Vinh Loc to release his last reserve, the 22d Ranger Battalion, but the II Corps commander was reluctant. Some American commentators have ridiculed this as an obsession with maintaining a "palace guard."[79] But was Vinh Loc's stance so absurd? Perhaps it is worthwhile to look at things from his point of view.

One of Vinh Loc's anxieties was that the Communists might be trying to trick him into denuding Pleiku of troops so that they could strike at, or even capture, the town.[80] Not merely a provincial capital but also home to a corps headquarters, Pleiku's capture would have been a dramatic success for Communist forces, even if they were unlikely to hold it for any length of time. Communist troops had, of course, struck the MACV compound and Camp Holloway the previous February, making dramatic worldwide headlines. This was good for Communist morale and very bad for that of the southern republic's defenders. Vinh Loc also had serious concerns about the challenge to government authority in the Highlands posed by FULRO, a movement about which he had recently written a very hostile book.[81] How far his perception of a FULRO threat to Pleiku affected his judgment about releasing 22d Ranger Battalion for the relief of Plei Me is not clear. But before ridiculing such an anxiety, it should be remembered that FULRO had seriously threatened Ban Me Thuot the previous year, and the movement was still very much alive.[82]

Plei Me was, of course, part of CIDG, a program that involved arming Highland troops in quasi-independent units, something of which many South Vietnamese officers were very suspicious. Nevertheless, on 20 October Vinh

Loc had released the bulk of his corps reserve for the camp's relief. Should he now, one day later, give up 22d Ranger Battalion as well? Other than RF troops, police, and a reserve CIDG company consisting largely of Nungs, this battalion was Pleiku's final defense. Admittedly, the Americans were now offering Vinh Loc a battalion of their recently arrived 1st Cavalry Division to defend Pleiku on the condition that he release 22d Ranger Battalion for operations to relieve Plei Me.[83] But was it appropriate for him to put the defense of the most important town in the Highlands (and that of his own corps headquarters) in the hands of foreign troops?

On Friday, 22 October, Major General Stanley "Swede" Larsen, commanding Field Force Vietnam based at Nha Trang, became actively involved in discussions on the relief of Plei Me. It is necessary here to explain Larsen's position and its relevance to the siege of Plei Me. Larsen's Field Force was, in reality, a corps organization, the first to be established, for the command of American divisions in Vietnam. American troops would, of course, be operating within ARVN corps tactical zones (CTZs), but the Americans had no intention of allowing them to be integrated into the ARVN command structure. To avoid confusion with preexisting ARVN corps, however, they decided to avoid the term "corps" in their own chain of command. US division commanders, such as Major General Harry Kinnard of the 1st Cavalry Division, would be responsible to and controlled by US Field Force commanders. On Monday, 18 October, as a result of discussions with Vinh Loc, who was sensitive about military protocol, Westmoreland made Larsen the ARVN II Corps senior adviser, with Mataxis as Larsen's deputy.[84]

Possibly drawn into the debate on the relief of Plei Me by Mataxis, Larsen flew to Pleiku on 22 October to put pressure on Vinh Loc to release the 22d Ranger Battalion for that purpose. As a result of the ensuing discussions, "1st Brigade, 1st Cavalry Division assumed responsibility for the protection of Pleiku city" on 23 October, and Vinh Loc finally released 22d Ranger Battalion to 24 STZ to help with Plei Me's relief. Some elements of the 1st Cavalry Division (collectively known as Task Force Ingram) were made available to help with the relief of Plei Me if the South Vietnamese requested them, but as far as ground forces were concerned, this was intended to be a predominantly ARVN operation.[85]

The 1st Cavalry Division (Airmobile) now entered the picture. This division would play a part (albeit a limited and subordinate part) in the relief of Plei Me, and it is necessary to say something about it here. In 1964 the US Army had conducted a series of airmobility exercises with an experimental formation called the 11th (Airmobile) Division. Some elements of what eventually became the 1st Cavalry Division (Airmobile) had taken part in those exercises. Much of the division, however, was rather hurriedly assembled in the summer of 1965. Most of it traveled to Vietnam by ship, with a large part of it leaving from Charleston, South Carolina. It arrived in installments between August and early October, a substantial element docking at Qui Nhon on the coast of central South Vietnam on 13 September. By that time, General Westmoreland had decided that the division headquarters and main base would be at An Khe, in Binh Dinh Province, on the eastern edge of the Central Highlands. Over the next few weeks, while the division built itself a base, Camp Radcliff, which included the world's biggest helipad, known as the Golf Course, some of its elements were committed to combat operations.[86]

The 1st Cavalry Division's commander, Major General Harry Kinnard, was an intensely ambitious officer determined to prove the concept of heliborne airmobility by achieving dramatic victories in Indochina. But in October 1965 his division was not an elite formation. Many of its personnel had played no part in the airmobility exercises of 1964 and had little experience working from helicopters. The division was untried in combat prior to its arrival in Vietnam, and American journalists covering some of its early operations were far from impressed. They made this clear in their articles and broadcasts, and Westmoreland and Kinnard, both very media conscious, were well aware of this initial bad publicity.[87] In all probability, it made Kinnard even more ambitious to achieve some striking success. He was increasingly attracted by the opportunities Plei Me offered in that regard.[88]

The Relief of Plei Me, 23–25 October

In the short run, however, the relief of Plei Me and the inevitable battle with Communist forces there were ARVN problems. On Friday, 22 October, Brigadier General Hon made the decision to airlift the 1st Battalion, 42d Infantry Regiment (already under his command), from Kontum to Pleiku. That battalion arrived at Pleiku's New Airfield at 1100 on 23 October and moved by truck to the Phu My area, where it joined the ATF. Including the 22d Ranger Battalion, Hon now had a force he considered sufficient: a total of 1,200 men, sixteen tanks, and fifteen armored personnel carriers (APCs). Hon ordered Lieutenant Colonel Luat to start moving the ATF from Phu My to Plei Me at 1400 on Saturday, 23 October.[89]

At 1400, as the ATF started its journey along Provincial Route 5, helicopters lifted 22d Ranger Battalion to an LZ just west of it, adjacent to the more distant of the two sites where 24 STZ predicted that Communist forces might be lying in ambush. From there, "it was to sweep East to the . . . road, destroy any VC found in the area and serve as a blocking force so that any VC along the road would be caught between [it] and the attacking ATF and destroyed."[90]

Preparatory air strikes, intended to suppress any opposition in and around 22d Ranger Battalion's LZ, caused horrific civilian casualties in a Jarai village. American advisers later arranged to have some of the worst cases taken to a hospital. The Rangers, however, landed without casualties and without opposition. There were, in fact, no Communist troops immediately to the east of the LZ, and they could have pushed forward to the road quickly and easily. Instead, they hardly moved from their LZ, remaining rather passive for the rest of the day. The explanation given, or at least implied, in some American accounts is that, while playing "palace guard" for Vinh Loc in Pleiku, the battalion had lost all appetite for combat. There are even hints that Vinh Loc may have ordered the 22d Rangers' commanding officer, Lieutenant Colonel Phuoc, to avoid heavy casualties by steering clear of any real fighting.[91] Such interpretations, however, are not the only ones possible.

Phuoc may well have thought that his 22d Ranger Battalion had been placed in extreme danger.[92] He may have suspected that it was being used as bait, a sort of tethered goat, to lure Communist troops away from the ATF. When the battalion (about 450 men, mostly lightly armed) landed at 1400, it was very isolated. A whole PAVN regiment was between it and the ATF to the north. Elements of another were probably between it and Plei Me to the south. The ATF would not join battle with the PAVN 32d Regiment for another three hours.[93] Had the 22d Ranger Battalion made its presence felt too early, there was a chance that, using a relatively small force to keep the road blocked to traffic from the north, most of PAVN 32d Regiment could have concentrated on destroying it. In the event, the 22d Rangers remained quiet until the PAVN 32d Regiment attacked the ATF. The Rangers then mortared the Communist positions they could see from the high ground near their LZ but made no attempt to close with the enemy.[94]

Based on subsequent investigations, it seems that the 32d Regiment's Colonel Khan became aware of the 22d Rangers' presence almost as soon as they landed. One of the 32d Regiment's battalions, the 966th, had been kept in reserve, and one of its missions was to deal with just such a heliborne threat. Given that the 22d Rangers remained passive, however, the North Vietnamese regimental commander decided to leave them alone and to concentrate on attacking anything that came down the road.[95]

The ATF's advance from Phu My was extremely cautious and by no means rapid. Though called an armored force, many of its troops were deployed as dismounted infantry, searching the roadsides as they advanced. The tanks and APCs could not exceed their walking speed. The force commander, Lieutenant Colonel Nguyen Trong Luat, was a determined, jovial, but battle-wise and cautious cavalryman in his mid-forties. American TV journalist John Laurence, who was with Luat a little later in the campaign, noticed his weather-beaten face, his thick neck, and the swagger stick he habitually carried.[96] On Saturday, 23 October, Luat had no doubt that he was taking his force into a stiff fight. To Bob Poos, another American TV journalist who accompanied him south from Phu My, he indicated fairly accurately where the Communist forces would be waiting in ambush.[97]

Having trained their crews himself, Luat had reason to be reasonably confident in his tanks and APCs. Since 20 October he had presumably given the 21st Rangers some idea of what he expected from them. But 1st Battalion, 42d Infantry, had joined him just a few hours earlier. Luat and that battalion had practically no time to get to know each other. In these circumstances, Luat could hardly expect brilliant interarm teamwork. He had to deploy his force in a way that seemed most appropriate and hope for the best. As an American after-action report described it:

> The APC troop and the tank company moved along the road supported
> on the left by the 1/42nd Inf Bn and on the right by two companies of the
> 21st Ranger Battalion. The trains [the ATF's logistical element carrying fuel
> and ammunition in soft-skinned vehicles] protected by [an element] of the
> 21st Ranger Battalion [and three M8 armored cars and accompanied by two
> 105mm artillery pieces] followed approximately 2 km behind the main attack
> force. At approximately 1700 hours the main force halted while a pre-planned
> air strike was conducted on a suspected VC position.[98]

When the air strike was over, the main part of the ATF, but not the train, proceeded down the road. At this point there was a misunderstanding between Luat and the officer who commanded the train. The latter apparently believed the advance had stopped for the day. He clearly did not appreciate that his vehicles might already be within the killing zone of the ambush, which was considerably wider than the South Vietnamese and their American advisers had anticipated. The vehicles of the train were not arranged for defense, and the troops with them started lighting fires to cook their evening meal.

At 1750 on Saturday, 23 October, the main body of the ATF came under intense fire from both sides of the road. We now know that the PAVN 32d Regiment's 635th Battalion was responsible for this. There was no panic among the ARVN troops in the main body. This fight was entirely expected. The tanks fired canister from their 76mm main armament, and both tanks and APCs opened up with their machine guns. Accompanying infantry joined in with their weapons. American F-100 jets then struck the PAVN 635th Battalion with cannon fire and napalm, and helicopter gunships attacked it with rockets and more machine gun fire. In such circumstances the North Vietnamese found it impossible to develop an effective assault on the ATF's main body.

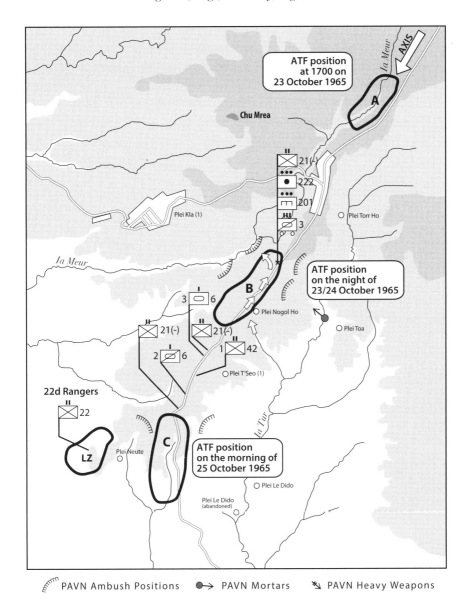

Plei Me relief operation: movements of the ATF

The firefight continued for about two hours, but it was extremely unequal, and it was the North Vietnamese who broke it off.[99]

Five kilometers back along Provincial Route 5, things had not gone so well for the ATF's supply train. Like the main body, and at about the same time, the train came under fire from west and east, from both sides of the road. The train became the focus of attack for the PAVN 32d Regiment's 344th Battalion.

Inevitably, the train had far less firepower than the main body of the ATF, and its soft-skinned vehicles were far more vulnerable. According to one account, there were "thunderous explosions" as fuel and ammunition trucks were hit by recoilless rifle, mortar, and rocket fire, and "columns of black smoke billowed up" into the evening sky. Then the "trains . . . were assaulted from the south by an estimated 2 to 3 company force. An immediate air strike was conducted on the attacking force but not before considerable damage was inflicted on the supply vehicles and [troops] of the 21st Ranger Bn." The main body of the ATF lost radio contact with the train. There were concerns that the rear column might have been overrun and completely destroyed. But that was not the case.

Before the PAVN onslaught began, Captain Paul Leckinger, American adviser to the 21st Rangers, accompanied by another officer, had gone back from the main body to find out what had happened to the train. When the attack started, they helped officers and men of the 21st Rangers form a perimeter around the train's vehicles that would continue to hold after dark.[100]

Leckinger's radio was damaged early in the action, and he had no means of communicating with the main body of the ATF or asking for air support. But Captain Hank Lang, who shared accommodations with Leckinger in the MACV compound in Pleiku, was flying over the battlefield in a Bird Dog light aircraft, operating as a forward air controller. Lang had been told that Leckinger was with the train, and he went to great lengths to save it. He was able to identify the positions of those trying to defend it after dark by the muzzle flashes of their weapons. He could make out the positions of the encircling North Vietnamese in the same way. Flying low, he used the landing lights on his aircraft as well as his radio to guide napalm strikes by two F-100s. These seem to have severely hurt the PAVN 344th Battalion, and its efforts against the train slackened.

Meanwhile, having repulsed the attack against it, the main body of the ATF withdrew 1 km to the north and formed a sort of defensive laager for the night. This was better organized and had much more firepower than the perimeter around the train. At 0300 on 24 October, however, after a short night march, the PAVN 32d Regiment's reserve battalion, the 966th, mounted an assault on the main body of the ATF from the north. But this soon wilted under ARVN fire. The ATF took few casualties during this phase.[101]

Overall, however, the fighting of 23–24 October had been costly for both sides. An after-action report on the campaign gives figures of 50 killed, 102 wounded, and 19 missing for anti-Communist forces on 23 October. Perhaps surprisingly, no American appears to have been hurt. Losses were almost certainly disproportionately heavy among the 21st Rangers defending the train, which also suffered the great bulk of the damage to equipment. Two M8 armored cars, two five-ton ammunition trucks, and two gasoline tankers were totally destroyed. Another M8 armored car, two 105mm guns, and some other logistical vehicles were damaged. But the tanks and APCs with the ATF's main body all survived, apparently without significant damage. The PAVN 32d Regiment had almost certainly suffered severe losses, but only 51 killed and 1 captured could be stated with any real certainty when this report was written. A history produced in Hanoi in the 1990s gives figures of 87 killed and 84 wounded.[102] They may well be too low.

Subsequent interrogations of captured North Vietnamese personnel indicate that on the morning of Sunday, 24 October, Colonel To Dinh Khan ordered the withdrawal of the bulk of his battered PAVN 32d Regiment to the west. Meanwhile, the ATF reorganized and licked its wounds. The 22d Rangers finally linked up with Luat's main body. Luat then withdrew the combined force back up the road until it linked up with the train; he then organized care for the wounded, having helicopters collect the more serious cases. Luat did not want to press on to Plei Me without adequate fuel and ammunition. There was, therefore, a logistical-operational pause that Sunday. The 1st Battalion of the 42d Infantry Battalion, the 22d Ranger Battalion, and the tank company established a defensive position roughly where the train had spent the previous night. The rest of the ATF went back to Pleiku to fetch the necessary supplies. The ATF apparently experienced no fighting in the daylight hours on 24 October.[103]

We now know that by the afternoon of 24 October, the road to Plei Me was largely clear. Not knowing this, however, Luat wanted all the artillery support he could get when he renewed the advance the following day. News of Luat's request for large-scale artillery assistance (passed on by Mataxis) was music to the ears of the senior officers of the 1st Cavalry Division. It gave them the opportunity to get the division's ground troops directly involved in the campaign. On 24 October helicopters rushed artillery pieces to positions from which fire support to the ATF could most effectively be provided.[104]

On Monday, 25 October, Luat irritated some Americans by his unhurried approach. He did not get the ATF moving until about 1300. At that point, however, artillery belonging to the 1st Cavalry Division put down a rolling barrage in front of that force, and it headed south to lift the siege. The ATF received a certain amount of small-arms fire a short way into the advance, possibly from rearguard elements of the PAVN 32d Regiment, or possibly from Communist district forces. In any case, air strikes and artillery fire quickly suppressed this opposition. The ATF reached Plei Me by dusk on 25 October, apparently without suffering any casualties that day.[105]

That evening, however, an incident occurred that did not augur well for relations between the Americans and their allies. According to journalist John Laurence, who witnessed these events, the CIDG and Vietnamese in the

camp's garrison cheered the ATF as it arrived. But when Luat strode over to
the main gate, he was confronted by the physically imposing figure of Charlie
Beckwith, who was apparently in a much darker mood. Although Beckwith
shook Luat's hand and thanked him, he did so, as he later admitted to Laurence, with serious reservations. He was peeved that Luat had not arrived days
ago "when he was needed."

Luat wanted to take his staff and some of his infantry into the camp. Beckwith refused. Thinking the camp already grossly overcrowded, he wanted the
ATF to form a defensive perimeter outside it. But Beckwith's point-blank
refusal to permit a superior officer of the host nation to enter a fortification he
had just relieved outraged the normally genial Luat. Swearing furiously in Vietnamese, French, and English, he threatened to shoot Beckwith. A group of
Americans standing with Beckwith flicked the safety catches off their weapons.
At that point, Luat had the good sense to walk away.[106]

It was an extremely ugly confrontation and surely quite unnecessary. In
terms of military protocol (which matters in such situations), Beckwith was in
the wrong. Not only was he the junior of the two; he was in the other officer's
country. Had he invited Luat into the camp for some refreshment and a talk,
it would surely have become obvious that there was no room for a substantial
number of extra troops. But tact was not Beckwith's strong suit. By his own
account, he had been extremely curt with Captain Moore, who had been in
command at Plei Me before his arrival. After being at least equally abrupt with
the officer who led the force that lifted the siege, he started hurling abuse at a
number of journalists who had accompanied that force. Behaving very incon-
sistently, however, he admitted the journalists to the camp.[107]

By nightfall on 25 October, the siege of Plei Mei was virtually over. General
Man's campaign in western Pleiku had completely failed in its initial objectives.
Two PAVN regiments had been badly battered. The ARVN, with a hastily
improvised force backed by American airpower, had (however hesitatingly)
won a considerable victory. The 32d Regiment had begun its retreat from Provincial Route 5 on 24 October. The bulk of the PAVN 33d Regiment started
to withdraw from the Plei Me area at 2200 on the night of 25 October.[108]

Plei Me had already become a big story. At some point that evening, Beckwith received a radio message of thanks and encouragement from his commander in chief, President Lyndon Johnson.[109]

Sting in the Tail: The Action on 26 October

On Tuesday, 26 October, the 3d Battalion of the PAVN 33d Regiment was
still lurking near Plei Me, acting as a rear guard to cover the other battalions'

retreat to their base area by the Chu Pong massif. That morning, Brigadier General Hon of 24 STZ ordered Lieutenant Colonel Luat to conduct a sweep of the Plei Me area. The ATF moved out from its night position just north of the main gate to perform a circuit of the camp. It advanced in a two-column formation, with the tank company and the 22d Ranger Battalion on the right and the APC troop, the 1st Battalion of the 42d Infantry Regiment, and the 21st Ranger Battalion on the left. At some point in the circuit (reports are confusing as to the exact location), the tanks and APCs found the terrain too rough to negotiate and turned back toward the camp. While the vehicles were turning, some of the accompanying infantry broke ranks to get water and take supplies from parachute drops. That was when, at about 1205, the 3d Battalion of the PAVN 33d Regiment opened up with intense mortar, rocket-propelled grenade, and small-arms fire. It was a perfectly timed surprise attack that caused some initial panic and killed, over the next hour, 27 ARVN soldiers and wounded another 80. The ATF called in artillery and air strikes and, recovering from its initial surprise and confusion, fought back. On the basis of body count, it claimed 148 PAVN soldiers killed, with many others carried away. The after-action report, however, concluded that many of the bodies the ATF found that afternoon were those of PAVN soldiers killed on previous days.[110]

For the ATF, the action on the afternoon of 26 October was probably the most traumatic of the campaign. Clearly, some of the ATF troops believed their mission had already been accomplished and the enemy, at least locally, had already been defeated. They had become complacent and were severely punished for it. The impact on ARVN morale was indicated by a couple of instances of unwounded men aggressively attempting to board helicopters summoned to take casualties to hospitals. Ultimately, PAVN troops may have sustained heavier casualties than the ARVN on 26 October, as they certainly had on 23–24 October. But, probably basing his judgment on its psychological impact, John Laurence reckoned this action an ARVN defeat.[111]

Some of the ARVN's casualties on Tuesday, 26 October, may have been the result of friendly fire. The camp as well as the ATF received PAVN mortar shells that afternoon. CIDG mortarmen in the camp had been trained to respond to incoming rounds with rapid return fire. It had become a conditioned reflex. It was difficult for the Americans in the camp (most of whom did not speak Jarai) to get CIDG soldiers to understand that the positions on which they were firing might be occupied by friendly troops. In at least one instance, an American used physical force to get a mortar team to stop shooting. According to 24 STZ's after-action report, this was not the only instance of "poor fire discipline" in the campaign. On previous occasions, ARVN units had apparently shot at each other in error.[112]

Also on 26 October, a reserve CIDG company consisting of Nung soldiers went by helicopter from Pleiku to the area where the ATF's train had been attacked. Its mission was to police the area and recover damaged equipment. Dense undergrowth and ten-foot-tall elephant grass near the side of the road made a thorough search practically impossible. But the Nungs found twenty-five dead Communist soldiers and collected twenty-nine weapons.[113]

Winding It Down, 27–29 October

By the morning of Wednesday, 27 October, the PAVN had largely cleared out of the area immediately around Plei Me. In sweeps around the camp that day, the ATF claimed just one Communist soldier killed, while suffering no casualties itself. At 1000 the 2d Battalion of the US 8th Cavalry arrived at Plei Me. That same day, Luat was ordered to start withdrawing the ATF to Pleiku, while the 1st Brigade of the US 1st Cavalry Division took responsibility for securing the vicinity of the camp. To help secure the route back along Provincial Route 5, II Corps summoned Marine Task Force Alpha from Darlac, and its two battalions flew up from Ban Me Thuot to Pleiku on 27 October. Starting on Thursday, 28 October, Luat conducted a very slow, methodical, cautious withdrawal, assisted by the Marines. At 1840 on the evening of Friday, 29 October, with most of the ATF units back in Pleiku, 24 STZ declared Operation Dan Thang 21, the mission to relieve Plei Me, at an end.[114]

Assessment

In retrospect, the Plei Me offensive looks like a belated and ill-judged Communist effort to reassert strategic initiative and regain operational momentum in the Central Highlands when the best season for such actions had passed. It may be true that factors beyond General Man's control (particularly the 33d Regiment's difficulties getting down the Ho Chi Minh Trail) had delayed the launch of his offensive. It is certainly true that, even given the late start, he and his men were somewhat unlucky with the weather. In western Pleiku the rainy season sometimes lasted into late October. But, as it happened, the skies were fairly clear most of the time, and there was no significant rain until the siege of Plei Me was over.[115] Even during the monsoon, the other side's airpower had helped deprive the Communists of any really big victory over the ARVN in the Highlands. In a generally clear, dry late October, it wrought bloody havoc with PAVN plans.

With hindsight (and perhaps without it), Man's whole "lure and ambush" scheme looks hackneyed and transparent. If the enemy chose to enter the killing zone of the PAVN ambush at all, there was a good chance it would do so in such strength and with so much air support that it could not be destroyed. Attacking under such circumstances was likely to cause the People's Army disproportionate losses. This had already happened to the 32d Regiment in the Duc Co campaign, and some of it had occurred at the hands of Luat's armor. Many of the 32d Regiment's soldiers had been left with serious "fears of enemy armored vehicles," as well as fears of artillery and airpower. Substantial numbers of them not only expected a repeat of Duc Co but also dared publicly to say so.[116] Elements of the 32d and its attached forces (especially the two antiaircraft machine gun companies) fought with great courage during the "maneuver ambush" on Saturday, 23 October.[117] But did the bulk of its personnel really believe in victory?

Reading between the lines of a history published in Hanoi in the 1990s, many members of the regiment, despite a rigorous campaign of political and military indoctrination while the operation was being planned and prepared, remained dubious about the feasibility of their mission. Like many Communist histories, this one contains elements of fantasy. After describing the planning and preparations for the ambush in an extremely detailed and convincing manner, it claims that the ATF was "essentially destroyed" on 23 October 1965, with six tanks and twenty-nine M-113s knocked out and 900 ARVN soldiers killed or wounded.[118] In fact, no tank or M-113 was even significantly damaged, and actual ARVN casualties were less than 20 percent of this figure.

This Hanoi history of the 32d Regiment's October 1965 "maneuver ambush" again becomes interesting, however, when it tries to explain why the victory was not complete, why the ATF was not totally annihilated. At critical moments, it concludes, both troops and commanders in the 32d Regiment "lacked determination and resolve." They "wavered and displayed hesitation." There were instances of subunits disobeying orders and seeking to avoid combat. Two specific cases are cited of entire PAVN companies withdrawing from the battle without permission and in violation of the spirit of their orders. A belief in the "shaky" morale of ARVN forces was one of the factors that had led PAVN planners to think victory was achievable. Yet this Communist account refers to some ARVN troops fighting with "insane fury" on 23 October, while some of the PAVN troops facing them "panicked" and were "too afraid to open fire."[119]

Some aspects of the 33d Regiment's conduct of the siege require explanation. From 20 to 22 October it mounted fierce attacks from both north and south. Yet it permitted a large CIDG patrol to reenter the camp, apparently without losses, on the night of Wednesday, 20 October. Similarly, Beckwith's Delta–Airborne Ranger force went in through the main gate in broad daylight on Friday, 22 October, with relatively few casualties.[120] How were these things allowed to happen?

The 33d Regiment evidently did not even try to keep the camp completely surrounded. Perhaps the regimental commander believed that maintaining a tight investment would excessively dissipate his strength. Most of the regiment's positions were constructed in a semicircular arc north, west, and south of the camp. For most of the siege, the camp remained accessible from the northeast. It was, moreover, almost certainly not General Man's intention for the 33d Regiment to capture Plei Me until the 32d had ambushed the relief force. But the personnel tasked to mount the assaults were probably not told this, and American Special Forces were convinced (as they were intended to be) that Communist forces were determined to take the camp and annihilate them.[121]

As the 33d Regiment's introduction to the war in the South, the siege of Plei Me was a nightmare. The regiment took heavy losses in its assaults and probes, but the worst ordeal was the relentless battering from the air, continuing for days after its ground attacks had ceased. The ARVN's relative slowness in relieving Plei Me merely prolonged the 33d's torture under the hammers and fires of American airpower—an agony vastly greater than that of those it besieged. By the end of the siege, two of the 33d Regiment's battalion commanders were reportedly dead, and the third had been wounded. All three battalions were severely battered, and the 2d Battalion had lost half its personnel. Five of the nine mortars in the regimental mortar company were wrecked, and half its men were dead.[122] It is truly astonishing that on Tuesday, 26 October, while operating as a rear guard, the 3d Battalion had sufficient nerve and stamina left to mount a surprise attack on the ATF. By doing so, however, it only drew down further destruction on itself.

By 27 October, both PAVN regiments involved in the campaign up to this point were badly cut up and in full retreat. Regardless of how Communist propaganda would later dress things up, it must have been obvious to every soldier that the Plei Me operation had been a failure. These troops would not have been human had they not been somewhat demoralized. Morale among the ARVN troops involved in the relief of Plei Me was also generally shaky, but a relatively fresh and exceptionally mobile and powerful American force was now entering the field.

12

Retreat, Search, and Pursuit, October–November 1965

Initiating the Pursuit: Kinnard and Westmoreland

The PAVN 32d Regiment began its retreat on the morning of 24 October, shortly after its last attack on Luat's Armored Task Force was defeated. The 33d Regiment ordered its 1st and 2d Battalions to abandon the siege of Plei Me at 2200 on 25 October. Although the 3d Battalion temporarily remained as a rear guard, it too had begun its retreat by last light on 26 October. The bulk of the 32d Regiment retreated to Plei The, on the northern bank of the river Drang just east of the Cambodian border. The 33d initially fell back in the direction of a village the North Vietnamese called Kro, about 15 km west and somewhat south of Plei Me.[1] From there, the regimental commander's intention may have been to retreat to the major Communist base in the Chu Pong massif–Ia Drang valley area. But when the US 1st Cavalry Division began its search and pursuit operations on 27 October, the only thing any American headquarters in Vietnam knew for sure was that the enemy's main force units in western Pleiku had broken contact and disappeared.

A common American criticism of their South Vietnamese allies was that they failed to follow up defensive successes with vigorous pursuits of their Communist enemies. In Western military theory, it is generally accepted that a beaten opponent should, if at all possible, be prevented from escaping, licking his wounds, and coming back to fight another day. When an advantage has been gained, it should be pressed, and momentum should be maintained; the opponent should be pursued and struck continuously until he is decisively defeated. All the military training, education, and experience of Major General Harry Kinnard would have recommended such a course with regard to the Communist forces retreating from the Plei Me fighting. In the 1st Cavalry Division (Airmobile), Kinnard was convinced he had the perfect tool for the job. Performing this mission successfully would prove the division's value and vindicate the "airmobile concept." In the process, it would increase Kinnard's personal reputation and prestige, making him a rising star among American generals. It was a mission he craved and for which he lobbied his superiors. By 28 October 1965, it had been granted to him.[2]

Like William Westmoreland, Harry Kinnard was in many respects a classic example of what some Americans call the "great generation," the age group that fought the Second World War. Born into a military family in Texas in 1915, he graduated from West Point in 1939. As an infantry officer and a keen athlete with an adventurous disposition, it was natural that he should join the Airborne forces when the US Army started to form them. He jumped into Normandy with the 101st Airborne Division on 6 June 1944, fought in Operation Market Garden in September, and, during the Ardennes offensive in December, helped defend Bastogne. At twenty-nine he was a full colonel. In the twenty years since the end of the Second World War, his career progression had been slower, yet his selection to command the experimental airmobile division reflected the continuing confidence of Maxwell Taylor, who had commanded the 101st Airborne Division in the Second World War and subsequently rose to be Chief of Staff of the Army and then chairman of the Joint Chiefs of Staff.[3]

The most notable thing about Kinnard upon his arrival in Vietnam in August 1965 was his sheer ambition: his desire for dramatic, potentially decisive roles for his division and thus for himself. Almost as soon as he arrived in the country he suggested to Westmoreland that the Air Cavalry should operate in Laos against the Ho Chi Minh Trail.[4] Finding an appropriate base in South Vietnam from which to do this was difficult, however, and Kinnard contemplated operating from Thailand. Convinced that the political problems would be insurmountable, Westmoreland did not encourage Kinnard to pursue this course. Westmoreland became increasingly concerned that Kinnard and his senior officers were developing a tendency to behave like prima donnas, always demanding special treatment. He must have found this particularly irritating, given that the division was much criticized by the American mass media for a lackluster performance in its initial Vietnam operations.[5]

In September Kinnard's division began to develop a base at Camp Radcliff near An Khe, the general location having been chosen by Westmoreland.[6] After his division's performance in some early operations had failed to win it many plaudits, the campaign developing around Plei Me caught Kinnard's attention as an opportunity to demonstrate its true powers. From limited beginnings, the division's involvement in that campaign grew rapidly.

On 22 October General Larsen of Field Force Vietnam ordered General Kinnard to dispatch a battalion-sized task force to the town of Pleiku to act as a reserve for ARVN II Corps. Kinnard immediately sent a force commanded by Lieutenant Colonel Earl Ingram comprising the 2d Battalion of the 12th Cavalry and an artillery battery. Apparently seeing an opportunity to get involved in major combat operations against the PAVN, on 23 October ,Kinnard obtained permission to shift his whole 1st Brigade, at that stage commanded by Lieutenant Colonel Harlow G. Clark, from operations around Binh Khe, just east of An Khe, to Pleiku. Caribou transport aircraft started lifting the extra troops to Pleiku that day.[7] When Luat requested greater artillery support on 24 October, this presented an opportunity to get the 1st Cavalry Division more actively involved, and Clark decided to move some of his men and guns to forward bases, closer to Plei Me. In the early days of its involvement, Clark's brigade established bases code-named Stadium (at the Catecka tea plantation), Field Goal, Field Goal South, and Homecoming, all located between the town of Pleiku and the camp at Plei Me.[8]

By Sunday, 24 October, Westmoreland was already considering whether, once the besieged camp at Plei Me had been relieved, he should give Kinnard a free hand to go after major Communist units in Pleiku Province.[9] One account indicates that he made the critical decision at a conference with Larsen and Kinnard on Tuesday, 26 October, at 1st Brigade's new forward command post at LZ Homecoming. In this version of events, after a discussion of the capabilities and potential of the 1st Cavalry Division, Westmoreland turned to Larsen and said, "Give Kinnard his head."[10] It is a good story that is partly supported by the 1st Cavalry Division's after-action report on the Pleiku campaign.[11] Westmoreland's own record of events, however, suggests that he spent that day in Saigon. He mentions no trip to the Central Highlands on 26 October and no discussion with anyone relating to the 1st Cavalry Division.[12]

There is no doubt, however, that by 27 October, if not earlier, Colonel Clark's 1st Brigade had commenced a search for Communist main force units in western Pleiku.[13] Westmoreland had clearly authorized this, presumably via Larsen and Kinnard, although he may have done so orally and informally. No written order has come to light. Westmoreland's notes for Thursday, 28 October, state:

> I flew up to Pleiku and thence out to the command post of the 1st Brigade of the . . . Air Cavalry Division [LZ Homecoming]. The Brigade commanded by Lt. Colonel Harlow Clark seemed to be in good morale and was attempting to locate VC in the environs of the Plei Me Camp. Although working hard they had not achieved much success. I urged them in several days to move to an area west towards the Cambodian border in the vicinity of the Duc Co Camp. My estimate is that the VC would in due time infiltrate back towards their base areas along the Cambodian border and the brigade might achieve some success in picking them up.[14]

Informal instructions of this nature were all that Clark and Kinnard would have needed. In later interviews with historians, Kinnard stated a preference for mission-style orders that gave as much latitude as possible.[15] The 1st Cavalry Division did eventually issue formal, written instructions to its 1st Brigade, but only on 2 November, several days into the search operation.[16]

Liaison, Cooperation, and Intelligence

Two vitally important, closely related issues with regard to the search and pursuit phase of the 1st Cavalry Division's 1965 Pleiku campaign are the sources of intelligence available to it and the extent of its liaison with other military organizations on the same side. It seems appropriate to address the second issue first. The Pleiku campaign is widely seen as an important step in the development of the American war effort. An offensive operation designed to search for and destroy enemy troops, it was unlimited in terms of time and (except by a somewhat ill-defined international border) space; this made it different from previous American ground operations in Vietnam, which had all been severely circumscribed in these respects.[17] To avoid accidental clashes, operations on the coastal plain had to be carefully coordinated with the South Vietnamese, who were still fielding the great majority of troops on the anti-Communist side. In the Highlands, however, there were large areas that contained no Saigon government troops, giving the Americans a greater opportunity to act independently.

At least in theory, however, American troops in Vietnam were still operating in an allied country in support of an allied government. The territory where the 1st Cavalry Division was mounting its campaign was, of course, part of the South Vietnamese II Corps' zone, and the government supremo in that area was Major General Vinh Loc, II Corps' commander. Westmoreland, however, regarded Vinh Loc as uncooperative and probably incompetent. American accounts of the Pleiku campaign mention no consultation with Vinh Loc about launching the 1st Cavalry Division's search and pursuit operation. Vinh Loc's own history of the campaign refers to a conference held at his Pleiku headquarters on 26 October at which he claims to have decided upon the pursuit.[18] But as Vinh Loc did not control the US 1st Cavalry Division, and as there is no indication that Westmoreland, Larsen, or Kinnard were present at this conference, it is difficult to imagine that any "decision" Vinh Loc made on this occasion had any impact.

There is no reason to doubt that Vinh Loc would have sanctioned the Americans' pursuit of the two Communist regiments involved in the Plei Me campaign had he been consulted. But the truth (so humiliating to someone of

Vinh Loc's temperament that he would not admit it in his published account) appears to be that the Americans initiated the search and pursuit operation in Pleiku without any reference to him or his staff. It may be that Vinh Loc was not the only one ignored in this respect; there is no definite indication that Westmoreland consulted with Vinh Loc's superiors (the JGS, Ky, or Thieu) before letting the 1st Cavalry Division loose.

An account of the campaign written by a former 1st Cavalry Division officer suggests not merely that the division completely disregarded ARVN II Corps when launching its search and pursuit but also that there was a good deal of tension between the Americans serving in the two organizations. As soon as the 1st Cavalry Division became involved in the Plei Me campaign, there was an influx of its officers into the MACV compound at Pleiku. This displaced advisory personnel and resulted in overcrowded accommodations. This naturally caused a degree of irritation. Some officers of the 1st Cavalry Division apparently arrived with the attitude that they would now be taking over the conduct of the war from the ARVN and its advisers; the latter had failed and were now practically redundant. Such arrogance exacerbated the situation and made relations worse.[19]

The Cavalry's tendency to ignore II Corps or ride roughshod over it was not just reprehensible as a form of bad military manners. The lack of a spirit of comradeship and cooperation seems to have had more serious consequences. II Corps and its subordinate headquarters, 24 STZ and Pleiku Sector, had all been taken by surprise by the start of the Plei Me campaign, but their intelligence picture developed rapidly from that point onward. They also had more background knowledge of II Corps' tactical zone, including the location of Communist base areas within it, than did the 1st Cavalry Division. The intelligence staff at II Corps knew of the existence of a major Communist base around the Chu Pong massif, adjacent to the valley of the river Drang.[20] Knowledge of this base area and the realization that at least some PAVN troops were likely to be retreating in its direction would have made the initial searches of Clark's brigade much more efficient and productive. Close liaison between 1st Brigade, 1st Cavalry Division, and ARVN II Corps would, therefore, have made good sense. But it does not appear to have happened.

Perhaps realizing that there were serious issues with the handling of intelligence during this campaign, the J-2 staff at MACV wrote an "intelligence history" of it, which indicates:

The Chu Pong base was known to exist well prior to the Plei Me attack and J2 MACV had taken this area under study in September 1965 as a possible B-52 target. On 13 September a returnee, who stated that he was from the 20th Transportation Bn of the 325th Division, revealed that an NVA [North

Vietnamese Army] Regiment was located in the vicinity of the Chu Pong mountain. He also stated that supply depots and a hospital were located between Duc Co and Chu Pong.[21]

MACV's intelligence history, however, gives no indication of whether its intelligence officers chose to vouchsafe this information to the 1st Cavalry Division or whether anyone in that division thought to ask MACV what relevant intelligence it had. Reading between the lines, it seems likely that neither of these things occurred.

Indeed, the general state of liaison on intelligence and reconnaissance matters on the anti-Communist side during 1st Brigade's search and pursuit operations in the Central Highlands (27 October–9 November 1965) appears to have been dismal. Westmoreland thought Beckwith's Project Delta teams might be helpful to Clark's brigade in finding PAVN troops in Pleiku, and for a while, Delta and the Cavalry tried to work together. In the absence of good background intelligence, however, Project Delta's personnel were perhaps little more likely to find the enemy than were the Cavalry's own. In any case, Delta and the Cavalry were unable to establish an effective working relationship. Beckwith thought the 1st Cavalry Division's helicopter pilots were far less competent than the Vietnamese pilots with whom Delta normally worked. Not known for his tact, he seems to have said so. Sometimes seen as prima donnas themselves, members of the Cavalry evidently considered Delta personnel far too demanding. Beckwith's people found no North Vietnamese for Clark's brigade, and the attempt at cooperation seems to have been short-lived.[22]

In the absence of intelligence that might have informed its search, the 1st Cavalry Brigade's initial operations amounted to a great deal of frenetic, ill-directed flying about in helicopters, followed by a lot of ineffective thrashing around in the jungle by the ground troops. The initial search areas (designated Shoe, Jim, and Earl) were generally too far to the north. Even American resources were not so superabundant that operations could be conducted as inefficiently as this without consequences. There was a logistical crisis within just a few days. Some of the most serious consequences, however, would emerge later in the campaign and would be visited on 3d Brigade.

1st Brigade: Organization, Tactics, and Operations, 27–30 October

When Kinnard first arrived in Vietnam, one of the things that most concerned him was that Westmoreland would send his three brigades to operate in widely separated areas. Kinnard insisted that, to get the best out of the division, it had to be kept together.[23] Only one of the division's three brigades would, however, participate in the Pleiku campaign at any given time. The division's helicopter fleet would probably have had great difficulty sustaining more than one brigade in the frenetic style of airmobile operations conducted in Pleiku in October–November 1965. An airmobile brigade operating in the Highlands at this time was, moreover, at the end of a long and precarious supply line. Supporting even one brigade operating as Clark's brigade was operating soon imposed a critical strain on the entire American logistical system in Vietnam.

Colonel Clark's 1st Brigade comprised the 1st Squadron, 9th Cavalry Regiment (1/9), and three battalions that, though belonging to "Cavalry" regiments, were acknowledged to be essentially infantry battalions: 2d Battalion, 8th Cavalry (2/8); 2d Battalion, 12th Cavalry (2/12); and 1st Battalion, 12th Cavalry (1/12), which was added to the brigade only on 28 October. Fire support was available from the 105mm howitzers of the 17th and 19th Artillery and the aerial rocket artillery of Battery A, 2d Battalion, 20th Artillery. An aerial rocket artillery battery consisted of twelve UH1 "Huey" helicopters mounting forty-eight 2.75-inch folding-fin aerial rockets—twenty-four on either side of the aircraft—and was controlled by the divisional artillery.

With the exception of the 1/9 Cavalry and the aerial rocket artillery battery, none of these units had their own helicopters. Their mobility depended on the lift companies allocated to 1st Brigade by division. At the outset of the campaign, the 1st Brigade was provided with two lift companies of the 227th Assault Helicopter battalion, each company consisting of four platoons with four model D Bell Iroquois UH1 "Huey" helicopters. Often known as "slicks," these machines were used to carry riflemen to patrol areas and battlefields. There was also an attached company of Huey UH1-B gunships that escorted the troop-carrying helicopters during assaults. The gunships, known as "hogs," were fitted with the XM-16 system, which had four 7.62mm M-60 machine guns and a seven-tube multiple rocket system on each side of the helicopter. To increase its lift capacity, the division also allocated 1st Brigade a company of medium-lift Chinook helicopters.[24]

At first, 1st Brigade's headquarters was at LZ Homecoming, but Colonel Clark soon realized that because it was accessible only by a dirt road and via a relatively small airfield, its maintenance imposed too much of a logistical strain. On 28 October he established a new headquarters at the base code-named Stadium, which was located at the Catecka tea plantation, 15 km from the town of Pleiku and accessible by way of both an all-weather road and an airfield capable of accommodating Caribou and C-123 Provider transport aircraft.[25]

The most mobile unit conducting the search in Pleiku—indeed, in the whole of 1st Cavalry Division—was the 1st Squadron of the 9th Cavalry, commanded by Lieutenant Colonel John Stockton. Stockton was a dynamic leader, a risk taker, and a colorful character whose attitude toward authority some-times bordered on insubordination.[26] His squadron consisted of three troops, each capable of operating independently. In the early days of the search, they conducted "aggressive aerial reconnaissance and surveillance west, south and east of the Plei Me," as "allied intelligence had no way of knowing which way the NVA forces went after they broke contact at the camp." In fact, as noted earlier, some intelligence officers on the anti-Communist side knew there was a big PAVN base area around the Chu Pong massif. It would have been rea-sonable to assume that at least some Communist forces would retreat in that direction after the siege of Plei Me. But it seems that the people capable of providing that sort of knowledge and advice (intelligence officers at II Corps, 24 STZ, and Pleiku Sector) were not consulted at this stage.

What was 1/9's modus operandi in conducting the search? Each of its three troops—each operating independently and searching a different area—was split into a scout (White) team, a gunship (Red) team, and a rifle platoon (Blue) team. White team pilots flew light Sioux H-13 helicopters, whose cockpits were designed to provide very good observation. White teams flew a little above treetop height and investigated clearings in the forest and jungle trails. If they attracted fire, the Red team UH1-B gunships, which were hovering higher up, would swoop down and deliver rockets and machine gun fire. If there seemed to be more than just a few stragglers in the area, the Blue team, the aerial rifle platoon, would land and investigate further. They sometimes established a patrol base from which they conducted night ambushes.[27]

The 1/9 was a specialist reconnaissance unit and was initially under 1st Brigade's command. In reality, from 27 October, all of 1st Brigade was ex-ecuting a reconnaissance mission. As the 1st Cavalry Division's after-action report put it:

> [The] concept was to conduct an intensive search for the enemy, looking
> everywhere—in the villages, in the jungles and along the stream beds. By
> wide-spread dispersion, made possible by excellent communications and heli-
> copter lift, the Brigade was to sweep large areas systematically. Each battalion
> was to be deployed with supporting artillery and was to further disperse its
> companies. Vigorous and intensive patrolling from company bases was to be
> conducted. When contact was first established, a rapid reaction force was to
> be assembled swiftly and lifted by helicopters to strike the enemy. Rapid air
> movement of artillery batteries, plus extensive use of tactical air strikes, would
> provide the fire support.
>
> Here was air mobility's acid test. The next few days [from 27 October]
> would reveal whether three years of planning and testing would bear the fruits
> of victory—for a concept and a division.[28]

How did 1st Brigade's three more conventional, infantry-type battalions operate during the search phase of operations? First, the brigade staff allocated each battalion a sector to search. The battalions normally arranged for their companies to be inserted by helicopter into particular subsectors. After leaving the helicopters, they would conduct their searches on foot. In 1965 American troops were not well equipped for lengthy jungle patrols. The 1st Cavalry Division went to war in heavy twill uniforms rather than lightweight jungle fatigues. They also lacked the large rucksacks that, later in the war, allowed troops to carry enough supplies to sustain them for several days. Instead, during 1st Brigade's search operations, infantry companies normally set up night positions in the late afternoon (at about 1640) and waited to be resupplied by a "log bird" or logistical helicopter, which brought in hot food, ammunition, and sometimes even mail before dark. This practice was "hideously wasteful of helicopter assets," but Kinnard justified it as necessary for the morale and efficiency of the division's ground troops.

Because the infantry was often shifted large distances by helicopter, the artillery also had to make frequent moves. The small, constantly shifting firebases were given little infantry protection—rarely more than a company's worth. At this stage, the divisional philosophy, as proclaimed by Kinnard, was that shifting firebases every forty-eight hours would keep the artillery safe. It would take the enemy longer than that to concentrate a force sufficient for an attack. This way of handling the artillery added to the 1st Cavalry Division's prodigious fuel consumption and to the enormous mechanical wear and tear on its helicopters.[29]

All this frenetic activity achieved practically no measurable military result for several days. The 1st Brigade found traces of the PAVN 32d Regiment's retreat to its base on the Cambodian border, but it searched those areas days after the North Vietnamese had passed through. The 33d Regiment had started its retreat later, so its units should have been much easier to catch. For several days, however, the focus of 1st Brigade's search was too far north to intercept them. From 27 to 29 October, most of 1st Brigade had no contact whatsoever with the North Vietnamese, although 1/9 claimed it had sighted a few PAVN soldiers from the air. On 29 October, for the third day running, the Cavalry recorded no enemy soldiers and no weapons captured. Enemy killed and wounded were "unknown." Thus, the Cavalry had nothing to show for the first three days of its search and pursuit.[30] To compound its embarrassment, its operations had already hit an acute logistical crisis.

The Logistical Crisis and Changes to Command and Control

The Cavalry had established a forward logistical base at Camp Holloway airfield and a helipad and refueling center known as the Turkey Farm, also near the town of Pleiku. The Turkey Farm was the base for the 5,000-gallon bladders that held the JP-4 and Avgas aviation fuels that powered the helicopters. The 1st Cavalry Division took responsibility for distributing fuel to its aircraft from Camp Holloway and the Turkey Farm, but getting the fuel as far as Camp Holloway was the responsibility of the army's logistical command. A major problem for the logisticians was that Highway 19 from Qui Nhon (on the coast) to Pleiku was still a precarious route. All but the most heavily defended convoys were vulnerable to ambush. The Cavalry had been granted use of the 17th Aviation Company, equipped with Caribou fixed-wing transport aircraft, and it was able to use some of these to ferry aviation fuel from Qui Nhon to the Turkey Farm. But not enough was getting through to keep the helicopters operational. On 27 October Kinnard asked the air force for assistance. There was no immediate improvement, however, and the following evening, Larsen's Field Force headquarters informed MACV that the fuel situation in the Highlands was "critical."[31]

Dealing with General Norton, the deputy commander of US Army, Vietnam (the organization set up to handle logistics and routine administration for MACV), Brigadier General Richard T. Knowles insisted that unless the fuel situation were addressed immediately, the 1st Cavalry Division's campaign in Pleiku would have to be closed down and its units returned to base, abandoning some of their equipment. Possibly at Westmoreland's personal insistence, the US Air Force made the delivery of JP-4 to the Highlands its highest priority, and operations continued.[32]

The logistical crisis apparently triggered some changes in command and control. The 1st Brigade's operations were putting the whole American supply system in Vietnam under serious strain, but until 1 November, there was practically nothing to show for them. Clark had made no obvious errors, but in the aftermath of the logistical crisis, he found his independence considerably curtailed. Kinnard's deputy, Dick Knowles, operating from a headquarters in the town of Pleiku, next to II Corps, increasingly directed the campaign. Knowles's forward headquarters took from Clark control of the 227th Assault Helicopter Battalion, which provided mobility for 1st Brigade's three infantry battalions and that of 1/9 Cavalry, the primary reconnaissance unit.[33]

Dick Knowles was forty-five years old, six feet three inches tall, and of slender build. Commissioned through the University of Illinois ROTC program, he had served with tank destroyers in Europe in the Second World War and had won a Silver Star in Korea. Active and enthusiastic, he was known for offering his subordinates good cigars when he visited them in the field.[34] It is not clear whether Knowles did anything in particular to bring it about, but as he took control of operations, 1st Brigade's luck seemed to change.

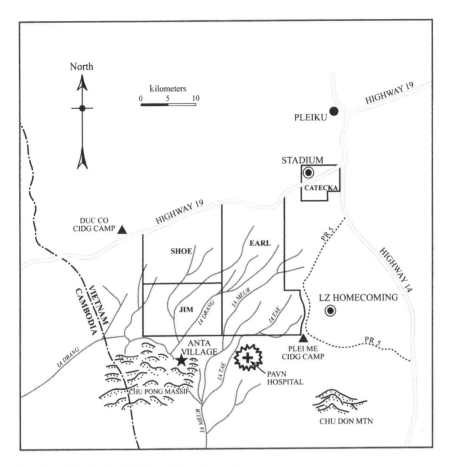

Location of the hospital firefight, 1 November 1965

The Hospital Firefight and Its Aftermath, 1–2 November 1965

Although there were some fleeting contacts on 30 and 31 October, not until 1 November did 1st Brigade's operations bear any substantial fruit. At about 0720 that morning, scouts belonging to Major Robert B. Zion's B Troop, flying from a base at Plei Do Rim near the Catecka tea plantation, spotted about a dozen PAVN soldiers about halfway between the Plei Me camp and their base camp at the foot of the Chu Pong massif. These were men of the 1st Battalion, 33d Regiment. They had been ordered to retreat almost a week earlier but were still only about 12 km west (and slightly south) of Plei Me.

The battalion had suffered about 40 percent casualties in the siege of Plei Me. Its retreat had been hampered by air strikes and by the need to carry some badly wounded men. The battalion had paused at a carefully concealed regimental aid post situated on a stream flowing into the Tae River, which in turn flowed south and west toward Cambodia. Most of its troops were now either defending the post or being cared for in it. The principal field fortification defending the post formed a *V* shape, with the apex of the *V* facing east toward Plei Me, the direction from which the threat was thought most likely to come. The North Vietnamese defending this position had 82mm mortars, 57mm and 75mm recoilless rifles, and heavy machine guns, as well as small arms.

The PAVN soldiers the Cavalry spotted on the morning of 1 November were immediately south of the aid post. After opening fire on them, B Troop's scouts and gunships sent for the aerial rifle platoon. Landing at 0808, this thirty-strong force moved toward the last-reported North Vietnamese positions, with scout helicopters acting as guides and as a protective screen. When they reached the streambed, the American riflemen clashed with a small group of North Vietnamese troops, killing five and capturing four. Moving on, they had soon captured the aid station itself and a considerable mass of valuable medical equipment and supplies. By 0955, another fifteen PAVN soldiers had been killed and fifteen captured.

Realizing that the captured medical equipment was extremely important to the North Vietnamese, 1/9 summoned helicopters to take it away. At about the same time, according to the division's after-action report, the squadron brought in its other two rifle platoons to reinforce the one that had captured the hospital. Colonel Stockton, who must have at least endorsed the decision to bring in the extra rifle platoons, was physically present at the aid station by early afternoon, but sources are vague as to the exact time of his arrival. The extra troops were soon needed. At 1410 scout helicopters reported a substantial PAVN force moving toward the squadron's positions from the northeast. The Air Cavalry's scout helicopters and gunships fired rockets and machine guns at the North Vietnamese, but they kept coming. From 1420 until 1800, a force of 100 to 200 PAVN troops kept 1/9's three rifle platoons continuously engaged. As the 1st Cavalry Division's after-action report expresses it:

> Time and again assaults were repulsed with just the organic weapons of the three platoons, since the enemy had pressed so close as to preclude the use of tactical air or aerial rocket artillery support. The position was, of course, well out of the range of tube artillery.

The use of the expression "of course" seems strange. The North Vietnamese field hospital was only about 12 km west of Plei Me, and the 1st Cavalry Division was proud of the mobility of its field artillery. It is clear that, even as late as 1 November, 1st Brigade's headquarters (and presumably Knowles's advance

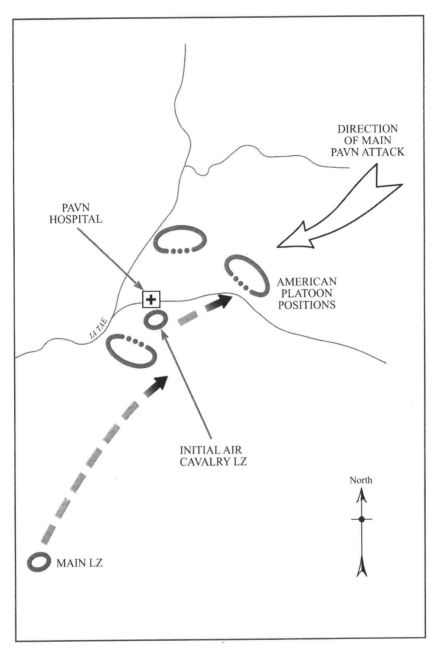

DIRECTION
OF MAIN
PAVN ATTACK

PAVN
HOSPITAL

AMERICAN
PLATOON
POSITIONS

IA TAE

INITIAL AIR
CAVALRY LZ

North

MAIN LZ

The hospital firefight, 1 November 1965

headquarters in Pleiku) still had little idea where to look for retreating PAVN troops. The bulk of the 1st Brigade, including its artillery, was still too far north.

During the course of the firefight, helicopters initially delivered ammunition and other supplies and evacuated the wounded using a small clearing immediately south of the aid station. But this landing zone was exposed to PAVN fire, and seven helicopters were hit, although none crashed. From 1500 onward, when single platoons from the 1/12, 2/12, and 2/8 Battalions arrived by helicopter to reinforce the three 1/9 platoons, they used a larger clearing, a kilometer or so farther south, as an alternative landing zone. Two additional platoons from 2/12 Cavalry arrived there in the early evening. By that time, however, the North Vietnamese had broken contact and disappeared.[35]

From the Cavalry point of view, 1 November was the best day yet in the search and pursuit phase of the Plei Me campaign. The intelligence summary given in the division's after-action report seems reasonable.

> The 33d Regiment sustained a major blow with the loss of its regimental aid station. Many of the patients were captured, along with many of the defenders and more importantly, medical supplies [of which the North Vietnamese were already critically short]. . . .
>
> The capture of the aid station was a major find for the division and besides the opportunity it provided for the destruction of NVA forces, it also yielded documents including one particularly valuable map, that revealed enemy supply and march routes. These in turn were converted into intelligence that led to further interdictory bombings by the Air Force.[36]

At 11 dead and 47 wounded, the 1st Cavalry Division's casualties in this little firefight were considerable. But it had inflicted substantially greater losses on the PAVN. On the basis of a body count, the division claimed to have killed 98 PAVN soldiers. It had also taken 44 prisoners. In addition to the medical supplies, it had captured 300 pounds of rice, three 75mm recoilless rifles, an 82mm mortar, and thirty-seven personal weapons, as well as grenades, some Bangalore torpedoes, and ammunition. The Cavalry's after-action report estimated that, in addition to the bodies counted, another 183 North Vietnamese had been killed and 208 wounded, although it is unclear how such specific figures were arrived at.

After a search and pursuit that had yielded almost no quantifiable results for several days, the events of 1 November must have come as something of a relief to Clark, Knowles, and Kinnard, despite the casualties sustained. Yet the firefight at the aid station demonstrated the 1st Cavalry Division's limitations as well as its strengths. It also illustrated the PAVN's continuing pugnacity and capacity for tactical adaptation.

Even on 1 November, no large body of North Vietnamese troops had been enveloped (vertically or otherwise). None had been forced to either fight or surrender. For a few hours, and to a limited extent, the tactical initiative was in American hands because the Americans had seized something of importance to the North Vietnamese. But the unwounded North Vietnamese in the vicinity of the hospital had fought only because their officers had decided to fight, and only for as long as they considered it feasible to do so. Once the Americans had built up their forces to a level at which a PAVN victory became impossible, the North Vietnamese had broken off the engagement and vanished again. Whatever its theoretical potential, the 1st Cavalry Division had shown little practical capacity to prevent the North Vietnamese from disengaging and disappearing in this way. They would do so several times in the course of this campaign.

When engaging American ground troops, moreover, the North Vietnamese were already beginning to find a pragmatic, partial solution to the problem of American firepower. They realized that if they got their infantry close enough to the American infantry, it became difficult for the latter fully to exploit their airpower and even their artillery (though the latter proposition was not tested on this occasion). Known as "grasping the belt," this tactic of engaging the enemy at very short range and pinning down his troops within yards of their own would become a standard method for all the Communist main force units in Vietnam, especially when dealing with the Americans.

On 2 November 2/12 Cavalry took charge of the situation at the PAVN aid station, while most of 1/9 returned to its base near 1st Brigade's Stadium headquarters. In searches around the hospital, 2/12 found another "29 large containers of medical supplies" and had a couple of firefights with small groups of PAVN troops, capturing six of them. At 0840, 1/9 was detached from 1st Brigade and went back to being a divisional asset under the control of Knowles's tactical headquarters at Pleiku. As the after-action report states: "The maps captured the day previously that depicted trails and movement all headed toward the CHU PONG–IA DRANG complex made the division commander and his assistants anxious to get something close to the Cambodian border. The Cav Squadron [i.e., the 1/9] was ideally suited for the task and this was to be its next mission."[37]

The Drang Valley Ambush and the
Attack on LZ Mary, 3–4 November 1965

On 3 November 1/9 Cavalry transferred its base of operations to the Duc Co CIDG camp, where it worked in conjunction with a CIDG Eagle Flight and A Company of 1/8 Cavalry. From Duc Co, it began helicopter reconnaissance

Chapter 12

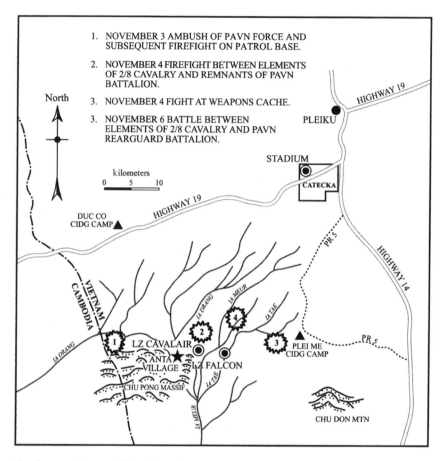

1. NOVEMBER 3 AMBUSH OF PAVN FORCE AND SUBSEQUENT FIREFIGHT ON PATROL BASE.

2. NOVEMBER 4 FIREFIGHT BETWEEN ELEMENTS OF 2/8 CAVALRY AND REMNANTS OF PAVN BATTALION.

3. NOVEMBER 4 FIGHT AT WEAPONS CACHE.

3. NOVEMBER 6 BATTLE BETWEEN ELEMENTS OF 2/8 CAVALRY AND PAVN REARGUARD BATTALION.

Cavalry operations, 3–6 November 1965

southward along the Cambodian border toward the valley of the river Drang. This reconnaissance into the Drang valley and the ambushes set there that afternoon were well to the west of the PAVN's main base in the area: Anta, at the foot of the Chu Pong massif. These moves were not well designed to intercept PAVN troops retreating from Plei Me. But the maps captured during the hospital firefight on 1 November showed trails leading all the way to the Cambodian border, and Knowles may have supposed that even if the PAVN paused at their Chu Pong base, their intention was to retreat into Cambodia and take sanctuary there. We now know that this supposition was wrong, but it was not unreasonable at the time.

With A Company of 1/8 Cavalry left at Duc Co as a reserve, at 1530 on 3 November B Troop of 1/9, together with the rifle platoons of the other two troops and the CIDG Eagle Flight, landed at a clearing just south of the Drang River, large enough to take five helicopters. Preselected during a personal reconnaissance by Stockton, the 1/9's dynamic but controversial commander, it was named LZ Mary after the wife of Charlie Black, a respected reporter covering 1/9's operations. At 1700 patrols went out from LZ Mary to establish three nighttime ambush positions; each was on a different jungle trail on a line running northwest to southeast, with the southernmost position being almost on the northwestern edge of the Chu Pong massif. The CIDG Eagle Flight laid the northwestern ambush, and the rifle platoon of B Squadron mounted another on a trail slightly to the south, about 800 meters from the Eagle Flight. C Squadron's rifle platoon manned the southernmost ambush, about 1,600 meters from B Squadron's. All the ambushes were ready before dark. At dusk the troops at all three sites were attacked by swarms of mosquitoes, but it was especially important for them not to fidget under this torment. It was a bright, moonlit night—reportedly as bright as if illuminated by parachute flares—and maintaining concealment would not be easy even if everyone remained still.[38]

It was at the southernmost ambush position, on a trail that skirted the northern edge of the Chu Pong massif, that "blood was drawn." According to the division's after-action report:

At 1930 hours [American lookouts] sighted a . . . heavily laden NVA unit of estimated company strength moving along an east-west trail. The column elected to take a break just 100 metres short of the ambush site and loitered just outside the killing zone for a full hour-and-a-half. At 2100 hours the NVA unit formed up and moved confidently and noisily along the trail. . . . The [American] platoon leader allowed the first element to pass through and sprung the trap on the weapons platoon, whose men were carrying machine guns, mortars and recoilless rifles. At 2105 eight Claymore mines set along a 100-meter kill zone belched fire and steel and troopers blazed away with M-16s for two minutes. Simultaneously, Claymore's [sic] sited both up and down the trail pumped death into the enemy column. There was no return fire.[39]

Captain Knowlen, commanding C Squadron of 1/9 Cavalry during the ambush, achieved a tactical success despite facing an unexpected and potentially unnerving situation. The decision of the North Vietnamese to take a break from their march just 100 meters short of his killing zone was purely a matter of chance. As things turned out, it made no difference to the outcome. On a bright, moonlit night, however, it was potentially very dangerous for the Americans, who were heavily outnumbered by their prospective victims.

Given the numerical imbalance, Knowlen had a difficult decision to make. He might have legitimately concluded that discretion was the better part of valor and refrained from springing the ambush. But he almost certainly knew that his commanding officer had been severely criticized a few nights earlier

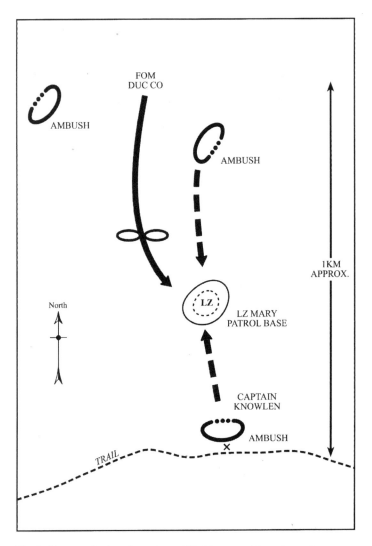

The Ia Drang ambush and attacks on LZ Mary, 3–4 November 1965

when a 1/9 rifle platoon had failed to engage the PAVN in similar circumstances. Stockton had defended the platoon commander's decision but had
been rebuked so harshly that he seemed in danger of being sacked.[40] Knowles
and Clark had evidently become so desperate to inflict casualties on the North
Vietnamese that they were prepared to take extreme risks with the lives of
their own men to do so. It also seems probable that, by 3 November, they had
instilled this attitude in their subordinates.

Apart from their sheer numbers and their worrying decision to pause just
before reaching the killing zone, two other things were disconcerting about

the North Vietnamese that Knowlen's platoon ambushed. First, they were moving in the opposite direction from the one expected—west-east, not east-west. Second, they did not seem to be shaken and demoralized, as troops of the 33d Regiment, retreating from the failed siege of Plei Me, were expected to be. Their morale appeared buoyant, their attitude almost casual.

In fact, Knowlen's platoon had attacked part of the 8th Battalion of the PAVN 66th Regiment, which had just arrived in South Vietnam. It was supposed to join the other battalions of the same regiment in the Communist Chu Pong–Ia Drang base area. The battalion had suffered considerable hardships while coming down the Ho Chi Minh Trail, and the men's spirits would have been lifted by the knowledge that they were approaching their new base area and nearing the end of their epic journey. Their lack of due caution and alertness is understandable, given that they thought they were making a logistical move through a Communist-controlled area. They did not believe they were yet in a combat zone.

Knowlen normally would have had his men "police up" the ambush site before departing, seizing weapons and equipment, counting bodies, and searching them for maps and documents that might be useful for intelligence purposes. Such action would have been considered mandatory under normal circumstances. But in the exceptional circumstances of this ambush, Knowlen decided to forgo any search of the killing zone. It was only a matter of time before the North Vietnamese platoon he had allowed to walk through the ambush recovered from its shock and counterattacked, and there was no way of knowing how many other PAVN troops were in the vicinity. He therefore ordered his men to move immediately to the planned post-ambush rendezvous point. From there, they went straight to LZ Mary. Their withdrawal was assisted by mortars based at LZ Mary, which put down heavy and accurate fire on the trail where the ambush had been sprung.[41]

Major Robert Zion, in overall command of LZ Mary, initially ordered the two other ambush patrols to stay put, hoping that the North Vietnamese fleeing from Knowlen's ambush might blunder into one of them. He later called in the other 1/9 patrol. But, reasoning that bringing in the Eagle Flight might risk a friendly fire incident, he decided to leave it where it was. As the after-action report explains, "The Eagle Flight wore different uniforms and, of course, spoke Vietnamese and Montegnard [sic]."[42] If any member of the US 1st Cavalry Division bothered to ask the Highland soldiers of the Eagle Flight what they thought of being left isolated while powerful North Vietnamese forces prowled the area seeking vengeance, their answer is not recorded.

Knowlen's suspicion that he had stamped on a tiger's tail soon proved valid. The mortar fire that covered his retreat was a strong indication that the Americans had a patrol base in the area, and it did not take the North Vietnamese long to find it. According to the division's report on the action, "The perimeter was assaulted at 2230 hours by an estimated two to three companies of enemy troops." The Americans at LZ Mary had dug no defensive positions, and their numerical strength was scarcely adequate, given the scale of attack they were facing. "At midnight," according to the after-action report, "the perimeter was under heavy seige [*sic*] and in grave danger of being overrun but reinforcements were on the way."[43]

"With the original force in the ambush base established by B Troop 1/9 Cav Sqdn insufficient to withstand the repeated assaults by the aroused NVA battalion," the report indicates:

> It became necessary to effect an immediate reinforcement. Shortly before midnight the rifle company standing by at Duc Co, A 1/8 Cav, was alerted. . . . Since the landing zone [LZ Mary] could handle only five ships at a time, it was decided to reinforce by platoon. The first platoon was on the ground at 0040 hours, followed by the remainder of the company in platoon lifts, closing by 0245 hours. It was the first time that a perimeter under heavy fire had been relieved at night by heliborne forces. It was also the first time that Aerial Rocket Artillery was employed at night and in very close support (50 meters) of friendly positions.
>
> By dawn the attacks by the enemy had slackened and incoming fire had diminished to occasional sniping from surrounding trees. At first light the remainder of the 1/8 Cav began moving into the L-Z and the 1/8 Cav assumed control of the position. Cav Squadron [i.e., 1/9] elements were extracted in outgoing lift ships.[44]

In the LZ Mary firefight, the Americans suffered four killed and fifteen wounded. The PAVN carried away nearly all its dead. Stockton, who briefly took command at Mary at first light, estimated seventy-two fatalities on the Communist side,[45] but this could only have been a guess. At some unspecified point during the firefight at LZ Mary or shortly afterward, one prisoner was collected. Although searches were conducted around LZ Mary until late afternoon, nothing more was found, and 1/8 Cavalry went back to its base at Stadium in the Catecka tea plantation.[46]

The Drang River ambush and the LZ Mary firefight were small American victories, but LZ Mary had been a close call. Springing an ambush on a significantly larger North Vietnamese force was an intrinsically dangerous thing to do and had led to a PAVN assault on an unfortified, weakly held landing zone. The whole episode was symptomatic of the increasing desperation of the senior officers of the 1st Cavalry Division to find and engage substantial numbers of the elusive North Vietnamese. Indeed, they had become so anxious to find the enemy that they seemingly did not give enough thought to how he might react if found. This attitude might be excused, at least in part, as long as intelligence indicated that the only PAVN forces in the operational area were the already battered regiments in retreat after the siege of Plei Me. According to both the division after-action report and MACV's intelligence history of the campaign, however, the capture of a North Vietnamese soldier after the LZ Mary firefight revealed the presence of the fresh PAVN 66th Regiment in the Drang valley.[47] There is little indication that this made these senior officers any more circumspect.

The main controversy that arose among the division's senior officers in the immediate aftermath of this firefight was Stockton's use of A Company, 1/8 Cavalry, to reinforce LZ Mary. Strictly speaking, Stockton had no authority to use this division reserve without asking Knowles. But the emergency occurred in the middle of the night, and getting Knowles on the radio might have taken a while. Stockton apparently ordered the company to go to LZ Mary on his own authority. Only then did he contact Knowles. By the time Knowles was aware of the situation, A Company had already started to move. Knowles nevertheless tried to get Stockton to countermand the order. But Stockton stuck to his guns. He reportedly told Knowles that he was the senior officer closest to the action and must have the freedom to act on his own judgment. Knowles considered the incident typical of Stockton's waywardness. He wanted Kinnard to sack Stockton immediately after the LZ Mary action. Kinnard thought sacking a senior officer after a successful firefight would be too controversial. He decided to hold off, at least for the time being. Stockton, however, found himself transferred to a desk in Saigon soon after the Pleiku campaign ended.[48]

On 3–4 November Stockton surely did nothing wrong. If he had not sent the reserve company to assist in the firefight at LZ Mary, the result might have been a minor military disaster for the Americans. Such a debacle would not have been of Stockton's making. In sending 1/9 to probe the western end of the Ia Drang in early November, he was merely obeying orders. Knowles's desire to sack Stockton after LZ Mary was apparently based on a clash of personalities and a history of minor insubordination on Stockton's part in matters such as unauthorized innovations in dress and the unauthorized movement of a unit mascot, matters not directly related to combat.[49]

1st Brigade's Final Days in the Pleiku Campaign

On the morning of 4 November, a reconnaissance platoon of 2/8 Cavalry was patrolling from a recently established landing zone and firebase called Cavalair, on a small plateau in the Drang valley just 4 km northeast of the PAVN assembly point at Anta village. Under the command of Lieutenant William A. Ward, the platoon was probing toward a suspected PAVN camp about 800 meters north of Cavalair. At 1130 the platoon made contact with an estimated two companies of North Vietnamese. Ward called for reinforcements. Two platoons of Alpha Company 2/8 were sent to join this fight at 1210, and additional reinforcements were thrown in over the course of the day. Early in the fight it proved difficult for the Americans to use their artillery and tactical airpower because the North Vietnamese were "grabbing the belt" (as they had at the hospital a few days earlier). They were too close to American troops and, in some places, interspersed with them.

Later that afternoon, however, 2/8 managed to disentangle its ground troops from those of the North Vietnamese and called in artillery and air support. "After taking punishing blows the NVA force broke contact, leaving 12 captives and 4 KIA on the battlefield" and carrying others away. Two Americans and an ARVN interpreter were killed. The combat lasted about six hours, with the PAVN pulling out only at 1730. It was later learned that the North Vietnamese troops belonged to the 1st Battalion of the PAVN 33d Regiment, a unit that fought well despite having been severely hurt during the siege of Plei Me.[50] It was another firefight in which the Cavalry failed to achieve the sort of substantial, clear-cut victory for which senior officers such as Clark, Knowles, and Kinnard were becoming increasingly desperate.

Also on 4 November, Bravo Company of 2/12 Cavalry clashed with North Vietnamese troops in a riverbed 7 km northeast of the hospital where fighting had occurred three days previously. The small PAVN force was apparently guarding a supply dump. After a firefight that killed three Americans and wounded fifteen, B Company found itself in possession of six heavy machine guns, three 75mm recoilless rifles, and two 82mm mortars, as well as some lighter weapons and a lot of ammunition. The PAVN also left behind a dozen dead. A North Vietnamese prisoner revealed that the 3d Battalion of the PAVN 33d Regiment (the rearguard battalion that had inflicted serious losses on the South Vietnamese ATF just outside Plei Me on 26 October) had just passed through the area on its way to the Chu Pong massif.[51]

On 5 November B Company of 2/8 Cavalry was operating between the Meur and Tae Rivers, about 6 km north and slightly west of the site of the PAVN hospital fought over four days previously. It established a base in the area that night. At 1000 on the morning of 6 November, one of its platoons clashed with a small number of North Vietnamese. The PAVN soldiers broke contact immediately, and the American platoon continued its patrol. By noon, however, all elements of B Company encountered what they initially believed to be an entrenched enemy company. They started to take serious casualties and became pinned down. Revising his estimate of enemy strength, B Company's commander now believed he faced a North Vietnamese battalion. With the PAVN probing for his flanks, he feared encirclement and called for both air support and reinforcement.

Lieutenant Colonel James Nix, commanding 2/8 Cavalry, ordered Charlie Company, operating about a kilometer to the west, to go to Bravo Company's assistance. C Company dutifully struggled through the dense jungle, but once it made contact with the North Vietnamese, it too started to take substantial casualties and soon became pinned down. The Americans called in artillery fire from 2/8's firebase at LZ Falcon and many more air strikes, but they were unable to execute any decisive maneuver. After dark, the bulk of the PAVN broke contact and disappeared—an old story by this point in the campaign. To discourage pursuit they left some troops as rear guards, and "these elements continued to pour automatic weapons fire into the Cavalry positions."

The fighting of 6 November cost the Cavalry twenty-six dead and fifty-three wounded. The 2/8 claimed it found seventy-seven PAVN bodies. It would be 1st Brigade's last firefight of the Plei Me–Ia Drang campaign. Over the next couple of days, 1st Brigade continued to look for the North Vietnamese that it had engaged on 6 November (almost certainly the 3d Battalion of the PAVN 33d Regiment), but with little success. For the Cavalry, the results of the firefight of 6 November were most disappointing. Despite the Americans' apparently huge advantages of firepower and mobility, a substantial body of North Vietnamese troops had once again put up a very good fight, inflicted considerable casualties, and, though suffering serious losses of its own, escaped destruction. The disappointment may have triggered Kinnard's decision to end 1st Brigade's participation in this campaign, a decision he made the following day. Colonel Thomas W. Brown's 3d Brigade would now take over.[52]

The Change of Brigades, 7 November 1965

Several reasons have been given for Kinnard's decision to replace 1st Brigade at this juncture. He later justified the move on the grounds that 1st Brigade was worn out and needed a rest. It had certainly been frenetically active, and portions of it were probably genuinely weary. But it had been conducting the search and pursuit for only twelve days, 27 October to 7 November, when the decision was made to withdraw it. None of its units had experienced more than a few days of actual fighting, and some had experienced none at all. Casualties had been relatively modest. The division as a whole (including 1/9, which was, for much of the time, listed as a divisional asset rather than part of 1st Brigade) had suffered just 59 dead and 196 wounded or injured in the first eighteen days of its involvement in the Pleiku campaign. Later in the war, brigades would be active in the field for far longer and suffer much heavier casualties without hope of relief.

The division's after-action report, an unofficial history of the division's participation in this campaign, and an article by Kinnard himself all put the best face on 1st Brigade's achievements. Harlow Clark even received a medal from the South Vietnamese after the campaign ended.[53] On 7 November, however, the real feeling about the brigade's performance at the division level and upward was most likely one of serious disappointment. It is doubtful that, at this juncture, many congratulations were coming Clark's way. Clark was only a lieutenant colonel and thus rather junior to be commanding a brigade. He had been placed in temporary command because his predecessor, Colonel Elvy Roberts, had suffered a leg injury and was temporarily absent while receiving medical attention. Did Kinnard now suspect that Clark had been put in command of a brigade too quickly and was not up to the job? There are definite hints in one insider's account that Kinnard and Knowles blamed Clark for not maneuvering his forces quickly and effectively enough to trap and destroy the substantial PAVN force engaged on 6 November.[54] This episode, moreover, was the culmination of nearly two weeks of frustration, relieved only slightly by the hospital firefight of 1 November.

Although he committed no such promise to paper, it is likely that Kinnard had assured Westmoreland that his division could intercept and destroy the PAVN forces that were in retreat after the failure of the Plei Me operation. This had not yet happened. It is unlikely that anyone outside the 1st Cavalry Division was impressed by the totality of its achievements up to this point in the Pleiku campaign.[55] A sense of frustration and disappointment almost certainly now hung over Knowles's and Kinnard's headquarters. There had been no dramatic vertical envelopments and no great masses of prisoners. Even the count of North Vietnamese bodies (a couple of hundred) was modest in relation to the effort expended and the American casualties sustained. In any case, as everyone knew, body counts could be exaggerated when senior officers wanted to put the best face on events.

The division's limited effectiveness in finding and intercepting the retreating North Vietnamese regiments between 27 October and 7 November was even more disappointing because the campaign had occurred at the ideal time of year in terms of weather and ground conditions. The skies were practically cloudless most of the time, temperatures were between 76 and 86 degrees Fahrenheit, nighttime humidity levels were low, and the ground was hard and dry.[56]

The 1st Cavalry Division had gained only the briefest contact with any part of the PAVN 32d Regiment.[57] Even in a published account in which he tried to put his division's performance in the best possible light, Kinnard did not claim that his troops had significantly interfered with that regiment's withdrawal. He did allege, however, that the 1st Cavalry Division was primarily responsible for the virtual destruction of the PAVN 33d Regiment: "This phase saw a North Vietnamese regular army regiment, operating [in] its own trackless 'stomping grounds' found, engaged and nearly destroyed by a new unit which had landed in Vietnam the month before."[58] It is perfectly true that, by 6 November, the 33d Regiment had been severely cut up.[59] But the claim that Kinnard's division was primarily responsible was massively misleading. Assuming that Kinnard was a man of above-average intelligence (which can scarcely be doubted), it must be considered intellectually dishonest.

Most of the PAVN 33d Regiment's casualties undoubtedly occurred during the siege of Plei Me, when it was obliged to stay in fixed positions that were relentlessly pounded by massive air strikes for almost a week. It is clear that the great majority of the 33d Regiment's casualties during the siege were inflicted by strikes by fixed-wing aircraft and in no way attributable to the 1st Cavalry Division. Artillery belonging to the division helped repel the attack by the 33d Regiment's 3d Battalion on Luat's ATF on 26 October. But with that exception, there was only fleeting contact between any element of Kinnard's division and 33d Regiment before 1 November. Up to that point, the great majority of the PAVN regiment's casualties, both during its retreat and during the siege, were almost certainly inflicted by fixed-wing aircraft, most of which belonged to the US Air Force.[60]

The 1st Cavalry Division's 1st Brigade engaged elements of the PAVN 33d Regiment on 1, 4, and 6 November. The engagement on 1 November, in which the aid station was overrun, was by far the most successful. But even on that occasion, the Cavalry failed to envelop or trap the PAVN forces engaging them. The PAVN broke off the engagement at will. The fighting of 4 November, like that of 1 November, netted an impressive amount of PAVN equipment, but 1st Brigade again failed to fix the North Vietnamese, who again broke contact when night fell. The combat of 6 November was the most disappointing of all. On all three dates, although the Cavalry deserves credit for finding the PAVN, the US Air Force, whose assistance was invariably called for, almost certainly inflicted a substantial proportion of North Vietnamese casualties.

Leaving aside the issue of who inflicted the most damage on the PAVN 33d Regiment, when Kinnard made the decision to change brigades on 7 November, no one had a clear idea of how much damage had been done. Most of what we now know about the 33d Regiment's dire condition—about half its original strength had been killed and was missing—was revealed only later. From beginning to end, a thick fog of war hung over 1st Brigade's operations in Pleiku.[61] This almost certainly contributed to a mounting sense of frustration in the division's headquarters and at higher levels and thus played a part in Kinnard's decision to change brigades.

The intelligence picture was no clearer at higher American headquarters' (such as Larsen's Field Force Vietnam at Nha Trang) than it was at 1st Brigade. Indeed, "it seemed the higher the headquarters, the more murky the intelligence waters."[62] When 3d Brigade first took over, its initial ideas about where to look for the North Vietnamese were just as vague and ill informed as those with which 1st Brigade had started its operations. Somewhat greater enlightenment would occur when an American staff officer had an interesting idea: Might not intelligence officers at the corps headquarters of the host nation's forces in the Central Highlands (which had, of course, been in the area somewhat longer) know a thing or two? Might it not be sensible at least to ask?

13

Catecka and X-Ray,
November 1965

3d Brigade and the Situation of the PAVN
in Western Pleiku, 9 November

The process of removing 1st Brigade's units from western Pleiku and substituting 3d Brigade's started on 9 November and took about four days, the last of 3d Brigade's battalions arriving on 12 November.[1] There were no substantial contacts between the Cavalry and the North Vietnamese during the changeover. By the end of this period, the PAVN 33d Regiment had completed its retreat to the Ia Drang–Chu Pong base area and had been provided with some fresh personnel. After a month-long series of grueling ordeals, it began what was bound to be a lengthy convalescence. During its withdrawal, it had lost perhaps another 200 or 300 personnel killed or taken prisoner, over and above the much heavier casualties suffered during the siege of Plei Me. The PAVN 32d Regiment had finished its withdrawal almost two weeks earlier, experiencing only the lightest contact with troops of the US 1st Cavalry Division.[2] If, therefore, that division's principal purpose in Pleiku since 27 October had been to intercept the retreat of the two PAVN regiments involved in the Plei Me fighting and destroy them before they got back to their bases, by 12 November, its chance had passed. The division's level of success in fulfilling this purpose, while by no means negligible, had been quite limited in relation to the effort expended.

By 12 November, however, the Americans, with the aid of their South Vietnamese allies, had identified the Chu Pong–Ia Drang area as a PAVN base. They had the means to make incursions into that area. But doing so was potentially far more dangerous than intercepting weakened and somewhat demoralized units in the process of retreat. Intelligence indicated that the Chu Pong massif now contained a fresh North Vietnamese regiment—one that had not been bloodied and battered in the siege of Plei Me.[3] Intense indoctrination had made at least some of its troops rather keen on killing Americans.[4]

It was the 1st Cavalry Division's 3d Brigade that would undertake any such incursion. Its commander, Colonel Thomas W. "Tim" Brown, had been born in West Point, New York, in 1919, the son of an army officer. Graduating from West Point in the accelerated wartime class of 1943, he had served in the 11th Airborne Division in the Philippines in 1944–1945 and had won both the Bronze Star and the Silver Star in Korea, where he commanded a battalion. Over six feet tall, Brown was thin, sandy-haired, and bespectacled. In manner he was quiet and undemonstrative but had the reputation of being a careful planner. His role in the Pleiku campaign has, however, occasioned little comment from historians. His freedom to maneuver his brigade was actually severely circumscribed by Colonel Richard Knowles, the deputy division commander, and in most accounts of the campaign's biggest firefight (at LZ X-Ray), his role is almost completely overshadowed, perhaps unjustly, by that of one of his subordinates, Harold Moore.[5]

Brown's deputy, Lieutenant Colonel Edward "Shy" Meyer, was widely regarded as a very talented officer, and 3d Brigade's staff as a whole was generally considered competent and effective. The brigade normally had just two battalions: 1st Battalion, 7th Cavalry (1/7), and 2d Battalion, 7th Cavalry (2/7). For operations in Pleiku, Kinnard assigned Brown a third battalion, the 2d Battalion, 5th Cavalry (2/5), transferred from Colonel Ray Lynch's 2d Brigade. The 1st Battalion, 21st Artillery, 3d Brigade's 105mm howitzer battalion would provide 3d Brigade with truly excellent fire support in its forthcoming operations.

Lieutenant Colonel Harold G. "Hal" Moore commanded 1/7 Cavalry. Born in Bardstown, Kentucky, in 1922, Moore had graduated from West Point in 1945, a little too late for active participation in the Second World War. Qualifying as a paratrooper, he served with the 11th Airborne Division in the American army of occupation in Japan. In the Korean War he commanded a company in the 17th Infantry Regiment of the 7th Infantry Division. Between then and assignment to the experimental air assault division, he earned a master's degree in international relations at George Washington University, doing his thesis on Laos. Tall, fair-haired, and charismatic, Moore was the most experienced combat leader and, some believed, the most effective battalion commander in the 1st Cavalry Division. Having commanded 1/7 for more than eighteen months, and having been selected for promotion to full colonel, he was due to leave the battalion shortly.

Lieutenant Colonel Robert McDade, who commanded 2/7 Cavalry, had led a rifle platoon in the South Pacific in the Second World War and a company in Korea. He had two Silver Stars and three Purple Hearts. For eighteen months he had been the G-1 (senior staff officer in charge of personnel) in division headquarters and had taken over the 2/7 only in October. Before that, it had been ten years since he had commanded troops. Lieutenant Colonel Robert Tully, commanding 2/5 Cavalry, was an Airborne officer like Moore. Like the other two battalion commanders, he had served in Korea, where he had done two combat jumps. By mid-November 1965, he had commanded his battalion for eighteen months and had thoroughly settled into the job.[6]

The Raid on Catecka, 12–13 November 1965

Colonel Brown decided to put his brigade command post in the Catecka tea plantation, code-named Stadium, where 1st Brigade's had previously been. In some respects, it was an appropriate and attractive location. The plantation house had its own water system and power generators and was set in land-scaped surroundings. There were usable roads radiating from it and airfields that could handle any traffic likely to be required. The French-owned plantation was, however, a profitable business that the South Vietnamese government regarded as important to the economic development of the Central Highlands. The 1st Cavalry Division was told not to disrupt its operation. This gave rise to security problems. The plantation manager was rumored to be paying "protection" money to local Communist forces to avoid assassination or kidnap and to ensure that trucks carrying his product were allowed to reach the coastal plain unmolested. Such arrangements almost certainly meant that local Communist forces had regular access to the plantation and knew their way around. To what extent Brown was aware of this situation when he decided to install 3d Brigade's command post at Stadium is unclear.

The former 1st Brigade command post at Stadium had never had an infantry company specifically tasked with its defense, and Brown did not initially organize one for 3d Brigade's. Instead, a provisional company-sized defense force was routinely provided from various supporting units based at Catecka: Charlie Battery of the 2d Battalion, 20th (aerial rocket) Artillery, with its twelve rocket-firing helicopters; a battery of the 6th Battalion, 14th Artillery, equipped with 175mm long-range guns; a radio intercept team; a prisoner interrogation team; a long-range patrol team; and a military police team. On 12 November Captain Riley McVeay, who commanded the 175mm artillery battery, also led the base defense force composed of these disparate elements. His second in command was Billy G. Wilson, a second lieutenant from his battery. About half an hour before midnight, the force's mettle was suddenly put to the test.[7]

Employing local Communist forces mainly to gather target intelligence and as guides, twenty-six members of the PAVN 952d Sapper Battalion (formed in early 1965 by amalgamating depleted units that had been in the South for some time) conducted this operation. It came in two parts. A battery equipped with 82mm and 60mm mortars (a total of four tubes), positioning itself on high ground some 450 meters to the north, opened up on a fuel dump and on aircraft on the ground, eventually firing an estimated 100 rounds. At the same time, sappers equipped with explosive charges delivered an assault from the north and west.

Riley McVeay's company offered stiff resistance to the assault, and although most of them took some hits getting up, seven aerial rocket artillery helicopters were in the air within about five minutes of the start of the action. Some of the helicopter crews soon identified the position of the Communist mortar battery from its muzzle flashes and suppressed it. Others engaged other targets. When the American perimeter was breached on its north side, McVeay's deputy, Billy Wilson, despite bleeding profusely from wounds inflicted by mortar shell fragments, organized a successful counterattack. The action was over within three-quarters of an hour. Seven Americans were killed and twenty-three were wounded. The Communist attackers left behind six bodies and apparently took others away. Relatively little material damage was done to the base—no aircraft were destroyed, and no fuel was ignited. But the attack made the brigade staff understandably nervous. From then on, Brown insisted on having an infantry company for night security.[8]

The Focus Shifts to the Chu Pong Massif, 10–13 November 1965

Only about thirty-six hours separated the fighting at Catecka from the beginning of the much larger and more famous firefight at LZ X-Ray at the foot of the Chu Pong massif. It is the immediate background to 3d Brigade's plunge into that part of the Drang valley that we must now examine.

On the instructions of the Field Force commander Major General Stanley "Swede" Larsen, as communicated through Knowles's forward division headquarters at Pleiku, 3d Brigade had begun its search for the North Vietnamese in the hill country east and south of Plei Me. All three of its battalions were initially employed in that area, with 2/5 Cavalry the furthest north, 1/7 in a central position, and 2/7 south of Plei Me. By 12 October, however, Knowles was pretty certain that this area was a "dry hole," and his attention became focused on the Chu Pong massif.[9]

On 10 November 1965 Meyer, Brown's deputy, sent Captain John Pritchard, an intelligence officer at 3d Brigade, to Pleiku to consult with the ARVN II Corps intelligence staff. Pritchard spoke to Captain Luong, who told him that, according to a number of North Vietnamese prisoners, the PAVN 66th Regiment was on the Chu Pong massif. Colonel Phuoc of the 24 STZ, whom Pritchard also met, confirmed this. The South Vietnamese claimed that they had already passed this information on to Colonel Lang, the 1st Cavalry Division's senior intelligence officer, but if so, Lang had not forwarded it to 3d Brigade. Pritchard, however, phoned it in to the 3d Brigade command post at Catecka, and it was duly entered in the brigade's intelligence summary. When he returned to Catecka on 13 November, Pritchard reported to Meyer in person and noted that a PAVN regiment had been marked on the Chu Pong massif on the brigade's intelligence map. According to Pritchard, Kinnard, Knowles, Brown, and Moore had all been informed of the PAVN 66th Regiment's presence on the Chu Pong massif before 1/7 Cavalry landed at the foot of that feature on 14 November.[10]

In 1968 Brown testified to a US Army official historian that before 3d Brigade took over the Pleiku campaign, the American advisers at II Corps (Mataxis's team) had briefed him on their understanding of the general situation in Pleiku Province. During the briefing Brown had noticed a prominent red star over the Chu Pong massif on II Corps' intelligence map. The II Corps advisers told him that Chu Pong was a major Communist base area and that no friendly force had been there for a considerable time. Brown, however, insisted to the same historian that he had "no tactical intelligence indicating the presence of any enemy force" on the Chu Pong massif, testimony that conflicts not only with Pritchard's evidence but also with 3d Brigade's after-action report on the campaign.[11] Possibly, after the passage of a few years, Brown had simply forgotten what intelligence had been available at this critical time. Perhaps he was not disposed to take seriously any intelligence emanating from South Vietnamese sources unless it had been confirmed by American observation. Or it may be that in the period from 12 to 14 November he was finding the whole situation so confusing and frustrating that he did not know what to believe.

Confusion and frustration seem to have been major ingredients in the atmosphere at all the major American headquarters involved in the Pleiku campaign at this stage. Intellectually and emotionally, it must have been difficult to accept that the most energetic efforts of the most modern and mobile division in the US Army had, over a period of two and a half weeks, produced such modest results. Even with all the latest American technology, it was proving most difficult to find and fix units of the army of a seemingly much less sophisticated opponent.

At some point on 12 November or on the morning of 13 November (accounts are inconsistent) Larsen paid a visit to 1st Cavalry Division's forward headquarters at Pleiku, where he spoke to Knowles. According to one version of events, Knowles first briefed Larsen about the attack at Catecka the previous night (which suggests that the visit occurred on the morning of 13 November). He then pointed out that 3d Brigade was drawing a complete blank in its searches east of Plei Me and that he had no real hope of finding anything there. Larsen demanded to know why all of 3d Brigade was searching that area if it seemed so unpromising. Knowles replied that he was merely obeying Larsen's orders. To this, Larsen reportedly responded that the overriding duty of the 1st Cavalry Division was to find and engage the enemy. On that basis, Knowles visited Brown later the same morning and told him to plan an air assault near the foot of the Chu Pong massif the following day.[12]

After Knowles's talk with Brown, 3d Brigade's operations officer, Major Henri G. "Pete" Mallet, drew three new operational areas for 3d Brigade: Area Maroon, immediately around Plei Me; Area Bronze, further west; and Area Lime, even further west, at the foot of the Chu Pong massif. On the same day, Brown ordered 2/5 Cavalry to reopen LZ Falcon, a firebase previously used by 2/8 Cavalry. On a plateau between the Meur and Tae Rivers, LZ Falcon was in artillery range of the eastern slopes of the Chu Pong massif and the adjacent Drang valley. By noon on 13 November, Battery C of the 21st Artillery was set up and firing from there, while two companies of the 2/5 Cavalry patrolled south along the Tae River, in a position to support the battery, should that be necessary.

On Saturday, 13 November, Hal Moore's 1/7 Cavalry was operating south and west of Plei Me. At 1700 that evening, Tim Brown flew south from Catecka to the command post of A Company 1/7, where he met Moore. Brown ordered Moore to conduct a battalion air assault into Area Lime the following morning. Moore was instructed to look for the North Vietnamese on the eastern edge of Chu Pong massif and to expect to remain in that area throughout 14 and 15 November. Moore had complete freedom in the selection of landing zones, and Brown assured him that he would get strong artillery support from LZ Falcon, as a second battery had been ordered to move there at 0800 the following morning.[13]

Moore Plans an Air Assault, 13–14 November 1965

Moore's memoirs confirm that he had received an intelligence briefing on the presence of the PAVN 66th Regiment in the area he was now ordered to probe, his testimony corroborating Pritchard's evidence.[14] There is, however, no indication in any source, including Moore's memoirs, that Moore protested that Brown's order would place his battalion at extreme risk. Nor is there much indication that Moore approached the new mission in a cautious or circumspect way—rather, the contrary. The difficulty of finding and fixing the enemy was causing senior American officers extreme frustration. Frustration tended to make them rash. So obsessed had they become with finding substantial concentrations of North Vietnamese troops in western Pleiku that they were not thinking carefully enough about how the North Vietnamese might react if found. A strong tendency to pursue contact regardless of risk was already apparent in some quarters at the time of the Ia Drang ambush on 3 November. By the middle of the month, it was becoming the dominant attitude among American commanders involved in this campaign, from Larsen's level down.

Perhaps the main exception to this superaggressive spirit was Tim Brown, the 3d Brigade commander. Brown had transmitted to Moore orders that were likely to place Moore's battalion in great danger. Yet, perhaps more than any other senior officer involved, he seems to have had a sense of just how acute that peril might be. He counseled Moore to be cautious and not to allow his companies to get separated—advice he would repeat the following morning.[15]

The risks to Moore's battalion were made significantly more serious by the relatively slender resources, in terms of both helicopters and personnel, that were available to him for this operation. Research has revealed no document providing a complete inventory of 1st Cavalry Division's aircraft on 13 November, indicating where they were and in what state of repair. Of the 435 helicopters on the division's establishment, however, only 24 "slicks" (troop-carrying Hueys) were assigned to Brown's 3d Brigade (responsible for the division's main effort), although some Huey gunships and Chinooks were also available. Brown reckoned that 2/7 and 2/5 Cavalry would need 4 slicks each just to keep operating at the most basic level. Moore, whose 1/7 Cavalry would be the point of the division's spear on 14 November, would have to manage with just 16.[16] The main reason for the extreme shortage of helicopters, especially slicks, at this critical moment was almost certainly the prodigious mechanical wear and tear caused by 1st Brigade's frenetic but, for the most part, rather ineffective operations of 27 October to 9 November.

As a result of sickness (especially malaria), the ending of some soldiers' enlistment periods before their replacements arrived, and the detachment of personnel for a variety of purposes, on 13 November 1/7 Cavalry was down to 431 personnel rather than its full complement of 633. Given the shortage of helicopters, however, even this fairly small number could not be picked up and moved all at once. Under most conditions, a Huey could lift eight infantrymen with full loads of equipment. In the relatively thin air of the Highlands, this was reduced to five. Sixteen slicks could therefore carry only eighty troops in the first lift. Although the exact time could not be calculated until a particular landing zone was selected, Moore's staff reckoned it would take about half an hour to fly from the airfield at Plei Me (the operation's starting point) to the eastern edge of the Chu Pong massif and back. Therefore, the first eighty men delivered to the landing zone would have to fend for themselves for thirty minutes without reinforcement, even if all went according to plan.[17]

Moore decided to ride in the first helicopter and land with the initial wave, quite literally leading his battalion into action, an approach reflecting his charismatic and somewhat flamboyant style. He intended to station his command helicopter, with his operations officer and fire support team, immediately over the LZ, enabling him to call in fire support and air strikes without delay. Normally, the first troops landed would concentrate on providing 360-degree protection of the LZ and wait for the next wave to arrive before starting offensive operations. Instead, Moore instructed that the first company to arrive at the LZ should immediately send one platoon toward the Chu Pong to look for the North Vietnamese; the remainder of the company would form up in an assault formation, presumably in order to be ready to attack as soon as the enemy was found. Clearly, this was a very offensively oriented approach.[18]

In his memoirs Moore quotes George Patton: "There are only three principles of warfare: Audacity, Audacity and AUDACITY."[19] It is at least possible that, at this stage in the campaign, Moore was excessively influenced by this questionable maxim and more concerned with attacking the North Vietnamese than with protecting his battalion's lifeline. Once the Americans had witnessed the violence of the PAVN reaction to their move to the edge of the Chu Pong base, such an attitude would seem less appropriate. It is, of course, perfectly normal for attitudes to change in the light of events.

After Brown's meeting with Moore on the evening of 13 November, Moore's S-3 (operations officer), Captain Gregory "Matt" Dillon, began searching the map for appropriate landing zones. At the same time, Moore contacted his companies to warn them of the next day's operation. At this stage, two of 1/7's companies were still in the field. They were told to concentrate their men at first light on 14 November for pickup and movement by helicopter. Another company, Captain John D. Herren's B Company, had been selected to guard the Stadium-Catecka base that night and had already been lifted there. Moore and his staff arranged for B Company to be picked up at first light on 14 November and lifted by Chinook helicopters (divisional assets) to Plei Me's airfield. Despite B Company's being on guard duty all night, Moore decided that it should be the first unit delivered to the edge of the Chu Pong massif.[20]

Final selection of the landing zone was delayed until the morning of Sunday, 14 November. Moore wanted to fly with his company commanders to review the possibilities before making a final decision. Captain Dillon had marked four possible landing zones on a map of the area: Tango, Whiskey, X-Ray, and Yankee. Moore and all four of his company commanders gathered at the Plei Me airstrip early on Sunday morning, and two Huey slicks, escorted by two Huey gunships, took them to inspect the possible landing zones. The flight plan was drawn up with deception in mind. They stayed at around 2,500 feet and at one point hovered for five minutes over Duc Co, not making it too obvious to the North Vietnamese that they were looking for landing zones near the Chu Pong. They were back at Plei Me by 0815.

After this reconnaissance flight, Moore decided that only three of the four possible landing zones were close enough to the Chu Pong massif to be usable. Of these, only two—X-Ray and Yankee—were sufficiently large. Before making a final decision, Moore sent a scout team from 1/9 Cavalry in their small, highly maneuverable OH-13 Sioux helicopters to take a closer look at X-Ray and Yankee and report back. The scouts flew lower than the reconnaissance mission had that morning, but they took no fire. They reported that Yankee contained many high tree stumps, a potential hazard. They had seen trails close to both potential landing zones and had observed what appeared to be communications wire just a couple of hundred yards west of X-Ray. In the end, Moore selected X-Ray partly because he thought it would present fewer hazards in terms of terrain and vegetation, but also because it seemed to offer the best prospect of early contact with the North Vietnamese.[21]

It is axiomatic that no plan survives, in any detail, first contact with the main body of the enemy. It would, however, be interesting to know, in general terms, how Moore imagined the operation developing in two of the most obvious contingencies: (1) The North Vietnamese would react to the American intrusion with an immediate and violent attack. (There was, after all, plenty of evidence that PAVN troops were sometimes capable of such a response.) (2) They would react by withdrawing up the Chu Pong massif. (Had the North Vietnamese preferred to retreat, it is difficult to see how Moore's battalion could have stopped them. His best hope in this contingency would have been to inflict as many casualties as possible by calling in artillery fire and air strikes.) But the transcript of the oral orders Moore issued to his battalion, his after-action report, and his book on the campaign all fail to provide any insight into how Moore imagined events unfolding once his troops made contact with the North Vietnamese. The whole operation was put together in such a rush that he had, perhaps, no time to think beyond his opening gambit. It is questionable, to say the least, whether such haste was necessary or appropriate when planning a probe into a long-established Communist base area where intelligence indicated that a fresh PAVN regiment was now ensconced. But the hurry was generated two or three command levels above Moore's. It would have been difficult for him to resist, even if he had been disposed to do so.

At Plei Me at 0845, Moore issued his operations order, giving his company commanders and helicopter pilots their final briefing for the imminent operation. He explained that one North Vietnamese battalion was likely to be in the immediate vicinity of the landing zone, with the possibility of others not far away. Thirty minutes before helicopters delivered the first wave of 1/7

Cavalry to X-Ray, artillery at Falcon would fire on Yankee and Tango for eight minutes to create a diversion. Then, for twenty minutes, the guns would turn on the area around X-Ray. As the tube artillery lifted, aerial rocket artillery and helicopter gunships would fire on the area immediately around the landing zone while the sixteen slicks delivered the battalion command group and the first troops of Captain John D. Herren's Bravo Company. As soon as all the troops of the first lift were on the ground, Herren would send out a platoon to patrol toward the Chu Pong massif, leaving the rest of the company on the landing zone in an assault formation. The balance of Bravo Company and part of Captain Ramon A. Nadal's Alpha Company would arrive in the second lift, followed by Companies C and D. Captain Robert H. Edwards's Charlie Company would initially form the battalion reserve but would then move west and northwest to search parts of the massif. Finally, Captain Louis R. Lefebvre's numerically weak Delta Company would arrive, taking charge of the battalion mortars and assuming the role of battalion reserve. Moore's briefing ended at approximately 0915. He intended the first wave to arrive at X-Ray at 1030.[22]

Colonel Brown was at Plei Me on the morning of 14 November. He approved Moore's plan, but he echoed the note of caution he had sounded the previous evening. He told Moore and Dillon to be extremely careful, to "stay tight," and not to allow 1/7 Cavalry's companies to become separated.[23] It was good advice but not altogether heeded.

X-Ray: The Initial American Landing, 1045–1120, 14 November

The second artillery battery sent to LZ Falcon, transported by the same Chinooks that had lifted Bravo Company from Catecka to the airfield at Plei Me earlier that morning, arrived a little late. That set the timing of the whole operation back slightly, with the "preparatory fires not commencing until 1017." Moore, however, observed from his position in the lead aircraft that the artillery fires were delivered "precisely where required" and were "beautifully timed with the lead elements of the assault company."[24] The explosion of a white phosphorus artillery round on the landing zone signaled the end of the tube artillery preparation.[25] The aerial rocket artillery helicopters "came in on the heels of the tube artillery fires and worked over the area for 30 seconds expending half their loads," and then they hovered over the area on call. As these helicopters finished firing and "banked steeply away," the four helicopter gunships escorting the sixteen troop-carrying UH-1Ds (all twenty helicopters belonging to the 229th Air Assault Battalion) dashed ahead and opened fire on the area around the landing zone, encouraging any North Vietnamese in the immediate vicinity to keep their heads down just before the first landings took place. As the slicks approached, the door gunners fired their machine guns into the trees and high grass. As they landed, the troops fired their M-16 automatic rifles at "likely enemy positions." The initial landing at 1048, eighteen minutes later than originally scheduled, was unopposed.[26]

The landing zone took the form of an "east-west oval almost pinched off in the middle by a grove of trees." It was covered by yellowish brown, waist-high plateau grass that also extended into the area around the landing zone, providing good cover for anyone attacking it and making it difficult for defenders to stay in touch. The grove of trees in the middle effectively divided X-Ray into two side-by-side landing zones each capable of holding four or five helicopters. Near the center of the grove was a termite mound about 10 feet high, 12 feet broad, and "hard as concrete." Moore decided to establish his command post at this central location. The command group consisted of Moore himself; Sergeant Major Basil Plumley; the battalion intelligence officer, Captain Thomas C. Metsker; two radio operators; and Mr. Nik, a Highlander who spoke good English and Vietnamese and had been sent from the brigade as an interpreter. Moore's operations officer Captain Dillon, his artillery liaison officer, his liaison officer with the helicopter lift company, and his forward air controller all remained in the command helicopter orbiting between the Ia Drang and Plei Me.

The heavily forested Chu Pong massif (or "mountain," as Moore and his troops tended to call it) did not look especially impressive from the air. Rising 500 meters above the floor of the Drang valley, however, it dominated X-Ray. From there, it looked huge and forbidding. For some of Moore's troops, the idea of attacking up the Chu Pong suddenly seemed rather daunting. Nevertheless, as soon as the first wave was on the ground, Captain Herren dispatched a platoon 100 meters or so west of the edge of the clearing in the direction of the massif. The rest of the personnel who arrived with the first lift remained on the landing zone for the time being.[27]

The Initial PAVN Reaction to the American Landing, 1048–1120, 14 November

Certain passages in Vietnamese Communist histories indicate that the PAVN deliberately and cunningly lured the Americans into a killing ground at the foot of the Chu Pong massif. Clearly, this is, or at one time was, the Party line. It is not inconceivable that fighting the Americans in this location genuinely was the PAVN's long-term intention. But there is also plenty of evidence in Vietnamese Communist accounts that the PAVN was ill prepared to deal with

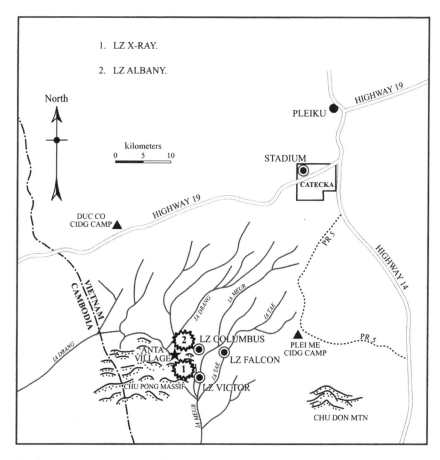

1. LZ X-RAY.

2. LZ ALBANY.

Cavalry operations, 14–17 November 1965

the actual American landing at X-Ray on 14 November 1965. A landing in force at this time and place took the North Vietnamese by surprise.[28]

The campaign in Pleiku (or Gia Lai, as the Communists called the province) was not going well for General Chu Huy Man and his Central Highlands (B3) Front. Despite claims to the contrary in Communist histories, Man's Plei Me "lure and ambush" gambit had been a terrible failure. It had achieved nothing substantial, and it had left two whole PAVN regiments very badly cut up. Admittedly, Man now had a fresh regiment, the 66th. But its arrival in the Highlands had only intensified logistical problems that were already acute. Despite its careful preparations for the Plei Me campaign, the PAVN was facing a food crisis in the Highlands by mid-November. Shortly before Moore's battalion landed at the foot of the Chu Pong, Man had, according to the memoirs of senior commissar Dang Vu Hiep, departed for Darlac with a view to procuring rice to supply his PAVN regiments in Pleiku.[29] Despite the seriousness of the logistical situation, it is difficult to believe that Man would have gone on a mission of this nature had he believed his forces were on the brink of the biggest battle the PAVN had yet fought with the Americans.

According to Hiep, shortly before leaving for Darlac, Man told his deputy, Lieutenant Colonel Nguyen Huu An, to establish a forward headquarters for the Central Highlands Front on the Chu Pong massif. With Hiep as his senior commissar, An was to take operational control of all PAVN forces in the area, including the battered and depleted 32d and 33d Regiments and the relatively fresh 66th Regiment, newly arrived from the Ho Chi Minh Trail. An was the sort of deputy to whom it was safe to delegate authority. Born in 1926 in Hanoi, he was a dedicated Communist and a very experienced combat leader who had served in many campaigns of the First Indochina War and had commanded a Viet Minh regiment at Dien Bien Phu.[30]

The Chu Pong massif had been part of a major Communist base area for years. But An's memoirs indicate that he, Hiep, and the thirty personnel they had been given to establish their command post arrived on the slopes of the massif only just before noon Hanoi time (1300 Saigon–US Army in Vietnam time) on 14 November. American ordnance was already exploding nearby.[31] All accounts from the Communist side indicate that An was able to exercise little or no command and control for several hours into the first day's battle. Even on subsequent days, his control of the units notionally under his command was evidently very limited. Yet Communist histories do not condemn or even criticize An. This would make sense if their authors appreciated that An arrived on the Chu Pong only after the battle had started and thus had little opportunity to establish his own headquarters, still less to establish communications with those of subordinate units.

To make matters worse for the North Vietnamese, the 66th Regiment—the principal battleworthy PAVN force that had battalions on and near the Chu Pong massif—had completed its march down the Ho Chi Minh Trail only in the last few days. The troops were still trying to get themselves organized by "building huts, digging fortifications and transporting rice and ammunition from the B3 Front's supply caches."[32] They were by no means ideally prepared for battle. As one study put it:

> 66th Regiment had only just arrived from North Vietnam; . . . units had not completed building their bivouac areas; the enemy situation was unknown; supplies of ammunition, rice and salt had not yet been built up to adequate levels; and our troops, whose health and physical condition had deteriorated during the long march down the trail, had not had a chance to rest and recuperate. . . . Generally speaking each unit was about 80% of its authorized strength.[33]

Authorized strength was 500 men per battalion, so the 66th Regiment's battalions were each probably about 400 strong, slightly numerically weaker than
Moore's battalion.

The PAVN 66th Regiment's headquarters and the 7th Battalion were biv-
ouacked in adjacent areas on the southeastern face of the massif. Located 5 km
away on the eastern face of the massif, barely 1 km west of X-Ray, was the
bivouac area of the main body of the 9th Battalion.[34] The 66th Regiment's
remaining battalion, the 8th, was on the other side of the Drang River in an
area called Ba Bi, half a day's march (perhaps 12 km) northeast of its regimental headquarters on the Chu Pong.[35] The 8th Battalion was the only one that
had previously encountered American ground troops. Elements of it had been
ambushed by a platoon of 1/9 Cavalry on the night of 3 November and had
participated in the firefight at LZ Mary later the same night. Other PAVN
units were in the vicinity. Most of what remained of the 33d Regiment was,
according to one source, dispersed in a 3 km line on the eastern side of Chu
Pong. The 32d Regiment, severely battered after its encounter with Luat's
Armored Task Force and American air support, was on the Cambodian border
about 15 km to the northwest.[36]

Even when fully deployed, the American 1/7 Cavalry would be outnumbered roughly 2:1 just by the two PAVN battalions on the massif, not counting
the one on the other side of the Ia Drang. Because of the small number of
helicopters allocated, it would take hours for the 1/7 to assemble all its troops,
so initially, the numerical disparity would be considerably greater than that.
The 66th Regiment's troops had the usual PAVN infantry weapons, including
a mix of SKS and AK-47 rifles, RPD machine guns, rocket-propelled grenades
(RPGs), 82mm mortars, and 75mm recoilless rifles—all very serviceable arms.
For an infantry fight at fairly close quarters, the North Vietnamese were as well
equipped, or almost so, as the Americans with their M-16 rifles, M-60 machine
guns, M-79 grenade launchers, and M-72 LAW shoulder-fired rockets.[37]

Given the numerical balance in their favor, the North Vietnamese had, in
theory, an opportunity to overrun X-Ray by a concerted attack as soon as the
first Americans landed. In practice, they were incapable of this. Their situation was far weaker than a purely numerical analysis makes it appear. Having
been taken by surprise, their command and control above the battalion level
practically failed to function in the first hours of the battle. When the first US
helicopters arrived, the 66th Regiment and 9th Battalion commanders were
surveying the terrain several kilometers away on the banks of the Drang River,
and the 66th Regiment's political commissar, La Ngoc Chau, was also away
from his office. The terrain of the Central Highlands looked about as strange
and forbidding to most North Vietnamese as it did to most Americans, and not
even the senior officers of the 66th Regiment were fully familiar with the lay

of the land on the Chu Pong. The regimental commander became hopelessly lost for a couple of days while trying to find his way back to his command post. The 9th Battalion's commander, who played a more active part in the battle, apparently did not find his command post until the battalion, in effect, had ceased to exist.

The 9th Battalion's forward outposts on the lower slopes of the eastern side of the Chu Pong, adjacent to X–Ray, were shattered by the artillery and aerial rocket fire the Americans delivered in support of the initial helicopter landing. Any survivors in these outposts seem to have been unable, whether because of physical incapacity or shock, to communicate with the main body of the battalion. The initial American probe up the Chu Pong massif thus caught the main body of the 9th Battalion unaware.[38]

A PAVN Prisoner and the American Advance up the Chu Pong Massif, 1120–1245, 14 November

At about 1120 a B Company patrol captured a North Vietnamese soldier whom the Americans thought might be a deserter. The prisoner reported that there were three PAVN battalions in the immediate vicinity and that they were looking forward to killing Americans. Having quickly interviewed the prisoner through his interpreter, Mr. Nik, Moore arranged for him to be picked up by his command helicopter and taken away for more detailed interrogation. As most of Captain Nadal's Alpha Company was now on the ground (the third lift having arrived at approximately 1210), Moore decided that Alpha could hold the landing zone. He ordered Herren to take all of Bravo Company, advance northwest up a finger-like ridge of the Chu Pong massif, and "develop the situation."[39]

In his book on the campaign, Moore explains that his order to B Company was motivated by a desire to push the North Vietnamese away from the landing zone until he had the whole of 1/7 Cavalry on the ground. Defense of the landing zone against the greatly superior enemy numbers reported by the prisoner was, according to Moore's published account, his overriding priority at this juncture. He chose to advance up the Chu Pong, he implies, only because, in these critical circumstances, that appeared to be the best method of defense.[40] No such explanation for sending Bravo Company up the Chu Pong massif is, however, offered in Moore's after-action report, written much sooner after the events it describes than his book. The North Vietnamese prisoner's information had, by Moore's own testimony, done little more than confirm the intelligence briefing he had received before planning the air assault. Up to this point, Moore's whole approach to the operation had been very aggressive.

There is no substantial evidence to suggest that his outlook had changed by 1220 on the afternoon of Sunday, 14 November.

Moore's order to Captain Herren at about 1220 that day, to take Bravo Company up the Chu Pong massif and "develop the situation," was surely motivated by a desire to find and fix the North Vietnamese and to bring on a battle with them as quickly as possible. Moore's orders to Captain Nadal a few minutes later (apparently sometime between 1220 and 1230) provide further evidence of a still resolutely aggressive, risk-taking state of mind. Moore told Nadal that as soon as enough of Charlie Company had arrived to take responsibility for the defense of X-Ray, Alpha Company should follow Bravo up the massif.[41] If Moore's principal concern, at this point, was the security of his landing zone, did it really make sense to send two of his three rifle companies in a probe up the Chu Pong?

After Captain John Herren briefed his platoon leaders in a creek bed on the northwestern side of the landing zone, Bravo Company began its advance at approximately 1230. Herren had two platoons leading and one following, with a platoon mortar in support.[42] The outpost line of the 9th Battalion of the PAVN 66th Regiment had already disintegrated, and the slopes of the Chu Pong were thickly forested; thus, the main body of the battalion did not know the Americans were coming until they were just 100 meters away. To the North Vietnamese, the Americans appeared to be attacking in two columns (possibly a reference to Herren's two leading platoons)—one headed directly at the 9th Battalion's 11th Company, and the other headed toward battalion headquarters. At this point, the battalion political officer who was the acting battalion commander panicked and ran away, leaving the 9th Battalion leaderless. As the battle started in earnest (at about 1245, according to American accounts), it seemed likely that the 9th Battalion might soon disintegrate.

The Development of a North Vietnamese Counterattack, 1245–1330, 14 November

In response to the leadership of its company commanders and some junior officers, the 9th Battalion rallied, and it was Herren's B Company that found itself in serious trouble. The 11th Company commander initially ordered all three of his platoons to open fire. He then ordered one platoon to "block the front of the enemy column while the other two platoons circled round to the rear." At the same time, First Lieutenant Nhoi, the staff assistant for operations, who found himself the highest ranking officer in the 9th Battalion's headquarters, boldly took charge of the situation. Calling for help from the nearby, as yet unengaged 13th Company, he ordered the battalion headquarters personnel, including cooks, runners, and medics, to grab weapons and fight. The 13th Company commander responded by sending "one platoon running to battalion headquarters to reinforce its defences and . . . another platoon to attack the left flank of the enemy attack column." At roughly the same time, "hearing the sounds of gunfire, on its own initiative 15th Company charged forward to join the fray." Gradually, all four companies of 9th Battalion became involved in the battle "as work details returned and commanders pieced together what was happening."[43]

B Company's 1st Platoon, moving to the left of the finger-like ridge that pointed northwest up the Chu Pong massif, was the first to become pinned down by North Vietnamese fire. Second Lieutenant Henry T. Herrick's 2nd Platoon was, on Herren's orders, maneuvering to the right of this ridge, hoping to clear the opposition in front of 1st Platoon, when it was surrounded and cut off. The two principal American books on the campaign, both by former members of the 1st Cavalry Division, give somewhat different accounts of how this happened. Moore's book pins the blame squarely on Herrick, whom it portrays as a glory seeker who was careless with the lives of his men—a portrayal, if anything, exaggerated in the Hollywood movie version, based largely on Moore's book. In this interpretation, Herrick, losing sight of his real mission, became carried away in a reckless chase after a group of North Vietnamese troops.[44] An earlier account written by J. D. Coleman, a publicity officer with the division, indicates, by contrast, that Henry Herrick was maneuvering in response to orders from his company commander, John Herren; that Herrick consulted Herren over the radio about each tactical move he made; and that his actions complied with both the letter and the spirit of his orders.[45]

Whichever version is believed, there can be no doubt of the outcome. Herrick's platoon first met stiff resistance from its front and then took fire from its flanks and became pinned down. Then, at some point between 1300 and 1330, as substantial numbers of North Vietnamese troops counterattacked downhill toward the American landing zone, they swept around and behind the platoon, surrounding it. Its position became increasingly critical as the afternoon wore on.

The saga of the lost platoon figures prominently in American histories of the X-Ray battle. From Moore's point of view, it played a large part in shaping the battle's course. There is, however, no reference to it in Vietnamese Communist accounts. This is not surprising. To the North Vietnamese, caught off guard and desperately trying to improvise counterattacks, this battle must have appeared even more chaotic than, for those caught up in them, battles normally do. They were fragmented. They apparently had no radio below the company level, and possibly none below the battalion level. Their ability to communicate detailed information in the heat of battle was thus much more limited than that of the Americans. It is therefore entirely possible that no PAVN officer above the company or even platoon level knew that an American platoon was surrounded. While cut off, Bravo Company's 2d Platoon received intense fire and was subjected to occasional assaults. But the latter may have been carried out by relatively small groups of North Vietnamese troops acting on local initiative. Given that PAVN commanders at the battalion level and above were seemingly unaware of 2d Platoon's predicament, it is unlikely that any large-scale, concerted effort was ever made to wipe it out.[46] That, together with the massive firepower the Americans were able to bring to bear in its support, probably explains why most of its members survived.

With the whole of B Company now fully engaged and Herrick's platoon isolated, Captain Herren realized that he was in serious trouble. A substantial North Vietnamese counterattack was in progress, and he urgently needed help. Organizing his men for defense as best he could, Herren radioed Moore at about 1330. This was a critical moment. Up to 1330, most of the evidence indicates that Moore thought he was conducting an offensive operation that, though meeting some resistance, was going reasonably well. After 1330 he realized he had a crisis on his hands. The initiative was slipping from his grasp. The landing zone might be at risk. The very survival of his battalion might be in jeopardy. At roughly the same time that Herren radioed Moore with his alarming report, the first PAVN mortar shells started exploding on LZ X-Ray.

On the basis of his radio conversation with Herren, Moore concluded that the main threat to X-Ray came from North Vietnamese troops sweeping around B Company's left flank while its other two rifle platoons moved right to try to rescue Herrick's. Moore therefore decided to commit Ramon Nadal's A Company on B Company's left and to assign one platoon from A Company to help B Company rescue its cutoff platoon. At the same time, he sent recently landed troops from Robert Edwards's C Company to cover A Company's left. In response to the mortar shells now hitting X-Ray, Moore requested massive artillery and air support.

The North Vietnamese Counterattack Continues, 1330–1615, 14 November

The hour between 1330 and 1430 on 14 November was pivotal in the battle's development. Although they got to within about 75 meters of it, the Americans were unable to rescue Herrick's platoon, which remained surrounded.

North Vietnamese efforts to envelop B Company by moving along a creek bed parallel to the edge of the landing zone also proved unsuccessful. The PAVN troops attempting this maneuver were taken in the flank by A Company as it moved forward to support B Company and were shot up. When it became clear that the effort to rescue Herrick's platoon had failed, Moore decided to pull the rest of B Company back to the creek bed. It appears to have been essentially the line of the creek bed that A Company and B Company were holding at 1430, blocking North Vietnamese efforts to get through to X-Ray from the west and northwest. C Company was covering A Company's left and protecting the landing zone from attacks from the south.[47]

For the next hour or so, however, roughly from 1430 to 1530, the situation for the Americans at X-Ray continued to appear alarming. Too thin on the ground to comply with fundamental principles, they did not have all-around defense, defense in depth, or any sort of reserve. The northern and eastern sides of the landing zone were almost totally undefended. Had the North Vietnamese been able to attack from those directions in real strength (using both the 9th and 7th Battalions), much of Moore's battalion might well have faced destruction.

The fifth lift of sixteen helicopters approached X-Ray at 1442. The first eight helicopters were able to land, bringing in almost all the remainder of Captain Edwards's C Company and D Company's reconnaissance platoon. But the intensity of enemy fire was such that Moore ordered the remaining eight not to attempt a landing at this time. The newly arrived members of C Company had no sooner entered the line with the rest of the company on the southwestern edge of the landing zone than they came under a fierce attack from an estimated 200 North Vietnamese. The fighting was savage and bloody, with heavy casualties on both sides. The Americans, however, were able to call in artillery and close air support, as well as using their infantry weapons. It was the North Vietnamese who, at about 1615, broke off the action on this sector of the battlefield.[48]

By 1520, the volume of fire being directed at X-Ray had lessened, making it possible for D Company to complete its landing, together with the battalion's reconnaissance platoon. Moore ordered Delta to take a position on the northwestern side of the landing zone, closing the gap between B Company and C Company. For the first time, something resembling a continuous defensive perimeter existed around the landing zone, and, using the reconnaissance platoon, Moore was able to establish a small battalion reserve. Rather than keeping the reserve in a central position near his command post, however, he positioned it near the numerically weak D Company, where he was most concerned that a breakthrough might occur.[49]

The American Attempt to Rescue the Isolated Platoon,
1620–1740, 14 November

As the crisis over the defense of the landing zone subsided in the late afternoon of 14 November, Moore decided to mount an attack to rescue the isolated platoon. It seems appropriate here to review that platoon's situation. At some point in the midafternoon Herrick suffered a bullet wound in the hip and soon died. Before losing consciousness, he turned over leadership to Sergeant Carl Palmer, who was killed within minutes. Shortly after taking over from Palmer, the second squad leader, Sergeant Robert Stokes, also suffered a fatal wound. At that point, Sergeant Clyde E. "Ernie" Savage took charge. All accounts give Savage much of the credit for saving what was left of the platoon. He ordered everyone to stay put and stay low. He used the radio to bring in friendly artillery fire all around the platoon's position, sufficiently close to give it real protection.[50]

Before launching A and B Companies into an attack designed to rescue the lost platoon (which was about 300 meters up the slope of the Chu Pong, northwest of the X-Ray perimeter), Moore pulled those companies back a short distance, under the cover of artillery fire, roughly from the line of the creek to the edge of the clearing. This allowed the companies to get medical attention for their casualties and to reorganize their remaining fighting strength. The American attack started from the creek bed at 1620, as scheduled, with A Company on the left and B Company on the right. Both tube and aerial rocket artillery provided fire support. The fire support, however, was delivered too far away from the start line of the American attack, presumably to avoid causing American casualties. Some North Vietnamese were "grabbing the belts" of the American ground troops, keeping very close to their forward edge, so the American supporting fires largely missed them. The American attack gained a maximum of only 150 meters before the North Vietnamese shot it down. By 1740, when Moore ordered both companies back to their start line, B Company alone had suffered a further thirty casualties.[51]

Paradoxically, and unknown to the Americans, the PAVN 9th Battalion (which had thus far done all the fighting on the Communist side in this battle) had reached the end of its endurance. As the Americans pulled back, it was in the process of disintegrating. The American withdrawal eventually caused the North Vietnamese considerable confusion and difficulty. As 66th Regiment's 7th Battalion approached the battle area for the first time that night, it had considerable initial difficulty in finding the American perimeter.[52]

North Vietnamese and American Perceptions and Realities, 1300–1700, 14 November

An authority on the Vietnamese Communist war effort has pointed out that this battle (indeed, the whole Pleiku campaign) offers classic illustrations of the phenomenon that Clausewitz called the "fog of war."[53] There was a great deal of confusion. Each side kept misunderstanding the other's immediate situation and intent.

In Vietnamese Communist accounts, the entire fight during the daylight hours of 14 November is perceived as essentially a defensive action by the PAVN. The Americans mounted an attack on the PAVN on the eastern slope of the Chu Pong; the PAVN reacted as best it could, counterattacking in an effort to wrest the initiative away from the Americans. After Bravo Company's push up the Chu Pong massif was stopped (roughly between 1300 and 1330), American accounts indicate that 1/7 Cavalry was thrown on the defensive and, from that point, was fighting merely to survive. Unaware of the issue of the isolated American platoon, the North Vietnamese, by contrast, perceived Moore's attempts to rescue it as renewals of the American drive up the slope of the massif. According to Vietnamese Communist histories, therefore, American efforts to storm the Chu Pong massif on 14 November continued until the early evening. In reality, it was about that time that the last effort to rescue the isolated platoon broke down.[54]

Some American accounts suggest that, after the North Vietnamese stopped Bravo Company's probe up the Chu Pong massif, 1/7 Cavalry was attacked by overwhelming numbers.[55] Histories published in Hanoi, however, indicate that a single battalion (which, at 80 percent strength, would have had about 400 troops) did all the fighting on the Communist side up to dusk on 14 November.[56] In the late afternoon, staff at the 66th Regiment's command post and the B3 Front's forward headquarters believed that the 9th Battalion had destroyed one American company and crippled another. This was a considerable exaggeration. The misperception apparently prompted An and Hiep to order an overambitious assault by the 7th Battalion that was almost bound to fail.[57] But the 9th Battalion's real achievements on 14 November were considerable. Not only did it successfully shield the newly arrived forward headquarters of the B3 Front and the headquarters of the 66th Regiment; it also put Moore's battalion under such serious pressure that Moore thought he needed substantial reinforcements just to hold the landing zone.[58]

The 9th Battalion achieved much of this under the direction of company commanders and junior officers acting on their own initiative. As noted, the battalion commander was down beside the Ia Drang when the action started.

Although he managed to find his battalion's 11th Company within an hour, at least according to some reports, he never made it back to his battalion command post and never regained full control of the battalion. By evening, the 9th Battalion was exhausted and demoralized, its troops "scattering in all directions." Only a small number of soldiers, apparently unaware that their comrades had withdrawn, remained in contact with the Americans. Predictably, during an inquest shortly after the campaign, higher authorities blamed the battalion commander for the 9th Battalion's disintegration, although he is treated more favorably in some accounts published since the war.[59]

Attempts by commanders above the battalion level to exercise some control of the PAVN's battle on 14 November were largely ineffective before evening, although Lieutenant Colonel An, at his recently established B3 Front forward headquarters, was trying hard to get a grip. The 66th Regiment's commander had managed to write himself out of the battle altogether. As already mentioned, he was down by the river Drang when the attack started. Trying to rejoin the regiment, he reportedly got completely lost and was missing for two days.[60] Pham Cong Cuu, who seems to have been the 7th Battalion commander at the start of the battle, operated as deputy regimental commander during its course. Though active throughout the battle, he was unable to exercise much influence until quite late. Cuu was at 7th Battalion headquarters when the American attack began. Together with a group of officers from the 7th Battalion and the battalion reconnaissance unit, he moved forward to the 9th Battalion's area in the early afternoon to find out what was going on. He found it in a state of confusion. The best information he could get came from the 9th Battalion's deputy political officer, referred to in the sources only as Comrade Tuy. By the time Cuu encountered him, Tuy had been wounded in both the head and an arm. He was moving to the rear to seek medical attention. Blood was oozing through his bandages as they conversed. Tuy reported that the 9th Battalion had been attacked by at least two companies of Americans. The Americans were well armed and, at first, very aggressive. They became less so when counterattacked. The 9th Battalion had taken losses but was fighting back hard.[61]

Accounts from both sides agree that the Americans started the battle very confidently. They also indicate that this confidence diminished somewhat as the battle progressed and the Americans developed an increasing respect for the ferocity and skill of the PAVN infantry. Moore's after-action report praises the quality of North Vietnamese field-craft, the high standard of marksmanship, and the extraordinary determination to engage at close quarters.[62] Vietnamese Communist accounts admit that PAVN troops and their commanders were generally apprehensive about meeting the Americans in battle for the first time. They admit too that North Vietnamese soldiers were initially impressed by the determination and aggression of American troops. These Communist histories (which undoubtedly contain a propagandistic element) indicate, however, that as the battle progressed, PAVN soldiers noticed considerable American weaknesses. Physically bigger and less agile than Vietnamese, Americans moved less fluently over ground and, in particular, through jungle. They made good targets. Being slower and less nimble, they were not so good at close-in fighting and seemed somewhat afraid of it. They sometimes seemed unnerved if charged with the bayonet. They were lazy about digging in. When nervous, they had a tendency to fire wildly, without aiming.

A PAVN consensus soon emerged that the Americans were nothing special as infantry, perhaps not significantly more formidable in that role than the "puppets," as the PAVN called the South Vietnamese armed forces. Tactics that worked against the "puppets" thus seemed likely to work against them. But American artillery firepower and airpower were another story. They were prodigious and seemingly limitless. The Americans seemed never to run out of shells and bombs. Even at a relatively early stage in the battle, American firepower was tearing up the vegetation and the landscape on the slopes of the Chu Pong and starting fires all over the place. (Much of the combustion was probably owing to the Americans' use of white phosphorus artillery ammunition, for which Moore had a particular penchant.) Engaging the Americans in the face of all that fire was a real test of nerve and a real strain on PAVN morale.[63]

PAVN Attempts to Organize a Night Attack, 1700, 14 November–0600, 15 November

At some point on the afternoon of 14 November, the 66th Regiment's political commissar, La Ngoc Chau, arrived in the 9th Battalion's area. Given the continued absence of the actual regimental commander, Chau tried to take control of the 9th Battalion's battle. He was unable to do so before the battalion disintegrated. At dusk Chau received an order from the B3 Front forward headquarters to attack the Americans that night with all available forces. In reality, the 7th Battalion was the only force over which 66th Regiment had any control, and its 3d Company was away fetching supplies of rice. Chau tried to bring the 7th Battalion to the battle area and link it with fragments of the 9th Battalion that were still battleworthy. Together with Cuu, the deputy regimental commander, he began to organize a night attack that Cuu was tasked to lead. These officers intended the attack to commence in the small hours of 15 November. But the troops' lack of familiarity with the terrain and the American artillery fire sweeping the area imposed delays:

Marching through the black jungle in spite of the greatest possible efforts our men just could not move any faster. When they reached open clearings, the enemy's aerial and artillery illumination flares made it easier to see, but the heavy enemy artillery fire and bombing attacks had completely altered the terrain, making it difficult for the guides to recognize landmarks. The troops had to work their way around bomb and artillery craters, so sometimes the troops moved in column and sometimes in a horizontal line but everyone sighted on the center of the area where enemy bombs and artillery were exploding and headed straight for it (the enemy usually bombarded the area around where their troops were located).[64]

Apparently, it was nearly dawn when the North Vietnamese reached the American perimeter.

Organizing American Reinforcements, the Evening of 14 November

By late afternoon on 14 November, Moore had asked to be reinforced with another rifle company. Colonel Tim Brown, commanding 3d Brigade, decided to send him Captain Myron F. Diduryk's B Company from 2d Battalion, 7th Cavalry, the company assigned as the "palace guard" for Stadium that night. The first 120 members of Diduryk's company arrived at X-Ray by helicopter not long after 1700, and platoons were inserted into the most vulnerable parts of the perimeter.

Moore also asked for continuous artillery fire and air strikes on the lower slopes of the Chu Pong massif, a request that Brown strongly endorsed and took steps to provide. Brown, however, did more than merely attend to Moore's explicit requests. He anticipated that the battle at X-Ray was likely to become even fiercer the following day. Brown believed that, having recovered from their initial surprise, the North Vietnamese would concentrate all their forces in the vicinity to destroy Moore's command. Brown thus concluded that Moore was likely to need far more reinforcements than the extra rifle company he had requested and was prepared to send Moore much of the rest of 3d Brigade.

Brown ordered the bulk of Lieutenant Colonel Tully's 2/5 Cavalry to move by helicopter to a clearing christened LZ Victor, about 3 km southeast of X-Ray. From there it would move overland to X-Ray early the next morning. Two companies of 2/5 had arrived at Victor by nightfall on 14 November, using four Hueys in relays; a third company remained at Falcon for the time being, providing security for the artillery there. That evening, A Company, 2/7 Cavalry, was shuttled by helicopter to Catecka, where it was to provide overnight security for the base; it would be lifted into X-Ray the following morning to join Diduryk's B Company. The remainder of Lieutenant Colonel McDade's 2/7 was to air-assault into another clearing, LZ Macon, about 4 km north of X-Ray, as soon as A Company had been delivered to X-Ray. Two batteries of 105mm guns would then be inserted at Macon, one of them newly supplied by the division. Largely organized by Major Mallet, the brigade operations officer, it "was an extremely complicated series of aerial moves, requiring exquisite timing on the part of air and ground commanders alike."[65]

That evening, Brown also requested that the 1st Cavalry Division send 3d Brigade another battalion. Knowles and Kinnard had reportedly anticipated that request some hours earlier. Once he knew that a major action was in progress at X-Ray (early in the afternoon), Brown had informed Knowles. Knowles had then flown from Pleiku to Catecka to get a full briefing from Brown. After his briefing, Knowles had radioed Kinnard and asked for another infantry battalion, more artillery, and more helicopters. Kinnard readily complied and, at Knowles's suggestion, flew from An Khe to Catecka, where Knowles briefed him. Apparently Kinnard was astonished to learn that a battle was in progress in the Chu Pong–Ia Drang area. It is indicative of the extraordinary extent to which Kinnard had delegated the conduct of the Pleiku campaign to Knowles that he had no idea that any part of his division was operating that far west. Kinnard was, however, glad that a large body of North Vietnamese had at last been found. He promised to help in any way he could. The largest body of reinforcements Kinnard sent—1st Battalion, 5th Cavalry—arrived at Camp Holloway on the evening of 14 November. The 3d Brigade made arrangements to fly the battalion to Catecka in Chinooks and Caribous early the following morning.[66]

American Activity, 14–15 November

The fighting around X-Ray having died down by around 1700, Hueys were able to bring in food, water, and ammunition and take out the wounded. There were no major assaults that night, although American troops reported that the North Vietnamese probed the perimeter with small groups of five to ten soldiers. The Americans thought the North Vietnamese were trying to identify the positions of their M-60 machine guns so that these could be dealt with by RPGs, mortars, or recoilless rifles. The Americans therefore tried to confine their response to fire from their M-16 rifles and M-79 grenade launchers. Meanwhile, American artillery, while carefully avoiding the isolated platoon, pounded the eastern slope of the Chu Pong to break up any major assaults that might be building. US Air Force A-1E Skyraiders bombed and strafed in support of Moore's perimeter, and a C-123 flare ship remained on station to provide illumination if required. An AC-47 fixed-wing gunship fired 12,000 rounds at high ground just west of the isolated platoon now led by Sergeant Savage. The platoon had an anxious night during which it reportedly repelled three North Vietnamese attacks. But no more members of the platoon were killed.[67]

The fate of the lost platoon continued to weigh heavily on Moore's mind, and he spent much of the night planning a major assault to rescue it the following morning. He intended to direct this operation personally and to use all three of his rifle companies. Meanwhile, Captain Dillon, who had landed at X-Ray that evening, would take charge of the defense of the landing zone.

Monday Morning, 15 November

At 0640 Moore ordered his company commanders to send patrols out 200 meters beyond the perimeter. Some of the American troops got no more than 50 meters before coming under intense fire. Moore's move triggered a North Vietnamese assault that was delivered at approximately 0650. PAVN troops had been crawling through the long grass, presumably hoping to launch their final assault from such a short distance that the Americans would have little time to react. Triggering the assault early undoubtedly worked to the Americans' advantage. Captain Edwards's C Company, holding the southern side of the perimeter, was initially the main focus of the North Vietnamese attack, but by 0715, D Company in the northeast was also under great pressure. Captain Edwards of C Company was seriously wounded and unable to stand, but when the officer to whom he had delegated authority was also hit, he was obliged to remain in command. At about 0745 Moore committed his one-platoon reserve at the junction of C and D Companies.[68]

The North Vietnamese attack persisted with undiminished ferocity, and by 0800, Moore was worried enough to request immediate reinforcement. The brigade told him he could have A Company from 2d Battalion, 7th Cavalry, as soon as the intensity of fire at X-Ray dropped to a point at which it was reasonably safe for helicopters to land. Meanwhile, Brown ordered Tully, commanding 2/5 Cavalry, to prepare to march from LZ Victor to LZ X-Ray.

The most immediate help, however, came from artillery, gunships, and fighter-bombers. These had been responding with constantly escalating force since the morning assaults began. For fear of fratricide, however, many of their munitions were expended farther from the perimeter than was ideal. The North Vietnamese were getting in very close, "grabbing the belt" of the Americans. For aircraft to deliver ordnance as close as possible to the perimeter

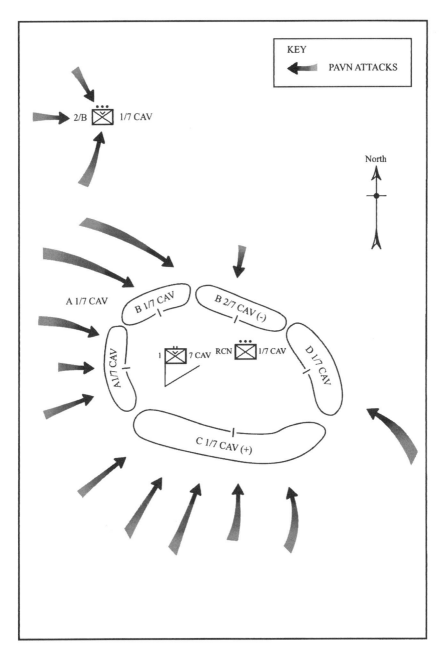

KEY

PAVN ATTACKS

2/B 1/7 CAV

North

A 1/7 CAV

B 1/7 CAV

B 2/7 CAV (-)

A 1/7 CAV

1 7 CAV   RCN 1/7 CAV

D 1/7 CAV

C 1/7 CAV (+)

Sketch of American dispositions in defense of LZ X-Ray, 14–15 November 1965

without causing American casualties, it was important to delineate the perimeter clearly. Moore therefore ordered his troops to detonate smoke grenades. At 0805 three F-100s arrived and, after dropping six napalm canisters and six other bombs, proceeded to execute strafing runs, firing 2,400 20mm cannon shells to within 100 meters of the perimeter. This seemed to help. But bringing air strikes so close was an intrinsically dangerous game. A little later that morning, napalm canisters from one F-100 fell within the perimeter, causing at least one American death.[69]

By 0900, the North Vietnamese fire had diminished, allowing Hueys to fly in the first batch of reinforcements: Captain Joel E. Sugdinis's A Company, 2/7 Cavalry. Moore sent these troops to reinforce the southern perimeter, where Edwards's C Company had suffered the heaviest losses. The immediate crisis was almost over. At about 0941 the North Vietnamese attacks on C Company and D Company of 1/7 Cavalry, on the southern and eastern parts of the perimeter, respectively, ceased. The majority of PAVN soldiers withdrew. Only harassing rifle fire persisted.

In the lull that followed, Moore decided to rearrange his defenses. Edwards's Charlie Company had taken the most severe battering, losing a total of forty-two dead and sixty-two wounded since arriving at LZ X-Ray. Moore pulled it out of the perimeter and made it the battalion reserve, putting Diduryk's B Company and one platoon of Sugdinis's A Company where Edwards's company had been. The rest of Sugdinis's company occupied what had formerly been Diduryk's position on the northern side of the perimeter.

While this reorganization was in progress, Tully's 2/5 Cavalry marched from LZ Victor to LZ X-Ray in company columns, with A Company on the left, B Company on the right, and C Company directly behind A Company. Although the distance was short, the move was cross-country, through long, dense grasses and brush. It was noon before the first of Tully's troops reached X-Ray. Their arrival without losses guaranteed the security of the landing zone.[70]

The Balance of Forces, Midday 15 November

Moore now had more than two battalions at X-Ray. The North Vietnamese had apparently fought the whole battle with just two battalions of the PAVN 66th Regiment—the 9th and 7th. As noted, the 9th did all the fighting in the daylight hours on 14 November, but in the evening it disintegrated. The 7th Battalion (minus its 3d Company, which was away fetching rice), assisted by a few surviving fragments of the 9th, did all the fighting on 15 November. By midday, however, the bulk of the 7th Battalion was shattered, with a high proportion of its personnel dead or wounded.[71]

Some American accounts indicate that two other Communist battalions (or the equivalent thereof) took part in the battle: elements of the PAVN 33d Regiment that had survived the siege of Plei Me and the subsequent American pursuit, and the H-15 Battalion.[72] Communist accounts agree that what was left of the 33d Regiment was in the general area. According to his memoirs, An did eventually try to bring this regiment into action, but late in the battle. He apparently had no radio contact with it and was unsure where to find its units. On the night of 15 November he sent a staff officer, Dong Thoai, to look for them. Thoai found 1st Battalion, 33d Regiment, and passed on An's order to attack American artillery positions (possibly those at LZ Columbus, where the batteries originally sent to LZ Macon were diverted when it was discovered that the ground at Macon was too soft). But the battalion got lost and failed to execute its mission.[73]

The H-15 Battalion was a provincial (i.e., local force) and not a main force unit, as indicated in some American accounts. Its firepower was limited, and it was not designed for prolonged high-intensity firefights. An essay in an important Vietnamese Communist collection on the Pleiku campaign outlines in some detail the contribution of local Party forces. The authors were evidently very eager to give all possible credit to local forces. Their account does discuss H-15's rather limited role. Had that battalion joined the fight at the foot of the Chu Pong, it is inconceivable that they would not have mentioned it. There is, however, no suggestion in this or any other published account from the Communist side that the H-15 Battalion became involved in the fighting at X-Ray.[74]

It is generally agreed that the PAVN 32d (aka 320th) Regiment took no part in the X-Ray fighting.[75] Lieutenant Colonel An seems never to have summoned it. It was a considerable distance away, and An was perhaps well aware of its condition. The 32d Regiment had been experiencing serious morale problems for months. Defeated around Duc Co in August, its morale had not altogether recovered, and this probably affected its performance during the attack on Luat's Armored Task Force on the road to Plei Me on 23–24 October. The 32d's heavy losses and further defeat in that action probably caused its morale to drop even more.

Another dog in the neighborhood had not yet barked. This was the 8th Battalion of the PAVN 66th Regiment, which was based only a few kilometers from the Chu Pong massif. An sent people to find it on the night of 15 November, as he did with the 33d Regiment. Apparently he wanted it to take part in the X-Ray battle. The battalion was eventually found (though perhaps not until the afternoon of 16 November), and it started to march. On 17 November it became involved in a battle with American troops, but not at X-Ray, and not until the fighting at X-Ray had long since ended.[76]

It seems quite likely that by midday on 15 November, as An's memoirs indicate, the numerical balance of ground troops on the X-Ray battlefield significantly favored the Americans.[77] American firepower, of course, massively outweighed anything available to the North Vietnamese.

The Rescue of the Lost Platoon, 1315–1615, 15 November

Moore remained in overall command of all troops at X-Ray, including Tully's battalion when it arrived around midday on 15 November. Rescuing the lost platoon had never been far from Moore's thoughts. At 1315 he mounted a three-company assault that employed Herren's B Company, 1/7 Cavalry, and A Company and C Company of Tully's 2/5 Cavalry, along with massive support from both conventional and aerial rocket artillery. Herren's company was employed in part because he knew the location of the lost platoon and would be able to guide the other companies. All accounts indicate that this American push met relatively little North Vietnamese resistance until the platoon, now commanded by Ernie Savage, was reached, so why it should have taken nearly two hours to cover about 300 meters is nowhere explained. After reaching Savage's platoon at 1510, according to Moore, the rescuers started to take more fire and were not inclined to hang around. According to Tully, "The platoon was in a real tight perimeter, they all looked tired and dirty, everyone appeared calm but it was obvious they were glad to see us!" He remembered that "carrying wounded men in the jungle with makeshift litters is no easy task." Transporting the casualties of the rescued platoon, plus a few wounded rescuers, took the greater part of two companies. Litter bearers had to be changed frequently. It was about 1615 before everyone was back at X-Ray.[78] Of the twenty-seven members of the platoon that Herrick had led into action, eight had been killed and another twelve wounded.[79]

Airpower at X-Ray: The Use of B-52s

As with the siege of Plei Me, the airpower the Americans brought to bear in defense of X-Ray was staggering in its immensity. In the course of 14 November, US Air Force A1-Es, F-100s, B-57s, and F-4s and US Marine A-4s were all employed.[80] On the morning of 15 November (sometime between 0600 and 0700) the forward air controller, Lieutenant Charlie Hastings, was so alarmed at the intensity of the North Vietnamese ground assaults that he used the code word "Broken Arrow," signifying that an American ground unit was in danger of being overrun and requesting all American combat aircraft in the theater to come to its support. By Hastings's own testimony, as reported in Moore's book, he had "aircraft stacked at 1,000-foot intervals from 7,000 feet to 35,000 feet, each waiting to receive a target and deliver their ordnance."[81]

In one particular respect, the air effort at this stage of the campaign went vastly beyond even that employed in Plei Me's defense. During the night of 14–15 November, someone requested that giant B-52 bombers be used against North Vietnamese positions on the Chu Pong massif. General William Westmoreland, who had become very interested in developments at X-Ray, certainly endorsed this request if he did not originate it. The B-52s were based on Guam and were not normally under MACV's control. Nevertheless, at 1600 on 15 November "18 B-52s, diverted from a bombing campaign farther south, dropped over 900 bombs into the enemy's area close to the fighting." According to the US Air Force official history, this was the first time in the war that these huge strategic bombers were used in direct support of ground forces. It was not possible to systematically assess the effectiveness of the B-52s on 15 November. Nevertheless, Westmoreland wanted to continue to use such strikes (known as Arc Lights) on successive days. By the time they ceased on 22 November, ninety-six sorties had been flown and nearly 5,000 bombs dropped.[82]

Relative Calm, the Evening of Monday, 15 November

There was a lull in North Vietnamese offensive efforts at X-Ray between the late morning of 15 November and the early hours of 16 November. The evening of 15 November was fairly quiet. Moore used the time to reorganize his defenses again, pulling D Company out of the perimeter so that it could join C Company as a reserve. Tully's battalion went into the perimeter to replace D Company, facing north and east. Artillery fired on the outer edges of the X-Ray perimeter all night, and some fire was also directed higher up the slopes of the Chu Pong massif, where secondary explosions were reportedly observed.[83]

The Last Fight at X-Ray, Tuesday, 16 November

On the night of 15–16 November the fog of war still hung thick over X-Ray. It caused the North Vietnamese to make some futile sacrifices. As noted, the PAVN 9th Battalion disintegrated on the evening of 14 November, and much of the 7th Battalion had been destroyed in the fighting on the morning of 15 November. At the B3 Front forward headquarters, An knew this. But he seems not to have fully appreciated the extent to which the Americans had reinforced

X-Ray, being unaware of the arrival of 2/5 Cavalry. He therefore ordered another attempt to overrun the landing zone, using 3d Company, 7th Battalion
(hitherto uncommitted, apparently because it had been away fetching rice),
and a surviving platoon of 1st Company as the main assault element, supported
by the 7th Battalion's heavy weapons (mortars and recoilless rifles). The 1st
Battalion of the 33d Regiment and the 8th Battalion of the 66th Regiment,
which An had summoned during the night, did not arrive in time to play any
part. The surviving elements of the 7th Battalion, attacking on their own, were
therefore grossly overmatched by the American defenders.[84]

Nevertheless, in darkness at approximately 0400, the North Vietnamese began probing the southern part of the perimeter held by Captain Diduryk's B
Company and one platoon of Captain Sugdinis's A Company, both of the
2/7 Cavalry. At 0422 they delivered a determined attack on Diduryk's sector from the southeast. But the area was illuminated by a flare ship, and four
artillery batteries fired in support of the defenders on the perimeter. In these
circumstances, it was practically impossible for the North Vietnamese to make
progress. They nevertheless continued to attack Diduryk's sector up to 0641,
when survivors were observed withdrawing, dragging corpses with them. It is
indicative of how overmatched the North Vietnamese were during that morning's fighting that they managed to inflict a mere seven casualties on Diduryk's
company, all of them only lightly wounded. After 0641 the fighting died away.

Moore, however, was not sure that the battle was finished. He ordered
everyone on the perimeter to fire for two minutes, starting at 0655, into any
vegetation immediately in front of or above their positions that might shelter
an enemy. When this was done, a number of North Vietnamese dropped
out of trees. The American flurry of fire also prematurely triggered a planned
PAVN assault on the northern sector of the perimeter, held by A Company
of 2/7 Cavalry. By American estimates, some thirty to fifty North Vietnamese crept to within 150 meters of this part of the American line. Possibly they
intended to creep further before delivering their attack. Apparently thinking
that they had been spotted, they rose to their feet to charge. They met such a
storm of fire from American infantry weapons and artillery that they stood no
chance. Those not cut down were compelled to retreat. This episode was over
in twenty minutes.

The X-Ray fighting as a whole was now almost finished. Between 0855 and
0955 there were no North Vietnamese attacks, but Moore was still reluctant
to take victory for granted. He ordered all units on the perimeter to patrol out
to a distance of 300 to 500 meters. According to Moore's after-action report:

The movement began at 0955 hours, however, after moving 50–75 meters B
Company, 2d Battalion, 7th Cavalry came under fire. One platoon leader was

seriously wounded. All movement was stopped. B Company, 2d Battalion, 7th Cavalry pulled back to the perimeter foxholes and close-in artillery and TAC air was called in. We then moved back out, eliminated all resistance and policed the area. 27 more PAVN were killed in this sweep.

Moore was now prepared to accept that the battle had ended.[85]

Immediate Results and Aftermath

The Americans lost 79 dead and another 121 wounded. Moore's officers officially claimed that they counted the bodies of 634 North Vietnamese and estimated that another 1,215 had been killed.[86] Given that only two under-strength PAVN battalions were involved, the American "body count" would indicate that about three-quarters of the North Vietnamese participating in the battle were dead by its conclusion. This seems extremely improbable. The other American estimate of PAVN fatalities should be dismissed as pure wishful thinking. In his published account, Moore admits the imprecision of both figures. Until the very end of the action, his officers had much more pressing priorities than counting cadavers. By then, the North Vietnamese had removed most of them.[87] It is clear that once the fighting started in earnest, its spirit became very savage on both sides. The Americans took only six prisoners.[88] The North Vietnamese apparently took none at all.

After the fighting ended, X-Ray was, in the short term, reinforced. In the late morning, two companies of Lieutenant Colonel McDade's 2/7 Cavalry, together with A Company of 1/5 Cavalry, began a 5-km march from LZ Columbus, arriving at X-Ray about noon. (The bulk of McDade's battalion had been lifted by helicopter to LZ Macon by 1305 on 15 November and was supposed to march from there to X-Ray. But because the Ia Drang was found to be unfordable where the 2/7 was originally intended to cross it, the battalion was lifted by helicopter to LZ Columbus, the move being completed by 1830 on 15 November.) The troops that left LZ Columbus on the morning of 16 November were replaced by two companies of 1/5 Cavalry flown by helicopter from Catecka. Soon after the fighting at X-Ray ended, someone decided that the troops who had been there the longest should immediately be withdrawn by helicopter for rest and recuperation. Who made the decision is unclear. There is no record of anyone's having disputed it. The process of removing by helicopter 1/7 Cavalry and the other most battle-weary subunits (Captain Diduryk's B Company, 2/7 Cavalry, and one platoon of Captain Sugdinis's A Company, 2/7 Cavalry) began at 1155. It was completed by 1500. These troops initially went to LZ Falcon before flying on to Camp Holloway.[89]

In an episode that would have seemed bizarre in any previous war, before leaving the battlefield, Moore was obliged to participate in a press conference. Captain J. D. Coleman, a 1st Cavalry Division publicity officer, had brought in (apparently on Colonel Knowles's instructions, or at least with his blessing) a Chinook-load of journalists, photographers, and cameramen. As he stood in front of the newsreel cameras, Moore was obviously tired to the point of exhaustion and so emotional that he was sometimes in tears. He attributed his battalion's survival in part to its possession of the fairly new, lightweight, fully automatic M-16 rifle. But the main things he wanted to convey were his enormous pride in and gratitude toward those who had served under his command. Jo Galloway, a young journalist and photographer who had been at X-Ray through much of the battle, was equally impressed with the dedication and courage of the American troops and equally eager to proclaim it to his colleagues in the press.[90]

Dick Knowles, who was at X-Ray for the press conference, told the journalists that the intention was to evacuate X-Ray completely the following day. Given that X-Ray is one of the most studied actions in American military history since 1945, it seems odd that who made this decision, when, and on what basis are all questions to which we have no definite answers. Even more curiously, the decision to abandon X-Ray the day after the North Vietnamese attacks upon it ceased, though baffling to some journalists at the time, has attracted little comment from historians.[91]

On 14 November Moore began the X-Ray action by attacking up the slope of the Chu Pong massif with a single company. With the benefit of hindsight, this move seems premature and reckless, and the force employed was far too small. By midday on Tuesday, 16 November, however, having smashed a sizable North Vietnamese force, the Americans could have had a brigade's worth of troops available to operate from X-Ray (had they not already commenced a withdrawal). Some of these troops were, of course, very weary and could have been left to guard the landing zone. But was it not now the logical move for the Americans to use their fresher troops to finish what they had started and consummate victory by storming the Chu Pong massif? Admittedly, they had no certainty at this stage that the forward headquarters of the North Vietnamese Central Highlands Front was on the massif. But they did know that the Chu Pong had been an important part of a major Communist base area for a long time. Was the massif not worth seizing and examining?

The American command at Westmoreland's level apparently appreciated the importance of this feature. Its response, however, was merely to work it over with B-52 strikes. Capturing the massif with American troops surely would have had a much more positive effect on American morale and done far greater damage to that of the North Vietnamese. Physically occupying a hurriedly evacuated headquarters might have offered significant intelligence benefits, with the possibility of captured documents or even personnel. That the Americans failed to storm the Chu Pong at this stage may be indicative of how much they were shaken—even shocked—by the fury of the PAVN response to their initial probe. It gives at least a modicum of credence to the Vietnamese Communists' claim that they had won a kind of victory.[92]

American military behavior at X-Ray was in many respects quite similar to that of their much less well armed, less well supported South Vietnamese allies in comparable circumstances in the recent past. Once their initial probe resulted in a violent Communist backlash, the Americans curled up into defensive perimeters and called in masses of artillery fire and air strikes. This was very much how the ARVN had often behaved in similar situations, although it had never been able to bring in supporting fires on the same scale as the Americans at X-Ray. The artillery and air support the Americans employed at X-Ray, moreover, supplemented the already fairly formidable firepower of the latest generation of American infantry weapons—weapons significantly better than those they supplied to the South Vietnamese. As noted, Moore credited the survival of his battalion at X-Ray to its possession of the M-16, a rifle that most of the ARVN would not get for several years.[93] As was sometimes the case with the South Vietnamese in similar circumstances, during a pause between Communist attacks, the Americans at X-Ray had engaged in just enough offensive action to link their main position with that of an isolated subunit. But when the North Vietnamese assaults finally ceased, the Americans merely heaved a collective sigh of relief and withdrew from the battlefield—exactly the sort of seemingly passive response for which they had often criticized the ARVN.

American ground troops conducted no decisive counterattack at X-Ray— indeed, no real riposte at all. Such a thing occurs only in the Hollywood version of Moore's book, in which Moore is depicted leading a bayonet charge up the Chu Pong massif and forcing the North Vietnamese commander to abandon his headquarters.[94] Hollywood is commonly said to be a dream factory, and some believe that dreams express the fulfillment of wishes. Some Americans may have wished that the X-Ray battle had ended in such a heroic manner. It is, however, the historian's duty to point out that nothing of the sort actually happened. On 17 November the US Army abandoned X-Ray, at least partly wasting the fruits of a hard-fought defensive victory.

14

Albany and After,
November–December 1965

The Background to LZ Albany:
American Decision Making, 16 November

Aspects of what happened in the Ia Drang on 16–17 November 1965 are still controversial, and some matters remain inadequately explained. At this stage in the Pleiku campaign, it is the decision making on the American side that is most difficult to interpret; that in the North Vietnamese camp seems like an open book by comparison. For one thing, it is not easy to determine who made the key American decisions. Who was really running the American campaign?

This question does not arise anew with regard to mid-November; it goes back to the deployment of 1st Brigade, 1st Cavalry Division, to Pleiku in late October. Harry Kinnard had lobbied hard to get his division involved in the Pleiku campaign. By 27 October at the latest, and until at least 17 November, this campaign was the most important thing the division was doing or had ever done. For reasons that have never been made clear, however, Kinnard showed very little inclination to direct it personally. Cavalry operations in Pleiku were largely run by a Tactical Operations Center (a forward division headquarters) under Kinnard's deputy, Dick Knowles. Kinnard left the conduct of operations in Pleiku to Knowles to such an extent that when a crisis arose at X-Ray on 14 November and Knowles had to ask Kinnard for greater resources, Kinnard was reportedly unaware that he had any troops in the Ia Drang.[1] Though only one of the 1st Cavalry Division's brigades was committed to the campaign at any given time, the independence of brigade commanders was quite limited. Knowles presumably allowed some decisions to be made at the brigade level, but it is not easy to determine which.

Knowles himself, was not, however, in complete control of the campaign. Harry Kinnard had the option of intervening whenever he chose, and he may have done so on occasion. More significantly, Knowles was subject to interventions, which amounted to orders, from Stanley "Swede" Larsen, the Field Force commander, who had precipitated the sudden, not very carefully planned plunge into the Ia Drang valley on 14 November.[2] William West-moreland and his MACV headquarters were also background presences, some-times trying to steer the general course of the campaign and occasionally inter-vening at the tactical level or at least trying to do so.[3]

According to one source, Knowles wanted to storm the Chu Pong massif when the attacks on LZ X-Ray ceased. Arguably, this was the logical move. The same source indicates, however, that it was ruled out because B-52 strikes against the Chu Pong massif had employed some delayed-action bombs, which would have presented a threat to American troops.[4] But who directed the US Air Force to use delayed-action ordnance? Who asked for B-52 strikes in the first place? To what extent, if at all, were Kinnard, Knowles, and Tim Brown, the 3d Brigade commander, consulted? There are no answers to these ques-tions in the official histories or in the relevant after-action reports. It seems likely, however, that these decisions were made over Knowles's and Brown's heads and perhaps over Kinnard's too.

No American headquarters intended, on 16 November 1965, to remove troops of the 3d Brigade, 1st Cavalry Division, from the Ia Drang altogether. Apparently perceiving the engagement at X-Ray to be a substantial and signif-icant victory, both the American and South Vietnamese high commands were eager to exploit it. The ARVN, indeed, had been eager to play a greater part in the Pleiku campaign for some time. According to Kinnard:

> Planning officers and commanders of several headquarters including MACV, Field Force I and the II ARVN Corps had held numerous discussions of var-ious operations . . . involving the commitment of ARVN units to the battle. These discussions had gone on for several days and included at various times Brigadier William E. Depuy, MACV's J3; General Larsen; Lieutenant General John A. Heintges, MACV's deputy commander, and General Westmoreland. On the ARVN side were General Vinh Loc, the II Corps commander, and various members of the ARVN high command.[5]

Kinnard's testimony on this matter is confirmed by other sources, including Westmoreland's notes for the same period. Apparently, the intention was that two ARVN Airborne battalions from the general reserve would operate south from Duc Co while the Americans pushed west and somewhat north along the Ia Drang valley. Reading between the lines, one might suppose that the principal target was the PAVN 32d/320th Regiment, which had been badly hurt during the monsoon offensive, especially around Duc Co and again in the attack on Luat's Armored Task Force as it went to relieve Plei Me. After that, however, the 32d/320th had managed to retreat, largely unmolested by the 1st Cavalry Division, to a base just north of the Ia Drang near the Cambodian border. The intention may have been for a joint operation by an ARVN Airborne battalion and the 3d Brigade of the 1st Cavalry Division to trap and destroy at least part of this PAVN regiment before it could withdraw across the Cambodian border. But it seems that these plans were still incomplete on 17 November.[6]

The bulk of Lieutenant Colonel Robert McDade's 2/7 Cavalry (but not B Company or one platoon of A Company, which had already left by helicopter), together with one company of 1/5 Cavalry and Lieutenant Colonel Robert Tully's 2/5 Cavalry, remained at X-Ray through the night of 16–17 November. They were due to leave the following morning and walk through the wilderness, each to a separate clearing.[7] The usual explanation of the need to leave X-Ray is that the Chu Pong massif was about to be subjected to further B-52 strikes. Theoretically, the safe distance was 3 km. But Arc Lights had apparently hit parts of the Chu Pong on 15 November, before the fighting at X-Ray had ended, without inconveniencing Moore's force. Indeed, a major reason for mounting these strikes was to help X-Ray's defenders.[8] Presumably, it had been decided to bring the Arc Light strikes significantly closer to X-Ray on 17 November than on previous days. But this issue has never been examined in detail in any published work.

Another question not answered in official accounts is why units of an airmobile division left X-Ray on foot. Admittedly, the distances were relatively short: less than 5 km to the northeast in the case of the clearing designated LZ Columbus, where 2/5 Cavalry was bound, and about the same distance almost due north in the case of the clearing designated LZ Albany, which was 2/7 Cavalry's destination.[9] But the essence of the 1st Cavalry Division was its fleet of helicopters. Earlier in the campaign, moves like this would have been made by air. Why not on 17 November? The likely answer is that after a few weeks of intensive heliborne operations, 1st Cavalry Division had, for the time being, largely ceased to be airmobile.

As early as 14 November, it had been possible to provide Moore with only sixteen serviceable slicks. Since then, there had been intense helicopter activity. During the X-Ray fight, very few helicopters had been shot down or even heavily damaged by North Vietnamese fire.[10] But it seems reasonable to suggest that, by 17 November, the mechanical wear and tear on airframes and engines had, at least temporarily, exceeded the capacity to make repairs, outstripped the supply of spare parts, or perhaps both.

We lack detail on these issues probably because the 1st Cavalry Division (which originated most of the official documents on this campaign to which historians have access) had no interest in providing the sort of data that would illustrate its weaknesses. It seems likely, however, that commanders and staffs at division and brigade levels knew by 16 November that a crisis had been reached with regard to the number of helicopters, particularly slicks, that were fit to fly. Some of these machines were no doubt still in good working order and others flyable in an emergency. But it seems a reasonable hypothesis that someone decided that, for the time being, helicopter flights should be kept to a minimum. Moves of less than a certain distance that did not look too danger-ous were to be made on foot.

Yet neither leaving X-Ray nor leaving it on foot was necessarily such a bad thing for the American units concerned. Certainly, the battalions that walked off X-Ray on the morning of Wednesday, 17 November, were tired; the 2/5 Cavalry, which had seen combat at X-Ray, was particularly so. But these bat-talions were not burdened with wounded and were not sick, malnourished, particularly demoralized, or otherwise in bad shape. Together, they would have been a formidable force for the PAVN to take on. The main problem was that the force was being divided, with the two battalions going to separate locations. Unless a substantial numerical superiority can be guaranteed, divid-ing one's forces in the presence of the enemy (especially an enemy as capable as the North Vietnamese had recently proved to be) is generally considered a dangerous thing to do. Sometimes it may be necessary. Sometimes it may be done profitably.[11] It should never be done lightly.

If, however, anyone believed that a serious risk was being run by separating these battalions and marching them to different destinations, no one seems to have said so. No one warned the commanders that they were involved in a dangerous maneuver. No one told them to be constantly on the alert.[12] Perhaps it was assumed that, as professional army officers, they would know these things without being told. But it also seems likely that whoever made the decision to separate the battalions assumed that the X-Ray fighting had drawn in and shattered all the battleworthy Communist units in the immediate area. There seems to have been an underlying assumption that no PAVN force ca-pable of mounting a significant attack remained in the vicinity.[13]

No one knows for certain who decided to divide the force leaving X-Ray. Quite likely, the decision was made at 3d Brigade by Colonel Brown and his staff. But it is conceivable that the matter was decided at Knowles's forward divisional headquarters or at a still higher level. Certainly, Brown was aware of this decision. He was at LZ X-Ray on the morning of Wednesday, 17 No-vember, to watch his troops begin their march. Brown regarded Albany as a mere stopover for 2/7 Cavalry. This unit was later intended to move to LZ Crooks, further west in the Ia Drang valley, from which base it would partic-ipate in joint operations with the South Vietnamese.[14] But like the decision to go to the foot of the Chu Pong in the first place, the decision on when to leave

X-Ray was almost certainly made above Brown's level, and Brown may also have been told where his battalions needed to go next.

Historical research into these issues has been impeded by the fact that the operations journals of 2/7 Cavalry and 3d Brigade have been missing at least since 1967.[15] Another complicating factor is that, as in many modern campaigns, a lot of decisions seem to have been made and orders given in face-to-face exchanges (a practice facilitated by commanders' ability to move by helicopter) or over the radio. The reasoning behind such decisions and orders was often committed to paper days, weeks, or months later, if at all.

The US Cavalry's March to Albany, 0900–1315, 17 November

It should be recognized that, although decisions made above battalion level put the battalions marching off X-Ray on 17 November at considerable risk, they condemned neither unit to disaster. A lot would depend on the decisions of the battalion commanders, and, as always in war, much would depend on luck.

The two battalions initially moved off X-Ray in the same direction, marching roughly northeast. X-Ray was in something of a basin, and they first marched to its eastern rim before going somewhat downhill to the landing zones that were their final destinations. The march, according to the official history and most other sources, commenced at 0900 with Lieutenant Colonel Tully's 2/5 Cavalry leading and Lieutenant Colonel McDade's 2/7 Cavalry following.[16] The 2/7 Cavalry after-action report, however, indicates that the march began an hour later,[17] a discrepancy that has gone largely unremarked.

Tully had his battalion move with two rifle companies up and the third following, which was essentially the same formation he had used on the way into X-Ray. During the march in, he had ordered artillery concentrations on areas where PAVN troops might be waiting in ambush. On the march out, he "used artillery to plunk a round out four hundred yards or so every half hour so we could have a concentration plotted. That way if we ran into problems we could immediately call for fire."[18] Judging by Tully's words, as quoted here, this was not a rolling barrage (a wall of exploding shells moving in front of the advancing troops), as some accounts suggest.[19] It was merely a matter of registering the supporting batteries from time to time so that they could deliver defensive fires quickly and accurately if this proved necessary. McDade's 2/7 Cavalry, following in the 2/5's wake, seems from most accounts to have been moving in a column, a less tactically robust configuration than Tully's. For the first 2 or 3 km, however, it had no particular problems.

At about 1100, according to the official history, about 3 km from X-Ray the two American battalions reached the point at which they would part. If this is correct, it had taken them roughly two hours to cover this distance.[20] (Nothing is straightforward about Albany, however, and 2/7 Cavalry's after-action report indicates not only that the march started at 1000, an hour later than stated in the official history, but also that their divergence occurred after only 2 km.)[21] The marching troops had been ascending slightly, but the gradient was not steep. Though the ground was forested and covered in tall grasses, it was not the sort of dense jungle that had to be hacked through with machetes. The ground was dry, and although it was hot and humid, the skies were clear and the sun was shining. The slow rate of movement suggests, therefore, not merely the tiredness of the troops but also the extreme care with which Tully's lead battalion advanced. Though Tully, like McDade, had received no intelligence brief before this march, he did not assume that his battalion's route was safe. Having fought at X-Ray, Tully had acquired a healthy respect for the North Vietnamese. He was taking no chances.[22]

From the point reached at 1100, Tully's battalion continued to move roughly northeast (practically straight ahead) to get to LZ Columbus. McDade's battalion had to turn about ninety degrees to the left to march the remaining distance to Albany, about 2.5 km. Within forty minutes, Tully's men had reached Columbus, where they were welcomed by Lieutenant Colonel Frederick Ackerson's 1/5 Cavalry and were soon enjoying an early lunch of hamburgers, mashed potatoes, and string beans.[23] For McDade's force, the immediate future was rather different.

Not all of 2/7 Cavalry had set off on the march to Albany. Having arrived at X-Ray earlier than the rest of the battalion, and having fought there, Bravo Company had been flown out by helicopter and was already back at Camp Holloway. The 3d Platoon of 2/7's Alpha Company had also fought at X-Ray, and it too was at Holloway on the morning of 17 November. To compensate 2/7 Cavalry for the loss of its Bravo Company, Colonel Brown had assigned it Alpha Company of 1/5 Cavalry. Because Alpha Company 2/7 was still a platoon short, however, McDade gave it the battalion's reconnaissance platoon to bring it to full strength.

Captain Joel Sugdinis's Alpha Company of 2/7 Cavalry led the advance of McDade's force. Most accounts indicate that it adopted a wedge formation and maintained fairly good order. Appropriately enough, Sugdinis had Second Lieutenant David P. Payne's reconnaissance platoon out in front, leading the advance. He had his other two rifle platoons advancing abreast, behind the reconnaissance platoon, with his command group between them. The mortar platoon formed the back of the wedge. Alpha Company 2/7 moved slowly and carefully, with its troops watching the trees for snipers. At the back of the column was Alpha Company 1/5 Cavalry, commanded by Captain George Forrest. The weight of evidence indicates that it too maintained good order, also moving in a wedge formation. But possibly because of the care with which it moved, it tended to lag slightly behind the rest of McDade's column. Taking a precaution that McDade seemingly neglected, Forrest made arrangements with the artillery to deliver defensive fires if required.

Companies C and D of 2/7 Cavalry, in the middle of the battalion column, were most vulnerable. C Company was, at least initially, ahead of D Company, according to most accounts. Charlie Company was commanded by Captain John A. Fesmire and Delta Company by Captain Henry B. Thorpe. Fesmire's company reportedly started moving in a tight wedge-shaped tactical formation, but this broke down as the march progressed. Both companies ended up with their platoons moving as platoon columns, one behind the other, leaving each company with long, unprotected flanks. Thorpe apparently failed to realize that he and his company were still in a combat zone and later testified that he considered the march to Albany merely a "walk in the sun."[24]

There is some controversy as to the position of McDade and his headquarters company during most of the march. According to some reports, it was near the back of the battalion column between D Company 2/7 and A Company 1/5; others place it immediately behind Sugdinis's A Company 2/7 or between C and D Companies 2/7. The precise order of march is not especially important. What is more significant is that McDade did not instill in his subordinates the need for vigilance, alertness, and discipline. Allowing each company commander to select his own formation, McDade apparently failed to notice that some of these were grossly inappropriate.

McDade later testified that he intended to "plow through" to Albany rather than "feel his way" there.[25] Had he "plowed through" quickly, even without exercising due caution, things might have worked out better. In reality, he exhibited a peculiar mixture of carelessness and hesitation. His carelessness allowed much of the column to become rather ragged and its general state of alert much too low. His hesitancy caused halts, one of them fairly lengthy. This allowed boredom and fatigue to set in and prevented the force as a whole from arriving at Albany and establishing a proper defensive perimeter there before disaster struck.

McDade called his lengthiest halt when the reconnaissance platoon at the front of the battalion column captured two prisoners—just 100 to 200 meters short of the clearing called Albany. The official history times this event at just before 1200. If so, McDade's force had speeded up significantly since diverging from 2/5 Cavalry at 1100 and had covered a lot of ground. Another account (Coleman's) puts the halt at 1240, which might be a better fit in terms of distance covered. The reconnaissance platoon leader, Second Lieutenant David Payne, took the prisoners to Captain Sugdinis of Alpha Company 2/7, who informed McDade by radio. McDade came forward with an interpreter and other members of his headquarters group to interview the prisoners. The two North Vietnamese claimed that, sick with malaria and demoralized by the B-52 strikes, they had deserted. They were probably telling the truth about being ill but, as some of their captors strongly suspected, lying about being deserters. One Vietnamese Communist history indicates that they were part of a five-man "helicopter ambush team" from 1st Company, 1st Battalion, 33d Regiment, sent to keep an eye on clearings the Americans might use as landing zones. The same source indicates that other members of this team got away and reported the American presence in the area.

The prisoners provided the Americans with no useful tactical intelligence. McDade's interrogation, however, took twenty or thirty minutes by Coleman's reckoning, longer according to the official history. During this time, the column was motionless. Most of the men sat or lay down. After losing a lot of sleep over the last couple of nights, and having been walking for hours in warm, humid weather, many began to doze. Some fell fast asleep.[26]

A few minutes after the column started moving again, Lieutenant Payne's reconnaissance platoon, leading the advance, reached Albany. Payne's men entered the clearing from east-southeast at 1307. Albany was roughly a square, but with very irregular sides measuring between 300 and 400 meters long. In the middle of the clearing was a substantial grove of trees and several large termite mounds. The grove effectively divided Albany in two. Just north of it was an area the size of a football field sloping slightly upward, the most suitable place for helicopters to land. The remainder of Sugdinis's Alpha Company 2/7 arrived at Albany just behind the reconnaissance platoon. The 1st Platoon went to the northern side of the clearing, and the 2d Platoon went to secure the southern side. The mortar platoon occupied the grove in the middle.

Sometime between 1309 and 1312, with Alpha Company 2/7 already at Albany and the rest of his force just about to arrive there, McDade decided to call a second halt. He wanted to instruct the other company commanders about how to dispose their troops on the objective, so he summoned them to the front of the column, which stood at the edge of the clearing. For three reasons, this proved to be a very bad decision. First, it fatally delayed the arrival of the rest of his force in the clearing at Albany. Had the whole force been together on the landing zone when the North Vietnamese attacked, a coherent battalion defensive perimeter would have been much easier to organize. Second, it left most of his force strung out in a column with its flanks exposed. Third, it detached the company commanders and their radio operators from their companies, seriously degrading command and control.

The company commander who had the greatest distance to travel was Captain Forrest, commanding A Company 1/5, at the back of the column. As he started to move forward to join McDade, Forrest noticed that most of the soldiers in his company were not behaving as if they were on an operation in contested territory. Rather, they were sitting on their packs as if they were "taking a break" while out on a "Sunday walk." He ordered his second in command to see to their dispersal and to keep them alert in his absence. It was about 1315 by the time Forrest reached the front of the column. But McDade's briefing on company deployments at Albany did not proceed as planned.[27]

The PAVN's Attack on Albany, 17 November

At approximately 1315 (Saigon–US Army Vietnam time) on 17 November, there was a ferocious North Vietnamese attack on McDade's force. It hit both Alpha Company 2/7, which was already at Albany, and, shortly thereafter, the stationary column waiting to enter the clearing. A nightmarish close-quarters battle ensued in which bayonets, rifle butts, and knives were employed. On some parts of the battlefield, fighting lasted well into the night.[28] The main North Vietnamese force involved was the 8th Battalion of the 66th Regiment, commanded by Le Xuan Phoi.

We know a considerable amount about the circumstances surrounding Phoi's attack. The numerous historical accounts published in Hanoi differ in the details but agree on the broad essentials. As noted in the earlier account of X-Ray, Lieutenant Colonel An was in command on the Chu Pong massif during that battle. He had grossly inadequate communications with most of the units supposedly under his command, and he evidently had none at all with 8th Battalion, 66th Regiment. This battalion was at Ba Bi, several kilometers north and west of the rest of the regiment and on the wrong (northwestern) side of the Ia Drang. Apparently preoccupied in the early stages of the battle with trying to get proper control of the units on the massif, it was not until the evening of 15 November, by his own account, that An sent a reconnaissance team ("two teams of runners," according to another account) to summon Phoi's battalion.[29]

We do not know exactly when An's dispatch reached Phoi. One Vietnamese Communist history indicates that it was the afternoon of 16 November,[30] which fits with the timing of other events. A PAVN senior officer's memoir gives the exact wording of the message and the name of the private soldier who delivered it (apparently a hero who died of wounds immediately afterward),[31] but it is possible that these are embellishments designed to add drama to the story. Separate accounts agree, however, that An intended Phoi's battalion to join the rest of the 66th Regiment (which Phoi knew was on the Chu Pong massif) while being prepared for battle with American units encountered en route. Evidently, An's main intent was that the 8th Battalion come and take part in attacks on the Americans at LZ X-Ray. If any American unit got in the way of his march, however, Phoi had the authority to attack it.[32]

The PAVN had only a limited number of radios available, and it was unwilling to site powerful sets in headquarters, for fear that the enemy would be able to get a fix on their positions and bring down air strikes or artillery fire.[33] Therefore, delegation of authority and independence of action on the part of middle-ranking officers like Phoi were crucial to PAVN operations. Phoi had the requisite experience to accept that kind of responsibility. Born in 1930 in Ninh Binh Province in North Vietnam, he had joined the Viet Minh army in March 1947 and served in several campaigns of the First Indochina War—notably, the northern Laos campaign of April 1953 and Dien Bien Phu. At Dien Bien Phu he initially led a heavy machine gun platoon but took command of an infantry unit when its commander was killed, and his superiors judged that he had performed well.[34]

In mid-November 1965 Phoi's 8th Battalion had three rifle companies—the 6th, 7th, and 8th—and a weapons company that would have been equipped with 82mm mortars and 75mm recoilless rifles. A 12.7mm heavy machine gun company (with six guns and a full combat load of ammunition) was attached to the battalion. Aware of the possibility of colliding with American units, Phoi had his battalion march in a combat formation designed for meeting engagements. Its march was, however, considerably disrupted by air and artillery strikes and became ragged at times, with the companies getting separated. After crossing the Ia Drang at the bridge at Ba Bi early on the morning of 17 November, the 8th Battalion paused to reorganize and to cook breakfast. It resumed its march at 0500 Hanoi time (0600 Saigon–US Army Vietnam time).[35] The details of how the battle with the Americans began that afternoon are presented somewhat differently in the various Vietnamese Communist accounts. The simplest and most straightforward (though not necessarily the most accurate) is from An's memoirs. At noon Hanoi-PAVN time (1300 Saigon–US Army time), according to An:

[The 8th Battalion was] resting and eating lunch beside the Ia Drang when reconnaissance reported to the battalion commander that "American troops are approaching." Battalion Commander Le Xuan Phoi directed his battalion to deploy quickly into positions to the front and on both sides of the enemy in order to surround and to squeeze the enemy force between the battalion's two pincer arms. After using our mortars to fire a quick preparatory barrage, our troops launched a valiant simultaneous assault that cut the enemy formation in two and engaged the enemy troops in hand-to-hand combat. Both sides were so interspersed with one another that they could only use assault rifles, bayonets and grenades.[36]

Other accounts suggest that troops from 1st Company, 1st Battalion, 33d Regiment, whom the 8th Battalion had encountered by chance during its march, first alerted Phoi's battalion to the proximity of McDade's force and that two companies of 1st Battalion, 33d Regiment, took part in the ensuing action.[37]

An important point on which all the Communist accounts agree is that Phoi and his 8th Battalion became aware of a marching American force during a march of their own. The 8th Battalion was on its way to join the rest of the 66th Regiment on the Chu Pong massif or perhaps to participate in the battle on the clearing the Americans called X-Ray. No one had ordered Phoi and his battalion to mount an attack in the vicinity of the clearing the Americans called Albany. How could they have done so? Albany had been empty when An sent his order to the 8th Battalion, and no one in the PAVN knew the Americans intended to occupy it. The North Vietnamese attack at Albany was, therefore, not a premeditated, carefully planned assault. Although the histories published in Hanoi are not totally consistent on the issue, the more analytical of them characterize the operation as a meeting engagement (*tran danh tao ngo*) rather than an ambush battle (*tran phuc kich*).[38]

An ambush, by definition, involves one party lying in wait for another in order to spring a trap. On the night of 3 November 1965, for example, the US 1/9 Cavalry had laid platoon-sized nighttime ambushes farther west in the Drang valley. As it happened, this American unit had sprung one such lethal trap on part of the 8th Battalion of the PAVN 66th Regiment, not quite the people it had intended or expected to ambush. A meeting engagement (*tran danh tao ngo*) or encounter battle is what happens when units on opposite sides clash accidentally. On 17 November 1965 the 8th Battalion had not been lying in wait for any length of time for McDade's or any other American force. Though running into an American unit was not totally unexpected, Phoi's force encountered McDade's unintentionally. If there was an element of an ambush about what happened next—and the term ambush (*mai phuc*) is used in one of the Vietnamese Communist histories[39]—it was a very hurriedly arranged ambush.

There is no doubt, however, that the North Vietnamese knew of the proximity of the American force before the Americans were aware of the North Vietnamese. One Vietnamese Communist account indicates that Phoi had as much as three-quarters of an hour between first becoming aware of the presence of McDade's force and the start of the fighting,[40] although other accounts suggest much less time.[41] Whatever Phoi's warning time, it was enough to allow him to deploy his subunits for battle and to seize the initiative—crucial advantages at the beginning of the action.

At least one American account indicates that Phoi believed he was attacking just an isolated American company.[42] This interpretation is not supported (or

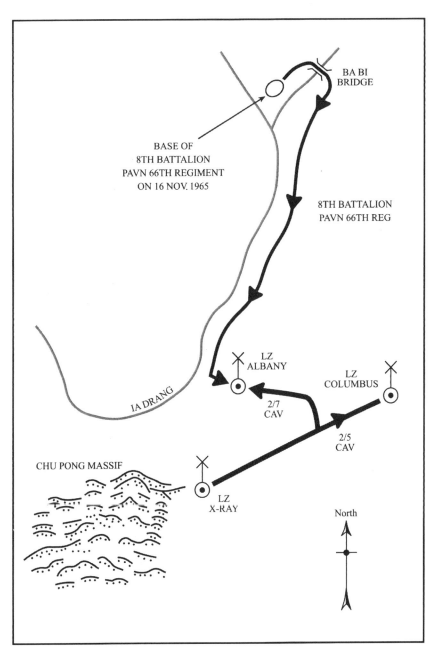

Meeting engagement at LZ Albany, 17 November 1965

even addressed) in Vietnamese Communist histories, and there appears to be
no way to determine the truth of the matter.

One account indicates that Phoi drew up his 6th Company (minus 3d Platoon) directly in the path of the American column, with the heavy weapons
of 10th Company in support. The 7th Company (with the addition of 3d
Platoon from 6th Company) was in reserve immediately to 6th Company's
rear. The 6th Company waited until the leading American platoons got within
30 to 40 meters before opening fire from its "ambush positions" (*tran dia mai
phuc*). The effect was devastating—many Americans in the lead platoons immediately dropping, either dead or wounded.[43] The battalion's 82mm mortars
also opened fire. The 6th Company then charged the most forward American
troops, who were now in a state of panic, and used "AK-47 fire and bayonets
to kill the enemy."[44]

The 8th Company, which had been ahead of the other companies on the
march, had to be called back to participate in the attack. Even though it had
only two rifle platoons (another platoon got lost before it reached the combat
area), it attacked into the flank of the American column and cut it in two. Phoi
then committed his reserve, sending "7th Company into the fight alongside 8th
Company." Acting on his own initiative, Comrade Luan, deputy commander
of 1st Battalion, 33d Regiment, successively committed his 1st and 2d Companies to the battle, with 2d Company joining in at 1300. The Hanoi histories
become rather difficult to follow at this point, but it is likely that some attacks
by 1st Battalion, 33d Regiment, came from the opposite side of the American
column. In one account, the Americans are described as being "surrounded
on all four sides."[45] It seems doubtful that Captain Forrest's Alpha Company,
1/5 Cavalry, at the rear, was ever fully surrounded, but the American column
probably was hit from both flanks as well as from the front.

Standard American accounts and graphic depictions, including those in the
US Army's official history, indicate that the initial North Vietnamese flank
attack on the American column (by 8th Company, 8th Battalion, 66th Regiment) came from the American right.[46] Vietnamese military maps of the Pleiku
campaign, however, show the attacks by 8th Battalion coming from the left
of the American column and the later attacks by 1st Battalion, 33d Regiment,
coming from the right—the opposite of standard American depictions. This is
another issue that cannot be resolved here, but there is at least a possibility that
the American versions are misleading. Before its encounter with McDade's
force, 8th Battalion was marching southwest along the southeastern bank of
the Ia Drang toward the Chu Pong massif. If the 8th Company was leading the
8th Battalion's march and had to be called back to participate in the attack, as
indicated by standard Vietnamese Communist accounts, it seems most likely

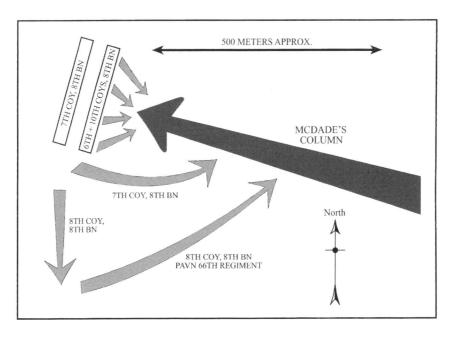

Initial attacks by 8th Battalion, 66th Regiment, on the American column at LZ Albany, 17 November 1965

that it would have struck the American column from the south and west, thus punching into its left flank.[47]

Phoi did not survive to tell us what he was thinking while launching this attack. Severely wounded within an hour of its commencement, he was dead by evening. The battalion's political officer, Nguyen Van Tuong, also suffered an early and serious wound, which meant he could not take over. Comrade Luan, deputy commander of the 33d Regiment, assumed command of all the PAVN troops when Phoi was wounded, but Luan also died that day. So, apparently, did a high proportion of PAVN officers involved. Indicative of the savage nature of the struggle, one account notes, "All cadres [officers] in 6th Company were killed or wounded, leaving only Deputy Political Officer Dinh Van De. Even though he himself was wounded, De determinedly remained in command, leading his men in combat and personally stabbing three American soldiers to death with his knife."[48]

Probably accepting that he would have little control once the battle began, Phoi committed the 7th Company, his only reserve, very early.[49] In this type of operation, delegation was crucial. Much would depend on inspiring leadership and ruthless aggression by rifle company commanders and platoon leaders. But once they had closed with the enemy, they too would largely lose control.

Phoi seems thus positively to have embraced chaos, accepting an uncontrollable melee in which friend and foe would be hopelessly mixed up.

If Phoi thought he was attacking a single American company, he might have hoped the action would be over quickly. If, however, he realized he was attacking a battalion-sized force, he must have accepted that it would be difficult to break off before nightfall and that both sides were bound to bleed profusely. A melee would nevertheless favor the PAVN more than most kinds of battle. It would significantly inhibit the use of American artillery and airpower, and it would play to the strengths of North Vietnamese troops. Their training and indoctrination made them particularly well suited for close-quarters combat in which individual initiative, skill at arms, and sheer ferocity were essentials.[50] In such a fight they might have at least a chance of inflicting as many casualties as they sustained.

American Reaction to the North Vietnamese Attack, 17 November

Chaos reigned over most of the Americans at and near LZ Albany as soon as the PAVN attack began. The tall grass made it impossible to see very far. North Vietnamese infantrymen seemed to be everywhere. Partly because they could not discern the direction of the attack, American troops became confused and disorganized. The most chaotic American subunits were C Company and D Company of the 2/7 Cavalry. As the US Army's official history describes it: "Men milled around and bunched up, making themselves inviting targets. Within moments, platoons and companies ceased to exist as fighting units. . . . Every man was on his own." At one stage, disoriented soldiers of C Company 2/7 were firing into A Company 2/7. Both C Company and D Company were without their commanders, though given how fragmented they became, this probably made little difference. Captain Thorpe and Captain Fesmire had been summoned forward with their radio operators to join Colonel McDade at the edge of LZ Albany. They had just reached him at 1315 when the attack started. Pinned down by North Vietnamese fire, they were unable to rejoin their companies.

Captain George Forrest of Alpha Company, 1/5 Cavalry, however, reacted with extraordinary speed. Like Thorpe and Fesmire, Forrest had barely reached McDade when the North Vietnamese struck. As soon as he heard the firing, and without pausing to ask the colonel's leave, he turned and ran back down the column, a distance of 500 to 600 meters, to join his company. Surviving this dash unwounded (though two radio operators with him were shot and killed), he resumed personal command of Alpha Company, pulled it back somewhat from the rest of the column, and formed a defensive perimeter.[51]

Within minutes, Forrest's company came under attack, but the attackers met stout resistance and did not press it home. Alpha Company, 1/5 Cavalry, sustained casualties, but fewer than the other companies serving under McDade that day. Forrest's leadership was certainly a factor, but probably not the main one. The North Vietnamese wrapped themselves around the front and flanks of the American force, but relatively few of them appear to have reached its rear. The scale and intensity of the PAVN attack on Forrest's company were, most accounts suggest, considerably less than that on the others in McDade's force.

Captain Sugdinis's Alpha Company, 2/7 Cavalry, located at Albany itself, was under intense pressure for the first hour of the battle and suffered severe losses. Sugdinis lost touch with his 1st Platoon early in the action and was forced to conclude that most of it had been wiped out. He and his command group took up position at a termite mound near the grove of trees in the middle of the landing zone, where the mortar platoon was also located. McDade and those immediately around him positioned themselves about 50 meters to the east, and the reconnaissance platoon led by Lieutenant Payne rallied around a mound on the north side of the grove. The three termite mounds and the officers and men clustered around them became the basis for a fairly solid triangular defensive perimeter, established by about 1345. With the middle of the column shattered, some members of Companies C and D tried to survive by working their way forward to Albany, and some of them too apparently ended up defending the termite mound perimeter.[52]

By about 1345, half an hour after the battle began, McDade had lost all communication with most of his battalion, but he could talk to the brigade. Colonel Brown, the brigade commander, was visiting LZ Falcon when the action started and apparently became aware of 2/7's crisis when the voices of panic-stricken personnel from Albany were heard over the radio. With his fire support officer, Captain Dudley L. Tademy, Brown then helicoptered over the battle area, trying to make sense of events.

In a radio conversation with Brown that afternoon, McDade reportedly played down the severity of the crisis, probably because he did not want to appear to a superior officer to be in a state of panic. At least according to some sources, however, he became totally ineffective as a commander. Certainly, he had no control over anything happening outside the landing zone. Command within the termite mound perimeter seems to have been a group effort involving McDade's deputy Major Frank Henry, Captain Sugdinis, and others; McDade himself apparently played little part. Brown and his fire support officer were for a considerable time so confused by what was going on beneath them that they were unable to be of any help.

A-1E Skyraiders of the 1st Air Commando Squadron based at Pleiku, summoned by the officers in the termite mound perimeter, were nevertheless approaching the battlefield within an hour of the initial North Vietnamese attack. Shortly before the aircraft arrived, the officers in the perimeter made a hard decision that turned out to be crucial for their own survival. Even though the area immediately around them might contain American wounded, the air force must be allowed to bomb and strafe it freely. Those inside the perimeter indicated its position by the use of smoke grenades. This allowed the Skyraiders, at 1415, to strafe and napalm a large body of North Vietnamese apparently forming up for an assault immediately to the east. This initial air strike ended the period of most acute crisis for the Americans at Albany itself. With their perimeter clearly defined, and having made the hard decision to sacrifice American survivors immediately around it, it was relatively easy to bring in supporting fires. Nevertheless, sniping and occasional probes continued until about 1800.[53]

About an hour into the battle, not long after the air strikes began, Le Xuan Phoi, the North Vietnamese commander, suffered the grievous wound that would kill him before nightfall. The memoirs of Dang Vu Hiep, the Central Highlands Front's senior commissar, are full of purple passages dealing with events he did not personally witness and thus must be treated with some caution. But his graphic account of this incident may be based on firsthand testimony and is worth quoting:

Another artillery round exploded nearby, and the soldiers saw Battalion Commander Le Xuan Phoi drop to his knees, his shirt ripped to shreds. Blood poured from his stomach, from which a section of intestine protruded from the gaping wound. With great difficulty Phoi forced his intestine back into the wound, using a piece of parachute cloth used for camouflage to tie the wound closed, and struggled to his feet. After stumbling a few steps forward, however, his legs buckled and he fell to the ground.[54]

Hiep indicates that the grave wounding of their commander inspired 8th Battalion troops to renew the vigor of their attacks. But the battlefield was so chaotic and PAVN communications so limited that it seems unlikely that most of them would have been aware of the incident.

Though fighting on some parts of the battlefield continued well into the night, it seems probable that the greatest slaughter of Americans happened in the first hour, roughly between 1315 and 1415. After that, the Americans "called in artillery and air strikes that flattened whole sections of the old-growth virgin forest. The sky itself seemed to have disappeared, replaced by swirling clouds of dust, smoke and ash. The air became difficult to breathe, filled with the stench of napalm and burning trees."[55] In such circumstances, the impetus of the PAVN attack was bound to diminish.

The Summoning and Arrival of US Reinforcements, 17 November

Colonel Brown tried to organize reinforcements from within 3d Brigade for those who had survived the initial North Vietnamese assaults, but they did not arrive quickly. The two groups of Americans who still had some coherent organization and were thus capable of receiving reinforcements were Forrest's company, at the back of the column, and those holding the termite mound perimeter at Albany. Initially, Forrest's Alpha Company seemed easier to reach. Shortly after 1400, Brown ordered B Company, 1/5 Cavalry, to march from LZ Columbus to join Forrest's A Company of the same battalion. B Company, commanded by Captain Walter B. Tully (a cousin of Colonel Tully, who commanded 2/5 Cavalry), set off on its westward march at 1442. Tully's men linked up with Forrest's at 1640. Together, they formed a landing zone big enough for a single helicopter and then called helicopters in to take the most seriously wounded men to the hospital. Brown's orders were for the two companies to advance toward Albany together and link up with McDade and the troops defending the termite mound perimeter. Captain Tully's company led. But after advancing about 400 meters it received quite intense small-arms, machine gun, and RPG fire. Tully ordered a quick attack that appeared to disperse much of the opposition, but not all of it. Given that it would be dark before long, Forrest's and Tully's companies proceeded to establish a perimeter for the night, intending to link up with McDade the following morning.

Even though Tully and Forrest did not get there that evening, some reinforcements did arrive at the Albany perimeter before darkness fell. On Colonel Brown's orders, Captain Diduryk's B Company, 2/7 Cavalry (which had fought at X-Ray and was down to eighty-three men), flew from Camp Holloway to the northern clearing at Albany and landed without incident at 1830. The fifteen slicks carrying Diduryk's men were able to take out some of the wounded on their return trip. The officers who had been in charge of the termite mound perimeter were now nearing total exhaustion, and Major Henry decided to put Diduryk in command. Diduryk integrated all the survivors at Albany into his own company and expanded the perimeter to cover the whole landing zone. Reinforced and well supported by artillery, it now seemed likely that the Americans at Albany could resist any night attack the North Vietnamese might mount.[56]

Those Americans within the two reinforced and defended perimeters had reason to feel more secure as the sun set, but the battlefield between them was still dangerous and filled with grim scenes. According to a PAVN account: "Enemy bodies lay in groups of three–five men each interspersed with the bodies of own troops. Many of the bodies of our soldiers lay on top of American bodies, their bayonets still stuck in the enemy chests. Some of our men were found still clutching hand grenades." American sources say much the same.[57]

Getting through the Night, 17–18 November

During the night, the North Vietnamese mounted no major attacks, but there are reports of groups of them scouring the battlefield looking for wounded Americans to kill. American troops defending the Albany perimeter heard others outside begging for mercy before shots rang out. One wounded American reportedly survived having a pistol fired inside his mouth, the bullet exiting through his neck without hitting the spinal cord or the spine.[58] But once the mayhem at Albany started, American troops seem to have given no more quarter than did their enemies. It is difficult to believe that no North Vietnamese wounded were left behind on the battlefield, yet there is no record of any being taken prisoner.

At about midnight a radio operator in the Forrest-Tully perimeter picked up a transmission from someone using the call sign "Ghost 4–6." This turned out to be Second Lieutenant Robert J. Jeanette, who had been wounded four times that day and was trying to stay alive. He and fifteen others were located in a small perimeter somewhere between the Forrest-Tully position and Albany. A platoon from Forrest's company, led by Sergeant Fred J. Kluge, went looking for this group. Kluge's platoon found them and many others nearby, about forty-five wounded Americans in all, and brought most of them back to the 1/5 Cavalry perimeter, some walking and some on litters. But eighteen men who were too badly wounded to walk had to be left behind because there were not enough litters to carry them. Specialist Five Daniel Torrez, the senior medic with Alpha Company 1/5, volunteered to stay behind to care for them. He remained with them for the rest of the night, treating their wounds and administering to their needs. Torrez had to interrupt this work from time to time to fire a machine gun at groups of North Vietnamese who were still prowling around, looking for wounded Americans to kill.[59]

Policing Up: The Immediate Aftermath, 18–20 November

By morning, the North Vietnamese had gone. Tully's and Forrest's men linked up with the Albany perimeter and started to police the battlefield, looking for American wounded, recovering equipment, and counting North Vietnamese bodies. This process was still incomplete at 1400 on 18 November when

Tully's and Forrest's companies were ordered back to LZ Columbus. What was left of 2/7 Cavalry continued to police the battlefield until the afternoon of Friday, 19 November. Helicopters then flew the unwounded survivors of 2/7 Cavalry to LZ Crooks, some 11 km to the northwest, where they remained for a day. The following day the same troops were flown from LZ Crooks to the 1st Cavalry Division base at An Khe.[60]

McDade's force had been about 400 strong when the North Vietnamese attack began. It suffered about 70 percent casualties, including 151 killed, 5 missing, and 121 wounded. The 1st Cavalry Division's after-action report indicated 403 PAVN dead "by body count" and another 100 enemy fatalities by "estimate." In fact, both figures were largely guesswork. No one actually counted anything like 403 North Vietnamese bodies. Figures for PAVN losses at Albany are not supplied in histories published in Hanoi, but these sources freely admit that Phoi, initially in command, and Luan, who assumed command an hour or two into the action, were both killed. Luan (of the 33d Regiment) assumed overall command, apparently because there was no one left in 8th Battalion, 66th Regiment, in a position to do so. This suggests that North Vietnamese casualties at Albany were considerably higher than those of the Americans. (Despite the scale of the carnage, McDade and all his company commanders survived.) The large amount of equipment left lying on the battlefield provides further evidence of heavy North Vietnamese casualties. The PAVN hated to abandon serviceable weaponry, but 212 assault rifles and carbines, 39 light machine guns, 8 rocket launchers, and 6 82mm mortars were recovered by the Americans at the end of the fighting.[61]

The Impact of Albany, 18–20 November

The fighting at Albany on 17 November 1965 has been deeply controversial for half a century now. In midmorning on 18 November, Rick Merron, an Associated Press photographer who had managed to hitch a ride on a helicopter out to Albany on the evening of 17 November, returned to Pleiku. Having seen a large number of American bodies, and reportedly white with shock, Merron allegedly dictated a "wild, nearly incoherent" story over the phone to his agency's Saigon desk. Merron was about to fly from Pleiku to Saigon with some film he had shot at Albany when he was intercepted and interviewed by Dick Knowles, the 1st Cavalry Division's deputy commander. Knowles evidently first got wind of the scale of the slaughter at Albany from Merron. (The reports received from 3d Brigade the previous day had played down what was happening. Only a relatively small number of casualties had been extracted the previous evening, and Merron apparently reached Pleiku before most of the American bodies did.) Knowles then flew to 3d Brigade at Catecka to get an explanation from Brown.[62]

Any ensuing conversation between Knowles and Brown was probably not very pleasant. Brown emerges quite well from the X-Ray episode, but Albany shows him in a much poorer light. Though this is not certain, he may have been responsible for the decision to separate McDade's battalion from Tully's, sending them to different locations and thus dividing his forces in the presence of the enemy. He cannot be blamed for the sloppy march discipline of McDade's battalion, but he had helicoptered rather helplessly over Albany for much of the afternoon, only managing to get reinforcements there in relatively small numbers and late in the day. His most grievous fault, however, was not keeping his superiors properly informed.

Just as McDade did not want to admit to Brown the severity of the crisis facing his unit, Brown had apparently not wanted to announce an emergency to his immediate superior, Knowles. According to one report, Brown had forbidden 3d Brigade staff officers to send any further reports to division headquarters. This may have been fatal for some Americans at Albany. The reinforcements Brown got into the Albany area in the late afternoon and evening of Wednesday, 17 November, were enough to secure a couple of perimeters but not the whole battlefield. Groups of North Vietnamese were thus able to roam the area at night, finishing off American wounded. Knowles reportedly believed that if the division's advance headquarters had been fully aware of the situation, it might have been able to move in sufficient reinforcements to secure the whole battlefield before night fell.[63]

On the evening of 18 November the 1st Cavalry Division held a press conference in Pleiku. Knowles presided, with Major E. C. "Shy" Meyer, Brown's deputy, starting the proceedings with an account of events at Albany. Rumors were already circulating among journalists that McDade's force had blundered into an ambush. The press wanted the division to admit this. The briefers refused to do so, insisting (correctly) that it had been a "meeting engagement." This term was probably unfamiliar to most of the journalists present, and many apparently perceived its use as nothing more than pompous military jargonizing and obfuscation. Vo Huynh, a respected Vietnamese cameraman working for NBC, became, however, a dissenter among the newspeople at this briefing. Rumored to have served with the Viet Minh in the First Indochina War, Huynh had more military knowledge than most of his colleagues, and he had been at Albany on the evening of 17 November. He denied that Albany had been an ambush. The North Vietnamese had not dug in. Some PAVN soldiers still had heavy packs on their backs, indicating that they had been in the middle of a march. There were rice bowls lying around, suggesting that some had been disturbed at lunch. Such subtleties seem, however, to have been lost on the majority of reporters present.

The press's failure to believe the 1st Cavalry Division on this issue was, however, largely the division's own fault. At the press conference on the evening of 18 November, Knowles claimed an American victory at Albany, indicating that 400 or more North Vietnamese had been killed, with "light to moderate casualties" on the American side.[64] The 400 figure was, at best, an optimistic guess; the "light to moderate" claim for American casualties was a blatant lie, and a ridiculously transparent one at that. Some reporters may have been uncertain about the difference between a meeting engagement and an ambush, but they had no difficulty discerning when they were being told insulting nonsense about American losses. Albany was therefore a significant episode in the decline of trust between the American military and the American media in this war. On the meeting engagement versus ambush issue, the journalists eventually won. Both the US Army and US Air Force official histories clearly state that the Americans at Albany walked into an ambush.[65]

According to Westmoreland's notes, he, like Knowles, discovered the truth about Albany in an odd and inappropriate manner. On the morning of 18 November, Westmoreland was involved in the parallel processes of celebrating the 1st Cavalry Division's victory at X-Ray and organizing its exploitation:

On Thursday, General Vien [Cao Van Vien, the newly appointed South Vietnamese chief of the Joint General Staff] and I flew up to Pleiku to visit 1st of the 7th Cavalry commanded by Lieutenant Colonel Hal Moore. In the presence of his staff, Moore briefed me on the operation that had taken place earlier in the week . . . I was tremendously impressed with . . . Moore, his staff, supporting elements and the general professionalism that was evident. Moore had the highest praise for his men and asked me if I would talk to them. After I visited several of the companies that had been badly hurt by the action, he assembled the battalion and I addressed them for about ten minutes at which time I told them that [they] were being recommended for a Presidential Unit Citation . . . I then flew down and visited the brigade commanded by Colonel Tim Brown. He gave me a briefing and we flew over the operational area.

Westmoreland does not say when he met Brown on Thursday, 18 November. We must assume that it was sometime before Knowles saw the 3d Brigade commander to remonstrate about his failure to pass critical information up the chain of command. Brown apparently compounded his offense of not properly briefing Knowles about the carnage at Albany on 17 November by not adequately informing Westmoreland of it on 18 November. After talking to Brown, Westmoreland still believed all was going well with the Pleiku campaign, and he proceeded to discuss plans for its further development with Vinh Loc and Larsen. It was only when he visited patients in the American military hospital at Qui Nhon later in the day that he realized there had been something of a setback:

> [The patients] were mostly personnel of the 1st Cavalry who had been wounded in the recent operation in Pleiku. While talking to them I began to sense I had not been given the full information when I visited the . . . Brigade CP [command post]. Several of the men stated that they had been in what they referred to as an ambush. Most of the men were from the 2d of the 7th Cavalry.

Westmoreland further noted that during the afternoon of 18 November, after returning to his Saigon office:

> Colonel [Ben] Legare [Westmoreland's press officer] came in and informed me that a story had been filed that was highly critical of the 1st Air Cavalry. This came as no great surprise to me since I had suspected it after talking to the men in the hospital. I then called General Larsen and told him to get the facts. It was ultimately revealed that nobody, to include the brigade commander, had knowledge of what actually happened. The next day [19 November] however we got the matter sorted out and determined that the 2d of the 7th got heavily involved with a PAVN outfit in their bivouac area and there was considerable close-in fighting. The PAVN got the worst of it and withdrew. . . . Some of our men were left on the battlefield during the course of the evening because of the high elephant grass, which made it very difficult to find the bodies.

Almost incredibly, Westmoreland seems to have accepted that, rather than deliberately withholding bad news from his superiors, Brown had merely been ignorant. Nor did Westmoreland consider that such a level of ignorance was worthy of dismissal in itself. The press conference that Westmoreland ordered Legare to organize was, of course, far too late to sterilize the story. Merron's sensational report had already been filed with Associated Press, and the 1st Cavalry Division's botched briefing of 18 November had made matters worse. Westmoreland noted, "Some unfortunate stories hit the headlines in the Washington papers, which we heard about the next day."[66] But no senior American officer's head rolled after Albany. Brown remained at 3d Brigade. Kinnard, who had appointed him in the first place, insisted that McDade remain in command of 2/7 Cavalry.[67]

While Westmoreland tended to minimize Albany in his historical notes, judging by his actions rather than his words, it shook him. He curtailed considerably plans for the continuation of the Pleiku campaign. His record for 19 November indicates:

General DePuy [his principal operations officer] returned from Pleiku where I sent him because of my concern that the 1st Air Cavalry and the airborne task force might get involved in more than they could handle, and a bloody nose for the ARVN general reserve would be adverse to government morale. Further, I feared that intense sustained combat would wear down the Cavalry Division to the point that it might not be capable of performing its mission during the next several weeks. I asked DePuy to look into all these matters and give me a report. After talking to all the commanders and advisors concerned, he recommended that the new phase of the operation be confined north of [the Ia Drang] since the river is unfordable and thus would reduce the risk of unsuccessful operations, particularly for the ARVN airborne.[68]

It is not easy to follow DePuy's and Westmoreland's reasoning here. Apparently, the original intention for the next phase of the campaign was for the 1st Cavalry Division to push west along the Ia Drang toward the Cambodian border while ARVN Airborne troops moved south from Duc Co, trapping PAVN forces between them. Albany, however, triggered doubts in the American chain of command. The upshot was that the ARVN Airborne Brigade proceeded to carry out (and considerably to expand) its part in the operation, while the 1st Cavalry Division's participation was confined largely to lending artillery support.[69]

The American press quickly seized on the winding down of 1st Cavalry Division involvement in the Pleiku campaign. At his monthly background session with the press at 1000 on Friday, 20 November, Westmoreland reviewed that campaign's progress. He then read a wire he had received from the Secretary of Defense that quoted "headlines from the *Washington Post* and *Star* implying the retreat and withdrawal of the 1st Cavalry Division." Westmoreland protested that, although he respected the press and had resisted demands for its censorship, if this sort of headline continued, it might ruin the morale of the American public and seriously degrade the war effort.[70]

The press, however, had been right that an American battalion had suffered a disaster at Albany, and they were right to think that the 1st Cavalry Division had initially tried to minimize it. The press was also correct that Westmoreland and the American military in Vietnam were reacting to this setback (and the critical news reports that followed it) not by renewing their military efforts in

Pleiku Province but by slackening them off. Indeed, J. D. Coleman, a public-
ity officer with the 1st Cavalry Division who wrote a standard account of the
Pleiku campaign, called his chapter on the post-Albany period "Winding It
Down." The Americans were now showing little enthusiasm for the vigorous
exploitation of the substantial overall victory won by anti-Communist forces
(South Vietnamese and American) in Pleiku.

At Albany, McDade's force had been unlucky enough to meet the last fresh,
fully combat-capable PAVN battalion in Pleiku. At a terrible cost to McDade's
troops, that battalion had now been largely destroyed. The three PAVN regiments that had fought in the Pleiku campaign, all physically and psychologically shattered, were on the point of withdrawing from South Vietnam into
Cambodia.[71] Perhaps reading the campaign better than Westmoreland did,
and being less concerned than he was about American newspaper reports, the
ARVN high command and the ARVN Airborne Brigade perceived an excellent opportunity and were eager to be on the PAVN's heels.[72] At this point in
the Pleiku campaign, the South Vietnamese were demonstrating a more acute
and refined killer instinct than their American allies.

LZ Crooks and LZ Columbus, 18 November

Before exploring the last phase of the Pleiku campaign, in which troops belonging to the ARVN Airborne Brigade played the leading role, it is necessary
to review the final actions fought by 3d Brigade, 1st Cavalry Division—a brigade that was about to be withdrawn from the campaign. On 18 November,
in the immediate aftermath of Albany, Colonel Brown sent Tully's 2/5 Cavalry
into an air assault designed to open up LZ Crooks, 18 km northwest of LZ Columbus and only 7 km northeast of the main concentration area of the PAVN
32d Regiment. The main purpose of opening this landing zone was to create
an artillery firebase from which the ARVN Airborne battalions due to head
south from Duc Co could be supported. The PAVN, presumably elements
of the 32d Regiment, probed Crooks that same night, but not very seriously.
One American was wounded. During a sweep of the perimeter the following
morning, the Americans found two North Vietnamese corpses.

Colonel An had tried to get the battalions of the 33d Regiment to attack
American firebases during the fighting at X-Ray. For whatever reasons, they
had not managed to do so. The fighting at X-Ray had ended on the morning
of 16 November. But the transmission of orders was not easy in the PAVN
at this time. It seems likely that, once issued, An's instructions were not re-
scinded. All the 33d Regiment's battalions had been very badly cut up in the
siege of Plei Me and the subsequent retreat. What was left of 1st Battalion

must have been bled white by participation in the action at Albany. On 18 November, however, the regiment summoned just enough strength to mount an attack on LZ Columbus. Whoever was in command at this stage may have been emboldened to do so by reconnaissance indicating that part of the garrison had left. Captain Tully's Bravo Company 1/5 had, as noted, marched off to Albany on the afternoon of 17 November. It did not complete its return march (accompanied by Forrest's Alpha Company) until 1700 on 18 November. The North Vietnamese attack started at 1745, coming mainly from the south and east, supported by heavy mortar and rocket fire. In addition to their infantry weapons, the defenders used the artillery on the base and called in air strikes. A firefight continued until midnight, after which time the PAVN broke contact, leaving behind twenty-seven bodies. Just three Americans were killed and thirteen wounded, probably indicating that the 33d Regiment was, for the time being, practically at the end of its combat power.[73]

ARVN–US Joint Operations, 18–27 November

We have few details of the joint planning of the Americans and the South Vietnamese for joint operations after X-Ray. Up to 17 November, the discussions appear to have centered around the employment of a couple of battalions from the ARVN Airborne Brigade, together with 3d Brigade.[74] After Albany, however, the continued use of 3d Brigade in Pleiku became problematic, to say the least. For the time being, the 2/7 Cavalry, which was supposed to play a role in joint operations with the ARVN, had ceased to exist as a usable unit. The 1/7 Cavalry was still very tired after X-Ray. Though nothing was said publicly, everyone in the American chain of command from Knowles's level up had almost certainly lost confidence in Tim Brown. Before Albany, there was apparently no discussion of a second change of brigades. After Albany, such a change happened quite quickly.

By noon on 20 November, Colonel William "Ray" Lynch and his 2d Brigade headquarters had replaced Brown and 3d Brigade. Lynch, like Brown before him, established a headquarters organization at Catecka but placed himself and some of his key staff at Duc Co, with the ARVN Airborne Brigade's forward headquarters. The ARVN Airborne Brigade would now play the leading role. Lynch would eventually have four battalions (1/5 Cavalry, 2/5 Cavalry, 2/12 Cavalry, and 1/8 Cavalry), plus the 1st Squadron of the 9th Cavalry for reconnaissance. But none of these troops were fresh. Two of Lynch's battalions (2/12 and 1/8 Cavalry) would be participating in the Pleiku campaign for the second time, having initially served with 1st Brigade. In addition to the weariness of its troops and Westmoreland's concerns about American casualties, the division's operations in the last phase of the Pleiku campaign were almost certainly severely restricted by a continuing shortage of flyable helicopters. In practice, Lynch's and the 1st Cavalry Division's support for the last phase of the Pleiku campaign would be artillery fire from firebases at LZ Crooks and LZ Golf. Lynch had two full artillery battalions—Lieutenant Colonel Smith's 1st Battalion, 77th Artillery, and Lieutenant Colonel Amos's 2d Battalion, 17th Artillery—to provide supporting fire in this last phase of the campaign.[75]

It seems likely that, after Albany, the Americans were obliged to confess to their South Vietnamese allies that the 1st Cavalry Division was in no position to undertake further offensive operations with its own troops (other than artillery) in Pleiku. Rather than abandoning the hope of conducting such operations, the South Vietnamese apparently responded with a hurriedly organized expansion of their own contribution to the campaign. Instead of the two battalions being discussed a few days earlier, the ARVN Airborne Brigade ended up employing two task forces with a total of five battalions.

The American after-action report on the ARVN Airborne Brigade's Operation Than Phong (Divine Wind) 7 indicates that the mission was to destroy Communist forces in a tactical area of responsibility extending from Duc Co south along the Cambodian border to the Ia Drang and to "provide a blocking force astride the Ia Drang river near the Cambodian border, for the first Cav Div operating to the East." The main enemy force in the vicinity was the PAVN 32d Regiment, with three battalions. It was thought that some reinforcements might be available to that regiment from the PAVN 66th Regiment and "local VC units."[76]

The operation was put together by the Airborne Brigade's headquarters under General Du Quoc Dong, with Lieutenant Colonel Ngo Quang Truong, the chief of staff, also playing a significant part in the planning. The concept of operations, as explained in an American adviser's after-action report, was that on D-day, 18 November, Airborne Task Force I, comprising the 3d, 5th, and 8th Battalions, would fly south from Duc Co, enter the Ia Drang valley by air assault, commence searching an area immediately north of the river, and prepare a crossing site. On D+1 Task Force II, comprising the 7th and 8th Battalions, would enter the operational area by helicopter, assume control of the area north of the river, and continue searching for the PAVN there. On D+3 Task Force I would cross the Ia Drang and search its southern bank. Although the Ia Drang was fast and unfordable this far west, the ARVN, ignoring Westmoreland's strictures, proposed to operate on both sides of it. Once five 500-man Airborne battalions were in the field, there does not appear to have been much fear of defeat in detail.[77]

The 5th Airborne Battalion was already at Duc Co on the morning of 18 November, and the 6th Airborne Battalion was already at Pleiku, so they had only a short distance to fly. Task Force I headquarters flew up to Duc Co from Saigon aboard USAF C-130s, arriving at about 0800. The 3d Airborne Battalion also came up from Saigon, apparently a little later, by the same means. A liaison officer from the 1st Cavalry Division arrived at Duc Co at 0930 to coordinate artillery support. But the task force did not receive a formal briefing on its mission by a liaison officer sent from the Airborne Brigade in Saigon until 1030. Helicopters for the intended air assault into the Ia Drang valley were provided by the US Army's 52d Aviation Battalion from Pleiku.

The 6th Battalion, the 3d Battalion, and part of the 5th Battalion had arrived on the northern side of the Ia Drang valley by 1745 on Thursday, 18 November. The movement was interrupted by nightfall, and the rest of 5th Battalion was brought in the following morning. Lieutenant Colonel Truong Quang An, Task Force I's commander, did not wait for all his troops to arrive before commencing search and clear operations. Elements of the 6th Airborne Battalion came under fire at 1530 as they crossed a small stream just south of the landing zone. In an action that continued the following morning, the battalion called in artillery fire, helicopter gunships, and air strikes against a hostile force thought to be about a company strong. Losing three killed and twelve wounded, 6th Battalion found the bodies of two soldiers from the opposing force and took a prisoner, who told them his unit had lost another forty dead as a result of the air strikes and artillery. Small firefights continued for much of Friday, 19 November.[78]

The main action during this phase of the campaign occurred on Saturday, 20 November, near Hill 185, about 1 km north of the river, not far from LZ Golf. A battalion-sized force of the PAVN 32d Regiment mounted an attack into the rear of the 3d Airborne Battalion, apparently not realizing the proximity of the 6th Airborne Battalion. The PAVN force became caught between two fires, as Task Force I commander ordered a pincer movement. According to the American after-action report:

> At 1515 hrs the 6th Bn left their positions and attacked the VC with three companies on line. Mortars, 4 A1Es and artillery were used to support the attack. The artillery was walked in front of the attacking troops to achieve maximum results. . . . By 1600 hrs all contact had been broken. . . . Twenty-eight weapons were captured and advisors counted 120 VC KIA. The unconfirmed body count was 200. The remainder of the day and evening were quiet.

During this brief action, the Airborne Brigade ordered 8th Battalion flown forward from Duc Co to join Task Force I on the northern side of the Ia Drang.

The 6th Airborne Battalion performed especially well in the action of 20 November. Not long afterward, probably sometime on Sunday, 21 November,

Major General Vinh Loc, the II Corps commander, flew down from Pleiku to give field promotions. He promoted the battalion commander, Nguyen Van Minh, from captain to major and similarly rewarded other members of the battalion, both officers and enlisted men, who had distinguished themselves.[79]

Between 0755 and 1000 on Monday, 22 November, Task Force II headquarters and the 7th Battalion joined the rest of the Airborne forces on the northern side of the Ia Drang, being shuttled down from Duc Co in twelve UH-1D helicopters of the 52d Aviation Battalion. Task Force II, commanded by Lieutenant Colonel Ngo Quang Truong,[80] assumed control of the 3d and 8th Battalions and remained on the north bank of the Ia Drang. Meanwhile, the other three battalions under the control of Task Force I crossed the river that afternoon, starting at 1445, using log and bamboo bridges prepared previously. Supported by artillery fire, the crossings were unopposed. Although the bridges kept breaking and it took hours to get everyone across, no drownings were reported.[81]

On 23 and 24 November there were small-scale actions on both sides of the river. During an attack mounted by the 6th Airborne Battalion on a fortified position south of the river on Wednesday, 24 November, PAVN demoralization was obvious. In the words of the American after-action report, "From the distribution of weapons and equipment it was apparent that the enemy had panicked and fled dropping much of their gear." On both sides of the river the ARVN found and destroyed a number of Communist camps, some of which had been heavily fortified. Over the next three days, 25–27 November, the operation wound down as the battalions returned, apparently on foot, to Duc Co, "clearing and searching as they went."[82]

On the basis of American advisers' body count, the operation was reported to have killed 265 Communist troops and captured 10, while 21 ARVN soldiers were killed and 50 wounded. There was also a good haul of captured weapons and documents. The American advisers judged that the "operation was quickly planned and rapidly executed. The maneuver plan was sound and the US artillery provided excellent fire support." The operation was based on good intelligence, which, according to one source, was partly owing to effective reconnaissance by the Airborne Rangers—the South Vietnamese Special Forces, who were often derided by the Americans.

US advisers to the ARVN Airborne Brigade regretted the absence of a psychological warfare team and aircraft equipped with loudspeakers, noting that in the later days of the operation: "The enemy was demoralized, hungry and broken into small scattered units. The use of loudspeaker aircraft might have induced significant numbers to surrender."[83] The American advisers may not have been aware of it, but according to a Communist officer in a good position to know, this type of intensive psychological warfare effort was employed against at least some PAVN forces in Pleiku in late November. Apparently, it was not without impact.

Kinnard later complained that his division was not allowed to consummate the victory by pursuing the North Vietnamese over the Cambodian border. Pursuing the PAVN regiments until they were utterly destroyed was the correct thing to do from a military point of view, and Cambodian neutrality was, of course, a sham: Sihanouk was actively helping the North Vietnamese. But even if Westmoreland had managed to get political permission to go after the PAVN in Cambodia, it seems likely that cross-border operations would have been confined to air strikes and, possibly, incursions by elements of the ARVN Airborne Brigade. Most of the evidence indicates that the 1st Cavalry Division had, for the time being, run out of steam. The bulk of its helicopter fleet appears to have been grounded for mechanical reasons,[84] and after 17 November, there is little evidence that its ground troops were seriously seeking contact with the North Vietnamese.

Impact of the Pleiku Campaign on PAVN Regiments

By the time all the ARVN Airborne battalions had returned to Duc Co on 27 November, both sides recognized that the Pleiku campaign was over. The last PAVN troops who were still functioning as part of any kind of coherent unit had crossed the border into Cambodia. By any normal standard, Chu Huy Man's October–November 1965 campaign in Gia Lai–Pleiku had not been merely a failure; for the PAVN regiments involved, it had been a catastrophe.

The memoirs of Dang Vu Hiep, the senior political commissar of Man's Central Highlands Front, to a certain degree uphold the Party line, stating that the campaign was, in some sense, a Communist victory. But they also graphically describe the desperate condition to which the PAVN regiments that had served in it were reduced by late November. Although Hiep's figures for battle casualties in the three regiments of the Central Highlands Front are likely far too low, his account of the impact of malnutrition and disease is extremely frank. The near total disintegration of morale that he describes meant, of course, a collapse of confidence in Party leadership, a matter of particular concern to a commissar:

From 19 October through 26 November 1965 320th Regiment lost 166 men killed and 197 wounded; 33d Regiment lost 170 men killed and 232 wounded; and 66th Regiment lost 208 killed and 146 wounded. In addition, because food rations were poor and we were short of medicine, the troops suffered severe malnutrition and disease spread, especially beriberi and acute malaria. The

combat strength of our units sank to only 50%. In some regiments as many as
400 men were out of action because of malaria and beriberi. One company
had 115 men but of this number only 33 men were in relatively good health.
At our hospitals and aid stations there were four sick soldiers for every soldier
that had been wounded. The enemy exploited this situation by sending aircraft to fly overhead day and night, dropping so many leaflets that the forest
was turned white and making loud broadcasts over loudspeakers appealing
to our soldiers to "rally" to the enemy side, using poisonous arguments that
included both enticements and threats. They said such things as, "North
Vietnamese soldiers! Do you believe that you were born in the North only to
be forced to die in the South? Come join our nationalist cause and you will be
well treated." Every night they made such broadcasts, and even broadcast the
sounds of children crying, dogs barking and pigs grunting in order to make
our men homesick for their villages and families and shake the morale of our
troops.

These problems had a not insignificant influence on the thoughts of our
soldiers. The units were enveloped in an atmosphere of gloom, which in some
places was quite serious. At meal times when they saw their comrades in arms
many men broke down and cried. In some units as many as two thirds of the
units' personnel spent all day lolling in their hammocks, discussing all kinds of
negative stories and subjects. Some men allowed themselves to become filthy
and refused to wash, even when they were near a stream. Many wrote letters
home saying that sooner or later the writer would die or become disabled, if
not from rifle bullets then from enemy artillery shells or bombs, if not from
hunger then from an acute attack of malaria. Tragic, negative, plaintive songs
appeared among the troops, such as:

"It is easy to get to the Highlands but hard to go home."

"The shortages of rice and salt numb a man's heart." . . .

Some people, in bitter and pessimistic words, compared themselves to crabs
on a chopping block—sooner or later they were going to die.

"The crab lies still on the chopping block

"Never knowing when the knife will fall."

Attempts by the officers ("cadre," in Communist parlance) to restore discipline were initially sometimes clumsy, ineffective, and even counterproduc-
tive. Hiep continues:

A number of our cadre engaged in arbitrary, militaristic actions that caused
tension between cadre and enlisted men, weakening the unit's spirit of solidarity, affection and willingness to fight and die together. The soldiers' ties
to their units weakened and they ignored orders from cadre. The more the

commanders shouted at them, the less willing they were to listen, driving the soldiers into a spirit of negativism and resistance. . . .

Soldiers stole from each other, took chickens from civilian homes and went round firing their weapons indiscriminately. Camp discipline broke down and there was an increase in troops failing to use the latrines and defecating indiscriminately all around the area where troops were quartered.[85]

Hiep goes on to point out that desertion had become a problem (despite the fact that most soldiers were many hundreds of miles from home and had little chance of getting back there alive). One young soldier, who was about to be honored as a "hero killer of Americans" deserted. In these circumstances, Man and Hiep realized that harsh discipline and exemplary punishment were not the answer. With regard to the young hero-deserter, Man was remarkably indulgent, commenting: "The kid is still young, hot-blooded and his mind is still unsettled. He is probably having flashbacks about the violence of the battle and is frightened." According to Hiep, Man ordered the young soldier to be found and brought back but not abused, denounced, or ridiculed. In political reeducation and self-criticism sessions held from 25 December 1965 to 5 January 1966, all who had served in the recent campaign were encouraged to admit their fears, failings, and weaknesses and to confess them in writing. Then Man, in a dramatic gesture of forgiveness and redemption, publicly burned the confessions. Everyone was to start over with a clean slate, provided, of course, they did so with a renewed spirit of loyalty to the Party and self-sacrifice for its cause.[86]

There was no comparable process of convalescence, self-criticism, and rebuilding for the units of the anti-Communist side. Even the most heavily damaged unit, 2/7 Cavalry, had its casualties replaced and was back in action within six weeks.[87]

Final Assessment of the Pleiku Campaign

Though he did his best to restore the spirit of his troops, Chu Huy Man must have struggled to maintain his own morale. As originally conceived, his Plei Me campaign had been a complete failure. The idea had been to lay siege to Plei Me in order to draw in and destroy whatever mobile and combat-capable troops the ARVN had in Pleiku Province before capturing Plei Me itself. After that, it was hoped that virtually the entire province would become a Communist base. But, despite some disagreements among them, Vinh Loc, his II Corps staff, and their American advisers understood the game Man was playing. They were reluctant to allow ARVN troops to be drawn into a relief operation for Plei Me until a force had been assembled that was too strong to be easily destroyed in an ambush. Ultimately, Luat's ARVN Armored Task Force, supported by American airpower, did much more damage to the PAVN 32d Regiment than the 32d did to the ARVN. Meanwhile, airpower (mainly American, but some of it South Vietnamese) inflicted appalling losses on the PAVN 33d Regiment besieging Plei Me. Failing to stop the relief force, the North Vietnamese were obliged to abandon the siege. Man's campaign was defeated before American ground troops (other than some Special Forces and 1st Cavalry Division artillery) had been committed to combat.

The PAVN 33d Regiment suffered from the attentions of the American 1st Cavalry Division and (probably much more seriously) from those of the US Air Force while trying to return to its base in the Ia Drang–Chu Pong area, even though the 32d Regiment's escape to a point further west in the Drang valley had been relatively untroubled. Meanwhile, despite the enormous effort put into planning and preparation, the logistics of the Central Highlands Front's campaign had broken down catastrophically. Reportedly trying to head off acute problems of malnutrition among his troops, Man was certainly in the wrong place and perhaps even in the wrong province when, in mid-November, the 1st Cavalry Division's 3d Brigade plunged into the Ia Drang valley and clashed with the still fresh troops of the PAVN 66th Regiment.[88]

Perhaps paradoxically, the PAVN's two big clashes with US 1st Cavalry Division troops in the Drang valley, on 14–16 and 17 November, respectively, were the episodes in this campaign on which the North Vietnamese could look back with the most pride and from which they could draw the most hope. The first battle was an American attack that came as a surprise, and the second was a meeting engagement on the march. In both cases, the North Vietnamese had acquitted themselves well. In terms of basic infantry skills such as field craft, camouflage, tactical use of terrain, digging in, fire control, marksmanship, and close-quarters fighting, accounts from the Communist side indicate that the North Vietnamese soldiers who survived these encounters believed that they were better than the Americans.[89]

Initially, at least, the determination and ferocity of PAVN troops made them, as many Americans would testify, extremely formidable. It was possible that in the future, in more carefully planned operations in which they enjoyed the initiative and were able to make fuller use of the "grabbing the belt" technique or were able to hit and run more cleanly, they might inflict more casualties than the Americans could endure. In this particular campaign, however, "grabbing the belt" provided the North Vietnamese with only limited protection. Most PAVN soldiers found the intensity of the American artillery fire and air strikes prodigious and terrifying. Having endured these sorts of fires during this campaign, it was not certain that they would willingly do so again, whatever they might plead at reindoctrination sessions.

On the one hand, PAVN battle casualties in this campaign, though certainly lower than US estimates, were probably much more severe than Vietnamese Communist writers such as Hiep were prepared to admit. On the other hand, Vietnamese Communist accounts reveal that levels of malnutrition and disease in the Central Highlands Front's PAVN regiments were more extreme than anything indicated in the standard American histories. Unless the supply of food and medicines could be massively improved, the Central Highlands would not, as Chuy Huy Man realized, be a suitable place for major PAVN offensives in the immediate future.[90]

The forces on the anti-Communist side, by any normal measure, collectively won a major victory in the Pleiku campaign. They not only foiled Man's plan to destroy the ARVN in Pleiku, capture Plei Me, and take control of the province; they also contributed to physically and morally shattering the equivalent of a PAVN division. For all his faults, if anyone on the anti-Communist side had a fairly clear idea of the scale and significance of what had been achieved, it seems to have been Vinh Loc. The II Corps commander proceeded to summarize the campaign in a short book, giving a generally balanced assessment of the contributions to the PAVN's defeat of the various forces involved.[91]

Among other generals on the anti-Communist side, Harry Kinnard also wanted to proclaim a major triumph. But his overriding aim was to give most of the credit to his 1st Cavalry Division and its concept of airmobility. He generated much controversy and considerable irritation within (and beyond) the American armed forces by exaggerating the achievements of his division in this campaign and by ignoring its weaknesses, failings, and mistakes. He claimed that its efforts had prevented the North Vietnamese from cutting South Vietnam in half, even though there is no evidence that the Communists had such a grandiose aim in the immediate future. He failed to acknowledge the colossal strain his division's airmobile operations had imposed on the entire US logistical system in Vietnam, depriving other forces of resources to keep the 1st Cavalry Division going.[92]

Kinnard also failed to admit that, despite frenetic helicopter movements, and despite his division's OV-1 Mohawk surveillance aircraft and the USAF's sideways-looking aerial radar and infrared scanning, his troops had often been unable to find the North Vietnamese. Only rarely had it been possible to bring the PAVN to battle against its will. Vertical envelopment, a maneuver much advocated by the prophets of airmobility, was never achieved against the PAVN in Pleiku. Kinnard also failed to acknowledge that by mid-November, his division had practically flown itself into the ground, the mechanical wear and tear on the helicopters grounding, at least temporarily, a high proportion of these machines. He made no admission that this temporary collapse of airmobility contributed to the disaster for 2/7 Cavalry at Albany and to the limited cooperation between the 1st Cavalry Division and the ARVN Airborne Brigade in the last phase of the campaign.[93] This campaign was many things, but a final and complete vindication of the concept of airmobility it certainly was not. Impressive as this aspect of American military technology was, it had failed to live up to the greatest expectations of its most vehement advocates. The failure of technology to live up to expectations, one influential historian has argued, is one of the major themes of modern military history.[94]

For many American newsmen, Albany and the 1st Cavalry Division's initially inept handling of the media made it difficult for them to provide an objective, balanced assessment of the Pleiku campaign. Albany and the media reaction to it somewhat unnerved Westmoreland and inhibited him from fully exploiting the successes of anti-Communist forces in the Pleiku campaign. Although the PAVN regiments involved suffered all the symptoms of catastrophic defeat, the North Vietnamese had proved that they could inflict sufficient losses on the Americans to cause them real distress. They had also exposed, if not yet entirely pierced, two American Achilles' heels: the much more limited American tolerance for casualties, and the difficult relations between the American military and the American news media. In that sense, the Vietnamese Communist Party line that the Plei Me–Chu Pong campaign was a victory for its forces cannot be entirely dismissed.

Summary and Conclusion

The Geneva Accords amounted to an armistice rather than a peace settlement. Everyone involved considered the renewal of large-scale violence in the near future a definite possibility.

As in other regions of the South, the Communists left stay-behind parties in the Central Highlands. Communist histories praise cadres so dedicated to the cause that they dyed their skins darker, filed their teeth, and put plugs in their earlobes in order to blend more easily into Highland communities. It is impossible to say how many Communist cadres were living among the civilian population in the Central Highlands in the mid- to late 1950s, how many Communist troops were present in remote base areas, or how many weapons were hidden in caches. But we can be sure they were there. Hundreds of Highlanders went to the North in 1954 to receive political training so they could return home and work within their own ethnic groups and, if the Party leadership considered it necessary, help organize them for armed struggle.

Diem was an extremely determined and, in some respects, an able political leader. The extent to which the writ of his regime extended across much of South Vietnam by 1956 surprised many people. But in the Central Highlands, as in the rest of the country, the policies and actions of his administration gave the Communists opportunities to mobilize a considerable portion of the population against him.

Though naturally authoritarian and frequently ruthless, Diem was not an evil man. A genuine and dynamic Vietnamese nationalist, he had a vision for his country's future that included developing the Central Highlands as a western land of opportunity, South Vietnam's new frontier. There is no evidence that Diem hated Highlanders or wished them any harm, provided they did not oppose his plans. He seems to have been happy for them to serve in his armed forces and in some civil government posts. But he also wanted Vietnamese people who supported his regime, including refugees from the North, to settle in the Highlands, and he wanted Highland provinces to make a positive contribution to the South Vietnamese economy, particularly by the growth of plantation crops for export.

In Diem's eyes, the future for the ethnic minorities of the Highlands was to abandon their primitive ways, become properly civilized in the Vietnamese way, and integrate themselves as fully as possible into South Vietnam's economy and society. Highlanders, however, feared they would be overwhelmed by the Vietnamese influx into their region, resulting in the loss of their lands and their identities as distinct peoples. Their feelings were inflamed by some government officials who treated them with contempt and some government troops who stole from them and engaged in sporadic acts of casual brutality.

Educated Highlanders, some of them employed by the government, were, of course, aware of these concerns and grievances. They formed the Bajaraka pressure group in an effort to redress them and to campaign for a degree of autonomy for the Central Highlands within South Vietnam. Diem's response was heavy handed. The great majority of the Bajaraka leaders were not Communists. They were only attempting to defend the well-being of their own peoples. Nevertheless, Diem sent several of them to jail. In some areas his government, fearing an uprising, confiscated from ordinary villagers the spears and crossbows they used for hunting. All this further antagonized Highlanders and provided excellent opportunities for the Communists to gain influence. The Party was able to motivate some Highlanders to resist the Saigon government's policies, join guerrilla units, and prepare to take part in insurrection.

By the late 1950s, local, small-scale oubreaks of violent revolt by Highlanders against the Diem government were already taking place. Some of these may have been spontaneous acts motivated by anger and frustration and may not have been instigated, organized, or controlled by the Communists. By mid-1960, however, a Communist-directed guerrilla war was undoubtedly in progress in the Central Highlands, and branches of the rapidly evolving Ho Chi Minh Trail (by which Communist cadres from the North, after traveling through Laos, could reach the coastal plain) were being established. Given the extreme remoteness of large parts of the region, the difficult terrain, and the cover afforded by the jungle, the Central Highlands was an obvious place to develop not just way stations on the Trail and guerrilla bases but also substantial Communist-controlled "liberated zones." In such zones it might be possible to accommodate and train large main force units for the war's decisive phase.

The establishment of a substantial Communist-controlled zone in the northern part of Kontum Province may have been the aim of the Communists' first major offensive in the Central Highlands during the Second Indochina War. This offensive, which started on 20 October 1960, was not just a matter of assassinations, hit-and-run raids, or small ambushes. It involved overrunning a considerable number of government posts in northern Kontum—a wave of assaults that triggered widespread guerrilla action in the Central Highlands as far south as Darlac. Reportedly the great bulk of Communist troops involved in this offensive, including those who assaulted the government posts in Kontum, were Highlanders, as were many of the Civil Guards defending them.

The Diem government's military response to this first major Communist offensive in the Highlands was rapid and effective. ARVN forces, including an Airborne battalion from the strategic reserve, counterattacked vigorously, and Communist forces in northern Kontum suffered heavy casualties. A sustained government counteroffensive over the next few months penetrated several Communist base areas. This caused acute morale problems among Highlanders who had hitherto been prepared to follow the Communist lead. At this stage, Communist forces in the Highlands were not as well armed as those of the South Vietnamese government. Artillery fire and air strikes in particular intimidated the Communist Highland troops. In late 1960 and for a considerable part of 1961, the Communist war effort in the Highlands stalled.

It may be that after October 1960 there was a clear reluctance on the part of Highland troops recruited by the Communists to mount attacks on government posts or to engage in stand-up battles with the ARVN. Or it may be that the Vietnamese Communist leadership lost faith in the capacity of their Highland recruits to cope with such fighting. For whatever reason, from this point onward, the Communist leadership tended to use units composed mainly of Highland troops to control Highland civilians in Communist base areas, to harass and attack defended villages affiliated with the other side, and to carry out small ambushes and other hit-and-run guerrilla work. For the tougher jobs, such as assaults on fortified posts defended by Civil Guard or ARVN troops or for attacks on substantial groups of troops in the field, the Communist command normally used ethnic Vietnamese main force units. Such units were not raised in the Central Highlands. They had to be brought in from the North through Laos or from the coastal plain.

Bringing ethnic Vietnamese main force units to the Highlands was a vital element in Communist efforts to restore the strategic initiative in 1961. In January the 200th Artillery Battalion arrived in Kontum from Laos and became the first main force unit in the Central Highlands. A hard-core PAVN unit, it included some Highlanders who had gone to the North in 1954, but most of its members were ethnic Vietnamese. Its function was to provide some of the firepower the Communists had so far lacked in this region. One small artillery unit would not, however, be enough to regain the initiative. For the Dak Ha offensive of September 1961, as the Communist history of their forces in the Highlands points out, they went to great trouble to bring in infantry units from both Laos and the coastal plain.

The Dak Ha offensive of September 1961 was a major episode in the war in the Central Highlands. We do not have all the details we would like on the fighting, but it is clear that the Communist offensive inflicted some heavy casualties on South Vietnamese government troops. Although the Communist main force units suffered significant casualties as well, their performance was impressive enough to restore morale among local force units on the Communist side, consisting mostly of Highlanders. There was an upsurge of guerrilla activity over much of Kontum and Pleiku and a corresponding decline of morale on the South Vietnamese government side.

There were enlightened ARVN officers in the Central Highlands. Hostile feelings toward the native peoples of the region were never universal in Diem's armed forces, which contained officers and men of Highland origin. But in the northern Central Highlands in late 1961, their sense of being surrounded by a hostile native population aggravated the racial prejudices of many ethnic Vietnamese ARVN officers. Some argued that, like the Indian tribes of the American West in the late nineteenth century, members of the Highland ethnic groups not actually in arms against the government should be rounded up and put on reservations. The rest should automatically be regarded as hostile. They thought that much of the Central Highlands should therefore be regarded as a free-fire zone. Some senior American officers accepted such a policy as the only practical solution.

By the second half of 1961, Communist strength was already substantial in Kontum and Pleiku and growing in Darlac, South Vietnam's largest province. To avoid losing control of the Central Highlands, the South Vietnamese government would have to take some fairly drastic steps, and quickly. Before opting for the reservation and free-fire zone approach, Diem's government (advised by some of its own officers and by some Americans, including William Colby of the CIA) decided to try some measures to win the support of the Highland population against the Communists. The Buon Enao experiment in Darlac was the most remarkable of these.

It has been said that 1962 was Diem's year. Across much of the country there was a dramatic fight-back by South Vietnamese government forces, aided and advised by the Americans. In the Central Highlands the shift in the strategic initiative and in the balance of forces was particularly dramatic. The Communists had a truly terrible year, with many of their troops suffering extreme physical privation and a corresponding crisis of morale.

In Darlac, as everyone who examined the project testified, the Buon Enao system of defended villages made a huge difference, denying influence to the Communists and giving Highlanders (especially the Rhade) renewed self-confidence. Had the Diem government continued this positive approach toward Highlanders, it might have developed a real partnership with the educated Highland elite. It might have been able to do this without offering formal autonomy to the Central Highlands. But no such positive outcome emerged.

Indeed, by the end of 1962, relations between the Diem government and the Highland ethnic groups were headed for another major crisis.

Given the extreme crisis the Communists encountered in the Central Highlands in 1962, Diem may have thought it unnecessary to court the goodwill of the Highlanders. To sustain their forces in the Central Highlands, the Communists made excessive demands on the Highland villages under their control. This tended to drive away the human resources they so desperately needed—the sea in which, to use Mao Zedong's famous analogy, they needed to swim. In many parts of the Highlands, people started to leave Communist-controlled areas in large numbers. But Highlanders were not moving to government-controlled areas in 1962 because the government was offering them anything positive. They were moving primarily to avoid the incessant Communist demands for food, labor, and military service and secondarily to avoid the occasional attacks mounted by the South Vietnamese air force on Communist-controlled villages.

In the Central Highlands in 1954–1965, the strategic importance of food can hardly be overstated. This was the least agriculturally productive area of South Vietnam, and traditional Highland communities normally lived not far above the basic subsistence level. Communist forces in this region perpetually suffered from malnutrition and were sometimes actually starving. The year 1962 seems to have been the worst, but the problem of food supply would impede the Communist war effort in the Central Highlands to the end of 1965 and beyond.

It is perhaps no coincidence that one of the most influential and effective leaders in the Central Highlands in late 1961 and 1962 was Dave Nuttle, an agriculture expert and amateur hunter who initiated and played the principal role in managing the Buon Enao project. Perhaps Buon Enao's greatest appeal to Highlanders was the sheer quantity and quality of the food it generated and its success in hanging on to that food, denying it to the Communists. At a higher level, the project gave Highlanders the feeling that they could deal with the modern world on their own terms, embracing its obvious benefits, such as superior agricultural science, medicine, and weaponry, while maintaining a strong sense of their own identity. But food was fundamental.

During 1962, however, the Diem government decided it did not need the Buon Enao program. Diem apparently thought the excessive demands being made on the Highlanders were sufficient to turn them against the Communists. At the same time, Buon Enao's very success made it dangerous to the government's authority. In a substantial part of Darlac, a large number of heavily armed Highlanders had achieved a sort of quasi-autonomy. While they were certainly keeping the Communists out of their area, they were also restricting the access of ARVN troops. This was unacceptable. Highlanders were developing ideas above their station. They needed to be put in their place.

From Diem's viewpoint, the fears engendered by the Buon Enao experiment were, to some degree, understandable. Yet the decision to close the project down was utterly negative and very damaging to the anti-Communist war effort in the Central Highlands. The closure of Buon Enao represented, indeed, Diem's authoritarianism at its worst. If the president troubled to make a risk assessment, he got it wrong. The Communists, not the Highlanders working with the Americans, were by far the greatest threat to his regime in this region. Significantly, some Vietnamese officers who were personally loyal to Diem thought that shutting down the Buon Enao experiment was a big mistake.

The closure of Buon Enao was in some ways linked with Operation Switchback, the US Army's takeover of CIDG from the CIA and the subsequent militarization of CIDG. Inter-American tensions and disputes over Switchback prevented the Americans from making a determined defense of what was quite clearly their most imaginative and successful counterinsurgency initiative anywhere in South Vietnam.

By the beginning of 1963, the process of transforming CIDG was well under way. Gradually, it ceased to be primarily a system of defending the villages of minority peoples against Communist penetration. Instead, it became essentially a program of recruiting indigenous mercenaries from minority groups, giving them American military training and pay, and putting them (sometimes accompanied by wives and families and sometimes not) in military outposts that might be remote from their native districts. Because the South Vietnamese government did not fully trust CIDG troops, it placed groups of Vietnamese Special Forces in every CIDG camp to keep an eye on them. Sometimes the presence of these Vietnamese personnel in CIDG camps was a serious source of friction.

Some of the problems with CIDG's new direction were illustrated by the attack on the Plei Mrong camp early in 1963. Though the camp was not entirely overrun, great damage and loss were inflicted, and the action amounted to a small Communist victory. The Plei Mrong attack was part of a determined Communist effort to restore a degree of initiative in the Central Highlands in 1963 after the nightmarish year the Party's forces had experienced in that region in 1962. As in late 1961, however, serious Communist offensive military efforts in 1963 depended on ethnic Vietnamese main force units recruited outside the region. This was the case with Plei Mrong, with Vic Klum, and with other little victories won in the first half of the year. A few small Vietnamese main force units were kept in the Highlands over the long term. Other larger units were brought in from the coastal plain on a short-term basis for particular missions.

But the small Communist victories in the Central Highlands in the first half of 1963 went against the general tide of the war in this region at this period. In general, the ARVN in the Central Highlands was becoming more aggressive and was mounting big operations against Communist base areas. Some of these operations had occurred in 1962, but both the scale and the frequency increased in the first half of 1963, especially in the northern part of the Highlands.

The Americans sometimes criticized such operations because the amount of contact achieved with Communist troops was often very limited (though the same would often be true of American operations later in the war). But getting involved in firefights with Communist soldiers was not the main point of incursions into Communist base areas. The principal purposes were to show Communist forces they were not completely safe anywhere, to deny them the strategic initiative by causing them massive disruption and by taking away and destroying the resources they needed. The destruction of crops and food stores, the killing or driving away of livestock, and the rounding up and removal of civilians were crucial in the Highlands. Such activities hit the Communists where it really hurt, forcing their troops to face the prospect of starvation.

Despite some small Communist victories, the initiative in the Central Highlands in the first half of 1963 was largely in South Vietnamese government hands. From July onward, however, the Diem government lost the military initiative in South Vietnam as a whole. The Communists staged a powerful offensive that lasted from July to early October and was renewed in November after Diem was overthrown. Exactly how and why the tide of the war turned at this time are questions that have not been answered or even fully addressed in these pages. It is quite clear that the shift in the fortunes of war occurred not initially or principally in the Central Highlands but in the lowlands, especially the Mekong Delta.

The failure of South Vietnamese government forces to deal adequately with the powerful Communist offensive of July–October 1963 has been attributed to the progressive American abandonment (indeed, progressive American subversion) of the Diem regime, to the Buddhist crisis, and to senior ARVN officers' preoccupation with internal politics and the plotting of a coup. These factors must have contributed to the military reverses suffered by government forces. Yet a full and proper evaluation is difficult. No historian writing in the English language seems to have attempted a detailed narrative and analysis of the actual fighting during this period of the war.

Most of the fighting in July–October 1963 occurred in areas other than the Central Highlands. Yet things started to go wrong for the South Vietnamese government there too. As many people had warned, the dismantling of the Buon Enao project and its replacement with a Strategic Hamlet Program, which in Darlac was underresourced and inadequate, massively demoralized

Highlanders who had earlier committed themselves to the anti-Communist side. Some Rhade had explicitly warned that, given the inadequate weaponry the government had left them with after the termination of the Buon Enao program, their people would not fight to deny Communist troops access to their villages. Indeed, in the latter half of 1963, Communist troops entered many villages in Darlac and carried off hundreds of weapons practically unopposed.

The Strategic Hamlet Program had, however, considerable importance in some parts of the Central Highlands, as it did on the coastal plain. In 1962 the ARVN 22d and 23d Divisions had developed ambitious programs to get most of the civilian population of the Central Highlands into strategic hamlets by 1963. Assessing the progress and the subsequent decline of the Strategic Hamlet Program in 1962–1964 is difficult because statistics on that program are known to be seriously unreliable where they are available at all. It is clear that after the coup of November 1963, the Communists attacked the program vigorously, especially in Kontum, Pleiku, Phu Bon, and Darlac, wrecking a substantial number of defended villages and in some cases removing their inhabitants.

The South Vietnamese administration and armed forces were plunged into chaos by the coup of November 1963, and the ongoing political instability diminished their effectiveness throughout 1964. In the Central Highlands, government control of the population tended to shrink significantly, and by the end of the year, it rarely extended far beyond the provincial capitals and district towns. Yet for most of 1964, the Communists had little military muscle in the Central Highlands—just three small battalions of ethnic Vietnamese main force troops in the whole region. Even counting their distinctly second- or third-rate units of Highland local force troops and militia, the Communist military forces in the Central Highlands were massively outnumbered. In the first half of 1964, moreover, some Communist bases in the Central Highlands were subjected to major incursions by the ARVN.

When Military Region 5 was called on to organize some military actions in the Highlands as part of the major Communist offensive of July 1964, the best it could manage was a big road ambush and an attack on the Special Forces–CIDG camp at Polei Krong. Both operations were executed by ethnic Vietnamese main force units recruited from outside the Central Highlands. Overrunning the extremely dysfunctional Polei Krong CIDG camp was by far the biggest Communist victory in the Central Highlands in 1964. In this region there was a huge gap between the aspirations of Le Duan and the high command in Hanoi (who wanted a speedy knockout blow against the Saigon government after the fall of Diem) and the actual situation on the ground.

Indeed, the most worrying event for the anti-Communist side in the Central Highlands in 1964 was not even a Communist military operation. The outbreak of mutiny in CIDG camps in Darlac in September 1964 was perceived by the Americans and the South Vietnamese as a major crisis. No one knew whether it was likely to spread to other CIDG camps in the Highlands or to what extent it might become a general armed uprising of the native peoples of the region. In the event, the mutiny was contained. In its aftermath, however, everyone became aware of the existence of FULRO, a Highland political movement much more radical that the earlier Bajaraka, of which the charismatic and prestigious Rhade leader Y-Bham was at least the figurehead. From this point onward, there was widespread suspicion among both American and South Vietnamese officers that the real political allegiance of many CIDG Strike Force members in the Central Highlands was to FULRO, not the Saigon government.

In 1964 the South Vietnamese government could not claim much real population control outside the provincial capitals and district towns of the Central Highlands. That does not mean, however, that the Communists controlled the rest of the population. In reality, large numbers of people lived in a sort of no-man's-land. The Communist Party's own statistics indicate that at the beginning of 1965, in the area the Party called Gia Lai (which included Pleiku Province and parts of Binh Dinh and Phu Bon), the Communists controlled only a modest proportion of the population. A dramatic increase in the number of people under Party control came only with the major military operations mounted after Tet, principally by PAVN regiments that had started moving down the Ho Chi Minh Trail in the last quarter of 1964.

The presence of relatively large, powerful Communist main force units in the Central Highlands in 1965, coupled with the fact that the withdrawal of troops in late 1964 had left II Corps exceptionally weak, threw South Vietnamese government forces on the defensive in that region to a greater extent than ever before. This allowed the Communists to get a real grip on much of the population outside the provincial capitals and district towns during the course of the year. Indeed, even some of the district towns fell into Communist hands. In Gia Lai the Party reckoned it controlled about 60 percent of the population in the last quarter of 1965, and this may have been close to the truth. But most of these people had fallen under Communist control only in the last few months. Given the exorbitant demands the Party made on them for food and labor to support Chu Huy Man's Plei Me campaign in October, it seems unlikely that many of them would have been keen for Communist control to continue.

This brings us back to the fundamental issue of food. Communist forces in the Central Highlands had encountered a devastating subsistence crisis in 1962. It may seem surprising that the high command in Hanoi considered it possible to have a number of PAVN regiments operating there in 1965. Between these dates, however, the PAVN had organized a major system of food purchase and transport in Cambodia that involved, among other things, the use of Vietnamese living in Cambodia and Cambodian army vehicles provided by that country's supposedly neutral regime. By the mid-1960s, the North Vietnamese were using a large part of the Cambodian rice crop to feed Communist forces in South Vietnam. They had established a depot in the triborder area, just inside Cambodia's supposedly neutral territory, from which they hoped to feed PAVN troops in the Central Highlands.

Nevertheless, the arrangements made in 1965 to sustain PAVN troops both on the Ho Chi Minh Trail and in the Central Highlands proved grossly inadequate. On the Trail the failure of storage arrangements seems to have been the main issue. In the Highlands the principal problem may have been a failure of the distribution system rather than an inadequate quantity of food having been accumulated. But this is largely speculation. What we can say with certainty is that virtually all the PAVN troops who operated in the Central Highlands for any length of time in 1965 suffered not just malnutrition but, at least at certain times, acute hunger. In addition, the inadequate supply of basic medicines (another long-term problem for Communist troops in this region) left a large proportion of them debilitated by tropical diseases, most notably malaria.

It seems to be a common American perception that the clashes between the PAVN and the US 1st Cavalry Division in the Ia Drang were the first substantial battles in the Central Highlands. In fact, whole PAVN regiments were in the region from January 1965 and started engaging in active offensive operations there in February. During heavy fighting in February–March and again in the monsoon offensive of May–August, PAVN regiments were sometimes joined by large Communist main force units from the coastal plain.

For the anti-Communist side, the presence of large Communist main force units in the Central Highlands in 1965 was extremely dangerous and difficult to deal with. As a result of Communist pressure elsewhere, II Corps' area as a whole, including the Central Highlands, had been left very weakly held. During phases of intense fighting in 1965, February–March and May–August, II Corps would draw heavily on Airborne and Marine units from the strategic reserve. Partly as a result of the assistance of these strategic reserve units, II Corps avoided any really crushing military defeats in the Central Highlands, even though it lost control of most of Kontum Province and large parts of Pleiku and Phu Bon.

To illustrate the relative scale of this fighting, it is worth pointing out that there may have been more Communist main force troops involved in the attack on the Special Forces–CIDG camp at Kannack on the night of 7–8 March 1965 than in either of the two principal Ia Drang clashes with the US 1st Cavalry Division in November of that year. Even though a US Army Special

Forces A-detachment was in the thick of it, the Kannack operation scarcely figures in most of the American literature on the war. Recent Vietnamese-language accounts make it clear, however, that it left deep psychological scars on some of the participants on the Communist side. In a relatively recent newspaper article, a former Communist officer is quoted as estimating the fatalities on his side at 400. This figure may be an overestimate, but it is also very unlikely that as many as 400 Communist soldiers died at either X-Ray or Albany. For the Communist side, it is at least possible that Kannack was the bloodiest of these encounters.

It was during the monsoon season of 1965, beginning in May, that the Communists had the best opportunities to cripple the ARVN in the Central Highlands, drawing in and destroying large parts of the South Vietnamese strategic reserve and achieving real dominance over a large section of the region. During the monsoon, the impact of the anti-Communist side's airpower was degraded to some degree. At the start of this period, moreover, the number of American troops in South Vietnam was still quite small. There was indeed a major Communist offensive in the Central Highlands during the 1965 monsoon season. But it is an episode of the war that neither American nor Vietnamese Communist histories have chosen to emphasize. It has been poorly written up and largely forgotten.

The campaign in the Thuan Man area of Phu Bon Province in late June and early July 1965 probably involved more troops on both sides than did either of the more famous clashes in the Ia Drang in November, and it may have been as bloody. Yet this campaign is practically unknown. In the West the military history of this war tends to be seen through American eyes, and only a relative handful of Americans were involved in ground operations in the Central Highlands during the 1965 monsoon season. From the point of view of the Vietnamese Communist Party, on the other hand, this is the "American War." Fighting against the Americans is easier to celebrate than fighting against other Vietnamese, especially when battles against the latter did not result in overwhelming victory. It is probably for that reason that the fierce fighting with the ARVN during the 1965 monsoon season seems to receive so little attention in modern Vietnam, compared with Chu Huy Man's Plei Me campaign and the ensuing clashes with the American 1st Cavalry Division in the Ia Drang.

What is most significant about the monsoon offensive is that, although main force Communist regiments badly battered South Vietnamese RF units and took control of a lot more territory, they generally failed to win the really big, decisive victories, annihilating or crippling large ARVN units, that the Communist high command was clearly seeking. Indeed, in a number of cases, most notably in the Thuan Man and Duc Co campaigns, Communist forces had the worst of it, sustaining by far the heavier casualties. Although only a small number of Americans were involved in this ground combat, American airlift and air strikes were often critical. The use of airlifts to get units from the strategic reserve to the right places at the right times was hugely important. And even during the monsoon, air strikes often played a key role in tipping the balance against Communist forces.

The Communists terminated their monsoon offensive in the Central Highlands in August, long before the season was actually over. The reason was almost certainly because the relatively large-scale intervention of the American army in the war was putting pressure on them in other areas of South Vietnam. PAVN regiments were therefore needed elsewhere. Of the four PAVN regiments operating in the Central Highlands (at least some of the time) between January and August, only the 320th/32d Regiment was still present for the Plei Me campaign in late October. Regiments 101A, 95A, and 18A had all left, although a fresh regiment, the 33d, had recently arrived.

The last major episodes of the war in the Central Highlands in 1965 were Chu Huy Man's Plei Me campaign and the US 1st Cavalry Division's efforts to pursue and destroy his regiments in its immediate aftermath. Although the Plei Me campaign has been celebrated in postwar Vietnam, it was badly misconceived. Even its opening date was dangerously close to the end of the monsoon season. The weather was dry and the skies clear through the vast majority of the fighting, giving the anti-Communist side a massive advantage. The "lure and ambush" scheme of operations, moreover, was transparent. Senior South Vietnamese and American officers soon developed a pretty good idea of what the Communists were up to.

A further problem was that Man's chosen instrument for delivering the campaign's decisive stroke was the 32d Regiment. Having been in the Highlands for the greater part of a year, the men of the 32d were malnourished, sick, psychologically battered, and, in some cases, demoralized. Its last big fight, near Duc Co in August, had ended in clear-cut defeat. Despite a serious South Vietnamese mistake that led to the ARVN relief force for Plei Me becoming divided, the 32d failed to destroy the relief force and suffered severe losses to its own troops. In the terms in which it was originally conceived, Man's Plei Me campaign was speedily defeated. Although a high proportion of the North Vietnamese casualties resulted from American air attacks, the PAVN was beaten without the involvement of American ground troops other than some Special Forces and some 1st Cavalry Division artillery.

Following Plei Me's relief, the initial aim of the US 1st Cavalry Division was to cut off and destroy the Communist forces involved in its siege and in the ambush of its relief force. Intelligence was still very vague as to what these forces were or where they were based. In reality, despite remarkably favorable conditions—clear skies and dry ground—the division's performance was initially rather embarrassing. The 1st Cavalry Division's operations in the Highlands made gigantic demands on the American logistical system in Vietnam, but far from being able to fix and destroy Communist forces in a series of vertical envelopments, it had enormous difficulty even finding them.

Its American pursuers achieved only the lightest contact with the PAVN 32d Regiment. Though in an extremely sorry state, that regiment got back to its base near the Cambodian border without fighting any major action against American ground forces. The 33d Regiment's retreat admittedly suffered a good deal more from the 1st Cavalry Division's interference. There were a number of contacts with retreating fragments of this force, the greatest success being the seizure of a small hospital for which some PAVN troops, for a few hours on 1 November, chose to fight. Even in this instance, however, the American airmobile forces were unable to fix their enemies, who broke contact within a few hours and disappeared.

The notion that helicopter mobility would allow the Americans to impose battle on big Communist units on American terms proved excessively sanguine and, as far as this campaign was concerned, almost entirely mistaken. Throughout the 1st Cavalry Division's 1965 campaign in Pleiku, it is difficult to point to anything that could meaningfully be termed vertical envelopment. Except in the case of 1/9 Cavalry's relatively small ambush of some PAVN 66th Regiment troops in the Ia Drang valley on the night of 3–4 November, PAVN forces generally fought the 1st Cavalry Division's troops when they chose to do so. Even in the case of the X-Ray action, when the Americans seized the initiative and achieved surprise, it would have been practically impossible to impose battle on the North Vietnamese had they collectively decided to refuse it. As it happened, PAVN troops of the 66th Regiment were all too willing to accept the American challenge.

American accounts tend to exaggerate the number of North Vietnamese involved in the X-Ray battle. It seems unlikely that Lieutenant Colonel Moore's force was ever under attack by many more than 400 PAVN troops at any given time. It also seems unlikely that more than about 800 were involved altogether. Yet the sheer intensity of the 66th Regiment's reaction to the American incursion into its Chu Pong–Ia Drang base area was enough to cause Moore serious anxiety at certain moments about the survival of his command. The PAVN's combination of ferocity with high levels of infantry skills shook the Americans. The PAVN, by contrast, was unimpressed with American infantry skills, which seemed not significantly greater than those of the South Vietnamese. The North Vietnamese were, however, very severely shaken by American firepower, especially by American artillery and airpower. At X-Ray the

PAVN was subjected to artillery fire and air strikes on a scale that neither it nor any southern Communist main force troops had ever experienced fighting the ARVN.

After being shaken by the ferocity of the North Vietnamese assaults on X-Ray, the Americans exhibited the same sort of cautious, somewhat passive behavior for which they had often criticized the South Vietnamese. Even though they were able to reinforce X-Ray massively during the course of the battle and in its immediate aftermath, they mounted no riposte when PAVN attacks ceased, undertaking no storm of the Chu Pong massif. Indeed, within a day of the end of the North Vietnamese assaults, they had completely evacuated the X-Ray position.

The fairly severe losses that the 1st Cavalry Division suffered in the subsequent encounter battle at Albany on 17 November (as well as the relatively small number of helicopters that were still flyable) led the Americans to curtail plans to continue the campaign by a joint operation with ARVN Airborne forces. Yet the ARVN went ahead with its part of this operation anyway, ultimately using five battalions. In the last episode of the Pleiku fighting of 1965, the ARVN Airborne Brigade, with American artillery support, inflicted considerable losses on the already battered and demoralized PAVN 32d Regiment. Subsequently, all three PAVN regiments under the command of Chu Huy Man's Central Highlands Front pulled out of South Vietnam to take refuge in "neutral" Cambodia.

It is sometimes suggested that the ultimate outcome of this war should have been obvious from events taking place relatively early in its course. This study has focused on the Central Highlands, and with regard to that region alone, it seems difficult to argue that developments up to the end of 1965 made the outcome of the war inevitable and obvious.

Certainly, the Diem regime made bad decisions and pursued mistaken policies that made it practically impossible to develop a trusting relationship between Saigon and the Highland peoples. Ideally, many politically conscious Highlanders, including those serving in the armed forces on the anti-Communist side, wanted a high degree of autonomy within South Vietnam, if not outright independence from it. Yet, with American mediation and guidance, the South Vietnamese government responded to the CIDG mutiny of September 1964 in a restrained and reasonably conciliatory manner. Highland troops continued to serve on the anti-Communist side. On occasion, as at Kannack in March 1965, they did so with distinction.

The Communists, in contrast, continued to make such extreme demands on Highlanders for food and labor that it is difficult to believe they were winning many hearts and minds. They may have controlled about 60 percent of the population in the area they called Gia Lai and perhaps 50 percent in the Central Highlands as a whole by October 1965. But most of that control had been gained as a result of offensives by PAVN units over the previous few months and was probably fairly fragile. The Communists continued to use units comprising mostly Highland troops for auxiliary tasks, generally not equipping them for or trusting them with major military operations.

The performance of South Vietnamese government troops in the Central Highlands up to the end of 1965 was very mixed. But the notion that it was universally poor is quite erroneous. There are too many references in Communist histories to ferocious, sometimes hand-to-hand fighting with South Vietnamese forces for such a simplistic view to be accepted. In 1965 the ARVN was generally reckoned to be at a low ebb. Yet Communist efforts to win decisive victories in the Highlands that would destroy substantial elements of the ARVN's strategic reserve had been failing even before the large-scale intervention of the American 1st Cavalry Division. During the last actions of the Pleiku fighting of 1965, American advisers reported that troops of the PAVN's 32d Regiment had dropped their weapons and fled during an assault by troops of the ARVN Airborne Brigade.

When the PAVN 32d, 33d, and 66th Regiments were withdrawn into Cambodia at the end of the Pleiku campaign, they were not only severely depleted but in a desperate state both physically and psychologically. Malnutrition and disease were, perhaps, almost as responsible for this state as losses in battle. We now know from the memoirs of their senior commissar that the collapse of morale and discipline among these troops was greater than anyone but the most extreme optimist on the anti-Communist side could have dared hope. In the whole of modern military history, there are few such graphic accounts of a collapse of this nature from someone with such a high degree of responsibility for the troops concerned. After Albany, much of 2/7 Cavalry must have been in a state of acute shock. But that was just one battalion. Even in that battalion, no one has suggested the degree of demoralization that Hiep describes as common among PAVN soldiers who had served in Pleiku–Gia Lai in October–November 1965.

In late 1965 the US 1st Cavalry Division was also withdrawn from the Central Highlands. As a result of wear and tear on its helicopters, the division had only limited airmobility at this stage. But the great bulk of its personnel were undoubtedly in much better shape physically and psychologically than the North Vietnamese involved in the same campaign.

All that could be predicted with much certainty in the Central Highlands at the end of 1965 was that a great deal of very hard fighting lay ahead. As is generally the case, victory might be expected to go to the side that avoided major operational and strategic errors and exhibited the greater resolve over the longer period. It is true that the Americans were already showing much more sensitivity to casualties than the North Vietnamese, and the American army was already having problems with the mass media that did not trouble the Communist side. But American losses were far lower than those of the North Vietnamese, and as far as troops who had fought in the Highlands were concerned, American morale was still much higher. Reading history backward must be avoided. It would have taken a reckless pundit to pick a winner at this stage.

Acknowledgments

A large number of people have assisted in the research and writing of this book—so many that I may not have been able to remember all. To any overlooked here I humbly apologize.

In December 2004 and January 2005 my Sandhurst colleague Ed Flint and I explored some of the routes of the old Ho Chi Minh Trail. In the northern part of the Central Highlands, we visited the towns of Kontum, Pleiku, and An Khe; the Catecka tea plantation; and the ruins of the Special Forces camp at Plei Me, all places that figure prominently in these pages. Conversations with Ed while touring these locations helped suggest the idea for this book. More recently, while he was serving at the Afghan military academy, Ed read and commented on several draft chapters. I have, therefore, a particular debt to him.

The basic idea of the book was discussed at an early stage with Professor Andrew Wiest of the University of Southern Mississippi, a friend and former colleague with whom I made my first trip to Vietnam back in 2000, and with Le Kim Huong, a former captain in the ARVN Rangers who has been my friend for almost thirty years. Conversations with CIA historians David Robarge and Clayton Laurie, during a chance meeting while the book was still just a vague conception, also proved helpful.

Early discussions with one of the US Army's current and one of its former official historians, Dr. Andrew Birtle and Dr. John Carland, respectively, were absolutely crucial. Andy Birtle was my gracious host at the Center of Military History in Washington, DC, on numerous occasions. Both he and John Carland helped me get access to documents I would not otherwise have seen. Dr. David Hogan, also of CMH, conversed with me about work he had done on Special Forces in the Highlands and commented usefully on some of my own writing on that subject.

Correspondence, in some cases extremely voluminous, with active participants in events described in this book proved vitally important. Dave Nuttle, Lawrence Arritola, Bonnie (Layton) Ensor, Hugh Murray, and Solomon Vaughn Binzer were all extremely helpful. I owe a particular debt to Dave Nuttle, who gave an immense amount of his time and who put me in touch with other participants. I had brief but useful e-mail exchanges, mainly relating to the siege of Plei Me, with writers Joseph Gallagher and John Laurence, both of whom witnessed at close quarters some of the bloodier episodes described in these pages.

Jon Strandquist, who became interested in Special Forces and counterinsurgency after his service as a US Army officer in Iraq, pointed me to a useful collection of records that I was previously unable to locate.

Merle Pribbenow provided a great mass of relevant Vietnamese Communist historical accounts in English translation. In a very long and voluminous e-mail correspondence he also offered the benefit of his vast knowledge of the Vietnam War, especially of Vietnamese Communist perspectives on it. My debt to him is inestimable.

All of the following read drafts and made helpful comments:

Lawrence Arritola, Solomon Vaughn Binzer, Dr. Gregory Fremont-Barnes, Dr. Andrew Birtle, Michael Briggs, Dr. John Carland, Dr. Christopher Duffy, Bonnie Ensor, Dr. Ed Flint, Courtney Frobenius, Dr. Thomas Goetz, John Hansen, Dr. John Hogan, Lieutenant Colonel Peter McCutcheon, Hugh Murray, Dave Nuttle, Merle Pribbenow, Dr. Christopher Pugsley, Jon Strandquist, Dr. Claus Telp, and Professor Andrew Wiest. I must give particular thanks to Andy Birtle and Merle Pribbenow, who read the entire book in draft and saw some chapters through multiple versions.

A large number of archivists and librarians gave crucial assistance. It seems appropriate to start with the Royal Military Academy Sandhurst's librarians, Andrew Orgill, John Pearse, and Ken Franklin, who provided practically all the secondary literature I asked for and pointed me to sources of which I was previously unaware. Ken was also constantly helping me out with IT.

At the US National Archives at College Park, Maryland, Dr. Mitchell Yockelson, whom I already counted as a friend from my days as a historian of the First World War, helped considerably. So did Richard Boylan, Martin Gedra, Jason Staton, Stan Fanaras, and many others.

Some debts incurred at CMH have already been acknowledged, but I must also thank James Tobias for his assistance in the library there. At the US Army Military History Institute at Carlisle, Pennsylvania, Dr. Conrad Crane was most welcoming, and I received considerable help from Michael Lynch, Guy Nasuti, Thomas Buffenbarger, and Richard Baker. I am grateful to Dr. John Prados for guidance concerning the resources of the National Security Archive at George Washington University and for an interesting conversation there about some relatively recent writings on the Vietnam War. The courtesy and consideration of its staff made a week spent at the Library of Congress very pleasant.

Conducting large-scale archival research on another continent presents challenges other than the purely intellectual. I owe thanks to my friend Dr. Tom Goetz for providing accommodation and to both him and Ken Eward for logistical and photographic assistance during some of my research trips. On some visits other friends, notably Dr. Bruce Gudmundsson and Jamie Hodge, also helped with transport, accommodation, and other practical matters.

I owe great thanks to the authorities at the Royal Military Academy Sandhurst, especially to the director of studies, Sean McKnight, for two sabbatical terms. Without them the project would have taken even longer. A lecturer's colleagues inevitably pick up extra teaching during his sabbaticals. I am grateful to the War Studies Department as a whole, particularly its head, Dr. Duncan Anderson, for the general willingness to assist in that way.

Gary Few gave major help with IT. My photo researcher, Amanda Carr, gave a level of assistance that was over and above the call of duty. Two firms, Alan Collinson's Geoinnovations and Christophe Wibaux's Business Maps, did their best to cope with my cartographic demands.

Conversations with friends and colleagues, especially Dr. Christopher Duffy and Dr. Klaus Schmider, sometimes over wine in the RMA's officers' mess, helped me preserve at least some outward appearance of mental balance at the more stressful stages of the book's development.

Last but certainly not least I must thank my publisher, the University Press of Kansas. Michael Briggs's expertise in the publishing of military history is well known to scholars in the field. He was involved with this project from an early stage and throughout, giving much encouragement. Kelly Chrisman Jacques and Jane Raese ably guided the book through the production process.

For whatever errors remain I am alone responsible.

Notes

Abbreviations

CMH	Army Center of Military History, Fort McNair, Washington, DC
FBIS	Foreign Broadcast Information Service
FRUS	*Foreign Relations of the United States*
MACV	Military Assistance Command, Vietnam
NARA	National Archives and Records Administration, College Park, MD
RG	Records Group
USAMHI	Army Military History Institute, Carlisle Barracks, PA
USASWS	Army Special Warfare School

Chapter 1. Vietnam and the Central Highlands to 1954

1. Vu Hong Lien and Peter D. Sharrock, *Descending Dragon, Rising Tiger* (London: Reaktion Books, 2014), 28–62.

2. Ibid., 62–125.

3. Ibid., 132–143.

4. Ibid., 153–175.

5. Ibid., 162–176. Joseph Buttinger, *The Smaller Dragon: A Political History of Vietnam* (New York: Praeger, 1958), 325–422.

6. Gerald C. Hickey, *Sons of the Mountains: Ethnohistory of the Vietnamese Central Highlands to 1954* (New Haven, CT: Yale University Press, 1982), 145–164, 207–259; Lien and Sharrock, *Descending*, 178.

7. Hickey, *Sons*, 78–120.

8. Ibid., 3, 144–189.

9. Ibid., 5–7.

10. Gerald C. Hickey, *Free in the Forest: Ethnohistory of the Vietnamese Central Highlands, 1954–1976* (New Haven, CT: Yale University Press, 1982), 1–89.

11. Hickey, *Sons*, 45–53.

12. Ibid., 7–9.

13. Ibid., 126–136.

14. Ibid., 263–271.

15. US Army Special Warfare School, *Montagnard Tribal Groups of the Republic of Vietnam* (Fort Bragg, NC, 1965), 1.

16. Ibid.

17. Ibid., 5. Hickey, *Sons*, 27–34.

18. USASWS, *Montagnard*, 11–12; Hickey, *Sons*, 23–27.

19. Hickey, *Sons*, 35–44.

20. Ibid., 290–384.

21. Ibid., 154–166.

22. Lien and Sharrock, *Descending*, 178; Hickey, *Sons*, 260–291.

23. Oscar Salemink, *The Ethnography of Vietnam's Central Highlanders: A Historical Contextualization, 1850–1990* (Honolulu: University of Hawaii Press, 2003), 73–99; Hickey, *Sons*, 292–308.

24. Hickey, *Sons*, 309–361; Salemink, *Ethnography*, 100–128.

25. K. W. Taylor, *A History of the Vietnamese* (Cambridge: Cambridge University Press, 2013), 532–534.

26. Hickey, *Sons*, 374–378.

27. William J. Duiker, *The Communist Road to Power in Vietnam* (Boulder, CO: Westview, 1996), 5–117; Lien and Sharrock, *Descending*, 184–188; Mark Moyar, *Triumph Forsaken: The Vietnam War, 1954–1965* (Cambridge: Cambridge University Press, 2006), 1–19.

28. Duiker, *Communist*, 117–131; Frederik Logevall, *Embers of War: The Fall of an Empire and the Making of America's Vietnam* (New York: Random House, 2012), 92–166.

29. Edgar O'Ballance, *The Indo-China War, 1945–54* (London: Faber & Faber, 1964), 54–55, 104–119.

30. Salemink, *Ethnography*, 129–130; Hickey, *Sons*, 403–407.

31. Hickey, *Sons*, 407–410; Research Analysis Corporation, "US Army Special Forces under the Civilian Irregular Defense Groups Program in Vietnam (1961–64) Appendix A: The Montagnards of South Vietnam: Their Military Value to the French," A6–A15, Historians' Files, CMH.

32. Hickey, *Sons*, 413.

33. Ibid., 429.

34. O'Ballance, *Indo-China War*, 187; Hickey, *Sons*, 427.

35. Hickey, *Sons*, 431–432.

36. Bernard B. Fall, *Street without Joy* (Mechanicsburg, PA: Stackpole Books, 1994), 184–250; Harold G. Moore and Joseph L. Galloway, *We Were Soldiers Once . . . and Young: Ia Drang, the Battle that Changed the War in Vietnam* (New York: Random House, 1992), 43.

37. Fall, *Street*, 184–250.

38. Hickey, *Free*, 1–89.

Chapter 2. The Diem Regime and the Central Highlands, 1954–1960

1. Gerald C. Hickey, *Free in the Forest: Ethnohistory of the Vietnamese Central Highlands, 1954–1976* (New Haven, CT: Yale University Press, 1982), xiii.

2. Ibid., xiii, xiv; Gerald C. Hickey, *Sons of the Mountains: Ethnohistory of the Vietnamese Central Highlands to 1954* (New Haven, CT: Yale University Press, 1982), 406, 410–413, 425–426.

3. Hickey, *Free*, 65; "Ethnic Area Development Concepts," 1 March 1963, 1; "Intell and Development Survey, D: Mountain-Cong System," sec. 3, 1, CIA-RDP78-06091A000100010001-4, CREST, Archives 2, NARA. The author of this CIA report believed that the Viet Cong were in the habit of promising to "help the mountaineer establish an independent nation."

4. Dennis J. Duncanson, *Government and Revolution in Vietnam* (London: Oxford Univer-

sity Press, 1968), 210–211; Thomas L. Ahern, *The CIA and the House of Ngo: Covert Action in South Vietnam, 1954–63* (Center for the Study of Intelligence), 24. Ahern indicates there is no evidence that the CIA influenced Bao Dai's offer of the premiership to Diem.

5. Duncanson, *Government,* 210–214; Mark Moyar, *Triumph Forsaken: The Vietnam War, 1954–1965* (Cambridge: Cambridge University Press, 2006), 211–214.

6. Joseph Buttinger, *The Smaller Dragon: A Political History of Vietnam* (New York: Praeger, 1958), 4–5. Moyar, *Triumph,* 32–37.

7. Thomas L. Ahern Jr., *Vietnam Declassified: The CIA and Counterinsurgency* (Lexington: University Press of Kentucky, 2010), 7; Moyar, *Triumph,* 33–34, 44–45.

8. Duncanson, *Government,* 217–222; Moyar, *Triumph,* 43–49.

9. Duncanson, *Government,* 210–232, 264–266.

10. Moyar, *Triumph,* 47–53; Carlyle A. Thayer, *War by Other Means: National Liberation and Revolution in Viet-Nam 1954–60* (Sydney: Allen & Unwin, 1989), 21–25, 37–39.

11. Moyar, *Triumph,* 49; Ahern, *Vietnam Declassified,* 16–17; Philip E. Catton, *Diem's Final Failure: Prelude to America's War in Vietnam* (Lawrence: University Press of Kansas, 2002), 10–11.

12. Ahern, *CIA and House of Ngo,* 77–92; Moyar, *Triumph,* 53–55; Thayer, *War,* 53.

13. Moyar, *Triumph,* 53–54; Duncanson, *Government,* 220–222; Thayer, *War,* 54–55, 57, 137.

14. Moyar, *Triumph,* 74, 58–59, 62–64; Duncanson, *Government,* 223–226; Thayer, *War,* 79, 92–96.

15. Moyar, *Triumph,* 57–58, 65–66; Ahern, *Vietnam Declassified,* 21–23; Thayer, *War,* 51–56.

16. Thayer, *War,* 142–145; Moyar, *Triumph,* 79–81; Jeffrey Race, *War Comes to Long An: Revolutionary Conflict in a Vietnamese Province* (Berkeley: University of California Press, 1972), 81–84, 97–104.

17. Ahern, *Vietnam Declassified,* 21; Duncanson, *Government,* 236–238; Moyar, *Triumph,* 71–76.

18. Race, *War Comes to Long An,* 130–131, 201–202. In his classic account of revolutionary warfare in the Mekong Delta, Race describes Major Nguyen Van Thanh, province chief of Long An, as an exemplary public servant who was honest, brave, and dynamic. Race indicates that the majority of public servants in this province in the early 1960s were essentially honest and that inappropriate policies were the real problem. Yet he also reports that "corruption was widespread" (46–47). Moyar, *Triumph,* 98, produces evidence from a former Communist cadre that an exceptionally honest and energetic district chief caused the Communists real problems in his area circa 1960. But Moyar also recognizes that there was widespread selfishness and corruption on the part of at least a substantial minority of officials of the Diem government.

19. Race, *War Comes to Long An,* 44–104; Moyar, *Triumph,* 91–98. Moyar is normally regarded as an admirer and defender of Diem. But in these pages he gives an interesting analysis of the Communists' superiority over the Diem government's leadership at the rice-roots level across much of South Vietnam in 1959–1961.

20. Duncanson, *Government,* 235–238.

21. Thayer, *War,* 21; Race, *War Comes to Long An,* 43–104; Catton, *Diem's Final Failure,* 25–71.

22. Race, *War Comes to Long An,* 5–43, 55–61; Catton, *Diem's Final Failure,* 51–71; Duncanson, *Government,* 240–247; Moyar, *Triumph,* 72–73.

23. Moyar, *Triumph,* 39; Duncanson, *Government,* 206–207; Vietnamese Affairs Staff of the Office of the Director of Central Intelligence, "The Highlanders of South Vietnam: A

Review of Political Developments and Forces," June 1966, 11–15, Historians' Files, CMH; hereafter cited as "Highlanders."

24. Race, *War Comes to Long An,* 25–28, 43, 89; Catton, *Diem's Final Failure,* 64–65; Moyar, *Triumph,* 65–66; Thayer, *War,* 55–56, 81–89, 114–119.

25. Brigadier General James Lawton Collins Jr., *The Development and Training of the South Vietnamese Army 1950–1972* (Washington, DC: Department of the Army, 2002), 12, 56; Race, *War Comes to Long An,* 71–72.

26. Race, *War Comes to Long An,* 105–140; Moyar, *Triumph,* 98–101; Ahern, *Vietnam Declassified,* 32–38.

27. "Highlanders," 10.

28. Colonel Le Ngoc Bon et al., *Nung Trang Sur Ve Vang Cua Luc Luong An Ninh Nhan Dan Viet Hung* [The glorious history of the heroic Vietnamese people's security forces], trans. Merle Pribbenow (Hanoi: People's Public Security Publishing House, 2006), 102–106. I thank Merle Pribbenow for bringing the Dong Van revolt to my attention.

29. "Highlanders," 10–11.

30. "Ethnic Area Development Concepts"; "Intell and Development Survey, D," 1–3; "Highlanders," 12.

31. "Highlanders," 12–13.

32. Ibid., 14–15.

33. Ibid., 15.

34. Thayer, *War,* 147–149.

35. Foreign Broadcast Information Service, trans., *Luc Luong Vu Trang Nhan Dan Tay Nguyen Trong Khang Chien Chong My Cuu Nuoc* [History of the Central Highlands people's armed forces in the anti-US war of resistance for national survival] (Hanoi: People's Publishing House, 1980), 9–12, Historians' Files, CMH; hereafter cited as FBIS, *Central Highlands People's Armed Forces* (page numbers refer to the English translation held at CMH, not to the Vietnamese original).

36. "Highlanders," 13. According to Douglas Pike, *Viet Cong: The Organization and Techniques of the National Liberation Front of South Vietnam* (Cambridge, MA: MIT Press, 1966), 205: "A Polish ship carried several thousand montagnards to North Vietnam during the 1954 partition; from these were selected agit-prop cadres to return to the South."

37. FBIS, *Central Highlands People's Armed Forces,* 10.

38. "Highlanders," 13.

39. Hickey, *Free,* 65–66.

40. "Ethnic Area Development Concepts"; "Intell and Development Survey, D," secs. 1–2, 1.

41. "Ethnic Area Development Concepts," 1; "Intell and Development Survey, D," sec. 3, 1–2.

42. "Ethnic Area Development Concepts," 1; "Intell and Development Survey, D," secs. 3–4, 2–3.

43. "Highlanders," 13–14.

44. Hickey, *Free,* 65.

45. Ibid., 49–53.

46. "Highlanders," 19–20.

47. Ibid., 20–22.

48. Ibid., 23–24.

49. Ibid., 24–25.

50. Ibid., 27.

51. Ibid., 28–29.

52. Ibid., 29–30.

53. E-mail correspondence with Dave Nuttle, 16 June 2013.

54. "Highlanders," 30.

55. "Resume of Information Concerning the Central Highlands Region of South Vietnam Prepared by Walter M. Forys USOM/PSD, Advisor to the Director of the National Police of the Central Highlands Region, July 1962," chart 2, "Viet Cong Incidents in the Central Highlands Region," Historians' Files, CMH.

Chapter 3. War in the Central Highlands, 1960–1961

1. Special National Intelligence Estimate (SNIE 63 1-60), 23 August 1960, "Short-Term Trends in South Vietnam," 1–4, in John K. Allen et al., *Estimative Products on Vietnam 1948–1975* (Pittsburgh, PA: US Government Printing Office, 2005); Mark Moyar, *Triumph Forsaken: The Vietnam War, 1954–1965* (Cambridge: Cambridge University Press, 2006), 101.

2. Not including the Diem government's other security forces (the National Police, the Civil Guard, and the Self-Defense Corps), the ARVN in late 1960 had seven infantry divisions and an Airborne Brigade. There were also three Marine battalions, a small air force, and a small navy. The total authorized strength of the national armed forces (army, air force, navy, and marines) was over 150,000, although they were somewhat below establishment. Brigadier General James Lawton Collins Jr., *The Development and Training of the South Vietnamese Army 1950–1972* (Washington, DC: Department of the Army, 1975), 17–20; "Command Histories and Historical Sketches of RVNAF Divisions," January 1974, enclosure to Airgram A-23, US Embassy Saigon to State Department, 6 February 1974, CMH.

3. On Diem's decision to create Ranger units (against US advice), see Collins, *Development,* 17, and Thomas L. Ahern Jr., *Vietnam Declassified: The CIA and Counterinsurgency* (Lexington: University Press of Kentucky, 2010), 35. According to the MAAG chief, Lieutenant General Lionel C. McGarr: "The original 65 Ranger companies were hastily formed in early 1960 and committed to operations without formal training." In 1961, however, MAAG was trying to rectify this, and the training of an additional twenty-one Ranger companies began in May. "First Twelve Month Report of MAAG Chief, Vietnam," 1 September 1961, 15, McGarr Papers, USAMHI. Former ARVN captain Le Kim Huong served with the 215th Ranger Company, formed from the 3d Regiment, ARVN 1st Division, in Quang Tri Province in July 1960. That company first saw action in the Mekong Delta in late August or September of that year. Telephone interview with and e-mail from Le Kim Huong, 8 August 2011.

4. Moyar, *Triumph,* 108–113. Moyar makes the point, also made by McGarr, that during a 1961 revolt, the bulk of the armed forces "quickly and positively rallied to the President" and demonstrated their "loyalty to the present government." See "First Twelve," 5.

5. Trinh Nhu, ed., *Van Kien Dang,* Tap 21 (Hanoi, 1960), 296–299, quoted in Moyar, *Triumph,* 101.

6. Mendenhall, Foreign Service dispatch, US Embassy Saigon to Department of State, Washington, 14 January 1961, "Viet Cong Attacks in Kontum Area," 1, 4–5, CMH; hereafter cited as "Attacks."

7. This order of battle material is drawn from two sources: Lt. Col. Walter D. Stevens, "Order of Battle Summary—Vietnam (South), 1 July 1961," CMH, and "Command Histories." The first source has useful material, but it was compiled some eight months after the

Kontum offensive of October 1960, and things were changing rapidly. The main changes that took place in the 22d and 23d Divisions between October 1960 and July 1961 can be ascertained from "Command Histories."

8. Foreign Broadcast Information Service, trans., *Luc Luong Vu Trang Nhan Dan Tay Nguyen Trong Khang Chien Chong My Cuu Nuoc* [History of the Central Highlands people's armed forces in the anti-US war of resistance for national salvation] (Hanoi: People's Publishing House, 1980), 14, Historians' Files, CMH; hereafter cited as FBIS, *Central Highlands People's Armed Forces* (page numbers refer to the English translation held at CMH, not to the Vietnamese original). On Military Region 5 and Inter-Zone 5, see Senior Colonel Tran Do, ed., *Tu Dien Bach Khoa Quan Su Viet Nam* [Military encyclopedia of Vietnam], trans. Merle Pribbenow (Hanoi: People's Publishing House, 1996), 477–478, 671, and Senior Colonel Tran Duong et al., *Lich Su Khu 6 (Cuc Nam Trung Bo-Nam Tay Nguyen) Khang Chien Chong My, 1954–1975* [History of Military Region 6 (extreme southern central Vietnam and the southern Central Highlands) during the resistance war against the Americans, 1954–1975], trans. Merle Pribbenow (Hanoi: People's Publishing House, 1995), 75–76.

9. "Attacks," 3–4; Gerald C. Hickey, *Free in the Forest: Ethnohistory of the Vietnamese Central Highlands, 1954–1976* (New Haven, CT: Yale University Press, 1982), 69; Vietnamese Affairs Staff of the Office of the Director of Central Intelligence, "The Highlanders of South Vietnam: A Review of Political Developments and Forces," June 1966, 31, Historian' Files, CMH; hereafter cited as "Highlanders."

10. "Attacks," 1.

11. Ibid., 2.

12. Ibid., 2, 4.

13. "Highlanders," 31.

14. "Attacks," 2–3.

15. Ibid., 3.

16. Ibid., 4.

17. "Highlanders," 31–32.

18. FBIS, *Central Highlands People's Armed Forces,* 15–16.

19. "Attacks," 5.

20. Nguyen Phung Minh, ed., *Nam Trung Bo Khang Chien, 1945–75* [Southern central Vietnam's war of resistance, 1945–1975], trans. Merle Pribbenow (Hanoi: National Political Publishing House, 1995), 282; "Highlanders," 33.

21. Telegram from the Embassy in Vietnam to the Department of State, 5 September 1961, in *FRUS, 1961–1963,* vol. 1, *Vietnam 1961* (Washington, DC: US Government Printing Office, 1988), 292.

22. The information about the use of the PAVN 19th Battalion in the Dak Ha offensive comes from Merle Pribbenow's translation of Senior Colonel Bui Bang Trang, ed., *History of the 305th Division* (Hanoi: People's Army Publishing House, 2009), 154, 272–274, which was received while this book was already in production. The information on other Communist units involved comes from FBIS, *Central Highlands People's Armed Forces,* 15–16.

23. Lieutenant General Nguyen Dinh Uoc and Senior Colonel Nguyen Van Minh, eds., *Lich Su Khang Chien Chong My Cuu Nuoc 1954–1975,* Tap III, *Danh Thang Chien Tranh Dac Biet* [History of the resistance war against the Americans to save the nation, 1954–1975, vol. 3, Defeating the special war], trans. Merle Pribbenow (Hanoi: National Political Publishing House, 1997), 137.

24. USARMA Saigon Viet-Nam to DA, 5 September 1961, and Lieutenant General Lionel McGarr (MAAG) to General Le Van Ty (ARVN Chief of Staff), 18 September 1961,

covering, "Analysis of Operations in II Corps Tactical Area 2–13 September 1961," CMH; telegram from Embassy in Vietnam to Department of State, 5 September 1961, *FRUS, 1961–1963*, 1:292; telegram from the Chief of Staff of the Military Assistance Advisory Group in Vietnam (McGarr) to the Commander in Chief Pacific (Felt), 10 September 1961, ibid., 296.

25. FBIS, *Central Highlands People's Armed Forces*, 16.

26. John J. Helble, American Vice-Consul in Hue, to State Department, Washington, "Security Conditions and Tribal Problems in Pleiku and Kontum Provinces," 12 October 1961, 1–2, CMH.

27. Ibid., 3.

28. On the government bombing of Highland villages, see Hickey, *Free*, 70–71. As early as October 1961 Lieutenant General Lionel McGarr, the overall MAAG commander in Vietnam at the time, was concerned about the apparently indiscriminate use of air strikes in II Corps, asking, "How do we know these villages were VC concentrations? Is ARVN using evaluated and factual intelligence information to plan and determine enemy strongholds as air targets before they are destroyed? As you know, indiscriminate destruction of people and property can lead to a most adverse affect [*sic*] on the Government of Vietnam and in turn on our own Government." McGarr to Wilbur Wilson (senior adviser II Corps), 9 October 1961, box 1, Wilbur Wilson Papers, USAMHI.

29. On "New Villages" in Malaya, see Richard Clutterbuck, *Riot and Revolution in Singapore and Malaya 1945–1963* (London: Faber & Faber, 1973), 175–178.

30. Helble, "Security Conditions," 3–5.

31. Ibid., 5.

32. Ibid., 5–7.

33. Embassy Saigon to State Department, Foreign Service Dispatch No. 131, "Provincial Notes: Darlac Province," 21 September 1961, 1–5, CMH; hereafter cited as "Darlac."

34. Ibid., 3–4. On the convoy ambush, see Hickey, *Free*, 70, and David Nuttle, "They Have Stone Ears Don't They" (unpublished account of Nuttle's activities in Darlac Province in the early 1960s), 2–3. Nuttle provided me with a copy of this memoir, but there are versions of it in US archives, including one under the title "Buon Enao" in the Colby Papers, Center for Study of the Vietnam War, Texas Tech University, referenced in John Prados, *Lost Crusader: The Secret Wars of CIA Director William Colby* (Oxford: Oxford University Press, 2003), 351 n. 22.

35. Ambassador Nolting's telegram from the US Embassy in Vietnam to the Department of State, 7 p.m., 26 September 1961, in *FRUS, 1961–1963*, 1:309–310.

36. "Darlac," 7.

37. A CIA report indicates that Diem considered the Rhade "more intelligent and sophisticated than other tribes" and therefore not as likely to "be influenced by the Viet Cong." This view of the Rhade was confirmed, in part, by American aid worker David Nuttle. "Highlanders," 32, 39.

38. Ahern, *Vietnam Declassified*, 39–42.

39. Ibid., 43–46.

40. Ibid. Ahern refers to Nuttle frequently in his discussion of the origins of the Buon Enao experiment, but always as "the volunteer" or "the NGO [nongovernmental organization] man," never by name. In Ahern's earlier work, *The CIA and the House of Ngo: Covert Action in South Vietnam, 1954–63* (Center for the Study of Intelligence), initially written as a CIA history for internal use, Nuttle is evidently referred to, but his name is redacted (toward the end of paragraph 3 on page 148 in the declassified online version). William Colby, *Lost Victory: A Firsthand Account of America's Sixteen-Year Involvement in Vietnam* (Chicago:

Contemporary Books, 1989), 89, refers to "a young American working for the International Voluntary Service" without naming him. But Nuttle is named elsewhere: "Highlanders," 39; Hickey, *Free,* 75–76; Shelby B. Stanton, *Green Berets at War: U.S. Army Special Forces in Southeast Asia 1956–1975* (London: Arms & Armour, 1986), 38; and Christopher K. Ives, *US Special Forces and Counterinsurgency in Vietnam: Military Innovation and Institutional Failure, 1961–1963* (London: Routledge, 2007), 15–17. His role is discussed most extensively and perceptively in Prados, *Lost,* 83–88; however, according to Nuttle (who was not consulted by any of the authors mentioned), Prados's version contains some inaccuracies, including the assertion that Captain Ronald Shackleton's A-113 was the first US Special Forces A-detachment at Buon Enao.

41. Nuttle, "Stone Ears," 1–2; Nuttle, e-mail correspondence with the author, June–July 2011.

42. David A. Nuttle, *Ede* (July 1962), an ethnological account of the Rhade, is contained in the CIA document "Ethnic Area Development Concepts," 1 March 1963, 90–120, CIA-RDP78-06091A00010001-4, CREST, Archives 2, NARA; Nuttle, "Stone Ears," 3–5; Nuttle correspondence; Prados, *Lost,* 84.

43. Nuttle, "Stone Ears," 2; Nuttle correspondence. The phrase "evident commitment to their welfare" is from Ahern, *Vietnam Declassified,* 45.

44. Nuttle, "Stone Ears," 5–6. Nuttle correspondence. Bonnie (Layton) Ensor, daughter of Gilbert Layton, has endorsed this part of Nuttle's account in e-mail correspondence and has provided me with some extracts from her father's unpublished account of Buon Enao.

45. Ahern, *Vietnam Declassified,* 45–46.

46. Nuttle, "Stone Ears," 8.

47. Frederick Nolting, *From Trust to Tragedy: The Political Memoirs of Frederick Nolting, Kennedy's Ambassador to Diem's Vietnam* (New York: Praeger, 1988), 1–31.

48. Nuttle, "Stone Ears," 8–9.

49. Ibid., 11–12; Hickey, *Free,* 73–75; Ahern, *Vietnam Declassified,* 45–48; Captain Ronald Shackleton, "Manual for Village Defense and Associated Development: Based on Experiences at Buon Enao, Ban Me Thuot, Vietnam, Darlac Province, 1 November 1961–1 July 1962," 8, in "Ethnic Area Development Concepts," 49–66.

50. Nuttle, "Stone Ears," 11–12; Nuttle correspondence.

51. Nuttle, "Stone Ears," 12; Nuttle correspondence; Ahern, *Vietnam Declassified,* 47.

52. Nuttle, "Stone Ears," 13; Prados, *Lost,* 86.

53. Ahern, *Vietnam Declassified,* 47; Nuttle correspondence. Ahern states that the Americans told village elders at Buon Enao that "any bug between the foot and the rug" would be crushed. Nuttle points out that the Rhade did not use rugs and would not have understood this concept. He used the elephant-grass analogy.

54. Nuttle, "Stone Ears," 13–14; Nuttle correspondence.

55. Shackleton, "Manual," 7; Ahern, *Vietnam Declassified,* 48; Nuttle, "Stone Ears," 13–15; Nuttle correspondence.

56. Nuttle, "Stone Ears," 14–15; Nuttle correspondence; Prados, *Lost,* 86; Ensor correspondence, containing extracts from her father's account of Buon Enao.

57. Prados, *Lost,* 87, indicates that Captain Ronald Shackleton's A-113 was the first US Special Forces A-detachment at Buon Enao, but Shackleton's team did not arrive until February 1962. Captain Larry Arritola's A-35 was present in December 1961, as both Nuttle and Arritola have confirmed. The exact date is uncertain. Ahern, *Vietnam Declassified,* 54, states 12 December. Nuttle has suggested 2 December. Perhaps the most likely date is 4 December, given in Colonel Francis J. Kelly, *US Army Special Forces: 1961–1971* (Washington,

DC: Department of the Army, 1973), 184, as the date Buon Enao opened as an American Special Forces camp. The notion that A-113 was the first at Buon Enao may derive from its commander's published account. Colonel Ronald A. Shackleton, *Village Defense: Initial Special Forces Operations in Vietnam* (Arvada, CO: Phoenix Press, 1975), does not mention Nuttle, Layton, the CIA, or any A-detachment before his own. Perhaps taking his cue from Shackleton, Charles M. Simpson III, *Inside the Green Berets: The First Thirty Years: A History of the U.S. Army Special Forces* (London: Arms & Armour Press, 1983), 102–103, states that A-113 was the first at Buon Enao. Prados apparently followed Shackleton and Simpson. The mistake is not universal, however. Hickey, *Free,* 77, identifies A-35 as the first at Buon Enao (although he states that it arrived from Laos when it actually came from Okinawa via Saigon). Kelly, *US Army Special Forces,* 25, and Ives, *US Special Forces,* 19, also identify A-35 as the first.

58. Nuttle, "Stone Ears," 15–17; Nuttle correspondence; Ahern, *Vietnam Declassified,* 51.

59. "Highlanders," 34–37; Hickey, *Free,* 77–78; Ahern, *Vietnam Declassified,* 62–68.

60. Memorandum from the Deputy Director of the Vietnam Task Force (Wood) to the Deputy Assistant Secretary of State for Far Eastern Affairs, 14 November 1961, "Viet Cong Infiltration: Nature and Extent," in *FRUS, 1961–1963,* 1:596.

61. Ibid., 597; "Highlanders," 40; Wilson to General Timmes, Chief Army Section MAAG, 24 November 1961, box 1, Wilbur Wilson Papers, USAMHI.

62. "Highlanders," 33. As early as November 1960, an armed patrol of the Cong An (Surete, or political police) reportedly encountered and killed, on the border of Darlac and Tuyen Duc Provinces, three Viet Cong cadres carrying 10,000 propaganda leaflets printed in the North. Walter M. Forys, Public Safety Adviser (Rural), to John F. McCabe, Public Safety Division, "Visit to the Central Highlands Region of Police and Surete Services in Vietnam," 2 October 1961, 3, CMH.

Chapter 4. Buon Enao and the Civilian Irregular Defense Group Program, 1962

1. The historian who has done the most to call attention to the Diem government's fight-back in 1962 is Mark Moyar in *Triumph Forsaken: The Vietnam War, 1954–1965* (Cambridge: Cambridge University Press, 2006), 148–185. Brigadier General James Lawton Collins Jr., *The Development and Training of the South Vietnamese Army 1950–1972* (Washington, DC: Department of the Army, 2002), 20–30, also emphasizes successes for the anti-Communist war effort by the end of 1962.

2. Moyar's use of the term "triumph" when referring to the Diem government's 1962–1963 counteroffensive in the title of his 2006 book on the Vietnam War is unfortunate. Although some well-placed witnesses perceived the anti-Communist side to be making progress or even "winning" in the latter half of 1962 and early 1963, they typically saw a longish road ahead with pitfalls along the way. An American report indicated: "The GVN is making progress against the VC but it is still too early to predict assured success in the counterinsurgency effort." "Status Report on Southeast Asia, Prepared by the Southeast Asia Task Force," 27 June 1962, in *FRUS, 1961–1963,* vol. 2, *Vietnam, 1962* (Washington, DC: US Government Printing Office, 1990), 478–479. The British counterinsurgency adviser Sir Robert Thompson took a similar line; see Ian F. W. Beckett, "Robert Thompson and the British Advisory Mission to South Vietnam, 1961–1965," *Small Wars and Insurgencies* 8, 3 (Winter 1997): 55–56. In January 1963 Colonel George C. Morton, commanding US Special Forces in Vietnam, noted: "It is a funny kind of war and fortune changes sides frequently. I feel we

are winning but it will take a long time." Morton to Colonel E. L. Mueller, Chief of Staff US Army Aviation Center, 18 January 1963, box 1, George C. Morton Papers, USAMHI. The Australian counterinsurgency guru Colonel F. P. "Ted" Serong indicated: "We can win this war. It will take several years yet. . . . However it is possible to lose it quite quickly, if certain mistakes are made." "Report . . . to General Paul D. Harkins, COMUSMACV: Current Operations in South Vietnam, October 1962," 2, Historians' Files, CMH. These individuals professed that victory for the anti-Communist side was *possible,* but it is hard to find anyone arguing in late 1962 or early 1963 that there was any overall "triumph" to forsake. Communist infiltration into South Vietnam apparently remained at a high level in 1962 and increased substantially between May and July of that year. See "Report on Increased Communist Infiltration into South Vietnam from Laos," memorandum from the Director of the Bureau of Intelligence and Research (Hilsman) to the Secretary of State, 16 July 1962, in *FRUS, 1961–1963,* 2:521. Communist numerical strength in South Vietnam reportedly remained relatively static for much of 1962 at about 20,000 "armed regulars." See "Viet-Nam—Assessment and Recommendations," para. 1, memorandum from the former Political Counselor of Embassy in Vietnam (Mendenhall) to the Deputy Assistant Secretary of State for Far Eastern Affairs (Rice), in *FRUS, 1961–1963,* 2:596. But in the II Corps area, the number of Communist troops apparently continued to rise: "On 1 January 1962, the G-2 II Corps held an estimated Viet Cong strength . . . of 10,824. During the year this figure rose to 18,113." "Year-End Report of Viet Cong Activity in II Corps Tactical Zone," 12 January 1963, para. 2b, box 2, Wilbur Wilson Papers, USAMHI.

3. See, for example, memorandum from the Officer in Charge of Vietnam Affairs (Heavner) to the Ambassador in Vietnam (Nolting), "Observations in Five Provinces," section 4, "Problems with ARVN," in *FRUS, 1961–1963,* 2:363. Serong makes some scathing criticisms of the ARVN, especially its officer corps, in Serong to Harkins, October 1962, 5–36, Historians' Files, CMH. Wilbur Wilson, the senior American adviser to II Corps, was moderately optimistic at the end of 1962 but thought II Corps needed to be much more active in 1963 if it were to gain decisive results. Wilson to General Dinh, "1963 Combat Posture of II Corps," 23 November 1962, box 2, Wilbur Wilson Papers, USAMHI.

4. On desertion as a serious problem in parts of the ARVN, see Col. Wilbur Wilson (senior MAAG adviser to ARVN II Corps) to General Dinh, "Training in the 9th Division," 25 June 1962, para. 1. Problems related to desertion and to soldiers in the 9th Division being absent without leave are also mentioned in Wilson to COMUSMACV, "Spot Report of ARVN Training and Intelligence and Planning Matters of Interest," 29 June 1962, para. 2. Wilson was constantly preoccupied with training; see Wilson to Major General Timmes (MAAG Chief), "Proposal for ARVN Officer Training Tour with U.S. Army Units in CONUS," 17 February 1962, para. 1: "ARVN requires training at every echelon. . . . The fact is that as a general rule ARVN officers know little about training and do not voluntarily initiate training in their units unless so ordered." Some of Wilson's later anxieties and aspirations concerning ARVN training are indicated in memoranda to General Dinh. See, for example, "Training," 1 October 1962; "Cadres for Civil Guard Training Centers," 18 October 1962; "Refresher Training for II Corps Separate Ranger Companies," 25 October 1962; and "Training Estimate of the 42nd Infantry Regiment," 28 November 1962. Although these reports tended to accentuate the positive, the "overall general status of training of the 42nd Infantry Regiment as of 17 November 1962," for example, was reported as merely "adequate." Serious problems were found with marksmanship and with the maintenance of weapons, clothing, and equipment. All the documents cited in this note are from box 2, Wilbur Wilson Papers, USAMHI.

5. On rumors, see "A Strategic Concept for South Vietnam: Paper Prepared by the Director of the Bureau of Intelligence and Research," 2 February 1962, in *FRUS 1961–1963*, 2:77. Two VNAF aircraft attacked the Presidential Palace on 27 February 1962, causing "renewed mistrust" between Diem and his officer corps. Airgram from the Embassy in Vietnam to State, 23 March 1962, A-257, ibid., 266. See also memorandum from the Vice-President's Military Aide (Burris) to the Vice President, "Re: Threats to Diem," 16 April 1962, ibid., 330–331. Burris believed that the bombing of the Presidential Palace had "set off full-scale plotting against Diem to the extent that there are now three principal groups which have been organised to take over the country at the slightest provocation or opportunity." Into June 1962 there were recurring reports that many American military personnel in Vietnam also favored a coup against Diem. See Embassy to State, 25 June 1962, 7 p.m., para. 3, ibid., 468–469.

6. On ARVN promotions based on political loyalty rather than military competence, see Col. Wilbur Wilson (Senior MAAG Adviser II Corps) to Lt. Gen. McGarr (MAAG Chief Vietnam), "Organizational Requirements for Success in the Conduct of the Pacification Campaign in Vietnam," 15 October 1961, para. 3, box 1, Wilbur Wilson Papers, USAMHI; US National Intelligence Estimate 53–63, "Prospects in South Vietnam," 17 April 1963, para. 21, 8, document 02405 in *US Policy in the Vietnam War*, pt. 1, *1954–1968: Guide and Index*, ed. Brandon, Byrne, and Battle, National Security Archive, George Washington University, Washington, DC. In October 1962 two of the ARVN divisions in II Corps were reported to have considerable "over-strengths" in their headquarters but a serious shortage of officers in their rifle companies. "Many infantry companies have only one officer. More than two is rare." See "Increasing Present for Duty Strength of Officers and NCO's," tab 8, box 2, Wilbur Wilson Papers, USAMHI. On the attractions of Saigon and the infantry's lack of appeal for many ARVN officers, see "Report by Colonel F. P. Serong, Special Advisor to General Paul Harkins, COMUSMACV: Current Operations in South Vietnam, October 1962," 5–6, CMH.

7. Vietnamese Affairs Staff of the Office of the Director of Central Intelligence, "Highlanders of South Vietnam: A Review of Political Developments and Forces," June 1966, 39–58, Historians' Files, CMH; hereafter cited as "Highlanders."

8. Dr. Smith, an American missionary working in the coastal provinces of central Vietnam, told Ambassador Nolting in June 1962 that "many US military advisers . . . whose work . . . he greatly admired, had said repeatedly . . . that anti-guerrilla war was being waged in the teeth of a predominantly hostile population, made so by the inefficiency and ineffectiveness of the GVN; and that on this basis military campaigns were bound to be unsuccessful or ineffective. He said that this was the almost universal theme of American military officers in his area." Nolting's telegram to the State Department, 25 June 1962, 7 p.m., para. 3, in *FRUS, 1961–1963*, 2:468–469.

9. For a favorable view of General Paul Harkins and his bullish optimism, see Moyar, *Triumph,* 165–168. Casting serious doubt on the validity of Harkins's sanguine outlook in 1962–1963, however, is that he seemingly exhibited the same rosy outlook well into 1964, when the situation of the anti-Communist side was deteriorating rapidly and becoming dire. Part 2 of "Fact Book: Brief Summary of Major Activities and Accomplishments February 62–June 64," Paul Harkins Papers, USAMHI (actually a collection of documents relating to his time at MACV) includes an unsigned document titled "T-1: Summary of the Situation in I Corps Area of Operations (TZ) as of 14 June 1964," which begins: "The pacification of I Corps Tactical Zone is progressing inexorably towards the final victory over the Viet Cong." This statement was scarcely supported by the rest of the report and was contradicted

by events. When reporting to Harkins, US military advisers apparently considered it advisable to at least start on a positive note.

10. Wilson's cautious optimism in late 1962 was expressed in Wilson to General Dinh, "1963 Combat Posture of II Corps," 23 November 1962, para. 1, box 2, Wilbur Wilson Papers, USAMHI: "1962 has largely been a training and planning year for II Corps, although I will be the first to agree that II Corps operations have become increasingly effective in the course of the year."

11. On Thompson's moderate optimism, see Beckett, "Thompson," 55, and Moyar, *Triumph*, 207. For a sympathetic portrait of Colonel Serong and his role in Vietnam, see Anne Blair, *There to the Bitter End: Ted Serong in Vietnam* (Crow's Nest, Australia: Allen & Unwin, 2001). For Serong's relative optimism at this time, see ibid., 35.

12. Communist sources and the views of Communist sympathizer Wilfred Burchett are quoted in Moyar, *Triumph*, 182–185. For an indication of the extreme pressure the Communists were under in the Central Highlands in late 1962, see Senior Colonel Tranh Duong et al., *Lich Su Khu 6 (Cuc Nam Trung Bo-Nam Tay Nguyen) Khang Chien Chong My, 1954–1975* [History of Military Region 6 (extreme southern central Vietnam and the southern Central Highlands) in the resistance war against the Americans, 1954–1975], trans. Merle Pribbenow (Hanoi: People's Publishing House, 1995), 198–202.

13. On the American wish for greater combat activeness on the part of government forces, see Col. Wilbur Wilson to General Dinh, "1963 Combat Posture of II Corps," 23 November 1962, box 2, Wilbur Wilson Papers, USAMHI. On American plans for the counterinsurgency effort in Vietnam and the Saigon government's reaction, see Graham A. Cosmas, *MACV: The Joint Command in the Years of Escalation, 1962–1967* (Washington, DC: Center of Military History, US Army, 2006), 75–77.

14. "Observations in Five Provinces," memorandum from the Officer in Charge of Vietnam Affairs (Heavner) to the Ambassador in Vietnam (Nolting), 27 April 1962, section 4, "Problems with ARVN," in *FRUS, 1961–1963*, 2:363.

15. On the ARVN's increased combat activity in 1962 compared with previous years, and especially on night operations in the latter part of the year, see Moyar, *Triumph*, 165–185.

16. Cosmas, *MACV*, 76–79; Philip E. Catton, "Counter-Insurgency and Nation Building: The Strategic Hamlet Program in South Vietnam, 1961–63," *International History Review* 21, 4 (December 1999): 918–940.

17. On breaking the links between the Communists and the rural population of South Vietnam, see "Decree by the President of the Republic of Vietnam, Special Instructions on the Plan to Restore Security in the Third Tactical Zone," articles 2 and 3, 16 March 1962, in *FRUS, 1961–1963*, 2:238–239. On food denial as a feature of the anti-Communist war effort in Malaya, see Richard Clutterbuck, *Riot and Revolution in Malaya and Singapore 1945–1963* (London: Faber & Faber, 1973), 212–249. On the Diem regime's obsession with food control, see Nolting's draft telegram from the Embassy in Vietnam to the Department of State, in *FRUS, 1961–1963*, 2:122–124, and airgram from the Embassy to State, 23 March 1962, "Assessment of Political and Economic Factors in Vietnamese War," section 5, "Economic," ibid., 266: "The GVN and the VC are engaged in a battle for rice, the main crop of South Vietnam." On Diem's insistent advocacy of spraying defoliants on crops in Communist-controlled areas, see telegram from the Embassy in Vietnam to the Department of State, 17 April 1962, 5 p.m., ibid., 331–332.

18. There were reportedly fifty-five strategic hamlets in Kontum and twenty-six in Pleiku in December 1962, and there were big plans to expand the Strategic Hamlet Program

in those provinces in 1963. "Plan for the Construction of Strategic Hamlets in 22nd DTA," 10 December 1962, CMH.

19. In July 1962 the Buon Enao experiment impressed the US Army chief of staff more than anything else in South Vietnam. Lt. Col. Kinnes (Special Warfare Branch, Pentagon) to Col. Morton, 19 July 1962, box 1, George C. Morton Papers, USAMHI. Buon Enao so impressed the DCI that he produced a history of it under his own name. John McCone's "History and Development of the Buon Enao Project," 28 August 1962, is referred to in Thomas L. Ahern Jr., *Vietnam Declassified: The CIA and Counterinsurgency* (Lexington: University Press of Kentucky, 2010), 384 n. 28. The document apparently went through a number of drafts, but all remain classified (see ibid., 385 nn. 38, 39). Information on Buon Enao as a center for VIP tourism comes principally from Dave Nuttle's e-mail correspondence with the author.

20. David A. Nuttle, "They Have Stone Ears, Don't They" (unpublished account of Nuttle's activities in Darlac Province in the early 1960s), 5–8; Nuttle correspondence.

21. Gerald C. Hickey, *Free in the Forest: Ethnohistory of the Vietnamese Central Highlands, 1954–1976* (New Haven, CT: Yale University Press, 1982), 76; Nuttle correspondence.

22. Nuttle correspondence.

23. Ibid.; Hickey, *Free,* 76.

24. Ahern, *Vietnam Declassified,* 51.

25. Nuttle, "Stone Ears," 15–16; Nuttle correspondence.

26. "Rhade Plant Nursery," in "Ethnic Area Development Concepts," 1 March 1963, 120, CIA-RDP78-06091A00010001-4, CREST Program (declassified CIA material), Archives 2, NARA; Hickey, *Free,* 75; Ahern, *Vietnam Declassified,* 46; Nuttle correspondence; Captain Ronald Shackleton, "Manual for Village Defense and Associated Development: Based on Experiences at Buon Enao, Ban Me Thuot, Vietnam, Darlac Province, 1 November 1961–1 July 1962," section 7, "Problems of Associated Development," 11–12, in "Ethnic Area Development Concepts," 61–62; Ronald A. Shackleton, *Village Defense: Initial Special Forces Operations in Vietnam* (Arvada, CO: Phoenix Press, 1975), 113–114.

27. Nuttle correspondence; Shackleton, *Village,* 114–115; Ahern, *Vietnam Declassified,* 57; John Prados, *Lost Crusader: The Secret Wars of CIA Director William Colby* (Oxford: Oxford University Press, 2003), 86.

28. Nuttle correspondence; Shackleton, *Village,* 95–101; Ahern, *Vietnam Declassified,* 57–58; "Highlanders," 42–44.

29. Ahern, *Vietnam Declassified,* 56.

30. Ibid., 56–57.

31. Nuttle correspondence; Shackleton, *Village,* 115.

32. Nuttle correspondence; extracts from Gilbert Layton's unpublished account of Buon Enao provided by his daughter, Bonnie Ensor, via e-mail.

33. Shackleton, *Village,* 116–117; Nuttle correspondence; Col. Wilbur Wilson to General Ton That Dinh, Commanding General II Corps, "Radio Stations Banmethuot and Dalat," 20 November 1961, box 1, Wilbur Wilson Papers, USAMHI.

34. Wilson to Dinh, "Radio," 20 November 1961, para. 6.

35. Shackleton, *Village,* 117.

36. Ibid., 120.

37. Nuttle correspondence; Shackleton, *Village,* 60–64.

38. Shackleton, *Village,* 55–59. On the Strike Force's function as a reserve, see Detachment A-113, Company A, 1st Special Forces Group (Airborne), "Monthly Operational Summary," 25 March 1963, para. 3a, in Records of A-Detachments, 5th Special Forces

Notes to Pages 90–102

Group Airborne, box 6, Ban Duon, Buon Enao, and Buon Tah, Darlac Province, II Corps, January 1963–July 1963, RG 472, Archives 2, NARA.

39. Nuttle correspondence.

40. Shackleton, *Village,* 14–19. A number of reports about Communist suspects interrogated at Buon Enao who provided information on Communist units, weapons, propaganda methods, and demands on Rhade villagers are included in 5th Special Forces Group (Airborne), Records of A-Detachments, box 40, Detachment A-223 (1st Special Forces Group), Buon Tah Mo, Darlac Province, II CTZ, September–December 1962, RG 472, Archives 2, NARA. See, for example, the "Inquiry" (interrogation report) dated 14 November 1962 of a Rhade Highlander known as Ama Y-Bham: "[During] June 1962 there was a group of rebels (4 Highlanders and 2 Vietnamese) carried 5 MAS-49 and 1 MAS 36, came in the village of Buon-Kuop, called the people and said our people are obliged to work hard in order to get so much rice to food [*sic*] us because we were . . . to battle against the Americans and Ngo Dinh Diem's Government."

41. Telegram from the Embassy in Vietnam to the Department of State, 7 p.m., 26 September 1961, in *FRUS, 1961–1963,* 1:309–310; Shackleton, *Village,* 16–17.

42. Christopher K. Ives, *US Special Forces and Counterinsurgency in Vietnam: Military Innovation and Institutional Failure, 1961–1963* (London: Routledge, 2007), 20, 22. Shackleton, *Village,* 118–119.

43. Shackleton, "Manual," section 5, "Area Growth Systems for Village Defense," 9–11; Nuttle correspondence.

44. "Highlanders," 43.

45. Ahern, *Vietnam Declassified,* 59.

46. Shackleton, *Village,* 105–106.

47. "After Action Report Buon Tang Ju," in "Ethnic Area Development Concepts," 234–235; Shackleton, *Village,* 18–21.

48. Ahern, *Vietnam Declassified,* 59; Shackleton, *Village,* 39–40.

49. Nuttle, "Stone Ears," 16.

50. Shackleton, *Village,* 21–23.

51. See "Weekly Report Buon Enao," section 2, "Operations," para. a, 13 May 1962, in "Ethnic Area Development Concepts," 227; Shackleton, *Village,* 109–112.

52. Roger Hilsman, "Memorandum for the Record by the Director of the Bureau of Intelligence and Research," 19 March 1962, in *FRUS, 1961–1963,* 2:246–247.

53. For background material on the Air Commandos, see Robert L. Gleason, *Air Commando Chronicles: Untold Tales from Vietnam, Latin America and Back Again* (Manhattan, KS: Sunflower University Press, 2000). On Air Commandos at Buon Enao, see Nuttle, "Stone Ears," 16; Ahern, *Vietnam Declassified,* 58–59; and Detachment A-113, "Monthly Operational Summary," para. 3c, "Air Support."

54. Shackleton, *Village,* 109–110; "Buon Enao Project October, 1962, as Related by Art Fields, Master Sergeant US Army Special Forces Team Leader, Bill Chambers, Captain USAF, Air Commando Pilot, Charlie Jones, Staff Sergeant USAF, Air Commando CCT/FAC," 1–2, http://www.glanmore.org/Buon Enao/Buon Enao.html.

55. Nuttle correspondence; Shackleton, *Village,* 91.

56. "Buon Enao Project," 2–8; e-mail correspondence with Hugh Murray, former CIA officer based at Buon Enao in October 1962.

57. Nuttle correspondence.

58. Chalmers B. Wood, "Memorandum: Impressions of Darlac, Pleiku, Kontum and Kien Hoa Provinces," 3–4, Enclosure No. 1 to Saigon Embassy to State Department Dispatch No. 496, 28 May 1962, CMH.

59. Wilson to Dinh, "Radio," 20 November 1961; Nuttle correspondence.

60. Nuttle correspondence; "Highlanders," 48–50. By September 1962, Nuttle was very apprehensive about Colonel Trong's efforts to take over direct control of the Buon Enao project. See Nuttle memo, "Conflict over Control of B. Enao Project," 11 September 1962, in 5th Special Forces Group, Records of A-Detachments, box 6, Detachment A-113 (1st Special Forces Group), Ban Don, Buon Enao and Buon Tah, Darlac Province, January 1963–July 1963, RG 472, Archives 2, NARA.

61. "Highlanders," 49–50.

62. Jack Benefiel to C/MOS (Gil Layton), "Meeting Held in Ban Me Thout [*sic*], 19 November 1962," 23 November 1962, p. 2, para. 7, 5th Special Forces Group (Airborne), Records of A-Detachments, box 6, RG 472, Archives 2, NARA.

63. Hickey, *Free,* 79–80.

64. Wilson to COMUSMACV (Harkins), "Analysis of Viet Cong Activity in II Corps Tactical Zone," 9 September 1962, p. 2, para. 3, box 1, Wilbur Wilson Papers, USAMHI.

65. On Vietnamese-Highlander relations, see "Highlanders," 10–31.

66. Hickey, *Free,* 73–84; "Highlanders," 7–11.

67. Ahern, *Vietnam Declassified,* 82; Nuttle correspondence.

68. Colonel Francis J. Kelly, *US Army Special Forces: 1961–1971* (Washington, DC: Department of the Army, 1973), 28–32.

69. Details of Morton's background are from "Biographical Sketch of George C. Morton, Col. U.S. Army-Ret.," box 2, George C. Morton Papers, USAMHI. Morton regarded the Buon Enao project as "our most successful undertaking in the CIDG effort," attributing the success to Shackleton and Cordell, two Special Forces captains. See Morton to Colonel Robert W. Garrett, 1st Special Forces Group (Airborne), 3 November 1962, box 1, Morton Papers. Morton claimed to have a "warm and cordial" relationship with "Mr. Richardson," the CIA station chief, indicating that "the problems occur with Layton and certain of his para-military staff who have been reluctant to relinquish the CIDG Program." Morton was cheered that "Layton leaves in a few days, for several months at least. Benefiel and other less desirable case officers have gone or are going." See Morton to Col. George Blanchard, Director of Special Warfare, ODCSOPS, Pentagon, 22 May 1963, ibid. On Morton's concern about "Air Commandos . . . encroaching in a field that belongs to the Special Forces of the US Army," see Morton to Lt. Col. Ralph Kinnes, GS, Special Warfare Branch ODCSOPS, Pentagon, 19 and 21 July 1962, ibid. Morton complained, however: "My biggest problem is that I have no aviation." See Morton to Col. Ed Mueller, Chief of Staff Army Aviation Center, Fort Rucker, Alabama, 16 November 1962, ibid. On Morton's insistence that Special Forces personnel wear proper uniforms, see Morton to Col. Robert W. Garrett, 1st Special Forces Group (Abn), 18 January 1963, ibid.: "I do realise that . . . as a result of the Army taking over this operation, there have been considerable changes in the control and direction of Special Forces personnel. The free wheeling days of cowboy suits and double holster pistol belts [a caricature of the sort of garb worn before Switchback] are over." On the green beret as impractical headgear, see "After Action Report of Det. A-2 for Period 9 Sep 62 to 24 Feb 63," 28 February 1963, section 4, "Problems Encountered," in 5th Special Forces Group (Airborne), Records of A-Detachments, box 6, Ban Don, Buon Enao and Buon Tah, Darlac Province, II Corps, RG 472, Archives 2, NARA: "The green beret was not adequate for patrolling. It proved too hot and did not shield the face from the sun or rain."

70. Shackleton produced two somewhat different documents on Buon Enao for his superiors: "Manual for Village Defense and Associated Development Based on Experiences at

Buon Enao" and "The Village Defense Program by Captain Ron Shackleton." The latter seems to have been written first and was attached as a sort of appendix to the former. Both appear in "Ethnic Area Development Concepts," 49–76. Neither is dated, but Shackleton's account of Buon Enao was attracting comment in the Pentagon by mid-July 1962. See Kinnes to Morton, 19 July 1962, box 1, George C. Morton Papers, USAMHI, which includes this comment: "Tell Capt. Shackleton that his operation impressed the C/S [Army chief of staff, General George H. Decker] more than anything else in SVN [South Vietnam]."

71. Richard D. Burke et al., *US Army Special Forces Operations under the Civilian Irregular Defense Groups Program in Vietnam (1961–64)* (McLean, VA: Research Analysis Corporation, 1965), vol. 1, 48–49, Historians' Files, CMH.

72. Nuttle memo, "Conflict over Control of B. Enao Project," 11 September 1962; "Memorandum for Colonel Le Quang Trong, Commanding Officer 23d Tactical Area: Approval of Concept of Operations," 12 September 1962, Wilbur Wilson Papers, USAMHI; Nuttle correspondence.

73. Nuttle correspondence.

74. Jack Benefiel to C/MOS (Gil Layton), "Meeting Held in Ban Me Thuot, 19 November 1962," 238/CSD, 23 November 1962, para. 6, 5th Special Forces Group (Airborne), Records of A-Detachments, box 6, RG 472, Archives 2, NARA; "Year-End Report of Viet Cong Activity in II Corps Tactical Zone," 12 January 1963, 2, "General," para. f, box 2, Wilbur Wilson Papers, USAMHI.

75. Kelly, *US Army Special Forces,* 30–35.

76. Jim Morris, *War Story* (Boulder, CO: Sycamore Island Books, 1979), 1–195. This officer's memoir of three tours with Special Forces in Vietnam is highly informative on the strengths and weaknesses of Special Forces A-teams in the early 1960s. See also Ives, *US Special Forces,* 101–104.

77. Kelly, *US Army Special Forces,* 37.

Chapter 5. Refugees, Strategic Hamlets, and ARVN Operations, 1962

1. On the increasing numbers of Communist troops in the Highlands and the resulting subsistence crisis, see Vietnamese Affairs Staff of the Office of the Director of Central Intelligence, "Highlanders of South Vietnam: A Review of Political Developments and Forces," June 1966, 44, Historians' Files, CMH; hereafter cited as "Highlanders." On Communist troops arriving from South Vietnam's lowlands as well as from Laos, see Ronald A. Shackleton, *Village Defense: Initial Special Forces Operations in Vietnam* (Arvada, CO: Phoenix Press, 1975), 19.

2. The constant battle for control of South Vietnam's food is discussed in an airgram from the Embassy in Vietnam to the Department of State, A-257, 23 March 1962, in *FRUS, 1961–1963,* 2:271. On the general abundance of food in South Vietnam, see memorandum from the Director of the Bureau of Intelligence and Research (Hilsman) to the Assistant Secretary of State for Far Eastern Affairs (Harriman), 28 July 1962, ibid., 561.

3. On the Communists' implicit threat of violence to obtain food from Highland villages, see the report of the interrogation of an eighteen-year-old woman, H'Ngon-Eban, who was suspected of working with the Communists at Buon Enao on 14 November 1962: "About February, 1962 there were 5 enemies (1 Highlander and 4 Vietnamese . . .) came in the village . . . and said . . . our people must work hard to get rice to food [*sic*] . . . soldiers who went to battle against the Americans and Ngo Dinh Diem's Government. People are

forbidden to supply the Government and become his soldiers—[those who wanted] to work for Americans and Ngo Dinh Diem . . . would be killed." 5th Special Forces Group, Records of A-Detachments, box 40, Detachment A-223 (1st Special Forces Group), Buon Tah Mo, Darlac Province, II CTZ, September–December 1962, RG 472, Archives 2, NARA; "Highlanders," 41.

4. John J. Helble (American Consul in Hue), Foreign Service Dispatch, 26 April 1962, "Recent Tribal Resettlement in Kontum and Pleiku," 2, Historians' Files, CMH; hereafter cited as Helble, "Tribal."

5. "Viet-Nam: Project for Crop Destruction," memorandum from the Secretary of State (Rusk) to the President (Kennedy), 23 August 1962, in *FRUS, 1961–1963,* 2:607–608. Rusk had heard it suggested that "the most effective way to hurt the Viet Cong is to deprive them of food. Food is scarce in their mountain strongholds and food destruction there can be most effective. . . . The Vietnamese have been burning Viet Cong crops with air dropped napalm for some months."

6. "Highlanders," 44.

7. Memorandum by Chalmers B. Wood, deputy director, Task Force, Viet-Nam, Washington, "Impressions of Darlac, Pleiku, Kontum and KienHoa Provinces," 4, attached to Foreign Service Dispatch 496, Saigon Embassy (Mendenhall) to Department of State, Washington, 28 May 1962, Historians' Files, CMH (hereafter cited as Wood, "Impressions"); "Highlanders," 42.

8. Helble, "Tribal," 1, para. 1.

9. Ibid., 2, paras. 2 and 3.

10. Ibid., 3–4.

11. Ibid., 3.

12. Ibid., 3–4.

13. "Status Report on Southeast Asia, Prepared by the Southeast Asia Task Force," Washington, 27 June 1962, "Viet-Nam: General Situation Evaluation," in *FRUS, 1961–1963,* 2:478.

14. Wood, "Impressions," 4.

15. Helble, "Tribal," 4.

16. Wood, "Impressions," 4–5.

17. "Status Report on Southeast Asia," 27 June 1962, para. 5, "Montagnard Program," in *FRUS, 1961–1963,* 2:480; US Embassy Saigon airgram A-19 to State Department, 9 July 1962, containing the report "Montagnard Refugees in Four Provinces" by William C. Truehart, Deputy Chief of Mission, Historians' Files, CMH.

18. On Nhu's interest in developments in the Highlands in 1962, see "Highlanders," 44. On Diem's visit to Highland tribes, see "Record of the Sixth Secretary of Defense Conference, Camp Smith, Hawaii," 23 July 1963, in *FRUS, 1961–1963,* 2:546. For the Joint Chiefs' comment on the movement of Highland refugees, see Joint Chiefs to the Secretary of Defense (McNamara), 28 July 1962 (JCSM-563-62), "Chemical Crop Destruction South Vietnam," para. 6, in *FRUS, 1961–1963,* 2:562–564.

19. Joint Chiefs to Secretary of Defense, 28 July 1962; memorandum from the Secretary of State (Rusk) to the President (Kennedy), "Viet-Nam; Project for Crop Destruction," 23 August 1962, in *FRUS, 1961–1963,* 2:606–609.

20. Memorandum from the Joint Chiefs of Staff's Special Assistant for Counterinsurgency and Special Activities (Krulak) to the Secretary of Defense (McNamara), "Support for Paramilitary and Irregular Elements in Vietnam," 30 July 1962, in *FRUS, 1961–1963,* 2:564.

21. "Highlanders," 44–45. On Koho refugees in Tuyen Duc Province, see also Col. Wilbur Wilson (senior adviser at II Corps) to Major General Timmes (MAAG chief,

Vietnam), "Various Matters of Interest," 25 June 1962, 1, para. 1, box 1, Wilbur Wilson Papers, USAMHI.

22. The connection between the Highland refugees and the establishment of strategic hamlets in the Highlands is emphasized in "Record of the Sixth Secretary of Defense Conference," 2:547.

23. "Plan for Construction of Strategic Hamlets in 22d DTA," 10 December 1962, Historians' Files, CMH; "Highlanders," 40; Wood, "Impressions," 4–5.

24. "Plan for Construction of Strategic Hamlets in 23 DTA," 1 December 1962, Historians' Files, CMH.

25. Christopher K. Ives, *US Special Forces and Counterinsurgency in Vietnam: Military Innovation and Institutional Failure, 1961–1963* (London: Routledge, 2007), 20.

26. "Highlanders," 46–49.

27. Wilson's administrative zeal as a corps-level adviser is indicated by the sheer quantity of documents from the 1961–1964 period bearing his signature and the care with which they are organized in his papers at USAMHI. He could, however, appear "abrupt, abrasive and threatening" to junior advisers. See Robert M. Bayless, *Vietnam: Victory Was Never an Option* (Oxford: Trafford, 2005), 54–56. Bayless served as an adviser under Wilson at ARVN III Corps in 1963.

28. Bayless, *Vietnam,* 56.

29. Colonel Wilson to General Dinh, "1963 Combat Posture of II Corps," 23 November 1962, box 2, Wilbur Wilson Papers, USAMHI.

30. "Order of Battle: Viet Cong Forces, South Vietnam," 1 October 1962, "Introduction to Viet Cong Order of Battle," 4–8, MACV Papers, USAMHI.

31. "Plan for Construction of Strategic Hamlets in 23 DTA," 1 December 1962; "Plan for Construction of Strategic Hamlets in 22d DTA," 10 December 1962.

32. Senior Colonel Tran Do, ed., *Tu Dien Bach Khoa Quan Su Viet Nam* [Military encyclopedia of Vietnam], trans. Merle Pribbenow (Hanoi: People's Publishing House, 1996), 671.

33. "Year-End Report of Viet Cong Activity in II Corps Tactical Zone," 12 January 1963, 1, sections 2(b), 11, box 2, Wilbur Wilson Papers, USAMHI.

34. "Order of Battle," 8.

35. "Order of Battle"; "Highlanders," 40.

36. For example, the Communists achieved a local and temporary superiority against the village of Buon Trap, in the Buon Enao complex, which they overran on 24 July 1962. Thomas L. Ahern Jr., *Vietnam Declassified: The CIA and Counterinsurgency* (Lexington: University Press of Kentucky, 2010), 59; Shackleton, *Village Defense,* 39–40.

37. "Year-End," 2(h), 2–3.

38. Ibid., 2(e), 2; Wilson to COMUSMACV (Harkins), "Analysis of Viet Cong Activity in II Corps Tactical Zone, August 1962," 9 September 1962, 1, paras. 1 and 2, box 1, Wilbur Wilson Papers, USAMHI.

39. "Year-End," 2(d), 2.

40. Ibid., 2(g).

41. Ibid., 7(d), 12.

42. The American medical missionary Dr. Gordon Smith, who was generally well trusted by the embassy, told Ambassador Nolting that many of his converts in the central coastal provinces were "bitterly anti-government." Telegram from the Embassy to the Department of State, 25 June 1962, in *FRUS, 1961–1963,* 2:468–469.

43. "Highlanders," 56–63.

44. "Year-End," 7(d).

45. "Plan for Construction of Strategic Hamlets in 22d DTA," 10 December 1962, 2.

46. "Year-End," 11.

47. Brig. Gen. H. K. Eggleston, Acting Chief, Headquarters, US Army Section, Military Assistance and Advisory Group, Vietnam, "Lessons Learned No. 3," 11 April 1962, #1 History Backup Files, 30 March 1962–November 1963, William C. Westmoreland Papers, CMH Library.

48. Eggleston, "Lessons Learned Number 11," 5 May 1962, #1 History Backup Files, 30 March 1962–November 1963, Westmoreland Papers.

49. On the 42d Regiment's find, fix, and destroy operations in Kontum from August 1962, see Wilson to COMUSMACV (Harkins), "Analysis of Viet Cong Activity in II Corps Tactical Zone, August 1962," 9 September 1962, 1, para. 2. On the pressure the Communists experienced as a result of ARVN operations against their Highland bases, see Lieutenant General Nguyen Dinh Uoc and Senior Colonel Nguyen Van Minh, eds., *Lich Su Khang Chien Chong My Cuu Nuoc 1954–1975*, Tap III, *Danh Thang Chien Tranh Dac Biet* [History of the resistance war against the Americans to save the nation 1954–1975, vol. 3, Defeating the special war], trans. Merle Pribbenow (Hanoi: National Political Publishing House, 1997), 158–159.

50. Tranh Duong et al., *Lich Su Ku 6 (Cue Nam Trung Bo-Nam Tay Nguyen) Khang Chien Chong My, 1954–1975* [History of Military Region 6 (extreme southern central Vietnam and the southern Central Highlands) during the resistance war against the Americans, 1954–1975], trans. Merle Pribbenow (Hanoi: People's Publishing House, 1995), 98.

51. Detachment A-134, "After Action Report," 29 April 1963, 5th Special Forces Group, Records of A-Detachments, box 27, Detachment A-134 (1st Special Forces Group) Krong No, Darlac Province, II CTZ, August 1962–May 1963, RG 472, Archives 2, NARA. On the commencement of Operation An Lac in Darlac Province, see also Wilbur Wilson to COMUSMACV (Harkins), "Analysis of Viet Cong Activity in II Corps 1–31 October 1962," 12 November 1962, box 1, Wilbur Wilson Papers, USAMHI.

52. Duong et al., *Lich Su Ku 6*, 98.

53. Ibid., 99.

54. Ibid., 99–100. On the identity of Highland ethnic groups affected by the An Lac campaign, see Detachment A-134, "After Action Report," 29 April 1963, 7.

55. Duong et al., *Lich Su Ku 6*, 100–101.

56. Ibid., 102.

57. "Year-End," 1.

58. Ibid., 6–9.

59. Ibid., annex A and incl. 1 to annex A.

60. Ibid., 3(i), 14(n).

61. Ibid., 11.

62. Wilbur Wilson to Ton That Dinh, "Serious Incident Report," 5 May 1962, box 2, Wilbur Wilson Papers, USAMHI. The report refers to the burning of part of a Bahnar village by a racially mixed group of ARVN soldiers on 3 May 1962. Wilson demanded an investigation and that the culprits be brought to justice. See also "Highlanders," 46.

Chapter 6. Reversal of Fortune, 1963

1. Lieutenant General Nguyen Dinh Uoc and Senior Colonel Nguyen Van Minh, eds., *Lich Su Khang Chien Chong My Cuu Nuoc 1954–1975*, Tap III, *Danh Thang Chien Tranh Dac*

Biet [History of the resistance war against the Americans to save the nation 1954–1975, vol. 3, Defeating the special war], trans. Merle Pribbenow (Hanoi: National Political Publishing House, 1997), 211.

2. Mark Moyar, *Triumph Forsaken: The Vietnam War 1954–1965* (Cambridge: Cambridge University Press, 2006), 186–209. Moyar's claim that Ap Bac was ultimately an ARVN victory seems questionable, but his arguments that the ARVN's severe tactical reverses there were untypical of operations in early 1963 and that the whole episode has been blown out of proportion in some accounts are valid.

3. On the reversal of military fortunes, see CIA Office of Current Intelligence, Current Intelligence Memorandum, "The Military Situation in South Vietnam," 18 November 1963, CIA-RDP79T00429A001200050024-6, and "Special Report: Trends of Communist Insurgency in South Vietnam," 17 January 1964, CIA-RDP7900927A004300080003-6, CREST, Archives 2, NARA. That the military reversal in 1963 was almost entirely owing to America's gradual abandonment and ultimate betrayal of Diem is Moyar's general thesis in *Triumph,* especially 206–287.

4. Maps showing "Old Tactical Territorial Division" and "New Tactical Territorial Division," undated but probably early 1963, Historians' Files, CMH.

5. "JOC Weekly Resume of RVNAF Activities, 161801–231800 August 1963," 26 August 1963, MACV Assistant Chief of Staff for Operations (J-3), Joint Liaison Group (MACJ3–12), JGS JOC Weekly Resume, 19 April 1963–9 October 1963, box 1, RG 472, Archives 2, NARA (unless stated otherwise, JOC Weekly Resumes subsequently cited are located here); "Darlac Province, 31st Divisional Tactical Area," 30 September 1963, Historians' Files, CMH.

6. "Command Histories and Historical Sketches of RVNAF Divisions, Prepared in January 1974," enclosure to Embassy Saigon to Department of State, E.O. 11652, 6 February 1974, Historians' Files, CMH.

7. Ibid.; Robert M. Bayless, *Vietnam: Victory Was Never an Option* (Oxford: Trafford, 2005), 56.

8. Boxes 3 and 4, Wilbur Wilson Papers, USAMHI.

9. Debriefing of Colonel Hal D. McCown, senior adviser, II Corps, 18 October 1963, USAMHI.

10. Uoc and Minh, *Lich Su Khang Chien,* 211.

11. Ibid., 211–212; Shelby B. Stanton, *Green Berets at War: U.S. Army Special Forces in Southeast Asia 1956–1975* (London: Arms & Armour, 1986), 54–57.

12. Nguyen Khac Tinh et al., *Phao Binh Nhan Dan Viet Nam: Nhung Chang Duong Chien Dau,* Tap II [People's artillery of Vietnam: combat history, vol. 2], trans. Merle Pribbenow (Hanoi: Artillery Command, 1986), 71; Nguyen Quoc Minh et al., *Lich Su Bo Doi Dac Cong,* Tap Mot [History of the sapper forces, vol. 1], trans. Merle Pribbenow (Hanoi: People's Publishing House, 1987), 105; Foreign Broadcast Information Service, trans., *Luc Luong Vu Trang Nhan Dan Tay Nguyen Trong Khnang Chien Chong My Cuu Nuoc* [History of the Central Highlands people's armed forces in the anti-US war of resistance for national salvation] (Hanoi: People's Publishing House, 1980), 15–17, Historians' Files, CMH; hereafter cited as FBIS, *Central Highlands People's Armed Forces* (page numbers refer to the English translation). These Communist histories are wildly inconsistent on both the geographic location of Plei Mrong and the date of the attack. But all agree that both the 200th Artillery Battalion and the 407th Sapper Battalion were involved. Stanton, *Green Berets,* 55–57, gives an account of the action from an American perspective.

13. "JOC Weekly Resume . . . 031801–101800 May 1963," 13 May 1963, appendix I: "Definition of Terms Used in This Report."

14. OPLAN Nhan Hoa, 22d Infantry Division, Kontum, Vietnam, 1 December 1962, Historians' Files, CMH.

15. II Corps Advisory Detachment Daily OPSUM, 9–10 March 1963, RG 0472, US Forces in Southeast Asia, 1950–1975, entry P1674, Vietnam Refiles, container 161, Archives 2, NARA. Dr. Birtle of CMH informed me that a number of boxes of OPSUM and INT-SUM (operational summary and intelligence summary) files were being returned by the historians at CMH to NARA's Archives 2 at College Park, Maryland. He was allowed to see these files, but they were still in a transitional state and had not yet been given a final NARA classification, still being regarded as "refiles."

16. "JOC Weekly Resume . . . 131801–201800 September 1963," 23 September 1963.

17. "VC Regiments and Battalions Area of Operations, Source: JGS OB, dated 30 June 1963" and "VC Strength by Province, Main Force Plus Regional Units, Source: JGS OB, dated 30 June 1963," enclosures 9 and 10 to "JOC Weekly Resume . . . 161801–231800 August 1963," 26 August 1963.

18. On Communist offensives in Phu Bon in 1965, see Theodore Mataxis, "The Monsoon Offensive in the Highlands," 11–15, Mataxis Papers, USAMHI.

19. II Corps Advisory Detachment Daily OPSUM, 17–18 February 1963, RG 0472, entry P 1674, Vietnam Refiles, container 161, Archives 2, NARA.

20. Ibid., 12–13 March 1963.

21. "JOC Weekly Resume . . . 261801 April–031800 May 1963," section I, "Ground Operations," 6 May 1963, and "JOC Weekly Resume 101801–171800 May 1963," section I, "Ground Operations," 21 May 1963; Uoc and Minh, *Lich Su Khang Chien,* 211.

22. "JOC Weekly Resume . . . 261801 April–031800 May 1963," section 1, "Ground Operations," 6 May 1963, and "JOC Weekly Resume 101801–171800 May 1963," section I, "Ground Operations," 21 May 1963; CINCUSPARC Ft Shafter Hawaii to AIG 731, ACSI, et al., BA SGs, Bangkok Thailand, 30 April 1963, Historians' Files, CMH.

23. "JOC Weekly Resume . . . 031801–101800 May 1963," section I, "Ground Operations," 13 May 1963.

24. Ibid.; "JOC Weekly Resume . . . 101801–171800 May 1963," section 1, "Ground Operations," 21 May 1963.

25. There is a reference to both the 200th Artillery Battalion and the 407th Sapper Battalion attacking the ARVN 42d Regiment "in the base area north of Cong Tum [Kontum]" during May 1963 in FBIS, *Central Highlands People's Armed Forces,* 17.

26. "JOC Weekly Resume . . . 141801–211800 June 1963," section 1, "Ground Operations," para. d, 24 June 1963.

27. According to MACV, the 145th Battalion (Heavy Weapons), a 180-man unit commanded by Captain Ngo Tan Thai, was based in Darlac. See MACV, Office of the Assistant Chief of Staff—J2, "Order of Battle Viet Cong Forces Republic of Vietnam," 60, USAMHI. It is difficult, however, to identify any such unit in Communist sources.

28. Operation An Lac, which had commenced in October 1962, was still running in January 1963 on the Darlac–Tuyen Duc borders. III Corps Adv. Det. OPSUM 6, 060001 to 062400 January 1963, and OPSUM 19, 190001 to 192400 January 1963, RG 472, entry P 1674, Vietnam Refiles, container 162, Archives 2, NARA.

29. Colonel Wilbur Wilson to General Ton That Dinh, 6 May 1963, box 4, Wilbur Wilson Papers, USAMHI.

30. "JOC Weekly Resume . . . 021801–091800 August 1963," section 7, "VC Food and Medical Shortages," 9 August 1963, and CIA Current Intelligence Memorandum, "The Military Situation in South Vietnam," 4, para. 12, 18 November 1963.

31. Richard D. Burke et al., "*US Army Special Forces Operations under the Civilian Irregular Defense Groups Program in Vietnam (1961–64)* (McLean, VA: Research Analysis Corporation, 1965), 35–48, Historians' Files, CMH; Stanton, *Green Berets,* 52–54.

32. Burke et al., *Special Forces,* 45–56; Vietnamese Affairs Staff of the Office of the Director of Central Intelligence, "The Highlanders of South Vietnam: A Review of Political Developments and Forces," June 1966, 51–52, Historians' Files, CMH, hereafter cited as "Highlanders."

33. Stanton, *Green Berets,* 47. Burke et al., *Special Forces,* 35–37, 46–48.

34. Burke et al., *Special Forces,* 46–48; Stanton, *Green Berets,* 60–62.

35. Burke et al., *Special Forces,* 48.

36. Stanton, *Green Berets,* 54–55.

37. Ibid., 56–57; Special Forces Investigating Team, "After Action Report—Attack on Plei Mrong," 6 January 1963, Historians' Files, CMH. Stanton's account does not agree in all the particulars with the after-action report, but Stanton apparently had access to some Special Forces documents that I did not.

38. "JOC Weekly Resume, 161801–231800 August 1963," 8–9, para. 5, "VC Activity," b. "Significant Attacks" (3), 8–9, 26 August 1963; Colonel Francis J. Kelly, *US Army Special Forces: 1961–1971* (Washington, DC: Department of the Army, 1973), 186. An appendix to Kelly's book refers to the closure of a camp called Plei Jar in Kontum on 23 August. It seems practically certain that this was the same camp referred to as Polei Jar in the JOC Weekly Resume.

39. Burke et al., *Special Forces,* 48–61; "Monthly Report—CIDG Program in RVN for December 1963," 8–18, 5th Special Forces Group (Airborne) Headquarters, Assistant Chief of Staff for Operations (S3) Command Reports—CIDG, 1963–1965, box 1, RG 472, Archives 2, NARA.

40. "Monthly Report—CIDG Program in RVN for December 1963," 8–18.

41. Douglas S. Blaufarb, *The Counter-Insurgency Era: US Doctrine and Performance 1950 to the Present* (New York: Free Press, 1977), 107.

42. On Layton's frustration with the Diem government, see Thomas L. Ahern Jr., *Vietnam Declassified: The CIA and Counterinsurgency* (Lexington: University Press of Kentucky, 2010), 60–61. For Morton's assessment of the Diem regime, see "Debriefing of Colonel George C. Morton," 6 November 1963, 5, para. 1, Historians' Files, CMH. Although this document is dated five days after the coup, it is clear from the context that Morton is referring to the Diem regime.

43. D. Nuttle, "Conflict over Control of B. Enao Project," 11 September 1962, 5th Special Forces Group (Airborne) Records of A-Detachments, box 6, Detachment A-113 (1st Special Forces Group) General Records, Ban Don, Buon Enao and Buon Tah, Darlac Province, II Corps, January 1963–July 1963 RG 472, Archives 2, NARA; "Memorandum for Colonel Le Quang Trong, Commanding Officer 23d Tactical Area. Subject: Approval of Concept of Operations," 12 September 1962, box 3, Wilbur Wilson Papers, USAMHI.

44. Colonel George C. Morton to Commander United States Military Assistance Command, Vietnam (COMUSMACV), "Position Paper—Darlac Province," 9 April 1963, paras. 1–2, Records of A-Detachments, box 6.

45. Colonel Layton to Colonel Morton, "Weapons Recovery in Darlac Province and Return of Capt. Terry to Okinawa," CSD/414, 14 January 1963, Records of A-Detachments, box 6.

46. Report by Colonel F. P. Serong to General Paul Harkins, COMUSMACV, "Current Operations in South Vietnam," October 1962, 43–44, Historians' Files, CMH.

47. Lt. Col. Eb W. Smith to Colonel Morton, "Memorandum for Commanding Officer, United States Army Special Forces, Subject: Weapons Pick up Buon Enao," 22 January 1963, para. 2, Records of A-Detachments, box 6.

48. Layton to Morton, "Weapons Recovery," 14 January 1963, Records of A-Detachments, box 6.

49. Lt. Col. R. J. Billado to Senior Adviser III VN Corps, Saigon, Vietnam, "Pick up of Weapons from Buon Enao Trained and Equipped Villages," 16 January 1963, Records of A-Detachments, box 6.

50. Wilbur Wilson to COMUSMACV (Harkins), 17 January 1963, Records of A-Detachments, box 6.

51. Smith to Morton, "Weapons Pick up Buon Enao," 22 January 1963, para. 3B.

52. Lt. Col. John J. Sawbridge to Senior Adviser, III Corps, Saigon, Vietnam, 26 March 1963, section 4, h(1), 4, Records of A-Detachments, box 6.

53. Report by Colonel F. P. Serong to General Paul D. Harkins, COMUSMACV, on the situation in South Vietnam, March 1963, 17, Historians' Files, CMH.

54. Colonel George C. Morton to COMUSMACV, "Position Paper—Darlac Province," 9 April 1963, Records of A-Detachments, box 6.

55. Draft notes on "Meeting with Darlac Province Chief Regarding Turnover of Buon Enao Project," 4 June 1963, Records of A-Detachments, box 6.

56. "Highlanders," 50–51.

57. Ibid., 53.

58. Ibid., 53–54.

59. Ibid., 55–58.

60. Headquarters U.S. Military Assistance Command, Vietnam, Office of the Assistant Chief of Staff—J2, "Order of Battle Viet Cong Forces, Republic of Vietnam," 1 October 1963, 1–7, USAMHI.

61. Maps showing "VC Regiments and Battalions: Area of Operations" and "VC Strength by Province: Main Force Plus Regional Units," based on JGS Order of Battle figures for 30 June 1963, enclosures 9 and 10 to "JOC Weekly Resume . . . 161801–231800 August 1963," 26 August 1963.

62. "Special Evaluation Team Report" to Senior Adviser III Corps, Saigon, Vietnam, 30 June 1963, box 4, Wilbur Wilson Papers, USAMHI.

63. Enclosures 9 and 10, "JOC Weekly Resume," 26 August 1963.

64. "Special Evaluation Team Report," III Corps, 30 June 1963.

65. CIA Current Intelligence Memorandum, "The Military Situation in South Vietnam," 18 November 1963, 1, para. 4.

66. Dennis J. Duncanson, *Government and Revolution in Vietnam* (London: Oxford University Press, 1968), 330–337; Moyar, *Triumph,* 206–208; John Prados, *Vietnam: The History of an Unwinnable War, 1945–1975* (Lawrence: University Press of Kansas, 2009), 77.

67. "JOC Weekly Resume . . . 161801–231800 August 1963," 26 August 1963, 1, section 1a.

68. Moyar, *Triumph,* 238–243.

69. Wilbur Wilson to Paul Harkins, "Counterpart Observations," 16 October 1963, box 3, Wilbur Wilson Papers, USAMHI. Wilson commented: "General Dinh is by nature an emotional, egotistical individual who is somewhat carried away by his own importance. He has not been available at III Corps since 5 October 1963; he stated that he is not on leave but has been engaged in 'important activities.'"

70. The upsurge in Communist military activity in 1963 can be dated from mid-July; see "JOC Weekly Resume . . . 121801–191800 July 1963," 22 July 1963, section 1b, 1. For

major ambushes and assaults on government bases, see "JOC Weekly Resume . . . 061801–131800 September 1963," 16 September 1963, section 1, 1–7.

71. "JOC Weekly Resume . . . 191801–261800 July 1963," 29 July 1963, sections 1b and e, 1, 3–4.

72. A report on Darlac from the end of September 1963 indicated: "This province had second highest incident rate in 31st DTA for third quarter. Fifty-two different harassments and armed attacks were reported." "Darlac Province, 31st Divisional Tactical Area," 30 September 1963, Historians' Files, CMH.

73. "JOC Weekly Resume . . . 091801–161800 August 1963," 19 August 1963, section 2c, 2.

74. On the decline in Communist offensive activity in early August 1963, see "JOC Weekly Resume . . . 021801–091800 August 1963," 12 August 1963, section 1, 1. On the upsurge later in the month, see "JOC Weekly Resume . . . 161801–231800 August 1963," 26 August 1963, section 1.

75. "JOC Weekly Resume . . . 301801 August–061800 September 1963," 9 September 1963, section 1a, 1, and section 5a and b, 7.

76. "JOC Weekly Resume . . . 061801–131800 September 1963," 16 September 1963, section 1, 1, 5–6.

77. "JOC Weekly Resume . . . 201801–271800 September 1963," 30 September 1963, 11, "Significant VC Attacks."

78. "JOC Weekly Resume . . . 271800 September–041800 October 1963," 7 October 1963, 1; "JOC Weekly Resume . . . 100001–162400 October 1963," 21 October 1963, 1, 9, 15, MACV Assistant Chief of Staff for Operations (J-3), Joint Liaison Group (MCAJ3–12), JGS JOC Weekly Resume, box 2, 10 October 1963–1 January 1964, RG 472, Archives 2, NARA.

79. "JOC Weekly Resume . . . 271800 September–041800 October 1963," 7 October 1963, 8, "Significant VC Attacks," 1; "JOC Weekly Resume . . . 170001–232400 October 1963," 28 October 1963, 1, 4–5, box 2, 10 October 1963–1 January 1964.

80. "JOC Weekly Resume . . . 31000–062400 November 1963," 11 November 1963, section 1c, 1–2, section 5, 8–10, and section 10, 12–13, box 2, 10 October 1963–1 January 1964.

81. On the chaos following the coup, see Moyar, *Triumph,* 275–287, and Anne Blair, *There to the Bitter End: Ted Serong in Vietnam* (Crow's Nest, Australia: Allen & Unwin, 2001), 64–74.

82. Minh et al., *Lich Su Bo Doi Dac Cong,* 105.

83. "JOC Weekly Resume . . . 28001 November–042400 December 1963," enclosure 12, map showing "Comparison of VC Activity (November 63)"; "JOC Weekly Resume . . . 19001–252400 December 1963," enclosure 8, "Comparison of VC Activity with Infiltration Routes (November 1963)," box 2, 10 October 1963–1 January 1964.

84. FBIS, *Central Highlands People's Armed Forces,* 18.

85. CIA Current Intelligence Memorandum, "The Military Situation in South Vietnam," 18 November 1963, para. 9, 3.

Chapter 7. The Central Highlands, January–June 1964

1. Mark Moyar, *Triumph Forsaken: The Vietnam War, 1954–1965* (Cambridge: Cambridge University Press, 2006), 274–391; David Kaiser, *American Tragedy: Kennedy, Johnson and the Origins of the Vietnam War* (Cambridge, MA: Belknap Press, 2000), 284–381.

2. Merle L. Pribbenow, trans., *Victory in Vietnam: The Official History of the People's Army of Vietnam, 1954–1975* (Lawrence: University Press of Kansas, 2002), 123–125.

3. Ibid., 125.

4. Lien-Hang T. Nguyen, *Hanoi's War: An International History of the War for Peace in Vietnam* (Chapel Hill: University of North Carolina Press, 2012), 63–65.

5. Ibid., 17–75.

6. JOC Weekly Resumes January–February 1964, Headquarters MACV, Secretary of the Joint Staff (MACJ03), Military History Branch, Historians' Background Material Files 206-02, box 19, RG 472, Archives 2, NARA; USMACV Military Reports, March–December 1964, microfilm, Madison Hall, Library of Congress. Colonel General Dang Vu Hiep et al., *Ky Uc Tay Nguyen* [Highland memories], trans. Merle Pribbenow (Hanoi: People's Publishing House, 2000), 22–23; Foreign Broadcast Information Service, trans., *Luc Luong Vu Trang Nhan Dan Tay Nguyen Trong Khang Chien Chong My Cuu Nuoc* [History of the Central Highlands people's armed forces in the anti-US war of resistance for national salvation] (Hanoi: People's Publishing House, 1980), 20–21, Historians' Files, CMH; hereafter cited as FBIS, *Central Highlands People's Armed Forces* (page numbers are to the English translation).

7. Hiep, *Ky Uc Tay Nguyen,* 23.

8. FBIS, *Central Highlands People's Armed Forces,* 13–18.

9. Fact sheets for Central Highlands provinces, 8 May 1964, Headquarters, MACV, Secretary of the Joint Staff (MACJ03), Military History Branch, Historians' Background Files 206-02, box 18, RG 472, Archives 2, NARA.

10. Hiep, *Ky Uc Tay Nguyen,* 25–26; FBIS, *Central Highlands People's Armed Forces,* 15–20.

11. Hiep, *Ky Uc Tay Nguyen,* 25.

12. FBIS, *Central Highlands People's Armed Forces,* 19.

13. Hiep, *Ky Uc Tay Nguyen,* 23; FBIS, *Central Highlands People's Armed Forces,* 19. I owe the explanation for the swift changes in the top two appointments at the CHF to Merle Pribbenow, who derived it by comparing the accounts in the various histories published in Hanoi.

14. Senior Colonel Tran Do, ed., *Tu Dien Bach Khoa Quan Su Viet Nam* [Military encyclopedia of Vietnam], trans. Merle Pribbenow (Hanoi: People's Publishing House, 1996), 556, 272–273.

15. FBIS, *Central Highlands People's Armed Forces,* 19.

16. The connections between the Central Highlands theater and events in Laos and Cambodia are also pointed out in Hiep, *Ky Uc Tay Nguyen,* 24.

17. Ibid., 24–25.

18. Robert Shaplen, *The Lost Revolution: Vietnam 1945–1965* (London: Andre Deutsch, 1966), 231–265; William Colby, *Lost Victory: A Firsthand Account of America's Sixteen-Year Involvement in Vietnam* (New York: Contemporary Books, 1989), 161–174; Moyar, *Triumph,* 275–349.

19. Fact sheet for Lam Dong and other Central Highlands provinces, 8 May 1964.

20. Dates of appointments to commands and information on the 25th Division's movement from II Corps to III Corps come from "Command Histories and Historical Sketches of RVNAF Divisions," pt. 2, "Short Historical Sketches of the Eleven Infantry Divisions, the Airborne Division and the Marine Division," January 1974, enclosure to A-23, American Embassy Saigon to State Department, 6 February 1974, CMH. Biographical information on ARVN commanders comes from the CMH and from Internet sources.

21. "Command Histories." On Do Cao Tri's views on the Highlander question, see Vietnamese Affairs Staff of the Office of the Director of Central Intelligence, "The Highlanders

of South Vietnam: A Review of Political Developments and Forces," June 1966, 61, Historians' Files, CMH; hereafter cited as "Highlanders."

22. Brigadier General James Lawton Collins Jr., *The Development and Training of the South Vietnamese Army 1950–1972* (Washington, DC: Department of the Army, 2002), 8–12, 41–43.

23. Information on Balthis comes from Lt. Col. Thomas W. Bowen, "Debriefing of Colonel Charles E. Balthis, Jr., Senior Adviser, II Corps, 8 October 1964," 17 October 1964, Headquarters, MACV, Secretary of the Joint Staff (MACJ03), Military History Branch, Historians' Background Files, box 17, RG 472, Archives 2, NARA.

24. Graham A. Cosmas, *MACV: The Joint Command in the Years of Escalation, 1962–1967* (Washington, DC: Center of Military History, US Army, 2006), 1–122.

25. Ibid., 122–125; Lewis Sorley, *Westmoreland: The General Who Lost Vietnam* (New York: Houghton Mifflin Harcourt, 2011), 1–90. Sorley's book amounts to a case for the prosecution. Engagingly written and aimed at a broad readership, its author arguably indulges in an excess of hindsight.

26. Cosmas, *MACV*, 123–125; Kaiser, *American Tragedy*, 284–311; Howard Jones, *Death of a Generation: How the Assassinations of Diem and JFK Prolonged the Vietnam War* (Oxford: Oxford University Press, 2003), 444.

27. FBIS, *Central Highlands People's Armed Forces*, 21.

28. Fact sheets for Central Highlands provinces, 8 May 1964.

29. "Highlanders," 60.

30. "JOC Weekly Resume . . . 060001–122400 February 1964," 17 February 1964, 8, (3) c, Headquarters, MACV, Secretary of the Joint Staff (MACJ03), Military History Branch, Historians' Background Material Files 06-02, box 19, RG 472, Archives 2, NARA.

31. "JOC Weekly Resume . . . 160001–222400 January 1964," 27 January 1964, 11, (3).

32. USMACV Military Report, 221601Z–281600Z March 1964, 24–25.

33. Ibid., 18.

34. USMACV Military Report, 111601Z–181600Z April 1964, 21–22.

35. USMACV Military Report, 051601Z–111600Z April 1964, 6–8.

36. Lieutenant General John Tolson, *Airmobility 1961–1971* (Washington, DC: Department of the Army, 1973), 3–62. On the Communist reaction to the employment of helicopters by their enemies, see Tolson's translation of a Communist instruction pamphlet on pp. 26–27. On the use of vertical envelopment by ARVN Rangers, see USMACV Military Report, 271601 June–01600Z July 1964, 8. See also Brigadier General J. Norton, "Critique of Counterinsurgency Airmobile Operations, Vietnam," 5 July 1965, William C. Westmoreland Papers, series II, Official Papers, COMUSMACV, History Backup Files 15–17 for 27 March–28 August 1965, box 37, USAMHI; J. D. Coleman, *Pleiku: The Dawn of Helicopter Warfare in Vietnam* (New York: St. Martin's Press, 1988), 1–32. Coleman's book is arguably the best to date on the Pleiku–Ia Drang campaign of 1965. But the intense fighting in Ia Drang came in November 1965, three years after the perceptive Communist analysis of heliborne warfare quoted in Tolson's book was written and disseminated. The Pleiku campaign of 1965 was therefore a very late "dawn."

37. USMACV Military Report, 051601Z–111600Z April 1964, 25.

38. Fact sheet, "Kontum," 8 May 1964.

39. Ibid., "Pleiku."

40. Ibid., "Phu Bon."

41. Ibid., "Darlac."

42. Ibid., "Tuyen Duc."

43. Ibid., "Quang Duc."

44. Ibid., "Lam Dong."

45. USMACV Military Report, 091601Z–161600Z May 1964, 36–37.

46. Ibid., 23–24.

47. USMACV Military Report, 231601Z–301600Z May 1964, 4–7.

48. *Quan Khu 5: Thang Loi va Nhung Bai Hoc Trong Khang Chien Chong My,* Tap I, [Military Region 5: victories and lessons learned during the resistance war against the Americans, vol. 1], trans. Merle Pribbenow (Hanoi: People's Publishing House, 1981), 54.

49. USMACV Military Report, 061601Z–1311600Z June 1964, 4–8.

50. FBIS, *Central Highlands People's Armed Forces,* 10.

51. Ibid., 18–19.

52. Hiep, *Ky Uc Tay Nguyen,* 26.

Chapter 8. Crisis in the Highlands, July–December 1964

1. *Quan Khu 5: Thang Loi va Nhung Bai Hoc Trong Khang Chien Chong My,* Tap I [Military Region 5: victories and lessons learned during the resistance war against the Americans], trans. Merle Pribbenow (Hanoi: People's Publishing House, 1981), 54; Merle Pribbenow, trans., *Victory in Vietnam: The Official History of the People's Army of Vietnam, 1954–1975* (Lawrence: University Press of Kansas, 2002), 76, 84, 127, 134–135; Lien-Hang T. Nguyen, *Hanoi's War: An International History of the War for Peace in Vietnam* (Chapel Hill: University of North Carolina Press, 2012), 60–71.

2. Pribbenow, *Victory,* 135; USMACV Military Report, 271601Z June–041600Z July 1964, 48, Library of Congress.

3. Colonel Francis J. Kelly, *US Army Special Forces: 1961–1971* (Washington, DC: Department of the Army, 1973), 70.

4. Captain John E. Williamson, Det. A-134 to Commanding Officer HQ USASFV, APO 40, U.S. Forces, "Debriefing Report," 1 May 1964, enclosure 2, "Intelligence" (S-2), 1, 1. "Weather and Terrain," d. "Topography," and enclosure 3, "Operations" (S-3), 1, 1.d. "Camp Site," 5th Special Forces Group (Airborne), Records of A-Detachments, box 28, Detachment A-134 (1st Special Forces Group), Polei Krong, Kontum Province, II CTZ, December 1963–May 1964, RG 472, Archives 2, NARA.

5. Ibid., enclosure 3, 2, 3.b. "Area of Influence"; Captain John E. Williamson, "Hamlet Information, Polei Krong Area," 5 January 1964, Records of A-Detachments, box 28, Detachment A-134, RG 472, Archives 2, NARA.

6. Williamson, "Debriefing Report," enclosure 2, section 4, "Counter-Intelligence Operations," 5, para. 6; enclosure 2, 4, section 4, "Counter-Intelligence Operations," e.; enclosure 2, 1, section 2, "Enemy Situation," d.

7. Ibid., enclosure 2, 2–4, esp. section 4, "Counter-Intelligence Operations," h.

8. Ibid., enclosure 2, 5, section 5.

9. Ibid., enclosure 3, 2, section 3, "Operations," a.

10. Ibid., enclosure 3, 3, section 4, "Additional Areas Pertaining to Operations and Training," a.

11. Ibid., enclosure 2, 2, section 4, "Counter-Intelligence Operations," c.

12. Ibid., enclosure 2, 5, section 4, "Counter-Intelligence," h.

13. Ibid., enclosure 2, 1–2, section 2, "Enemy Situation," b, d, and e.

14. Ibid., enclosure 2, 5, section 9, "Conclusions and Lessons Learned."

15. *Quan Khu 5,* 54; Nguyen Quoc Minh et al., *Lich Su Bo Doi Dac Cong,* Tap Mot

[History of sapper forces, vol. 1], trans. Merle Pribbenow (Hanoi: People's Publishing House, 1987), 111–112.

16. Foreign Broadcast Information Service, trans., *Luc Luong Vy Trang Nhan Dan Tay Nguyen Trong Khang Chien Chong My Cuu Nuoc* [History of the Central Highlands people's armed forces in the anti-US war of resistance for national survival] (Hanoi: People's Publishing House, 1980), 20, Historians' Files, CMH; hereafter cited as FBIS, *Central Highlands People's Armed Forces* (page references are to the English translation).

17. Captain William Johnson, "After Action Report," Detachment A-122, 1st SFG, 8 July 1964, 1–2, 5th Special Forces Group (Airborne), Records of A-Detachments, box 17, Detachment A-122 (1st Special Forces Group), Polei Krong, Kontum Province, II CTZ, May–October 1964, RG 472, Archives 2, NARA.

18. Ibid., 2–3.

19. Minh, *Lich Su Bo Doi Dac Cong,* 111; Johnson, "After Action Report," 4–5.

20. Johnson, "After Action Report," 5–6.

21. Ibid., 7.

22. Captain William D. Johnson, Detachment A-122, 1st SFG, "Monthly Operational Summary," 21 July 1964, 5th Special Forces Group (Airborne), Records of A-Detachments, box 17, Detachment A-122 (1st Special Forces Group), Polei Krong, Kontum Province, II CTZ, May–October 1964, RG 472, Archives 2, NARA; USMACV Military Report, 041601Z–111600Z July 1964, 24.

23. The claim that four companies were "destroyed" in this action is found in *Quan Khu 5,* 54. The claim of nine Americans killed is made in Minh, *Lich Su Bo Doi Dac Cong,* 111, and FBIS, *Central Highlands People's Armed Forces,* 20.

24. Johnson, "After Action Report," 7.

25. Major Ton That Hung, "Lessons Learned from the Loss of a Special Forces Camp on the Night 3–4 July 1964," 18 July 1964, 2, 5th Special Forces Group (Airborne), Records of A-Detachments, box 28, Detachment A-134 (1st Special Forces Group), Polei Krong, Kontum Province, II CTZ, December 1963–May 1964, RG 472, Archives 2, NARA. Hung's report on the disaster at Polei Krong seems to have been misfiled. Logically, it should be with Johnson's report in box 17 of this series, which deals with Polei Krong in May–October 1964. But there is little logic to this system, in which the bulk of the material included in box 17 comes chronologically after the material in box 28, and both boxes deal entirely with Polei Krong.

26. Richard D. Burke, R. P. Joyce, et al., "*US Army Special Forces Operations under the Civilian Irregular Defense Groups Program in Vietnam (1961–64)* (McLean, VA: Research Analysis Corporation, 1965), vol. 2, appendix D, 7–11, "Polei Krong: The Attack, Retreat, VC Activity, Findings of Subsequent ARVN Investigation," Historians' Files, CMH.

27. FBIS, *Central Highlands People's Armed Forces,* 20.

28. "Draft DCI Briefing for Vinson Subcommittee," 1 August 1964, 1–2, CIA-RD-P82R00025R000400160008-7, CREST, Archives 2, NARA; USMACV Military Report, 041601Z–111600Z July 1964, 25–28; Burke et al., *Special Forces,* appendix D, 11–14.

29. USMACV Military Report, 041601Z–111600Z July 1964, 30–31.

30. USMACV Military Report, 111601Z–181600Z July 1964, 27; Vietnamese Affairs Staff of the Office of the Director of Central Intelligence, "The Highlanders of South Vietnam: A Review of Political Developments and Forces," June 1966, 64–65, Historians' Files, CMH; hereafter cited as "Highlanders."

31. USMACV Military Report, 11601Z–181600Z July 1964, 43–44.

32. USMACV Military Report, 181601Z–251600Z July 1964, 25, 28–29.

33. "Highlanders," 64–65.

34. USMACV Military Report, 251601Z July–011600Z August 1964, 1; USMACV Military Report, 011601Z–081600Z August 1964, 1.

35. USMACV Military Report, 011601Z–081600Z August 1964, 18.

36. USMACV Military Report, 291601Z August–051600Z September 1964, 1, 24, 25; USMACV Military Report, 121601Z–191600Z September 1964, 50.

37. USMACV Military Report, 051601Z–121600Z September 1964, 20, 27.

38. USMACV Military Report, 121601Z–191600Z September 1964; USMACV Military Report, 201601Z–261600Z September 1964, 1.

39. "Highlanders," 60–61; Gerald C. Hickey, *Free in the Forest: Ethnohistory of the Vietnamese Central Highlands, 1954–1976* (New Haven, CT: Yale University Press, 1982), 94–95.

40. "Highlanders," 61–62.

41. Ibid., 60.

42. Ibid., 62.

43. Ibid., 62–63.

44. Ibid., 62–64.

45. Ibid., 66; "The Montagnard Uprising September 1964," 1–2, 5th Special Forces Group (Airborne) Headquarters, Organizational History 1961–1966, box 1, RG 472, Archives 2, NARA (hereafter cited as "Uprising"); Hickey, *Free*, 99. "Uprising" is anonymous and undated, but it is the clearest narrative of events.

46. Hickey, *Free*, 99–101; "Highlanders," 66. On events at Buon Brieng, see also Captain Vernon Gillespie Jr., "After Action Report: CIDG Revolt at Camp Buon Brieng," 30 September 1964, 5th Special Forces Group (Airborne) Headquarters, Organizational History 1961–1966, box 1, RG 472, Archives 2, NARA.

47. "Uprising," 2.

48. On General Co's role in the FULRO uprising, see "Highlanders," 68; Hickey, *Free*, 104. Material on Co's wider career and reputation with the Americans was supplied by CMH.

49. Information supplied by Dr. Andrew Birtle from files held at CMH.

50. "Uprising," 3–4.

51. "Highlanders," 68.

52. "Uprising," 3.

53. "Highlanders," 66–67; General William C. Westmoreland, *A Soldier Reports* (New York: Dell, 1976), 99–100.

54. "Uprising," 5.

55. Ibid., 6–19; Lieutenant Colonels Brownlee and Mullen, *Changing an Army: An Oral History of General William E. DePuy*, 126–128, box 29, William DePuy Papers, USAMHI; Hickey, *Free*, 99–109. All the quotations in this section are from "Uprising."

56. Brownlee and Mullen, *Changing*, 126–128.

57. "Highlanders," 69–70.

58. Ibid., 69.

59. Ibid., 68–73.

60. Hickey, *Free*, 109; Lt. Col. Thomas W. Bowen, "Debriefing of Colonel Charles E. Balthis, Jr., Senior Advisor, II Corps, 8 October 1964," "a. General Situation in II Corps," 17 October 1964, Headquarters, MACV, Secretary of the Joint Staff (MACJ03), Military History Branch, Historians' Background Files, box 17, RG 472, Archives 2, NARA.

61. Nguyen, *Hanoi's War*, 71–74.

62. Lieutenant General Nguyen Dinh Uoc, *Lich Su Khang Chien Chong My Cuu Nuoc*

1954–1975, Tap III, *Danh Thanh Chien Tranh Dac Biet* [History of the resistance war against the Americans to save the nation 1954–1975, vol. 3, Defeating the special war], trans. Merle Pribbenow (Hanoi: National Political Publishing House, 1997), 326–327.

63. USMACV Military Report, 031601Z–101600Z October 1964, 1, 2, 24, 26–28; US-MACV Military Report, 171601Z–241600Z October 1964, 18.

64. "Command Histories and Historical Sketches of RVNAF Divisions," pt. 2, 33, enclosure to American Embassy Saigon airgram to State Department, A-23, 6 February 1974, Historians' Files, CMH.

65. USMACV Military Report, 151601Z–211600Z November 1964, 4.

66. Pribbenow, *Victory,* 105; John Prados, *Vietnam: The History of an Unwinnable War, 1945–1975* (Lawrence: University Press of Kansas, 2009), 109.

67. Mark Moyar, *Triumph Forsaken: The Vietnam War, 1954–1965* (Cambridge: Cambridge University Press, 2006), 336–339.

68. MACV, "Monthly Evaluation Report, January 1965," 36, USAMHI.

69. USMACV Military Report, 051601Z–121600Z December 1964, 24, 27, 32; US-MACV Military Report, 191601Z–261600Z December 1964, 1–3.

70. Moyar, *Triumph,* 356; Ang Chen Guan, *The Vietnam War from the Other Side: The Vietnamese Communists' Perspective* (Oxford: Routledge, 2002), 87–89.

Chapter 9. An Escalating War, January–March 1965

1. Merle L. Pribbenow, trans., *Victory in Vietnam: The Official History of the People's Army of Vietnam, 1954–1975* (Lawrence: University Press of Kansas, 2002), 142.

2. Lien-Hang T. Nguyen, *Hanoi's War: An International History of the War for Peace in Vietnam* (Chapel Hill: University of North Carolina Press, 2012), 74–75.

3. MACV, "Monthly Evaluation Report, January 1965," 23 February 1965, 1–4, 9–12, USAMHI.

4. Theodore C. Mataxis, "The War in the Highlands: Attack and Counter-Attack on Highway 19," *Army,* October 1965, 51.

5. Pribbenow, *Victory,* 137–138; Major W. P. Boyle and Major R. Samabria, "The Lure and the Ambush: An Account of the Opening Battle of Stage Three in the Struggle for the Highlands, 19 October 1965–26 November 1965," 2, 14, Historians' Files, CMH.

6. Boyle and Samabria, "Lure," 2.

7. Pham Gia Duc, *Su Doan 325,* Tap II [325th Division, vol. 2], trans. Merle Pribbenow (Hanoi: People's Publishing House, 1986), 39–40.

8. Ibid., 40–46.

9. Ibid., 47.

10. Ibid., 48.

11. General William C. Westmoreland, *A Soldier Reports* (New York: Dell, 1976), 135–138.

12. Nguyen Huu An, *Chien Truong Moi* [New battlefield], trans. Merle Pribbenow (Hanoi: People's Publishing House, 2002), 9–12; Mark Moyar, *Triumph Forsaken: The Vietnam War, 1954–1965* (Cambridge: Cambridge University Press, 2006), 356.

13. Duc, *Su Doan 325,* 49.

14. Nguyen Van Thuy et al., *Trung Doan 95 Thien Thuat (1945–1995)* [The 95th Thien Thuat Regiment (1945–1995)], trans. Merle Pribbbenow (Hanoi: People's Publishing House, 1995), 92.

15. Duc, *Su Doan 325,* 49.

16. An, *Chien Truong Moi,* 13.

17. Duc, *Su Doan 325,* 323.

18. An, *Chien Truong Moi,* 13.

19. "The Liberation Army's Millionaire 'Boss' in Cambodia," http://vietnamnet.vn /vn/kinh-te/-ong-chu-trieu-do-cua-quan-giai-phong-tren-dat-chua-thap.html (accessed 28 April 2015 and translated by Merle Pribbenow on the author's behalf); Dong Si Nguyen and Nguyen Duy Tuong, eds., *Lich Su Bo Doi Truong Son Duong Ho Chi Minh* [History of the Annamite Mountain troops of the Ho Chi Minh Trail], trans. Merle Pribbenow (Hanoi: People's Publishing House, 1994), 139; Dang Phong, *5 Duong Mon Ho Chi Minh* [Five Ho Chi Minh Trails], trans. Merle Pribbenow (Hanoi: Intellectual Publishing House, 2008), 257–258. The term "requisition-purchase" is used in Foreign Broadcast Information Service, trans., *Luc Luong Vu Trang Nhan Dan Tay Nguyen Khang Chien Chong My Cuu Nuoc* [History of the Central Highlands people's armed forces in the anti-US war of resistance for national survival] (Hanoi: People's Publishing House, 1980), 21, Historians' Files, CMH.

20. David Chandler, *The Tragedy of Cambodian History: Politics, War and Revolution since 1945* (London: Yale University Press, 1991), 122. On the importance of Cambodian resources for the Vietnamese Communist war effort and, specifically, requisition purchasing in Cambodia, see also *Tong Ket Cong Tac Hau Can Chien Truong Nam Bo—Cuc Nam Trung Bo Trong Khang Chien Chong My* [Review of rear services operations for the Cochin China battlefield], trans. Merle Pribbenow (Hanoi: General Department of Rear Services, People's Army of Vietnam, 1986), 30, 46, 47, 128.

21. Mataxis, "War," 50–51; MACV, "Monthly Evaluation Report, January 1965," 9–11.

22. Mataxis, "War," 51.

23. MACV, "Monthly Evaluation Report, January 1965," 23; Captain Michael D. Mireau to Commanding Officer, Detachment C-2, 5th SFG (Abn), 1st SF, "Initial Area Assessment—Camp Suoi Doi," 5 February 1965, 5th Special Forces Group (Airborne), Records of A-Detachments, Detachment A-214, box 184, RG 472, Archives 2, NARA.

24. MACV, "Monthly Evaluation Report, January 1965," 23; Lt. Col. L. W. Hale to Commanding Officer, 5th Special Forces Group (Airborne), 1st Special Forces, "Action Near Mang Yang Pass, 20 February–1 March 1965," 26 March 1965, 6, para. 13, Report no. 13 in MACV J3, After Action Reports, box 1, RG 472, Archives 2, NARA; Shelby B. Stanton, *Green Berets at War: U.S. Army Special Forces in Southeast Asia 1956–1975* (London: Arms & Armour, 1986), 93.

25. MACV, "Monthly Evaluation Report, January 1965," 11.

26. USMACV Military Report, 311601Z–061600Z February 1965, 2, Library of Congress.

27. MACV, "Monthly Evaluation Report, February 1965," 1–4.

28. Major General Milton B. Adams, USAF, "Report of Investigation Pleiku Incident," section 6, 13–14, "The Attack and Reactions to the Attack," Historians' Files, CMH.

29. Pribbenow, *Victory,* 142.

30. Article in 19 May 2012 edition of *Binh Dinh* newspaper on a reunion of personnel of the 409th Sapper Battalion, http://www.baobinhdinh.com.vn/chinhtri-xahoi/2012/5 /126877/ (accessed and translated by Merle Pribbenow on the author's behalf).

31. Military Region 5 Headquarters and Tran Quy Cat, eds., *Lich Su Bo Doi Dac Cong Quan Khu 5 (1952–1975)* [History of Military Region 5 sapper troops (1952–1975)], trans. Merle Pribbenow (Hanoi: People's Publishing House, 1998), 142.

32. Nguyen Tri Huan et al., *Su Doan Sao Vang* [The Yellow Star Division], trans. Merle

Pribbenow (Hanoi: People's Army Publishing House, 1984), 15; USMACV Military Report, 061601Z–131600Z February 1965, 27.

33. Adams, "Report of Pleiku Incident," 14.

34. Pribbenow, *Victory,* 142–143; John Prados, *Vietnam: The History of an Unwinnable War, 1945–1975* (Lawrence: University Press of Kansas, 2009), 110–113.

35. MACV, "Monthly Evaluation Report, February 1965," 2–5, 11–14.

36. Nguyen Dinh Uoc and Nguyen Van Minh, eds., *Lich Su Khang Chien Chong My Cuu Nuoc 1954–1975,* Tap III, *Danh Thang Chien Tranh Dac Biet* [History of the resistance war against the Americans to save the nation 1954–1975, vol. 3, Defeating the special war], trans. Merle Pribbenow (Hanoi: National Political Publishing House, 1997), 349.

37. Duc, *Su Doan 325,* 55.

38. USMACV Military Report, 061601Z–131600Z February 1965, 2–5.

39. Ibid., 3.

40. W. G. Leftwich Jr. "Bong Son Operation," 29–31, Theodore Mataxis Papers, USAMHI. This article was apparently published in a US Marine Corps journal, but the details are unclear.

41. USMACV Military Report, 201601Z–271600Z February 1965, 5.

42. Summary of Mataxis's career in Mataxis Papers, USAMHI.

43. Mataxis, "War," 50.

44. Captain Michael D. Mireau to Commanding Officer, Detachment C-2, 5th Special Forces Group (Abn), 1st Special Forces, "Narrative Report of Ambush of Regional Force Convoy Vicinity of Mang Yang Pass on Highway 19, 15 February 1965," 15 February 1965, 1–2, Suoi Doi Camp Folder, 5th Special Forces Group (Airborne), Records of A-Detachments, Detachment A-214 (5th Special Forces Group), box 184, RG 472, Archives 2, NARA; Lt. Col. Joseph R. Ulatoski to Senior Adviser II Corps, "After Action Report of Operations in Mang Yang Pass, Pleiku and Binh Dinh Sectors, 14 February to 21 March 1965," 19 April 1965, cover letter to Hale, "Action Near the Mang Yang Pass, 20 February–1 March 1965," 26 March 1965.

45. Mataxis, "War," 51.

46. Duc, *Su Doan 325,* 54.

47. Thuy, *Trung Doan 95,* 93.

48. Moyar, *Triumph,* 354.

49. Hale, "Action," 1; Stanton, *Green Berets,* 93.

50. Hale, "Action," 2.

51. Ibid., 3; Stanton, *Green Berets,* 94.

52. Hale, "Action," 3–4; Mataxis, "War," 52.

53. Hale, "Action," 4; Captain Ilmar H. Dambergs to Senior Adviser, II Corps, "Combat Operations After Action Report," 9 March 1965, attached to Hale, "Action."

54. 1st Lieutenant Alanson D. Bartholomew to Senior Adviser II Corps, "Combat After Action Report," 9 March 1965, 3–4, attached to Hale, "Action"; Hale, "Action," 5.

55. Hale, "Action," 5–6.

56. Mataxis, "War," 53.

57. Bartholomew, "Combat," 6.

58. Lt. Col. Joseph E. Ulatoski to Senior Adviser II Corps, "Summary of Mang Yang Extraction Operation," 9 March 1965, attached to Hale, "Action"; Mataxis, "War," 53–54.

59. Bartholomew, "Combat," 6.

60. Mataxis, "War," 54.

61. Thuy, *Trung Doan 95,* 94.

62. Ulatoski, "After Action," 1; Hale, "Action," 7; Bartholomew, "Combat," 7.

63. Hale, "Action," 7.

64. Colonel Francis J. Kelly, *US Army Special Forces: 1961–1971* (Washington, DC: Department of the Army, 1973), 50, 69; Stanton, *Green Berets,* 96; Lt. Col. Robert B. Rheault to Brig. Gen. William E. DePuy, "CIDG Forces Successfully Defend from Hard Core VC Attack," 11 March 1965, 1, 5th Special Forces Group (Airborne), Records of A-Detachments, Detachment A-231, box 49, RG 472, Archives 2, NARA. Two more detailed accounts of the defense of Camp Kannack are attached to Rheault's report to DePuy: Major General Peers, "Defense of Kannack CIDG against Major VC Assault on 8 March 1965," 11 March 1965, 1–3, and an unsigned and undated briefing document or lecture typed in block capitals and titled "Camp Kannack," 1–5. Captain Viau's more formal "After Action Report, Attack 8 March," is dated 26 March, ibid.

65. Article in the 24 July 2009 edition of *Gia Lai* newspaper, http://www.baogialai.com.vn/channel/1624/200907/tran-danh-don-ka-nak-7-3-1965-khuc-trang-ca-giua-dai-ngan-1713482/ (accessed 26 January 2014 and translated by Merle Pribbenow on the author's behalf as "The Attack on Ka Nak Outpost, 7 March 1965: Heroic Saga in the Vast Jungle").

66. Vietnamese military history website, http://www.vnmilitaryhistory.net/index.php?topic=16770.0 (accessed 26 January 2014 by Merle Pribbenow and translated on the author's behalf as "The Battle of Ka Nak," section 1, "General Situation"); Military Region 5 and Cat, *Lich Su Bo Doi Dac Cong Quan Khu 5,* 158.

67. Rheault, "CIDG," 1–2; "Camp Kannack" briefing document, 1.

68. Vietnamese military history website, "The Battle of Ka Nak," section 1, "General Situation."

69. Rheault, "CIDG," 1–2; "Camp Kannack" briefing document, 2.

70. Military Region 5 and Cat, *Lich Su Bo Doi Dac Cong Quan Khu 5,* 158; Vietnamese military history website, "The Battle of Ka Nak," section 1, "General Situation"; "Attack on Ka Nak Outpost," *Gia Lai,* 24 July 2009.

71. "Camp Kannack" briefing document, 1–3.

72. Vietnamese military history website, "The Battle of Ka Nak," section 2, "Progress of the Battle and Results of the Battle."

73. "Camp Kannack" briefing document, 4.

74. Vietnamese military history website, "The Battle of Ka Nak," section 2, "Progress of the Battle and Results of the Battle."

75. Military Region 5 and Cat, *Lich Su Bo Doi Dac Cong Quan Khu 5,* 158.

76. Various attachments to Rheault, "CIDG," in the Camp Kannack folder.

77. "Attack on Ka Nak Outpost," *Gia Lai.*

78. Military Region 5 and Cat, *Lich Su Bo Doi Dac Cong Quan Khu 5,* 158; Vietnamese military history website, "The Battle of Ka Nak," section 2, "Progress of the Battle and Results of the Battle."

79. Article in the 1 August 2008 edition of *An Ninh The Gioi* newspaper, http://antg.cand.com.vn/News/PrintView.aspx?ID=67003 (accessed 28 January 2014 and translated by Merle Pribbenow on the author's behalf as "The Giai Lai Province People's Committee and People's Public Security Newspaper Begin Construction of Memorial to the Knak Martyrs: Expressing Gratitude for the Noble Service of These Heroic Martyrs").

80. Thuy, *Trung Doan 95,* 94.

81. Ulatoski, "After Action," 1.

82. MACV, "Monthly Evaluation Report, February 1965," 1–2, 11–15.

83. Duc, *Su Doan 325,* 55–56; Uoc and Minh, *Lich Su Khang Chien Chong My Cuu Nuoc,* 349.

84. Moyar, *Triumph,* 365.

85. MACV, "Monthly Evaluation Report, February 1965," 3.

Chapter 10. The Monsoon Offensive, April–August 1965

1. Ang Cheng Guan, *The Vietnam War from the Other Side: The Vietnamese Communists' Perspective* (Oxford: Routledge, 2002), 85; Lien-Hang T. Nguyen, *Hanoi's War: An International History of the War for Peace in Vietnam* (Chapel Hill: University of North Carolina Press, 2012), 74.

2. Mark Moyar, *Triumph Forsaken: The Vietnam War, 1954–1965* (Cambridge: Cambridge University Press, 2006), 339–340.

3. MACV, "Monthly Evaluation Report, February 1965," 1–4, 11–12, MACV Papers, USAMHI.

4. Theodore C. Mataxis, "War in the Highlands: Attack and Counter-Attack on Highway 19," *Army,* October 1965, 54, copy in Mataxis Papers, USAMHI.

5. Moyar, *Triumph,* 357–358.

6. Merle Pribbenow, trans., *Victory in Vietnam: The Official History of the People's Army of Vietnam, 1954–1975* (Lawrence: University of Kansas Press, 2002), 142; John Prados, *Vietnam: History of an Unwinnable War, 1945–1975* (Lawrence: University of Kansas Press, 2009), 113–114.

7. General William C. Westmoreland, *A Soldier Reports* (New York: Dell, 1976), 159.

8. Pribbenow, *Victory,* 143; Westmoreland, *Soldier,* 173–183.

9. Nguyen, *Hanoi's War,* 74.

10. On Le Duan's obsession with a mass uprising in the South, see Nguyen, *Hanoi's War,* 65, 76.

11. Pham Gia Duc, *Su Doan 325,* Tap II [325th Division, vol. 2], trans. Merle Pribbenow (Hanoi: People's Publishing House, 1986), 48–49.

12. Pribbenow, *Victory,* 143–144; Nguyen, *Hanoi's War,* 75–76.

13. Westmoreland, *Soldier,* 169–177; Moyar, *Triumph,* 368–369.

14. Pribbenow, *Victory,* 142–144, 156; Moyar, *Triumph,* 365.

15. The effectiveness of the southern republic's armed forces was diminished owing to "the consummate interest in politics of key senior officers." See MACV, "Monthly Evaluation Report, February 1965," 3. On Khanh's initial efforts to appeal to a broad spectrum of opinion, see CIA, "The Situation in South Vietnam," 20 February 1964, section 2, "The Saigon Regime," 4–5, folder 01, box 01, Central Intelligence Agency Collection, The Vietnam Center and Archive, Texas Tech University, http://www.vietnam.ttu.edu/virtual archive/items.php?item=0410101005 (accessed 17 September 2014); Moyar, *Triumph,* 295–297, 343–347.

16. Westmoreland, *Soldier,* 120–121; Moyar, *Triumph,* 333–335, 350–351.

17. Westmoreland, *Soldier,* 121–124, 177; Moyar, *Triumph,* 363–365.

18. Moyar, *Triumph,* 368; CIA SC No. 04464/65, CIA-DIA Memorandum, "An Assessment of Present Viet Cong Military Capabilities," 21 April 1965, paras. 11 and 2, http://academic.brooklyn.cuny.edu/history/johnson/65vn-3.htm (accessed 17 September 2014).

19. MACV, "Monthly Evaluation Report, January 1965," 1–2, 9–12.

20. MACV, "Monthly Evaluation Report, February 1965," 2–5, 11–13; Mataxis, "War," 53–55.

21. Doan Them, *1965—Viec Tung Ngay* [1965—daily chronicle of events], trans. Merle Pribbenow (Saigon: Phan Quang Khai Publishing, 1968), 54, 57.

22. Theodore C. Mataxis, "Monsoon Offensive in the Highlands," n.d., 1–4, Mataxis Papers, USAMHI.

23. CIA, "Assessment of Present Viet Cong Capabilities," 21 April 1965; CIA, Office of Current Intelligence, Intelligence Memorandum SC No. 07361/65, "The Viet Cong Campaign in Vietnam's Central Highlands," 9 July 1965, 2, 3, National Security Archive, George Washington University, Washington, DC.

24. On munitions deliveries to the Central Highlands, see Guan, *Vietnam War,* 87–88. PAVN troops in northern Kontum Province in March 1965 were surviving on 250 grams of rice per person per day. Foreign Broadcast Information Service, trans., *Luc Luong Vy Trang Nhan Dan Tay Nguyen Trong Khang Chien Chong My Cuu Nuoc* [History of the Central Highlands people's armed forces in the anti-US war of resistance for national salvation] (Hanoi: People's Publishing House, 1980), 22, Historians' Files, CMH; hereafter cited as FBIS, *Central Highlands People's Armed Forces* (page numbers refer to the English translation).

25. Mataxis, "Monsoon," 5–7.

26. FBIS, *Central Highlands People's Armed Forces,* 19.

27. Ibid., 27.

28. Mataxis, "Monsoon," 7–11.

29. Ibid.

30. Ibid., 11–13.

31. Ibid., 13–14; Nguyen Dinh Uoc and Nguyen Van Minh, eds., *Lich Su Khang Chien Chong My Cuu Nuoc 1954–1975,* Tap III, *Danh Thang Chien Tranh Dac Biet* [History of the resistance war against the Americans to save the nation 1954–1975, vol. 3, Defeating the special war], trans. Merle Pribbenow (Hanoi: National Political Publishing House, 1997), 376.

32. Mataxis, "Monsoon," 15.

33. Ibid., 16; Duc, *Su Doan 325,* 58.

34. Mataxis, "Monsoon," 17.

35. Ibid., 17–19.

36. Le Thanh Canh, ed., *Lich Su Dang Bo Tinh Gia Lai,* Tap I [History of the Gia Lai Province Party committee chapter, vol. 1], trans. Merle Pribbenow (Hanoi: National Political Publishing House, 1997), 294; Nguyen Quoc Minh et al., *Lich Su Bo Doi Dac Cong,* Tap Mot [History of the sapper forces, vol. 1], trans. Merle Pribbenow (Hanoi: People's Publishing House, 1987), 116; Word Press Vietnamese Military History website, http://quansuvn.net/wordpress/p=316 (accessed 14 May 2014 and translated by Merle Pribbenow on the author's behalf).

37. Mataxis, "Monsoon," 20.

38. Uoc and Minh, *Lich Su Khang Chien,* 377.

39. Mataxis, "Monsoon," 21.

40. Ibid.; Minh et al., *Lich Su Bo Doi Dac Cong,* 116; Canh, *Lich Su Dang Bo Tinh Gia Lai,* 294.

41. Mataxis, "Monsoon," 21–22.

42. Ibid., 24–25.

43. Westmoreland, *Soldier,* 177–178; CIA, "The Situation in South Vietnam," 17 June 1965, 2, para. 5, folder 05, box 02, Larry Berman Collection (Presidential Archives Research), The Vietnam Center and Archive, Texas Tech University, http://www.vietnam.ttu.edu/virtualarchive/items.php? item=0240205002 (accessed 17 September 2014); CIA, "The Situation in South Vietnam," 17 June–23 June 1965," 1–6, ibid., http://www.vietnam.ttu.edu/virtualarchive/items.php?item=0240205003.

44. General H. Norman Schwarzkopf, *It Doesn't Take a Hero* (New York: Bantam, 1992),

126, 128–129; Vinh Loc, *FULRO: The So-Called Movement for Autonomy* (Pleiku and Ban Me Thuot, 1965); Westmoreland, *Soldier*, 417–424; "General Westmoreland's History Notes Vol. I," 29 October 1965, 91–92, Westmoreland Collection, CMH Library.

45. Information provided by Le Kim Huong, a former ARVN Ranger officer and long-time friend of the author.

46. Tin Nguyen, *General Hieu, ARVN: A Hidden Military Gem* (Lincoln, NE: Writer's Club Press, 2003), 23–27. Hieu, clearly a talented officer, served as chief of staff at II Corps under both Co and Vinh Loc. Tin Nguyen's book on his brother contains valuable material, even if one must be skeptical of the assessment of Hieu as both military genius and saint.

47. In Mataxis's narrative, this meeting is not dated. It is presented as if it happened before or at the beginning of the monsoon season. But Mataxis indicates that Vinh Loc was commanding II Corps at the time, and Vinh Loc did not take over until June. Mataxis, "Monsoon," 3–5.

48. Ibid., 22–23.

49. Ibid., 25–27; Uoc and Minh, *Lich Su Khang Chien*, 377; CIA, "Viet Cong Campaign in Central Highlands," 4, para. 10.

50. Nguyen Van Thuy et al., *Trung Doan 95 Thien Thuat (1945–1995)* [The 95th Thien Thuat Regiment (1945–1995)], trans. Merle Pribbenow (Hanoi: People's Publishing House, 1995), 94. This account indicates that it was the 95A Regiment that besieged and ultimately captured Thuan Man.

51. Mataxis, "Monsoon," 28.

52. Major William N. Ciccolo, Airborne Brigade Advisory Detachment to COMUS-MACV, "Combat Operations After Action Report: Trung Doan 58, 27 June–1 July," 26 July 1965, sections 5, 6, 11, MACV, Assistant Chief of Staff for Operations (J3) Evaluations and Analysis Division (MACVJ3–05), After Action Reports, box. 1, Report No. 9–Report No. 130, RG 472, Archives 2, NARA.

53. Ibid., sections 7, 8, 11; Mataxis, "Monsoon," 28–30.

54. Ciccolo, "After Action Report: Trung Doan 58," sections 7, 11; Mataxis, "Monsoon," 31.

55. Nguyen Tri Huan et al., *Su Doan Sao Vang* [The Yellow Star Division], trans. Merle Pribbenow (Hanoi: People's Army Publishing House, 1984), 15, 17. By 3 August 1965, the South Vietnamese and Americans had identified the main Communist force that attacked the 1st Airborne Task Force as the 2d Regiment. See Major W. G. Leftwich Jr. to Commander, U.S. Military Assistance Command, Vietnam (USMACV), "Combat After Action Report (MACV/RCS/J3/32) Trung Doan 58, 1400, 30 June to 100, 4 July 1965," 3 August 1965, 1–2, section 8, MACV, Assistant Chief of Staff for Operations (J3) Evaluation and Analysis Division (MACVJ3–05), After Action Reports, box 1, Report No. 9–Report 130, RG 472, Archives 2, NARA.

56. Thuy et al., *Trung Doan 95*, 94.

57. Duc, *Su Doan 325*, 58.

58. Uoc and Minh, *Lich Su Khang Chien*, 376. After acknowledging the strength of ARVN resistance during 30 June, the same source claims that at 0100 on 1 July Communist forces mounted a concerted nighttime attack that annihilated the 1st Airborne Battalion. This claim appears to be pure fiction. Ciccolo's after-action report mentions no night attack, and 1st Airborne Battalion was certainly not annihilated.

59. Mataxis, "Monsoon," 31; Duc, *Su Doan 325*, 58.

60. Mataxis, "Monsoon," 32–33; Leftwich, "After Action Report: Trung Doan 58," 1–2, sections 6–11.

61. Mataxis, "Monsoon," 33.

62. Leftwich, "After Action Report: Trung Doan 58," 2–3, sections 11, 15.

63. Ciccolo, "After Action Report: Trung Doan 58," sections 11, 12.

64. Leftwich, "After Action Report: Trung Doan 58," 2, section 11.

65. Mataxis, "Monsoon," 33–35.

66. Leftwich, "After Action Report: Trung Doan 58," 1–2, section 8.

67. Mataxis, "Monsoon," 36.

68. Ibid., 36–38.

69. Major W. G. Leftwich Jr. to Commander, USMACV, "Combat Operations After Action Report (MACV/RCS/J3/32) 8–14 July 1965," 4 August 1965, MACV, Assistant Chief of Staff for Operations (J3), Evaluation and Analysis Division (MACV J3–05), After Action Reports, box 1, Report No. 9–Report No. 130, RG 472, Archives 2, NARA; CIA, "Viet Cong Campaign in Central Highlands," 4, para. 10.

70. Mataxis, "Monsoon," 39.

71. Vinh Loc, "Road-Clearing Operation," *Military Review* 46, 4 (April 1966): 23.

72. Ibid., 23–27; Major W. G. Leftwich Jr. to Commander USMACV, "Combat Operations After Actions Report (MACV/RCS/J3/32) Dan Thien 109, 14–24 July 1965," 4 August 1965, 1–2, sections 1–11, MACV, Assistant Chief of Staff for Operations (J3), Evaluation and Analysis Division (MACV J3–05), After Action Reports, box 1, Report No. 9–Report No. 130, RG 472, Archives 2, NARA.

73. Major William N. Ciccolo to COMUSMACV, "Combat Operations After Action Report, Operation Free Way, 15 July to 25 July 1965," 17 August 1965, 1–4, sections 1–11, MACV, Assistant Chief of Staff for Operations (J3), Evaluation and Analysis Division (MACV J3–05), After Action Reports, box 1, Report No. 9–Report No. 130, RG 472, Archives 2, NARA.

74. Leftwich, "After Action Report: Dan Thien 109," 2–3, section 11.

75. Ciccolo, "After Action Report: Free Way," 9, section 13.

76. Vinh Loc, "Road-Clearing," 28.

77. Leftwich, "After Action Report: Dan Thien 109," 4, section 15.

78. Mataxis, "Monsoon," 40; Colonel Francis J. Kelly, *US Army Special Forces: 1961–1971* (Washington, DC: Department of the Army, 1973), 50, 69; J. D. Coleman, *Pleiku: The Dawn of Helicopter Warfare in Vietnam* (New York: St. Martin's Press, 1988), 53.

79. A-224/215, "Monthly Operational Summary for Month of February 1965," 28 February 1965, 5th Special Forces Group (Airborne), Records of A-Detachments, box 46, Detachment A-224, Duc Co, Pleiku Province, II CTZ, November 1964–March 1965, RG 472, Archives 2, NARA; Mataxis, "Monsoon," 40–41; Coleman, *Pleiku,* 55.

80. Schwarzkopf, *It Doesn't Take a Hero,* 126–130.

81. Lt. Colonel Robert J. Craig, Senior Adviser, 24 STZ to COMUSMACV, "Combat Operations After Action Report (MACV/RCS/J3/32) Dan Thang 4, 5, 6 and 7," 13 September 1965, 1–3, sections 1–9, MACV, Assistant Chief of Staff for Operation (J3), Evaluation and Analysis Division (MACJ3–05), After Action Reports, box 1, Report No. 9–Report No. 130, RG 472, Archives 2, NARA.

82. Craig, "After Action Report: Dan Thang," 1, 3, sections 6, 7, 11; Ha Mai Viet, *Steel and Blood: South Vietnamese Armor and the War for Southeast Asia* (Annapolis, MD: Naval Institute Press, 2008), 22.

83. Craig, "After Action Report: Dan Thang," 3, section 11c; Mataxis, "Monsoon," 41.

84. Craig, "After Action Report: Dan Thang," 4, section 11f.

85. Schwarzkopf, *It Doesn't Take a Hero,* 137.

86. Craig, "After Action Report: Dan Thang," 4, section 11f.

87. Mataxis, "Monsoon," 43; Craig, "After Action Report: Dan Thang," 4, section 11g.

88. Craig, "After Action Report: Dan Thang," 3, sections 10c, 10d.

89. Mataxis, "Monsoon," 43–46; Craig, "After Action Report: Dan Thang," 2, sections 7a, 7b.

90. Craig, "After Action Report: Dan Thang," 4, section 11h.

91. Ibid., sections 11n, 11o.

92. Coleman, *Pleiku,* 54–55; Craig, "After Action Report: Dan Thang," 5, section 11p.

93. Craig, "After Action Report: Dan Thang," 5, section 11q.

94. Ibid., 5, section 11r; 2, section 7d; 6, section 11w.

95. Mataxis, "Monsoon," 49.

96. Shelby B. Stanton, *Green Berets at War: U.S. Army Special Forces in Southeast Asia 1956–1975* (London: Arms & Armour, 1986), 110.

97. Craig, "After Action Report: Dan Thang," 5, sections 11t, 11u, 11v, 11w.

98. Mataxis, "Monsoon," 49–52.

99. Ibid., 52–54.

100. FBIS, *Central Highlands People's Armed Forces,* 24.

101. Mataxis, "Monsoon," 55.

102. Ibid.

103. Stanton, *Green Berets,* 110.

104. Mataxis, "Monsoon," 57; Major W. G. Leftwich to Commander USMACV, "Combat Operations After Action Report (MACV/RCS/J3/32) Than Phong 3, Road Security, 22 August through 1 September 1965," 3 September 1965, and Major W. N. Ciccolo to Commander USMACV, "Eagle 3, 24 August to 1 September 1965," 13 September 1965, MACV, Assistant Chief of Staff for Operations (J3), Evaluation and Analysis Division (MACJ3–05), After Action Reports, box 1, Report No. 9–Report No. 130, RG 472, Archives 2, NARA.

105. Mataxis, "Monsoon," 57.

106. Gia Lai Province Party Committee, "Vai Tro va Nhuug Dong Gop cua Luc Luong Vu Trang Dia Phuong Tinh Gia Lai Trong Chien Dich Play Me 11–1965" [The role and contributions of Gia Lai local armed forces in the Plei Me campaign, November 1965], in *Chien Thang Plei Me: Ba Muoi Nam Sau Nhin Lai (Tai Lieu Hoi Thao Kha Hoc),* ed T. V. Hong et al. [The Plei Me victory: looking back after thirty years (a scientific conference document)], trans. Merle Pribbenow (Hanoi: People's Publishing House, 1995), 81; Mataxis, "Monsoon," 59.

107. One Communist history claims that in Gia Lai the Communist Party controlled a total of 226,000 people by the late monsoon season (September–October). Of these, 117,000 had been "liberated" in the spring (roughly February–May) of 1965, and 50,000 in the summer (May–October). These figures are interesting, in that the number of people the Communist Party claimed to control in Gia Lai at the end of 1964 was remarkably small. See Gia Lai Province Party Committee, "Vai Tro va Nhuug Dong Gop," 79. Another Communist history claims that at the end of the summer of 1965 the Party controlled a little less than 60 percent of the population of Gia Lai. See Canh, *Lich Su Dang Bo Tinh Gia Lai,* 297. Mataxis's claim that the South Vietnamese government still controlled more than half the total population of the Central Highlands at the end of the monsoon season is not necessarily incompatible with that Communist claim, especially if southern provinces such as Quang Duc, Tuyen Duc, and Lam Dong are included in Mataxis's assessment. Even if these southern provinces are left out, the gap between the official postwar Communist

claim regarding population control in Gia Lai (almost 60 percent) and Mataxis's claim for government control (more than 50 percent) are not vastly different readings of the situation.

Chapter 11. Plei Me: Background, Siege, and Relief, August–October 1965

1. Theodore C. Mataxis, "Monsoon Offensive in the Highlands," 57, Mataxis Papers, USAMHI; Foreign Broadcast Information Service, trans., *Luc Luong Vu Trang Nhan Dan Tay Nguyen Trong Khang Chien Chong My Cuu Nuoc* [History of the Central Highlands people's armed forces in the anti-US war of resistance for national salvation] (Hanoi: People's Publishing House, 1980), 24–25, Historians' Files, CMH; hereafter cited as FBIS, *Central Highlands People's Armed Forces* (page numbers refer to the English translation).

2. Pham Gia Duc, *Su Doan 325,* Tap II [325th Division, vol. 2], trans. Merle Pribbenow (Hanoi: People's Publishing House, 1986), 56. This work indicates that in February–March 1965 in Kontum Province, the infantry of PAVN Regiment 101A was living on "only 250 grams of food per day" and that personnel "assigned to staff organizations voluntarily reduced their own daily rations in order to increase the daily rations being supplied to front-line units." Mataxis, "Monsoon," 50–52, gives details of a captured document indicating acute malnutrition and sickness in the PAVN 32d Regiment at the time of the Duc Co campaign in July–August 1965. According to an unpublished American paper, some 40 percent of the personnel in the 33d Regiment's rifle companies were sick at the time of the siege of Plei Me. Major William Boyle and Major Robert Samabria, "The Lure and the Ambush," 5, Historians' Files, CMH.

3. The involvement of part of the 95A (aka 10th) Regiment in the disastrous Communist attack on the Special Forces camp at Kannack on the night of 7–8 March 1965 is frankly discussed in "Attack on Ka Nak Outpost . . . Heroic Saga in the Vast Jungle," *Gia Lai* (Vietnamese provincial newspaper), 24 July 2009, http://baogialai.com.vn/channel /1624/200907/tran-danh-don-ka-nak-7-3-1965-khuc-trang-ca-giua-dai-ngan-1713482/ (accessed 26 January 2014 and translated by Merle Pribbenow on the author's behalf). The defeat of the 32d Regiment at Duc Co is outlined in Mataxis, "Monsoon," 46–49.

4. Duc, *Su Doan 325,* 61. After the action at Dak Sut, the 101A Regiment went to Cochin China, the southern portion of South Vietnam. At roughly the same time, the 95A Regiment was ordered to go to the Phu Khanh lowlands in MR 5, and the 18A Regiment went to Binh Dinh, where it formed the basis of 3d Division, which would subsequently operate in northern Binh Dinh and southern Quang Ngai.

5. Boyle and Samabria, "Lure," 2–3.

6. Ibid., 2–6; Mataxis, "Monsoon," 46–49; Colonel Nguyen Van Bieu, *Mot so Tran Danh cua don vi thuoc Binh doan Tay Nguyen,* Tap V [A number of battles fought by units of the Central Highlands corps, vol. 5], trans. Merle Pribbenow (Hanoi: People's Publishing House, 1996), 37.

7. J. D. Coleman, *Pleiku: The Dawn of Helicopter Warfare in Vietnam* (New York: St. Martin's Press, 1988), 51–53. Coleman was a staff officer with the US 1st Cavalry Division and dealt principally with publicity matters during the Plei Me–Ia Drang campaign. He had access to the division's papers and some captured documents. His account does not include source references, but it remains the standard book-length study of the campaign as a whole. His analysis of its place in Communist strategy, however, is taken word for word from Boyle and Samabria, "Lure," 3, and is very much open to question.

8. Boyle and Samabria were US Army majors serving in Vietnam in 1965 as intelligence

officers: Boyle at ARVN II Corps, and Samabria with 1st Brigade, 101st Airborne Division. Their "Lure" paper is based on captured documents and interrogation reports, is fully referenced, and was used as a source for the US Army's official history: John M. Carland, *Stemming the Tide: May 1965 to October 1966* (Washington, DC: Center of Military History, US Army, 2000), 96, 99. The "Lure" paper generally stands up well in relation to other sources that are now available. But the account of the Communist strategy that led to the campaign appears to be based on the interrogation of a single PAVN political officer with the rank of first lieutenant—a flimsy foundation for such a grandiose analysis. I am grateful to Merle Pribbenow for pointing out that this part of Boyle and Samabria's paper does not fit with what we know about Communist strategy from postwar Communist publications and makes little sense in relation to the war's course at that time.

9. Communist forces' concerns about their ability to cope with American troops and technology are outlined in FBIS, *Central Highlands People's Armed Forces*, 29, and Gia Lai Province Party Committee, "Vai Tro va Nhung Dong Gop cua Luc Long Vu Trang Dia Phuong Tinh Gia Lai Trong Chien Dich Play Me 11–1965" [The role and contribution of Gia Lai Province local armed forces in the Plei Me campaign, November 1965], in *Chien Thang Plei Me: Ba Muoi Nam Sau Nhin Lai (Tai Lieu Hoi Thao Kha Hoc),* ed. Trinh Vuong Hong et al. [The Plei Me victory: looking back after thirty years (a scientific conference document)], trans. Merle Pribbenow (Hanoi: People's Publishing House, 1995), 81.

10. Bieu, *Mot so Tran Danh,* 32.

11. Communist planners anticipated that "one or two US battalions" might be assigned as reserves for the ARVN battle groups charged with the relief of Plei Me. See "Combat Order for an Ambush by the 32d Regiment, Prepared at Regimental Headquarters, Plei-Luo-Chin at 1500 hours, 12 October 1965," para. 1, annex B to Boyle and Samabria, "Lure." The Communists' standard one-volume military history of the war indicates that a principal aim of the Plei Me campaign was "to study the fighting methods of the Americans in actual combat." See Merle Pribbenow, trans., *Victory in Vietnam: The Official History of the People's Army of Vietnam 1954–1975* (Lawrence: University Press of Kansas, 2002), 158. But, as Pribbenow has pointed out, the North Vietnamese did not deliberately lure American forces into their base area in order to destroy them; the arrival of the US 1/7th Cavalry in the area of the Chu Pong massif on 14 November 1965 took PAVN forces by surprise. Merle L. Pribbenow, "The Fog of War: The Vietnamese View of the Ia Drang Battle," *Military Review* 81, 1 (January–February 2001): 94.

12. Boyle and Samabria, "Lure," 3, 5; Coleman, *Pleiku,* 53–55.

13. Boyle and Samabria, "Lure," 2–3.

14. On the familiarity of ARVN forces and their US advisers with Communist "lure and ambush" methods by October 1965, see John Laurence, *The Cat from Hue: A Vietnam War Story* (New York: Public Affairs, 2002), 236–237. See also Vinh Loc, *Why Plei Me* (Pleiku and Ban Me Thuot, 1966), 53–67, USAMHI.

15. Mai Hong Linh, "A Number of Issues Relating to Party and Political Activities during the Plei Me Campaign—1965," in Hong, *Chien Thang Plei Me,* 110; Pribbenow, "Fog," 93; Bieu, *Mot so Tran Danh,* 38.

16. Coleman, *Pleiku,* 60–62; Bieu, *Mot so Tran Danh,* 34.

17. "Target Folder: Special Forces Camp, Plei Me, Prepared by II Section, 55 MI Det., Oct. 65," 5th Special Forces Group (Airborne), Records of A-Detachments, box 187, Detachment A-217, Plei Me, Pleiku Province, II CTZ, May 1965–January 1966, RG 472, Archives 2, NARA. Other information on crew-served weapons at Plei Me was provided by Solomon Vaughn Binzer, who served as a captain in Pleiku sector headquarters in 1965.

18. "Inclosure 1 (CIDG in Camp Defense) to Quarterly Command Report for Period Ending 31 December 1965," HQ, 5th SFG (Abn), 1st SF, 10 January 1966, para. 1 (b), Historians' Files, CMH (hereafter cited as "Camp Defense"); "Plei Me Psyops Estimate" (undated), 5th Special Forces Group (Airborne), Records of A-Detachments, box 187, Detachment A-217, Plei Me, Pleiku Province, II CTZ, May 1965–January 1966, RG 472, Archives 2, NARA; Colonel Francis J. Kelly, *US Army Special Forces: 1961–1971* (Washington, DC: Department of the Army, 1973), 50, 70.

19. "Comrade Siu Sir, Deputy Village Military Unit Commander, spent two months directing the local militia in cooking rice and transporting food to supply our reconnaissance personnel watching the Plei Me outpost." "Vai Tro va Nhung," in Hong, *Chien Thang Plei Me,* 85.

20. Boyle and Samabria, "Lure," 5.

21. Article by Colonel Do Dac Yen in *Quan Doi Nhan Dan* (People's Army) newspaper, 7 December 2014, http://qdnd.vn/qdndsite/vi-vn/61/43/khoa-hoc-nghe-thuat-quan-su/chuan-bi-chu-dao-va-linh-hoat-baodam-can-ky-thuat-cho-chien-dich/335186 (accessed 7 December 2014 and translated by Merle Pribbenow as "Meticulous Preparation and Flexible Logistics-Technical Support for the Campaign").

22. "Vai Tro va Nhung," in Hong, *Chien Thang Plei Me,* 81; Le Thanh Canh, ed., *Lich Su Dang bo tinh Gia Lai,* Tap I [History of the Gia Lai Province Party committee chapter, vol. 1], trans. Merle Pribbenow (Hanoi: National Political Publishing House, 1996), 297.

23. "Vai Tro va Nhung," in Hong, *Chien Thang Plei Me,* 79.

24. Ibid., 83.

25. Gerald C. Hickey, *Sons of the Mountains: Ethnohistory of the Vietnamese Central Highlands to 1954* (New Haven, CT: Yale University Press, 1982), 314–315.

26. "Vai Tro va Nhung," in Hong, *Chien Thang Plei Me,* 84.

27. Ibid., 84–85.

28. Canh, *Gia Lai,* 319; "Vai Tro va Nhung," in Hong, *Chien Thang Plei Me,* 83.

29. "Vai Tro va Nhung," in Hong, *Chien Thang Plei Me,* 86.

30. Boyle and Samabria, "Lure," 4.

31. Ibid., 5–6; Bieu, *Mot so Tran Danh,* 43. This 1990s Hanoi history confirms that the 32d Regiment had two antiaircraft companies instead of the usual one.

32. Bieu, *Mot so Tran Danh,* 33–35, 39–46; Boyle and Samabria, "Lure," 4–5.

33. "Camp Defense," 1, para. 1(a).

34. Colonel Archie D. Hyle, Senior Adviser Special Tactical Zone 24, "Combat Operations After Action Report (MACV/RCS/J3/32) Operation Dan Thang 21 (Plei Me) 20 October thru 29 October 1965," 5 December 1965, 3, section 8, "Intelligence," para. a., MACV J3, After Action Reports, Report No. 9–Report No. 130, box 1, RG 472, Archives 2, NARA.

35. USMACV, Assistant Chief of Staff J-2, "Intelligence Aspects of the Plei Me/Chu Pong Campaign 20 October–20 November 1965," 6, MACV Papers, USAMHI.

36. "Camp Defense," 1, para. 1(a); W. Beene, "Plei Me Fight Stands as War Turning Point," *Stars and Stripes,* 27 December 1965.

37. Beene, "Plei Me."

38. Coleman, *Pleiku,* 71.

39. Boyle and Samabria, "Lure," 4.

40. "Camp Defense," 1, section 2(a).

41. Ibid., section 2(b).

42. "The Siege at Plei Me," 24 February 1966, HQ ACAF, Tactical Evaluation Center, Project CHECO, 2, Historians' Files, CMH; "Camp Defense," 1, section 2(b).

43. "Camp Defense," 2, section 2(c); Shelby B. Stanton, *Green Berets at War: U.S. Army Special Forces in Southeast Asia 1956–1975* (London: Arms & Armour, 1986), 114.

44. "Camp Defense," 2, section 2(d).

45. Ibid.; Charlie A. Beckwith, Major Inf. Commanding Detachment B-52, 5th Special Forces Group (Airborne), 1st Special Forces, "Sequence of Events for the Plei Me Operation for Period 20–28 October 1965," 15 November 1965, Inclosure 22 to Quarterly Command Report, 31 December 1965, 1.

46. "Camp Defense," 2, section 2(e).

47. Laurence, *Cat,* 258; Charles Beckwith and Donald Knox, *Delta Force: The US Counter-Terrorist Unit and the Iranian Hostage Rescue Mission* (London: Arms & Armour, 1984), 14–44.

48. Beckwith, "Sequence," 1; Beckwith and Knox, *Delta,* 63–64.

49. Beckwith, "Sequence," 2; Beckwith and Knox, *Delta,* 64.

50. Beckwith "Sequence," 2; Coleman, *Pleiku,* 78; Beckwith and Knox, *Delta,* 64.

51. Beckwith, "Sequence," 2; Beckwith and Knox, *Delta,* 65–66; Laurence, *Cat,* 259.

52. Beckwith, "Sequence," 2; "Camp Defense," 2; Beckwith and Knox, *Delta,* 66–67; Laurence, *Cat,* 260.

53. Beckwith, "Sequence," 3; "Camp Defense," 2(f); Coleman, *Pleiku,* 79.

54. Beckwith and Knox, *Delta,* 67.

55. Laurence, *Cat,* 260–261.

56. Laurence indicates that the camp was filthy and its defenders extremely grimy when he got there at the end of the siege. Laurence, *Cat,* 262–263, 270.

57. "Camp Defense," 3–4.

58. "General Westmoreland's History Notes, Vol. I: 29 August 1965–1 January 1966," 88–89, Tuesday, 26 October 1965, CMH Library.

59. "Camp Defense," 2–4; Beckwith, "Sequence," 3–4.

60. Beckwith and Knox, *Delta,* 68.

61. Beckwith, "Sequence," 3.

62. Ibid.; Beckwith and Knox, *Delta,* 68. Beckwith's account of this episode in his memoirs is somewhat different from that in his after-action report. I follow the after-action version here.

63. Beckwith and Knox, *Delta,* 69; Laurence, *Cat,* 282.

64. "Camp Defense," 4, section 3(b).

65. "Siege at Plei Me," 1; John Schlight, *The War in South Vietnam: The Years of the Offensive 1965–1968* (Washington, DC: Office of Air Force History, US Air Force, 1988), 101.

66. "Siege at Plei Me," 3–4; "Camp Defense," 3, section 3(h), 4, section 3(b).

67. Beckwith and Knox, *Delta,* 68–69.

68. Beckwith, "Sequence," 3–4.

69. Ibid., 4.

70. Laurence, *Cat,* 258–267. The Beckwith TV interview can be found online by going to YouTube and entering "Plei Me."

71. "Camp Defense," 3, section 2(i), 4, section 4.

72. Beckwith and Knox, *Delta,* 71.

73. Ibid.; Beckwith, "Sequence," 4.

74. Coleman, *Pleiku,* 75, 78. Coleman is slightly inconsistent about the number of Airborne Rangers sent to Plei Me but indicates somewhere between 135 and 150. "Camp Defense," 4, section 4.

75. "Camp Defense," 4, section 4.

76. Beckwith, "Sequence," 4; "Camp Defense," 3, section 2(j).

77. Hyle, "After Action Report: Dan Thang 21," 3, section 8(a)–8(e).

78. Ibid., sections 9–11(b); Ha Mai Viet, *Steel and Blood: South Vietnamese Armor and the War for Southeast Asia* (Annapolis, MD: Naval Institute Press, 2008), 26.

79. Hyle, "After Action Report: Dan Thang 21," 6, section 11(b); Coleman, *Pleiku,* 75–76.

80. Coleman, *Pleiku,* 76; Laurence, *Cat,* 236.

81. Coleman, *Pleiku,* 60; Vinh Loc, *FULRO: The So-Called Movement for Autonomy* (Pleiku and Ban Me Thuot, 1965).

82. There were serious FULRO-organized disturbances in parts of the Central Highlands in December 1965. Memorandum from Lt. Col. Jay B. Durst to Brig. Gen. William E. DePuy, "FULRO," 20 December 1965, 5th Special Forces Group S-3 Command Reports, box 3, RG 472, Archives 2, NARA; Vietnamese Affairs Staff, Office of the Director of Central Intelligence, "The Highlanders of South Vietnam: A Review of Political Developments and Forces," 79–97, Historians' Files, CMH.

83. Hyle, "After Action Report: Dan Thang 21," 6, section 11(b).

84. Coleman, *Pleiku,* 63, 75–76; Major General George S. Eckhardt, *Command and Control: 1950–1969* (Washington, DC: Department of the Army, 1974), 52–54; "Westmoreland's History Notes," 31, Monday, 20 September 1965, 71, Monday, 18 October 1965; General William C. Westmoreland, *A Soldier Reports* (New York: Dell, 1976), 201.

85. Coleman, *Pleiku,* 76, 80; Carland, *Stemming,* 101; Hyle, "After Action Report: Dan Thang 21," 6, sections 11(b), 11(d).

86. Shelby B. Stanton, *The 1st Cav in Vietnam: Anatomy of a Division* (Novato, CA: Presidio Press, 1987), 1–43; Carland, *Stemming,* 57–63; "Westmoreland's History Notes," 13 September 1965; Coleman, *Pleiku,* 62–69.

87. On Kinnard's ambition, see "Westmoreland's History Notes," Sunday, 29 August, and Tuesday, 31 August 1965. On unfavorable publicity for the 1st Cavalry Division and Westmoreland's communication with Kinnard about it, see ibid., Sunday, 17 October, and Thursday, 21 October 1965.

88. Coleman, *Pleiku,* 80.

89. Hyle, "After Action Report: Dan Thang 21," 6, sections 11(c), 11(d).

90. Ibid., section 11(d); Vinh Loc, *Why Plei Me,* 64.

91. Laurence, *Cat,* 237–245; Coleman, *Pleiku,* 83–85.

92. Some of Phuoc's concerns were explained to Laurence by Vietnamese cameraman Vo Huyn. At the time, Laurence believed Phuoc was too cautious; however, once he gained more war experience, he was less sure. Laurence, *Cat,* 243.

93. Hyle, "After Action Report: Dan Thang 21," 6, section 11(d).

94. Laurence, *Cat,* 240–241.

95. Boyle and Samabria, "Lure," 7–9; Coleman, *Pleiku,* 82.

96. Bieu, *Mot so Tran Danh,* 52; Laurence, *Cat,* 254–256.

97. Coleman, *Pleiku,* 82.

98. Hyle, "After Action Report: Dan Thang 21," 6, section 11(d). See also Vinh Loc, *Why Plei Me,* 64.

99. Hyle, "After Action Report: Dan Thang 21," 6, section 11(d); Coleman, *Pleiku,* 83.

100. Ibid.

101. Boyle and Samabria, "Lure," 9; Coleman, *Pleiku,* 84–85.

102. Hyle, "After Action Report: Dan Thang 21," 7, section 11(d), 9–10; Bieu, *Mot so Tran Danh,* 59.

103. Hyle, "After Action Report: Dan Thang 21," 7, section 11(e).

104. Boyle and Samabria, "Lure," 9; Coleman, *Pleiku,* 85–87.

105. Hyle, "After Action Report: Dan Thang 21," 7, section 11(f); Coleman, *Pleiku,* 87.

106. Laurence, *Cat,* 255–257.

107. Ibid., 257.

108. Boyle and Samabria, "Lure," 10.

109. Laurence, *Cat,* 268.

110. Hyle, "After Action Report: Dan Thang 21," 7, section 11(g), 12, section 11 (k)3(f).

111. Ibid.; Laurence, *Cat,* 274–282.

112. Laurence, *Cat,* 276–277; Hyle, "After Action Report: Dan Thang 21," 9, section 11(k)d.

113. Hyle, "After Action Report: Dan Thang 21," 7, section 11(g).

114. Ibid., 7–8, sections 11(h), (i), (j); Coleman, *Pleiku,* 89–90; Beckwith, "Sequence," 5; Major William G. Leftwich Jr. to COMUSMACV (Westmoreland), "Combat Operations After Action Report (MACV/RCS/J3/32), Dan Thang 21, Road Security, 1600 27 October to 1630 29 October 1965," 1 November 1965, MACV, Assistant Chief of Staff for Operations (J3), After Action Reports, box 1, RG 472, Archives 2, NARA.

115. Bieu, *Mot so Tranh Danh,* 33–34; FBIS, *Central Highlands People's Armed Forces,* 31.

116. Pribbenow, "Fog," 93; Bieu, *Mot so Tran Danh,* 38, 39, 41. The latter account refers to many "heated arguments and tense debates" between "positive thinking and negative thinking" members of the 32d Regiment when, less than a month after Duc Co, it received orders to participate in the Plei Me campaign. It also refers to particular "fears of enemy armored fighting vehicles."

117. Laurence, *Cat,* 241–242.

118. Bieu, *Mot so Tran Danh,* 58.

119. Ibid., 57–61.

120. "Camp Defense," 2, 3.

121. Laurence, *Cat,* 264–265.

122. Boyle and Samabria, "Lure," 10.

Chapter 12. Retreat, Search, and Pursuit, October–November 1965

1. William P. Boyle and Robert Samabria, "The Lure and the Ambush," 9–10, Historians' Files, CMH.

2. John Schlight, *The War in South Vietnam: The Years of the Offensive 1965–1968* (Washington, DC: Office of Air Force History, US Air Force, 1988), 101–102; Shelby B. Stanton, *The 1st Cav in Vietnam: Anatomy of a Division* (Novato, CA: Presidio, 1987), 50; John M. Carland, *Stemming the Tide: May 1965 to October 1966* (Washington, DC: Center of Military History, US Army, 2000), 104.

3. Stanton, *1st Cav,* 25.

4. "General Westmoreland's History Notes," vol. 1, 29 August–1 January 1966, 1, Sunday, 29 August 1965, CMH Library.

5. General William C. Westmoreland, *A Soldier Reports* (New York: Dell, 1976), 135–137; "Westmoreland's History Notes," 1, 4, 69, 80, 121.

6. J. D. Coleman, *Pleiku: The Dawn of Helicopter Warfare in Vietnam* (New York: St. Martin's Press, 1988), 46–47; Stanton, *1st Cav,* 45.

7. Carland, *Stemming,* 101.

8. Coleman, *Pleiku,* 88–98.

9. Carland, *Stemming,* 104.

10. Coleman, *Pleiku,* 92.

11. "1st Cavalry Division (Airmobile) Combat Operations After Action Report, Pleiku Campaign, Pleiku Province, Republic of South Vietnam, 23 Oct–26 Nov 1965," 28, "Addendum," USARV Command Historian After Action Reports, box 24, RG 472, Archives 2, NARA.

12. "Westmoreland's History Notes," 87–89, Tuesday, 26 October 1965.

13. Carland, *Stemming,* 105.

14. "Westmoreland's History Notes," 90, Thursday, 28 October 1965.

15. Carland, *Stemming,* 104.

16. Lt. Col. Earl K. Buchan, ACofS, G3, order dated 021165, 1–2, 1st Cavalry Division, Assistant Chief of Staff G-3, Operations Planning Files, Fragos 1965 to Oplans 1968, box 1, USARV, RG 472, Archives 2, NARA.

17. Coleman, *Pleiku,* 92–93; Carland, *Stemming,* 104–105.

18. On Westmoreland's attitude toward Vinh Loc, see "Westmoreland's History Notes," 92, 166. On Vinh Loc's "decision" to mount a pursuit, see Vinh Loc, *Why Plei Me* (Pleiku and Ban Me Thuot, 1966), 73–74.

19. Coleman, *Pleiku,* 27–28.

20. Col. Thomas W. Brown to Major John A. Cash, 8 August 1967, 1, and John Pritchard to John Cash, 8 April 1968, Historians' Files, CMH.

21. USMACV, Assistant Chief of Staff, J-2, "Intelligence Aspect of Plei Me/Chu Pong Campaign, 20 October–20 November 1965," 6, MACV Papers, USAMHI.

22. Charles Beckwith and Donald Knox, *Delta Force: The U.S. Counter-Terrorist Unit and the Iranian Hostage Rescue Mission* (London: Arms & Armour, 1984), 73–75.

23. Stanton, *1st Cav,* 39.

24. Carland, *Stemming,* 95; Coleman, *Pleiku,* 95.

25. "1st Cavalry Division After Action Report," 33; Coleman, *Pleiku,* 98.

26. Stanton, *1st Cav,* 51; Coleman, *Pleiku,* 41–42.

27. Coleman, *Pleiku,* 98–99.

28. "1st Cavalry Division After Action Report," 28, para. 5, "Addendum."

29. Coleman, *Pleiku,* 103–106.

30. Ibid., 106; "1st Cavalry Division After Action Report," 31, 34, 37.

31. Coleman, *Pleiku,* 95–97, 106–107; Carland, *Stemming,* 105.

32. Ray L. Bowers, *Tactical Airlift* (Washington, DC: Office of Air Force History, 1983), 213–214; Coleman, *Pleiku,* 107–108; Carland, *Stemming,* 105–106.

33. Coleman, *Pleiku,* 95–96; "1st Cavalry After Action Report," 48.

34. Lieutenant General Harold G. Moore and Joseph L. Galloway, *We Were Soldiers Once and Young: Ia Drang, the Battle that Changed the War in Vietnam* (New York: Random House, 1992), 19; information from CMH, courtesy of Andy Birtle.

35. Captain Joseph M. Tupas and SP4 Morris H. Brown, "History of the First Squadron, Ninth Cavalry Regiment, 1 July to 31 December 1965," 33–34, 14th Military History Detachment, Historians' Background Files, History/1st Sqn, 9th Cav Regt 1965–Binh Dinh Pacification Campaign 1966, RG 472, Archives 2, NARA; "1st Cavalry Division After Action Report," 45; Coleman, *Pleiku,* 111–112; Carland, *Stemming,* 106–107; "1st Cavalry Division After Action Report," 4; Steve Yarnell, "The Hospital Battle," in *Hunter Killer Squadron: Aero-Weapons, Aero Scouts, Aero-Rifles, Vietnam 1965–1972,* ed. Matthew Brennan (Novato, CA: Presidio, 1990), 5–11.

36. "1st Cavalry Division After Action Report," 46.

37. Ibid., 48.

38. Ibid., 51; Coleman, *Pleiku,* 140.

39. "1st Cavalry Division After Action Report," 51.

40. Coleman, *Pleiku,* 102.

41. Tupas and Brown, "History of First Squadron," 36–37; "1st Cavalry Division After Action Report," 51; Coleman, *Pleiku,* 141–142.

42. "1st Cavalry Division After Action Report," 51; Lt. Col. John B. Stockton to Commanding General 1st Air Cavalry Division, "Drang River Ambush," 6 November 1965, 1–2, Headquarters, United States Army Vietnam Command Historian After Action Reports, box 9, Davy Crockett/1st Cav Div–Duc Lap/1 Field Force Vietnam, RG 472, Archives 2, NARA.

43. Stockton, "Drang," 1–2; "1st Cavalry Division After Action Report," 51.

44. "1st Cavalry Division After Action Report," 54; Colonel Kenneth D. Mertel, *Year of the Horse: 1st Air Cavalry in the Highlands 1965–1967* (Atglen, PA: Schiffer Military History, 1997), 113–124.

45. Stockton, "Drang," 2, para. 3.

46. "1st Cavalry Division After Action Report," 54.

47. Ibid., 52; "Intelligence Aspect of Plei Me/Chu Pong Campaign," 28. Strangely, the MACV's "Intelligence Aspect" paper, which appears to be largely direct plagiarism of the "1st Cavalry Division After Action Report," disagrees about which battalion of the PAVN 66th Regiment was involved in the Ia Drang ambush of 3 November. The division's report indicates the 8th Battalion, and the MACV indicates the 9th Battalion. This may represent no more than incompetent plagiarism.

48. "1st Cavalry Division After Action Report," 54; Stockton, "Drang," 1–2; Coleman, *Pleiku,* 151.

49. Coleman, *Pleiku,* 48–49.

50. "1st Cavalry Division After Action Report," 54–55; Coleman, *Pleiku,* 155–160. These two sources disagree as to the number of PAVN bodies found after this firefight. Coleman states twenty-two, but the division reports only four.

51. "1st Cavalry Division After Action Report," 54–55.

52. Ibid., 57–58, 60–61; Carland, *Stemming,* 110–111; Coleman, *Pleiku,* 163–169, 17, and 175.

53. "1st Cavalry Division After Action Report"; Coleman, *Pleiku,* 175, and photo caption facing 153; Harry Kinnard, "A Victory in the Ia Drang: The Triumph of a Concept," *Army,* September 1967, 77–84.

54. Coleman, *Pleiku,* 81, 153, 169–170.

55. On the morning of 1 November there was some excitement about the capture of the PAVN aid station. Vinh Loc, Mataxis, Larsen, and Knowles all flew in to visit the site before the North Vietnamese counterattack developed in the early afternoon. Carland, *Stemming,* 106. The excitement turned to disappointment on subsequent days.

56. Stanton, *1st Cav,* 50.

57. Coleman, *Pleiku,* 100–101.

58. Kinnard, "Victory," 84.

59. Boyle and Samabria, "Lure," 11–12.

60. Ibid., 15. At the end of their account of the North Vietnamese side of the Pleiku campaign, Boyle and Samabria analyze the casualties sustained by the three PAVN regiments involved, supposedly based on PAVN sources. They do not estimate the number of casualties inflicted on 33d Regiment during its pursuit by 1st Brigade, but the figures they do provide suggest that the great majority of its losses occurred during the siege of Plei Me.

61. For a discussion of the Clausewitzian theme of the fog of war in relation to the Pleiku campaign, see Merle L. Pribbenow, "The Fog of War: The Vietnamese View of the Ia Drang Battle," *Military Review* 81, 1 (January–February 2001): 93–97.

62. Coleman, *Pleiku,* 179.

Chapter 13. Catecka and X-Ray, November 1965

1. "1st Cavalry Division (Airmobile) Combat Operations After Action Report, Pleiku Campaign, Pleiku Province, Republic of Vietnam, 23 October–26 November 1965," 69–79, Headquarters, United States Army Vietnam Command Historian After Action Reports, box 24, RG 472, Archives 2, NARA; John M. Carland, *Stemming the Tide: May 1965 to October 1966* (Washington, DC: Center of Military History, US Army, 2000), 111; J. D. Coleman, *Pleiku: The Dawn of Helicopter Warfare in South Vietnam* (New York: St. Martin's Press, 1988), 173–181.

2. "1st Cavalry Division After Action Report," 69–79; William P. Boyle and Robert Samabria, "The Lure and the Ambush," 10–11, 15, Historians' Files, CMH; Lieutenant General Harold G. Moore and Joseph L. Galloway, *We Were Soldiers Once . . . and Young: Ia Drang, the Battle that Changed the War in Vietnam* (New York: Random House, 1992), 50.

3. John Pritchard to John Cash, 4 April 1968, Historians' Files, CMH.

4. Moore and Galloway, *We Were Soldiers,* 63.

5. Information from CMH, courtesy of Andrew Birtle; Moore and Galloway, *We Were Soldiers,* 19–20; Coleman, *Pleiku,* 175.

6. Coleman, *Pleiku,* 20, 175–176, 186–187; Moore and Galloway, *We Were Soldiers,* 207.

7. Coleman, *Pleiku,* 176–177; Moore and Galloway, *We Were Soldiers,* 34–35.

8. "1st Cavalry Division After Action Report," 78; Merle L. Pribbenow, "The Fog of War: The Vietnamese View of the Ia Drang Battle," *Military Review* 81, 1 (January–February 2001): 93; Nguyen Huu An (as told to Nguyen Tu Duong), *Chien Truong Moi* [New battlefield], trans. Merle Pribbenow (Hanoi: People's Publishing House, 2002), 31; Major Leon McCall Jr. to Commanding General 1st Air Cavalry Division, "Command After-Action Report, Operation Silver Bayonet, 9–20 November 1965," 4 December 1965, 1–2, section 8, "Intelligence," para. c, Historians' Files, CMH; Coleman, *Pleiku,* 181–183.

9. Captain George C. Johnson to Commanding Officer 3d Brigade, 1st Cavalry Division (Airmobile), "After Action Report—Operation Silver Bayonet—12–21 November 1965," 24 November 1965, 1; "Activity for the Period 12–21 November 1965," 1–2, Headquarters United States Army Vietnam Command Historian, After Action Reports, box 30, RG 472, Archives 2, NARA; McCall, "After-Action Report: Operation Silver Bayonet," 2, section 8, 2, "Intelligence," para. D; Coleman, *Pleiku,* 178–181.

10. Pritchard to Cash, 4 April 1968, Historians' Files, CMH.

11. Brown to Cash, 8 August 1967, Historians' Files, CMH; McCall, "After-Action Report: Operation Silver Bayonet," 1, section 8, "Intelligence," para. B.

12. Carland, *Stemming,* 114; Moore and Galloway, *We Were Soldiers,* 83; Coleman, *Pleiku,* 181.

13. Moore to Commanding Officer, 3d Brigade, 1st Cavalry Division, "After-Action Report, Ia Drang Valley Operation, 1st Battalion, 7th Cavalry, 14–16 November 1965," 9 December 1965, 1, section 2, "Background," para. B, Historians' Files, CMH; Coleman, *Pleiku,* 183–185.

14. Moore and Galloway, *We Were Soldiers,* 39, 55, 63.

15. Ibid., 36, 58.

16. Coleman, *Pleiku,* 185; Carland, *Stemming,* 114.

17. Moore, "After-Action Report: Ia Drang," 2, section 2, "Background," para. D; Carland, *Stemming,* 114; Moore and Galloway, *We Were Soldiers,* 39, 215.

18. Moore and Galloway, *We Were Soldiers,* 40–41; Coleman, *Pleiku,* 186; written transcript of oral operations order issued by Lieutenant Colonel Harold G. Moore, commanding officer, 1st Battalion, 7th Cavalry, 14085, November 1965, 1, Historians' Files, CMH.

19. Moore and Galloway, *We Were Soldiers,* 119.

20. Coleman, *Pleiku,* 185; Moore, "After-Action Report: Ia Drang," 1–2, section 2, "Background," para. C.

21. Moore, "After-Action Report: Ia Drang," 2–3, section 3, "Operations on 14 November: A. The Air Recon. and Results"; Moore and Galloway, *We Were Soldiers,* 55–57; Coleman, *Pleiku,* 187–188.

22. Moore, "After-Action Report: Ia Drang," 2–3; Moore, written transcript of oral operations order, November 1965; Carland, *Stemming,* 115–117.

23. Moore and Galloway, *We Were Soldiers,* 23.

24. Moore, "After-Action Report: Ia Drang," 3, section 3, "Operations on 14 November: B. The Initial Assault."

25. Coleman, *Pleiku,* 193.

26. Moore, "After-Action Report: Ia Drang," 3.

27. Coleman, *Pleiku,* 193; Moore, "After-Action Report: Ia Drang," 3–4.

28. Pribbenow, "Fog," 94.

29. Dang Vu Hiep et al., *Ky Uc Tay Nguyen* [Highland memories], trans. Merle Pribbenow (Hanoi: People's Publishing House, 2000), 56.

30. Moore and Galloway, *We Were Soldiers,* 48.

31. An, *Chien Truong Moi,* 31–32.

32. Pribbenow, "Fog," 94.

33. Pham Dinh Bay, "Tran Van Dong Trong Thung Lung Ia Drang Cua Trung Doan Bo Binh 66 Va Trieu Doan 1 Trung Doan 33 Tu Ngay 14 Den 17 Thang 11 Nam 1965" [Mobile attacks conducted by the 66th Infantry Regiment and 1st Battalion, 33d Infantry Regiment in the Ia Drang valley 14–17 November 1965], in *Nhung Tran Danh Trong Khang Chien Giai Phong,* Tap V [Battles during the liberation war, vol. 5], trans. Merle Pribbenow (Hanoi: People's Army Publishing House, 1996), 7–23.

34. Pribbenow, "Fog," 94.

35. Hiep, *Ky Uc Tay Nguyen,* 58.

36. Moore and Galloway, *We Were Soldiers,* 51.

37. Pribbenow, "Fog," 94; Coleman, *Pleiku,* 186.

38. Pribbenow, "Fog," 94; Nguyen Huy Toan and Pham Quang Dinh, *Su Doan 304,* Tap II [304th Division, vol. 2], trans. Merle Pribbenow (Hanoi: People's Army Publishing House, 1990), 29.

39. Moore, "After-Action Report: Ia Drang," 4.

40. Moore and Galloway, *We Were Soldiers,* 63.

41. Moore, "After-Action Report: Ia Drang," 4.

42. John A. Cash, "Fight at Ia Drang," in John A. Cash, John Albright, and Allan W. Sandstrum, *Seven Firefights in Vietnam* (Washington, DC: Center of Military History, US Army, 1970), 13; Moore and Galloway, *We Were Soldiers,* 65–66.

43. Toan and Dinh, *Su Doan 304,* 29; Pribbenow, "Fog," 94. All the quotations in this paragraph are from Toan and Dinh, except for the last, which is from Pribbenow.

44. Moore and Galloway, *We Were Soldiers,* 68–72. The movie based on the Moore and Galloway book, directed by Randall Wallace and entitled *We Were Soldiers,* was released by Paramount Pictures on 1 March 2002.

45. Coleman, *Pleiku,* 194–196.

46. I thank Merle Pribbenow for information on PAVN radio availability. George C. Herring, "The 1st Cavalry and the Ia Drang Valley, 18 October–24 November 1965," in *America's First Battles 1776–1965,* ed. Charles E. Heller and William A. Stoft (Lawrence: University Press of Kansas, 1986), 318, suggests that most of the lost platoon survived in part because of the "enemy's ignorance of the platoon's plight."

47. Moore, "After-Action Report: Ia Drang," 4–5.

48. Ibid., 5; Carland, *Stemming,* 123.

49. Moore and Galloway, *We Were Soldiers,* 124; Carland, *Stemming,* 124.

50. Coleman, *Pleiku,* 203.

51. Moore, "After-Action Report: Ia Drang," 6–7; Carland, *Stemming,* 124–125.

52. Pribbenow, "Fog," 94; Pham Cong Cuu (as told to Le Nhu Huan), "Trung Doan 66 Tieu Diet Tieu Doan 2 Ky Binh Bay My o Thung Lung Ia Drang (tu 14 den 17 thang 11 nam 1965)" [The 66th Regiment's annihilation of the US 2d Air Cavalry Battalion in the Ia Drang valley (14 to 17 November 1965)], in *Chien Thang Plei Me: Ba Muoi Nam Sau Lai (Tai Lieu Hoi Thao Kha Hoc),* ed. Trinh Vuong Hong et al. [The Plei Me victory: looking back after thirty years (a scientific conference document)], trans. Merle Pribbenow (Hanoi: People's Publishing House, 1995), 100. Despite its title, much of Cuu's article actually deals with the X-Ray battle.

53. Pribbenow, "Fog," 93–97; Cuu, "Trung Doan 66," 100.

54. Toan and Dinh, *Su Doan 304,* 29.

55. Coleman, *Pleiku,* 201, indicates that Moore realized by 1500 on 14 November that he was under attack by at least two battalions. In his after-action report Moore was more modest, claiming that his battalion engaged 500 to 600 enemy troops. Moore, "After-Action Report: Ia Drang," 6, para. 6. Moore's after-action report is nearer the mark but probably represents an overestimate of 20 to 50 percent.

56. Cuu, "Trung Doan 66," 98–100; Toan and Dinh, *Su Doan 304,* 29–31; An, *Chien Truong Moi,* 32–33; Hiep, *Ky Uc Tay Nguyen,* 60–64.

57. Pribbenow, "Fog," 94; Toan and Dinh, *Su Doan 304,* 30.

58. Moore, "After-Action Report: Ia Drang," 6.

59. Pribbenow, "Fog," 94. In Toan and Dinh, *Su Doan 304,* 30, the 9th Battalion commander is named as Comrade Lien and is praised. An hour into the battle, "Comrade Lien . . . who had run all the way from the banks of the Ia Drang River, arrived at 11th Company's position. Along the way he had collected and brought with him 11 soldiers from 12th Company and one 82mm mortar. From this point onward Comrade Lien personally took command of the battalion in the battle. . . . Lacking adequate communications equipment, the 9th Battalion commander lost contact with some subordinate units."

60. An, *Chien Truong Moi,* 32–33; Pribbenow, "Fog," 94.

61. Hiep, *Ky Uc Tay Nguyen,* 61; Pribbenow, "Fog," 94.

62. Moore's profound respect for the martial qualities and skills of the PAVN as a result of X-Ray is outlined in Moore, "After-Action Report: Ia Drang," 17, section 9, "Comment," para. F, "The PAVN Enemy."

63. Hiep, *Ky Uc Yay Nguyen,* 61–63; An, *Chien Truong Moi,* 38–39; Nguyen Quoc Dung, "Chien Thang Play Me: Mot Loi Giai Dap ve Thang Bai trong Chien Tranh Viet Nam" [Plei Me victory: an answer to the question of victory or defeat in the Vietnam War], trans.

Merle Pribbenow, in Hong et al., *Chien Tang Plei Me,* 131–132. On the American use of white phosphorus, see Moore, "After-Action Report: Ia Drang," 7, paras. 2, 3.

64. Hiep, *Ky Uc Tay Nguyen,* 61–65.

65. Coleman, *Pleiku,* 210–211.

66. Brown to Cash, 8 August 1967, Historians' Files, CMH; Carland, *Stemming,* 125–126; Coleman, *Pleiku,* 202, 210.

67. Moore, "After-Action Report: Ia Drang," 8, section 4, "Activities during the Night of 14 November"; Carland, *Stemming,* 126–127.

68. Moore, "After-Action Report: Ia Drang," 9–11, section 4, "Activities during the Night of 14 November," para. D, section 5, "Enemy Attacks of 15 November"; Carland, *Stemming,* 128–129.

69. Moore, "After-Action Report: Ia Drang," 9–10, section 5; Carland, *Stemming,* 129; Moore and Galloway, *We Were Soldiers,* 161–163.

70. Johnson, "After Action Report—Operation Silver Bayonet," 2; Lt. Col. Robert B. Tully to Commanding Officer 2d Brigade, 1st Cavalry Division (Air), "After Action Report of Silver Bayonet," 5 December 1965, 2, Headquarters, United States Army Vietnam Command Historian, After Action Reports, box 30, RG 472, Archives 2, NARA; Tully to Cash, 6 September 1967, Historians' Files, CMH; Carland, *Stemming,* 129.

71. Toan and Dinh, *Su Doan 304,* 31–34; Pribbenow, "Fog," 95.

72. Harry Kinnard, "A Victory in the Ia Drang: The Triumph of a Concept," *Army,* September 1967, 86. Kinnard indicates that on the morning of 15 November, Moore's force was assailed by three PAVN battalions: the 7th and 9th of the 66th Regiment and "a composite battalion" of the 33d Regiment. Interestingly, before the publication of this article, Moore warned Kinnard that he might be stretching things a bit. "I do not know what captured enemy documents reveal, or what the 1st Cav Div. G-2 later estimated, but I felt that we were attacked by no more than a reinforced battalion on 15 Nov—possibly as many as five enemy companies." This quotation is from Moore, "Memorandum for General Kinnard: The Battle at X-Ray," 16 November 1966, 2, Historians' Files, CMH. In Moore and Galloway, *We Were Soldiers,* 96, the authors quote An as saying that the 33d Regiment participated early in the X-Ray action. But there is no reference to this in An's memoirs or in the large volume of other material published in Hanoi on this campaign that Merle Pribbenow translated and made available to me. The claim that the H-15 Battalion became involved in the battle on the morning of Monday, 15 November, is made in Moore and Galloway, *We Were Soldiers,* 149. But the main basis for it seems to be that some Communist soldiers were reportedly wearing black rather than the khaki normally associated with the PAVN.

73. An, *Chien Truong Moi,* 34.

74. Gia Lai Province Party Committee, "Vai Tro va Nhung Dong Gop cua Luc Luong Vu Trang Dia Phuong Tinh Gia Lai Trong Chien Dich Play Me 11–1965" [The role and contributions of Gia Lai Province local armed forces in the Plei Me campaign, November 1965], trans. Merle Pribbenow, in Hong et al., *Chien Thang Plei Me,* 79–90. The H-15 Battalion is mentioned on page 82, but there is no indication that it fought at X-Ray.

75. Coleman, *Pleiku,* 209.

76. An, *Chien Truong Moi,* 34–35.

77. Ibid., 34.

78. Moore, "Memo for General Kinnard: Information on X-Ray Battle," 3 November 1966, and Tully to Cash, 5 September 1967, Historians' Files, CMH; Moore, "After-Action Report: Ia Drang," 11, section 6, "The Relief of the Surrounded 2nd Platoon, Company B and Redisposition of the Perimeter"; Moore and Galloway, *We Were Soldiers,* 178–179.

79. Coleman, *Pleiku,* 203.

80. John Schlight, *The War in South Vietnam: The Years of the Offensive 1965–1968* (Washington, DC: Office of Air Force History, US Air Force, 1988), 104.

81. Moore and Galloway, *We Were Soldiers,* 149.

82. Schlight, *War,* 104–105; Carland, *Stemming,* 130.

83. 2/5 Cavalry, Tully After Action Report, 2; Carland, *Stemming,* 131.

84. Pribbenow, "Fog," 95; Toan and Dinh, *Su Doan 304,* 33.

85. Johnson, "After Action Report—Operation Silver Bayonet," 2; Moore, "After-Action Report: Ia Drang," 11–12, section 7, "Enemy Night Attack, 0400–0630 Hours, 16 Nov"; Carland, *Stemming,* 131.

86. Moore, "After-Action Report: Ia Drang,"13, section 8, "Enemy, Friendly Casualties, Captured."

87. Moore and Galloway, *We Were Soldiers,* 199.

88. Moore, "After-Action Report: Ia Drang," 13.

89. Johnson, "After Action Report—Operation Silver Bayonet," 2; Carland, *Stemming,* 134.

90. Coleman, *Pleiku,* 225–226. A brief clip of Moore speaking to the camera at the end of the X-Ray fight can be accessed on YouTube by typing "Moore" and "Ia Drang."

91. Herring, "1st Cavalry and Ia Drang," 323.

92. Toan and Dinh, *Su Doan 304,* 34–35.

93. General William C. Westmoreland, *A Soldier Reports* (New York: Dell, 1976), 204–205; Lewis Sorley, *Westmoreland: The General Who Lost Vietnam* (New York: Houghton Mifflin Harcourt, 2011), 131–132. Whether it was Westmoreland's fault (as Sorley alleges) that M-16s were not widely issued until after the 1968 Tet Offensive is not the issue here. The key fact is that few of them had this weapon at this point in the war.

94. *We Were Soldiers* (Paramount Pictures, 2002).

Chapter 14. Albany and After, November–December 1965

1. J. D. Coleman, *Pleiku: The Dawn of Helicopter Warfare in Vietnam* (New York: St. Martin's Press, 1988), 202.

2. Lieutenant General Harold G. Moore and Joseph L. Galloway, *We Were Soldiers Once . . . and Young: Ia Drang, the Battle that Changed the War in Vietnam* (New York: Random House, 1992), 33; Coleman, *Pleiku,* 181–182.

3. "General Westmoreland's History Notes," vol. 1, 29 August 1965–1 January 1966, 90, 95, Thursday and Sunday, 28 and 31 October 1965, CMH Library; Moore and Galloway, *We Were Soldiers,* 185. According to Moore, MACV demanded that he leave his battalion in the middle of the X-Ray battle to brief Westmoreland in Saigon. Moore declined the invitation.

4. Coleman, *Pleiku,* 229–230.

5. Harry Kinnard, "A Victory in the Ia Drang: The Triumph of a Concept," *Army,* September 1967, 89.

6. "Westmoreland's History Notes," 126, Thursday, 18 November 1965.

7. T. Brown to J. Cash, 8 August 1967, Historians' Files, CMH; John M. Carland, *Stemming the Tide: May 1965 to October 1966* (Washington, DC: Center of Military History, US Army, 2000), 134.

8. H. Kinnard, "Commander's Narrative," 16, in 1st Cavalry Division, Assistant Chief of

Staff G-3, Operations Reports—Lessons Learned, RG 472, Archives 2, NARA; Coleman, *Pleiku,* 229–230; John Schlight, *The War in South Vietnam: The Years of the Offensive, 1965–1968* (Washington, DC: Office of Air Force History, US Air Force, 1988), 104–105.

9. Coleman, *Pleiku,* 230.

10. Lt. Col. H. Moore, "After Action Report, Ia Drang Valley Operation 1st Battalion, 7th Cavalry 14–16 November 1965," 9 December 1965, 8, section E, para. 1.

11. A classic case of the deliberate and successful division of forces in the face of a superior enemy force is that carried out by Robert E. Lee at Chancellorsville to allow corps commander Thomas Jackson to mount a flank attack that proved to be decisive. See S. W. Sears, *Chancellorsville* (New York: Houghton Mifflin, 1996), 230–235.

12. Moore and Galloway, *We Were Soldiers,* 217.

13. Merle L. Pribbenow, "The Fog of War: The Vietnamese View of the Ia Drang Battle," *Military Review* 81, 1 (January–February 2001): 95.

14. Moore and Galloway, *We Were Soldiers,* 216.

15. Carland, *Stemming,* 145.

16. Lt. Colonel R. Tully, 2d Battalion, 5th Cavalry, "After Action Report of Silver Bayonet," 5 December 1965, 2, Headquarters United States Army Vietnam, Command Historian, After Action Reports, box 30, RG 472, Archives 2, NARA; Carland, *Stemming,* 134; Moore and Galloway, *We Were Soldiers,* 215; Coleman, *Pleiku,* 231.

17. Captain George C. Johnson, 2d Battalion, 7th Cavalry, "After Action Report—Operation Silver Bayonet—12–21 November 1965," 24 November 1965, 3, Headquarters United States Army Vietnam, Command Historian, After Action Reports, box 30, RG 472, Archives 2, NARA; William Triplett, "Chaos in the Ia Drang," *VVA Veteran* 6, 10 (October 1986): 20, also gives 1000 as the time of the departure from X-Ray.

18. Moore and Galloway, *We Were Soldiers,* 215–216.

19. Carland, *Stemming,* 134, refers to "marching artillery fire." Coleman, *Pleiku,* 231, indicates that "Tully had artillery crashing in front of his lead unit . . . as it marched through the jungle." This sounds like a creeping or rolling barrage. But Tully's laconic after-action report does not mention this, and a rolling barrage is not what Tully described to Moore and Galloway during the research for their book on X-Ray and Albany.

20. Carland, *Stemming,* 134; Tully, "After Action Report of Silver Bayonet," 2.

21. Johnson, "After Action Report—Operation Silver Bayonet," 3.

22. Moore and Galloway, *We Were Soldiers,* 215–223.

23. Tully, "After Action Report of Silver Bayonet," 2; Coleman, *Pleiku,* 230–231; Moore and Galloway, *We Were Soldiers,* 223; R. E. Towles, "The Tears of Autumn: Air Assault Operations and Infantry Combat in the Drang Valley, Vietnam" (Ph.D. diss., Kent State University, 2000), 270, USAMHI.

24. Johnson, "After Action Report—Operation Silver Bayonet," 2–3; Coleman, *Pleiku,* 231; Carland, *Stemming,* 134–135; Moore and Galloway, *We Were Soldiers,* 219–222.

25. Coleman, *Pleiku,* 231; Carland, *Stemming,* 135.

26. Carland, *Stemming,* 135–136; Coleman, *Pleiku,* 234–235; Towles, "Tears," 275–279; Johnson, "After Action Report—Operation Silver Bayonet," 3; Pham Dinh Bay, "Tran Van Dong Tien Cong Trong Thung Lung Ia Drang Cua Trung Doan Bo Binh 66 Va Tieu Doan 1 Trung Doan 33 Tu Ngay 14 Den 17 Thang 11 Nam 1965" [Mobile attacks conducted by the 66th Infantry Regiment and 1st Battalion, 33d Infantry Regiment, in the Ia Drang valley 14–17 November 1965], in *Nhung Tran Danh Trong Chien Tranh Giai Phong,* Tap 5 [Battles during the liberation war, vol. 5], trans. Merle Pribbenow (Hanoi: People's Army Publishing House, 1996), 16.

27. Johnson, "After Action Report—Operation Silver Bayonet," 3; Towles, "Tears," 279–282; Carland, *Stemming,* 136.

28. Nguyen Huy Toan and Pham Quang Dinh, *Su Doan 304,* Tap II [304th Division, vol. 2], trans. Merle Pribbenow (Hanoi: People's Army Publishing House, 1990), 35–40; Moore and Galloway, *We Were Soldiers,* 230–291.

29. Nguyen Huu An, *Chien Truong Moi* [New battlefield], trans. Merle Pribbenow (Hanoi: People's Publishing House, 2002), 34; Bay, "Tran Van Dong," p. 17.

30. Toan and Dinh, *Su Doan 304,* 35.

31. Dang Vu Hiep, *Ky Uc Tay Nguyen* [Highland memories], trans. Merle Pribbenow (Hanoi: People's Publishing House, 2000), 70.

32. Ibid.; An, *Chien Truong Moi,* 34; Bay, "Tran Van Dong," 17; Toan and Dinh, *Su Doan 304,* 35.

33. Nguyen Quang Cuong and Vu Anh Hien, *Lich Su Bo Doi Thong Tin-Lien Lac,* Tap II, *1954–1975* [History of communications troops, vol. 2, 1954–1975], trans. Merle Pribbenow (Hanoi: Communications Command, 1986), 166.

34. There is a brief account of Phoi's military career in Dang Van Lam, "Tim Hai Cot Anh Hung Le Xuan Phoi Tai Thung Lung Ia Drang" [The remains of hero Le Xuan Phoi found in the Ia Drang valley], trans. Merle Pribbenow, in *Quan Doi Nhan Dan* [People's army newspaper], 26 August 2006, http://www.qdnd.vn/qdnd/baongay.psk.nhanvat.2270 .qdnd (accessed 28 August 2006).

35. Toan and Dinh, *Su Doan 304,* 35–36.

36. An, *Chien Truong Moi,* 35.

37. Toan and Dinh, *Su Doan 304,* 36; Hiep, *Ky Uc Tay Nguyen,* 71.

38. Bay, "Tran Van Dong," 16–17.

39. Toan and Dinh, *Su Doan 304,* 37.

40. Ibid., 36. This account indicates that Phoi became aware of the proximity of American forces at about 1130 Hanoi time (1230 Saigon–US Army time). American accounts generally agree that the fighting started at about 1315 Saigon–US Army time.

41. Bay indicates that Phoi became aware of the American presence at about 1200 Hanoi time (1300 Saigon time) and that the battle started twenty minutes later. Based on these times, it is inevitable that Bay characterizes the operation as a meeting engagement rather than an ambush. Bay, "Tran Van Dong," 17.

42. Coleman, *Pleiku,* 236.

43. Toan and Dinh, *Su Doan 304,* 37; Bay, "Tran Van Dong," 17; Hiep, *Ky Uc Tay Nguyen,* 72.

44. Hiep, *Ky Uc Tay Nguyen,* 72.

45. Toan and Dinh, *Su Doan 304,* 37; Bay, "Tran Van Dong," 18; Towles, "Tears," 291. Towles acknowledges here that 8th Company, 8th Battalion, 66th Regiment, struck the left flank of the American column.

46. Carland, *Stemming,* 137–140, including map 11.

47. All three copies of the campaign maps and diagrams from Vietnamese Communist publications in my possession show the attacks on the American column at Albany by 8th Battalion, 66th Regiment, as coming from the west—that is, from the left of the column—and the 1st Battalion, 33d Regiment, attacking from the right. These include the campaign diagram accompanying the article "Chien Dich Play Me" [The Plei Me campaign], in *Tu Dien Bach Khoa Quan su Viet Nam,* ed. Senior Colonel Tran Do [Military encyclopedia of Vietnam], trans. Merle Pribbenow (Hanoi: People's Publishing House, 2004), 191. I am grateful to Merle Pribbenow for making these maps and diagrams available to me.

48. Toan and Dinh, *Su Doan 304,* 38–39.

49. Ibid., 37.

50. Towles, "Tears," 41–49.

51. Carland, *Stemming,* 137–138; Towles, "Tears," 282–299.

52. Carland, *Stemming,* 138–143; Coleman, *Pleiku,* 238–239.

53. Towles, "Tears," 318–321; Carland, *Stemming,* 140, 142–143.

54. Hiep, *Ky Uc Tay Nguyen,* 75.

55. Ibid., 72–73.

56. Coleman, *Pleiku,* 240–242; Moore and Galloway, *We Were Soldiers,* 264–267.

57. Hiep, *Ky Uc Tay Nguyen,* 76; Coleman, *Pleiku,* 245.

58. Coleman, *Pleiku,* 243–244.

59. Moore and Galloway, *We Were Soldiers,* 292–302; Coleman, *Pleiku,* 244–245.

60. Carland, *Stemming,* 143–145.

61. Ibid., 145; Toan and Dinh, *Su Doan 304,* 38; Hiep, *Ky Uc Tay Nguyen,* 72–77; Coleman, *Pleiku,* 248–249.

62. Coleman, *Pleiku,* 246–248.

63. Ibid., 248.

64. Moore and Galloway, *We Were Soldiers,* 305–306; Coleman, *Pleiku,* 250–251.

65. Carland, *Stemming,* 136–147; Schlight, *War,* 105.

66. "Westmoreland's History Notes," 126–128, Thursday, 18 November 1965.

67. Coleman, *Pleiku,* 251.

68. "Westmoreland's History Notes," 130, Friday, 19 November 1965.

69. Coleman, *Pleiku,* 250–266; Major William N. Ciccolo, "Combat Operations After Action Report, Than Phong 7, 17 November 1965 to 26 November 1965," 17 December 1965, 3 sections 8, 9, MACV, Assistant Chief of Staff for Operations (J3), Evaluation and Analysis (MACVJ3–05), After Action Reports, box 1, Report Nos. 9–137, RG 472, Archives 2, NARA.

70. "Westmoreland's History Notes," 131–132, Saturday, 20 November 1965.

71. William P. Boyle and Robert Samabria, "Lure and the Ambush," November 1965, Historians' Files, CMH; Hiep, *Ky Uc Tay Nguyen,* 86–94; Carland, *Stemming,* 146–147.

72. Coleman, *Pleiku,* 250–253; Vinh Loc, *Why Plei Me* (Pleiku and Ban Me Thuot, 1966), 97–102; Ciccolo, "After Action Report, Than Phong."

73. Coleman, *Pleiku,* 252–257. Coleman attributes the 18 November attack on LZ Columbus to the H-15 Battalion, but this is not supported by Vietnamese Communist sources. Foreign Broadcast Information Service, trans., *Luc Luong Vu Trang Nhan Dan Tay Nguyen Trong Khang Chien Chong My Cuu Nuoc* [History of the Central Highlands people's armed forces in the anti-US war of resistance for national salvation] (Hanoi: People's Army Publishing House, 1980), chap. 2, credits the 33d Regiment with this attack but grossly exaggerates the success achieved.

74. Kinnard refers rather vaguely to "two or more ARVN airborne battalions." Kinnard, "Victory," 89.

75. Ibid.; Coleman, *Pleiku,* 256–258; Ciccolo, "After Action Report, Than Phong,"2, section 7.

76. Ciccolo, "After Action Report, Than Phong,"3, sections 8, 9.

77. Ibid., section 4, "Control Headquarters," 1, section 10, "Concept of Operations," 3; "Chien Dich Ia Drang" [Ia Drang campaign], 16–18, posted 28 December 2012 on the "Nhay Du" [Airborne] website, http:/nhaydu.com/index83hgfiles/leftfiles/T-Chien /1965ChienDichIaDrang.pdf (accessed and translated by Merle Pribbenow, 9 February

2015); General H. Norman Schwarzkopf, *It Doesn't Take a Hero* (New York: Bantam, 1992), 140–144.

78. Ciccolo, "After Action Report, Than Phong," section 11, "Execution," 18 and 19 November 1965, 3, 4.

79. Ibid., 20 November 1965, 5–6.

80. "Chien Dich Ia Drang," 18.

81. Ciccolo, "After Action Report, Than Phong," section 11, "Execution," 22 November 1965, 6.

82. Ibid., 23–27 November 1965, 6–7.

83. Ibid., section 14, "Advisory Analysis," 8.

84. Moore and Galloway, *We Were Soldiers,* 341–342; Coleman, *Pleiku,* 258–264. Coleman suggests on page 264 that the 1st Cavalry Division coped successfully with its mechanical problems, although he admits that spare parts were an issue. On page 258, however, he gives two examples of whole battalions moving by truck convoy in the last days of this campaign, in areas that were by no means totally secure. This strongly suggests that flyable helicopters were in short supply.

85. Hiep, *Ky Uc Tay Nguyen,* 86–88.

86. Ibid., 88–94.

87. Coleman, *Pleiku,* 251.

88. Hiep, *Ky Uc Tay Nguyen,* 55–56. Hiep states that before the battle for LZ X-Ray, Man had gone to Darlac in an effort to fix the logistical crisis.

89. Ibid., 62, 80; An, *Chien Truong Moi,* 38–39; Nguyen Quoc Dung, "Chien Thang Play Me: Mot Loi Giai Dap ve Thang Bai trong Chien Tranh Viet Nam" [Plei Me victory: an answer to the question of victory or defeat in the Vietnam War], in *Chien Thang Plei Me: Ba Muoi Nam Sau Nhin Lai (Tai Lieu Hoi Thao Kha Hoc),* ed. Trinh Vuong Hong et al. [The Plei Me victory: looking back after thirty years (a scientific conference document)], trans. Merle Pribbenow (Hanoi: People's Army Publishing House, 1995), 131.

90. Chu Huy Man with Le Hai Trieu, *Thoi Soi Dong* [Time of upheaval], trans. Merle Pribbenow (Hanoi: People's Army Publishing House, 2004), 439–440.

91. Vinh Loc, *Why Plei Me.*

92. Kinnard, "Victory"; Carland, *Stemming,* 147–148.

93. Kinnard, "Victory," 88–91.

94. See Paddy Griffith's seminal work on the development of tactics, *Forward into Battle: Fighting Tactics from Waterloo to Vietnam* (Strettington, UK: Bird, 1981), 143.

Bibliography

Archival Sources

The following archive centers were visited during the research for this book:

US National Archives and Records Administration (NARA), Archives 2, College
   Park, Maryland
US Army Center of Military History (CMH), Fort McNair, Washington, DC
US Army Military History Institute (USAMHI), Carlisle Barracks, Pennsylvania
Library of Congress, Washington, DC
National Security Archive at George Washington University, Washington, DC

The great majority of the documents consulted at Archives 2 came from the vast Records Group (RG) 472, which deals with the US armed forces in Southeast Asia during the era of the Second Indochina War. From College Park the author also obtained copies of records made available through the CREST program. Consisting of declassified CIA documents, CREST material is available via computer terminals owned by the Agency and kept on an upper floor at Archives 2.

By courtesy of Dr. Andrew Birtle and Dr. John Carland, the author was allowed privileged access to Historians' Files at the Center of Military History at Fort McNair. Historians' Files are documents being used, or that have been used, in the writing of US Army official histories. They include both official records that will eventually be open to the public at NARA's Archives 2 and the official historians' correspondence. The author also consulted the William Westmoreland Collection, accessible in the library of the Center of Military History, at Fort McNair.

The collections consulted at the US Army Military History Institute, Carlisle, Pennsylvania, included the US Military Assistance Command, Vietnam (MACV) Papers, William DePuy Papers, Paul Harkins Papers, Theodore Mataxis Papers, Lionel C. McGarr Papers, George C. Morton Papers, William Westmoreland Papers, and Wilbur Wilson Papers.

A sequence of MACV Weekly War Reports for 1964 that could not be found in the MACV collections at Archives 2 or USAMHI was located in the Library of Congress (Madison Hall), where the author spent about a week.

The National Security Archive at George Washington University has cataloged and made electronically available a broad range of documents related to American politico-strategic policy making on the Vietnam War, the hard copies of which are inconveniently scattered among archive centers distributed over an extremely wide geographic area. A brief visit to the National Security Archive was most useful.

511

Published Primary Sources

Several volumes of the *Foreign Relations of the United States* (*FRUS*) series were consulted. They are listed here in chronological order of the historical period covered in each volume.

Landa, Ronald D., and Charles S. Sampson, eds. *Foreign Relations of the United States, 1961–1963*, vol. 1, *Vietnam, 1961*. Washington, DC: US Government Printing Office, 1988.

Glennon, John P., David M. Baekler, and Charles S. Sampson, eds. *Foreign Relations of the United Sates, 1961–1963*, vol. 2, *Vietnam, 1962*. Washington, DC: US Government Printing Office, 1990.

Keefer, Edward C., and Louis J. Smith, eds. *Foreign Relations of the United States, 1961–1963*, vol. 3, *Vietnam, January–August 1963*. Washington, DC: US Government Printing Office, 1991.

Keefer, Edward C., ed. *Foreign Relations of the United States, 1961–1963*, vol. 4, *Vietnam, August–December 1963*. Washington, DC: US Government Printing Office, 1991.

Keefer, Edward C., and Charles S. Sampson, eds. *Foreign Relations of the United States, 1964–1968*, vol. 1, *Vietnam, 1964*. Washington, DC: US Government Printing Office, 1992.

Also consulted were the following works:

Allen, John K., et al. *Estimative Products on Vietnam 1948–1975*. Pittsburgh, PA: US Government Printing Office, 2005. This volume and the accompanying CD contain declassified intelligence reports on Vietnam from several branches of the US intelligence community.

Sheehan, Neil, ed. *The Pentagon Papers as Published by the* New York Times. New York: Bantam, 1971.

American Official Histories

Birtle, Andrew J. *US Army Counterinsurgency and Contingency Operations Doctrine 1942–1976*. Washington, DC: Center of Military History, 2006.

Bowers, Ray L. *Tactical Airlift*. Washington, DC: Office of Air Force History, 1983.

Carland, John M. *Stemming the Tide: May 1965 to October 1966*. Washington, DC: Center of Military History, US Army, 2000.

Cash, John A. "Fight at Ia Drang." In John A. Cash, John Albright, and Allan W. Sandstrum, *Seven Firefights in Vietnam*, 3–40. Washington, DC: Center of Military History, US Army, 1970.

Collins, Brigadier General James Lawton, Jr. *The Development and Training of the South Vietnamese Army 1950–1972*. Washington, DC: Department of the Army, 2002.

Cosmas, Graham A. *MACV: The Joint Command in the Years of Escalation, 1962–1967*. Washington, DC: Center of Military History, US Army, 2006.

Eckhardt, Major General George S. *Command and Control: 1950–1969*. Washington, DC: Department of the Army, 1974.

Futrell, Robert F. *The Advisory Years to 1965*. Washington, DC: Office of Air Force History, US Air Force, 1981.

Kelly, Colonel Francis J. *US Army Special Forces: 1961–1971*. Washington, DC: Department of the Army, 1973.

Schlight, John. *The War in South Vietnam: The Years of the Offensive 1965–1968.* Washington, DC: Office of Air Force History, US Air Force, 1988.

Spector, Ronald H. *Advice and Support: The Early Years.* Washington, DC: Center of Military History, US Army, 1985.

Tolson, Lieutenant General John. *Airmobility 1961–1971.* Washington, DC: Department of the Army, 1973.

Van Vien, General Cao, et al. *The US Adviser.* Washington, DC: US Army Center of Military History, 1977.

Vietnamese Official Histories Not Published in English

The use of translated Vietnamese Communist official histories was very important in the writing of this book. Merle Pribbenow's published English translation of the one-volume official history of the war by the People's Army of Vietnam (PAVN) is listed under secondary sources. The Vietnamese histories listed below have never been published in English (and in most cases probably never will be). In all but one case, Merle Pribbenow was the translator, and he supplied the relevant material in the form of e-mail attachments. The single exception is the following:

Foreign Broadcast Information Service, trans. *Luc Luong Vu Trang Dan Tay Nguyen Trong Khang Chien Chong My Cuu Nuoc* [History of the Central Highlands people's armed forces in the anti-US war of resistance for national salvation]. Hanoi: People's Publishing House, 1980. A copy of this document is held in the Historians' Files at the CMH.

When the above document is cited in the notes, page numbers refer to the typescript English translation held at CMH, not the original Vietnamese book. In Pribbenow's translations, however, the page number in the original Vietnamese published work is always cited.

The authors of official Vietnamese publications are not always named. Another complication is that in Vietnamese names, the family name is normally written first. In the case of Ngo Dinh Diem, for example, the family name is Ngo. However, even in an official context, he was addressed as President Diem, not President Ngo. Similarly, General Vo Nguyen Giap was General Giap, not General Vo. Vietnamese works are therefore listed here alphabetically by the author's last name, the name by which the individual would have been known and addressed, rather than by the first (family) name.

Pribbenow's unpublished translations used in this book include the following:

An, Nguyen Huu. *Chien Truong Moi* [New battlefield]. Hanoi: People's Publishing House, 2002.

Bay, Pham Dinh. "Tran Van Dong Trong Thung Lung Ia Drang Cua Trung Doan Bo Binh 66 Va Trieu Doan 1 Trung Doan 33 Tu Ngay 14 Den 17 Thang 11 Nam 1965" [Mobile attacks conducted by the 66th Infantry Regiment and 1st Battalion, 33d Infantry Regiment, in the Ia Drang valley 14–17 November 1965]. In *Nhung Tran Danh Trong Khang Chien Giai Phong,* Tap V [Battles during the liberation war, vol. 5]. Hanoi: People's Army Publishing House, 1996.

Bieu, Nguyen Van. *Mot so Tran Danh cua don vi thuoc Binh doan Tay Nguyen,* Tap V [A number of battles fought by units of the Central Highlands corps, vol. 5]. Hanoi: People's Publishing House, 1996.

Bon, Colonel Le Ngoc, et al. *Nhung Trang Su Ve Vang Cua Luc Luong An Ninh Nhan Dan Viet Nam* [The glorious history of the heroic Vietnamese People's Security Forces]. Hanoi: People's Security Publishing House, 2006.

Canh, Le Thanh, ed. *Lich Su Dang Bo Tinh Gia Lai,* Tap I [History of the Gia Lai Province party committee chapter, vol. 1]. Hanoi: National Political Publishing House, 1997.

Cuong, Nguyen Quang, and Vu Anh Hien. *Lich Su Bo Doi Thong Tin-Lien Lac,* Tap II, *1954–1975* [History of communications troops, vol. 2, 1954–1975]. Hanoi: Communications Command, 1986.

Do, Senior Colonel Tran, ed. *Tu Dien Bach Khoa Quan Su Viet Nam* [Military encyclopedia of Vietnam]. Hanoi: People's Publishing House, 1996.

Duc, Pham Gia. *Su Doan 325,* Tap II [325th Division, vol. 2]. Hanoi: People's Publishing House, 1986.

Duong, Tranh, et al. *Lich Su Khu 6 (Cuc Nam Trung Bo-Nam Tay Nguyen) Khang Chien Chong My, 1954–1975* [History of Military Region 6 (extreme south central Vietnam and the southern Central Highlands) during the resistance war against the Americans, 1954–1975]. Hanoi: People's Publishing House, 1995.

Hiep, Dang Vu, et al. *Ky Uc Tay Nguyen* [Highland memories]. Hanoi: People's Publishing House, 2000.

Hong, Trinh Vuong, et al., eds. *Chien Thang Plei Me: Ba Muoi Nam Nhin Lai (Tai Lieu Hoi Thao Kha Hoc)* [The Plei Me victory: looking back after thirty years (a scientific conference document)]. Hanoi: People's Publishing House, 1995.

Huan, Nguyen Tri, et al. *Su Doan Sao Vang* [The Yellow Star Division]. Hanoi: People's Army Publishing House, 1984.

Man, Chu Huy, with Le Hai Trieu. *Thoi Soi Dong* [Time of upheaval]. Hanoi: People's Army Publishing House, 2004.

Military Region 5 Headquarters and Tran Quy Cat, eds. *Lich Su Bo Doi Dac Cong Quan Khu 5 (1952–1975)* [History of Military Region 5 sapper troops (1952–1975)]. Hanoi: People's Publishing House, 1998.

Minh, Nguyen Phung, ed. *Nam Trung Bo Khang Chien, 1945–1975* [Southern central Vietnam's war of resistance, 1945–1975]. Hanoi: People's Publishing House, 1995.

Minh, Nguyen Quoc, et al. *Lich Su Bo Doi Dac Cong,* Tap Mot [History of the sapper forces, vol. 1]. Hanoi: People's Publishing House, 1987.

Nguyen, Dong Si, and Nguyen Duy Tuong, eds. *Lich Su Bo Doi Truong Son Duong Ho Chi Minh* [History of the Annamite Mountain troops of the Ho Chi Minh Trail]. Hanoi: People's Publishing House, 1994.

Phong, Dang. *5 Duong Mon Ho Chi Minh* [Five Ho Chi Minh Trails]. Hanoi: Intellectual Publishing House, 2008.

Quan Khu 5: Thang Loiva Nhung Bai Hoc Trong Khang Chien Chong My, Tap I [Military Region 5: victories and lessons learned during the resistance war against the Americans, vol. 1]. Hanoi: People's Publishing House, 1981.

Thuy, Nguyen Van, et al. *Trung Doan 95 Thien Thuat (1945–1995)* [The 95th Thien Thuat Regiment (1945–1995)]. Hanoi: People's Publishing House, 1995.

Tinh, Nguyen Khac, et al. *Phao Binh Nhan Dan Viet Nam: Nhung Chang Duong Chien Dan,* Tap II [People's artillery of Vietnam: combat history, vol. 2]. Hanoi: Artillery Command, 1986.

Toan, Nguyen Huy, and Pham Quang Dinh. *Su Doan 304,* Tap II [304th Division, vol. 2]. Hanoi: People's Army Publishing House, 1990.

Tong Ket Cong Tac Hau Can Chien Truong Nam Bo—Cuc Nam Trung Bo Trong Khang Chien

Chong My [Review of rear services operations for the Cochin China battlefield]. Hanoi: General Department for Rear Services, People's Army of Vietnam, 1986.

Uoc, Nguyen Dinh, and Nguyen Van Minh, eds. *Lich Su Khang Chien Chong My Cuu Nuoc 1954–1975,* Tap III, *Danh Thang Chien Tranh Dac Biet* [History of the resistance war against the Americans to save the nation 1954–1975, vol. 3, Defeating the special war]. Hanoi: National Political Publishing House, 1997.

Other Secondary Sources Published in English

Ahern, Thomas L., Jr. *Vietnam Declassified: The CIA and Counterinsurgency.* Lexington: University Press of Kentucky, 2010.

Bayless, Robert M. *Vietnam: Victory Was Never an Option.* Oxford: Trafford, 2005.

Beckett, Ian F. W. "Robert Thompson and the British Military Advisory Mission to South Vietnam, 1961–1965." *Small Wars and Insurgencies* 8, 3 (Winter 1997): 41–63.

Beckwith, Charles, and Donald Knox. *Delta Force: The U.S. Counter-Terrorist Unit and the Iranian Hostage Rescue Mission.* London: Arms & Armour, 1984.

Beene, W. "Plei Me Stands as a War Turning Point." *Stars and Stripes,* 27 December 1965.

Blair, Anne. *There to the Bitter End: Ted Serong in Vietnam.* Crow's Nest, Australia: Allen & Unwin, 2001.

Blaufarb, Douglas S. *The Counter-Insurgency Era: U.S. Doctrine and Performance 1950 to the Present.* New York: Free Press, 1977.

Brennan, Matthew. *Headhunters: Stories from the 1st Squadron, 9th Cavalry in Vietnam, 1965–1971.* Novato, CA: Presidio, 1987.

———, ed. *Hunter Killer Squadron: Aero-Weapons, Aero Scouts, Aero-Rifles, Vietnam 1965–1972.* Novato, CA: Presidio, 1990.

Buttinger, Joseph. *The Smaller Dragon: A Political History of Vietnam.* New York: Praeger, 1958.

Catton, Philip E. "Counter-Insurgency and Nation-Building: The Strategic Hamlet Program in South Vietnam, 1961–1963." *International History Review* 21, 4 (December 1999): 918–940.

———. *Diem's Final Failure: Prelude to America's War in Vietnam.* Lawrence: University Press of Kansas, 2002.

Chandler, David. *The Tragedy of Cambodian History: Politics, War and Revolution since 1945.* London: Yale University Press, 1991.

Cheng, Christopher C. S. *Air Mobility: The Development of a Doctrine.* London: Praeger, 1994.

Colby, William. *Lost Victory: A Firsthand Account of America's Sixteen-Year Involvement in Vietnam.* New York: Contemporary Books, 1989.

Coleman, J. D. *Pleiku: The Dawn of Helicopter Warfare in Vietnam.* New York: St. Martin's Press, 1988.

Clutterbuck, Richard. *Riot and Revolution in Singapore and Malaya 1945–1963.* London: Faber & Faber, 1973.

Daddis, Gregory A. *Westmoreland's War: Reassessing American Strategy in Vietnam.* Oxford: Oxford University Press, 2014.

Duiker, William J. *The Communist Road to Power in Vietnam.* Boulder, CO: Westview, 1996.

Duncanson, Dennis J. *Government and Revolution in Vietnam.* London: Oxford University Press, 1968.

Fall, Bernard B. *Street without Joy.* Mechanicsburg, PA: Stackpole Books, 1994.

Freedman, Lawrence. *Kennedy's Wars: Berlin, Cuba, Laos and Vietnam.* Oxford: Oxford University Press, 2000.

Gleason, Robert L. *Air Commando Chronicles: Untold Tales from Vietnam, Latin America and Back Again.* Manhattan, KS: Sunflower University Press, 2000.

Griffith, Paddy. *Forward into Battle: Fighting Tactics from Waterloo to Vietnam.* Strettington, UK: Bird, 1981.

Guan, Ang Cheng. *The Vietnam War from the Other Side: The Vietnamese Communists' Perspective.* Oxford: Routledge, 2002.

Halberstam, David. *The Best and the Brightest.* New York: Random House, 1969.

Herring, George C. "The 1st Cavalry and the Ia Drang Valley, 18 October–24 November 1965." In *America's First Battles 1776–1965,* ed. Charles E. Heller and Wiliam A. Stoft, 300–326. Lawrence: University Press of Kansas, 1986.

Hickey, Gerald C. *Free in the Forest: Ethnohistory of the Vietnamese Central Highlands, 1954–1976.* New Haven, CT: Yale University Press, 1982.

———. *Sons of the Mountains: Ethnohistory of the Vietnamese Central Highlands to 1954.* New Haven, CT: Yale University Press, 1982.

Ives, Christopher K. *US Special Forces and Counterinsurgency in Vietnam: Military Innovation and Institutional Failure, 1961–1963.* London: Routledge, 2007.

Jacobs, Seth. *Cold War Mandarin: Ngo Dinh Diem and the Origins of America's War in Vietnam, 1950–1963.* Oxford: Rowman & Littlefield, 2006.

Jones, Howard. *Death of a Generation: How the Assassination of Diem and JFK Prolonged the Vietnam War.* Oxford: Oxford University Press, 2003.

Kaiser, David. *American Tragedy: Kennedy, Johnson, and the Origins of the Vietnam War.* Cambridge, MA: Belknap Press, 2000.

Kinnard, Harry. "A Victory in the Ia Drang: The Triumph of a Concept." *Army,* September 1967, 71–91.

Krepeinevich, Andrew F., Jr. *The Army and Vietnam.* Baltimore: Johns Hopkins University Press, 1986.

Laurence, John. *The Cat from Hue: A Vietnam War Story.* New York: Public Affairs, 2002.

Lewy, Guenter. *America in Vietnam.* New York: Oxford University Press, 1978.

Lien, Vu Hong, and Peter D. Sharrock. *Descending Dragon, Rising Tiger.* London: Reaktion Books, 2014.

Loc, Vinh. *FULRO: The So-Called Movement for Autonomy.* Pleiku and Ban Me Thuot, 1965.

———. "Road-Clearing Operation." *Military Review* 46, 4 (April 1966): 23–27.

———. *Why Plei Me.* Pleiku and Ban Me Thuot, 1966.

Logevall, Frederik. *Embers of War: The Fall of an Empire and the Making of America's Vietnam.* New York: Random House, 2012.

Luan, Nguyen Cong. *Nationalist in the Viet Nam Wars: Memoirs of a Victim Turned Soldier.* Bloomington: Indiana University Press, 2012.

Mataxis, Theodore C. "War in the Highlands: Attack and Counter-Attack on Highway 19." *Army,* October 1965.

McMaster, H. R. *Dereliction of Duty: Lyndon Johnson, Robert McNamara, the Joint Chiefs of Staff and the Lies that Led to Vietnam.* New York: HarperCollins, 1997.

Mertel, Colonel Kenneth D. *Year of the Horse: 1st Air Cavalry in the Highlands 1965–1967.* Atglen, PA: Schiffer Military History, 1997.

Moore, Lieutenant General Harold G., and Joseph L. Galloway. *We Were Soldiers Once . . . and Young: Ia Drang, the Battle that Changed the War in Vietnam.* New York: Random House, 1992.

Morris, Jim. *War Story.* Boulder, CO: Sycamore Island Books, 1979.

Moyar, Mark. *Triumph Forsaken: The Vietnam War, 1954–1965.* Cambridge: Cambridge University Press, 2006.

Neese, Harvey, and John O'Donnell, eds. *Prelude to Tragedy: Vietnam 1960–1965.* Annapolis, MD: Naval Institute Press, 2001.

Nguyen, Lien-Hang T. *Hanoi's War: An International History of the War for Peace in Vietnam.* Chapel Hill: University of North Carolina Press, 2012.

Nguyen, Tin. *General Hieu, ARVN: A Hidden Military Gem.* Lincoln, NE: Writer's Club Press, 2003.

Nolting, Frederick. *From Trust to Tragedy: The Political Memoirs of Frederick Nolting, Kennedy's Ambassador to Diem's Vietnam.* New York: Praeger, 1988.

O'Ballance, Edgar. *The Indo-China War, 1945–54.* London: Faber & Faber, 1964.

Pike, Douglas. *Viet Cong: The Organization and Techniques of the National Liberation Front of South Vietnam.* Cambridge, MA: MIT Press, 1966.

Prados, John. *The Blood Road: The Ho Chi Minh Trail and the Vietnam War.* New York: John Wiley & Sons, 1999.

———. *Lost Crusader: The Secret Wars of CIA Director William Colby.* Oxford: Oxford University Press, 2003.

———. *Vietnam: The History of an Unwinnable War, 1945–1975.* Lawrence: University Press of Kansas, 2009.

Pribbenow, Merle L. "The Fog of War: The Vietnamese View of the Ia Drang Battle." *Military Review* 81, 1 (January–February 2001): 93–97.

———, trans. *Victory in Vietnam: The Official History of the People's Army of Vietnam, 1954–1975.* Lawrence: University Press of Kansas, 2002.

Race, Jeffrey. *War Comes to Long An: Revolutionary Conflict in a Vietnamese Province.* Berkeley: University of California Press, 1972.

Rust, William J. *Before the Quagmire: American Intervention in Laos 1954–1961.* Lexington: University Press of Kentucky, 2012.

Salemink, Oscar. *The Ethnography of Vietnam's Central Highlanders: A Historical Contextualization, 1850–1990.* Honolulu: University of Hawaii Press, 2003.

Scales, Robert H. *Firepower in Limited War.* Novato, CA: Presidio, 1995.

Schwarzkopf, General H. Norman. *It Doesn't Take a Hero.* New York: Bantam, 1992.

Sears, S. W. *Chancellorsville.* New York: Houghton Mifflin, 1996.

Shackleton, Ronald A. *Village Defense: Initial Special Forces Operations in Vietnam.* Arvada, CO: Phoenix Press, 1975.

Shaplen, Robert. *The Lost Revolution: Vietnam 1945–1965.* London: Andre Deutsch, 1966.

Simpson, Charles M., III. *Inside the Green Berets: The First Thirty Years: A History of the U.S. Army Special Forces.* London: Arms & Armour Press, 1983.

Sorley, Lewis. *Westmoreland: The General Who Lost Vietnam.* New York: Houghton Mifflin Harcourt, 2011.

Stanton, Shelby B. *The 1st Cav in Vietnam: Anatomy of a Division.* Novato, CA: Presidio, 1987.

———. *Green Berets at War: U.S. Army Special Forces in Southeast Asia 1956–1975.* London: Arms & Armour, 1986.

Summers, Harry. "The Bitter Triumph of the Ia Drang." *American Heritage,* February–March 1984, 51–58.

Taylor, K. W. *A History of the Vietnamese.* Cambridge: Cambridge University Press, 2013.

Thayer, Carlyle A. *War by Other Means: National Liberation and Revolution in Viet-Nam 1954–60.* Sydney: Allen & Unwin, 1989.

Triplett, William. "Chaos in the Ia Drang." *VVA Veteran* 6, 10 (October 1986): 18–22.

Veith, George J. *Black April: The Fall of South Vietnam 1973–75.* New York: Encounter
    Books, 2012.
Viet, Ha Mai. *Steel and Blood: South Vietnamese Armor and the War for Southeast Asia.* Annapo-   •
    lis, MD: Naval Institute Press, 2008.
Westmoreland, General William C. *A Soldier Reports.* New York: Dell, 1976.
Wiest, Andrew. *Vietnam's Forgotten Army: Heroism and Betrayal in the ARVN.* New York:
    New York University Press, 2008.

Unpublished Secondary Sources

Hansen, John P. "Armed Social Work: US Army Special Forces Operations in Vietnam
    1961–1963." Diss., Virginia Military Institute, April 2014. Copy in author's possession.
Mataxis, Theodore C. "Monsoon Offensive in the Highlands." N.d. Apparently intended
    for publication but for some reason never published, this article is a crucial source on
    the monsoon offensive of 1965 in the Central Highlands. It can be found in the Mataxis
    Papers, USAMHI.
Nuttle, David. "They Have Stone Ears Don't They." N.d. This is an account of the initia-
    tion of the Buon Enao experiment; copy in author's possession.
Towle, Robert L. "The Tears of Autumn: Air Assault Operations and Infantry Combat in
    the Ia Drang Valley, November 1965." Ph.D. diss., Kent State University, 2000. A copy
    is held at the USAMHI library.

Online Sources

This bibliography does not list every online document consulted. However, the following
book referred to in the notes is available only online (released to the public on 19 February
2009), having never been published in hard copy:

Ahern, Thomas L. *The CIA and the House of Ngo: Covert Action in South Vietnam 1954–63.*
    Center for the Study of Intelligence.

It also seems worthwhile to list some of the historical websites consulted:

The Retired Air Commandos have established a site dealing with their role in Buon
Enao. See "Buon Enao Project October 1962," http://www.glanmore.org./Buon Enao
/Buon Enao.html.

When researching the action at Kannack on 8 March 1965, Merle Pribbenow consulted a Vietnamese military history website: http://www.vnmilitaryhistory.net/index
.php?topic=16770.0 (accessed 26 January 2014).

While researching PAVN logistics in the Central Highlands in 1965, Merle Pribbenow
consulted another Vietnamese site: http://vietnamnet.vn/vn/kinh-te/-ong-chu-trieu-do
-cua-quan-giai-phong-tren-dat-chua-thap.html (accessed 25 April 2015).

Participants and Correspondents

The following were participants in some of the events described in this book and provided
information via e-mail correspondence:

Lawrence Arritola

Vaughn Binzer

Bonnie Ensor

Hugh Murray

Dave Nuttle (the author's correspondence with Nuttle was exceptionally detailed and voluminous and extended over several years)

Index